SCHOOL CRIME AND JUVENILE JUSTICE

School Crime and Juvenile Justice

Second Edition

Richard Lawrence
St. Cloud State University

New York   Oxford
Oxford University Press
2007

Oxford University Press, Inc., publishes works that further Oxford University's objective of excellence in research, scholarship, and education.

Oxford   New York
Auckland   Cape Town   Dar es Salaam   Hong Kong   Karachi
Kuala Lumpur   Madrid   Melbourne   Mexico City   Nairobi
New Delhi   Shanghai   Taipei   Toronto

With offices in
Argentina   Austria   Brazil   Chile   Czech Republic   France   Greece
Guatemala   Hungary   Italy   Japan   Poland   Portugal   Singapore
South Korea   Switzerland   Thailand   Turkey   Ukraine   Vietnam

Published by Oxford University Press, Inc.
198 Madison Avenue, New York, New York 10016
http://www.oup.com

Oxford is a registered trademark of Oxford University Press

Library of Congress Cataloging-in-Publication Data

Lawrence, Richard (Richard A.)
   School crime and juvenile justice / Richard Lawrence.—2nd ed.
      p. cm.
   ISBN-13: 978-0-19-517290-4 (alk. paper)
   ISBN-10: 0-19-517290-6 (alk. paper)
   1. School violence—United States—Prevention.   2. Juvenile delinquency—United States
   —Prevention.   3. Juvenile justice, Administration of—United States.   I. Title.
   LB3013.3.L38 2006
   371.5′8—dc22
                                                                    2005054656

Printing number: 9 8 7 6 5 4 3 2 1

Printed in the United States of America
on acid-free paper

To my wife, Dorothy, for your unconditional love and support throughout this time-consuming project; and to my daughter, Stephanie. You have made your father so proud, in so many ways. My love and appreciation to you both.

Contents

12 School-Based Programs for Delinquency Prevention   272

Preface

The first edition of *School Crime and Juvenile Justice* was written before the highly publicized school shootings in Littleton, Colorado, and other tragic school shooting incidents around the United States. Much has happened since the publication of the first edition. Before 1998, very few books had been written on the subject of school crime and violence. School crime was given very little attention by the public, legislators, or police. A number of violent incidents in schools the past several years changed that. Contrary to what many believe, however, the number of assaults, injuries, and even deaths at schools has *not* significantly increased in the past 10 years. In fact, most types of school crime have actually decreased since 1993. What has changed is the recognition that "everyday" school crime is more serious than originally believed. Bullying, for example, has been a dreaded part of school attendance for thousands of students. Bullying, harassment, and teasing were unfortunately not recognized as serious problems in U.S. schools until recently. The problem of bullying has been studied extensively for decades by researchers in Norway, Great Britain, and other European countries. The recognition that "normal" student behaviors such as teasing and bullying often escalate to more serious incidents, such as school shootings, has instigated considerable public concern, media attention, and research on the problem. Thus, the increased attention on school crime and violence is due not to a significant increase in the problem, but to the recognition that any amount of school crime creates fear that disrupts the education environment for teachers and students and must not be tolerated.

This second edition is written with the same multiple objectives as the first:

•How extensive and serious is school crime?

•Who commits school crime?

•Who are the victims?

•What are the characteristics of schools with more crime?

•What are the characteristics of youths who commit crime in and around schools?

•To what extent do school experiences contribute to delinquent behavior?

•What can schools do to help prevent delinquency?

•How can schools, students, parents, police, and juvenile justice agencies combine their efforts to reduce delinquency?

The second edition draws upon the numerous sources and research findings generated since the publication of the first edition. Recent school shooting incidents attracted media attention as no other single school problem has ever done. Demands from the public to make schools safe brought immediate attention from police, legislators, federal departments and bureaus, and even the White House. Funding was made available to more carefully examine the causes and factors related to school violence. When the first edition was published we could only report on a few federal initiatives to address school crime and delinquency. In the past few years the federal government has committed numerous resources and funding to address school violence. We have witnessed for the first time a close collaboration between the U.S. Departments of Education and Justice in gathering data on the extent and nature of school violence and in publishing annual reports on "Indicators of School Crime and Safety." The revisions and updates in this second edition report on the advances made in attempting to better understand and prevent the causes of school crime and violence. The greater challenge, however, is not a lack of understanding the sources and causes of the problem as much as our willingness and determination to implement violence-prevention policies and practices that are feasible and have been shown to work, based on research findings.

Comments from colleagues and reviewers of the first edition have confirmed my original belief that studying crime and delinquency in schools can help us better understand crime in communities. The school is a focal point in many theories of delinquency, so the reader new to this material will find the introductory discussion of criminology theories to be helpful. Schools have close ties with both criminology and criminal justice. First, school experiences help explain crime causation for some juveniles; second, schools are one of the locations where juvenile crime occurs and where the juvenile justice process often begins. An understanding of the balance between school rules and school law, on one hand, and students' rights and responsibilities, on the other, can serve as a starting point by which we may better understand the effectiveness of laws and their enforcement in society. Innovations such as community policing, restorative justice, and mediation as alternatives to traditional crime control and retributive forms of justice have been effectively implemented in schools. As primary institutions of education and socialization, schools are a proper starting point for delinquency prevention and community justice practices.

This second edition has been extensively revised and updated, with two new chapters that reflect the increased emphases on attempting to understand, predict, and prevent school violence. Chapter 6 discusses the school environment and how school size, structure, and related factors affect school crime and safety. Chapter 7 addresses the recent research on attempting to identify and predict students who may be at risk of committing school violence. The original chapters on explaining the causes of juvenile delinquency and the role of police, courts, and corrections in the administration of juvenile justice have been expanded and updated to reflect the latest available research and resources.

It is my hope that this second edition will contribute to a better understanding of school crime and violence, the development of more effective prevention strategies, and more fair and just policies and practices for responding to delinquent and violent children and youth.

Acknowledgments

This book is a product of more than 35 years of studying and writing about the juvenile justice system. I have learned much and owe a debt of gratitude to many friends and colleagues during years of working in the system, doing research, and teaching. A number of colleagues contributed to this book through their reviews and comments on the first edition, offering encouragement and suggestions that culminated in what has become an entire revision and expansion of the previous edition. I am grateful to David Mueller for his helpful suggestions and to Frank Hagan who urged me to write this second edition. Friends and colleagues from the National Center for Education Statistics who offered helpful comments and suggestions include Kathryn Chandler, Jill DeVoe, Mike Planty, and Lynn Addington. Kris LaMar and Janet Steverson helped in the section on legal and constitutional rights of juveniles. The work of Howard Snyder and Melissa Sickmund enabled me to compile and discuss statistical reports of juvenile arrests, court cases, and juveniles in corrections. Ron Stephens and June Arnette of the National School Safety Center assisted in providing current information on school shootings and deaths and on school violence-prevention programs.

A number of colleagues have contributed to my understanding of school crime and juvenile justice. I am grateful to Rolando del Carmen, Delbert Elliott, Barry Feld, Denise and Gary Gottfredson, David Huizinga, Steve Lab, Joe Sanborn, Jackson Toby, Wayne Welsh, and John Whitehead. Thanks also to David Cole, Katherine Newman, and those authors above and their publishers who allowed me to cite their work and research findings.

I am grateful for the support and encouragement of my colleagues at St. Cloud State University, who have contributed to creating an academic environment where scholarly research and writing are valued and made possible. My thanks go to Richard Lewis, Ronald Farrell, C. W. Seefeldt, Deb Yorek, and my colleagues in the Criminal Justice Department.

Peter Labella, Senior Editor at Oxford University Press, made this second edition possible and deserves special thanks for his patience and tolerance as I took more time than anticipated in order to include updates on the numerous developments in school violence and prevention in the past several years. I want to also express my profound appreciation to the fine editorial staff at Oxford University Press: Sean Mahoney, Shiwani Srivastava, Erika Wise, and Barbara Mathieu. They provided expert editorial assistance in bringing this revised and expanded second edition to press.

My life has been enriched and blessed by parents and family members who have valued the importance of education. I dedicated the first edition of this book to my parents, who were both public school teachers. I have dedicated this book to my wife, Dorothy, and my daughter, Stephanie. I am especially grateful to Dorothy for her unconditional love and support through this lengthy and time-consuming writing endeavor. She deserves a special statement of gratitude for her 34 years as a junior high school teacher, where she became all too familiar with the changes and challenges faced by educators. My daughter, Stephanie, is following in her footsteps as a teacher in elementary education. It has been a great pleasure as a proud father to watch her grow and develop while contributing so much to those around her. I have written this book in the hope that all teachers and students will be able to work productively together in a safe learning environment, free of threats and victimization, and that citizens, taxpayers, government, and justice officials will support them in that endeavor.

R. L.
St. Cloud, Minnesota

1

Juvenile Crime in Society and in Schools

Juvenile crime and violence are problems throughout society and in schools. Crime seems to be pervasive throughout society. It generally ranks as one of the top concerns of Americans, based on the results of polls. Crime news and crime stories pervade the news and information media, including newspapers, news magazines, radio, and television. Young people appear to be disproportionately involved in delinquent and criminal activities. Although statistical data indicate that most juvenile crime tends to be nonviolent—involving theft, substance abuse, and minor petty offenses—news media and public attention tend to focus on violent delinquent behavior because it is shocking and newsworthy. Crimes that occur in schools tend to receive special attention. Schools are a central educational and social institution in every American city, from the smallest towns to major metropolitan areas. We expect children and teachers to be safe in schools and are shocked at news of another violent incident in the classrooms and hallways.

Metropolitan inner-city schools have traditionally been viewed as dangerous places where assaults, drugs, and weapons are common. That perception is supported, for the most part, by official police reports and victimization surveys. A higher proportion of school crime is reported in public schools located in urban inner-city areas. Students and teachers in such schools report a greater amount of disorder, threats, and fighting than in suburban or rural schools. School crime and violence are not restricted to inner-city schools, however. School officials from suburban and smaller city schools are now reporting an increasing number of crimes. Shooting incidents that have occurred in suburban and small city schools have attracted national attention and caused concern about school safety. The shootings involving multiple fatalities in Jonesboro, Arkansas (1998), and at Columbine High School in Littleton, Colorado (1999), have dramatically illustrated that school violence is not limited to inner-city schools. The extensive media coverage has tended to inflate the risk of violent victimization in schools (Lawrence and Mueller, 2003), but the national attention has also served to highlight the presence of bullying, threats, and disorder, which often lead to violence.

The types of crimes most often committed in schools involve drugs, alcohol, theft, and vandalism. School equipment and property are vulnerable to theft, and administrators have had to step up security precautions to prevent vandalism. Verbal harassment, threats, and bullying have existed in schools for decades but have only recently been perceived as serious problems. A small percentage of students carry weapons to school for self-protection, and there is evidence that a number of tragic school shooting incidents were triggered by bullying and victimization experiences.

Public Views of Juvenile Crime

Most Americans' knowledge and opinions of crime and justice are based on what they see on television and read in the newspapers (Warr, 2000). A national crime survey found that 96 percent of citizens relied on the news media to learn about crime and criminals (Flanagan and McGarrell, 1986). Media critics believe that there is cause for concern when news reports are the sole source of information about crime, because the information the public receives about crime and public safety is often exaggerated and lacks a balanced perspective. The mass media exaggerates the true nature and extent of violent crime and presents a distorted picture of criminals, victims, the causes of crime, and the criminal justice system (Surette, 1998). Television, newspaper, and magazine stories regularly draw attention to crimes committed by teenagers. Media portrayals of youth crime tend to overgeneralize and exaggerate the problem in at least two ways: (1) by not reporting the variations in crime in different cities, schools, and regions of the country; and (2) by not reporting the *rates* of crime (number of crimes per 100,000 population). Television and news stories also tend to portray an image of the juvenile delinquent today as a hardened, ruthless criminal and dramatically portray the youth crime problem as pervading all cities and most suburbs. Numerous television reports and newspaper and magazine articles have increased the public awareness of school crime and violence. Violent crimes committed by youth are newsworthy events primarily because they are relatively uncommon and often shocking (Lawrence and Mueller, 2003). The shooting incident at Columbine High School was reported in the print and electronic media for months and years after the incident. Television and newspaper reports of school violence present exaggerated and distorted views of students' risk of being seriously attacked or harmed at school. The extensive media coverage of shooting incidents at schools throughout the United States have presented the image of school violence as fairly common and likely to happen anywhere, anytime.

The widely publicized news stories suggesting that school shooting incidents were increasing and that students were more at risk of violent victimization in schools certainly contributed to a greater fear of school violence among students and parents. A Gallup poll conducted 1 year after the Columbine shootings found that 63 percent of K–12 parents believed that a similar tragedy was very likely or somewhat likely to occur in their community, and 70 percent agreed that the shooting made them more concerned about their child's safety at school (Gillespie, 2000). Data from the School Crime Supplement (SCS) to the National Crime Victimization Survey (NCVS) indicate that students were slightly more fearful after Columbine (Addington, 2003).

To say that media stories are exaggerations is *not* to deny that youth crime is a serious problem about which one should be concerned. But inaccurate reports of the true extent and nature of youth crime often lead to targeting of certain youths and attacking the perceived problem with extreme policies. Accurate measures provide the basis for a more reasoned, rational approach to reducing violence in society and in schools. It is important that we have accurate and reliable reports on the extent and seriousness of juvenile crime in order to properly inform the public.

Some Historical Perspective

The public concern about juvenile crime in society and in schools is not a new or recent phenomenon. Bernard (1992) notes several beliefs about juvenile delinquency and juvenile justice that have stayed the same for over two hundred years, including the belief that juveniles, especially young males, commit more crime than other groups, and that the current group of juveniles commit more frequent and more serious crimes than juveniles in the past—that is, there is a "juvenile crime wave" at the present time (Bernard, 1992: 21). These beliefs pervaded American society whether the actual rates of juvenile crime were remaining stable or decreasing. Public beliefs about a juvenile crime wave and concerns that lenient juvenile justice policies were to blame led to frequent changes in those policies in what Bernard (1992) referred to as "the cycle of juvenile justice."

One of the first major federal government initiatives in juvenile delinquency assessment and prevention initiatives was the 1967 President's Commission on Law Enforcement and Administration of Justice that produced a series of reports, one of which was the "Task Force Report: Juvenile Delinquency and Youth Crime" (President's Commission on Law Enforcement and Administration of Justice, 1967). The report made a contribution to our understanding of delinquency, informed legislators and government officials about the nature and sources of juvenile crime, and urged policymakers to allocate funding and resources for delinquency-prevention programs.

Measures of Crime

Measures of crime were originally limited to *"official" reports* of police, courts, and correctional agencies. Official crime statistics, however, are not a precise measure of the true extent of crime, because many crimes are not reported to police or other criminal justice agencies. The problem of unreported crime led criminologists to devise other "unofficial" methods of measuring crime. *Self-report measures* and *victimization surveys* are the two most common. In self-report measures, samples of youth are asked to report on their own involvement in delinquent activities whether or not they were ever caught. Self-reports provide a more complete picture of juvenile delinquency, but are not completely error-free because they depend on subjects' honesty and reliability of memory. Victimization surveys, administered to a sample of the population, ask respondents whether and how often they have been victims of crime. These surveys may also ask about the perpetrators and circumstances of the crime, and they have the advantage of asking if the crime was reported and, if not, why it was not reported. Fewer than 50 percent of all violent crimes are reported to the police, and almost 35 percent of all police departments in the United States fail to completely report their arrest data to the Federal Bureau of Investigation (FBI) (Lynch, 2002: 3). Crimes are not reported for several reasons. In many property crimes there is no victim or witness present, and persons are reluctant to report crimes for which they believe the police are unlikely to find the perpetrator. "Victimless" or "consensual" crimes such as drug use, possession, and sales are unlikely to be reported to police as long as the incidents go undetected. Victimization surveys of crime are not perfect, error-free measures, nor are they intended to replace official police statistics. They do, however, serve as a valuable supplement to official statistics, and provide information about crime that is not available from police and court statistics. Each of the crime measures has strengths and weaknesses, but together they provide the best available measures of crime in society and in schools.

Police Measures of Juvenile Crime

The FBI compiles data on the number of crimes reported to local, county and state police and publishes an annual report, *Crime in the United States*, more commonly known as the Uniform Crime Report (UCR) (Federal Bureau of Investigation, 2005). While the UCR is considered the official report on crime in the United States, we should remember that it is at best an estimate, since many crimes are not reported to police. Official reports of juvenile arrests are summarized in Table 1–1.

Law enforcement agencies arrested an estimated 2.2 million juveniles in 2003. Juveniles (under 18 years of age) accounted for 16 percent of all violent crimes cleared by arrest (5 percent of murders, 12 percent of rapes, 14 percent of robberies, and 12 percent of aggravated assaults) (Snyder, 2005). The number of arrests of juveniles for murder has been declining since the peak year of 1993, when there were 3,790 juvenile arrests for murder; in 2003 there were 1,130 juvenile arrests for murder, about one-third of the number in 1993. The juvenile violent crime arrest rate in 2003 was lower than it had been since 1980, and nearly half what it was in 1994. The total of 1,550 murder victims under age 18 in 2003 was the smallest number since 1984 (Snyder, 2005: 2–3).

Juvenile arrests disproportionately involve minorities. Of juvenile arrests for violent crimes in 2003, 53 percent involved white youth, 45 percent involved black youth, 1 percent involved Asian American youth, and 1 percent involved American Indian youth; for property crime arrests, the arrests involved 69 percent white youth, 28 percent black youth, 2 percent Asian American youth, and 1 percent American Indian youth. In comparison, the racial composition of the juvenile population in 2003 was 78 percent white, 16 percent black, 4 percent Asian/Pacific Islander, and 1 percent American Indian (Snyder, 2003: 9). A comparison of the arrest rates per 100,000 juveniles in the racial groups shows the racial disparity even more dramatically. In 2003 the Violent Crime Index arrest rate (per 100,000) for black juveniles was 752, which is four times greater than for whites (arrest rate of 186 per 100,000). For Property Crime Index arrests, the rate for black juveniles (2,352) was almost double the rate for white juveniles (1,237) (Snyder, 2005: 9). The black–white disparity in juvenile arrest rates has declined significantly during the past 20 years, but it is still very high.

The juvenile arrest rates for violent crimes in 2003 continued the declining trend (an), along with decreases (between 1994 and 2003) of 62 percent for motor vehicle theft, and 41 percent for weapons law violations; but there were increases in that same time period for juvenile arrests for drug abuse violations (19 percent) and driving under the influence (33 percent) (Snyder, 2005: 3).

Table 1–1
Juvenile Arrests, 2003

Most Serious Offense	2003 Estimated Number of Juvenile Arrests	Percent of Total Juvenile Arrests		Percent Change		
		Female	Under Age 15	1994– 2003	1999– 2003	2002– 2003
Total	**2,220,300**	**29%**	**32%**	**–18%**	**–11%**	**0%**
Violent Crime Index	92,300	18	33	–32	–9	0
Murder, manslaughter	1,130	9	11	–68	–18	–10
Forcible rape	4,240	2	37	–25	–11	–9
Robbery	25,440	9	25	–43	–8	3
Aggravated assault	61,490	24	36	–26	–9	0
Property Crime Index	463,300	32	37	–38	–15	–3
Burglary	85,100	12	35	–40	–15	–1
Larceny-theft	325,600	39	38	–35	–15	–3
Motor vehicle theft	44,500	17	25	–52	–15	–4
Arson	8,200	12	61	–36	–12	–3
Nonindex						
Other assaults	241,900	32	43	10	5	5
Forgery, counterfeiting	4,700	35	13	–47	–36	–8
Fraud	8,100	33	18	–29	–37	–9
Embezzlement	1,200	40	6	15	–30	–17
Stolen property	24,300	16	27	–46	–19	–5
Vandalism	107,700	14	44	–33	–11	2
Weapons	39,200	11	36	–41	–6	11
Prostitution, vice	1,400	69	14	31	23	11
Other sex offense	18,300	9	51	2	3	–3
Drug abuse violations	197,100	16	17	19	–3	4
Gambling	1,700	2	15	–59	46	1
Offenses against the family and children	7,000	39	35	19	–24	19
Driving under influence	21,000	20	2	33	–9	–4
Liquor law violations	136,900	35	10	4	–22	–6
Drunkenness	17,600	23	13	11	–19	–6
Disorderly conduct	193,00	31	41	13	–0	6
Vagrancy	2,300	25	25	–50	–20	9
Curfew and loitering	136,500	30	29	–1	–18	–8
Runaways	123,600	59	36	–42	–18	–2

Source: Snyder, Howard N. 2005. "Juvenile Arrests 2003." *OJJDP Juvenile Justice Bulletin.* Washington, DC: U.S. Department of Justice.

The juvenile arrest rates for females have increased for several crimes. Females accounted for 24 percent of juvenile arrests for aggravated assault and 32 percent of simple assaults and intimidations, far more than their involvement in other types of violent crimes. More than half (59 percent) of juvenile arrests for runaway involved a female, and females accounted for 30 percent of arrests for curfew and loitering law violations (Snyder, 2005: 3).

Juvenile Court Cases

According to the most recent available report on juvenile court cases, U.S. juvenile courts processed an estimated 1,633,300 delinquency cases involving juveniles charged with criminal law violations (Puzzanchera et al., 2004) (Table 1–2). These estimates are based on data from nearly 2,000 courts with jurisdiction over 70 percent of the U.S. juvenile population.[1] The number of delinquency cases handled by juvenile courts increased 43 percent between 1985 and 2000. During this time, the number of drug law violation cases increased 164 percent, public order offense cases increased 106 percent, person offense cases increased 107 percent, and property offense cases decreased 3 percent (Puzzanchera et al., 2004: 6).

Table 1–2
Delinquency Cases in Juvenile Courts, 2000

		Percent Change		
Most Serious Offense	*Number of Cases*	*1991–2000*	*1996–2000*	*1999–2000*
Total	**1,633,300**	**16**	**−9**	**−2**
Total person offenses	**375,600**	**35**	**−1**	**−3**
Criminal homicide	1,700	−32	−39	−16
Forcible rape	4,700	−15	−25	11
Robbery	22,600	−29	−41	−12
Aggravated assault	51,200	−23	−36	−5
Simple assault	255,800	79	15	−1
Other violent sex offense	12,500	42	20	9
Other person offense	27,200	32	35	−15
Total property offenses	**668,600**	**−21**	**−23**	**−4**
Burglary	108,600	−21	−27	−5
Larceny–theft	303,200	−6	−24	−13
Motor vehicle theft	38,300	−46	−29	−3
Arson	8,300	14	−7	−2
Vandalism	106,800	−5	−13	−3
Trespassing	49,400	−17	−25	−15
Stolen property offense	25,200	−15	−22	−4
Other property offense	28,900	−9	−7	9
Drug law violations	**194,200**	**197**	**5**	**2**
Public order offenses	**395,000**	**79**	**11**	**2**
Obstruction of justice	179,200	142	20	5
Disorderly conduct	90,200	54	0	1
Weapons offense	37,500	12	−15	−6
Liquor law violations	27,000	126	110	37
Nonviolent sex offenses	14,900	31	23	8
Other public order offenses	46,200	46	−4	−11

Source: Puzzanchera, Charles, Anne L. Stahl, Terrence A. Finnegan, Nancy Tierney, and Howard N. Snyder. 2004. *Juvenile Court Statistics 2000*. Pittsburgh, PA: National Center for Juvenile Justice.

Age

In 2000, 58 percent of the juvenile delinquency cases processed involved a juvenile younger than 15 years of age at the time of referral. Juveniles aged 15 years or younger accounted for a smaller proportion of drug and public order cases than of person and property offense cases. The juvenile court case rate per 1,000 juveniles increases for each age group. For example, the case rate for 10-year-olds was 5 per 1,000, compared with 21 at age 12, 65 at age 14, 86 at age 15, 105 at age 16, and 112 per 1,000 for 17-year-olds. The case rate for most age groups increased significantly between the years 1985 and 2000 (Puzzanchera et al., 2004: 9).

Gender

About three-fourths (75 percent) of juvenile court cases in 2000 involved a male, and 25 percent involved females (Puzzanchera et al., 2004: 14). This represented an increase from 1985, when females accounted for 19 percent of the total. Male juveniles outnumber females in juvenile court cases by at least four to one, but the rate of increase for females has been greater than that for males. Between 1985 and 2000 the rate of increase of female cases was greater than the rate of increase of male cases for person offenses (185 percent vs. 88 percent), property offenses (28 percent vs. −11 percent), and public order offenses (144 percent vs. 96 percent). The rate of increase for male drug offenses in court was greater than the rate of increase for female cases in court between 1985 and 2000 (166 percent vs. 152 percent, respectively) (Puzzanchera et al., 2004: 12).

Race

In 2000, approximately 79 percent of the juvenile population in the United States was white and 15 percent was black. (Juveniles of Hispanic ethnicity are usually included in the white racial category.) White juveniles were involved in 68 percent (1,140,500) of the delinquency cases that juvenile courts handled, and black juveniles were involved in 28 percent (476,500). White juveniles were involved in 71 percent (135,900) of drug law violation cases, 70 percent (494,600) of property offense cases, 69 percent (267,400) of public order offense cases, and 63 percent (242,500) of person offense cases. Black juveniles were involved in 34 percent (133,300) of person offense cases, 28 percent (109,500) of public order offense cases, 27 percent (50,900) of drug law violation cases, and 26 percent (182,700) of property offense cases (Stahl, 2003). Between 1990 and 1999 the number of cases involving white youth increased 30 percent, while cases involving black youth increased 20 percent (Puzzanchera et al., 2003: 15). Cases involving black youth comprise a disproportionate number of juvenile court cases. This is seen most dramatically when we compare the case rate: the number of juvenile court cases per 1,000 juveniles in the general population. The total case rate for black juveniles in 1999 was 106 per 1,000 juveniles—more than twice the rate for white juveniles, which was 49 per 1,000 (Puzzanchera et al., 2003: 15).

Self-Report Measures

Many crimes are not reported to police, so official statistics of juvenile delinquency do not provide a complete and accurate measure of the true extent of juvenile crime. Criminologists have used self-report studies such as the National Youth Survey to obtain a more accurate measure of the true extent of delinquency (Elliott et al., 1985). Self-report surveys provide a more comprehensive measure of delinquency than police reports, but they are susceptible to weaknesses that may not yield accurate results. The samples used are relatively small and may not be representative of the population of juvenile offenders, therefore, the results may underreport juvenile crime. Self-report studies are also vulnerable to response errors because subjects may overstate or underreport their offending behavior. Self-report measures do, however, offer an important supplement to official measures of delinquency and provide a more complete picture of the true extent of juvenile crime. Police patrols and encounters with juvenile offenders tend to be focused more in certain neighborhoods that have a reputation for higher levels of disruptive and deviant behavior. Those neighborhoods also tend to be inhabited chiefly by lower-class residents, often comprised of racial and ethnic minorities. These youth, therefore, tend to be disproportionately represented in police reports. Results of self-report measures show that delinquent behavior is spread more equally among youth of all social classes, and in fact white middle-class youth report involvement in offenses such as drug violations to a greater extent than lower-class and minority youths (see, e.g., Elliott et al., 1985). Self-report measures are very important in providing a more complete picture of delinquent behavior. Findings that some delinquent behavior is nearly universal among all youth regardless of social class or ethnic and racial group led to the development of additional research and theories to explain delinquent involvement of middle-class youth and females.

Victimization Surveys

The National Crime Victimization Survey (NCVS) is the second type of "unofficial" measure that provides a more complete picture of juvenile crime. As with self-report measures, the NCVS includes a significant portion of offending behavior that is not reported to police. Victimization measures also have some advantages over self-report surveys (Lynch, 2002). First, the NCVS uses larger samples than self-report surveys, therefore, the results are believed to be more accurate estimates of the true nature of offenses. Second, although the NCVS is likely to have some response errors, there is reason to believe that the errors are less serious than those in self-report surveys. Third, the NCVS includes more detailed information about victimization and individual crime incidents than either police reports or self-report surveys (Lynch, 2002). The NCVS does have limitations in estimating rates of offending by youth, a measure that can be made more accurately with self-report measures. The NCVS asks few questions about the characteristics of offenders. Some researchers question the ability of victims to provide reliable information on offenders, even for person crimes (Lynch, 2002). Offenders themselves can obviously provide more detailed and accurate information in self-report measures. Despite some limitations, the NCVS provides important additional information on youthful offending through the SCS, discussed further later in the chapter.

Measuring School Crime

Public concern about school disorder and crime can be traced back to the origins of the public school system in America (Crews and Counts, 1997). More nationwide emphasis was focused on the relationship between schools and delinquency with the *Task Force Report* by Schafer and Polk (1967), and the Office of Education of the U.S. Department of Health, Education, and Welfare offered recommendations as to how schools could help reduce delinquency. Congressional hearings reflected the public concern about school disorder, and the testimony at these hearings confirms an image of deviance and disorder in schools (U.S. Senate, 1975). Public officials have periodically responded to the concerns of citizens and parents expressing alarm about problems of school disorder and violence. Criminologists and education researchers have attempted to identify the sources, characteristics, and effects of school crime for more than 30 years (Polk and Schafer, 1972; McPartland and McDill, 1977; Rubel, 1977; Baker and Rubel, 1980).

The Safe School Study

The first major federal initiative dedicated solely to examining the extent and nature of school crime and violence began in 1974, when Congress passed legislation and funded a 3-year, $2.4 million study to assess the nature and extent of crime, violence, and disruption in the nation's schools. The nationwide survey gathered data on school crime from principals, teachers, and students in thousands of schools.[2] Findings of the nationwide survey were published in a report entitled *Violent Schools—Safe Schools: The Safe School Study Report to the Congress* (National Institute of Education, 1977, 1978). The Safe School Study was the first comprehensive assessment of the extent and nature of school crime in the United States. The report provided a wealth of descriptive data and a sound basis for further research, despite some weaknesses in the research methods and statistical analyses.[3] Gottfredson and Gottfredson (1985) reexamined the Safe School Study data to statistically control for community and demographic characteristics while examining the relative contribution of school governance, school climate, and other school characteristics. The Safe School Study focused on in-school variables such as student characteristics, school governance, and rule enforcement. A major theme running through the report is the role of administrators and teachers in reducing school disruption. The message of the report is that school administration and policies make a difference. Although the National Institute of Education (NIE) study acknowledged that schools with more disruption and crime were located in communities with more crime, the report virtually ignored community factors and focused on the school variables. In their reanalysis of the data, the Gottfredsons combined a number of variables in an index of social disorganization and found that schools with high rates of teacher victimization are located in communities characterized by poverty and disorganization and are in central cities. They found significant associations between the community factors in which schools are located and the level of disruption within the schools. The findings supported previous research indicating that community social disorganization is a major causal factor of crime and delinquency. The results of the Safe School Study are still relevant for examining the factors related to school crime, even though the data are now nearly 30 years old. The study concluded that schools can do more to reduce school violence and disruption through policies such as (1) increasing efforts in student governance and rule enforcement, (2) treating students fairly and equally, (3) improving the relevance of subject matter to suit students' interests and needs, and (4) having smaller classes, with teachers instructing a smaller number of students (National Institute of Education, 1977: A13–A14). The Safe School Study report set a precedence for what has become an increasingly important role of the federal government in assessing school crime and violence and developing recommendations, resources, funding, and technical assistance for local schools and justice agencies in responding to the growing concerns about juvenile crime in communities and schools (Lawrence, 2002).

Are School Crime Measures Accurate?

Measuring and reporting on the extent of school crime has suffered the same difficulties as noted above regarding the questionable accuracy of crime reports in general. Imprecise and incomplete methods of reporting on crime incidents in and around schools have been used. As mentioned, police records do not maintain special reports on crime in schools, and most crimes that occur in schools are not reported to the police. Many students do report the incidents to school officials, but those reports are not always passed on to the police. Bullying, harassment, and verbal threats traditionally have not been viewed as incidents worthy of referral to legal authorities. Physical altercations and minor fights at school were not viewed as assaults that required police intervention. Thefts of student or teacher possessions have often been handled within schools as disciplinary infractions.

No widely accepted criteria for identifying and recording the kinds and incidents of school crime were at first established (Garrett, Bass, and Casserly, 1978). In recording incidents of vandalism, some school systems included damages that may have been accidental, while others did not; some included all incidents of damage and destruction, while others included only acts for which a perpetrator is identified; and some excluded from reports any damages covered by insurance.

Similar variations exist for the reporting of weapons in schools. Some schools have subjected students found with weapons in their backpacks or lockers to in-school suspension; others with a "zero-tolerance" policy reported the incidents to police and suspended students for a period of days or even expelled them for the remainder of the school year. Significant variations exist in discipline-reporting practices in schools throughout the nation. This is true among different school districts in the same metropolitan area and among urban, suburban, and rural school districts in the same state (Lawrence, 1998). There are a number of explanations for the lack of uniformity in counting school crime incidents and disciplinary reports. State departments of education have slightly different policies, definitions, and criteria to determine which crimes and disciplinary incidents are required to be reported. School officials also feel under pressure to maintain safe and crime-free schools and therefore are often reluctant to report all incidents out of a concern that it will make the school appear unsafe and raise questions as to whether the school personnel are sufficiently in control of maintaining order and discipline. School administrators in the past have been reluctant to involve law enforcement officials in incidents that they felt could be handled by the schools. They feared that the presence of police vehicles at schools would send a message to the community that the school was unsafe.

Steps Toward Accurate and Uniform Reports

More uniform reporting practices are necessary in order to monitor the seriousness of school crime incidents. Accurate information as to the extent of the school crime problem is necessary in order to implement appropriate prevention strategies. The imprecise and incomplete methods of measuring school crime continue to be a problem that must be addressed by school districts and state departments of education and has recently been addressed at the federal level. The National Center for Education Statistics has recognized the importance of collecting complete and accurate data on school crime and discipline incidents. A book entitled *Safety in Numbers: Collecting and Using Crime, Violence, and Discipline Incident Data to Make a Difference in Schools* (Hantman et al., 2002) was designed to be used by school, district, and state staff to improve the collection and use of disciplinary incident data. Hantman and her associates provide recommendations as to what types of data to collect, why it is critical to collect such data, and how the data can be used effectively to improve school safety and answer policy questions relating to school improvement and student safety. Comprehensive and accurate collection of data on school violence and disciplinary incidents is essential for school districts to comply with required state and federal incident reports. Most state education departments have required school districts to report the number of disciplinary incidents, the reasons for them, and the number of suspensions and expulsions related to those incidents. The federal government focused on reporting with passage of the No Child Left Behind Act of 2001, which was signed into law January 8, 2002. The Act includes requirements for reporting crime incidents and the identification of "dangerous schools" and focuses on school district accountability to assure safe schools with the possible consequence that students may transfer out of those schools if adequate steps to assure safety are not taken.

Measures of School Crime and Safety[4]

The methods used to measure school crime and safety have multiplied in the past decade. The Safe School Study (National Institute of Education, 1978) was the first nationwide study of school crime and the community and school factors related to the problem. It was more than 10 years later that the SCS to the NCVS was conducted (Bastian and Taylor, 1991). Those were important measures because official police records reported by the FBI's UCR did not include locations of reported crimes (such as in or around schools). Federal reports on school crime and safety are now published regularly, some on an annual basis. Following the tragic school shooting incident at Columbine High School, President Clinton mandated annual reports on school crime and safety, to be published through a collaborative effort of the Departments of Education and Justice. Reports of school crime and safety are not comparable in all respects, however, to other reports of general crime, because of the wider range of behaviors being measured and reported.

Definition Problems: School Disorder, Crime, and Violence

The literature on school crime has used a variety of terms to describe the problem, ranging from "school conflict, disorder, crime, and violence." Some authors have included bullying, peer harassment, and verbal threats in definitions of "violence," while other reports limit violent acts to assault, robbery, sexual assault, and murder, which have been traditionally categorized as violent crimes by the FBI in the UCR. The lack of agreement and consistency in definitions has resulted in widely varying measures of school crime.

School disorder, crime, and violence have been reported in the literature based on at least five measures: (1) students' and teachers' self-reported victimization, (2) students', teachers', and administrators' perceptions of disorder, (3) school security incidents, (4) school disciplinary data, such as suspensions and expulsions, and (5) self-report measures of misconduct or serious offending by students (Welsh, 2001).[5]

Victimization Reports

The primary sources of information on school crime are self-reports of victimization. The Safe School Study (National Institute of Education, 1978) first reported on student and teacher reports of victimization. The SCS was added to the NCVS in 1989 (Bastian and Taylor, 1991) and was repeated in 1995 (Chandler et al., 1998), and 1999 (Addington et al., 2002). For the SCS, the NCVS gathers survey data from a nationally representative sample of households of (10,000 students ages 12–19 from 43,000 households in the 1999 sample). Any household member between 12 and 18 years of age was given an SCS interview (Addington et al., 2002). Students were asked to respond to questions regarding victimization at school, drug availability, street gangs, fear of being attacked, and whether or not they reported crimes to police. As with results of the NCVS, most crimes that occur in and around schools are not reported to police. Results of the SCS show that 88 percent of the crimes were not reported (Addington et al., 2002: 11). Reasons for not reporting most school crimes to police include that the students reported them to school officials, students viewed the crimes as minor or unsuccessful, they did not believe the police could do anything, and school officials in turn did not report the crimes to police but handled the matters informally within the school (Addington et al., 2002: 12).

Observations and Perceptions of Disorder

A second type of measure is students' observations of bullying, threats, and similar forms of victimization directed at other students and their perceptions of the school as disorderly or unsafe (DeVoe et al., 2003). Included in this category are seeing or knowing about the presence of guns and other weapons in school, the presence of street gangs, hate-related words or graffiti, and the availability of alcohol or drugs in school. Regardless of whether a student has been personally victimized, knowing about or having observed school disorder and victimization against other students creates a perception of disorder and a feeling that school officials are not in control and that the school is unsafe. Observing or knowing about crime and disorder in school increases students' fear of being victimized, which in turn may lead to students avoiding certain places in school or even avoiding school altogether on given days.

Welsh (2001) has noted that measures of fear often do not differentiate between perception (e.g., witnessing the victimization of others), cognition (e.g., believing one is at risk based on others' victimization), and emotion (e.g., feelings about victimization) (Welsh, 2001: 914). Most experts agree that fear of victimization is primarily an emotion, something that Warr (2000: 453) has referred to as "a feeling of alarm or dread" caused by a person's awareness of or expected risk of danger. Warr suggested that measures of fear and measures of perceived risk do not measure the same thing. What is perhaps more relevant in relation to school crime measures is a behavioral indicator of fear, such as student avoidance of places perceived as dangerous. There is still a limitation on assessing behavior that may be based on a perception or emotional feeling, since students' responses are based on individual perceptions and circumstances. Research evidence does suggest that students have avoided places in school (hallways, restrooms, stairways) because they feared that they may be a victim of assault (DeVoe et al., 2003).

Reports by Police and School Officials

A third measure of school disorder and crime includes reports by school principals and law enforcement officers. In 1999–2000 an estimated 1.5 million violent incidents occurred in public schools (K–12). One or more violent incidents were reported by 71 percent of school officials, and 36 percent of schools reported one or more such incidents to the police (DeVoe et al., 2003: 24). Twenty percent of schools experienced one or more serious violent crimes (rape or other sexual assault; physical attack, fight, or threat of attack with a weapon; and robbery with or without a weapon). One or more thefts were reported in 46 percent of schools (DeVoe et al., 2003: 24). These statistics depict a serious crime problem in schools, but likely do not report the true extent of the problem. School crimes are underreported, as noted above, because not all crimes are reported to principals and the crimes reported to principals are not always reported to police, but rather handled within the school (Addington et al., 2002). Official reports of school crimes also reflect the policies and practices of teachers, principals, and school districts (Welsh, 2001). Official school crime reports are nevertheless useful as one measure of school crime and disorder.

School Disciplinary Data

A fourth measure of school crime and disorder is principals' reports of disciplinary problems, suspensions, or expulsions. During the 1999–2000 school year, about 54 percent of public schools reported one or more disciplinary problems. Of disciplinary actions taken, 83 percent were suspensions lasting 5 days or more, 11 percent were removals with no services (i.e., expulsions), and 7 percent were transfers to specialized schools (DeVoe et al., 2004: 28). The types of violations and percentage of schools that took disciplinary actions for those violations included:

•Fights: 35 percent

•Threats: 22 percent

•Possession or use of illegal drugs or alcohol: 20 percent

•Possession of weapons other than firearms: 19 percent

•Insubordination: 18 percent

•Distribution of illegal drugs: 10 percent

•Use of weapons other than firearms: 5 percent

•Possession of a firearm or explosive device: 4 percent

•Use of a firearm or explosive device: 2 percent

As a measure of school crime and disorder, school disciplinary records are inconsistent and unreliable (Gottfredson and Gottfredson, 1985). Record keeping is not a high priority among all schools, and teachers may be discouraged from reporting disciplinary problems to principals because it may indicate their inability to handle problems themselves (Welsh, 2001). There is considerable variation in discipline policies among school districts and even between schools in the same district. One study of suspensions for discipline problems reported significant differences between school districts in the same metropolitan area. A school district located in a relatively low-crime suburban area reported significantly more suspensions for violations, including weapon possession, than the larger inner-city school district that had more reported incidents of street gangs and weapon possession in the neighborhoods around the schools (Lawrence, 1998). Disciplinary reports clearly represent individual school district policies more than reliable measures of school crime and disorder. They are, nevertheless, a useful indicator of school crime and safety, particularly when used in combination with other more reliable measures.

The School Survey on Crime and Safety (SSOCS) is the most recent measure of school crime and disorder (Miller and Chandler, 2003). The survey was first administered in 2000 to a nationally representative sample of principals in 2,270 public elementary, middle, and secondary schools. SSOCS was designed to provide an overall picture of school crime and safety in the United States by asking school principals about the frequency of crime and violence, violent deaths at and near schools, the characteristics of school disciplinary policies, school violence-prevention programs, disciplinary problems and actions, and other factors associated with school crime and disorder. Principals from 71 percent of the schools reported at least one violent incident (sexual assault, physical attacks, fights with or without a weapon, and robbery) during the 1999–2000 school year (Miller and Chandler, 2003).

Student Self-Reports

A fifth measure of school crime and disorder is student self-reports. As discussed previously in this chapter, self-report measures have an established record of providing a more accurate and complete picture of juvenile crime than official reports of police. Self-report measures such as the National Youth Survey (NYS) have been widely used by researchers (Elliott, Huizinga, and Ageton, 1985); and have been administered in schools to examine differences in self-reported delinquent behavior of students, and to test theoretical explanations for school crime and disorder (Lawrence, 1985). Standardized self-report measures of school crime and disorder are not as common, but have been done (Welsh et al., 1999). Self-report measures of school crime unfortunately do not always clearly distinguish between misconduct (such as disrespect to teachers or school rule violations) and serious offending (such as assault, theft, or robbery). It is important for researchers to clearly define the behaviors measured by student self-reports and differentiate between criminal or delinquent offenses and less serious acts of school disorder (Welsh, 2001).

These measures together have been valuable in providing fairly accurate and reliable reports on the extent of school crime and disorder in American schools. While they are cross-sectional measures, repeated administration of some of the measures (such as the NCVS School Crime Supplement) over several years has enabled researchers to document changes in the frequency and serious of school crimes. *Indicators of School Crime and Safety* (DeVoe et al., 2004) compiles data from various sources to report on the most currently available information on school crime. This report and others are summarized in Table 1–3.

What is important is not that we adopt a single definition or measure, but that we make clear what it is that we are measuring and exactly what behaviors are included as well as the method and subjects used. Measures of school crime should not be limited to the law violations included in the UCR. Many acts of violence and law violations that occur in schools are precipitated by less serious conflicts, disorder, and threats. In order to assess the overall levels of school crime and safety, it is important to include a variety of disorderly and threatening behaviors that disrupt the learning environment and create a climate of fear among students and teachers. This book discusses a variety of measures of school disorder and crime. It is important for the reader to note the definitions of the behaviors being measured and the methods and sources used.

Table 1–3
Measures of School Crime

Measure of School Crime	Summary of Data	Source (Dates)
National Crime Victimization Survey (NCVS)	The most extensive measure of criminal victimization; number of incidents, location, and age of respondent, 12 years and older. Provides frequency and rates of school crime.	U.S. Bureau of Justice Statistics (1972–present)
School Crime Supplement (SCS) to the NCVS	Questions about the school environment (security, discipline, drug use, gang presence), victimization, bullying and fear, in past 6 months. Provides prevalence of school crime.	U.S. Dept. of Justice (1989, 1995, now every other year)
Youth Risk Behavior Survey (YRBS)	Asks about criminal behavior and possession of firearms, within the last 30 days.	Centers for Disease Control (1993–2001)
School and Staffing Survey (SASS)	Teacher and school staff victimization measure.	U.S. Dept. of Education (1993–1994; 1999–2000)
Principal/School Disciplinarian Survey on School Violence (FRSS)	Principals' reports of disciplinary measures taken (suspensions, expulsions, for school violations).	U.S. Dept. of Education (1996–1997)
School Survey on Crime and Safety (SSOCS)	Nationally representative sample of public schools. Principals' reports of school crimes, discipline problems, and school violence prevention programs.	U.S. Dept. of Education (2000)
School-Associated Deaths	Annual (school year) reports of homicides and suicides in school, on school grounds, and on the way to school. Compiled from official and newspaper sources.	National School Safety Center (1992–present)
School-Associated Violent Death Study (SAVD)	Studies reporting all deaths that occur at school or at school-sponsored events; not limited to students.	Kachur et al., 1996; Anderson et al., 2001

Sources: Kachur et al., 1996; Heaviside et al., 1998; Anderson et al., 2001; DeVoe et al., 2003: 133–141; Miller and Chandler, 2003; National School Safety Center, 2005.

Nonfatal Student Victimization

It is helpful to review findings of the Safe School Study so that we have some perspective on and basis for comparison of the trends of crimes against students in schools. According to in 1976, theft was the most common type of school crime, with 11 percent (2.4 million) of the nation's secondary school students reporting that something worth more than $1 was stolen from them in a month (items such as money, sweaters, books, notebooks, and similar property found in lockers). Only one-fifth of the reported thefts involved money or property worth $10 or more (National Institute of Education, 1977: 2).

An estimated 1.3 percent (282,000) of secondary school students reported that they were attacked at school in a typical 1-month period. Twice as many (2.1 percent) junior high students reported attacks. About two-fifths of the reported attacks resulted in some injury, but only 4 percent involved injuries serious enough to require medical treatment. Only 0.5 percent (about 112,000) of students reported being robbed (money or property taken by force, weapons, or threats) (National Institute of Education, 1977: 2). When the amount of time spent at school is taken into account, the risk of violence to teenagers is greater in school than elsewhere. While youth spend up to 25 percent of their waking hours in school, 40 percent of the robberies and 36 percent of the assaults on urban teenagers occurred in schools (National Institute of Education, 1977: 2).

Current reports on school crime based on the NCVS show that students aged 12–18 were victims of about 2 million nonfatal crimes (theft plus violent crime) while at school and about 1.7 million crimes while away from school in 2001. These figures represent victimization rates of 73 crimes per 1,000 students at school and 61 crimes per 1,000 students away from school (DeVoe et al., 2003: 6). Thefts are the most frequently occurring crimes at school. In 2001, about 1.2 million thefts occurred at school and about 913,000 away from school. Students aged 12–18 were victims of about 603,000 simple assaults (fighting, hitting, kicking, and punching that do not result in serious injury). About 107,000 students were victims of violent crimes (rape, sexual assault, robbery, and aggravated and) at school. Students were victims of about 161,000 serious violent crimes (rape, sexual assault, robbery, and aggravated assault) at school and 290,000 serious violent crimes away from school. During most of the period from 1992 to 2001, the victimization rates for violent crime and serious violent crime were lower at school than away from school. Fighting or simple assaults occurred more frequently at school, and serious violent crimes more often away from school. The victimization rates for students both at and away from school declined for thefts and violent crimes during 1991–2001. Rates of crime at school are similar among urban, suburban, and rural students, but rates of serious violent crimes away from school are higher for urban students. Younger students (ages 12–14) were more likely than older students (15–18) to be victims of crime at school, whereas older students were more likely than younger students to be victimized away from school (DeVoe et al., 2003: 6). The most recent available measures of crimes against students are summarized in Table 1–4.

Fatal Student Victimization

Serious violent crimes involving fatalities draw considerable attention and have been the subject of national concern regarding school safety. Violent deaths in schools are shocking and tragic events that affect the families and friends of the victims involved as well as the entire school and community. *School-associated deaths* include homicides, suicides, legal intervention involving law enforcement officers, or unintentional firearm-related deaths in which the fatal injury occurred on the school grounds, at a school-sponsored event, or going to or from school. Victims include students, staff members, and other nonstudents. The FBI reports of crimes known to police do not indicate the location of a crime, therefore, data on school-related fatalities were drawn from a number of data sets. Reports on violent deaths in schools are available in the *Indicators of School Crime and Safety* (DeVoe et al., 2004) and have been published in the *Journal of the American Medical Association* (Kachur et al., 1996). Perhaps the best ongoing available report on school-associated deaths is provided by the National School Safety Center (NSSC) (2005). School-associated deaths

Table 1–4

Number and Rate of Nonfatal Crimes Against Students Ages 12–18 Occurring at School or on the Way to or from School, by Type of Crime and Student Characteristics, 2001[a]

Student Characteristics	Total	Theft	Violent[b]	Serious Violent[b]
Total	2,001,300 (73)	1,237,700 (45)	602,800 (22)	160,900 (6)
Sex				
Male	1,105,600 (78)	680,900 (48)	335,900 (12)	88,800 (6)
Female	895,700 (67)	556,600 (42)	266,900 (9)	72,200 (5)
Age (yr)				
12–14	997,500 (82)	573,900 (47)	415,160 (15)	84,400 (7)
15–18	1,003,700 (66)	663,600 (43)	263,600 (10)	76,500 (5)
Race/ethnicity[c]				
White	1,399,800 (79)	888,100 (50)	423,100 (15)	88,600 (5)
Black	274,100 (63)	165,300 (38)	78,300 (3)	30,500 (1)[d]
Hispanic	269,100 (64)	130,700 (31)	99,100 (4)	39,300 (9)
Other	58,300 (51)	53,400 (46)	2,400 (<1)[d]	2,500 (<1)[d]
Urbanicity				
Urban	551,900 (73)	330,000 (44)	169,500 (6)	52,500 (7)
Suburban	1,092,000 (76)	685,600 (48)	325,300 (12)	81,100 (6)
Rural	357,300 (66)	222,000 (41)	108,100 (4)	27,300 (<1)[d]

[a] Rate per 1,000 students in parentheses. Rate based on 27,380,000 students in 2001. (Note: Numbers are rounded to the nearest 100.)
[b] Violent crimes include simple assault (fighting, hitting, kicking, punching). Serious violent crimes include rape, sexual assault, robbery, and aggravated assault. Total crimes include theft, violent crimes and serious violent crimes.
[c] Other includes Asians, Pacific Islanders, and American Indians (including Alaska natives).
[d] Estimate based on fewer than 10 cases.

Source: Adapted from DeVoe et al., 2003. *Indicators of School Crime and Safety: 2003*, pp. 58, 62.

as reported by the NSSC include any death (including accidental and suicide) that occurs on school property, on the way to or from school, including on a school bus, or while attending a school-sponsored event whether on or off school property. All victims are included, regardless of age, including teachers, other school staff, and nonstudents. Most of the victims over the years have been students 10–18 years of age, but these reports of school deaths show higher numbers than other reports that include only homicides and only victims who are students or school staff members. The school-associated deaths by year and reasons for deaths for the school years 1992–2005 are summarized in Table 1–5.

News Media Reporting of School Violence

School shooting incidents resulting in deaths and serious injuries have drawn a considerable amount of news media coverage and public attention. They are newsworthy events primarily because they are relatively rare and because of the fact that they occur in schools, which are expected to be safe places. School shootings, such as the tragic incident at Columbine High School in Littleton, Colorado, receive media coverage for months and even years after the incident, and lead people to believe that such tragic incidents could happen anywhere, even at their schools. School shootings are actually rare events, and students are safer at school than in most other places in the community. Compared with the 32 school-associated deaths (24 homicide and 8 suicide) during the 1999–2000 school

Table 1–5
School-Associated Deaths by Year and Reasons for Deaths[a]

School Year	Total	Accidental	Homicide	Suicide	Unknown
1992–3	56	2	36	9	9
1993–4	53	4	21	7	21
1994–5	21		10	4	7
1995–6	36	1	16	6	13
1996–7	26	1	16	1	8
1997–8	44		26	9	9
1998–9	31	1	20	5	5
1999–2000	32	3	7	10	12
2000–01	24	2	5	6	11
2001–02	5	0	2	2	1
2002–03	22	0	8	9	5
2003–04	42	1	19	4	18
2004–05	23	1	8	3	11
Totals	413	16	194	75	130

[a] School-associated deaths includes any death that occurs on school property, on the way to or from school including on a school bus, while attending a school-sponsored event whether on or off school property. All victims are included, regardless of age. Most of the victims were 10–18 years of age, but some were older, and included teachers and other school staff, and nonstudents.

Source: Adapted from National School Safety Center, 2005.

year, there were 2,124 homicides and 1,922 suicides of youths aged 5–19. Compared with the total number of school-aged youths (ages 5–19) at school during 1999–2000, this equals only about one homicide or suicide of a school-aged youth at school per million students (DeVoe et al., 2003: 2). Lawrence and Mueller (2003) compared the number of students killed at school and away from school and found that school-associated deaths of youth represent a very small percentage (1–2 percent) of the total number of juvenile murder victims each year. They also compared the news media coverage of school shooting incidents and found that the small number of school homicides draw a greatly disproportionate amount of news coverage, particularly when the shootings occur in suburban or rural schools and the victims are white. Numerous research studies have documented how the news reporting selection process results in greater attention to what are considered more newsworthy crimes. Of a total of about 2,000 homicides each year involving youth, the stories that receive the most news coverage are the school shooting incidents in suburban and small city schools involving white, middle-class victims. Researchers have found that more television and newspaper coverage was given to white victims than to black victims (Romer et al., 1998; Weiss and Chermak, 1998) despite the fact that minority youths suffer a higher rate of violent victimization than white, middle-class youths. The concern among social scientists is that the news media coverage does not present an accurate picture of the frequency and locations of crime incidents and victimization (Surette, 1998). This is particularly important because the majority of the public receive most of their information on crime and safety from the news media. Research evidence suggests that news media emphasis on school shootings may elevate public concerns and fear concerning school violence. Data from the SCS to the NCVS indicate that a sample of students from schools throughout the United States were more fearful of being victimized in schools after the Columbine school shooting incident than before it occurred (Addington, 2003).

Table 1–6
Recommendations for Accurate Reporting of School Violence

Recommendations for news media
  Expand sources beyond law enforcement personnel to include school administrators and staff, counseling psychologists, youth advocates, and academics specializing in criminology and criminal justice.
  Use a variety of sources; provide context and background factors to news reports of school shootings and other violent incidents.
  Provide statistics and graphic presentations to inform readers as to local and regional crime and school violence trends in comparison with national data.
  Examine the selection process for covering crime stories and establish a set of criteria for reporting incidents.

Recommendations for educators and juvenile authorities
  School administrators and professionals who work with youth can build closer working relationships with journalists and be available to provide information for more complete news stories.
  Help ensure more accurate reporting by providing information to reporters, including school discipline policies, disciplinary actions taken.
  Academics and researchers in criminal justice and criminology can offer additional perspectives for news stories based on their study and research in specialized areas.
  Educators and youth advocates can become more active participants with news editors and television reporters about news coverage, both as consumers and contributors to more complete and accurate coverage.

Sources: Dorfman and Schiraldi, 2001; Lawrence and Mueller, 2003: 340–342.

School violence is a problem that must be taken seriously, and all realistic means must be implemented to provide safe schools. School safety strategies, however, must be based on accurate assessments of the true extent of threats to student safety. An important step in that direction is to provide more complete and accurate information on school crime and safety. Because the newspapers and television media are the primary sources for public information about crime and justice, more efforts should be made to give them access to the most accurate and complete information. A number of recommendations have been made to the news media, school officials, and law enforcement authorities to provide a proper balance and perspective in reporting on school violence (Dorfman and Schiraldi, 2001; Lawrence and Mueller, 2003). These recommendations are summarized in Table 1–6.

Serious school violence resulting in injuries and deaths understandably draw the most media and public attention, but bullying, threats, harassment, and fights occur far more frequently in schools throughout the United States and other countries. Many students face these types of victimization on a weekly and even daily basis. They have been referred to as "everyday school violence" by one author (Toby, 1994).

Threats and Injuries with Weapons

In the Youth Risk Behavior Survey (YRBS), students (grades 9–12) were asked whether they had been threatened or injured with a weapon on school property during the preceding 12 months. In the survey years from 1993 to 2001, 7–9 percent of students reported being threatened or injured with a weapon such as a gun, knife, or club. Males reported more victimization than females, and those in lower grades reported more victimization than those in higher grades (13 percent of 9th graders, 9 percent of 10th graders, 7 percent of 11th graders, and 5 percent of 12th graders) (DeVoe et al., 2003: 12). The percentage of students who reported carrying a weapon anywhere declined from 22 percent in 1993 to 17 percent; and those who reported carrying a weapon at school declined from 12 percent to 6 percent 2001 (DeVoe et al., 2003: 34).

Physical Fights

According to the YRBS, 33 percent of students (grades 9–12) reported being in a physical fight anywhere, and 13 percent reported being in a fight at school. This is a decline from 1993, when 42 percent reported being in a fight anywhere and 16 percent were in a fight at school. More males than females reported being in a fight. In 2001, 43 percent of males were in a fight anywhere and 18 percent on school property; 24 percent of females reported being in a fight anywhere and 7 percent on school property. More students in lower grades reported being in a fight. In 2001, 17 percent of 9th graders reporting being in a fight on school property compared with 8 percent of 12th graders reporting the same (DeVoe et al., 2003: 14).

Bullying at School

The problem of bullying is now recognized as one of the most serious victimization problems in school for a number of reasons. Despite being viewed in the past as just normal teasing and adolescent behavior, there is evidence that bullying has very serious effects on youth, both emotionally and physically. Furthermore, bullying has long-lasting consequences, affecting persons for months and years after the victimization. Educators and behavioral and social scientists in America have only recently focused their research efforts on bullying. The foremost researcher on bullying was Dan Olweus, a Norwegian researcher, who began documenting the problems of bullying in Scandinavian schools in the 1980s (see Olweus, 1979, 1994). Others (Farrington, 1993; Juvonen and Graham, 2001) have added to our knowledge and understanding of the causes, extent, and consequences of bullying in schools.

In the SCS to the NCVS, students aged 12–18 were asked if they had been bullied (picked on or made to do things they did not want to do) at school. In 2001, 8 percent of students reported that they had been bullied at school in the last 6 months, up from 5 percent in 1999 (DeVoe et al., 2003: 16). Males were more likely than females to report being bullied in 2001 (9 vs. 7 percent). Bullying varied by race and ethnicity of students. White students were more likely than black students to report being bullied (9 vs. 6 percent), and 8 percent of Hispanic students reported being bullied in school in 2001. Bullying was reported more frequently among lower- than upper-grade students. In 2001, 14 percent of 6th graders, 9 percent of 9th graders, and 2 percent of 12th graders reported that they had been bullied at school (DeVoe et al., 2003: 16).

Crimes Against Teachers

Teachers are also targets of threats, theft, and violence in schools. In the first national study of school crime, survey data from the Safe School Study estimated that 12 percent of secondary school teachers had something worth more than $1 stolen from them, about the same proportion as students (11 percent) (National Institute of Education, 1977: 3). One out of every 200 secondary school teachers (about 5,200) was physically attacked at school each month. About 1,000 (20 percent) of the attacks on teachers each month required medical treatment (compared to only 4 percent of assaults on students) (National Institute of Education, 1978: 75). Attacks on teachers occurred predominantly in urban schools, and junior high schools showed higher percentages than senior highs. Teachers were more likely to be victimized if they had large classes with more low-ability students, under-achievers, and behavior-problem students; with higher proportions of minority students; and with classes exceeding 30 pupils.

Recent data from the NCVS show that teachers continue to be targets of school violence. During the 5-year period from 1997 to 2001, teachers were the victims of about 1.3 million nonfatal crimes at school, including 817,000 thefts, 425,000 simple assaults (hitting, kicking, punching), and 48,000 serious violent crimes (sexual assault, robbery, and aggravated assault) (DeVoe et al., 2003: 28). The rate of teacher victimization was 21 simple assaults per 1,000 teachers and 2 serious violent crimes per 1,000 teachers annually. Male teachers were victimized more than female teachers (39 vs. 16 violent crimes per 1,000 teachers), and senior high and middle/junior high school teachers were victimized more than elementary school teachers (31 and 33, respectively, vs. 12 violent crimes per 1,000 teachers). Teachers in urban areas were more at risk of violent victimization than teachers in suburban or rural schools (28 vs. 13 and 16 per 1,000 teachers, respectively). Teachers in urban schools were also more likely to be victims of theft than those in rural schools (42 vs. 26 thefts per 1,000 teachers) (DeVoe et al., 2003: 28).

Teachers are also victims of verbal threats and harassment. Insults and threats against teachers are associated with increased risks of victimization, particularly in urban, junior high schools. The Safe School Study report noted that in schools with serious disorder and disruption, hostility and conflict are likely to be part of a pattern of general turbulence in which violent acts are common. Extensive personal violence in such schools is likely to be just one part of a negatively charged social environment in which many things go wrong (National Institute of Education, 1978: 71). Junior high school students show more overt hostility toward teachers than do older students. Two-thirds of secondary school teachers in large urban settings report that students swore or made obscene gestures at them in 1 month, compared with 41 percent of rural and 48 percent of suburban secondary school teachers. The study found that 90 percent of all assaulted teachers also reported having been sworn at in the previous month. These hostile encounters affect teachers' responses to student misbehavior. The teachers were asked whether they hesitated to confront misbehaving students out of fear for their own safety, and 12 percent indicated that such an incident had happened at least once or twice in the past month. A higher percentage of teachers in urban areas experienced fear and hesitated to confront students. There was no difference between junior high and senior high teachers, in spite of more verbal abuse in junior highs. It is likely that the greater age and size of senior high youth increases the fear and hesitation of teachers (National Institute of Education, 1978: 70–71).

In the more recent Schools and Staffing Survey, teachers were asked whether they had been threatened with injury by a student in the previous 12 months. Survey results showed that 9 percent of teachers were threatened with injury by a student in the 1999–2000 school year (a decrease from 12 percent in the 1993–1994 school year). Teachers in central city schools were more likely (11 percent) to be threatened with injury than teachers in urban fringe and rural schools (8 percent). Secondary school teachers were more likely to be threatened with injury than elementary school teachers (10 vs. 8 percent), and public school teachers were threatened more than private school teachers (10 vs. 4 percent) (DeVoe et al., 2003: 30).

Crimes Against School Property

Victimization against students and teachers is not the only crime problem in schools. In the 1977 Safe School Study the principals' reports focused primarily on offenses directed at the school building and property, rather than persons. The most frequent property offenses reported were trespassing, breaking and entering, theft of school property, and deliberate property destruction, or vandalism. Data indicated that in the late 1970s one in four schools was vandalized, at an average cost of $81 per incident. One in 10 schools were broken into, at an average cost of $183 per incident. Schools were about five times as likely to be burglarized as commercial establishments. Estimates of the annual cost of school crime ranged from about $50 to $600 million, with most estimates being in the $100–$200 million range (National Institute of Education, 1977: 3).

Unfortunately, no current national statistics are available on the costs of school crime. Robert Rubel, an authority on school crime and former director of the National Alliance for Safe Schools, noted that the Safe School Study was the last national research effort to collect data on the costs of school property crime. National estimates are difficult to obtain because of the many variables involved and the different measures used by school districts across the country in counting damage, glass breakage, and vandalism (Rubel, 1996). Peter Blauvelt, an expert on school security and currently Executive Director of the National Alliance for Safe Schools, has noted that individual school districts have estimates of the cost of school crime and vandalism, but no state or national figures are available. The National Center for Educational Statistics stopped collecting damage and cost measures in the early 1980s, and no state or federal legislation requires the reporting of costs of damage and theft of school property (Blauvelt, 1996). Among the states that do collect data on vandalism, there is an indication that vandalism is on the rise (Goldstein and Conoley, 1997).

A number of school districts have developed programs to reduce vandalism and arson. The most effective programs are those that have been jointly developed with local police and fire departments and that involve students, teachers, and school staff members. Vandalism and arson must be treated as serious crimes, with penalties ranging from school expulsion to police arrest and judicial action. Improved security practices can reduce the incidents of vandalism and arson. School efforts that help students develop a sense of pride and ownership in their school will help reduce property damage and theft. The tremendous cost of school property damage is an additional drain on tight school budgets. School districts should develop a school safety task force to carefully analyze the problem and develop possible solutions in collaboration with police, the fire department, parents, and community organizations (see National School Safety Center, 1990). To reduce the extent of school vandalism, increased security measures have been recommended, such as limiting access to school property through continuous monitoring by personnel or security devices (Trump, 1998).

Graffiti is a form of vandalism that defaces and devalues school property, requiring time and money to remove and restore the property. Graffiti also has a social and personal impact on students and school staff. The 1999 SCS to the NCVS asked students if they had seen any hate-related graffiti at school in the last 6 months. A total of 36 percent of students reported seeing hate-related graffiti at school. Graffiti was more common in public schools (33.8 percent) than in private schools (20.6 percent) (Addington et al., 2002: 51). In the SSOCS, school principals were asked how many incidents of vandalism occurred at their school during the 1999–2000 school year. More than half (51 percent) of the principals reported incidents of vandalism, and the number of incidents reported was 211,002 (Miller and Chandler, 2003: 67). The survey did not assess the extent of the vandalism incidents or the cost to repair the damages. The findings show evidence that vandalism continues to be a serious problem for many schools, disrupting the educational process and increasing the cost of maintaining safe schools.

Alcohol, Drugs, and Gangs in Schools

The presence of alcohol and other drugs in school are crimes that adversely affect the school environment and school safety. Substance use and possession, along with gang presence may, lead to other more serious crimes in and around schools (DeVoe et al., 2003). Students in grades 9–12 were asked in the YRBS whether they had consumed alcohol on school property. In 2001, 5 percent of students reported they had consumed at least one drink of alcohol on school property in the past 30 days. More males (6 percent) than females (4 percent) admitted drinking at school. There was no difference among students' grade levels (9–12) and their reports of drinking (DeVoe et al., 2003: 46). In 2001, 29 percent of all students in grades 9–12 reported that drugs were made available to them on school property (someone had offered, sold, or given them an illegal drug). More males (35 percent) than females (23 percent) reported the availability of drugs. Availability of drugs on school property remained about constant over the school years from 1993 to 2001 (DeVoe et al., 2003: 50). Students were also asked whether they had used marijuana at school or anywhere in the past 30 days. In 2001, about one-fourth (24 percent) of students in grades 9–12 reported having used marijuana anywhere, and 5 percent of students reported using marijuana on school property. More males (8 percent) than females (3 percent) reported using marijuana at school. The reported use of marijuana on school property has remained about the same between 1993 and 2001 (DeVoe et al., 2003: 48).

Students were asked in the SCS to the NCVS if street gangs are present in their schools. In 2001, 20 percent of students aged 12–18 reported that there were gangs at their schools. Students in urban schools were the most likely to report the presence of street gangs at school (29 percent), followed by suburban (18 percent) and rural students (13 percent) (DeVoe et al., 2003: 42). Street gangs are often involved in drugs, weapons trafficking, and violence. Their presence in school can be disruptive because they are likely to create fear among students and increase the level of violence in school (Laub and Lauritsen, 1998).

The Effects of School Crime and Violence

School crime clearly affects the intended victims, but the impact goes far beyond the immediate victims. School violence affects the entire school environment, creating fear in students and disrupting their ability to learn and focus on schoolwork. In the SCS to the NCVS, students aged 12–18 were asked how often they were afraid of being attacked at school or on the way to or from school during the previous 6 months. In 2001, 6 percent of students reported that they were fearful about their safety at school. Slightly fewer (5 percent), reported fear of being attacked away from school. More black and Hispanic students (9 and 11 percent) reported fear for their safety than white students (5 percent). Students in lower grades were more fearful than those in higher grades (for example, 11 percent of 6th graders, 6 percent of 9th graders, and 3 percent of 12th graders). The location of schools was also related to students' fear of crime. More students in urban schools (10 percent) reported fear of attack than those in suburban (5 percent) or rural (6 percent) schools (DeVoe et al., 2003: 36).

When students fear being attacked and feel unsafe at schools, many of them avoid places they perceive as being most risky. In the SCS to the NCVS, students aged 12–18 were asked whether they had avoided certain places in school, such as any hallways or stairs, parts of the cafeteria, restrooms, or locker rooms, during the previous 6 months. Five percent of students reported that they had avoided one or more places in school. The characteristics of students who avoided places in school resemble those who feared being attacked. Black and Hispanic students (7 and 6 percent) reported certain areas more than white students (4 percent). Likewise, 6th-grade students (7 percent) were more likely to avoid certain areas than 12th graders (3 percent); and students in urban areas (6 percent) avoided areas more than suburban or rural students (4 percent) (DeVoe et al., 2003: 38).

In summary, research clearly indicates that crime and violence is a problem that affects virtually all schools. The extent of the problem varies according to school size, location, and racial/ethnic background as well as the age of the students. Regardless of size and location of the schools, however, a majority of school officials report some crimes occurring every year. Some teachers report being victims of personal and property crimes, but the majority of crimes in schools involve students as victims and perpetrators. The most recent available measures of school crime and violence in the United States indicate that the problems have *not* increased significantly in the past several years. In fact, some serious incidents such as school shootings, assaults involving injuries, physical fights, and weapon possession have actually decreased slightly. An increased sensitivity to and concern about school crime and safety has resulted in more extensive and frequent measures to assess students' reported victimization by behaviors such as threats, bullying, gang presence, alcohol and drug availability, and hate-related graffiti. Survey results show that a significant percentage of students experience these problems in their schools. Continuing the practice of annual measures and reports on school safety will help to determine whether the frequency of reported victimization occurs simply because more students are sensitized to the problem, and therefore reporting more, or because the problems in fact are increasingly common in too many schools.

International Measures of School Crime and Violence

School crime is not limited to the United States. We noted earlier in this chapter that bullying was recognized as a serious problem in schools in Scandinavia, Great Britain, and Europe long before American criminologists and educators focused on it. There are difficulties however, in comparing school violence among countries for a number of reasons. Many countries do not collect national information about reported school violence, and among those that do there are differences in reporting practices. Countries also use different definitions of school violence, and the language and cultural differences make it difficult to compare even similar behaviors (Shaw, 2001; Smith et al., 1999). In addition, other countries have faced most of the same challenges as the United States when attempting to get complete and accurate measures of school crime. The sources range from small self-report school studies to area surveys of victimization to police or school reports of incidents. The sources vary among different ages of students, types of schools, and time periods; students face peer pressure to not report incidents; and schools are often reluctant to admit the presence of crime problems (Shaw, 2001: 5). In other countries, there is little agreement on what exactly constitutes school violence. Much of what is called school violence in other countries is bullying, and most of the bullying behavior is non-physical. What other countries have in common with the United States is an increase in reported incidents in schools. School officials are also reporting more incidents to police than was the case a decade ago.

Bullying is a common type of victimization in schools and has been the subject of studies in other countries for many years. Bullying is embedded in adolescent peer culture. It has been underreported, perhaps because it is considered by many to be a "normal" part of adolescent behavior. Bullying has also been overlooked and under-reported because it may include a wide variety of behaviors. A widely used definition describes bullying as an aggressive act with an imbalance of power, which may include physical acts, verbal harassment, threats, or "put-down's", and even nonverbal actions such as social exclusion (Shaw, 2001: 9). Studies on bullying have been widely reported in Norway, Britain, Spain, Australia, Germany, and Japan (Shaw, 2001: 9). Bullying is a focal point for any discussion of school violence, because it occurs in all types of schools, among all types of students, has serious and long-term effects on victims, and has links to more serious school violence, including fatal school shootings. It is for this reason that increased reports of bullying in all types of schools are now taken very seriously and more efforts and resources are being directed toward prevention programs to reduce bullying and improve school safety.

Despite some differences in defining and reporting bullying and similar forms of school violence, it is possible to measure and compare the extent of the problem in the United States and other nations. International attention on school bullying has increased in the past decade, evidenced by an international symposium on bullying held in Japan in 1996. Experts from Japan, Holland, Norway, England, and Australia exchanged research finings on the nature and prevention of school bullying (Akiba et al., 2002; see also Smith et al., 1999). The European Commission, the administrative body of the countries in the European Union, launched a Violence in Schools Initiative in 1997 in response to growing concerns about school safety. That was followed in the same year by a Safer Schools conference held in Utrecht, Holland, and in 1998 by a European Conference on Initiatives to Combat School Bullying, held in London. Following the leadership of Olweus (1993), who introduced successful antibullying projects in Norway, bullying prevention has become a major area of intervention. The European Network on the Nature and Prevention of Bullying is developing a 4-year comparative project in German, Italy, Portugal, Spain, and Britain (Shaw, 2001).

Despite the growing international concern about school violence, there is little comparative research on the levels and characteristics of the problem in different countries.

One study was done using student and teacher survey data from the Third International Math and Science Study (TIMSS). The dataset provides several indicators of types of school violence and other delinquent behaviors from 37 participating nations. The researchers found that the United States does not have high rates of school violence when compared to other nations, that rates of general crime in nations are not good predictors of school violence, and that factors inherent in the educational system are more powerful predictors of school violence (Akiba et al., 2002: 831). Compared with other nations, reported school victimization of 7th- and 8th-grade students in the United States fall below the international mean. Based on student reports, U.S. schools are about in the middle of the nations surveyed by TIMSS, and U.S. 7th- and 8th-grade students do not appear to be either more or less likely to worry about violence in schools than their peers around the world. For example, 80 percent of Hungarian students reported that their friends were the victims of school violence, and students in Canada, Australia, Korea, Israel, and New Zealand reported higher levels of school violence than U.S. students (Akiba et al., 2002: 839). Results of teachers' reports of school disruption and violence were similar as the student reports. The United States fell just above the international average on whether teachers thought their teaching was limited by disruption, but below the mean on teachers' perceived threats to their own or students' safety. Akiba and associates (2002) have made a significant contribution to our understanding of levels of school violence and factors related to the problem in schools around the world. A summary of their findings is worth noting:

•School violence is widely prevalent among the 37 nations studied.

•School violence rates are not related to general crime rates in those nations.

•School violence rates are related to some social indicators such as absolute deprivation and age distribution but not to income inequality or social integration.

•School violence rates are related to school system variables (Akiba et al., 2002: 846).

We examine further some of the factors associated with school crime and violence in a discussion of school structure and environment in Chapter 6. We will discuss various school violence prevention and school safety strategies in Chapter 12.

Summary

Crime and violence in schools are serious problems that have changed the climate and environment of schools and affect the quality of education. Many students fear being victimized in or around schools and often avoid places in the school building, or even stay away from school because of bullying and threats. Despite the fact that students and teachers are safer at school than most other places in society, schools have come to be perceived as dangerous places. A number of highly publicized school shooting incidents have helped to increase the perception of schools as dangerous, increased concerns among the public, and led to demands for policies to increase school safety. School crime is a serious problem, but it is important to place it in perspective in comparison with crimes throughout society.

Notes

1. The report includes youth who are juveniles under the statutes of each state. In most states the upper age of juvenile jurisdiction is 17, but it ranges from 15 to 18. Juvenile court statistics are compiled from the National Juvenile Court Data Archive, which is maintained by the National Center for Juvenile Justice for the Office of Juvenile Justice and Delinquency Prevention.

2. The study was completed in three phases. Phase I was a mail survey of 5,578 schools selected through a probability sample, representing a profile of all the nation's schools. School principals responded to a questionnaire on illegal or disruptive activities and prepared reports on incidents during a 1-month period. Phase II included on-site surveys of 642 junior and senior high schools. Phase III consisted of detailed, qualitative case studies of 10 schools in which problems of violence had dramatically and rapidly decreased. Survey return rates were very high. In Phase I, 97 percent (3,910) of the principals returned their questionnaires. In Phase II, 91 percent (582) of the schools returned incident reports; 23,895 teachers (76 percent) returned their questionnaires; 31,373 students (81 percent) responded to questionnaires; and 6,283 students (83 percent) responded to in-depth interviews. [See also Robert J. Rubel. 1978). "Analysis and Critique of HEW's Safe School Study Report to the Congress." *Crime & Delinquency* 24: 257–265; and Jackson Toby. 1994. "Everyday School Violence: How Disorder Fuels It." *American Educator* (Winter): 4–9, 44–48.]

3. Criticisms include poor conceptualization of "seriousness" of crimes, survey methods that have questionable validity and reliability, and reliance on cross-tabulation statistical analyses, which can analyze data only categorically and provide a weak basis for sound policy recommendations.

4. The author acknowledges the assistance of Lynn Addington (American University), Kathryn Chandler (National Center for Education Statistics), and Jill DeVoe and Mike Planty (Education Statistics Services Institute) for their advice and suggestions in writing this chapter.

5. Portions of this summary of measures of school disorder and crime are from Wayne Welsh (2001), and the author acknowledges the helpful suggestions of Professor Welsh in writing this chapter.

2

Justice for Juveniles

Juvenile justice in America has evolved and developed over more than a century through numerous differences in philosophy, legal opinions, and policies. The question of whether juvenile offenders should be tried and sentenced differently from adult offenders elicits strongly held opinions from citizens, policymakers, and professionals. The first juvenile court was established in Chicago, Illinois, in 1899, but a century later there is considerable debate over the goals and the legal procedures for dealing with juvenile offenders. The juvenile justice system was established on the principle of individualized justice and focused on rehabilitation of youthful offenders. While due process protections were considered important, they were considered secondary in importance given the court's emphasis on care, treatment, and rehabilitation for juveniles. It was believed that youths could be held responsible for their unlawful behavior and society could be protected through an informal justice system that focused on treatment and "the best interests of the child." For the majority of juvenile offenders, this approach may still be appropriate and effective. The majority of juvenile crimes range from status offenses, property offenses, and drug offenses. The juvenile justice system has come under increasing scrutiny, however, as a growing number of juveniles are involved in violent crimes, especially school violence, gang-related violence, and assaults with weapons resulting in fatalities and serious injuries. Despite the fact that juveniles are involved in a proportionately small number of murders each year, violent crime committed by juveniles elicits widespread media coverage. The public and political/legislative response to juvenile violence has been to demand more accountability and punishment, resembling that of the criminal justice system. One century after the development of the first juvenile court, the system faces a multitude of challenges and questions.

Historical Overview of Juvenile Justice

Legal codes have distinguished between adult and juvenile offenders for centuries. The Code of Hammurabi some 4,000 years ago (2270 B.C.) included reference to runaways, children who disobeyed their parents, and sons who cursed their fathers. Two thousand years ago, Roman civil law and canon (church) law distinguished between juveniles and adults based upon the idea of "age of responsibility." In early Jewish law, the *Talmud* set forth conditions under which immaturity was to be considered in imposing punishment (Cox et al., 2003). Moslem law also called for leniency in punishing youthful offenders, and children under the age of 17 were to be exempt from the death penalty (Bernard, 1992). Under fifth-century Roman law children under the age of 7 were classified as infants and not held criminally responsible. Youth approaching the age of puberty who knew the difference between right and wrong were held accountable. The legal age of puberty (age 14 for boys and 12 for girls) was the age at which youth were assumed to know the difference between right and wrong and were held criminally accountable.

Roman civil law and canon law had a major influence on Anglo-Saxon common law that dates back to the eleventh and twelfth centuries in England. This has particular significance for American juvenile justice because it has its roots in English common law. The Chancery courts in fifteenth-century England were created to consider petitions of those in need of aid or intervention, generally women and children who were in need of assistance because of abandonment, divorce, or death of a spouse. Through these courts the king could exercise the right of *parens patriae* ("parent of the country"), and the courts acted *in loco parentis* ("in place of the parents") to provide services in assistance to needy women and children. The principle of *parens patriae* later became a basis for the juvenile court in America. The doctrine gives the court the authority over juveniles in need of guidance and protection, and the state may then act *in loco parentis* (in place of the parents) to provide guidance and make decisions concerning the best interests of the child (Cox et al., 2003).

Juvenile Justice in America

Juvenile offenders have not always been processed through a separate system of justice. Following the tradition of English law, children who broke the law in Eighteenth-century America were treated much the same as adult criminals. Parents were responsible for controlling their children, parental discipline was very strict, and punishments were harsh. Youth who committed crimes were treated much the same as adult criminal offenders. The law made no distinction based on the age of the offender, and there was no legal term of "delinquent." The American judicial procedures in the nineteenth century continued to follow those of England, subjecting children to the same punishments as adult criminals. Some punishments were very severe. Youth who committed serious offenses could be subjected to prison sentences, whipping, and even the death penalty. During the nineteenth century, criminal codes applied to all persons, adults and children alike. No provisions were made to account for the age of offenders. Originally there were no separate laws or courts and no special facilities for the care of children who were in trouble with the law.

During the nineteenth century, a number of developments paved the way for a separate system of justice for juveniles. An increase in the birth rate and the influx of immigrants brought a new wave of growth to American cities. With this growth came an increase in the numbers of dependent and destitute children. Many urban youth and children of immigrants were perceived to be prone to deviant and immoral behavior. The term "juvenile delinquent" was first used in New York City in 1818, linking troubled youths to a cause of pauperism (Cox et al., 2003). In 1825 the Society for the Prevention of Juvenile Delinquency advocated for the separation of juvenile and adult offenders. Prior to this, only children under the age of 7 were held not criminally liable, and juveniles past the age of puberty (12–14 years) were treated the same as adults.

Official intervention in the lives of wayward youth was based on doctrine of *parens patriae*. Parents were expected to supervise and control their children, but when it became apparent that parents were not properly controlling and disciplining their children, the state was given the authority to take over that responsibility. The doctrine of *parens patriae* was first tested in the Pennsylvania Supreme Court case of *Ex parte Crouse* in 1838. The father of Mary Ann Crouse argued that his daughter was illegally incarcerated without a trial. The court denied his claim, stating that the Bill of Rights did not apply to juveniles. The court stated that when parents are found to be "incompetent" in their parental duties, the state has the right to intervene and provide their child with guidance and supervision. The *Crouse* ruling was based on what the court believed was the best interests of the child and the entire community, with the assumed intentions that the state could provide the proper education and training for the child. As states intervened in more juvenile cases, especially ones involving minor misbehavior, the concept of *parens patriae* would later meet more legal challenges.

The New York House of Refuge was established in 1825 to take in delinquent youths under the concept of *in loco parentis*. Other houses of refuge in Boston and Philadelphia were soon established, and these were followed shortly thereafter by reform schools for vagrant and delinquent juveniles. State reform schools opened in Massachusetts in 1847, in New York in 1853, in Ohio in 1857, and the first State Industrial School for Girls was opened in Massachusetts in 1856 (Law Enforcement Assistance Administration, 1976: 65). The early juvenile reform schools were intended for education and treatment, not for punishment, but hard work, strict regimentation, and whippings were common. Discriminatory treatment against blacks, Mexican Americans, American Indians, and poor whites remained a problem in the schools. Sexual abuse and physical attacks by peers (and sometimes staff members) was also a problem.

Institutional abuses against incarcerated juveniles came under increasing criticism by the last half of the 1800s. The practice of taking custody of troubled youths under the concept of *parens patriae* led many by the mid-1800s to question whether most youths benefited from the practice. There is evidence that the state is not in fact an effective or benevolent parent and that there is a significant disparity between the promise and the practice of *parens patriae*. A review of the *Ex parte Crouse* ruling and subsequent legal decisions revealed that judges in the nineteenth century were committing minors to reformatories for noncriminal acts on the premise that the juvenile institutions would have a beneficial effect (Pisciotta, 1982). In theory, reformatories were "schools" that provided parental discipline, education, religious instruction, and meaningful work for incarcerated youth. Examining the records, annual reports, and daily journals of superintendents, Pisciotta (1982) found a significant disparity between the theory and practice of juvenile incarceration. He noted that discipline in the juvenile reform schools was more brutal than parental, and inmate workers were exploited under an indenture or contract labor system. The schools were marked by institutional environments that had a corrupting influence on the residents, as evidenced by assaults, homosexual relations, and frequent escapes (Pisciotta, 1982).

Critics of this extensive state intervention argued against intervention of youth over minor, noncriminal behavior, and claimed that reformatories were not providing the kind of parental care, education, or training that was promised under the parens patriae doctrine. In a legal challenge in *People v. Turner*, the Illinois Supreme Court ruled that "we should not forget the rights which inhere both in parents and children. . . . The parent has the right to the care, custody, and assistance of his child" [*People v. Turner*, 55 Ill. 280 (1870)]. The court ruled that the state should intervene only after violations of criminal law and only after following due process guidelines. The ruling actually did little to change the prevailing practices in most other states, however. It would take later court decisions to clearly define the rights of children and their parents in state intervention.

The "Child-Saving" Movement

The failure of the houses of refuge and early reform schools aroused more interest in the welfare of troubled youth who were abandoned, orphaned, or forced to work under intolerable conditions. In the latter half of the nineteenth century following the Civil War period, humanitarian concerns were directed toward troubled children and their treatment. A pivotal point in the development of the juvenile justice system in America was what became known as the "child-saving movement" (see Faust and Brantingham, 1979; Law Enforcement Assistance Administration, 1976). The child-savers were a group of reformers that included philanthropists, professionals, and middle-class citizens who expressed concerns about the welfare of children. They pushed for state intervention to save at-risk children through shelter care and educational programs. The result of this child-saving movement was to extend government intervention to youth behaviors that had previously been the responsibility of parents and families. The leading advocates in the child-saving movement believed that such youth problems as idleness, drinking, vagrancy, and delinquent behaviors threatened the moral fabric of society and must be controlled. If parents could not or would not control and properly supervise their own children, then the government should intervene. They pushed for legislation that would give courts jurisdiction over children who were incorrigible, runaways, and committed crimes.

The First Juvenile Court

The reform movement in the latter part of the nineteenth century following the Civil War eventually led to the development of a separate juvenile court for juveniles. Some states, including Massachusetts in 1874 and New York in 1892, had passed laws providing for separate trials for juveniles (Cox et al., 2003). The first juvenile court was established in Cook County (Chicago), Illinois, in 1899. The *parens patriae* doctrine was the legal basis for court jurisdiction over juveniles and was central to the juvenile court philosophy, because children who violated laws were not to be treated as criminals. Because children were considered less mature and less aware of the consequences of their actions, they were not to be held legally accountable for their behavior in the same manner as adults. Under the juvenile justice philosophy, youthful offenders were designated as delinquent rather than as criminal, and the primary purpose of the juvenile justice system was not punishment but rehabilitation (see Davis, 1980; Mennell, 1972).

In replacing treatment for punishment as the stated purpose, the courts sought to turn juvenile delinquents into productive citizens. Juvenile court objectives were clearly stated in the laws that established the courts, clearly distinguishing their purpose as different from the adult penal codes. A ruling by the Pennsylvania Supreme Court in the case of *Commonwealth v. Fisher* in 1905 supported the juvenile court's purpose and illustrates how the court's role in training delinquent children superseded the rights of children and their parents.

> The design is not punishment, nor the restraint imprisonment, any more than is the wholesome restraint which a parent exercises over his child. . . . Every statute which is designed to give protection, care, and training to children, as a parental duty, is but a recognition of the duty of the state, as the legitimate guardian and protector of children where other guardianship fails. No constitutional right is violated [*Commonwealth v. Fisher*, 213 Pa. 48 (1905)].

The Pennsylvania Supreme Court therefore supported the juvenile court's treatment objectives over the rights of the juvenile or the parents. For the next 50 years juvenile courts continued the practice of legal interventions over a broad range of juvenile cases, from status offenses to criminal code violations. The focus on offenders' needs for supervision and rehabilitation more than on offenses committed had an impact on judicial procedures and decisions. Decisions of what cases would go to court was made by a juvenile court intake division, unlike criminal court, where district attorneys made the decision. Juvenile court intake considered extralegal as well as legal factors in deciding how to handle cases and had discretion to handle cases informally, diverting cases from court action (Snyder and Sickmund, 1999).

This first step in processing juvenile offenders separately from adults was the culmination of the reform efforts discussed above. Because the purpose of the juvenile court was the protection and treatment of the child and not punishment, the juvenile proceeding was more civil than criminal. Since the juvenile legal process was purportedly "in the best interests of the child," the hearing was more informal, unlike the more formal, adversarial criminal court process. It was believed that children did not need the same formal procedural legal rights as adults in criminal court; thus, children were denied many of the legal rights of adults, such as formal notice of the charges and the right to legal counsel. The juvenile reform efforts were also based on the growing optimism that application of the social sciences was more appropriate for handling juvenile offenders than the law. Delinquency was viewed more as a social problem and a breakdown of the family than a criminal problem. Thus, social workers, probation officers, and psychologists took the place of lawyers and prosecutors. They examined the background and social history of the child and the family environment to assess the child's needs and then developed a treatment plan that was intended to change delinquent juveniles. The juvenile court judge was expected to be more like a father figure than a legal jurist (Davis, 1980). The focus was on offenders and not offenses, on rehabilitation and not punishment, and this was to be accomplished through individualized justice for juvenile offenders (Snyder and Sickmund, 1999).

The juvenile court movement grew rapidly in the first half of the twentieth century and introduced what has been referred to as the "era of socialized juvenile justice" in the United States (Faust and Brantingham, 1979: 139). By 1910, 32 states had established separate courts and/or probation services for juveniles, and by 1925, all but two states had developed juvenile courts (Snyder and Sickmund, 1999). For the first half century after it was first developed, the juvenile court system went largely unchallenged in the manner in which juvenile cases were processed. Despite some differences among states and jurisdictions, there was general agreement on the goals and objectives of juvenile justice and how it should be similar to, and distinct from, the criminal justice system.

Comparison of Juvenile and Criminal Court

Distinctions between juvenile and adult offenders are based on English common law, which formed the basis for a separate juvenile justice system. At the core of this distinction is the question of what age and under what circumstances children are capable of forming *criminal intent*. More than 1,000 murders are committed by juveniles every year. Many citizens and policymakers react to what is perceived as a growing trend toward more juvenile violence with demands to punish violent juvenile offenders like adult criminals. Under law, however, two elements are necessary in order to find a person guilty of a crime. The most attention is focused on the first element, the criminal act itself. The second element, criminal intent, is equally important, although often overlooked. In weighing evidence against a suspect, a court must determine that there is sufficient evidence for both a criminal act and criminal intent, known as *mens rea*, or "guilty mind." The critical question is at what age is a child capable of understanding the differences between right and wrong and of comprehending the consequences of a criminal act before it occurs. The answer to the first question appears clear to most persons, who would argue that even very young children know that killing a person is wrong. It is less clear whether children charged with violent crimes have carefully weighed the consequences of their actions, however, or whether they have formed criminal intent comparable to that of an adult. Laws and policies that place limitations on youths' drinking, driving, marrying, and entering into other contracts illustrate our belief that they are not as prepared as adults to responsibly engage in these activities. Based on the belief that youths do not have equal capacity for careful thinking and awareness of the consequences of their behavior, young people are treated differently and allowed limited responsibility under the law for most other critical decisions while they are minors. Judicial experts generally agree that legal sanctions for criminal behavior should be consistent with laws limiting juveniles' legal rights in other areas. Distinctions between legal procedures for juveniles and adults therefore stem from the differences in juveniles' maturity, limited knowledge of the law and its consequences, limited legal responsibility, and the belief that youths should be processed separately from adults throughout the judicial system.

Legal and Procedural Distinctions: Juvenile Versus Criminal Justice

Juvenile justice grew out of the criminal justice system, so there is common ground between the two. The main features that have distinguished juvenile court proceedings from criminal court proceedings may be summarized as follows:

•*Absence of legal guilt.* Because juveniles are generally less mature and often unaware of the consequences of their actions, they are not held legally responsible for their actions to the same extent as adults. Legally, juveniles are not found guilty of crimes, but are "found to be delinquent." Juvenile status, generally being less than 18 years of age, is a defense against criminal responsibility, much like the insanity defense. Exceptions are made in cases of more mature juveniles who have committed serious offenses. The juvenile court may waive jurisdiction and transfer the case to criminal court.

•*Treatment rather than punishment.* The stated purpose of the juvenile court is treatment of the child and community protection, not punishment as for adult felony offenders in criminal court.

•*Informal, private court proceedings.* Juvenile court hearings are more informal, and in many states they are not open to the public, with usually only the child, parents, attorneys, and probation officer present. Hearings are often held in the judge's chamber. The majority of hearings are informal, noncontested, nonadversarial proceedings that take less than 10 minutes. This practice is rooted in the original child-saving philosophy that the purpose of the court was for treatment, not punishment. Proceedings for more serious juvenile offenders are now often open to the public.

•*Separateness from adult offenders.* Juvenile offenders are kept separate from adult offenders at every stage of the juvenile process, from arrest (or "taking into custody") to detention, pretrial and court proceedings, to probation supervision and institutional corrections. All juvenile records are also maintained separately from adult criminal records, including in computerized information systems.

•*Focus on a juvenile's background and social history.* A juvenile's background, the need for and amenability to treatment are considered of equal importance with the offense committed when making decisions on handling each case. This is consistent with the stated purpose of treatment rather than punishment. The assumption that court officers can assess and treat juveniles' needs is open to question. Basing the length of "treatment" on the child's needs as well as the offense has come under criticism. Children committing relatively minor crimes but with "greater needs for treatment" are often supervised for longer periods of time than more serious offenders who have been determined to be less "in need of treatment."

•*Shorter terms of supervision and incarceration.* The terms of probation supervision, confinement in a detention center, or commitment to a correctional facility are usually shorter in duration than for adult offenders—generally not much longer than one to two years, on average. In recent years many states have revised their juvenile statutes, extending jurisdiction and length of incarceration over violent juvenile offenders.

•*Distinctive terminology.* Consistent with the need to treat juveniles differently from adults because of their immaturity and limited legal accountability, different terms are used when handling juveniles at each stage of the process. Juveniles are taken into custody, not arrested; transported to a detention center, not booked into jail; a petition for delinquency is filed with the court, not a criminal indictment; the result is an adjudication of delinquency rather than conviction of a felony or misdemeanor crime.

Jurisdictions vary as to the extent of the distinctions between juvenile and criminal justice. Some of the distinctions are less visible today as states modify the juvenile laws. There has been considerable discussion recently about the possibility of merging the juvenile and criminal justice systems. An understanding of the similarities and differences, and the assumptions behind them, is important for forming opinions and making decisions on proposed changes to juvenile justice laws and procedures (see Snyder and Sickmund, 1999: 94–96).

Challenges and Changes in Juvenile Justice

By the 1960s many had begun to question the ability of the juvenile court to succeed in rehabilitating delinquent youth. Juvenile justice professionals were committed to the goals of rehabilitation, but the resources were not always available, and the treatment techniques were not equally effective for all delinquents. There was also a growing concern about the number of juveniles who were institutionalized in the name of treatment, but who received little if any education, training, or treatment services. Under the guise of treatment and decisions intended to be "in the best interests of the child," juveniles were not accorded due process rights under the constitution, nor were they provided with the benevolent treatment programs and services promised. In response to these concerns, the juvenile court has been undergoing significant changes and reforms. As confidence in the treatment model waned, due process protections were introduced.

The reform movement began with a number of U.S. Supreme Court decisions in the 1960s, in which the Court required most of the same due process protections provided for adults in criminal courts. Juveniles were provided notice of the charges, right to counsel, and protection against self-incrimination and unlawful searches. The high Court stopped short of giving juveniles the right to bail and a jury trial. Accompanying the court decisions that focused on juveniles' due process rights, federal and state legislation more clearly defined age limits for juvenile court jurisdiction and modified sanctions and dispositional alternatives for serious and violent offenders.

U.S. Supreme Court Decisions

Kent v. United States

Morris Kent, age 16, was on probation when, in 1961, he was charged with rape and robbery. He confessed to the offense, and his attorney filed a motion requesting a hearing on the issue of jurisdiction, because he assumed that the District of Columbia juvenile court would consider waiving jurisdiction to criminal court. The judge did not rule on the motion for a hearing, but waived jurisdiction after making a "full investigation," without describing the investigation or the grounds for the waiver. Kent was found guilty in criminal court and sentenced to 30–90 years in prison. Appeals by Kent's attorney were rejected by the appellate courts. The U.S. Supreme Court ruled that the waiver without a hearing was invalid, and that Kent's attorney should have had access to all records involved in the waiver, along with a written statement of the reasons for the waiver. *Kent* is significant because it was the first Supreme Court case to modify the long-standing belief that juveniles did not require the same due process protections as adults because treatment and not punishment was the intent of the juvenile court. The majority statement of the justices noted that juveniles may receive the "worse of both worlds"—"neither the protection accorded to adults nor the solicitous care and regenerative treatment postulated for children" [383 U.S. 541, 86 S.Ct. 1045 (1966)].

In re Gault

Gerald Gault, age 15, was on probation for a minor property offense when he and a friend made what was described as obscene comments in a telephone call to a neighbor woman. Gerald was picked up by police and held in a detention facility until his parents were notified the next day. Gerald was not represented by counsel at his court hearing. The victim was not present, and no evidence was presented regarding the charge, but Gerald was adjudicated delinquent and committed to a training school. (The maximum sentence for an adult making an obscene phone call would have been a $50 fine or 2 months in jail.) An attorney obtained later by the Gault's filed a writ of habeas corpus that was rejected by the Arizona Supreme Court and the appellate court, but was eventually heard by the U.S. Supreme Court. The Court found that Gerald's constitutional due process rights had been violated and ruled that in hearings that could result in commitment to an institution, juveniles have the right to notice and counsel, to question witnesses, and to protection against self-incrimination [387 U.S. 1, S.Ct. 1428 (1967)].

In re Winship

Samuel Winship, age 12, was accused of stealing money from a woman's purse in a store. A store employee stated that Samuel was seen running from the store just before the money was reported missing, but others in the store disputed that account, noting that the employee was not in a position to see the money actually being taken. At the juvenile court hearing, the judge agreed with Winship's attorney that there was some "reasonable doubt" of Samuel's guilt, but New York juvenile courts (like those in most states) operated under the civil law standard of "preponderance of evidence." Winship was adjudicated delinquent and committed to a New York training school. Winship's attorney appealed the case on the issue of the standard of evidence required in juvenile court. The Supreme Court ruled that the standard of evidence for adjudication of delinquency should be "proof beyond reasonable doubt" [387 U.S. 358, 90 S.Ct. 1068 (1970)].

McKiever v. Pennsylvania

Joseph McKeiver, age 16, was charged with robbery and larceny when he and a large group of other juveniles took 25 cents from three youths. At the hearing, the judge denied his attorney's request for a jury trial, and McKiever was adjudicated and placed on probation. McKiever's attorney appealed the case to the state supreme court, which affirmed the lower court. The case was then appealed to the U.S. Supreme Court, which upheld the lower court rulings. The Court argued that juries would not enhance the accuracy of the adjudication process and could adversely affect the informal atmosphere of the nonadversarial juvenile court hearing process [403 U.S. 528, 91 S.Ct. 1976 (1971)].

Breed v. Jones

Gary Jones, age 17, was charged with armed robbery and appeared in Los Angeles juvenile court, where he was adjudicated delinquent. At the disposition hearing, the judge waived jurisdiction and transferred the case to criminal court. Jones's attorney then filed a writ of habeas corpus, arguing that the waiver to criminal court after adjudication in juvenile court violated the double jeopardy clause of the Fifth Amendment. The court denied the petition on the basis that juvenile adjudication is not a "trial." The case was appealed to the U.S. Supreme Court, where the Justices ruled that adjudication is equivalent to a trial, because a juvenile is found to have violated a criminal statute. Jones's double jeopardy rights had therefore been violated, and the Court ruled that double jeopardy applies at the adjudication hearing as soon as any evidence is presented. A juvenile court waiver hearing must therefore take place before or in place of an adjudication hearing [421 U.S. 519, 95 S.Ct. 1779 (1975)].

Schall v. Martin

Gregory Martin, age 14, was arrested and charged with robbery, assault, and possession of a weapon. He and two other youths reportedly hit a boy on the head with a loaded gun and stole his jacket and shoes. Martin was detained pending adjudication because the court officials believed he posed a serious risk and might commit another crime if he was not detained. Martin's attorney challenged the fairness of preventive detention of a juvenile, and the lower appellate court agreed and reversed the juvenile court's detention order on the basis that it amounts to punishment before an adjudication hearing. The U.S. Supreme Court upheld the constitutionality of preventive detention of juveniles, stating that it serves a legitimate juvenile court objective to protect both the juvenile and society and is not intended to punish the juvenile. The Court noted that preventive detention decisions should be supported by a statement of the facts and reasons for detention and a probable cause hearing [467 U.S. 253, 104 S.Ct. 2403 (1984)].

Federal and State Legislative Changes

The President's Commission on Law Enforcement and Administration of Justice (1967) recommended narrowing the range of offenses going before the juvenile court, and groups such as the American Bar Association–Institute of Judicial Administration (1982) called for an end to adjudicating and incarcerating status offenders in juvenile institutions. The U.S. Congress in the Juvenile Delinquency Prevention and Control Act of 1968 recommended that children charged with noncriminal or status offenses be removed from formal adjudication and commitment to detention centers and juvenile institutions. Juvenile lockups and training schools housed many youths whose only "crime" was disobeying their parents, running away, or school truancy. Advocates of such practices argued that involvement in status offenses was the first step toward more serious delinquency and early intervention might prevent serious delinquency. Opponents noted the unfairness of punishing youths for minor deviant behavior and voiced concerns about the adverse effects on status offenders being housed with older, hard-core juvenile offenders. Congress passed the Juvenile Justice and Delinquency Prevention Act of 1974, which required as a condition for receiving formula grants the deinstitutionalization of status offenders and nonoffenders as well as the separation of juvenile delinquents from adult offenders. In the 1980 amendments to the 1974 Act, Congress added a requirement that juveniles be removed from adult jail and detention facilities. The reforms that began in the 1960s continued into the 1970s, as community-based programs, diversion, and deinstitutionalization became the highlights of juvenile justice policy changes (Snyder and Sickmund, 1999). The major provisions of the Juvenile Justice and Delinquency Prevention Act are summarized in Table 2–1.

The Cycle of Juvenile Justice

Juvenile justice has undergone numerous statutory and procedural changes in the past 40 years. The system has evolved from a time when juveniles older than 7 years were held accountable for crimes and punished much the same as adult criminals, to a focus on rehabilitation and treatment, to changes in the juvenile system that blurred the lines

Table 2–1
Major Provisions of the Juvenile Justice and Delinquency Prevention Act

Year	Major Requirements of the Juvenile Justice and Delinquency Prevention Act
1974	The "deinstitutionalization of status offenders and nonoffenders" requirement specifies that juveniles not charged with acts that would be crimes for adults "shall not be placed in secure detention facilities or secure correctional facilities."
1974	The "sight and sound separation" requirement specifies that, "juveniles alleged to be or found to be delinquent and [status offenders and nonoffenders] shall not be detained or confined in any institution in which they have contact with adult persons incarcerated because they have been convicted of a crime or are awaiting trial on criminal charges." This means that juvenile and adult inmates cannot see each other and no conversation between them is possible.
1980	The "jail and lockup removal" requirement states that juveniles shall not be detained or confined in adult jails or lockups. Exceptions: juveniles being tried as a criminal for a felony or who have been convicted as a criminal felon; 6-hour grace period to temporarily hold juveniles until other arrangements can be made; jails in rural areas may hold delinquents up to 24 hours.
1992	The "disproportionate confinement of minority youth" requirement specifies that states determine the existence and extent of the problem in their state and demonstrate efforts to reduce it where it exists.
1996	Regulations modify the Act's requirements: (1) in nonresidential areas in jails, brief, accidental contact is not a reportable violation; (2) permit time-phased use of nonresidential areas for both juveniles and adults in collocated facilities; (3) expand the 6-hour grace period to include 6 hours both before and after court appearances; (4) allow adjudicated delinquents to be transferred to adult institutions once they have reached the state's age of full criminal responsibility, if such transfer is expressly authorized by state law.

Source: Adapted from Snyder and Sickmund, 1999: 88

of distinction between how we handle juvenile and adult offenders. Despite what appear to be significant changes in how we view juvenile delinquents, Bernard (1992) noted that there are *five beliefs or assumptions* about juvenile delinquency and juvenile justice that have stayed the same for at least 200 years:

1. Juveniles, especially young males, commit more crime than other groups.
2. There are special laws that only juveniles are required to obey.
3. Juveniles are punished less severely than adults who commit the same offenses.
4. Many people believe that juveniles today commit more frequent and serious crime than juveniles in the past—that is, there is a "juvenile crime wave" at the present time.
5. Many people blame juvenile justice policies for the supposed "juvenile crime wave," arguing that they are too lenient (serious offenders laugh at "kiddie court") or that they are too harsh (minor offenders are embittered and channeled into a life of crime) (Bernard 1992: 21).

These beliefs or assumptions about juvenile delinquency and juvenile justice have been strongly espoused for many years and are factors that led to changes in juvenile justice laws and policies in the past several decades. Bernard was making two points in referring to the "cycle of juvenile justice." First, these are "beliefs" and "assumptions" because they are not necessarily based on research data or scientific evidence on the extent of delinquency or the most effective policies for delinquency prevention. Second, because the beliefs and assumptions have been expressed for more than a century, they are part of a cycle.

Juvenile offenders have always been treated more leniently than adults who commit the same offenses. Some juveniles who commit minor offenses and receive lenient treatment go on to commit other, more serious crimes. Many people believe that these crimes would not have occurred if the juvenile had been punished more severely for the previous offenses. They argue that juveniles simply laugh at a justice system that is lenient and are not deterred from committing more crimes. Justice officials then respond to these views and "toughen up" the response to juvenile crime. Because fewer "lenient" responses are then available, some minor offenders receive harsh punishments, and others are released because some officials believe the harsher punishments are ineffective and may promote rather than deter juvenile crime. Despite the "get tough" policies, juveniles continue to commit a disproportionate amount of crime and juvenile crime rates remain high. Many people believe that the current "juvenile crime wave" is a recent problem, is worse than years ago, and that it can be solved through better juvenile justice policies. We noted in Chapter 1 that most juvenile crime has remained fairly stable over the years and that juvenile involvement in violent crime has *not* increased every year, but in fact has seen some dramatic decreases from previous years. People who are not aware of the long-term trends in juvenile crime continue to believe that better justice policies can reduce juvenile crime. The cycle of juvenile justice cannot be broken by implementing another new policy, because people remain convinced that juvenile crime is too high and is getting worse, despite the changed policies (Bernard, 1992). The juvenile justice system is limited in the extent to which laws and official interventions can prevent delinquency. In subsequent chapters we will address the multiple factors that contribute to delinquency and examine the role of schools and other social institutions in delinquency prevention.

Current Juvenile Justice Trends and Reforms

Following the federal statutory guidelines and the U.S. Supreme Court decisions of the 1960s and 1970s, the pendulum began to swing toward law and order in the 1980s. In response to public perceptions that serious juvenile crime was increasing and that the system was too lenient with offenders, many state legislators responded by passing more punitive laws. Some laws removed juvenile offenders charged with violent crimes from the juvenile system; other laws required the juvenile justice system to be more like the criminal justice system and to treat more serious juvenile offenders as criminals but in the juvenile court. The result is to exclude offenders charged with certain offenses from juvenile court jurisdiction or to face mandatory or automatic waiver to criminal court. In some states, concurrent jurisdiction provisions give prosecutors the discretion to file certain juvenile cases directly in criminal court rather than in juvenile court (Snyder and Sickmund, 1999).

The trend continued through the 1990s as state legislatures continued to pass more punitive laws in an effort to deal more harshly with juvenile crime. Five areas of change have emerged as states passed laws to crack down on juvenile crime. Most of the statutory changes involved expanding eligibility for criminal court processing, sentencing juvenile offenders to adult correctional supervision, and reducing confidentiality protections that have been customary for juvenile offenders. Between 1992 and 1997, all but three states changed laws in one or more of the following areas:

•Transfer provisions—Laws in 45 states made it easier to transfer juvenile offenders from the juvenile to the criminal justice system.

•Sentencing authority—Laws in 31 states gave criminal and juvenile courts expanded sentencing options.

•Confidentiality—Laws in 47 states modified or removed traditional juvenile court confidentiality provisions by making records and proceedings more open.

•Victims' rights—Laws in 22 states increased the role of victims of juvenile crime in the juvenile justice process.

•Correctional programming—As a result of new transfer and sentencing laws, adult and juvenile correctional administrators developed new programs (Snyder and Sickmund, 1999: 89).

The changes in juvenile justice laws reflect the belief that leniency in juvenile court processing accounted for what many perceived to be dramatic increases in juvenile crime. The tougher laws are based on the assumption that juveniles who commit "adult-like" crimes are equally culpable as adult offenders, that is, juveniles who commit crimes that are treated more seriously in criminal court when committed by adults should be processed more like adult offenders. The tougher laws were also intended to send the message to serious or chronic juvenile offenders that they will be held more accountable.

Juvenile justice experts have differing opinions on the results and consequences of the statutory changes in juvenile justice. Research evidence is mixed as to whether tougher laws are likely to have much effect on reducing juvenile crime. The laws have clearly resulted in more juvenile offenders being waived to criminal court prosecution and sentencing, and more juvenile offenders serving time in adult correctional facilities. What is not clear is whether the tough laws have any significant deterrent effect on juvenile offenders. We will discuss more of the changes and reforms in the juvenile court and changes in correctional processing in later chapters.

As long as society relies solely on tougher laws and their enforcement to respond to juvenile crime, we are unlikely to see any changes in the current trends of increasing numbers of young people committing crimes. Legal institutions will continue to respond to the juvenile crime problem, but social institutions such as the family, schools, and community agencies are essential for helping prevent the problem before it occurs. In the following chapters we examine the causes of juvenile delinquency and how those causes relate to problems in the family, among peers, and in schools.

Summary

The juvenile justice system has had a relatively brief history in the United States but has experienced dramatic growth and development in the past 100 years. From its origins in English common law, through the "child-saving" movement, to the U.S. Supreme Court cases that called into question many of the original legal procedures of the juvenile court, the juvenile justice system continues to meet challenges. One current issue is whether the juvenile court should be retained as a separate court for juvenile offenders, or whether young offenders might receive a better quality of justice with due process safeguards that are more common in adult criminal courts. Other current trends are to treat juvenile offenders more harshly, and to subject serious juvenile offenders to adult prison sentences— even death sentences. We will continue to examine these issues and trends throughout the book.

3

Explaining Delinquency
and School Crime

Most persons have opinions about what causes crime and delinquency. Those include poverty, unemployment, family problems and a loss of traditional family values, rational choices by "bad" persons, or laws and punishments that are not tough enough. Social scientists have sought for years to better understand and explain the complex origins and etiology of crime and delinquency. Explanations have ranged variously from those that focus on the individual to those that place the origins of crime in society. In the process of attempting to explain crime, social scientists have come up with a number of theories—ideas and observations that help to explain facts. Theories are constantly being developed, tested, and revised based on research studies that may either support or question their accuracy. The best theories are ones that are (1) clear and simple, (2) testable, (3) based on observations and research data, and (4) logically consistent.

The number and complexity of theories explaining crime and delinquency can be overwhelming, as criminologists seem to be competing with each other for the most correct and comprehensive theoretical perspective. In reality, however, the diversity of theories attempting to explain crime and delinquency attests to the complexity of the problem and its variation among subcultures and social classes and across gender, ethnic, and racial lines. No single theory can adequately explain all the reasons behind deviant behavior and delinquency of youth, but the predominant theories, considered together, are able to explain most delinquent behavior. Several criminologists have developed integrated theories of crime, which combine the best features of several theories.

Why Study Theories of Crime and Delinquency?

Crime is a problem that affects society and the quality of life of every citizen. Even persons who are not actual victims of crime have a fear of being victimized, and this affects our everyday behavior. Crime costs local, state, and federal governments billions of dollars. A problem of this magnitude demands our utmost attempts to understand its origins and causes. Social scientists have spent years studying the varieties of criminal behavior and the factors that seem to underlie the problem. The study of crime theories is not simply an academic or intellectual exercise. Understanding the causes of crime is essential in order to make rational, informed responses to the problem of crime. All policies, laws, and crime-prevention programs are based on some beliefs about what causes the problem. Those who argue in favor of passing tougher laws to combat crime assume that offenders are acting rationally and may be deterred by tougher laws and harsh punishment. On the other hand, those who argue for more rehabilitation and treatment programs assume that some underlying psychological problems, or alcohol or other drug abuse have impaired offenders' judgment or caused them to commit crime. Both of these explanations and responses are correct and appropriate for some offenders in given circumstances and cases. To assume, however, that one crime-prevention strategy will work effectively for all offenders under all circumstances is naive and doomed to fail. Thus, like any problem facing society, it is incumbent upon us to attempt to understand the origins and causes of crime in order to make policy decisions that are more realistically in line with the true nature of the problem. Of course, no single explanation can account for the variety of delinquent behaviors of youth, and in fact most of the major explanations of delinquency do offer accurate descriptions for why youths become involved in delinquency under different circumstances. Just as there are a variety of causes, therefore, policymakers must also take a variety of approaches to deal with the problem.

Types of Crime Theories

Explanations of crime and delinquency fall into one of two broad categories: rational theories and positivist theories.[1] According to *rational theories of crime*, persons commit crime simply because they made a voluntary, rational decision to do so. The theory originated as the "classical school of criminology" in eighteenth-century Europe and England with Cesare Beccaria and Jeremy Bentham. Their primary concern was not so much to explain criminal behavior, but to develop a legal system by which the punishment would fit the crime. It was assumed that since crime was a rational choice, criminal offenders could be deterred by punishment. Punishment was justified because of its practical usefulness in preventing crime. Classical theory has thus been referred to as a utilitarian approach to crime. Rational explanations of crime currently receive wide support among those who believe that crime occurs when an offender decides that the probable gain from illegal behavior outweighs the possible costs of getting caught, convicted, and punished.

Rational choice theory has become one of the most popular theoretical approaches in criminology, economics of crime, political science, and law (see, e.g., Cornish and Clarke, 1986; Akers, 1990). This explanation assumes that crime results from a rational process in which offenders make decisions and choices, often planning their criminal activity so as to maximize the benefits and avoid the risks (see Cornish and Clarke, 1986: 1–2). Lawrence Cohen and Marcus Felson (1979) developed a version of rational theory called "routine activity theory" to explain trends and cycles in the crime rate since the 1960s. They concluded that crime is closely related to the interaction of three variables associated with the "routine activities" of everyday life: the availability of suitable targets of crime, the absence of capable guardians, and the presence of motivated offenders. Thus, as more homes are unoccupied while their inhabitants are at work (and fewer neighbors, family members, or relatives are looking after them), they are more likely to be targeted by unemployed teens or young adults. The routine activity approach links delinquency to social changes that increase the opportunities for crime and emphasizes the role that the victim's lifestyle and behavior have in the crime process. Felson (1994) described how social changes in large and small cities and large versus small schools have increased the likelihood of crime occurring.

Critics of rational choice theory question the degree to which criminal behavior is always a rational, free-will process. Ronald Akers (1990) questioned whether offenders really make rational decisions to commit crime based on knowledge of the law and possible punishments and whether their decision was made in the absence of any situational factors that tend to influence crime. Rational choice proponents do not always hold to a strict definition of rationality, but acknowledge that situational factors do affect individuals' choices, and there are efforts to integrate rational choice theory with other explanations (see, e.g., Felson, 1986; Hirschi, 1986). Certainly many crimes reflect rational choices of persons, and this holds true especially for so-called white-collar crimes often committed in workplace situations that pose relatively little risk of detection, conviction, or punishment. Much juvenile crime reflects rational choice, especially when youths perceive that their chances of being caught are low; many are well aware that the punishment for juvenile crime is often much less than for comparable crimes committed by adults.

Rational Theories and Punishment

We noted at the beginning of this chapter that all legal and social responses to crime are based on some assumptions about the causes. The logical response to crime as rational behavior is tougher punishment as a deterrent. Deterrence theory holds that punishment has a *general* effect, discouraging the general public from engaging in criminal activity by striking fear in them by the threat of punishment. *Specific deterrence* discourages offenders from repeating their crimes by threatening to punish them more harshly the next time. Punishment, and the threat of punishment, are effective as deterrents against crime: most persons (including offenders), after all, do obey most of the laws most of the time. The effectiveness of punishment as a deterrent to crime, however, depends on three factors: certainty, speed, and severity. Offenders will only be deterred from crime if they believe they are likely to be caught, convicted, and punished. Furthermore, punishment is more effective if it is administered soon after the violation and if it is sufficiently severe. The last requirement, severity, is the one that lawmakers rely on the most and is relatively easier to achieve than the first two. It is more difficult to increase the certainty of police arrest and court conviction, however. That would require additional funding for hiring more police to increase the certainty of arrest and more judges and attorneys to process more cases through the courts. Tougher laws are only effective when they are accompanied by a higher probability of quick and certain enforcement. This is a difficult task, and one that generates heated debate throughout the political process at all levels of government and among citizens. Many persons attribute students' disrespect and disruption in schools to teachers' and principals' limited ability to punish students. Lack of support from superintendents, school boards, and parents often limits the ability of teachers to maintain discipline in their classrooms.

Positivist theories form the second category of delinquency explanations. These theorists hold that behavior is determined, or caused, by factors over which individuals have little or no control. Positivist explanations originated with the nineteenth-century criminologist Cesare Lombroso, who was the first person credited with using the scientific method to study crime. Lombroso was an Italian physician who noted what he believed to be distinguishing physical characteristics of criminals in prison. Lombroso documented his findings in *The Criminal Man* in 1876, in which he described certain characteristics— or "stigmata"—such as an irregularly shaped head and face, a large jaw, protruding ears, and receding chin. He linked such stigmata to "atavism," a lower stage of biological development, and believed these to be related to criminal tendencies. Lombroso's original findings have since been largely discounted, but the influence of his early work provided the incentive for subsequent criminologists to apply the scientific method to studying criminals.

Positivist theorists have developed explanations of delinquency based on individual factors, such as heredity, intelligence, and psychological characteristics; on social structures within society and social processes within groups of persons; and on political and economic structures of society. Proponents of positivist theories argue that much criminal behavior is not the result of rational choice, but stems from a variety of individual and social factors that influence delinquent behavior. Because crime according to these theorists is not a rational choice but instead results from conditions over which individuals have little or no control, they are critical of overreliance on punishment for deterring crime. Focusing laws and policies primarily on legal sanctions and punishment as the single best answer to crime reduction assumes that most illegal activity is a rational choice. Positivists question that assumption and the tendency of lawmakers to focus on legal sanctions and harsher punishment as the primary response to crime. They believe that individual and social factors that cause crime must be addressed, and many of them have been instrumental in pushing for educational and social programs as alternative means of crime prevention.

Individual Explanations for Delinquency

Following the initial work of Lombroso, others have posited biological causes of crime. In the 1930s, Earnest Hooton, an American anthropologist, compared physical measurements of 10,000 male prisoners with those of noncriminals and discovered some distinctive differences. The physical differences, such as ear shapes, eye colors, or hair distributions, had no clear connection to crime other than a statistical correlation, however. In the 1940s, William Sheldon (1949), a physician, developed a system for classifying human physique types (endomorphy, mesomorphy, and ectomorphy) and found that these have some correlation with personality and temperament. Mesomorphs tend to be characterized by high activity levels, restlessness, and aggressiveness and tend to seek adventure and danger. Sheldon reported that male and female offenders tended to be mesomorphs.

Genetic influences on delinquency have been examined through studies of twins and adopted children. Glenn Walters (1992) analyzed 38 family, twin, and adoption studies on the gene–crime relationship and found that only the older, poorly designed studies claim to show a relationship. The newer (1975–1989) better-designed studies provide less support for the gene–crime hypothesis. Rather than viewing criminal behavior as a product of nature *or* nurture, it seems preferable to examine the relative contributions of genetic and environmental concerns (Walters, 1992: 608). David Rowe and D. Wayne Osgood (1984) view genetic factors as contributing to certain individual differences, which in turn interact with specific sociological and environmental conditions that influence delinquent behavior.

Individual explanations of delinquency and school crime have been focused primarily on the subjects of intelligence, learning problems, psychological characteristics, and biochemical factors.

Intelligence and Delinquency

The relationship between IQ and delinquency received much attention in the early part of this century. Henry Goddard (1920) found that some juveniles in training schools were what he called "feebleminded," and he created much debate when he concluded that half of all juvenile delinquents were mentally defective. Relatively few studies were published on the topic again until the 1960s and 1970s. D. J. West and D. P. Farrington (1973) conducted a longitudinal study of 411 English boys and found that those who later became criminals had lower IQ scores than those who did not become criminals, leading them to conclude that intelligence is a predictive factor of future delinquency. Lis Kirkegaard-Sorensen and Sarnoff Mednick (1977) conducted a similar longitudinal study of 311 Danish children. Results on intelligence tests supported the West and Farrington study: adolescents who later committed criminal acts had a significantly lower tested intelligence than their more law-abiding peers (1977: 271). Travis Hirschi and Michael Hindelang (1977) examined several research studies, including Hirschi's data from his California study, Wolfgang and associates' data from the Philadelphia studies, and Weis's data from studies in Washington. They concluded that IQ is more important than race or social class for predicting delinquency. The findings of these studies were supported by analyses of data on Danish students, which demonstrated that low IQ is related to delinquent involvement independently of the effects of socioeconomic status (Moffitt et al., 1981: 155). The authors suggest that the IQ–delinquency relationship is likely explained in part by the lower verbal ability of children with low IQ, who experience frustration and failure in school. The frustrating school experiences may contribute to delinquency by creating a negative attitude toward authority, by leading the failing student to seek rewards in less socially desirable settings, or by making the student more vulnerable to during a period in which peers provide a source of self-esteem (Moffitt et al., 1981: 155). Wilson and Herrnstein (1985) believe there is clear evidence for an association between intelligence and crime. A student who is struggling academically in the classroom may feel justified in engaging in theft, violence, and other illegal behavior outside of school. School failure increases students' feelings of unfairness and in turn increases their chances of delinquent involvement. Failure in school also predicts a likelihood of failure in the workplace. Young people who fail in school find it hard to get jobs and are more likely to yield to the tempting rewards of criminal behavior.

Others have questioned the IQ–delinquency relationship. Rosenbaum (1976) argued that the practice of curriculum tracking may depress IQ of students placed in the lower tracks, and Simons (1978) suggested that IQ can change in response to environmental factors and is therefore unstable over time. Scott Menard and Barbara Morse (1984) believe that school practices of tracking that tend to generate failure may affect IQ itself and confound the relationship between IQ and academic performance. They concluded from an analysis of longitudinal data of San Diego high school students that the correlation of IQ with delinquency is not because IQ has a causal effect on delinquent behavior. Rather, it is one of many individual characteristics that schools tend to select for differential treatment among students.

Proponents of the IQ–delinquency hypothesis nevertheless insist that there is ample evidence to support a statistically significant relationship. Robert Gordon (1987) compared delinquency prevalence rates and concluded that the higher arrest rates and court appearance rates of minority males are best explained by differences in IQ—not by geographical location, city size, or socioeconomic status. Gordon concludes that because there are differences in IQ between black and white students before they enter school and the differences remain throughout schooling, we should seriously consider race differences in IQ when confronting the crime problem (Gordon, 1987: 91–92). Wilson and Herrnstein (1985) suggest that intelligence makes a difference in the types of crimes committed by offenders, in that more intelligent offenders tend to commit crimes having a lower risk of arrest and prosecution and that involve preparation and planning. Less intelligent offenders, on the other hand, are more likely to commit crimes with an immediate payoff or gratification—generally crimes of violence that are acted on impulsively (1985: 166–167).

Empirical evidence from research studies does indicate that there is a relationship between intelligence and types of crimes committed by delinquents. Anthony Walsh (1987) analyzed IQ and offense data from the files of male delinquents and concluded that those with lower IQs commit impulsive and spontaneous crimes which offer instant gratification, while more intelligent offenders are more "future-oriented" as they tend to commit crimes that require planning and offer deferred gratification, but also lead to more valuable pay-offs (1987: 288–289). Longitudinal research provides additional evidence of a relationship between early intelligence scores and later involvement in delinquent behavior. Paul Lipsitt, Stephen Buka, and Lewis Lipsitt (1990) analyzed data of 3,164 children involved in the Brown University cohort of the National Collaborative Perinatal Project. Children who scored lower on IQ tests at ages 4 and 7 had a significantly higher risk of later delinquent involvement. Their findings suggest that children with lower IQs who are identified as disruptive and behavior problems at an early age may be helped to avoid further delinquent behavior in adolescence if they receive early intervention from school counselors and family therapists (see Gordon, 1990: 207).

Learning Disabilities and Delinquency

Juvenile justice practitioners have noticed that delinquent youth seem unable to learn effectively in normal classroom settings. The idea that learning disabilities may be a cause of delinquency originally stemmed from anecdotal evidence of persons who worked with delinquent populations. Learning disabilities refer not to lower intelligence, but to difficulties in the use of spoken or written language and the ability to focus and attend to verbal tasks. According to the National Advisory Committee on Handicapped Children in 1975, children with special learning disabilities have a disorder in the psychological process involved in understanding or using spoken or written languages. The disability may involve a problem of listening, thinking, talking, reading, writing, spelling, or arithmetic. Conditions may include brain injury, minimal brain dysfunction, dyslexia, or aphasia (Podboy and Mallory, 1978). Learning disabilities do *not* include visual or hearing handicaps, mental retardation, or emotional disturbance. Research has established a link between low academic achievement and delinquency (see Maguin and Loeber, 1996), but that is not the same as a delinquency–learning disability connection, which has come under question because of methodological concerns.

Many researchers claim to have evidence supporting a relationship between learning disabilities and juvenile delinquency. Several explanations have been offered for the apparent link between learning disabilities and delinquency (Post, 1981; Malmgren et al., 1999). One is the *susceptibility rationale*, which suggests that because of to neurological and intellectual impairment along with impulsiveness and hyperactivity, learning-disabled (LD) children are less receptive to social cues and may not learn from experience as well as other youth. Their learning disability leads to uncontrollable antisocial behavior, and they develop negative self-images as they are then grouped with children who perceive delinquent behavior as part of their expected roles. The second is the *school failure* explanation, which posits that youths with learning disabilities experience academic failure and may be labeled by teachers and other students as school failures. In spite of how hard they may try, LD children are faced with failure each day in the school setting. The daily experience of failure and frustration leads such children to withdraw and not participate in class work. They may attempt to gain recognition by acting out in the classroom. The LD child is labeled as a problem, which results in a negative self-image and is reinforced by both adults and peers. These youths are then more likely to be truant, drop out of school, and thereby increase their interaction with other dropouts and delinquent peers and involvement in delinquency.

A third explanation is the *differential treatment* hypothesis. Studies show that a higher proportion of LD children are arrested and incarcerated. It is estimated that about 10 percent of children in the general population have learning disorders, and estimates of learning disabilities among adjudicated delinquents range from 26 to 73 percent (Zimmerman et al., 1981). Some have suggested that such disproportionate representation is additional support for the relationship between learning disabilities and delinquency. Others suggest, however, that youths with learning disabilities engage in no more serious or frequent delinquency than other youth, but are more likely to be arrested and adjudicated (Malmgren et al., 1999).

John Podboy and William Mallory analyzed intelligence test and aptitude test scores of 250 juveniles in a detention facility in California and found that 12.9 percent were developmentally disabled and 48.9 percent were learning disabled (1978: 31). The juveniles with learning disabilities tended to come from larger families, had poorer school performance, poorer English grades, and were likely to have been in a remedial reading class. Their findings led them to conclude that approximately 13 percent of those who enter the juvenile justice system may be below average in IQ, and close to 50 percent of the juvenile delinquent population may be LD (1978: 33). One type of learning disability is attention deficit and hyperactivity disorder (ADHD). David Offord and associates (1979) compared 31 delinquent children who were also hyperactive with 35 delinquents who were not hyperactive. The hyperactive delinquents had more antisocial symptoms with earlier onset, and they were characterized as being more reckless and irresponsible and more involved in fighting and drug abuse than the nonhyperactive delinquents. The two groups did not differ in socioeconomic status, IQ, or school performance prior to the onset of antisocial behavior.

Terrie Moffitt (1990) analyzed longitudinal data of a birth cohort of 435 boys, comparing self-reported delinquency scores and assessments for attention deficit disorder (ADD).

She found that delinquents with ADD began life with significant motor skills deficits and more family adversity; they had difficulty meeting the demands of school, experienced reading failure soon after entering school, and fell further behind their peers in reading as they approached high school. The antisocial behavior of the ADD boys was more persistent than non-ADD boys and became significantly worse over the years. The link between ADD and delinquency appears to be highlighted by the finding that the greatest increase in antisocial behavior of the ADD boys coincided with their entry into school and identified reading failure (Moffitt, 1990). Britt Klinteberg, David Magnusson, and Daisy Schalling (1989) analyzed longitudinal data including scores on personality and impulsiveness scales for subjects in their teens and again at age 26–27 years and found that early indications of hyperactive behavior was an important predictor of adult impulsivity. They suggested that boys who were hyperactive at an early age are at high risk for delinquency at a young adult age.

Studies that show a link between delinquency and learning disabilities have also been criticized for methodological weaknesses, however. Robert Pasternack and Reid Lyon (1982) found no support for the contention that the majority of juvenile delinquents exhibit learning disabilities. They found no significant difference between prevalence of LD youth from a juvenile delinquent sample and the public school population when age was held constant. They suggested that the contradiction between their results and those of previous studies supporting a juvenile delinquency–learning disability link stems from differences in definitions of learning disabilities and in the diagnostic procedures used to identify them (1982: 11). Malmgren, Abbott, and Hawkins (1999) conducted a 7-year longitudinal study to examine whether the presence of learning disabilities increases a youth's risk of becoming a juvenile delinquent. They studied self-report data and official court records for 515 students, 51 (10 percent) of whom were LD youth. When controlling for demographic variables, their findings did not support any direct relationship between learning disabilities and delinquency. Malmgren and associates (1999) suggest that findings of an learning disability–delinquency relationship by other researchers may actually be explained by confounding effects of age, ethnicity, or socioeconomic status. It may be that LD youths are not involved in more delinquent behavior than non-LD youths, but they may be more likely to be arrested, adjudicated, and incarcerated than other youth.

In summary, while there are some questions about the exact association between juvenile delinquency and learning disabilities, it is clear that many children with learning disabilities do fail in school, many of them do act out in response to their experience of failure and frustration, and many of them do find their way into the justice system. The delinquent behavior of many of these youths justifiably brings them to the attention of juvenile authorities, but it is also apparent that decisions of juvenile justice officials to process them through the system may be influenced by the learning problems and school failure as well as by the antisocial behavior.

Psychological Explanations of Delinquency

Personality characteristics and individual differences in learning are the major emphases of psychological explanations of delinquency. August Aichhorn (1936) drew upon the psychoanalytic theories of Sigmund Freud and suggested that juvenile delinquents had difficulty conforming to parental and societal expectations because they had not developed a healthy superego. Fritz Redl and David Wineman (1951) also argued that juvenile delinquents had an inadequate superego and so tended to follow the impulses and drives of the id. Psychoanalytic theories have been criticized because it is impossible to establish a causal relationship between a person's mental state and delinquent behavior.

Sheldon and Eleanor Glueck (1950) compared 500 juvenile offenders and 500 non-offenders and found that the delinquents were more defiant toward authority, extroverted, resentful, hostile, suspicious, and defensive than the nondelinquents. Conger and Miller (1966) found that delinquents were more emotionally unstable, impulsive, suspicious, hostile, irritable, and egocentric than nondelinquents. Other researchers have found no conclusive evidence of personality differences between delinquents and nondelinquents (see Schuessler and Cressey, 1955; Waldo and Dinitz, 1967; Tennenbaum, 1977).

Psychological learning theories include behaviorism, social learning, and moral development. According to B. F. Skinner (1953), behavior is conditioned by the reinforcements and punishments that it produces. Reinforcements increase the likelihood that the behavior will be repeated, and punishments decrease the probability of the behavior being repeated. Skinner is regarded as the most influential psychologist of the twentieth century. *Behaviorism* has contributed a great deal to understanding human behavior, but critics contend that it falls short of explaining the role of cognitive mental processes involved in behavior. *Social learning theory* attempts to explain why some adolescents engage in delinquent behavior while others, in similar environments, do not. According to this theory, behavior is a reflection of people observing and imitating other persons (see Bandura, 1977). Evidence suggests that some delinquent behavior is a result of observing the actions of others, and many believe that television and movie viewing may affect aggressive and violent behavior (Josephson, 1987). Social learning theory is a popular explanation for delinquent behavior, but it has been criticized because it does not account for the role of free will and it does not completely examine the relationship between thought processes and behavior. *Moral development theories* (see Piaget, 1932; Kohlberg, 1964) focus on how children learn social rules and make judgments on the basis of those rules. In terms of Kohlberg's theory, delinquents are at a lower level of moral development than nondelinquents. They are more likely to define right and wrong in absolute terms, and they focus more on external consequences, act to avoid punishment, and show little concern for the feelings of others. Nondelinquents, in contrast, have internalized societal rules and expectations. Research comparing the moral judgments of delinquents and nondelinquents shows mixed results. Critics note that Kohlberg's work focused on reasoning, not behavior, and moral and immoral behavior is inconsistent and situation-specific. Psychologists discovered that children at different stages of moral development behave similarly and those at the same stages of moral development behave differently. In other words, psychological theories of delinquency are difficult to test and verify, and the relationship between personality factors and delinquent behavior has not been well supported by research.

Biochemical Explanations of Delinquency

Biochemical factors focus on chemical imbalances in the body that may influence delinquent behavior. Researchers have found evidence that chemical imbalances in the body bring about changes in perception and hyperactivity (Hoffer, 1975). The connection between nutrition and delinquent behavior has received considerable attention in the juvenile justice system (Schauss, 1981). Stephen Schoenthaler and Walter Dorza (1983) observed that a reduction in the sugar intake of institutionalized youths brought about a corresponding reduction in the number of assaults, fights, thefts, and defiant acts. In another study they found that improving the diets of public school students was correlated with improved school performance (Schoenthaler et al., 1986).

Researchers have discovered that exposure to toxic substances such as lead interferes with brain functioning and affects behavior. Herbert Needleman and colleagues (1979) found that children with higher dentine lead levels had lower IQ test scores and exhibited more attention difficulties that resulted in poor classroom performance. Research on the long-term effects on many of the same lead-contaminated children indicated that they were more likely to have a reading disability, lower class standing in high school, and increased absenteeism and were more likely to have dropped out of high school (Needleman et al., 1990). In a recent study Needleman and associates found a relationship between lead poisoning and delinquency (Needleman et al., 1996). The most common cause of lead poisoning is exposure to lead-based paint. Although it is no longer produced, lead-based paint is still on the walls, woodwork, and windows of many older homes and apartment buildings. The children of lower-income families are more likely to suffer the effects of lead toxicity. Fortunately, lead poisoning as a cause of school failure and delinquency is preventable. Knowledge of the dangers of lead poisoning and proper building maintenance can minimize this source of learning and behavior problems among children.

The relationship between drugs and behavior is a third biochemical factor in delinquency. Pharmacology experts know that drugs affect human emotions, but drugs have not been proven to cause aggressive behavior. Persons react differently to the influence of drugs, and certain personality types are affected more by drugs (McCardle and Fishbein, 1989). Whether a person engages in aggressive or antisocial behavior while under the influence of drugs depends on individual and environmental conditions (Fishbein, 1990). Alcohol and drugs are clearly associated with aggressive behavior and violent crimes, but criminologists do not agree on the exact causal relationship. Studies have not clearly demonstrated that alcohol and drug use are a cause of crime and delinquent behavior (Huizinga et al., 1994). Relatively few juvenile offenders have reported committing a crime while using drugs, and most youths appear to commit crime for reasons other than drug use (Altschuler and Brounstein, 1991). Elliott, Huizinga, and Ageton (1985) concluded that delinquent peer associations increase the likelihood of delinquency and drug use, that is, youths who associate with friends who use drugs and engage in delinquency are more likely themselves to use drugs and commit crime. In summary, psychological and biochemical factors are associated with delinquency, but whether they cause individuals to commit crime depends on environmental circumstances and social influences.

Social Structure Theory

Social structure explanations of delinquency focus on the social and cultural environment in which adolescents grow up or on the subcultural groups in which they become involved. Social structure theorists, relying on official statistics as the primary measure of crime, claim that such forces as cultural deviance, social disorganization, and status frustration lead lower-class youths to become involved in delinquent behavior. Three categories of social structure explanations are social disorganization theory, strain theory, and cultural deviance theory.

Social disorganization theory originated in what was referred to as the Chicago School after Clifford Shaw and Henry McKay (1942), of the Chicago School of Urban

Criminology, and Walter Miller (1958a), a social anthropologist from the University of Chicago. They studied Chicago's urban development and noted changes in the quality of life as industrialization changed the city. Large numbers of European immigrants were moving to the city and taking advantage of jobs available in the factories, businesses, and stockyards. Juvenile delinquency was commonly believed to be a problem of "morally inferior" ethnic groups, and many upper-class citizens believed in the stereotype that foreign immigrants had low moral values and were responsible for the increase in crime. The Chicago School sociologists challenged this prejudiced view by a scientific approach to the study of delinquency. Urban growth produced a condition of social disorganization characterized by urban density, overcrowding, substandard housing, low income, unemployment, poor schools, and family problems. The increase in crime that occurred with urban growth resulted not from immoral, crime-prone immigrants but from social disorganization and conditions over which individuals had little control.

Strain theory, the second type of social structure theory, emphasizes that most people share similar values, goals, and aspirations, but that many people do not have an equal ability or the means to achieve those goals, such as economic or social success. The discrepancy between what persons want and their limited opportunities to achieve them produces frustration, or "strain." Because opportunities for success are more open for the middle and upper classes, strain is experienced most by those in the lower socioeconomic class, for whom quality education and employment opportunities are more limited. The strain and frustration resulting from blocked opportunities increases the likelihood that some individuals will use deviant and illegitimate means to achieve their goals. Strain theory explains why many lower-class youths resort to theft, drug dealing, and other delinquent behavior when they perceive fewer legitimate means and opportunities to achieve their goals. Strain and social disorganization are similar because they emphasize the relationship between social variables, such as poverty, economic opportunity, and available goods and services, and crime and delinquency. Strain is more common among lower-class persons who live in inner-city urban areas characterized more by social problems and crime.

Robert Merton (1957) was the foremost criminologist who formulated strain theory around the concept of "anomie" or "normlessness." Social disorganization leads to uncertainty, confusion, and shifting moral values, referred to as anomie or normlessness. Conditions of anomie exist when the rule of law is weakened and becomes powerless to maintain social control. Under conditions of anomie, crime may be considered a "normal" response to existing social conditions. Merton applied the concept of anomie to rapidly changing conditions in U.S. society in which competition for success, wealth, and material goods is highly valued. Persons with little formal education and few economic resources are denied the ability to acquire the goals of American society, producing a sense of alienation, hopelessness, and frustration. Merton claimed that this sense of anomie often leads to attaining socially desired goals through criminal or delinquent means.

Robert Agnew (1992) extended Merton's theory of strain and anomie to better explain varieties of delinquent behavior through a "general strain theory." Agnew identified three sources of strain:

1. Strain caused by the *failure to achieve positively valued goals*, basically the same as Merton's theory of anomie.
2. Strain caused by the *removal of positively valued stimuli* from the individual. Examples include the loss of a girl- or boyfriend, death of a loved one, divorce or separation of parents, or leaving friends and moving to a new neighborhood or school.

3. Strain as the *presentation of negative stimuli*, such as child abuse and neglect, physical punishment, family and peer conflict, stressful life conditions, school failure, and criminal victimization (Agnew, 1992: 57).

Agnew's general strain theory has made an important contribution to explaining delinquency. The theory helps to explain how stressful incidents and sources of strain in the life course influence patterns of offending. There is ample research support for the general strain theory. Youth who report being "hassled" by peers, have bad peer relationships, or experience victimization or similar "negative life events" are also the persons most likely to engage in delinquency (Agnew and White, 1992). Research shows that indicators of strain such as family breakup, unemployment, moving, feelings of dissatisfaction with friends and school, are positively related to delinquency (Paternoster and Mazerolle, 1994).

Cultural deviance theory, also referred to as "subcultural theory," is the third type of social structure theory. Subcultural theorists point to observations that values and attitudes of lower-class youth differ from mainstream middle-class values. Youths from socially disorganized neighborhoods marked by unemployment, poverty, and social problems develop values and attitudes of that subculture. Cultural deviance theory suggests that youths violate the law because they follow the values of their lower-class community. Honesty and hard work make little sense to youths growing up in a neighborhood where poverty, unemployment, and crime are part of life. Drug dealing and prostitution are viewed by many lower-class youths as a way to overcome unemployment and poverty. They learn to value being tough and "street smart." Threats and physical attacks are preferred over verbal negotiation for resolving conflicts in some subcultures.

Walter Miller (1958a) described a number of "focal concerns" that dominate lower-class cultures and often run counter to lawful, middle-class behavior:

1. *Trouble*: Getting into trouble and being able to handle trouble are valued, therefore, troublemaking behaviors such as fighting, drinking, and sexual misconduct are accepted.
2. *Toughness*: Surviving in lower-class subcultures requires toughness, so physical strength, fighting ability, and mental toughness are valued over being soft and sentimental.
3. *Smartness*: Formal education is not valued as much as being "street smart" and able to outsmart or "outcon" one's opponent.
4. *Excitement*: Similar to "trouble," members of the lower class seek to enliven their tough life through exciting activities such as gambling, fighting, getting drunk, and sexual activity.
5. *Fate*: Members of the lower class believe there is little they can do to change their course in life and that any good that may come their way is simply through luck and good fortune.
6. *Autonomy*: Lower-class youths learn to value being independent and not depend on anyone else, particularly authority figures such as police, parents, and teachers (Miller, 1958a).

Miller's "focal concerns" accurately describe the attitudes and behaviors of many lower-class (and middle-class) youth today. Getting in trouble is common among youths, and a reason given for much delinquent activity is a search for excitement ("because we were bored"). Poor school performance among lower-class students may be explained by the value placed on "street smarts" over being smart in the classroom, and one's life success being ruled by fate more than by personal goals and achievements. Many youths carry guns in order to protect themselves, thus displaying their toughness and autonomy. Street-smart youths take care of themselves and do not depend on police for protection. The primary reason for weapons in schools is that students who feel threatened and fearful believe they cannot depend on school officials for protection and must take matters into their own hands.

Albert Cohen (1955) developed a theory of delinquent subculture that specifically emphasized the role of the school. Cohen focused on lower-class youths and the strain or frustration of attending schools based on middle-class values and standards. Cohen believed that delinquency is a protest against middle-class norms and values and against the perceived unfairness of being disciplined and evaluated according to a "middle-class measuring rod." Four assumptions of Cohen's theory are:

1. Many lower-class youths (especially males) do poorly in school.
2. School performance is related to delinquency.
3. Poor school performance is a result of a conflict between the dominant middle-class values of the school system and youth's lower-class values.
4. Lower-class male delinquency is largely gang delinquency and a means of gaining positive self-concept and maintaining antisocial values.

Cohen's first assumption is generally true: more lower-class youth do perform poorly in school compared to middle-class youth. Cohen's second thesis has also been supported by research. School performance is related to delinquency, but scholars disagree as to the causal ordering of school problems, dropout, and delinquency. Elliott and Voss (1974) studied the school performance and delinquency records of 2000 California youths and found that, while those who dropped out did have higher rates of delinquency, the rates of delinquency were higher before dropping out and declined after leaving school. Thus, dropping out may reduce, rather than cause delinquency. Thornberry and associates (1985) failed to replicate the Elliott and Voss study, however, finding that arrest rates of school dropouts increased soon after dropping out. Thornberry et al. concluded that their results did not support Cohen's theory, but did support control theory.

Cohen's claim that school problems were class-related has received only mixed research support. Middle-class values and norms purportedly related to school performance include punctuality, neatness, cleanliness, drive and ambition for achievement and success, individual responsibility, willingness to postpone immediate gratification of desires, courtesy and self-control, and control of violence and aggression. Polk, Frease, and Richmond (1974) examined the relationship between social class, school experience and delinquency and found that school failure, but *not* social class, is directly related to delinquency. They found that boys who do poorly in school, regardless of their social class, are more likely to be delinquent than those who are performing adequately at school. Their results showed that white- and blue-collar adolescents who had low grade point averages also had higher rates of delinquency (Polk et al., 1974).

Cohen's contention that lower-class delinquency is a gang phenomenon by which youth reduce their frustration and gain a more positive self-concept has received mixed research support. There is little question that delinquency tends to be group behavior, but the extent to which delinquency (lower- or middle-class) is associated with structured, deviant gangs or whether gang membership increases youths' self-esteem is questionable (Jensen and Rojek, 1980).

In summary, social structure, strain, and cultural deviance explanations claim that delinquent acts are often an expression of frustration because of limited educational and employment opportunities, particularly of lower-income and disadvantaged youth. Opportunity-structure theorists note that most young people accept middle-class goals and aspire toward a middle-class lifestyle, but those from disadvantaged backgrounds often find illegitimate means for achieving those goals, which have been blocked to them. Barriers include unequal educational and vocational opportunities. Whether or not there is out-right discrimination, the verbal and social skills, family reputation, and social contacts necessary to compete educationally and vocationally often exclude children from poor families.

Delinquent acts are viewed as reactions to the frustration caused by blocked opportunity. Disruption in school classrooms often results from such frustration. Because schools present barriers and are sources of frustration to many youths, they are easy targets for youthful aggression. Vandalism, theft, and assaults at schools are thus seen as resulting from the frustration of restricted opportunities. Social structure and strain theories are supported by considerable research evidence explaining a great deal of delinquent behavior.

Social Process Explanations

Social process explanations of delinquency focus not on societal structures but on social interactions between individuals and environmental influences that may lead to delinquent behavior. Differential association theory holds that delinquency is a learned behavior as youth interact closely with other deviant youth. Control theory is a social process explanation that specifically includes school experiences as a variable in delinquency. Control theories explain delinquency as evolving from the nature of juveniles' social interactions.

Differential association theory was developed by Edwin Sutherland, who believed that delinquency is learned behavior as youths interact with each other. The theory is founded on a number of propositions (Sutherland, 1947):

1. Criminal behavior, like other behavior, is learned.
2. Criminal behavior is learned as youths are involved and communicate with each other, primarily through intimate groups.
3. The learning process includes methods of committing crimes, and the motives, drives, rationalizations, and attitudes to support criminal behavior.
4. A youth becomes delinquent because of an excess of definitions favorable to violation of law over definitions unfavorable to violation of the law.
5. The differential association process varies in frequency, duration, priority, and intensity.

Sutherland's differential association theory remains an important explanation for juvenile delinquency. It is difficult to argue against a theory that maintains that crime is learned like other behaviors. This explanation also has a positive appeal in that it holds that youths are changeable and can be taught prosocial behavior. Delinquency-prevention efforts may be effective when they are directed at reducing the criminal influence among groups of antisocial youths. Sutherland's differential association theory has stimulated considerable research on delinquent behavior. Burgess and Akers (1966) reformulated the differential association theory according to operant conditioning principles, and Akers (1985) further developed an explanation of deviant behavior according to a social learning approach.

Control theories begin with the premise that the way to understand delinquency is to know the characteristics of persons who conform and do *not* do delinquency. The focal question therefore is not "Why do youths become delinquent?" but rather "Why do most youths *not* engage in repetitive, serious delinquency?" Control theorists are informed by self-report measures of delinquency, and therefore an assumption of control theories is that some deviance and delinquency are to be expected among most youth. The basic idea of control theory is that human behavior is guided by various controls: some within the person, and some outside the person. An internal source of control, for example, is one's self-concept, and external sources include the family and the school. Walter Reckless (1961) posited that internal factors such as self-control and external factors such as parental supervision, discipline, and social institutions help to "insulate" or "contain" persons from crime. Reckless and associates' primary contribution was the emphasis on inner containment, or self-concept, which they believed was a major variable in steering youth away from delinquency (Reckless et al., 1956: 744–746). While there are problems in operationalizing and measuring self-concept, studies have confirmed that the greater the self-esteem, the less likely a youth is to become involved in delinquent behavior (Jensen, 1973).

Travis Hirschi (1969) holds that four elements of the social bond explain delinquency: attachment, commitment, involvement and belief. *Attachment* refers to the ties of affection and respect that youths have to parents, teachers, and friends, which will help them avoid the temptation to commit delinquent acts. *Commitment* to socially acceptable activities and values, such as educational and employment goals, likewise helps youths avoid delinquency by increasing the cost and risks involved. *Involvement* in conventional activities keeps youths occupied and reduces their opportunities to commit deviant acts. *Belief* refers to respect for the law and societal norms and derives from close relationships with other positive role models, especially parents. Hirschi tested and supported his control theory by giving a self-report survey to more than 4,000 junior and senior high school youth in California. The theory has generated a considerable amount of research.

Control theory has several strengths. It has clear concepts that lend themselves to empirical research and testing. Others have used the social control model to develop integrated theories patterned on the social bond (Elliott et al., 1979). Hirschi's control theory has made valuable contributions in understanding the relationship between delinquency and the major social institutions of family and the school. He examined the role of attachment to parents and the relative importance of peer relationships as youth mature. The theory addresses educational aspirations and goals, student–teacher relationships, and the role of school performance and behavior in delinquency.

Control theory does have some weaknesses. The measure of the social bond is limited, and the delinquency measure lists only a few relatively minor behavior problems. Second, the chain of events that weaken the social bond is not clearly defined, and the division of youth into socialized or unsocialized tends to ignore the wide range of delinquent activities. Finally, many causal factors of delinquency are not explained by social control variables. Nevertheless, social control theory has more empirical support than any other explanation of delinquency.

Parents, Peers, and School

A major emphasis of control theory is the role of parents, peers, and school experiences in explaining delinquency. Hirschi found that students who perform poorly in school lose interest in school and related activities, increasing the likelihood of their committing delinquent acts. Students' perceived academic ability and actual performance affect their bond to school, and Hirschi's data show that these are associated with delinquent involvement (1969: 120). Students with weak attachments to parents tend to show less respect for teachers and to dislike school (Hirschi, 1969: 131–132).

The nature of peer relationships has an intervening effect on parental attachment, school experiences, and delinquency. Attachment to peers does not necessarily mean less attachment to parents. It appears to depend on to whom one is attached and the nature of one's peer attachments. Linden and Hackler (1973) found that self-reported delinquency was inversely related to ties to parents and conventional peers, but positively related to ties to deviant peers. Others suggest that parental attachment affects delinquency, which affects school performance, which in turn affects parental attachment (Liska and Reed, 1985: 556–557). Parents, not school, are the major institutional sources of delinquency control for lower class more than for middle class youth (Liska and Reed, 1985: 557–558). According to Hirschi's control theory, delinquents are less dependent on peers than are nondelinquents, a finding that has been supported by other research. In a study comparing the personality factors of nondelinquent high school students and adjudicated delinquents, the delinquents scored higher on the "self-sufficiency" personality factor, whereas nondelinquents scored higher on "group dependence" (Lawrence, 1985: 77).

The role of parents, peers, and school as factors in promoting or preventing delinquent behavior deserves careful examination, particularly for practical and policy implications. One study of school performance, peers, and delinquency analyzed self-report data from the National Youth Survey, comparing youths' school attachment and how many of their friends had committed delinquent acts (Lawrence, 1991). The results indicated that peer relationships have a greater influence on delinquent behavior than attachment to school. Measures of school attachment included items such as "How important has school work been?", "How important is it to have teachers think of you as a good student?", "How do teachers think you are doing?" and "How important is a high grade point average?" Youths who had fewer friends who had committed delinquent acts reported less delinquent involvement themselves, regardless of high or low school attachment. Youths with more friends who had engaged in delinquent behavior reported a higher number of delinquent acts, and this held true even for students with higher school attachment. Those with more delinquent friends and lower school attachment reported the highest self-reported delinquency rate. These findings indicate that peer relationships are more important than school attachment in explaining delinquent behavior (Lawrence, 1991).

School involvement tends to reduce involvement in delinquency. Boys in Hirschi's sample who felt they had nothing to do were more likely to become involved in delinquent acts. He theorized that lack of involvement and commitment to school releases youth from a major source of time-structuring (1969: 187–196). Hirschi's claim for the positive benefit of involvement has been supported by other studies. The results of a self-report survey of 1,400 high school students in San Antonio, Texas, showed that, compared to delinquents, nondelinquents tend to participate in or attend more extracurricular school activities (Lawrence, 1985). There appears to be an interactive relationship between involvement in school activities, school attachment, and school performance, as well as with positive parental and peer relationships. School extracurricular involvement requires parental support and, in turn, offers opportunities for positive peer relationships. There is considerable research evidence and theoretical support for the school–delinquency relationship. Sampson and Laub postulate that weak school attachment and poor school performance have the strongest mediating effects on delinquency (1993: 101–102). Gottfredson and Hirschi (1990) explain that the relationship stems from the school system's rewards and discipline, which also increases a young person's level of self-control. Schools require students to be in a certain place on time and to be orderly and attentive, and they reward good behavior and performance. Gottfredson and Hirschi note however that the discipline, structure, rewards, and greater self-control provided by schools can only happen when students have parental support and regularly attend school (1990: 162). Parents and schools share an interdependent and reciprocal relationship as the two most important factors that enable most youths to avoid chronic and serious involvement in delinquency.

Developmental and Life-Course Theories

Recent developments in explaining delinquency question the traditional sociological theories for explaining crime and delinquency (Thornberry, 1997; Sampson and Laub, 1997). Theories that explain delinquency as being a function of social structures, cultural deviance, or learning and social process fail to recognize that delinquent involvement is not constant throughout childhood, adolescence, and adulthood. Delinquent involvement varies with age, and youthful offenders vary as to the onset of delinquency and whether their offending persists into adulthood. Sampson and Laub (1993) point to evidence that delinquency varies by age; although delinquency tends to peak in the teenage years, there is an early onset of delinquency, as well as continuity of criminal behavior over the life course. Sociological criminology has failed to recognize age variations in delinquency, therefore recent theorists have turned to developmental psychology to better understand delinquency over the life course. Moffitt (1993) studied the psychological development of children and youth and offers evidence that most adolescents who engage in delinquency do not persist into adult crime. Social factors may diminish their tendency to continue delinquent careers, in contrast to "life-course–persistent" delinquents, who are likely to continue deviant, antisocial, and criminal conduct as adults. Developmental or life-course explanations attempt to account for differences among delinquents who begin offending at an early age and continue to offend and those who begin in adolescence and seem to grow out of it. There is a distinction, for example, between "adolescent-limited" antisocial behavior, that is, temporary normative behavior among teens, and "life-course–persistent" delinquent behavior, typified by a smaller group, whose antisocial behavior begins early in life and develops into an adult career in crime (Moffitt, 1993: 696). Others have noted the differences between early and late starters in delinquency and the different effects of parenting and deviant peers on these two types of delinquents (Simons et al., 1994). The developmental, life-course perspective points to the importance of longitudinal studies of antisocial behavior beginning in infancy and childhood. While most adolescents do not persist in delinquent careers, most adults who engage in antisocial and criminal behavior are the same persons whose antisocial behavior began in early childhood.

General and Integrated Theories

Most criminological research has proceeded with the assumption that delinquency is the result of a social environment or social processes common to all delinquents. Criminologists now acknowledge that no single theoretical orientation can adequately explain the multiple variables and factors that cause delinquent behavior. Some have examined whether there are multiple paths to the same types of delinquency. For example, some youths may run away from home because of a poor family environment, some because they are pushed out, and others may run away for fun and excitement (Huizinga et al., 1991). A number of criminologists have taken the best parts of different theories and combined them in a single general or integrated theory. Strain, social control, and social learning theories have been combined into an integrated theoretical explanation of delinquency and drug use (Elliott et al., 1979, 1985).

Gottfredson and Hirschi (1990) combined the strong points of the classical traditional (otherwise referred to as the "rational-choice" model) and positivist theories that crime is caused by biological, psychological, or socioeconomic factors. In the general theory of crime they begin with the question, "What is crime?" rather than "What causes crime?" They claim that crime in fact bears little resemblance to criminological theories or to explanations offered by law enforcement or the media. Crimes are illegal acts that are for the most part simple, trivial, and mundane. Gottfredson and Hirschi even describe homicides as "mundane" and easily explainable, because most involve acquaintances, alcohol, or drugs and are often impulsive crimes of passion with little rational gain (1990: 32). In an extension of Hirschi's (1969) control theory, they describe the offender as an individual who lacks self-control and tends to be impulsive, insensitive, physical (more than mental), a risk taker, short-sighted, and nonverbal. These traits predispose the individual to pursue immediate pleasure, including criminal acts and noncriminal behavior such as smoking, drinking, drug use, gambling, and illicit sex (1990: 90). The general theory of crime aptly describes juvenile delinquents whose lack of self-control draws them to criminal acts that offer excitement, risk, deception, and power, and criminal or antisocial adults whose lack of self-control results in unstable marriages, friendships, and jobs (1990: 89).

Social Reaction Theories: Labeling and Conflict

Social reaction theories focus more on how society, social institutions, and government officials react to crime and delinquency than on why offenders commit crime. The theories we have discussed so far explain juvenile delinquency as a function of individual choices or characteristics, social structure, or social processes that influence delinquent involvement. Social reaction theories are different in that they see crime as a result of how laws are written and enforced and how social institutions and justice agencies react to crime and criminals. Unlike the biological, psychological, and sociological explanations that have been developed and tested for many years, social reaction theories first developed in the 1960s and 1970s. Agencies of government and justice were being scrutinized and criticized in the years following the Vietnam War and the Nixon administration. Critical scholars noted that criminal laws and their enforcement tended to focus more on crimes committed by the lower class, while many "white-collar" crimes were ignored or punished lightly. They contended that laws were written by those in power to serve their own interest and to keep the lower class in its place. Theorists also point to the stigmatizing effect of the judicial and correctional processes, whereby offenders tend to be labeled and restricted from reintegration back into society even after serving their sentence. Despite not being as popular or having as much research support as many other theories, labeling and conflict theories do offer interesting insights into societal reactions to crime and how changes in laws and policies will help reduce crime.

Labeling Theory

Labeling theory begins with the understanding that most youths engage in some deviant acts, and labeling theorists use findings from self-report studies to support that contention.

Initial deviant and delinquent activities of youth have many varied causes. The primary assumption of the labeling perspective is that repeated delinquent behavior is caused by society's reaction to minor deviant behavior. Frank Tannenbaum (1938) first suggested that the very process of identifying and segregating deviant persons as criminals increased the likelihood that the behavior would continue. Lemert (1951) and Becker (1963) are the other major proponents of labeling theory. Lemert differentiated between "primary deviance," referring to behavior of the individual, and "secondary deviance," resulting from society's response to that behavior, which resulted in a status, role, or individual identity. Becker proposed that those in society who make and enforce the rules "create" deviants by labeling persons, who in turn tend to act out the deviant behaviors consistent with their new identity.

There has been limited research support for labeling theory. Jensen (1972) found that having a delinquent record was related to having a delinquent self-concept for young white males (but not for black youth). Jensen concluded that an official label of delinquency may not affect black youth because such labels are more common and because the label is given by outsiders. Ageton and Elliott (1974) studied youths over a 6-year period and concluded that police contact was followed by a greater delinquency orientation among both lower- and upper-class boys. Other studies show mixed or negative support for labeling theory. Foster, Dinitz, and Reckless (1972) found no changes in personal relationships or parental attitudes toward boys following a juvenile court appearance. Most (90 percent) of the boys showed no evidence of being negatively labeled; they believed their official delinquency record would not pose difficulties with their finishing school. Hepburn (1977) compared the self-concepts and attitudes of nondelinquent and delinquent males. He found that the delinquents did have greater definitions of themselves as delinquents, more commitment to future delinquency and to other delinquents, lower self-concepts, and less respect for the police. However, when other variables such as socioeconomic status and self-reported delinquency were considered, he found that an arrest record had no direct effect on self-concept or delinquent identification.

Labeling theory does have a number of strengths. It provides an explanation for why many youths who become involved in minor deviant acts often continue offending and may escalate to more serious delinquent acts following initial contact with police and juvenile authorities. The theory emphasizes the important role of rule making, power, and reactions of society and justice system authorities. As part of the symbolic interactionist perspective, labeling theory points out that some persons *do* tend to take on the roles and self-concepts expected of them.

Labeling theory has many weaknesses. It lacks clear-cut definitions and testable hypotheses (Gibbs, 1966). It does not explain why youths initially commit deviant or delinquent acts and tends to minimize the importance of delinquency. The theory appears to excuse the behavior of the delinquent and make society the culprit. The reasons or motives for why youths engage in delinquency are not explained. Overall, labeling theory has been widely criticized and has little empirical support. The theory nevertheless does have some important applications to school practices.

Labeling Theory and School Tracking. A common practice in schools is to classify students according to their learning ability and place them into groups, or "tracks," of students who supposedly perform similarly. Educators believe that students learn better in groups that are similar to themselves and that placing students into tracks enables teachers to direct their efforts at the appropriate ability level for slower and faster learners. After an extensive study of a sample of 25 elementary, junior high and senior high schools throughout the United States, Oakes (1985) took issue with the assumed benefits of tracking and claimed to have found no evidence that students benefit educationally from the practice. Her findings supported those of other studies—that the learning of average and slow students tends to be negatively affected by homogeneous placements—and she is confident that bright students are not held back when they are in mixed classrooms, as many parents and educators believe.

Tracking has been criticized for a number of reasons: more minority and lower-income students are in the basic or low-ability tracks; placement in the tracks tends to be permanent, with little movement up or down in spite of students' learning and progress; and tracking has a labeling and stigmatizing effect, so that teachers expect less of the lower-track students, and frequently their expectations are correct. Schafer, Olexa, and Polk (1972) found that even when IQ and previous ability factors were controlled, blacks and low-income students were still more apt to be found in the basic or low-ability tracks. They also found that track assignment was virtually irreversible, operating much like a rigid caste system. Kelly and Grove (1981) claim that race, social class, and other nonacademic factors (such as the father's occupation or student misconduct) are criteria for tracking. They cite evidence that students are routinely assigned to a low-ability track not according to IQ or current ability and performance, but their past academic record. School tracking affects students in at least three ways: (1) *personal identity* (how an individual views oneself), (2) *public identity* (how others view the individual), and (3) *self-image* (how the individual evaluates him- or herself) (Kelly and Pink, 1982: 55). Teachers, peers, parents, and others come to expect less from students in low-ability tracks, whereas more is expected of students in high-ability tracks. The expectations are often fulfilled. Misconduct and behavior problems are also often expected of students in lower tracks. Kelly and Pink (1982) suggest that students who engage in school crime are probably living up to teacher, peer, parental, and self-expectations and are also striving to obtain some measure of success and well-being in deviant ways to compensate for school failure. Students' misbehavior serves to confirm their initial diagnosis and labeling as potential troublemakers. William Pink (1984) maintained that the practice of placing slow learners in a lower track resulted in virtually withholding essential skills from students, failing to help those students develop a sense of competence and status, and thereby creating greater vulnerability to delinquent involvement.

Research consensus seems to be that tracking is not in the best interests of most students; and does not appear to be related to increasing academic achievement or promoting positive attitudes and behavior. Poor and minority students seem to have suffered most from tracking, and these are the students on whom we place so many educational hopes. The very students who seem to need the most appear to be getting the fewest quality schooling experiences to help promote learning in the areas of academics, vocational, social, and personal growth. One of the goals of public education is to provide access to economic, political, and social opportunity for those who are denied equal access. School tracking, however, appears to seriously interfere with that educational goal (Oakes, 1985). Samuel Lucas (1999) studied recent tracking practices by analyzing data from the High School and Beyond longitudinal survey. Lower-class and minority students disproportionately take courses categorized as remedial, business, and vocational as opposed to the college-preparatory courses taken by middle- and upper-class students. He found that social class clearly plays an important role in students' attainments. The lower-class students were less likely than others to pursue advanced instruction because they had failed to take the prerequisite courses. Lucas (1999) found racial, ethnic, and gender differences among students not taking academic and college preparatory courses, and not staying in school.

Unfortunately but perhaps not surprisingly, inequality in America's schools reflects the inequality in society. Labeling students based on perceived ability and academic success and placing them in lower tracks appears to be perpetuating that inequality. The challenge for schools is to avoid alienating or labeling any students, especially those who are slow learners or score lower on aptitude tests. Braithwaite (1989) describes integrative schools as those where all students can "be someone" and can earn positive reputations. Integrative schools will help to minimize deviance and delinquency by developing a school environment that avoids competition among students and helps all students attain some skills and achieve some success through positive group contributions (1989: 176).

Conflict Theory

Conflict theory shares a similarity with labeling theory in its focus on social and political institutions as causes of crime, rather than individual characteristics and criminal tendencies of offenders. Conflict theorists point to the presence of conflict and competition among social classes and groups in society (Quinney, 1974). Examples that come to mind are the differences in values and beliefs between gender, race, ethnicity, political parties, and religious groups. Conflict results when competing groups vie for power and attempt to implement laws and policies that support their views. Nowhere is this conflict more evident than in the criminal justice system, where law enforcement practices, judicial sentencing policies, and correctional trends have changed dramatically over the years. Competing groups try to convince others that their beliefs and policies offer the best answer to solve what they believe to be the most urgent crime problems in the nation. Conflict theory offers an explanation as to why certain deviant and illegal behaviors are enforced and punished more severely. It explains why the number of persons arrested, convicted, and sentenced to prison has increased with criminal law and sentencing changes, despite the fact that criminal and deviant behavior has remained fairly stable over the years: certain laws "criminalize" behavior that is not a crime in other countries, that was not a serious crime in this country in the past, and that are considered by some persons to be more of a medical or social deviance problem than a crime. A clear example is the emphasis placed on drug enforcement in America. Certain drugs have been identified as dangerous and addicting drugs, and the use, possession, and sale of those drugs results in severe sentences, including jail and prison time. Other drugs, such as tobacco and alcohol, despite causing serious medical, behavioral, and social problems, do not receive the same severe criminal sanctions as marijuana and other drugs. Conflict theorists claim that economic forces, business interests (such as the alcohol and tobacco lobbies), and public sentiment of those in power are responsible for the differential enforcement of drug use. Criminal laws and their enforcement tend to focus more on crimes committed by the lower class, whereas many "white-collar" crimes are ignored or punished lightly. Critical or conflict theorists contend that laws written by those in power are done so in order to serve their own interest and to keep the lower class in its place. An examination of the crimes committed by the thousands of persons in our growing prison population is evidence that conflict theorists have raised a critical issue in the administration of justice in America (see Reiman, 1990). Most prisons and jails in America today house more persons convicted of drug offenses than of property or violent offenses.

Race, Social Class, and Delinquency. Conflict theorists view juvenile delinquency and juvenile justice in terms of a capitalist, class-structured society. They point to economic and social inequities that increase the probability of lower-class youth turning to crime because so few opportunities are open to them. Critical criminologists contend that the origin of the concept of "delinquency" and juvenile justice in America is based on economic and class differences. Anthony Platt (1974) argued that the role of the "child savers" in creating a separate system of juvenile justice was not so much to save wayward children, but an effort by wealthy upper-class individuals to maintain the existing class structure and control the behavior of lower-class youth. Conflict theorists view schools as social control institutions whose primary purpose is to prepare young people for entry into the work world and to assure that they conform to the existing capitalist structure. Lower-class and minority youth do not enjoy the same social, economic, and educational opportunities as middle- and upper-class white youths in America (Ferguson, 2000). Most youths and families look to education as the primary means by which they can compete for good jobs and improve their social standing. Equal quality education is not available to all youths, however, as differences in school funding have resulted in what one critic described as "savage inequalities" in schools throughout the United States (Kozol, 1991). Conflict theorists argue that competition among social classes restricts equal quality education and employment opportunities for some youth.

Race is a factor in delinquency, juvenile justice, and school policies. African Americans and other racial and ethnic minorities are disproportionately lower class with fewer social and economic opportunities. There is evidence that black Americans suffer disproportionately both as victims and as offenders. A higher proportion of blacks live in high-crime areas, where they face a higher probability of being victims and of witnessing crime as an everyday fact of life. Young black males growing up in a high-crime neighborhood are more likely to join a gang and to engage in antisocial and delinquent behavior. Ferguson (2000) noted that school disciplinary practices such as after-school detention, suspension, and expulsion are disproportionately enforced against black males. Teachers tend to view the attitudes and behaviors of African American males as threatening and intimidating, and their behavior is monitored more closely so that minor infractions may result in sanctions while similar misbehavior of white youths is overlooked or treated more leniently. Ferguson notes that black males are not totally innocent and play an active role in this labeling process, for they view challenging teachers or the school rules as a way to enhance their own "bad boy" image. Ferguson's observations offer at least a partial explanation for the disproportionate alienation, academic failure, and dropout rates of racial minorities.

News media depictions of crime and criminals tend to focus more on blacks as offenders (Lawrence and Mueller, 2003). Newspapers are more likely to identify race in a crime story when an African American is the suspect (Dorfman and Schiraldi, 2001), and minorities are overrepresented as perpetrators of crime (Romer et al., 1998; Weiss and Chermak, 1998). Despite higher rates of black victimization, white victims are shown at a much higher rate on television news and in newspaper coverage (Romer et al., 1998; Sorenson et al., 1998; Weiss and Chermak, 1998). Persons of color are shown primarily for their role as perpetrators of crime, whereas whites are shown primarily for their role as victims of crime (Romer et al., 1998). School violence and shooting incidents are more prominently covered by the media when they involve white victims than when minorities are victims (Males, 2000). News media researchers explain this phenomenon as a focus on those events that are most "newsworthy," meaning those that are most shocking, surprising, or unexpected. The implication is that crime and violence involving blacks and other minorities are considered normal, everyday events in lower-class communities. This may explain what conflict theorists believe to be a differential response by law enforcement and the judicial system to blacks and other racial and ethnic minorities. Race has played a prominent role in recent legislative changes in juvenile laws and in juvenile court practices (Feld, 1998, 2003). In an analysis of historical events, political developments, and media studies, Feld (2003) argues that recent get-tough-on-crime policies have unfairly targeted blacks so that they are overrepresented at every stage of the justice process despite federal mandates to examine and reduce the disproportionate confinement of minorities in detention and correctional facilities.

Feminism and Delinquency. The feminist perspective on delinquency is a form of conflict theory that focuses on victimization of women, gender differences in crime, and differences in judicial and correctional policies for women offenders. Research and theory in criminology and criminal justice have traditionally focused on male offenders and ignored women. Feminist theory is critical of traditional criminological theories that focus almost exclusively on male crime and delinquency and fail to adequately account for gender differences. Feminist theory claims that the patriarchal structure of society and the justice system results in laws and policies that are unfair to women. It claims that the male-oriented system creates gender bias, fails to protect women victims, and oppresses women offenders through unfair sentencing policies and unequal correctional resources and services (Chesney-Lind, 1989; Chesney-Lind and Shelden, 1992). Chesney-Lind (1989) maintains that juvenile laws and the application of them by police, the courts, and prisons reinforce women's place in male society. Female delinquency frequently begins with victimization experiences in the home. Girls are victims of sexual abuse to a greater extent than boys. Leaving home to avoid victimization brings the likelihood of being arrested as runaways and places them at risk of other crimes perceived as necessary for street survival, such as theft, dealing drugs, and prostitution. A double standard is still applied to young women in the belief that they need protection more than boys. As a result, a major reason for girls' referral to juvenile court was that their parents insisted on their arrest (Chesney-Lind, 1989). Feminist theory points to the differences in male and female delinquency, emphasizing that the discrepancies are primarily a result of paternalistic responses by parents and the justice system.

Female Delinquency

Most juvenile crimes known to police are committed by boys. Crimes committed by girls are less frequent and less serious than those by boys, but the rate of increase of female juvenile arrests has been greater than for boys. An estimated 2.2 million juveniles were arrested in 2003, and female juveniles accounted for 643,000 (29 percent) of the arrests. Females accounted for 24 percent of juvenile arrests for aggravated assault, 39 percent of the larceny-theft arrests, and 35 percent of liquor law violations (Snyder, 2005: 3). Between

1994 and 2003, arrests of juvenile females increased more than male arrests in most categories. The percent increase in female juvenile arrests in that ten-year period was 36 percent more arrests for simple assault, 56 percent increase for drug abuse violations, and 26 percent more liquor law violations (Snyder, 2005: 8). This is a marked increase from past years. From 1965 to 1977, arrest statistics from the Uniform Crime Reports indicated that females were not catching up with males in the commission of violent, masculine, or serious crimes, but there were rising levels of female delinquency in the categories of larceny, runaway, and liquor law violations (Steffensmeier and Steffensmeier, 1980: 80). Girls' share of all juvenile arrests remained fairly steady over that time period, ranging from about 15 to 29 percent (1980: 66). The ratio of male-to-female arrests is 3.4 to 1, but self-report studies report a male-to-female ratio of only 2:1 (Cernkovich and Giordano, 1979; Canter, 1982). Cernkovich and Giordano (1979) found that while males report more delinquent acts than females, the differences in self-reported delinquency are considerably smaller than those for arrest rates. They found no significant gender differences for school problems, suspension, and expulsion; status offenses such as truancy, defying parents' authority, and running away; and drug-related offenses such as smoking marijuana, using and selling hard drugs, and driving under the influence of hard drugs.

The types of offenses for which most youths are arrested are less serious crimes. The index crime for which most juveniles, especially girls, are arrested is larceny/theft (usually shoplifting).

Status offenses (so called because they are linked to the status of age and are not crimes if committed by adults) play a major role in girls' official delinquency. Status offenses accounted for 24.1 percent of all girls' arrests in 1990 but only about 8 percent of boys' arrests (Chesney-Lind, 1995: 74). Arrests of juveniles for status offenses declined during the 1970s with the passage of the Juvenile Justice and Delinquency Prevention Act (JJDPA) in 1974, which called for diversion and deinstitutionalization of youths arrested for non-criminal offenses. Arrests of juveniles, especially girls, for status offenses began increasing again in the 1980s, however. Meda Chesney-Lind (1995) suggested that girls are arrested disproportionately more often than boys for such status offenses as running away and curfew violations because of a tendency to sexualize their offenses and to control their behavior under the patriarchal authority of the juvenile justice system. There is evidence that many young women run away to escape sexual victimization at home, and once on the streets they are vulnerable to further sexual victimization (Chesney-Lind, 1995: 83).

Little attention has been paid to female delinquency, primarily because delinquency is generally associated with boys. Most research and explanations of the juvenile crime problem in fact focus on boys. Except for some early work (Lombroso, 1903; Thomas, 1923), research and writing on delinquency involving girls was virtually nonexistent until the past 50 years (Pollok, 1950; Konopka, 1966). Much more attention has been given to female delinquency since a dramatic increase in arrests of girls beginning in the 1970s. Freda Adler (1975) believed that the increase in female crime could be explained by a "liberation hypothesis," suggesting that as women have become more active and taken advantage of opportunities outside the home and in the workplace, they have begun to engage in more crimes originally committed almost entirely by men. Rita Simon (1975) proposed that as women have become more liberated and work more often outside the home, they have had more opportunities and incentives to commit property crimes.

Other researchers have found only partial support for the liberation hypothesis to explain the increase in female delinquency. Giordano and Cernkovich (1979) surveyed girls in three high schools and two state institutions to examine their attitudes on traditional versus liberated feminist views and found that the more delinquent girls were less liberated and held more traditional views of marriage and children. Rankin (1980) interviewed 385 students in several Wayne County (Detroit), Michigan, high schools to examine their attitudes toward education and involvement in delinquency. He found that negative attitudes toward school and school performance were associated with more delinquency involvement for both boys and girls, but surprisingly, the relationship was stronger for girls than for boys (1980: 431). The findings seem to indicate that with more women in the workforce today, the perceived occupational consequences of negative attitudes toward education or poor grades seem to be just as serious for girls as for boys. Rankin suggests that school factors may inhibit female delinquency as much as male delinquency (1980: 432).

John Hagan and associates (1985) developed a power–control theory to explain variations of delinquency among males and females. The theory examines social class, whether husbands and wives work outside the home, and the degree of power and control they have in the workplace. According to the theory, in the "patriarchal" family with traditional gender role definitions, mothers have the primary socializing role and a daughter is more controlled than a son. Gender differences result because girls, more than boys, are taught to avoid risks in general, and particularly illegal behavior. Thus girls appear to be more easily deterred by the threat of legal sanctions, an effect that Hagan et al. believe is produced more through maternal than through paternal controls (1985: 1156). In an "egalitarian" family, control over daughters and sons is more equal, and both are encouraged to be more open to risk taking. That is, daughters are encouraged to be more decisive and willing to take control and assume responsibility, although risk taking may have unintended consequences, such as involvement in delinquency (1987: 793). Thus, in egalitarian families daughters are more like sons in their involvement in risk taking behaviors, including some delinquency.

Rosenbaum and Lasley (1990) analyzed data for 1,508 adolescents from the Seattle Youth Study and found support for the power–control theory in explaining male–female differences in the school–delinquency relationship. Positive attitudes toward school and achievement produced stronger reductions in delinquency for boys than girls, whereas involvement in school activities and positive attitudes toward teachers led to more delinquency reduction for girls than for boys (1990: 510). They also found social class differences and suggested that school conformity is instilled socially in females and in middle/upper-class youths more strongly than in males and lower-class youths. Chesney-Lind is critical of the power–control theory as an explanation of variations in female delinquency. The argument that mothers' employment leads to daughters' delinquency in more egalitarian families is little more than a variation on the earlier liberation hypothesis, but "now, mother's liberation causes daughter's crime" (1995: 81–82)! She also notes methodological problems with the theory and a lack of evidence to suggest that girls' delinquency has increased along with women's employment. A reanalysis of the 1981 National Survey of Children indicated that gender differences in delinquency were present regardless of patriarchal or egaliltarian family structures (Morash and Chesney-Lind, 1991: 347), and female delinquency has declined or remained stable in the last decade as women's employment in the labor force has increased (Chesney-Lind, 1995: 82). Morash and Chesney-Lind argue for a feminist theory of female delinquency, noting that children (boys or girls) who identify with a nurturing parent who cares for others are likely to be more caring and have concern for others, rather than harm others. They believe that nurturing roles are not gender-specific: sons can identify with a nurturing parent as readily as daughters and can learn prosocial behaviors (1991: 351). A significant amount of female delinquency can be accounted for by patriarchal tendencies of the juvenile justice system. Girls' delinquent involvement is often a result of physical and sexual abuse, since running away from victimization experiences leads to more serious criminal involvement. They are referred to juvenile court for behaviors that parents and authorities generally ignore or overlook when committed by boys out of a perceived need to protect girls from engaging in more serious delinquency (see Chesney-Lind, 1995: 82–85).

Further research is needed to more clearly explain the causes of female delinquency and the extent to which girls' involvement in crime is different from boys. Boys still commit more serious and violent offenses, but girls' involvement in property and drug-related offenses is a matter of concern. More research is needed on how differences in family and school factors contribute to female delinquency. Finally, further research is needed to examine how the juvenile justice system responds to female delinquency, from police referral to juvenile court decisions.

Applying Theories to School Crime and Justice

Crime is a problem that affects society and the quality of life of every citizen. Even persons who are not actual victims of crime have a fear of being victimized, and this affects our everyday behavior. Crime costs local, state, and federal governments billions of dollars. A problem of this magnitude demands our utmost attempts to understand its origins and causes. Social scientists have spent years studying the varieties of criminal behavior and the factors that seem to underlie the problem. The study of crime theories is not simply an academic or intellectual exercise. Understanding the causes of crime is essential in order to make rational, informed responses to the problem of crime. All policies, laws, and crime-prevention programs are based on some beliefs about what causes the problem. Those who argue in favor of passing tougher laws to combat crime assume that offenders are acting rationally and may be deterred by tougher laws and harsh punishment. Those who argue for more rehabilitation and treatment programs assume that some underlying psychological problems or alcohol or other drug abuse have impaired offenders' judgment or caused them to commit crime. Both of these explanations and responses are correct and appropriate for some offenders in given circumstances and cases. To assume, however, that one crime-prevention strategy will work effectively for all offenders under all circumstances is naive and doomed to fail. Thus, like any problem facing society, it is incumbent upon us to attempt to understand the origins and causes of crime in order to make policy decisions that are more realistically in line with the true nature of the problem. Of course, no single explanation can account for the variety of delinquent behaviors of youth, and in fact most of the major explanations of delinquency do offer accurate descriptions for why youths become involved in delinquency under different circumstances. Just as there are a variety of causes, therefore, policymakers must also take a variety of approaches to deal with the problem.

Summary

Explanations of delinquency fall into one of two broad categories: classical or rational theories, and positivist or determinist theories. We have summarized and briefly discussed those theories in reference to school problems. Individual explanations focus on the biological, genetic, and psychological causes of delinquency. The major sociological theories include social structure or strain, subcultural, and social process and social control theories. While all of the major theoretical explanations make some contribution to our understanding of delinquent behavior, control theory has received the most extensive research support. A measure of a good theory is not only how well it explains the causes of delinquency, but also whether it provides clear, workable strategies for delinquency prevention.

Note

1. The explanations of delinquency presented here are not intended to be a complete and comprehensive discussion of all major criminological theories. I have provided only an overview and general explanation of crime theories, and focused on those that explain delinquent behavior in the context of school experiences. Readers are encouraged to review Shoemaker (2004) and other books that provide a more complete discussion of criminological theories.

4

Family, Peers, Gangs, and Delinquency

The nature and quality of the social interactions and experiences normally encountered by adolescents in the process of growing up make a significant difference in the likelihood of their avoiding trouble with the law or engaging in delinquent behavior. The theories of delinquency and research findings discussed in the previous chapter include many of those childhood experiences. In this chapter we examine more closely some of the correlates of delinquency. Factors such as the parent–child relationship, family experiences, peer relations, gang involvement, drug use, and school experiences are important in determining whether or not youths engage in delinquent behavior. These factors are called correlates rather than causes because every young person experiences them in varying degrees during the normal process of growing up. Despite being exposed to some family problems, negative peer influence, or drug use, for example, most youths do not become serious delinquents. The difference is in the nature and extent of their exposure to these problems and how they cope with or respond to these factors through the childhood and adolescent development process.

The Family

The family is the most important source of nurturance and socialization in a child's life. Parents are role models for children, providing examples for interacting with others, for ethical and legal behavior, for instilling work habits, and for fulfilling responsibilities. Nurturing parents who are positive role models and who maintain a positive home environment provide support to help children resist negative peer influence in schools and on the streets. Good parents and nurturing families provide the kind of home environment that helps youth succeed in school and resist antisocial behaviors even when growing up in high-crime neighborhoods.

On the other hand, children who grow up in families marked by parental conflict and tension or with parents who are absent, are neglectful, and frequently engage in verbal abuse are predisposed to factors that promote antisocial and delinquent behavior. There is little question that family problems contribute to school problems, absenteeism, and failure and to deviant and delinquent behavior. The nature of parent–child relations also affects youths' relations with their peers and their selection of friends. At some point in every youth's life, friends begin to have an equal or greater influence than their parents. Youths who feel rejected by their parents often turn to peers for support. The emergence of juvenile gangs is a manifestation of youths' need for acceptance and a sense of belonging. The kind of friends with whom they associate therefore has great importance. Parental and peer relationships differ for boys and girls, and there are gender differences in how parental neglect leads to school problems and delinquent behavior. There is little question that family problems and peer influence are major contributing factors to juvenile delinquency. Exactly how and under what conditions the process occurs is not agreed upon by researchers. This chapter examines the role of the family, peers, gangs, and drugs in juvenile delinquency.

Changes in Family and Parental Roles

The American family has undergone many changes in the last few decades and is faced with serious problems. Among those problems are divorce, single-parent families, teenage mothers bearing children outside of marriage, unemployment, poverty, alcohol and drug abuse, verbal abuse, family conflict, and violence.

The divorce rate in this country has had a major impact on family life. One in four of our nation's youth now live with only one parent, typically the mother, and among black families, more than half of young people do not have a father in the home (Dryfoos, 1990: 17). This increase in female-headed households presents a dramatic contrast with what Americans have viewed as the "ideal family"—a father at work, mother at home, with considerable "quality time" together after dad returns from work and the kids return home from school. In countless homes today, the father lives elsewhere, mother is at work, and the kids return home from school (if they have attended!) to an empty home.

Female-headed households face special difficulties, beginning with below-average income levels as a result of unemployment or underemployment. Census Bureau figures for 2002 indicate that 12.1 million (16.7 percent) of children under 18 are in families with incomes below the poverty level, up from 11.7 million in 2001 (U.S. Census Bureau, 2004). Female-headed families have a higher percentage of poverty than married-couple families. In 2002, 7.2 million families (9.6 percent) lived in poverty, and the number of female-headed households was 3.6 million, or 26.5 percent (U.S. Census Bureau, 2004). Being raised in a single-parent family or in poverty does not necessarily cause a child to become delinquent, but those factors certainly place stress on the family environment and may increase the tendencies and temptations to become involved in deviant and delinquent behaviors. There is substantial evidence that children raised in poverty and under adverse conditions have a higher probability of becoming delinquent.

The Family and Delinquency

The role of parents and families is important in explaining delinquent behavior. The problem seems clear to juvenile justice officials, policymakers, and concerned citizens. Juvenile probation officers often remark that they work with as many "delinquent parents" as they do delinquent children. The Office of Juvenile Justice and Delinquency Prevention (OJJDP) has recognized the importance of effective parenting and stable families in preventing delinquency. The office has funded several research and program development initiatives with the goal of providing information, resources, and technical assistance to juvenile justice agencies to help strengthen families (Kumpfer and Alvarado, 1998; Thornberry et al., 1999). Numerous resources for parents and caregivers have been made available through the OJJDP and the National Criminal Justice Reference Service (NCJRS) as well as electronically (http://ojjdp.ncjrs.org).

Criminologists have not consistently focused on the role of the family in delinquency. After some extensive research in the 1950s and 1960s, less attention was given to studying the family in efforts to understand delinquency. There seem to be at least two reasons for this. First, attention turned more to social structure and social problems that seemed to lend themselves to change, such as gangs and drugs. Second, more emphasis was placed on those factors that seemed amenable to change in reducing delinquency, and it was unclear whether family intervention or training could be done and whether it would have any effect on delinquency.

Different explanations have been offered for the association between family problems and delinquency. Some criminologists believe that family structure (whether one or two parents are present and family size) is important in explaining delinquency. Others argue that "functional" factors or "quality of family life" is more important. They contend that factors such as family relationships, parent–child interactions, and the quality of supervision and discipline are more important in determining whether children become delinquent (Wilkinson, 1974; Rosen, 1985). Researchers have developed a sizable body of literature in attempting to explain family structure, processes, and the relationship with juvenile delinquency (see Gove and Crutchfield, 1982; Lincoln and Straus, 1985; Loeber and Stouthamer-Loeber, 1986; Pope, 1988). The difference between functional and structural factors may not be so clear-cut, and there is a relationship between them. In addressing family disruption and delinquency, criminologists have examined the impact of "family transitions" (Thornberry et al., 1999). Family transitions refer to the number of changes in families, such as whether parents were separated or divorced within the past year, whether they changed residence, or whether a child was sent to live with a relative or other caregiver for a period of time. These are primarily "structural" factors, but have a direct effect on the quality of family relationships. Thornberry and associates analyzed data from three longitudinal studies (the Rochester, Denver, and Pittsburgh Youth Surveys) and found that the number of family transitions had an effect on the prevalence of delinquency and drug use among affected youth. The findings have implications for the prevention of delinquency and drug use. Social agencies and schools, for example, may help to provide some stability and structure in the lives of young people experiencing family transitions.

The Broken Home

The "broken home" refers to a family structure that has been disrupted by separation, divorce, or death of a parent. Research by Sheldon and Eleanor Glueck (1950) showed that 60 percent of delinquents, but only 34 percent of nondelinquent youth, came from broken homes. There is evidence that a broken home increases the probability that some types of youth will participate in delinquency (Datesman and Scarpitti, 1975; Rankin, 1980). In a longitudinal study of men who had been involved in a delinquency-prevention program, McCord found that over half of the fathers of boys reared in broken homes were known to be alcoholics or criminals and close to half of the sons of alcoholic or criminal men had been convicted for serious crimes (1982: 123). The lack of supervision in these broken homes accounted for much of the criminal behavior of children raised by only one parent. Absence of the father was not found to be important in explaining the boys' criminal behavior, however. The quality of home life rather than the number of parents is most important in explaining youths' criminal behavior (McCord, 1982: 124). Gove and Crutchfield (1982) noted gender differences in family variables relating to delinquency. Boys in single-parent homes are more likely to be delinquent, but marital variables have little impact on girls' delinquency. For boys in intact families, delinquency was strongly related to marital interaction, and physical punishment was strongly related to delinquency. Marital status has little effect on girls, but the quality of the parent–child interaction and parental control (including knowledge of friends) is more strongly related to misbehavior among girls. The parents' feeling toward their children was most strongly related to delinquency (Gove and Crutchfield, 1982: 316). Other research indicates that the broken home is only associated with running away and truancy (Rankin, 1977, 1980); there is a moderate relationship with status offenses (Van Voorhis et al., 1988), but a weaker relationship for serious delinquent behavior (Wells and Rankin, 1991). Several studies have challenged the notion of the broken home as a cause of delinquency. Cernkovich and Giordano (1987) believe that broken homes have no effects on delinquency, rather that family-interaction variables such as caring, trust, control, and supervision are more important than family structure.

Researchers have concluded that there is a relationship between official measures, but not self-report measures of delinquency, and the broken home (Wilkinson, 1980; Johnson, 1986; Laub and Sampson, 1988). Laub and Sampson (1988) reanalyzed the Gluecks' data and concluded that their original conclusion of a relationship between delinquency and broken homes is not supportable. The Gluecks' data were based on official delinquency measures, not on self-report data. Self-report measures of delinquency show few if any differences between youth from intact homes and those from broken homes. Decisions by school and juvenile justice officials are often influenced by family status. Youths from single-parent homes are believed to be in greater need of intervention and supervision than those with two parents, and officials often process cases that might be dropped for youths with two parents who are perceived less in need of court intervention. Thus, youths from broken homes are disproportionately represented in referrals to the justice system (Johnson, 1986; Laub and Sampson, 1988).

In summary, the reemergence of research on the broken home has contributed to our understanding of one- versus two-parent families and delinquent behavior. The exact connection between broken homes and delinquency remains unclear, however, and involves more than simply the dichotomous description of broken versus intact homes (Wells and Rankin, 1986, 1991). Nevertheless, the percentage of parents who are divorced and the percentage of households headed by women are among the most important predictors of crime rates. Since 1970, the proportion of American households that have children who live with both parents has declined substantially. In 1970, 64 percent of African

American children lived with two parents, compared with 35 percent in 1997; comparable figures for white children are 90 percent and 74 percent, respectively (Lugaila, 1998). Most studies indicate that children from intact homes have lower crime rates than children from broken homes. It would be an oversimplification to claim that broken homes are a cause of delinquency, however. Most youths from broken homes after all are not delinquent, and intact families are not a guarantee against delinquent involvement of youth. Rather it is the quality of the parent–child relationship, whether there are one or two parents, that is more important in explaining youth involvement in delinquent behavior. When all else is equal, one parent is sufficient for child-rearing. However, "all else" is rarely equal (Hirschi, 1983: 62). Single-parent families do face more difficulties in discipline, supervision, and economic pressures. The single parent (usually a woman) faces considerable responsibilities to maintain employment and a household and to devote time to numerous child-rearing tasks, often without the psychological, social, and financial support of a former spouse. Given the high rate of divorce in this country, it is appropriate that family courts and legislative bodies have placed a high priority on the well-being of the child in custody and support decisions. More attention has been given lately to enforcing child-support responsibilities of the noncustodial parent. This is an important step in minimizing the difficulties faced by children of broken homes.

Family Size

The number of children in a family is also related to delinquency and, as with the broken home, this variable also needs explanation. A sizable number of youths who come in contact with police are from larger families. Loeber and Stouthamer-Loeber (1986) suggest three reasons for this apparent relationship: (1) it is harder for a parent to discipline and supervise a larger number of children; (2) parents often delegate the authority to supervise younger children to their older siblings; and (3) larger families are often associated with other social problems such as illegitimacy, poverty, and crowding in the home (1986: 100–101). Families of any size with adequate financial means, quality parent–child relations, and good discipline and supervision are less likely to have children who are involved in delinquent behavior. Studies indicate that a broken home is less important than the quality of the parent–child relationship in explaining delinquency (Matsueda and Heimer, 1987; Laub and Sampson, 1988).

Family Relationships

Broken homes, large families, and working mothers seem to many persons to be obvious causes of juvenile delinquency. Research fails to show much support for this belief, however, and directs us to examine the quality of family relationships. Nye (1958) suggested that the quality of the parent–child relationship was more important than whether there were one or two parents present in the home. Parental rejection describes parent–child relationships that are lacking in warmth, love, affection, and appreciation of parents for their children. Loeber and Stouthamer-Loeber found that 12 of 15 studies measuring parent–child relations reported a significant relation between rejection and delinquency and aggression (1986: 55). Rosen (1985) found lower delinquency rates among African American youths who had more father–son interaction. Hirschi (1969) contends that delinquency is less likely among youths who have a positive "attachment" with their parent(s). More recent research support the theory that the quality of family life and degree

of parental attachment are more important predictors of delinquency than family structure (Laub and Sampson, 1988; Rankin and Kern, 1994). Parents influence their children's
behavior through positive interaction, emotional closeness, and gaining respect. Parents
are positive role models. Children who feel loved and respect their parents and identify
with them are less likely to get into trouble.

Discipline and Supervision

Parents differ greatly in parenting skills. Some parents are inconsistent in their
discipline, and when they do correct their child they are nagging or too harsh. Parents
who are preoccupied with their own concerns often neglect their children, fail to monitor
their whereabouts, do not know their children's friends, or are simply too lenient or
inconsistent in their discipline. Parents in "broken homes" and in large families face more
difficulties administering consistent discipline and supervision. Nye (1958) found a slight
causal relationship between mothers' employment and delinquent behavior of their children. Hirschi (1969) found slightly higher delinquency rates for children whose mothers
were employed outside the home and suggested that they were less able to closely supervise the children's activities and behavior. Inconsistent parental discipline and limited supervision are strong predictors of delinquent behavior (Patterson and Stouthamer-Loeber, 1984;
Cernkovich and Giordano, 1987). Other research has noted a stronger relationship
between lack of supervision and official delinquency than between lack of supervision
and self-reported delinquency (Loeber and Stouthamer-Loeber, 1986: 61). Wells and Rankin
(1988) concluded that direct parental controls such as close supervision and monitoring
of youngsters' behavior have as great an impact on delinquency as that of indirect controls such as "attachments" or positive parent–child relations.

Do Parents Cause Delinquency?

Research clearly shows that parents play a vital role in helping their children grow and
mature through a healthy and normal child development. What do we know about the
consequences of ineffective parenting? Parents are blamed for their child's misbehavior
despite the fact that the child may be acting out behavior learned from playmates and
peers or from watching television. To what extent should parents be held accountable for
their children's misbehavior, and is there evidence that parents may actually contribute
to their children's delinquent behavior? We review in this section what psychologists
and other social scientists know about parenting styles and family functioning and
the effects on youths' crime and victimization experiences. Parents cannot shield their
children from all antisocial behavior and deviant influences from peers, popular culture,
and the media. Parents can, however, reduce the risk that their child will be victimized
or engage in deviant and delinquent behavior by following at least three effective parenting practices:

•*Awareness*: Be aware of popular culture and peer influences on youth.

•*Communication*: Maintain communication, encourage sharing, listen as much as (or more than)
  talking.

•*Engagement*: Practice a combination of the above, remaining in touch with youths, their issues and
  concerns, school progress and problems, and decisions they are expected to make.

A number of studies and research findings illustrate the importance of these three effective parenting practices and the consequences of ineffective families and parents. The universal importance of a healthy parent–child relationship is illustrated by cross-cultural and international research. A study of Australian children examined peer relations and family and parental background factors in explaining bullying and victimization experiences at school (Rigby, 1993). Poor family functioning and relations and negative attitudes toward parents was predictive of bullying behavior for both boys and girls when controlling for age. The tendency for girls to be victimized by peers at school was associated with poorer family functioning and negative attitudes toward mothers, and negative relationships with absent fathers in single-parent families characterized boys who reported being victimized at school (Rigby, 1993). Olweus (1980) found that among Norwegian children, mothers' negativism or lack of warmth toward their sons was a significant factor in the development of aggressiveness and tendency toward bullying behavior in boys.

Awareness and Communication

The level of communication and quality of parent–child relationships is important in youths' pro-social development and avoidance of drugs and delinquency. Parents' awareness of youth problems and behavior is essential in order for meaningful communication, monitoring, and parental supervision to take place. A study of parents' and their children's knowledge, attitudes, and perception of drug abuse issues was conducted in Malaysia (Low et al., 1996). Teenagers knew more about the causes as well as the treatment and rehabilitation for drug addiction than their parents. Youths reported that not being loved or treated fairly by parents, having unfulfilled needs, and not being respected or recognized for one's capabilities all contributed to drug abuse. The authors suggested that differences in youths' and parents' knowledge and awareness of drug abuse were issues that must be addressed as a part of any meaningful drug abuse–prevention program (Low et al., 1996). A statewide survey of parents and their adolescent children examined associations between parenting strategies and self-reported teen drinking (Haynie et al., 1999). Less teen drinking was associated with parents' reports of checking to see if other parents would be present at teen parties, particularly among white parents. Parents who reported more awareness and monitoring of their teens' involvement with alcohol expressed more competence in taking a proactive approach. Research has also established a relationship between parental influences on students' aggressive behaviors and weapon carrying. Orpinas, Murray, and Kelder (1999) examined the association between family variables and fighting and weapon carrying among 8,865 6th, 7th, and 8th graders from eight urban schools in Texas. Parental monitoring, positive parent–teen relations, and lack of parental support for fighting had an inverse relationship with aggression, fighting, and weapon carrying. Students who lived with both parents were less likely to report aggression. Youths' perception of parents' attitudes toward fighting was the strongest predictor of aggression (Orpinas et al., 1999).

Parental Engagement

The quality of the parent–child relationship is important in helping children form positive peer relationships, make a commitment to education, avoid use of tobacco, alcohol, and other drugs, and avoid involvement in delinquent behavior. In a study of more than 20,000 American teenagers from nine high schools, researchers found that adolescents who had the most problems came from families in which parents were hostile, aloof, or uninvolved (Steinberg et al., 1996; Steinberg, 2000). Steinberg and associates found that children from homes characterized by negative parenting were at risk for problems regardless of their ethnicity or income and regardless of whether their parents were married, divorced, single, or remarried. The quality of the parent–child relationship therefore matters much more than the social demographics of the household (Steinberg, 2000: 35). The most worrisome finding of their research was what they described as the high level of *parental disengagement* they saw in their sample (Steinberg, 2000: 35). Examples of parental disengagement cited by Steinberg were:

- One-fourth of students were allowed to decide what classes to take in school without discussing the decision with their parents.
- Thirty percent of parents did not know how their child was doing in school.
- One-third of parents did not know how their child spends his or her spare time.
- One-fourth of the students said their family "never" did anything together for fun.
- Only 30 percent of the students said their parents spend some time talking with them each day.

Based on their study of 20,000 youth, Steinberg estimated that 25–30 percent of families with teenagers nationally may be characterized by some degree of parental disengagement (Steinberg, 2000: 35). These findings have important implications for adolescent development and safe schools. Adolescents from disengaged homes were more likely to show psychological immaturity and adjustment difficulties, such as less self-reliance, lower self-esteem, and diminished social competence. Youths from such homes were less interested and less successful in school and more likely to become involved in misconduct, drug use, and delinquency (Steinberg, 2000: 36). Parental involvement in their children's lives is one of the most important, if not *the* most important, contributors to children's healthy psychological development. Steinberg believes that job demands and work stress are only partial explanations for parents' disengagement from their children. Other factors are parental mental health problems, lack of community support for families, and misinformation about parenting. Many parents believe that their children do not need them after they reach adolescence or that parents don't really matter after that age because children's development is determined by factors outside the family. These beliefs are wrong and are contradicted by scientific data. Steinberg asserts that we need a public health campaign in America to make sure that all parents know how to raise psychologically healthy children and are willing to take responsibility for doing this (2000: 37).

Child Abuse and Neglect

Child abuse is a serious problem in America and has a long history. It has endured because harsh discipline, corporal punishment, and cruelty to children have not always been recognized as serious problems. Dr. C. Henry Kempe first brought attention to child abuse when he reported survey results of medical and law enforcement agencies that showed high rates of child abuse. He originated the term "battered child syndrome" to describe the numerous incidents of nonaccidental physical injuries of children by their parents or guardians (Kempe et al., 1962). Kempe and associates have since dropped the term "battered child" and recommended the terms child abuse and neglect, which are more inclusive in referring to physical abuse and failure to properly care for children's development and emotional well-being (Helfer and Kempe, 1976). The initial revelation of the problem of child abuse prompted a quantity of research in the 1960s and 1970s. Several states have passed laws requiring mandatory reporting of child abuse and neglect cases. The U.S. Congress passed the Child Abuse and Prevention Act and established the National Center on Child Abuse in 1974.

Definitions of Child Abuse and Neglect

Child abuse includes neglect and physical beating. The terms describe physical or emotional trauma to a child where no reasonable explanation, such as an accident or acceptable disciplinary practices, can be detected. Child abuse is usually a pattern of behavior rather than a single beating or act of neglect. Its effects are cumulative, and the longer it persists, the more severe are the physical and emotional effects on the child. *Neglect* refers to parental deprivation of children, such as lack of food, shelter, clothing, care, and nurturance. Neglect is more passive in nature, which over time results in emotional or physical problems. Abuse is more overt, physical mistreatment of a child, often resulting in injuries requiring medical care. The two terms are often used interchangeably and often occur together in the same family (see Helfer and Kempe, 1976; Kempe and Kempe, 1978).

The Extent of Child Abuse

The American family and the home setting have been called one of the most violent institutions in the nation (Straus et al., 1980). Americans face the greatest risk of assault, physical injury, and even murder in their own homes, by their own family members. Straus and associates (1980) conducted a nationwide survey of families and found that an astounding number of parents interviewed in 1975 reported that they kicked, punched, bit, beat, or threatened their children with a gun or a knife. About three parents in 100 kicked, bit, or punched their child; 1 percent had beat up their child in the past year, and 4 percent had done that at some point in the child's life. Three of 100 children have had a parent threaten to use a gun or knife on them some time in their lives, and one in 1,000 children faced a gun or knife threat from parents during 1975. Straus and associates estimated that between 3.1 and 4 million children have been kicked, bitten, or punched by a parent at some time in their lives; between 1 and 1.9 million were kicked, bitten, or punched in 1975 (1980: 62). The survey showed that physical abuse in these families was not a single occurrence, but happened four to nine times in the course of a year. The national survey showed that family violence was not limited to children. Straus et al. (1980) found that the extent of spousal assaults and intrafamily violence was so great that they reported on domestic abuse in general and not just child abuse. The National Center on Child Abuse and Neglect in 1982 estimated that each year 3.4 children per 1,000 were victims of some physical abuse in this country; 5.7 per 1,000 were victims of some type of emotional, physical, or sexual abuse; and 5.3 per 1,000 had experienced educational, emotional, or physical neglect (see Gray, 1988). The 1985 National Family Violence Survey found that each year about 1.5 million children were kicked, bitten, punched, beaten up, burned or scalded, or threatened or attacked with a knife or gun (Gelles and Straus, 1988). In 1996, the U.S. Department of Health and Human Services estimated that the number of child abuse and neglect reports had nearly doubled between 1986 and 1993, rising 98 percent from 1.42 to 2.81 million, and the number of seriously injured children nearly quadrupled, increasing from 141,700 in 1986 to 565,000 in 1993 (Bavolek, 2000: 2). An average of three children die of child abuse and neglect each day in the United States (National Clearinghouse on Child Abuse and Neglect Information, 1998).

Victims of child abuse and neglect suffer the worst forms of family conflict and parental rejection. Neglect and abuse have serious effects on a child's emotional development. Abused children often act out through truancy and disruptive behavior in school, run away from home, and use alcohol and other drugs. Abuse causes self-rejection and low self-esteem that youths may attempt to deal with through substance abuse, attention-getting behavior in school, or association with other deviant peers. The parent–child relationship is so damaged that parents do not have the respect of their children, so are not accepted as role models or positive authority figures. Children who have been victims of physical aggression often act out later with aggressive violent behavior (see Zingraff and Belyea, 1986).

There is research evidence that abused and neglected children have greater difficulty in school. Kempe and Kempe believe that many abused children face academic and social problems as soon as they enter school (1978: 25). Broadhurst reviewed studies that show the detrimental effects of abuse and neglect on school performance (1980: 19–41). Teachers who have worked with abused and neglected children say that these children "have difficulty in concentrating, are aloof, have little or no confidence, frequently have emotional outbursts, have not internalized rules, and are often destructive of property" (Bartollas, 1993: 279). As a result, abused and neglected children are often labeled as disruptive in schools, are assigned to special classes, and in this way are set up for failure.

The relationship between child abuse and delinquency has been widely accepted. Curtis (1963) suggested that "violence breeds violence." Abused and neglected children often act out as juveniles and young adults with acts of violence. The process by which child abuse often leads to delinquency has been described as a "cycle of violence" (Widom 1989b: 3). Several studies document a relationship between child abuse and aggressive, delinquent, and violent behavior (see Zingraff and Belyea, 1986; Gray, 1988). Alfaro (1981) studied children in eight New York counties who had been abused and found that 10 percent of them later had a record of being delinquent or ungovernable, compared to only 2 percent for all children in the counties during the same period. Kratcoski (1982) found no significant differences between abused and nonabused youth in the frequency of violent offenses, but delinquents who had been abused were more than twice as likely (45 percent vs. 18 percent) to engage in violence against family members, as opposed to other acquaintances or strangers. Family violence—physical fighting between parents and among siblings—is associated with youth accepting attitudes toward violence as a part of life and committing a violent crime in adult life (Fagan et al., 1983). A large proportion of juvenile female offenders have been victims of physical or sexual abuse or exploitation. Bergsmann (1989) reviewed an American Correctional Association study reporting that 62 percent of female juveniles said they were physically abused. Forty-seven percent reported 11 or more incidences of abuse, 30 percent said the abuse began between 5 and 9 years of age, and 45 percent said the abuse occurred between 10 and 14 years of age. Parents were the abusers in most of the cases (Bergsmann, 1989: 73). Other studies failed to show a strong relationship between abuse and later violent behavior. Fagan et al. (1983) found only a low incidence of child abuse and parental violence among violent offenders compared with nationwide rates. In most studies, in fact, the majority of abused children became neither delinquent nor violent offenders (Widom, 1989b).

In a study of street gangs on the West Coast, Fleisher (1995) found that, almost without exception, members of the Crips and Bloods grew up in "dangerous family environments." Most of the youth joined gangs in order to escape violence at home or because they were abandoned or neglected by their parents. They developed what Fleisher calls a "defensive world view," which he characterizes as (1) a feeling of vulnerability and a need to protect oneself, (2) a belief that no one can be trusted, (3) a need to maintain social distance, (4) a willingness to use violence and intimidation to repel others, (5) an attraction to similarly defensive people, and (6) an expectation that no one will come to their aid (Fleisher, 1995: 103–107; see also Wright and Wright, 1994: 15).

Other researchers have argued that there is a relationship between child abuse and later adult criminal behavior. Persons who have been victims of abuse or have witnessed abusive family environments purportedly view violence and aggression as an appropriate way to deal with problems. Zingraff and Belyea (1986) reviewed a number of studies documenting cases in which offenders convicted of murder reported having been physically or emotionally abused by their parents. Many offenders convicted of first degree murder had been severely abused by their parents, 85 percent of a group of 53 murderers reported that they experienced severe corporal punishment during their early childhood, and a group of 112 felons reported significantly more abusive treatment than a comparison group of 376 noninstitutionalized male adults (Zingraff and Belyea, 1986: 52). In their study of the social histories of 18,574 inmates in North Carolina prisons, Zingraff and Belyea found that only 9 percent reported experiencing abuse as children, and there were few statistically significant differences between abused and nonabused inmates serving time for violent crimes. Their findings cast doubt on the notion that "violence breeds violence." There is some evidence that abuse breeds abuse, however. Widom (1989b) reviewed studies that showed a higher likelihood of abuse among parents who were abused themselves, although the majority of abusive parents were not themselves abused as children. She estimated that about a third of the persons who were abused as children will abuse their own children (Widom, 1989b: 8). A connection has also been made between abuse, neglect, and delinquency. Various studies reported that between 8 and 26 percent of delinquents had been abused; Widom (1989b) reported that delinquency occurs in fewer than 20 percent of those who had been abused or neglected. Widom (1989a) compared a large group of persons with histories of abuse or neglect with a matched control group and found that 28.6 percent of the abused and neglected subjects compared to 21.1 percent of the control group had an adult criminal record (1989a: 260). For both men and women, a history of abuse or neglect significantly increased their chances of having a criminal record as an adult. However, while 29 percent of the abused and neglected subjects had adult criminal records, 71 percent did not; therefore, having a history of childhood abuse or neglect does not inevitably lead to criminal behavior as an adult (Widom, 1989a).

In summary, we know there is some connection between child abuse and neglect and later criminal behavior as juveniles or adults. We know that many abused children become abusive parents. However, most abused children do *not* become abusive parents, juvenile delinquents, or violent adult criminals (Widom, 1989a; Wright and Wright, 1994).

Parents, School Problems, and Delinquency

There is considerable research evidence showing a relationship between parents' lack of support for education and children's school problems and between school misconduct, school failure, and involvement in delinquent behavior (see Patterson and Dishion, 1985; Spivak and Cianci, 1987). Offord studied a sample of boys and girls placed on probation by the Juvenile Court of Ottawa, Canada, and found that families of delinquents with early school failure (repeating a grade, special class placement) tended to be more disorganized, nonintact, poorer, the mothers had a history of being on welfare, and many of the fathers had been involved with the law (1982: 134, 136). Simons et al. (1991) suggested that ineffective parenting and a coercive interpersonal style causes youngsters to experience difficulties with peers and authority figures at school and that these difficulties lead to negative labeling and rejection by conventional peers. School problems do not have a direct effect on delinquency according to their explanation, but contribute indirectly to delinquent behavior because youth with school problems are more likely to associate with deviant peers. A coercive parenting style is important in explaining delinquent involvement, and Simons and associates found that it increases delinquency involvement independent of peer influences. Inept and coercive parenting includes attempts to control a child through threats, power plays, abstinence, or ploys to make the child feel guilty and when the parent persistently complains, nags, or criticizes the child (Simons et al., 1991: 652–653). The link between parenting practices, school problems, and delinquency led to the development of school programs directed at improving parenting skills.

Family and School Involvement

Given the importance of the family in explaining delinquency, family training is logically considered by many to be a necessary step toward delinquency prevention (see Wilson and Loury, 1987). Some believe that schools are the most appropriate settings for early intervention efforts in delinquency prevention (Hirschi, 1983; Zigler and Hall, 1987; see also Patterson, 1986; Hawkins and Lam, 1987).

Educators generally complain that schools have been expected to take on many additional responsibilities that were traditionally the responsibility of parents. Furthermore, teachers and principals complain that many of the teaching and discipline problems they face could be alleviated if they had more support from parents. Their complaints certainly have merit. Many discipline problems could be minimized if parents would help to instill respect for teachers and support educators in disciplinary sanctions when their children have violated school regulations. Parents can help improve their children's school achievement by inquiring regularly about their required assignments and what they are studying week to week, by encouraging them to complete homework, and by providing a place and a quiet time in the home to complete homework.

Many educators, however, do not welcome the idea of parental involvement in the schools. Sara Lawrence Lightfoot (1978) noted the irony of families and schools sharing the complementary task of educating and raising young people, yet finding a great deal of conflict with one another. According to Lightfoot, teachers tend to be defensive about their professional status, their occupational image, and their special skills and abilities. Teachers generally develop a better awareness of the educational abilities and needs of children than most parents. Parents' fears tend to grow as they lose control of their child's daily life and as someone else becomes the expert and judge of their child's abilities. Teacher evaluations of a child's attention, study habits, discipline, or general school performance are often met with defensive reactions by parents. Teachers have difficulty with parents who do not seem to value their special competence and skills (see Lightfoot, 1978: 20–42).

Many teachers and school administrators believe that parents have no right to exert influence on the schools. Gene Maeroff (1982) suggested that some school procedures seem to intentionally exclude parents and keep them uninformed. Parents have no role in the selection of teachers for their children or the assignment of principals to schools, for example, and most schools do not involve parents in decisions regarding curriculum development and selection of textbooks (1982: 208). Other examples of schools' failure to involve parents are in setting regulations for dress and behavior, report cards that are complex and unintelligible or so simple that they report little about a child's progress, and meetings that are scheduled during the day with little regard for parents' work schedules (Maeroff, 1982: 208). Many schools do encourage parental involvement and have implemented a number of programs and policies to maintain close communication with parents aimed at a cooperative team approach to enhance educational progress for children. In addition, parents may become involved in schools through parent–teacher organizations and through decisions and policies of school boards.

There is evidence that parental involvement in their children's education makes a difference in school achievement. To determine why children of some low-income families were more successful in school, teams of teachers and principals visited the homes of successful students. Three common factors in the homes were: (1) the parents knew what was happening in school and kept in touch with teachers to know what was expected of their children; (2) the parents viewed school as the key to their children's upward mobility and encouraged regular attendance; and (3) in addition to the parent there was usually another adult, such as a grandparent, neighbor, or aunt, who provided addition emotional and psychological support (Maeroff, 1982: 227). The combination of these three factors resulted in a strong emphasis on regulated television viewing, completing assigned chores around the house, and doing homework. The organization and structure that began in these children's lives at home apparently carried over into the classroom.

The School and Parent Training

The role of the school in promoting child-rearing practices is worth pursuing. Although schools already have many responsibilities beyond basic education, this expectation may not place many additional demands on schools. The school is already involved in child-rearing in terms of promoting social expectations, setting limits, and providing structure to students' lives. The promotion of communication and mediation skills with opportunities for social interaction with teachers and positive peers are important factors in child-rearing, particularly in the absence of close parental relations and supervision. Most educators' values and practices seem close to those of successful parents (Hirschi, 1983: 67). Hirschi suggests that schools have some advantages over the family, in that teachers care about the behavior of children (disruption makes their lives more difficult), school monitoring of behavior is very efficient, and teachers are probably more expert than parents in recognizing deviant behavior (1983: 67). Granted, the school's role in child-rearing does have limitations. It depends on students' regular attendance and to some extent on parents' support for schooling. To the extent that the child and parent are not committed to or regularly involved in the educational process, the ability of the schools to make an impact is limited. Nevertheless, the inability of schools to affect those who are less involved in education should not obscure the fact that schools do very well with many students. The difficulties in working with some students should not minimize the potential that schools have for helping families improve their child-rearing practices (Hirschi, 1983).

J. David Hawkins and associates (1987) have been active in developing and evaluating the effectiveness of a school-based parent-training program in Seattle. They found that to be effective, parent training must reach the parents of children who are most at risk of delinquent behavior and the training must involve parents before the children's misbehavior has become serious. The parent training can be implemented as early as when the children are in the first grade (1987: 196–197). Others have suggested that intervention efforts may have little impact on "antisocial" families marked by criminality and family violence and that interventions with youth from such families would more effectively be focused in schools and with their peers (Fagan and Wexler, 1987: 665). An outstanding program designed to deal with family problems before they result in delinquency is the Oregon Social Learning Center developed by Gerald Patterson and associates (Patterson, 1986). They believe that many parents do not know how to deal with their children effectively and that antisocial behavior in the home and at school is associated with poor parenting skills. Children whose parents ignore their misbehavior one moment and then overreact another time with explosive anger are not provided the consistent discipline that they need. The Oregon program teaches parents to use effective disciplinary techniques that emphasize firmness and consistency and encourages the use of positive reinforcement for good behavior while discouraging ineffective discipline such as yelling, humiliating remarks, or hitting. Similar programs patterned after the Oregon program have proven successful.

Parent training has been among the most promising approaches for dealing with misbehavior of young people, especially very young children. There are a number of limitations to parent training as a primary means of delinquency prevention, however. Existing programs are quite expensive; they do not reach many families, some of whom could most benefit from them; many parents (some of whom most need training) are unwilling to participate; and it is not clear how long the beneficial effects of training last (Loeber, 1988). The role of government in family intervention and training has become a regular topic of discussion. The role of the government in parenting training is by necessity limited. Just as government efforts in crime prevention are limited, so also are they limited in preventing family problems. Laws and government policies have by nature been "reactive" more than preventive. Some in fact believe that governmental interventions into family life may do more harm than good. Some social service and social welfare programs, for example, may contribute to the breakup of families that otherwise would have remained together. Government programs that may be more effective are those aimed at the environment in which children grow up by improving schools, housing, and nourishment (Loeber, 1988). It is not clear whether such programs have much impact on keeping families together or keeping children from becoming delinquent.

Peer Relationships and Delinquency

Youths' relationships with peers and the kinds of friends with whom they associate are very important in their school performance and behavior and in whether they become involved in delinquent behavior (Lawrence, 1991). As they reach the teenage years, peer group influence often interferes with parental and family ties, encouraging alienation between them and their parents. Next to the family, the school is the most important social insti-tution in preparing young people for a career and a satisfying life that is free of social and legal problems. The role of parents, peers, and the school are thus closely related in the emergence of delinquent behavior. Youths who do not have parental support and attach-ment are less equipped to deal with school demands and the resulting frustration of school failure. They are more likely to violate laws when they are with their friends, especially if ties with their parents are weaker; they are more vulnerable to the temptations and pressures of peers. It is little wonder then that many youth turn to disruptive and delin-quent behavior in school. When parents and schoolteachers are unable to get them involved in productive school performance and behavior, they often turn to delinquent friends who are experiencing similar problems. Associations with delinquent peers pro-vide the acceptance and the support that they are not getting from parents and the school.

The tendency for young people to turn away from their parents and seek closer ties with their peers has long been recognized. According to Riesman (1950), the American family began changing in the 1950s. The family was a closely knit unit where parents had a great deal of respect and authority. Today parents have less power, less confidence, and more doubts about how to raise their children. Children are influenced by the media and by their friends, and they put pressure on their parents to go along with these norms. Riesman argued that peers were becoming more important influences on a child than parents. Junior and senior high schools actually play a major role in drawing youth away from their parents and other adults. Schools draw hundreds of youth together, and as a result teenagers create their own subculture, with language, behaviors, and values that are distinctly different from that of adults. In the past American children and youth spent more time with adults, but today children spend a large portion of their time at school, going to and from school, at school events, and with their peers. Bronfenbrenner (1970) argued that society has become age-segregated and parents and other adults want it this way. They do not want to spend much time with their children, but prefer that their children spend time with their peer group instead. Problems arise when young peer groups pro-mote negative values and deviant behavior, and Bronfenbrenner cautioned that this alien-ation of youth from adults was likely to result in more violence among the younger generation (1970: 121). David Greenberg (1977) also noted the age segregation of youth and empha-sized that as youth have become excluded from adult work and leisure activities, they have been forced to associate mostly with one another. They thus have less influence from adult role models, and the result is greater peer influence (1977: 196). As youths spend less time with their parents and other adults and much more time with their peers, their decisions and lifestyles begin to reflect the expectations of their peers. This heightened sensitivity to peers and weakened attachments to parents also explains the increased likelihood of some youths engaging in delinquent behavior (Greenberg, 1977: 196).

The nature and extent of peer influence on young people varies according to a num-ber of factors. First of all, the influence of peers varies depending on the behavior or atti-tude in question. Peers play an important role in young peoples' alcohol and substance use, but Ronald Akers emphasized that the process is not one of peer pressure but of peer *influence* (1985: 115). Akers found that for the majority of teenagers, peers are more likely to reinforce conforming behavior than deviant behavior, most of them reported feeling no pressure from peers to use any substances, and they said parents were more important than peers as sources of influence and knowledge in their decisions whether or not to use tobacco, alcohol, and other drugs (Akers, 1985: 117).

The importance of peer relationships tends to vary by gender and race. Peer group influence has a greater impact on delinquency among males than among females (Johnson, 1979). Giordano, Cernkovich, and Pugh (1986) examined friendship patterns between male and female adolescents and found that females have closer relationships with peers than do males. Girls are more likely to commit a delinquent act when they are in a group of other girls and boys than when alone (Giordano, 1978: 127). The researchers also found that white females seem to have closer relationships with peers than do African American females. The African Americans felt less caring and trust and less pressure from their peers to behave in certain ways (Giordano et al., 1986: 1195). Merry Morash (1986) found that adolescent females belong to fewer delinquent groups than males, partially explaining their lower levels of delinquent involvement. Female characteristics of being less aggressive and having more empathy also restrains them from engaging in delinquent and violent behavior with peers (Morash, 1986). Herman and Julia Schwendinger (1985) compared peer groups in working-class and middle-class communities in southern California and found distinct differences. Both groups were preoccupied with leisure activities and disliked or were at least indifferent to school, but the middle-class youth tended to avoid violent and aggressive roles more than the working-class ones; the latter were also more involved in drug use, possession, and sale. Mark Colvin and John Pauly (1983) claimed that the difference in peer relationships between working-class and middle- or upper-class youths was explained by their parents' workplace experiences. Lower-class workers tend to experience a coercive working environment, which reduces their capacity as parents to deal with their children in any other way than a repressive manner, using harsh verbal or physical punishment. The coercive family environment places a strain on parent–child relations. Colvin and Pauly further argued that these children are more likely to be placed in coercive school control situations, which leads them to associate more with other peers who feel alienated from their parents and school. The resulting peer group associations increase the likelihood of their becoming involved in delinquent activities and violent behavior (Colvin and Pauly, 1983: 542–543).

Travis Hirschi (1969) developed a social control theory of delinquency in which he held that delinquency is more likely when an individual's attachment or bond to society is weak (1969: 16). Hirschi maintained that youths who are most closely bonded to social groups such as the family, the school, and peers are less likely to commit delinquent acts (1969: 16–34). An individual's attachment to conventional others and sensitivity to other persons relates to the ability to internalize norms and to develop a conscience (1969: 18). Attachment to others also refers to the affection and respect that children have for parents, teachers, and friends; these are important considerations when youth are tempted to engage in delinquent behavior. Hirschi tested his theory on 4,077 junior and senior high school students in California, using a self-report survey along with school and police records. He found that youths with a greater attachment to parents reported less delinquent involvement. Young people with weak ties to parents reported little concern for the opinions of teachers and disliked school, and those with less attachment to school and poor school performance were more likely to become involved in delinquent behavior (1969: 110–134). Hirschi found that attachment to peers does not imply a lack of attachment to parents. Youths in his study who were close to and respected their friends were least likely to have committed delinquent acts, but he also found that delinquents were less dependent on peers than were nondelinquents, suggesting that youths' decisions whether or not to conform to the law affect their choice of friends rather than the other way around (1969: 135–161).

The peer attachment–delinquency relationship as explained by social control theory has received a great deal of support among criminologists. Some have obtained findings that further specify and clarify the relationship between peer attachment and delinquency. Hindelang (1973) found a direct relationship between peer attachment and self-reported delinquency among rural males and females and concluded that it appears to depend on the kinds of friends youths have and the characteristics of their peer associations. Linden and Hackler (1973) studied youths' relationships with parents, conventional peers, and deviant peers and found that those who had closer relationships with deviant peers than with their parents and conventional peers had the highest rates of self-reported delinquency. Liska and Reed (1985) concluded that peers can be either a positive or a negative influence and that parents, more than school, are the major sources of delinquency control (1985: 558). Burkett and Warren (1987) found that deviant peer associations, through lowered religious commitment, make youth more vulnerable to marijuana use. Positive peer influence, on the other hand, tends to reduce the likelihood of young peoples' drug use. Johnson, Marcos, and Bahr (1987) found that associations with peers rather than with parents seems to matter most in adolescent drug use. They disagreed with the idea of peer influence, that friends' drug use makes it seem right or safe, but argued that youths use drugs "simply because their friends do" (1987: 336). Others have emphasized the interactive and reciprocal nature of peer relationships and delinquency, in that association with delinquent peers leads to delinquent conduct, but delinquent conduct also increases association with delinquent peers. Thornberry (1987) proposed an interactional theory with a focus on attachment to parents, commitment to school, and association with delinquent peers. He concluded that associating with delinquent peers, not being committed to school, and engaging in delinquent behavior are contradictory to parents' expectations and therefore tend to diminish the attachment between parent and child. Adolescents who fail at school, who associate with delinquent peers, and who engage in delinquent conduct adversely affect the bond with their parents (1987: 874). Commitment to school also affects peer relationships, so students who are committed to doing well in school are unlikely to associate with delinquent peers (Thornberry, 1987: 875). Agnew (1991) analyzed data from the National Youth Survey and concluded that peer attachment strongly affects delinquency when an adolescent spends much time with serious delinquents, feels they approve delinquency, and feels pressure to engage in delinquency (1991: 64). Gerald Patterson and Thomas Dishion (1985) proposed a model to explain the process by which parents and peers contribute to delinquency. During preadolescence a breakdown in family management procedures leads to an increase in a child's antisocial behavior and disrupts the development of social and academic skills, placing the child at risk for rejection by normal peers and likely academic failure. During adolescence, poor parental monitoring practices and poor social skills further the likelihood of contact with a deviant peer group. The combined effects of association with deviant peers, poor parental monitoring, and academic failure contribute to the likelihood that these youth will engage in delinquent behavior (Patterson and Dishion, 1985: 63–64).

It is clear that peer associations play an important role in delinquent behavior. Youths whose friends are positive and law-abiding are at less risk of delinquent involvement than those who associate with peers having a higher level of self-reported delinquency. Close relationships with parents and family reduce delinquent influences, but they alone are not enough. Commitment to school helps reduce delinquency, but analyses of data from the National Youth Survey show that the influence of delinquent friends is more important than school attachment in explaining delinquent behavior (Lawrence, 1991: 66). Research

findings of the effects of peer associations on delinquent involvement have important implications for parents, schools, and juvenile correctional programs. Elliott, Huizinga, and Ageton
(1985) suggested that treatment approaches that use adolescent peer groups or "group
processes" may actually have the unintended effect of contributing to closer delinquent
friendships. They believe it is not reasonable to expect pro-social values and norms to
result from group processes involving serious juvenile delinquents. Incarceration of juvenile
offenders together in institutional settings inevitably results in closer ties among serious
young offenders, but Elliott et al. emphasized that juvenile correctional programs do not
have to perpetuate this practice, and they recommended efforts to integrate high-risk youth
into conventional peer groups (1985: 149–150). Gary Gottfredson (1987) reviewed studies
of the effects of peer group interventions conducted in schools (e.g., guided group interaction, positive peer culture, peer group counseling) and arrived at a similar conclusion. He
found no difference in police contacts between experimental groups (who had participated
in peer group interventions) and control groups. Except for elementary school students,
he found no support for the benefit of peer group treatment; for high school students the
effects even appeared harmful in that such groups may weaken students' bonds with their
parents, which serve as some restraint against adverse peer group influence (1987: 709).
Gottfredson suggested that it might be better to seek ways to avoid delinquent peer interaction entirely rather than to try to change its nature (1987: 710).

In summary, parents should be concerned about their children's friends and closely
monitor what their children do, where they go, and with whom. Schools may unintentionally be promoting the development and adverse influence of deviant peer groups
by the practice of tracking and placing at-risk, disruptive, and marginally performing
students together (see Elliott et al., 1985: 150). Placing troublesome students together in
special classes increases their association with each other and may increase discipline
problems and failure. Research evidence seems to indicate that, whenever possible, dispersing problem students among different teachers and classrooms is preferable. Singling
out problem students should be seen as a short-term, temporary solution, with the ultimate objective being reintegration into the regular classroom. Juvenile detention centers
and training schools have for decades been viewed as "schools for crime." Association
with delinquent peers is inevitable in these institutional settings. Increased emphasis on
the use of community residential alternatives is clearly more appropriate for those youths
who do not require a secure setting for the protection of themselves and others. Parents,
schools, and correctional programs cannot entirely control or eliminate associations with
delinquent peers. The evidence is clear that failure to minimize such associations promotes delinquency, however (see Lawrence, 1991: 67). The more effective delinquency-
prevention strategies are those that encourage stronger attachments to family, school, and
nondelinquent friends. Coordinating the efforts of school and juvenile justice personnel
with parents and developing community programs that accomplish collaborative efforts
is a worthwhile goal for effective delinquency prevention.

Gangs and Delinquency

We have seen that peer associations take on great importance for adolescents, for most
of whom these friendships are positive and supportive, indeed a normal part of adolescent
development. Youths who have poor relationships with their parents and family, on the
other hand, are likely to experience school problems and to associate with delinquent friends.

The resulting negative peer influence leads to involvement with delinquency and drugs, even to serious criminal and violent behavior. The formation of juvenile gangs is an extension of adolescent peer groups, and youths join gangs for a variety of reasons: a need for peer acceptance, belonging, and recognition or for status, safety or security, power, and excitement (see Spergel et al., 1994b: 3). Youths who are especially drawn to gangs include those raised under socially deprived conditions, those who are failing in school and not involved in school activities, and those who are unemployed with few if any perceived job goals or opportunities.

Gangs and crime committed by gang members are evident in many American cities. A National Institute of Justice (NIJ)–sponsored survey of metropolitan police departments in the 79 largest U.S. cities showed that in 1992 all but seven were troubled by gangs, as were all but five departments in 43 smaller cities (Curry et al., 1994). In 110 jurisdictions reporting gangs, the survey found that during the previous 12-month period there were:

•249,324 gang members

•4,881 gangs

•46,359 gang-related crimes

•1,072 gang-related homicides (Curry et al., 1994: 1)

A gang problem of this magnitude clearly presents a challenge for law enforcement and calls for a concerted community-wide effort to respond to the problem.

Definitions and Characteristics of Gangs

Despite the existence of youth gangs since the early part of this century, delinquency experts have not been able to agree on a precise definition of a "gang." The term is sometimes used (even by some youth themselves) to describe any group of teenagers who participate together in deviant and delinquent activities. Police departments and researchers generally prefer a narrower definition of gangs to include violent behavior, group organization, leadership, and territory (see Horowitz, 1990; Curry et al., 1994). Jeffrey Fagan (1989) defined gangs according to their primary purpose and activities: some are basically social groups, involved in few delinquent activities and little drug use; some gangs are involved in drug use and sales, and in vandalism; other gangs have members who are serious delinquents, and are extensively involved in property and violent offenses (1989: 649–651). In a study of gangs in Cleveland and Columbus, C. Ronald Huff (1989) identified three types of gangs: (1) informal hedonistic gangs, whose primary interest was in "getting high" and "having a good time"; (2) instrumental gangs, who commit property crimes for economic reasons; and (3) predatory gangs that commit robberies, street muggings, and are actively involved in drug use and sales (Huff, 1989: 528–529).

Gangs appear to be more structured than delinquent groups, but some loosely organized groups may still be regarded as gangs. Most gangs tend to be organized on a geographical basis, such as neighborhoods, and many are focused around racial or ethnic origin, age, or gender. Males make up the vast majority of gang membership, but female participation in gangs is increasing (Campbell, 1990). Gangs tend to be concentrated in communities such as low-income, public-housing projects and poor black and low-income Hispanic sections of the city (Curry and Spergel, 1988: 399).

Gangs and Delinquency

Most delinquency is committed by youths who are not gang members, and gang membership is not necessarily synonymous with delinquent behavior. Huff (1989) observed that gang members spend more time in deviant adolescent behavior (skipping school, disobeying parents), and only the more delinquent gangs and gang members engage in serious criminal behavior. Jeffrey Fagan (1990) surveyed samples of students and dropouts in Chicago, Los Angeless, and San Diego and observed that the involvement of both gang and nongang youths in delinquency and drug use suggests that gangs are only one of several deviant peer groups in inner cities, but gang members in his sample were more heavily involved in both delinquency and substance use than non–gang members. City police departments in the NIJ survey reported far more gang members than gang-related incidents. The Los Angeles Police Department reported 503 gangs and 55,258 gang members but only 8,528 gang-related crimes in 1991, and the Chicago Police Department reported that 29,000 gang members in 41 gangs accounted for only 4,765 gang incidents in 1991 (Curry et al., 1994: 7). Thornberry and associates (1993) conducted a longitudinal study to compare youths' crime patterns prior to, during, and after gang involvement. They found that gang members did not have higher rates of delinquency or drug use before entering the gang, but once they became members their rates increased substantially, and the rates of delinquency decreased when gang members left the gang. Esbensen and associates had similar conclusions from their studies of youths in high-risk urban neighborhoods. Gang members are already delinquent before joining the gang, but gang membership does slightly increase their delinquent activity (Esbensen and Huizinga, 1993). Gang members were found to be similar to youths who were self-reported serious offenders but were not members of a gang (Esbensen et al., 1995).

Why Youth Join Gangs

Gangs are more widespread and diverse than the stereotypical group of lower-class minority youth from inner-city urban areas. Gangs are now found in smaller cities, suburban areas, and even youths in small town and rural communities are emulating gang behavior. It is still true, however, that the majority of gangs are located in larger cities, primarily in the lower socioeconomic urban areas. However, because most youth from those areas do *not* join gangs, additional factors are required to explain gang membership. Researchers have identified a number of characteristics or risk factors are associated with gang membership (Esbensen, 2000).

1. *Individual and family demographics*: Gang members are primarily male, although females may account for up to one-third of youth gang members (Esbensen and Winfree, 1998) and join gangs and participate for reasons that differ from those of male members (Campbell, 1990). Gangs in urban areas are believed to be primarily African American or Hispanic, but whites accounted for 30 percent of gang members in small cities and rural counties (Esbensen, 2000: 3). Some gang youth do come from two-parent families, but gangs are made up primarily of minority members residing in single-parent households.
2. *Personal attributes*: Gang members have more antisocial beliefs (Hill et al., 1999), and more delinquent self-concepts (Maxson et al., 1998). Gang members tend to be more impulsive, engage in more risk-seeking behavior, be less committed to school, and have less communication and attachment with their parents (Esbensen, 2000).
3. *Peer group, school, and community factors*: The strongest predictor of gang membership is a high level of interaction with and influence by antisocial peers (Battin-Pearson et al.,

1998). Gang youth are less committed to school than non-gang youth (Maxson et al., 1998; Hill et al., 1999). Community factors predominate in gang research, and studies indicate that poverty, unemployment, the absence of meaningful jobs, and social disorganization contribute to the presence of gangs (Fagan, 1990; Huff, 1990). Gangs are clearly more prevalent in urban areas and are more likely to emerge in neighborhoods characterized by economic distress and social disorganization (Esbensen, 2000).

Gangs in Schools

A youth gang member is likely to have done poorly in school and is not involved in school activities. Most gang members are bored with school and feel inadequate in class. They have not developed effective learning skills and therefore experience frustration and failure in school. They do not identify with teachers and tend to dislike and distrust them (Spergel et al., 1994a, 1994b). Gang members reported significantly more negative labeling by their teachers than did a comparison group of street offenders (Esbensen and Deschenes, 1998).

Gang problems in schools often begin in the streets as students who are gang members bring gang attitudes and behaviors into the school. Gang violence generally does not occur in schools, although gang recruitment and planning of gang activities may occur on school grounds. Gang members may claim parts of the school as their turf, leave their marks with graffiti, and intimidate and assault other students (Spergel et al., 1994a, 1994b).

Results of school crime victimization surveys indicate a relationship between gang presence in schools and students' reports of fear and victimization. In 1989, 15 percent of students reported "street" gangs in their school (Bastian and Taylor, 1991). By 1993, 35 percent of students reported that "fighting" gangs were present in their schools (National Center for Education Statistics, 1993). Results of these two surveys indicate that:

•Gangs are not limited to inner-city, urban schools. Minority and white students from urban and suburban schools report gangs in their schools.

•Gang presence in schools is strongly associated with increased student reports of victimization and fear.

•Gang presence, not a student's race or ethnicity nor whether the student lives in an urban area, accounts for most of the differences in students' reports of fear and victimization at school (National Center for Education Statistics, 1995).

Data from the School Crime Supplement (SCS) of the National Crime Victimization Survey (NCVS) show that gang presence in schools has actually declined slightly but support earlier findings that gangs are still a problem and are associated with higher levels of school violence and gun possession. The percentage of students who reported that street gangs were present at school dropped from 28 percent in 1995 to 17 percent in 1999 (Addington et al., 2002: 27). The authors suggest that the decrease may be a reflection of the overall decline in the number of gangs and gang members and because the average age of gang members has increased to 18 years (National Youth Gang Survey, 2000; Addington et al., 2002: 33). More Hispanic (28 percent) and black students (25 percent) reported gang presence than did white students (13 percent). More students from urban schools (25 percent) reported that street gangs were present in school than students from suburban (16 percent) or rural areas (11 percent); and gangs were more prevalent in public schools (19 percent) than in private schools (4 percent). Schools with more gang presence have higher levels of crime and victimization. The 1999 SCS data show that 36 percent of students reporting violent victimization and 25 percent of those reporting property victimization said that gangs were in their school. Gangs in schools are also associated with guns at school; 45 percent of students who reported gang presence also reported knowledge of another student bringing a gun to school, and 58 percent of students actually saw a student with a gun at school (Addington et al., 2002: 27–33). Not all schools, even some in high-crime areas, are affected by the presence of gangs. Schools that have strong leadership and a positive learning environment have been able to maintain students' commitment to education and control gang problems and youth crime.

Responding to Gang Problems

Five strategies have been variously used in dealing with youth gangs: (1) neighborhood mobilization, (2) social intervention, (3) providing social and economic opportunities like special school and job programs, (4) gang suppression and incarceration, and (5) special police gang units and specialized probation units (Spergel et al., 1994b).

There are limits to what schools can do about family and community factors that contribute to youth gang problems, but there is much they can do in cooperation with community agencies. Public schools, especially middle schools, are among the best resources for preventing and intervening early in youth gang problems. The peak period for recruitment of new gang members occurs between the 5th and 8th grades among youth who are doing poorly in class and are at risk of dropping out (Spergel et al., 1994b). One suggested approach is the delivery of a flexible curriculum targeted to youth gang members who are not doing well in their classes. The goal is to enhance the students' basic academic and work-related problem-solving skills (Spergel et al., 1994a). Experts have made several recommendations for an effective gang control and suppression strategy by schools:

•Inform and prepare teachers and administrators to recognize and respond to gang problems in schools.

•Make a clear distinction between gang- and non–gang-related activity so as not to exaggerate the scope of the problem.

•Develop clear guidelines and policies for responding to gang behavior; controlling intimidation, threats, and assaults among students; and strictly forbidding any weapons.

•Enforce rules and regulations through open communication and positive relationships between school personnel, students, and parents.

•Work closely with police and probation agencies, communicating regularly and sharing information for monitoring gang activity (see Huff, 1989: 53–55; Spergel et al., 1994a: 18–19).

The most recent comprehensive effort to respond to the youth gang problem is the Gang Resistance and Education Training (G.R.E.A.T.) Program funded by the NIJ, developed by the Bureau of Alcohol, Tobacco and Firearms and the Phoenix, Arizona, police department. Objectives of the program are to reduce gang activity and teach youths to set goals for themselves, to resist peer pressure, to resolve conflicts, and the consequences of gang involvement (Esbensen and Osgood, 1999). The program is offered to middle school students (primarily 7th graders) and taught by law enforcement officers. A national evaluation involving more than 5,000 8th-grade students reported small but positive effects on students' attitudes and their ability to resist peer pressure. The G.R.E.A.T. students reported less delinquency and had lower levels of gang affiliation, higher levels of school commitment, and greater commitment to prosocial peers (Esbensen and Osgood, 1999; Esbensen, 2000).

Many other gang intervention and prevention programs are conducted in schools throughout the United States. A survey of school-based gang prevention and intervention programs conducted on a national sample of schools estimated that there were 781,800 gang prevention activities and 159,700 gang intervention activities underway in the nation's schools (Gottfredson, 2001). Most of the programs were not limited to gang prevention but also covered other forms of problem behavior. The quality and effectiveness of the programs varied greatly, but research findings show that school-based gang prevention programs can have a positive impact on the gang problem.

Drugs and Delinquency

Drug use among young people continues to be a serious problem despite some downturns in use levels. Youth alcohol and drug abuse may lead to other problems, including antisocial behavior, school problems, delinquency, and health-related issues. Those who begin drug use at a younger age are more likely to develop drug problems later in life (Office of National Drug Control Policy, 2004).

Extent of Drug Use

According to the 2003 Monitoring the Future Survey, 24 percent of 12th graders reported using illegal drugs in the past month, 39 percent in the past year, and 51 percent during their lifetime (National Institute on Drug Abuse, 2003). Results of the 2003 Youth Risk Behavior Surveillance System indicated that 40 percent had used marijuana during their lifetime and 22 percent reported current use (Centers for Disease Control and Prevention, 2004). In 2001, state and local law enforcement agencies reported 139,238 drug abuse arrests of juveniles under 18. Juvenile drug arrests represented about 9 percent of all arrests of juveniles under 18 and about 13 percent of drug arrests among all age groups (Federal Bureau of Investigation, 2002). The FBI's Uniform Crime Report reported that 116,781 juveniles under 18 were arrested for drug abuse violations in 2002 (Federal Bureau of Investigation, 2003). Juvenile courts in the United States in 1998 handled an estimated 192,500 delinquency cases in which a drug offense was the most serious charge. Drug offense cases accounted for 11 percent of all delinquency cases during the year. This was a significant decrease since 1989, when 36 percent were drug cases. Also during 1998, 23 percent of all juvenile delinquency cases involving detention were drug-related cases (Office of National Drug Control Policy, 2003). A census of juvenile offenders in residential placement in October 1999 indicated that there were 9,882 juvenile offenders in custody for drug offenses—about one-third of them for drug trafficking. According to preliminary data from the Arrestee Drug Abuse Monitoring (ADAM) program, about 60 percent of male juvenile detainees and 46 percent of female juvenile detainees tested positive for drug use in 2002 (Office of National Drug Control Policy, 2004).

Alcohol and Drugs in Schools

The presence of alcohol and drugs at school affects students' perceptions of their school environment. Results of one survey showed that 20 percent of students blamed drugs for the level of violence in their schools (Arnette and Walsleben, 1998). In the 1999 SCS, 20 percent of students ages 12 through 18 reported that alcohol was available at school, and 37 percent reported that drugs were available (Addington et al., 2002: 18). Alcohol was reported to be available in school more by white students (23 percent) than by black and Hispanic students (14 and 15 percent, respectively). More white students (40 percent) than black or Hispanic students (34 and 31 percent, respectively) reported that drugs were available. Likewise, more high school than junior high and middle school students reported availability of drugs and alcohol. More students from higher-income households reported alcohol and drug availability. For example, 24 percent of students from households with incomes of $50,000 or more reported that alcohol was available, compared with just 9 percent of students from households with an income less than $10,000; 41 percent of students from $50,000 households reported drugs available, compared with just 23 percent of students from the $10,000 households. More students from suburban (22 percent) and rural schools (23 percent) than students from urban schools (15 percent) reported that alcohol was available. Drug availability showed a similar trend, with slightly more suburban students (40 percent) than urban students (34 percent) reporting availability of drugs at school (Addington et al., 2002: 20). Marijuana was the drug reported to be most available by students at school (35 percent), whereas other drugs such as crack and cocaine (13 percent), uppers/downers (16 percent), LSD (11 percent), and PCP and heroin (6 percent) were reported to be available by fewer students. The presence of alcohol and drugs in schools is associated with other problems, such as the presence of gangs, victimization, and student reports of knowing about a student who brought a gun to school. According to the 2000 School Survey on Crime and Safety (SSOCS), 12 percent of public school principals (K–12) reported some distribution of illegal drugs at their school, and 27 percent reported possession or use of illegal drugs by students at school (Miller and Chandler, 2003). Possession or use of alcohol and illegal drugs was much higher in middle and secondary schools and in larger schools. An estimated 52 percent of middle school and 77 percent of high school principals reported some possession or use, and 73 percent of principals in schools with enrollments of 1,000 or more reported some drug use or possession. No significant differences were reported in drug possession based on city size, crime level where students lived, or percentage of minority enrollment. In other words, 25–30 percent of principals reported some drug possession incidents in urban, suburban, and rural schools; schools in both high- and low-crime areas; and where minority enrollments ranged from less than 20 percent to more than 50 percent (Miller and Chandler, 2003: 67). Alcohol and illegal drug possession or use was associated with more discipline problems, disruptions, and students absent without excuses. Twice as many principals who reported some alcohol or drug possession also reported problems with discipline, disruption, or absenteeism (Miller and Chandler, 2003: 69).

Effects of Drug Abuse

Persistent substance abuse by young people often leads to academic difficulties, health-related problems including mental health, family conflicts, poor peer relationships, and involvement with the juvenile justice system (Office of National Drug Control Policy, 2004). Results from the 2001 National Household Survey on Drug Abuse show that the earlier in life people begin drug use, the more likely they are to develop a drug problem. Greater use of cigarettes, alcohol, or any illegal drug had a negative effect on students' grades (Substance Abuse and Mental Health Services Administration, 2002). Estimates indicated that substance abuse and addiction would add at least $41 billion to the costs of elementary and secondary education for the 2000–2001 school year. The costs include truancy (and resulting reduction of per pupil funding of education), drug testing, employee training to increase alcohol and drug awareness, and special education programs for students with substance abuse problems (Office of National Drug Control Policy, 2004).

Drugs and Delinquency

Alcohol and substance use is a form of deviant behavior to which most young people are exposed from late childhood through adolescence. Possession and use of alcohol and illegal drugs are of course delinquent acts in themselves, which may result in arrest and referral to juvenile court. For those who avoid police arrest and judicial sanctions, drug use has adverse effects on their lives. Youths who take drugs do poorly in school, have high dropout rates, and continue to use drugs after they leave school (Krohn et al., 1995). We have discussed drug use in this chapter as one of the many "correlates" of delinquency—one of the factors along with family problems, peer influence, and gang involvement associated with delinquency. It is unclear, however, whether drug use is a cause of delinquency. Elliott and associates have studied delinquency and drug use for many years using the National Youth Survey (Elliott et al., 1985). In longitudinal studies of self-reported delinquency and drug use, they found a strong association between the two but believe that drug abuse is a type of delinquent behavior and not a cause of it (Huizinga et al., 1989). They found that most youths engage in delinquent acts before they begin using drugs, and they concluded that both delinquency and drug use appear to reflect a developmental problem that is part of a disturbed socialization process and lifestyle. Their research findings have important implications for drug abuse and delinquency prevention. Programs targeted solely at substance abuse prevention may have little effect on delinquency rates because drug use is a symptom and not a cause of delinquent behavior.

Summary

Parents and families play a major role in the development of young people. Research evidence shows that the chances of children becoming involved in delinquent behavior are greater when they have experienced problems in parent–child relations, inconsistent supervision and discipline, parental rejection, and abuse. Peers have a significant influence on a youth's behavior, and association with negative peers is more likely when there are problematic relations with parents. Youth gangs often provide a feeling of acceptance and belonging for young people lacking a positive family relationship and who are experiencing problems in school. Alcohol and substance abuse adversely affect their family and peer relationships and school performance and are associated with delinquent involvement. These factors are correlates of delinquency that may or may not cause delinquency, but place young people at greater risk of delinquent involvement.

5

Dropout and Delinquency

School problems and low academic achievement have been linked to deviant and delinquent behavior. Students who are not committed to school and who are not positively involved in school activities are at risk of school failure and antisocial behavior. The academic demands and discipline of school are frustrating for many students. Those who do not receive support and encouragement from parents, siblings, and peers are at risk of absenteeism and truancy. School truancy is considered to be the first step to a lifetime of problems (Garry, 1996) and is associated with substance abuse, gang involvement, and delinquency (Dryfoos, 1990; Bell et al., 1994; Huizinga et al., 1995). Truancy has been linked to higher rates of crime, which increase the cost of law enforcement. Additional costs attributed to truancy are for revenues lost to school districts based on attendance figures from federal and state funds, higher welfare costs to taxpayers, and costs to businesses that must pay to train uneducated workers (Garry, 1996). There is evidence that truancy may have long-term effects. Adults who were frequently truant as teenagers are more likely to have poorer physical and mental health and lower paying jobs, to live in poverty, to depend on welfare support, to have children with problem behaviors, and to have an increased risk of incarceration (Dryfoos, 1990; Bell et al., 1994).

School attendance and satisfactory academic performance are perhaps the most important factors for personal and social development, helping youths to become productive adults and to avoid antisocial behavior. Failure to address truancy problems early can have significant negative effects on students, schools, and society. Students who skip school fall behind in their classes, and many of them eventually drop out of school. School dropouts are at risk for drug use and delinquency (Thornberry et al., 1985; Jarjoura, 1993). Research has established a relationship between dropout and delinquency, but it is unclear whether dropout causes delinquency or delinquency causes dropout. In this chapter we examine the school dropout problem, its causes and consequences, and research on dropout and delinquency, and we conclude with a discussion of truancy and dropout-prevention programs.

Perspectives on Truancy and Dropout

On any given school day in the United States, as many as 10–30 percent of students are absent from school. In the New York City public school system, about 150,000 (15 percent) of the 1 million public school students are absent on a typical day; the Los Angeles school district reports an average of 62,000 (10 percent) of students are out of school each day (Garry, 1996). Although the school dropout rate has gradually declined over the years, it is still a serious problem. The problem is particularly acute in inner city urban schools. School principals have rated absenteeism and tardiness as among the worst discipline problems they face. In a nationally representative sample of principals in public elementary, middle, and secondary schools during the 1996–1997 school year, student tardiness (40 percent) and student absenteeism (25 percent) were among the discipline issues most often cited as serious or moderate problems in their schools (Heaviside et al., 1998).

Compulsory School Attendance

Placed in historical perspective, the proportion of American youth who attend school and graduate is better than it was 100 years ago. Compulsory school attendance laws were introduced in state legislatures in the late nineteenth century, following the lead of Massachusetts in 1852. By 1890, 27 states and territories required parents or guardians to send their children to school, and by 1918, each legislature had enacted such a law (Rippa, 1980: 170). The age stipulations of early laws generally applied to children age 8–14 years, with some states extending the law to the age of 16. In some states children were allowed to leave school after completing a stated number of grades, regardless of age. The majority of youth at the turn of the century were leaving school after age 16 and not completing high school. The National Association of Manufacturers complained that 60–65 percent of students in 1914 dropped out by the end of the 5th or 6th grade, with no vocational preparation or working skills. The Association advocated for more vocational training in public schools, both as a way to encourage youth to complete high school and to assure that graduates had more useful vocational and work skills (Rippa, 1980: 159).

Enforcement of compulsory school attendance laws has generally not been given high priority among law enforcement agencies and juvenile courts. As with other status offenses, such as running away, curfew violations, disobeying parents, and incorrigibility, police officers generally do not intervene or take into custody youths who are out of school during school hours unless parents or school officials have made a specific complaint or the juvenile is suspected of having committed another, more serious crime. Juvenile courts in the United States likewise focus primarily on misdemeanor and felony offenses for which juveniles can be adjudicated delinquent. Status offenses including truancy generally come to the juvenile court's attention when juveniles under court-ordered probation supervision are brought back for a revocation hearing for violating rules or conditions of probation, including school attendance. Law enforcement and juvenile court policies are, however, dependent upon community priorities and individual problems and needs.

When citizens, school officials, and justice authorities collectively agree that a significant number of youths are involved in school truancy, curfew violations, or loitering, they may choose to focus on selective enforcement of those activities. Such policy decisions are particularly justifiable if there is reasonable suspicion that such status offenses are contributing to increased incidents of drug dealing, petty theft, property damage, and graffiti. At the conclusion of this chapter we will discuss several truancy-reduction strategies developed precisely for those types of problems.

Truancy Statutes and Court Procedures

Every state juvenile code includes a provision defining school attendance requirements under the compulsory attendance laws, along with procedures and sanctions for children and their parents who violate the law. Parents are held legally responsible for assuring that their children attend school. Legal sanctions are directed at the juvenile only after the parent(s) are able to show that they have discharged their responsibility by doing all within their power to get their child to school (generally supporting school attendance, getting them up in time, assuring they are up and out the door to the school bus, etc.). Clear parental violations are cases in which children are expected to care for younger siblings at home or to help at work outside of school. In Great Britain, under the 1944 Education Act, when a child fails to attend school it is the parents who are legally responsible (Berg et al., 1988). Under Britain's Child and Young Persons Act of 1969, failure to attend school may result in a "care order" by the court. This procedure is similar to the statutes and procedures of American juvenile courts, whereby a parent or guardian is presented with a notice that their child is a continuing truant. Unless there is a valid excuse for the child's absence, the parent and the child may be subject to juvenile court proceedings if the truancy persists. Juvenile courts do not generally intervene in truancy cases until other options are first tried. Under Minnesota Statutes (Chapter 260A), for example, truant children and their parents are first referred to community-based truancy projects and service centers that offer counseling, testing, psychological evaluations, tutoring, mentoring, and mediation. In some jurisdictions the county attorney's office may establish a truancy mediation program for the purpose of resolving truancy problems without court action. Children under the age of 16 who are persistently absent without an excuse may be required to appear in juvenile court with their parent or guardian. Under the Minnesota Truancy Statutes (Chapter 260C), the child may be declared a "child in need of protection or services" (CHIPS). Similar statutes in other states refer to a "child (or person) in need of supervision" (CHINS or PINS). The terms are intended to differentiate between an adjudication of delinquency for the commission of criminal behavior. The court procedure addresses the question of whether the parent or guardian is capable of providing care and supervision of the child, and the result may be removal of the child from the parent's custody and placement with a relative, other guardian, or foster care.

Only a small proportion of juvenile court cases involve truancy. The number of youths who are truant and who drop out of school has remained stable or declined in most states. Overall statistics indicate that a greater percentage graduate from high school. Nevertheless, there is still a concern about the truancy and dropout problem today. Several explanations have been suggested for this increased concern:

1. The long-term trend of dropping out has declined, but the short-term trend has remained steady and even increased, especially for some groups.

2. Minority populations, who have always had higher dropout rates than the white population, are increasing in public schools.
3. Many states have recently passed legislation to raise academic course requirements for graduation to motivate students and improve performance, but others might be more inclined to drop out.
4. There is a widespread belief that the educational requirements for employment will increase in the future, leaving dropouts even more disadvantaged in the job market.
5. There is increased political pressure on schools because state and federal education officials have begun to judge schools' performance by a series of "indicators" like dropout rates and test scores (Rumberger, 1987: 101–2).

The slight improvements in graduation rates are encouraging, but there is still cause for concern. A disproportionate number of the youths who do not complete a high school education are blacks, Hispanics, and Native Americans from households characterized by poverty and unemployment. Young people who drop out of high school will not have the minimum skills and qualifications necessary to function in an increasingly complex society and technological workplace.

Defining and Measuring Dropout

Studying the dropout problem is complicated by the absence of a uniform definition of dropout and a standard system of measuring the extent of the problem. There are at least two methods of measuring the dropout rate. Defining a dropout necessarily involves a time dimension. A student who stops attending school for a time but returns later is not considered a dropout. Some students leave school and may return. Some of those who return may stay and complete a high school degree. Some who do not return may later complete an equivalency diploma. Thus, national data sources have variously reported a dropout rate, a graduation rate, or completion rate (Pallas, 1987). They are not the same. Dropout statistics compiled by the U.S. Census Bureau and the U.S. Department of Education have been the two predominant national sources of data. The methods of computing these statistics differ, so the reported dropout and graduate rates are also different. States also differ as to definitions of dropout, high school completion, and whether or not equivalency diplomas are counted. Caution must therefore be exercised when comparing states. The available data sources do, nevertheless, provide fairly accurate measures that seem to represent the lower and upper limits of the rates of dropout and high school completion in America.

The Extent of Absenteeism and Dropout

Our discussion of dropout and high school completion rates will be limited here to those compiled by the U.S. Department of Education. The National Center for Education Statistics (NCES) reports a variety of annual data on schools. The NCES compiles data on enrollments by grade, dropout statistics, and numbers of high school graduates originally collected by state education agencies. Only public schools are included, and the data reported are only for regular day school graduates. Students who receive a certificate of general educational development (GED) or other nonregular day school credentials are excluded.

High School Dropouts

The NCES defined a dropout as an individual who:

1. was enrolled in school at some time during the previous school year (e.g., 1999–2000); and
2. was not enrolled at the beginning of the current school (e.g., 2000–2001); and
3. has not graduated from high school or completed a state- or district-approved educational program; and
4. did not transfer to another school district or private school, was not in a correctional facility, and was not temporarily absent due to suspension or an excused illness (Young, 2003: 1–2).

The *dropout rate* (also referred to as the "event" dropout rate) is the number of dropouts for a school year divided by the number of students enrolled at the beginning of that school year. A total of 45 states met the NCES definition of dropouts and provided data (dropout data were not available for California, Colorado, Indiana, and Michigan). The 9th-through 12th-grade dropout rate in the reporting states ranged from 2.2 in North Dakota to 10.9 in Arizona. The median rate of the reporting states was 4.2 (Young, 2003: 2). The highest and lowest state dropout rates are summarized in Table 5–1.

The numbers of dropouts varied greatly among the states because of differences in population size and partly because of population demographic differences such as racial and ethnic composition. States that had a dropout rate of less than 3.0 in 2000–2001 were Iowa, New Jersey, North Dakota, and Wisconsin. States with dropout rates of more than 8.0 were Alaska, Arizona, and Louisiana. Dropout rates were lowest for white and Asian/Pacific Islander students and highest for American Indian/Alaska native, black, and Hispanic students. More than 15 percent of American Indian/Alaska native high school students dropped out in Arizona, Minnesota, and South Dakota. Twelve states had a dropout rate of 10 percent or higher for American Indian/Alaska native students. Eight states reported dropout rates of 10 percent or more among black high school students; and 11 reporting states had dropout rates of 10 percent or higher for Hispanic high school students. Higher dropout rates were reported in school districts in large or midsize cities, and lower dropout rates were reported in rural areas. Nine reporting states had dropout rates of more than 10 percent in large city school districts (Young, 2003: 3–4).

Table 5–1
Summary of States with Highest and Lowest Dropout Rates

State	Total 9–12 Graders	Number	Rate 9–12 Graders	9th	10th	11th	12th
Lowest rates							
North Dakota	36,230	784	2.2	1.1	2.4	2.5	2.7
Wisconsin	259,047	6,002	2.3	1.8	1.6	1.9	4.2
Iowa	158,050	4,193	2.7	1.5	2.4	3.2	3.7
New Jersey	351,496	9,882	2.8	2.9	2.8	2.9	2.6
Highest rates							
Arizona	234,367	25,632	10.9	11.3	10.2	11.0	11.3
Louisiana	196,141	16,361	8.3	9.1	8.2	7.7	8.2
Alaska	38,914	3,177	8.2	6.6	8.4	8.5	9.8

Source: Adapted from Young, Beth A. 2003. *Public High School Dropouts and Completers from the Common Core of Data: School Year 2000–01.* Washington, DC: National Center for Education Statistics.

The NCES also reports *status dropout rates*, which represent the proportion of young people ages 16–24 who are out of school and who have not earned a high school credential. Status rates are higher than event rates because they include all dropouts in this age range, regardless of when they last attended school. In 2000, some 3.8 million (10.9 percent) 16- to 24-year-olds were not enrolled in a high school program and had not completed high school. This is a decline from the 1970s, but the number has remained fairly stable with little improvement since the 1980s. The status dropout rate for Hispanic young adults was the highest at 27.8 percent, followed by 13.1 percent for blacks, 6.9 percent for Whites, and Asian/Pacific Islanders were the lowest at 3.8 percent (National Center for Education Statistics, 2002).

High School Completers

The NCES uses the term "high school completers" (rather than "graduate rate") to include both high school graduates who receive a diploma and other high school completers, such as those who receive a certificate of attendance. The latter was included in order to make data as comparable as possible across states. Students who receive a GED-based equivalency credential were not included, because not all states report these. The high school graduation rate (or more accurately, completer rate) is the rate of students who were enrolled in the 9th grade and graduated (or completed) 4 years later.[1] States with the highest and lowest graduation rates are reported in Table 5–2.

As with the dropout rates, numbers of high school completers also varied widely by state, primarily because of the varying sizes of public school populations. California, the state with the largest public school population, also had the most high school completers (316,124); the District of Columbia, with the smallest public school population had the fewest high school completers (3,043). Seven states had more than 100,000 high school completers: California, Florida, Illinois, New York, Ohio, Pennsylvania, and Texas (Young,

Table 5–2
Summary of States with Highest and Lowest High School Completion Rates

States	*2000–2001*	*1999–2000*	*1998–1999*
Highest			
Connecticut	86.6	86.5	83.7
Iowa	89.2	88.8	88.3
Maine	86.5	86.2	86.4
Massachusetts	86.3	85.5	86.0
New Jersey	88.0	86.7	85.2
North Dakota	90.1	88.9	89.7
Wisconsin	90.0	89.3	89.7
Lowest			
Arizona	68.3	—	63.2
Georgia	71.1	70.7	68.9
Louisiana	65.0	62.6	61.5
Nevada	73.5	70.2	66.9
New Mexico	74.4	73.0	70.6

Source: Adapted from Young, Beth A. 2003. *Public High School Dropouts and Completers from the Common Core of Data: School Year 2000–01*. Washington, DC: National Center for Education Statistics.

2003: 5). To calculate a high school completion rate, 4 years of dropout data are needed. For the 2000–2001 school year, only 39 states had complete data. California and Texas were two of the states without sufficient dropout data to calculate high school completion rates. As noted in Table 5–2, the completion rates varied from a high of 90.1 in North Dakota to a low of 65.0 in Louisiana for the states with complete data. The seven states with completion rates of 85 percent or more were Connecticut, Iowa, Maine, Massachusetts, New Jersey, North Dakota, and Wisconsin. Five states had completion rates of less than 75 percent: Arizona, Georgia, Louisiana, Nevada, and New Mexico (Young, 2003: 5).

Although GEDs are not considered equivalent to a high school degree by most educators and are not included in the high school completion rates, some reports indicate that a growing number of teenagers are getting GEDs. The GED was originally created to help World War II veterans earn the equivalent of a high school diploma; it was intended to be a second chance for adults and not a substitute for a high school education. The proportion of teenagers getting GEDs has increased in the past several years. In 2002 teenagers accounted for 49 percent of those earning GEDs, up from 33 percent 10 years earlier; in New York City 37,000 school-age students were in GED programs run by the school system, up from 25,500 2 years earlier (Arenson, 2004). The GED is not an educational program but a set of five tests covering reading, writing, mathematics, social studies, and science (called Tests of General Educational Development and administered by the American Council on Education). Students are not required to enroll in any classes before taking the tests, but most do need some help to pass them, and a variety of preparation programs are run by school districts, colleges, and community organizations. In 2001, about 2.8 million students earned traditional high school diplomas, while about 648,000 GEDs were awarded, including 266,000 to teenagers (Arenson, 2004). Some education experts believe that the increase in students getting the GED may be attributable to school reforms requiring exit exams, which have resulted in many students dropping out before graduation or taking the GED rather than completing high school. There is evidence that state-mandated minimum course requirements cause some students to drop out (Lillard and DeCicca, 2001). Some believe that under the federal No Child Left Behind (NCLB) law and state reform efforts to hold schools more accountable, some students are "pushed out" by school administrators who encourage them to seek GEDs instead.

Factors Associated with Dropping Out

Research studies have identified several factors associated with dropping out of school. The most prominent factors noted by the majority of studies include race, ethnicity, and gender; family, parents, and peers; school-related factors; economic factors; and individual factors (Rumberger, 1983, 1987; Ekstrom et al., 1986; Dunham and Alpert, 1987; Drennon-Gala, 1995).

Race, Ethnicity, and Gender

Members of racial and ethnic minorities are more likely to drop out than white students, and males drop out at a slightly higher rate than females. It is not that racial or ethnic minorities are inherently dropout prone, but these groups tend to be characterized by more of the social factors associated with dropping out. Socioeconomic status is actually a better predictor of which students drop out and which ones complete high school

(Dryfoos, 1990). Students whose families are below the poverty level or on welfare have higher dropout rates, regardless of racial or ethnic background.

Family Background and Structure

Parents who value education and offer support and encouragement for their children's education are important factors in preventing dropout. In a study of truants in Great Britain, Farrington (1980) noted that truant students were more likely to have fathers who were unemployed or had erratic job histories; parents who had criminal records and siblings had delinquent records; or parents who had poor child-rearing skills, practiced erratic or overly harsh discipline, and engaged in marital conflict. Other documented parent and family factors that increase a student's risk of dropping out include:

•Single-parent families

•Low parental educational and occupation levels

•The absence of learning materials and opportunities in the home

•The absence of parental supervision and monitoring

•Fewer opportunities for non–school-related learning

•Mothers with lower levels of formal education

•Mothers with lower education expectations for their children

•Speaking a language other than English in the home (Ekstrom et al., 1986; Rumberger, 1987; Dryfoos, 1990)

Influence of Peers

Many students drop out because of peer influence (Dryfoos, 1990); their friends were doing poorly in school, had low educational expectations, began skipping school, and dropped out. Although many dropouts have friends who have also dropped out, it is difficult to determine how much influence their friends have had on their decision to leave school. Dropouts often feel alienated from school life, and they tend to have friends who have lower educational aspirations and also feel alienated from school. It is not clear whether the friends had a negative influence on their dropping out or whether these friendships developed after dropping out through associations outside of school and as a means of social support.

School-Related Factors

Many students who drop out have performed poorly in school as measured by grades, test scores, and grade retention. Behavior problems in school, absenteeism, truancy, and having a record of frequent disciplinary actions are associated with dropping out. School misbehavior is a factor in dropout and is interrelated with students' school performance, whether they like school and are involved in activities, and whether they feel alienated from school. Behavior problems are closely associated with a pattern of absenteeism and truancy, which often culminates in dropping out.

School quality is an important factor in dropout rates. Most of the research on dropout has focused more on individual students' behavior and academic performance than on school structure, discipline policies, and teaching quality. Dropout rates tend to be higher in segregated schools, those with high student-to-teacher ratios, in larger schools with larger class sizes, and in schools that place emphasis on tracking and testing (Dryfoos, 1990). School safety, school discipline, grading policies, amount of homework assigned, and the extent to which students receive resources and support are factors that affect the dropout rate (Toles et al., 1986). School-related factors deserve more attention, and many of these factors can be changed through improved school policies and practices. A number of measures might be taken to prevent student misbehavior and increase the level of involvement of at-risk students in school. Many dropouts have left schools with poor facilities and inadequate teaching staffs, suggesting that the lack of resources affected their performance and decision to drop out (Fine, 1986). Wehlage (1986) suggested that large schools with too many students and not enough teachers and counselors to give students the attention and encouragement they need may exacerbate the dropout problem. He described one student dropout's experience and why she left school. She hated her school because it was over-crowded, the teachers didn't seem to care, students walked out and acted up, and no one did anything to change the situation. She never knew who her counselor was and received no advice or assistance. She began sleeping in class, then skipping class and walking the halls; finally, she decided to drop out of school and hang out on the streets (Wehlage, 1986: 20). Large class size make it impossible for school personnel to give the time and atten-tion to students who are failing, frustrated, and at risk of leaving school. Dropping out is a way of avoiding negative school experiences for some students. Teachers and principals grow impatient with misbehaving and truant students and often attempt to get rid of them through transfers to another school or encourage them to drop out (Bowditch, 1993).

Economic Factors

About 20 percent of dropouts have reported that they left school because of financial difficulties and they felt that they had to work to help out their families (Rumberger, 1983: 201). It is not clear whether financial necessity really precipitated dropping out, whether they decided to work after already dropping out, or whether the pressures of working and attending school at the same time led to dropping out. Students from lower socioeconomic backgrounds have a much higher dropout rate, and the combination of difficulties faced by lower-income families places more pressure on these youth. Mann (1987) cited studies showing that work-related reasons account for 21 percent of boys and 9 percent of girls dropping out. Paid employment poses a tough choice for students already at risk and frus-trated with school. Working up to 14 hours a week has little effect on schoolwork, but 15–21 hours a week depletes a student's time and energy and increases the dropout rate by 50 percent (Mann, 1987: 6).

Individual Factors

How students feel about themselves and whether they like or dislike school depends on parents, peers, economic factors, and the quality of their school. Students who stay in school generally have support and encouragement from their parents and a positive influence from peers, and their school performance and involvement is satisfying to them. Truant students have been rated as "troublesome" by parents and teachers, dishonest, and unpopular with positive peers (Farrington, 1980). In a study of truants in Great Britain, Farrington (1980) reported that primary school teachers described truants as lazy, lack-ing concentration, restless, difficult to discipline, not careing about being a credit to their parents, and not clean or tidy on arrival at school (1980: 53).

Dropouts tend to have lower self-esteem and less sense of control over their lives than other students. They have poor attitudes about school and low educational and occupational aspirations (see Ekstrom et al., 1986; Wehlage and Rutter, 1986; Rumberger, 1987; Dunham and Alpert, 1987). Many students who eventually drop out see little or no relevance of school classes to their future or success in life. Vocational education programs might help to retain many of these marginal students, but such programs are not available to many of the students who could most benefit from them. Many girls drop out because they are pregnant, some boys and girls leave school to get married, and others report dropping out to help support their family (Rumberger, 1987; Ekstrom et al., 1986). Alpert and Dunham (1986) compared a group of "marginal" students who stayed in school and dropouts from the same schools and identified five factors that differentiated the two groups. The marginal students who remained in school had avoided misbehavior, believed that school had relevance to their future jobs, had experienced some success in school, had parents who monitored their school performance, and avoided peers who dropped out.

Consequences of Dropping Out

Dropping out of school clearly has serious consequences for one's educational and employment prospects. High school graduation is seen as a minimal educational requirement today for entry into most jobs. A diploma is a symbol of a young person's academic success and ability to meet the expectations of the workplace. There is evidence that dropping out has negative consequences for the employment and economic prospects of the individual dropout, but there may be personal and social consequences for the individual, family members, and society. Levin identified seven social consequences of the failure to complete high school:

1. Forgone national income
2. Forgone tax revenues for the support of government services
3. Increased demand for social services
4. Increased crime
5. Reduced political participation
6. Reduced intergenerational mobility
7. Poorer levels of health (Levin, 1972: 41–48)

To learn more about the consequences of school truancy, Robins and Ratcliff (1980) selected a sample of African American men from St. Louis public school records and followed them into their thirties. They were able to compare the subjects based on records of school attendance and evaluate the effects of school truancy. They found that high school truancy was a predictor of poor occupational opportunities, very low earnings, low self-esteem, depressive and anxiety symptoms, and adult deviance. They suggested that low earnings might also encourage theft to increase income and substance abuse to overcome feelings of alienation and low self-esteem. Robins and Ratcliff noted that truancy is similar to other forms of childhood deviance such as drinking, fighting, and delinquency and that they may be early indicators of later adult deviance. What sets truancy apart, however, is that it is readily identifiable by school teachers and from school records and is usually the earliest form of childhood deviant behavior. Truancy is an early indicator of school and behavior problems and therefore presents opportunities for early intervention. They found that boys who had graduated from high school despite truancy problems had considerably better adult outcomes than those whose truancy led to dropping out. These findings led them to suggest that strategies to encourage truants and at-risk youth to complete high school should be encouraged (Robins and Ratcliff, 1980).

Despite recent criticism of the quality of public school education, schools *do* make a difference in students' cognitive development (Alexander et al., 1985). Graduates overall are able to secure more steady jobs with better pay. Compared to high school graduates, dropouts have higher unemployment rates and earn less money when they do eventually find work (Kaufman et al., 2001). According to a report on the working poor, more than twice as many school dropouts (14.3 percent) than workers with a high school degree (6 percent) were below the poverty level (Bureau of Labor Statistics, 2001). School dropouts are more likely to receive public assistance than high school graduates. This is particularly true for young women who drop out of school, who are more likely to have children at younger ages and more likely to be single parents than high school graduates (Kaufman et al., 2001). There are individual consequences of dropping out beyond the employment and economic factors. Rumberger (1987) suggested that dropping out of school may lead to poor mental and physical health through its effects on employment and income; he cited a study that found that increased unemployment was associated with increases in total mortality, suicides, and admissions to state mental hospitals (1987: 113). As they encounter more unemployment, and financial difficulties, high school dropouts are likely to need more social services such as welfare, unemployment, and medical assistance. Unemployment and financial pressures also increase the temptation to engage in shoplifting, petty theft, and more serious criminal behavior. With little or no improvement in the unemployment rate and increased importance placed on education and job skills, it is likely that the social consequences of dropping out will be even greater in the future.

Truancy, Dropout, and Delinquency

There is clearly a relationship between dropout and delinquency, but there is disagreement as to the exact causal order of the association. In other words, it is unclear whether dropout causes delinquency, whether delinquency causes dropout, or whether other social factors may be responsible for truancy, dropout, and delinquency. There are two theoretical views on this association. *Strain theory* holds that the frustration of school failure leads to delinquency and in turn to dropout. After dropping out, delinquency is likely to decline as the dropout no longer experiences the "strain" of school failure. *Control theory*, in contrast, holds that school involvement provides a protective social bond that helps youth avoid delinquency. Weakening or severing that social bond through truancy or dropout increases the probability of drug use and delinquency. A number of studies have examined the relationship between delinquency and dropout. The major research questions examined are whether delinquency increases or decreases following dropout and which variables best explain dropout and delinquency. Researchers have tested both theoretical explanations. Using reliable self-report data from large representative samples of youth, criminologists have found support for both the strain and control theories.

Delinquency Causes Dropout

According to *strain theory*, delinquency is a response to the frustrations or strains of school experiences. Cohen (1955) noted the frustration of working-class youths trying to meet middle-class school standards and explained delinquency as a response to the frustration of students who were failing in school. Elliott and Voss (1974) also hypothesized that dropping out occurred after school failure led to frustration. Feeling alienated from successful achievers and students who are positively involved in school activities, the failing students associate with peers who are also failing, dislike school and are skipping classes. Based on this reasoning, Elliott and Voss believed that delinquent behavior occurs more frequently while youth are in school and declines after they drop out. The theoretical framework guiding their research was the strain theory of Cloward and Ohlin (1960), in which delinquency is a response to the frustration of limited opportunities to attain desired goals. Dropping out was believed to be an alternative response to school failure (Elliott and Voss, 1974: 27). They conducted a longitudinal study of 2,617 students from eight schools in California and compared rates of police contacts and self-reported delinquency for both high school graduates and for dropouts. Delinquency rates for the dropouts were higher and increased more while they were in school than those for high school graduates. After the students dropped out, the rates of delinquency declined. The decrease in delinquency following dropout occurred regardless of the age of the student at the time of dropout and could not be explained by class or gender differences. The dropouts had consistently higher police contact rates than graduates for every period they were in school. Their involvement in delinquency increased prior to leaving school, but once they dropped out of school their involvement in serious offenses declined and the total number of reported offenses declined slightly (Elliott and Voss, 1974: 128). Elliott and Voss concluded that their findings supported a strain theory explanation that delinquency is a response to the frustration of negative school experiences and that dropping out diminishes both the frustration of school and involvement in delinquency. This first major study on dropout and delinquency provoked considerable attention, and the findings raised policy questions about the wisdom of compulsory school attendance, especially for young people 16 years or older who were failing and exhibiting problem behavior in the school and community. One weakness of the study that raised questions about the findings was the failure to control for the influence of age. Studies indicate that delinquent behavior tends to decline as persons get older, and this might explain the decline in delinquency among the 16- to 18-year-old dropouts.

Other studies have supported strain theory in explaining school dropout. Agnew (1985) suggested that students who drop out often experience worse relationships with their parents, which may add to the likelihood of delinquency. Farnworth and Leiber (1989) cited evidence that youths who want a good, high-paying job but are unlikely to complete the college education required may become involved in delinquent behavior.

Dropout Causes Delinquency

Social control theorists emphasize factors that help youths avoid delinquent involvement. Delinquency takes place when young peoples' bonds to conventional society are weak (Hirschi, 1969). Individuals who are attached to conventional social institutions (of which school is one of the most important) and to nondelinquent peers are less likely to become delinquent. Youths who believe school has positive benefits for them, who have high educational aspirations, and who are involved in school are less likely to be involved in delinquent behavior.

Thornberry, Moore, and Christenson (1985) sought to replicate the Elliott and Voss research design to determine whether delinquency declined after dropout (strain theory) or increased after dropping out (control theory). They analyzed longitudinal data from a sample ($N = 975$) of the Philadelphia birth cohort of 1945 (males born that year who lived in Philadelphia from ages 10 to 18). In addition to reviewing arrest histories, they interviewed 567 (62 percent) of the sample. Youths who dropped out at 16 and 18 years of age had significantly more arrests following dropout than during the previous year while they were still in school. There was a slight decrease in arrests (22 percent) for those who dropped out at seventeen, but much less than the 55 percent decrease for all graduates. Results of their analysis offered little support for a strain model explanation—that delinquent behavior preceded dropping out of high school and then declined. The dropouts in their sample did not show a reduction in criminal activity, and they interpreted the results to be consistent with a control perspective (Thornberry et al., 1985: 12). Their analyses also showed that criminal involvement declines with people in their early twenties, both graduates and dropouts. Even controlling for age, however, their results indicated that dropping out was positively associated with later criminal behavior. Thornberry et al. (1985) also controlled for social status, race, marriage, and employment and found that these variables made no difference in their finding that dropout status has a positive impact on criminal involvement. Other studies supported the social control findings of Thornberry and associates. Farrington and associates (1986) extended the analysis of dropout to include unemployment and delinquency and found some association with criminal involvement after school dropout if youth were unemployed. Students who stayed in school committed fewer offenses, and the research suggests that unemployment may be a more important factor in crime than is school dropout. Hartnagel and Krahn (1989) suggested that unemployment and dropout may lead to criminal behavior because youths do not have enough money to buy what they need or want. They suggested that increased involvement in deviant behavior for unemployed dropout males may be a normal part of their lifestyle, because the social controls of a job are absent, negative peer group influences are stronger, and free time and boredom increase the opportunities for and temptations to engage in deviant behavior (Hartnagel and Krahn, 1989: 440). Fagan and Pabon (1990) administered surveys to a sample of 2,467 high school students and dropouts from inner-city metropolitan areas in the East, the South, and on the West Coast. Comparisons of the findings showed that delinquency and substance use were more frequent and serious among the school dropouts, but they could not establish a causal relationship between substance use, delinquent involvement, and school dropout from this cross-sectional designed study.

Other Factors May Cause Delinquency and Dropout

Jarjoura (1993) analyzed data from the 1979 and 1980 National Longitudinal Survey of Youth to study delinquency and dropout, and controlled for previous offending of dropouts, which was not accounted for in the Thornberry et al. (1985) study. Previous delinquency involvement is important to consider in analyses, because dropouts have higher delinquency rates than those who graduate, which often predicts dropping out. Besides controlling for gender, race, and age, Jarjoura included prior misconduct, school experiences, and performance as control variables. He found that those who dropped out because they disliked school and those who were expelled for school misconduct had the highest probabilities of involvement in theft and selling drugs after dropping out. Dropping out for personal reasons, such as marriage or pregnancy, had no effect on later involvement in drugs or theft, but was significantly related to future violent behavior. Jarjoura suggested that this unexpected finding might be due to an aversive home environment in which violence is directed at a spouse or child. Whereas youths who were expelled reported more involvement in delinquent behavior than graduates, Jarjoura found that the differences in later criminal behavior were explained by prior misconduct, not by dropping out. Jarjoura noted that while dropouts were more likely to have higher levels of involvement in delinquency than graduates, it was not always because they dropped out. He concluded that dropouts are not more likely to engage in delinquency as a result of leaving school before graduating, but subsequent delinquent behavior depended on the reasons for leaving school (Jarjoura, 1993). In subsequent analyses, Jarjoura (1996) noted that dropout is more likely to be associated with higher levels of involvement in delinquency for middle-class than for lower-class youths. He found that for youths living in poverty, dropping out of high school does not increase involvement in violent offenses. For middle-class youths, dropping out of high school for school-related or personal reasons significantly increased their participation in violent offenses compared with high school graduates, but dropping out for economic reasons was not associated with increased involvement in violent offenses. The findings seemed to support strain theory because middle-class youth are under more expectations and pressure to complete high school and succeed. The strain of failing to meet expectations places them at risk of criminal involvement. The findings may also support a social control explanation. Jarjoura (1996) noted that dropouts are not a homogeneous group; they differ by social class, reasons for dropping out, and the level of criminal involvement after dropping out. The existing research shows that multiple factors are associated with dropout and delinquency. The theoretical explanation for leaving school depends on the student's gender, social class, and reasons for dropping out. Strain and control theories offer the best explanation, but no single criminological theory provides an adequate explanation of dropout and delinquency. The findings of Jarjoura (1996) suggest that different approaches to dropout prevention may be appropriate based on the youth's social class, but it seems clear that improving graduation rates may lead to a reduction in offending.

Policy Implications of Delinquency and Dropout

Although there is not total agreement on the exact nature of the causal relationship between delinquency and dropout, it is clear that the two are associated. Researchers, school officials, and juvenile justice authorities have been concerned about the most appropriate policies to prevent school dropout and delinquency. Dropping out of school before graduation by itself has undeniably serious consequences for the individual and for society. To the extent that dropping out is either a cause or consequence of delinquency, the problem is further magnified. Efforts to encourage at-risk students to stay in school and graduate would certainly improve their chances of employment, and reduce social costs and might prevent crime and additional justice system costs. Four policies have been at the center of discussions concerning school dropout and delinquency: compulsory school attendance laws, school policies and "pushouts", expulsion of disruptive students, and school reforms that raise academic requirements.

Compulsory School Attendance

There is no question that compulsory school attendance laws have been beneficial to individuals and to society in encouraging young people to obtain a high school diploma.

Many youths who dislike school and see little value in a high school education have been deterred from dropping out, only afterwards to realize the value of their education. Compulsory school attendance laws may, however, unintentionally contribute to disruptive and delinquent behavior in school. Enforcing compulsory attendance on students who do not want to attend is likely to increase strain and frustration, which in turn may lead to acting out and disruptive behavior. The presence of disruptive youth adversely affects the learning environment for students desiring to learn and complete school. Worse, it may increase the probability of delinquency. Elliott and Voss (1974) questioned attempts to raise the age of compulsory attendance and efforts by probation officers and court officials to encourage delinquent dropouts to return to school. Juvenile probation requirements to attend school are based on the assumption that the school functions as a positive form of social control and assists youths in adjusting to life. The findings of Elliott and Voss are at odds with this policy and suggest that school aggravates the problems of some students rather than alleviating them. They posited that compulsory school attendance facilitates delinquency by forcing students to remain in what is sometimes a frustrating situation in which they are stigmatized as failures. Therefore, it was not surprising that youth who felt trapped in schools rebelled or attempted to escape what was perceived as a negative experience (Elliott and Voss, 1974: 207). They did not suggest that all students who are frustrated by school experiences be encouraged to drop out, but that the law should not restrict dropping out in cases where leaving may be the most appropriate alternative. A preferable strategy is one that would change the school structure, with new learning environments in which competition is minimized and failure is reduced.

Jackson Toby (1980) noted that a major factor in schools becoming less orderly is the pressure to keep children in school longer. While acknowledging that rising educational levels is a positive side of this trend, he maintained that compulsory attendance laws have resulted in retaining disruptive students who do not want to be in school. Toby noted that the negative aspect of compulsory-school-attendance laws and of informal pressure to stay in school longer was that youths who did not want further education were compelled to remain in school. Being required to attend against their will means that some feel like prisoners and became troublemakers (Toby, 1980: 29). Toby has suggested that compulsory school attendance laws be changed so that only younger students are required to attend. This would allow students who do not want to stay in school to drop out and would presumably diminish the extent of disruptive and violent behavior by those who do not want to be in school. There is no denying that misbehavior and threats of violence from a small number of students is a serious disruption in schools. Allowing students to simply leave school does present a dilemma, however. While this alleviates the school problem, dropouts present a continuing problem for society in terms of unemployment, loitering, and troublemaking in the community. The dilemma also raises the question of how far the school is expected to extend its educational function. Schools should be expected to create a positive learning environment that attempts to retain at-risk students who experience failure and frustration. But schools are limited in their ability to deal with disruptive and violent youth. Toby has suggested that one reason school have become less orderly is the decreased help with discipline problems from the juvenile courts (Toby, 1980: 30; see also Toby, 1993: 44). School truancy and ungovernable behavior are no longer sufficient grounds for court action and incarceration in most states. Adjudicated juveniles on probation supervision in the community are generally required to attend school and to obey school rules and regulations. Very few students are on probation, however, so tougher enforcement of probation rules is unlikely to make much difference in the extent of school disruption and crime.

School Policies and "Pushouts"

School structure, rules, and policies often result in students leaving school. Mann (1987) noted that young peoples' school experience is the most frequently cited reason for quitting early. He suggested that when students fail to learn and leave school early they are called "dropouts", but when schools fail to teach students and to make an effort to retain them, they are called "pushouts." Elliott and Voss (1974) found that a sizable number of students left school out of frustration after they were denied access to regular school programs. They found that approximately one-fifth of the dropouts in their sample were pushed out of school and concluded that the phenomenon of dropout cannot be viewed strictly in terms of personal decisions of students to leave school. Pushout resulted from the enforcement of rules prohibiting pregnant girls, married students, and troublesome 18-year-old students from attending the regular day-school program (Elliott and Voss, 1974). Few of the students in their sample dropped out to go to work, and they saw little evidence that dropouts rejected the benefits of a high school diploma. They suggested that restrictive school policies and the failure to accommodate all students amounted to a practice of pushing some students out of school.

Mann (1987) noted that students in his study blamed the school less for their failures than might be expected. The reason given for dropping out by one-third of boys was "because I had bad grades" or "because I did not like school," while only 13 percent were expelled. Mann believes those statistics underestimate the extent to which schools make a willful decision not to teach all children. He claimed that referrals to special education have become a common way to solve class-control problems by pushing some youth out of the mainstream. Mann acknowledges that to say schools push out some students is a harsh statement about the responsibilities and difficult decisions schools must make. If every student were given a diploma, such as with social promotion, school officials would inevitably be criticized for not fulfilling their educational responsibilities. Maintaining minimum standards is more likely to preserve the significance of the high school diploma but will mean that some students may be "pushed out."

Bowditch (1993) analyzed the routine disciplinary activities in an inner-city high school and found that the policies and practices encouraged school workers to "get rid of" students deemed to be "troublemakers." She noted that the indicators used to identify "troublemakers" were the same "risk factors" that emerge in research on dropouts. Through observations made in the boys' discipline office, her study examined how routine administrative decisions and actions affect a student's passage through high school and the disciplinarian's role in selecting students who will be "dropped." The discipline office had two strategies to get rid of students identified as troublemakers. One was to transfer the student for disciplinary reasons, and disciplinarians would document all incidents of misbehavior and disruptive incidents in order to justify the decision. The second strategy was through dropping a student from the roll. This could be done if the student was 17 years of age and therefore beyond the compulsory school attendance requirement. The discipline office interpreted this to mean that the school no longer had to keep the student. The observations of Bowditch (1993) led her to conclude that the same factors that predict dropout (frequent absences, truancies, or suspensions; failing classes;

and being overage in grade) are the indicators that disciplinarians used to define trouble-makers and that led to suspensions, disciplinary transfers, and involuntary drops. The clear implication of her conclusions is that the preferred option of many school officials dealing with troublemakers is to push them out rather than work at correction and retention.

Expulsion of Disruptive Students

The most severe sanction available to school officials for dealing with disruptive students is expulsion. Expulsion is the involuntary removal of a student, generally for the remainder of the school year. A student generally can only be expelled for clearly stated rule violations that are thoroughly documented by school officials. Expulsion is an appropriate sanction for students who have brought a weapon to school, who have a history of violent behavior, or who continue to engage in disruptive and delinquent behavior after school officials have resorted to suspensions and other sanctions short of expulsion. Toby (1980) suggested that school officials be allowed to use expulsion more freely, especially with the small percentage of violent students who have proved that they cannot be controlled. Curtailing these students' rights to an education is justified when their behavior interferes with the rights of the majority of students to a safe educational environment. He acknowledges that expulsion is a last resort to maintain safe and orderly schools. Home instruction and alternative schools will be often be available for expelled students, but the likelihood is that they will not make much further academic progress. Toby nevertheless believes that schools must have the option to give up on students who are threatening the educational opportunities of their classmates. His suggestions would surely help rid schools of the most troublesome students. Changing compulsory school attendance laws to apply only to younger students and allowing school officials to expel disruptive students surely alleviates many school problems. Others disagree with Toby about compulsory attendance and expulsion.

Gary and Denise Gottfredson (1985) have expressed concern that such policy reforms lead schools in the wrong direction and do not address the fundamental problems. The findings of their reanalysis of the "Violent Schools–Safe Schools Study" indicated that school disorder tends to be greatest in schools serving communities characterized by social disorganization and largely minority populations. They are concerned that lowering the age of compulsory school attendance and expelling more disruptive students would only compound the problem of educational inequality of minority groups and perpetuate social disorganization in their communities. Many educators agree that suspension and expulsion should be used only as a last resort. Susan Black (1999) described a school district in which suspension and expulsion are rare. The goal is to keep every student in school so that they can learn. Before resorting to suspension or expulsion, she believes that school officials should provide discipline options such as counseling and alternative schools. Others have noted that the unintended consequences of suspension and expulsion when students have no educational alternative may include further alienation from school, delinquency, and substance abuse (Taras et al., 2003).

There is reason to question any drastic actions in revising compulsory school attendance laws and expulsion policies. School failure and misconduct often result from youths' lack of attachment to school and lack of parental support for education, both of which are more common among parents who have attained less education. Parents with less education—who are disproportionately poor and minorities—often fail to wholeheartedly support their children's educational performance and may not offer enough support for school officials in attendance and conduct problems. Youths who do not do well in school are the ones who more frequently drop out and commit delinquent behavior. Changing state attendance laws and expulsion policies is likely to perpetuate problems of educational deficiency and delinquent conduct among those students. Kozol (1991) documented the "savage inequalities" of unequal educational opportunities among poor and minority youth. Students in many inner-city urban schools are placed at a severe disadvantage when their schools lack adequate classroom space, textbooks, lab and computer equipment, and the well-paid and qualified teachers more common in suburban schools. These students are also more at risk of losing interest in school, dropping out, and engaging in deviant or delinquent behavior.

The issues of compulsory attendance, "pushout," and expulsion present difficult dilemmas that are unlikely to be settled in the near future. Available research studies do not offer sufficiently conclusive findings on which to base policies for students who do not want to attend school or those who disrupt the classroom. The Gottfredsons (1985) acknowledge that we do not know if compelling young people to remain in school would increase their rebellion or decrease it, nor are we certain whether compelling young people to remain in school would enhance their career prospects or decrease them. We have discussed previously in this chapter the social and economic consequences of leaving school before graduation, and there is ample evidence that persistence in school pays off in terms of occupational attainment and income. These factors make a strong case for taking efforts to prevent dropout and increase retention and graduation rates of students.

Jackson Toby does make a very convincing case for taking a tougher approach with disruptive students. In schools throughout the United States, compulsory school attendance is treated as more important than promoting an orderly school environment (Toby, 1983: 43). Today teachers are commonly confronted with disruptive behavior and verbal harassment that two or three decades ago would have resulted in immediate suspension or expulsion. Many teachers complain about not being supported by principals. School administrators are often not supported in their disciplinary efforts by school board members, who often come under pressure from parents. Parents too often are reluctant to accept teachers' reports of their child's misbehavior. Some have gone so far as to challenge school suspensions or expulsions through court action. Legal action is certainly appropriate when a student's constitutional rights have been violated. Challenging school disciplinary actions that have been administered fairly and following proper procedures, however, sends the wrong message to young people. In order to maintain an orderly and safe school environment for teachers and students, it is essential that a proper balance be maintained between students' rights and responsibilities. Toby has suggested lowering the age of compulsory attendance (to age 14 or 15), and requiring that students meet minimum behavioral standards. Lowering the age of compulsory attendance, in his opinion, would not result in a significantly greater number of youth leaving school. Most youth do want to attend school. School attendance offers valued peer associations, and school enrollment carries a more positive status than being a dropout. Students who simply attend school but make no effort to learn present a problem for teachers and other students. Students who are not interested in education and who disrupt the educational process would temporarily lose their enrollment status. They would be encouraged to return to school as soon as they are willing to comply with behavioral and educational expectations (Toby, 1983: 44). A school district policy whereby chronically misbehaving students are expelled or pushed out represents a shift in educational philosophy. Schools generally attempt to retain students until the compulsory school attendance age. The unsafe environment and disruptive conditions in some high schools, however, makes such a policy seem worth considering. School districts that have alternative schools or special programs offer school officials more discipline options that may better support educational goals.

Most researchers and policymakers in the fields of education and juvenile delinquency have pushed for dropout and delinquency-prevention programs before resorting to a policy of excluding students. Most believe that it makes more sense to look at alternative solutions and policies, rather than simply allowing more students to drop out and expelling those who are disruptive. Rather than excluding problem students, some changes in school structure and teaching methods may help schools retain at-risk students.

School Reform and Dropout

There has been considerable concern about the poor academic skills of students in the past few decades. A report entitled *A Nation at Risk: The Imperative for Educational Reform* stated that the United States was falling behind in commerce, industry, science, and technological innovation because of reduced educational quality and lower standards (National Commission on Excellence in Education, 1983). Numerous federal and state commissions have criticized the quality of public education and pushed for school reforms and higher graduation standards. Similar to the complaints a century ago, the business community has expressed concerns about the skills and working habits of high school graduates. Mann (1987) cited a report by the Committee for Economic Development noting that if schools tolerate excessive absenteeism, truancy, tardiness, or misbehavior, we cannot expect students to meet standards of minimum performance or behavior either in school or as adults. He found it not surprising that a student who is allowed to graduate with numerous unexcused absences, regular patterns of tardiness, and a history of uncompleted assignments will make a poor employee (Mann, 1987: 224).

Most states have raised high school graduation standards, and many have instituted some form of minimum competency tests for students before they can earn a diploma. School reform measures generally include a demand for higher standards in three areas: the academic content of courses, the use of time for schoolwork, and student achievement (McDill et al., 1987). There is general agreement that higher standards are needed for high school graduates to meet the requirements of college or the demands of business. But there are concerns about what some refer to as the "high costs of high standards." Raising academic standards may not bring about the desired skills and academic performance among marginal students who are most at risk of truancy and dropout. McDill, Natriello, and Pallas (1987) believe that the result of higher standards for these students may not be increases in cognitive achievement but rather notable increases in absenteeism, truancy, school-related behavior problems, and dropping out. They believe that substantial additional assistance and resources must also be provided in order to help at-risk students attain the higher standards and stay in school. While this will add to the costs of education, failure to take measures to reduce the dropout rate will result in even greater costs to the nation. Raising standards without also providing additional resources for schools and assistance for at-risk students is not likely to significantly reduce school failure, truancy, and dropout.

The "No Child Left Behind" (NCLB) law is the most recent school reform effort by the federal government. Signed into law in January 2002 by President George W. Bush, the law is a reauthorization of the 1965 Elementary and Secondary Education Act (ESEA) and is the primary mechanism through which federal tax dollars are funneled to state departments of education. The law covers a wide range of issues related to education standards and reform, but the provision most pertinent to the present discussion is the demand for regular assessment and greater accountability for student academic performance. The NCLB law requires schools to administer standardized tests and requires virtually all students to test at their grade level for math and reading. Schools that do not measure up for 2 years in a row have to provide more tutoring or let students transfer to better schools. Many state and local school administrators have objected to provisions of the law for a number of reasons. First, average assessment test scores for schools are based only on students who take the test, and in the past there was no minimum number of students who had to take the test, so many schools actually discouraged lower-performing students from taking the tests. Under NCLB a school could be placed on the probationary list of those not meeting minimum standards if absentee students brought the participation below 95 percent on the day of the test. Second, educators and state legislators object to unfunded mandates or federal initiatives not backed by enough money. They maintain that local schools are required to meet minimum standards without sufficient federal funds to hire and train the most qualified teachers and provide the extra educational resources to help academically deficient students improve their performance and pass the tests. Schools in states and cities with more minority and immigrant students are likely to face additional challenges to meet the new standards. Congressman George Miller (D-CA) a member of the House Committee on Education and the Workforce, who had a role in passing the NCLB law, was critical of an Education Department regulation that is likely to overlook increased dropout rates that may result from the higher standards. The original intent of the law was that "no child be left behind" and that schools would be help accountable for retaining and helping all students meet educational standards. Miller charged that the federal Education Department regulation would certify schools as making "adequate progress" even if they had high numbers of dropouts among poor and minority students. Ignoring dropout rates would enable schools to receive inflated test scores (Miller, 2002).

The goal of the NCLB law was to improve the quality of education for all students. Some question whether using punitive sanctions to meet educational standards is the most effective means of achieving the goal. Some state officials believe the federal mandate is not sufficiently funded to help local schools meet the educational standards. Congressman John Boehner (R-Ohio), Chairman of the House Committee on Education and the Workforce, believes that the law is improving education and cites *Washington Post* columnist Jay Matthews, who claims that the law has raised educational expectations (Matthews, 2003). Other state education officials report that the law has had a positive impact on school performance and that it has the support of many citizens and parents who demand that schools be held accountable for providing quality education for all students.

Truancy and Dropout-Prevention Programs

Truancy and dropout affect thousands of students each year. They are considered to be the first step to a lifetime of problems (Garry, 1996), are associated with substance abuse, gang involvement, and delinquency (Bell et al., 1994), and result in lost revenues to school districts, higher welfare costs to taxpayers, and costs to businesses that must pay to train uneducated workers (Garry, 1996). Because of the seriousness of the problem and its consequences, priority has been given to reducing truancy and dropout, ranging from local school districts to federal agencies. Multiple efforts have been introduced throughout the nation to encourage young people to stay in school. Educators are aware that they must make special efforts to retain at-risk students and improve the rate of high school graduation.

The factors associated with truancy and dropout are varied, so prevention programs must address these multiple factors. Truancy-intervention programs have generally been directed at the individual truant, the family, and the schools (Bell et al., 1994). Student-based interventions are directed at conduct disorders, attitudes toward school, academic abilities, and motivation. Showing students the personal consequences of truant behavior and what can be done to solve their school problems has proven to be helpful in many cases. Family-based interventions attempt to alter dysfunctional family situations, encourage more parental involvement in their child's education, and bring parents and teachers together to work on ways to improve students' school performance and attendance. School-based interventions include reward systems for good attendance and contracting with students to emphasize that attendance is their responsibility. Schools have revised their attendance policies and installed better systems for monitoring and recording absences. Teachers are encouraged to set good examples, maintain accurate attendance records, create a class-room attendance reward system, and consider individual students' capabilities. Based on their overview of truancy intervention programs, Bell et al. (1994) believe that a multi-modal approach that targets those three areas will be most effective. In support of the role of parents, Rumberger (1995) noted a number of home factors associated with students who completed high school: the presence of study aids, high educational expectations and aspirations, and parental monitoring and participation.

Because truancy and dropout have multiple causes and consequences, multiple government agencies are involved in promoting and funding prevention programs. Likewise, experts and researchers from several professional and academic fields have been involved in research on the causes and correlates of truancy and dropout and the most effective intervention strategies. Professional and academic disciplines represented in research efforts include education, counseling, medicine, psychology, criminology, and criminal justice. The U.S. Departments of Education and Justice have promoted funding, research, resources, and technical assistance for truancy and dropout interventions. Most of the available published studies and resources can be found in publications and on internet sites associated with either education or criminology and criminal justice.

Educational Research and Programs

Wehlage, Rutter, and Turnbaugh (1987) developed and implemented an effective dropout-prevention program in several Wisconsin high schools. They kept the programs small, with close teacher–student relationships and individualized instruction. Teachers were encouraged to give at-risk students a renewed opportunity to learn and to take on an "extended role" with students, confronting home, community, peer group, or substance abuse problems. The program was voluntary, but students had to apply for admission and admit that attitude and behavior changes were necessary for success. Students were expected to commit themselves to rules, work expectations, standards of behavior, and consequences for breaking rules. The curriculum and courses were individualized, with clear objectives and means for ongoing assessment of students' progress. Teachers were expected to offer prompt feedback and to emphasize an active role for students. Finally, experiential learning was required to offer youths opportunities to work with responsible adults, develop a positive work ethic, and introduce them to vocational opportunities. Students were involved as volunteers in daycare centers, nursing homes, hospitals, and social service agencies. Results indicated that special school interventions with at-risk youth can produce some positive benefits (Wehlage et al., 1987: 72–73).

Educational researchers have attempted to identify the types of interventions and programs that are most effective in reducing truancy and dropout. McPartland (1994) identified four essential components: providing opportunities for success in schoolwork, creating a caring and supportive environment, communicating the relevance of education for future endeavors, and helping with students' personal problems. The National Dropout Prevention Center at Clemson University has identified several strategies associated with reduced dropout rates. The most effective strategies fall into four general approaches: early intervention, basic core strategies, making the most of instruction, and making the most of the wider communities (Schargel and Smink, 2001). The National Dropout Prevention Center has conducted and analyzed research, sponsored workshops, and collaborated with educators to further its mission of meeting the needs of at-risk students and reducing America's dropout rate.

The U.S. Department of Education awarded numerous grants to school districts to address the dropout problem. Results of evaluation research suggested that alternative schools for middle-school students and GED programs have promise for reducing school dropout (Dynarski and Gleason, 1999). The General Accounting Office (2002) noted that despite the presence of many federal, state, and local dropout-prevention programs over the last two decades, few have been carefully evaluated for effectiveness. The authors of the GAO report called for additional funding to review and evaluate the effectiveness of state and local programs and to disseminate the results and information on the most effective programs. Lehr et al. (2003) reviewed several dropout-prevention programs and noted that we need better ways to accurately identify students at risk of dropping out, clearly describe dropout interventions and outcome variables, implement more experimental design studies, and conduct evaluative studies that can identify for which students under what conditions dropout-prevention strategies may be most effective (Lehr et al., 2003).

Juvenile Justice Programs and Research

School truancy and dropout are violations of the compulsory school attendance laws in every state and in most other countries that require youth to attend school until a given minimum age. As discussed at the beginning of this chapter, school truancy is considered a status offense and therefore generally not given the highest priority by law enforcement and juvenile courts, unless special policies and programs have been implemented to focus police and court resources on truancy and the related delinquency and social problems believed to accompany truancy and dropout. We have discussed the legal procedures that may be taken by juvenile courts to enforce compulsory school attendance laws. Courts attempt to hold parents accountable for their child's school attendance, and after trying precourt remedies a habitual truant may be declared a "child in need of protection or services." Until recently there has been little available research on the effectiveness of court intervention in truancy cases. A study in Great Britain found that even the threat of a juvenile court appearance appeared to improve the school attendance of habitual truants (Berg et al., 1988). Similar to procedures in American juvenile courts, the British court viewed court intervention as a last resort. Efforts were made by education welfare officers and a school attendance subcommittee to improve truants' attendance records before resorting to court intervention. Findings indicated that bringing habitual truants to court did have at least a short-term effect on school attendance and had a significant effect on reducing the commission of offenses. Berg et al. acknowledged that the finding does seem to be at odds with the views that all efforts should be concentrated on diverting children from court (1988: 122).

Research has established a link between truancy, dropout, and delinquency, so one of the priorities of the Office of Juvenile Justice and Delinquency Prevention (OJJDP) in the past decade has been truancy and dropout prevention programs. One of the first dropout prevention initiatives that was publicized by the OJJDP was Communities in Schools (CIS), a network of local, state, and national partnerships working together to help prevent youth from dropping out of school (Cantelon and LeBoeuf, 1997). CIS has brought together businesses and public and private agencies into schools to assist at-risk students and their families. Examples of collaborative efforts in schools include welfare and health professionals, employment counselors, social workers and recreational leaders, clergy, and youth organizations. Findings indicated that 80 percent of the students who participated in CIS services between 1989 and 1991 were still in school or had graduated in 1993, 70 percent of absentee students improved their attendance, and 60 percent improved their low grades (Cantelon and LeBoeuf, 1997: 7). Families and Schools Together (FAST) is a program that provides support to parents so that they can better help their children avoid school failure, prevent alcohol and other drug abuse in the family, and reduce the stress that parents and children often experience in daily family life. The FAST program has resulted in improvement in classroom and home behavior and more parental involvement in the schools. The program has been highly recognized throughout the United States (Cantelon and LeBoeuf, 1997).

Criminal justice agencies have become involved in truancy-reduction efforts as a way of reducing gang involvement, delinquency, and drug offenses. Truancy-reduction programs have been implemented by county attorneys' offices, law enforcement agencies, as juvenile court diversion programs, and with probation officers working in schools. Concentrated efforts by the Dallas Police Department to enforce truancy and curfew laws had a positive impact on reducing gang violence (Fritsch et al., 1999). Results of a combined school law enforcement Truant Recovery Program in California showed slight improvements in attendance, behavior, and grades a year after the program began (White et al., 2001). The Pima County Attorney's office in Arizona developed ACT Now, a truancy diversion program to enforce attendance laws and to hold parents accountable. The program offered services to address the root causes of truancy and threatened sanctions for students who failed to attend school regularly or failed to complete the diversion program successfully (and their parents). School districts participating in the program showed decreases in the number of truancies ranging from 64 percent in the largest school district to 4 percent in the smallest (Baker et al., 2001: 6). A Truancy Reduction Demonstration Program (TRDP) was initiated in 1998 through the combined resources of the OJJDP, the Justice Department's Weed and Seed program, and the Safe and Drug-Free Schools Program of the Education Department. Funded programs include a probation officer working with truants in a school in Contra Costa County, CA; a precourt diversion program for truants in Jacksonville, FL; a program in Honolulu, Hawaii, in which attendance officers work with the Honolulu police department to provide Saturday truancy workshops for truant youth; a probation officer in Suffolk County, New York, who works with school personnel to help improve truant students' attendance; a Houston program that combines efforts of the mayor's Anti-Gang Office, community police officers, and school case managers working with chronically truant students; and programs in Seattle and Tacoma, Washington, that combine efforts of law enforcement, juvenile court, and school personnel in working with truant students (Baker et al., 2001: 8–9). A national evaluation of the TRDP is ongoing. Initial overall assessments indicate positive collaborative involvements of schools, courts, and law enforcement. Underlying issues relating to truancy that have been identified by the projects include family poverty, less education by parents, substance abuse, cultural variation in the valuing of public education, and pressures on the youth to work and provide child care for younger siblings (Baker et al., 2001: 13). Mueller and Giacomazzi (2003) reported on a truancy-reduction program in Idaho that aimed at changing poor attendance habits through early, nonpunitive intervention. In an evaluation of the program, school officials reported that in 77 percent of the cases referred for truancy problems the students' attendance record had improved, and in 73 percent of the cases the students' grades had improved. A truancy-reduction program in three elementary schools in a Midwestern city was initiated by concerns about unsupervised children, juvenile crime, loitering, and graffiti (McCluskey et al., 2004). Youths identified as chronic truants were visited at their homes by a school attendance officer and a community policing officer, who impressed upon them the seriousness of truancy and offered assistance of school and outside agency resources. Analyses of the percentage of days absent before and after intervention showed significant reduction in truancy, suggesting that the program was successful in reducing elementary school absenteeism.

Truancy presents challenges for both educators and justice officials. It is an education problem but also has direct and indirect effects on crime and delinquency. Keeping students actively engaged in school, attending regularly, and making educational progress through meaningful and good-quality teaching is the primary responsibility of educators. We have noted, however, that many if not most of the reasons for truancy and dropout lie outside the school. Family problems and lack of parental support, economic pressures and social problems in the community, and influences from peers, pop culture, and media exposure are factors related to truancy and dropout. Truancy-reduction strategies, therefore, require the collaborative efforts of schools, the community, and justice agencies.

We have seen a shift recently toward greater participation of law enforcement and juvenile justice professionals in the schools. Indicators of this shift include the job titles and role descriptions of officials working in schools and a change in school environment, which now places more emphasis on suppression and control of criminal activities (Trulson et al., 2001). Police officers assigned to schools were originally called "resource officers" or "school liaisons," and their defined roles were educational as much as law enforcement. Today it is not uncommon to have assigned to schools "security officers" and "guards," whose primary duties are law enforcement and crime control (Bazemore et al., 2004). The role of the juvenile court in truancy has also changed. Supreme Court decisions and the Juvenile Justice and Delinquency Act of 1972 minimized the juvenile court's jurisdiction over truancy and other status offenses and discouraged the detention and institutional commitment of juvenile status offenders. The policy of nonintervention with status offenders has changed since the 1990s, as law enforcement officials have claimed that truancy is linked to criminal behavior. The number of truancy cases in juvenile courts is still small but has increased significantly from 22,000 cases in 1989 to 41,000 cases in 1998—an 85 percent increase (Baker et al., 2001: 2). These changes are indicative of a trend toward law enforcement and juvenile court authorities taking a more active role in enforcing school attendance.

Gordon Bazemore and associates (2004) evaluated a truancy intervention program in a southeastern county that was initiated by the sheriff's department and involved sheriff's deputies and officers from a municipal police department taking students who were absent without an excuse to a central truancy unit, where they were processed and assessed by social service professionals to determine the need for follow-up and remedial programs. The program evolved into one with a narrow deterrence strategy, so Bazemore et al. examined the program's effectiveness in improving school attendance and reducing delinquency of truant youths. Evaluation of the program revealed mixed results. Youths processed through the program had some short-term improvement in attendance, but those with attendance problems who were not processed through the truancy center actually had better attendance afterwards. Bazemore et al. suggest that a possible reason for the mixed outcomes might be the limited long-term effectiveness of a law enforcement and control-oriented deterrence approach to truancy prevention. The project began as a multiagency partnership with a broader focus than law enforcement, but the sheriff's department staff eventually took the primary leadership, and the program moved away from a multidimensional model toward a crime-control model. Time spent with truant students, for example, was void of positive interaction beyond "just-the-facts" questioning and warnings to sit still and be quiet. Officers did not seem to take much interest in understanding or supporting the services or the remedial education component of the program. The officers spent very little time in informal interaction with the youth, their families, or school personnel. Their primary motivation seemed to be to make as many truancy arrests as possible, exemplified by "sweep day." On the first Wednesday of the month the school resource officers presented a show of force and made large-scale pickups that resulted in four to five times more students processed. Sweep day resembled a quota system that supported a crime-control approach to truancy.

The results of this study raise some important questions about the most effective strategies for dropout and truancy prevention and whether a formal law enforcement approach is the best strategy for dealing with this problem. Bazemore and associates (2004) believe that the findings raise concerns about the relationship between formal and informal social control in dealing with school problems. They suggest that zero-tolerance policies and rhetoric have weakened the informal authority and decision-making discretion of educational professionals and have been replaced by the formal controls of police and juvenile justice authorities. Truancy and dropout are not violations that warrant a petition for delinquent behavior. Formal police intervention in truancy cases is common in many cities for at least two reasons: evidence that truancy and dropout are factors in delinquent behavior and the belief that early intervention may prevent more serious delinquent behavior, and the fact that truancy is a status offense in most state juvenile codes that may result in a juvenile court finding of "child in need of supervision." Formal police intervention in status offenses raises two concerns: teachers and principals are likely to feel absolved of responsibility for problem students at risk of truancy and dropout, and there is a tendency to criminalize behaviors that were once viewed as simply troublesome and that are primarily violations of school rules (Bazemore et al., 2004: 296–297). Giving precedence to formal control by police and juvenile probation officers tends to weaken and replace the informal controls of education professionals (see Clear and Karp, 1999). We have already seen a trend in which educators take on parenting and socialization responsibilities that were traditionally the responsibility of parents. Parents now expect schools to provide drug and sex education, training in moral development, in addition to the standard school curriculum, and they expect police to control their children. As police have been willing to exert more formal controls in schools, school officials seem to have gotten the message that social control is no longer their primary responsibility (Clear and Karp, 1999; Bazemore et al., 2004).

A running theme of this book is that juvenile crime is the responsibility of the community as well as the formal justice system. Delinquent behavior in schools and in the neighborhoods around schools is not likely to be reduced without the cooperative participation of citizens, parents, educators, and justice officials. We turn in the next chapter to how schools are a factor in disruption and delinquency and how they may contribute to academic failure, dropout, and delinquency.

Summary

More Americans complete high school today than 50 years ago, but the dropout rate shows little improvement, particularly among minorities, individuals from lower socioeconomic groups, and urban inner-city youth. There are problems in defining and measuring dropout rates, and the two major national measures of school dropout differ slightly. Research studies have examined the causes and consequences of dropout and the relationship between dropout and delinquency. School dropout has serious economic and personal consequences for young people and the future of the nation. Research has established a link between dropout and delinquency, but there is some disagreement on the exact causal relationship. The school dropout problem raises a number of social and political issues, such as compulsory attendance laws, school structure, and policies such as expulsion, school reform, and equitable funding of schools. Dropout-prevention programs are being instituted throughout the country, and many show promise of effectively reducing the dropout rate.

Note

1. The high school completer rate is calculated by dividing the high school completers in year 4 by the sum of the dropouts in grades 9 + 10 + 11 + 12 + the high school completers in year 4 (see Young, 2003: 4). The completion rate is not the same as a graduation rate, which is the proportion of a cohort of 9th grade students who graduate 4 years later.

6

School Environment, Crime, and School Safety

If one were to ask a citizen, a probation officer, or a teacher which American institution is most responsible for crime and delinquency, he or she would likely answer "the family." If we asked a criminologist involved in delinquency theories and research, on the other hand, he or she would likely respond that the American institution most responsible for crime is "the school" (Gottfredson and Hirschi, 1990: 159). Experiences in a young person's life course influence the likelihood of engaging in delinquent behavior, and the institution that has the greatest impact next to the family is the school (Sampson and Laub, 1993). School experiences are critical as adolescents are developing morally, socially, and psychologically and are most at risk of delinquent involvement. Schools can be a turning point in a young person's life, and education can reduce the potential for criminal behavior and risk of imprisonment (Arum and Beattie, 1999).

The social institution responsible for educating children has not always been viewed as holding out promise for at-risk youth. Stinchcombe (1964) argued that youths' rebellious behavior was a reaction to the school itself and to its empty promises, and he suggested that schools had nothing to offer working-class adolescent males. Schools have long been criticized for the repressive environment and punitive methods of teachers, which tend to minimize the possibility of learning. Schools have been compared to prisons, for example, based on the treatment of students, the appearance and physical structure, and the regimented activities (Haney and Zimbardo, 1975). Most prisons and many schools are characterized by a stark physical appearance on the outside. They are surrounded by fences and have dull, endless, uniform hallways on the inside. Like prisoners, students' movement is regimented and controlled by roll calls and bells. Both institutions have regulations as to what prisoners and students can wear, the length of their hair, when they may go to the toilet, when they may eat, and when they may go outside. Strict discipline, corporal punishment, and the use of detention are used to maintain control. Haney and Zimbardo noted that because both prison guards and teachers are greatly outnumbered, they often resort to techniques to divide their subjects to keep them from uniting in solid opposition to authority. Corrections officers often turn prisoners against each other by the discriminatory use of privileges. Educators divide students into separate groups based on perceived ability and future educational or career goals and thereby set up rivalries based on rank and status within the school. Schools also promote competition between students on the premise that it will promote motivation and better performance, but it also creates barriers between students. The overall result of this prison-like school structure is humiliation that engenders hostility and a tendency for students to either act out disruptively or withdraw into themselves.

It is important to examine the effects that schools have on students and teachers. As social institutions they have a powerful influence on human behavior. Schools are expected to provide students with the critical skills and personal values necessary to function in a democratic society. Schools that are repressive and that mimick prisons are counterproductive to the goals of education in America. The purpose of this chapter is to examine school structure, organization, and environment and their relationship with academic performance, school disorder, and delinquency.

Schools have a central and important role in society. As an important social institution, high expectations are placed on the school to prepare young people to be productive and responsible citizens in a democratic society. Schools are an integral part of the community and often reflect the values and the social problems of the community. Evidence points to a relationship between crime in the community and crime in schools, so it is important to examine the factors that may affect the ability of schools to provide a quality education in a safe environment.

School Crime: Community Problem or School Problem?

A number of nationally publicized shooting incidents in schools in the past few years has spawned the belief that crime in schools is a recent phenomenon and that school violence is a problem throughout the nation. Explanations for this perceived increase in school disorder are often directed at inconsistent or "soft" discipline policies and inadequate school security procedures. This view is not shared uniformly. Some have suggested that school violence is simply one manifestation of an urban society in which conflict and violence are more common occurrences. The question therefore is whether school crime is simply a reflection of crime in the community or whether it is a function of problems within the school itself. In other words, the question is whether school crime is an internal or an external problem.

A School Problem

According to the Safe School Study, school crime is not merely a reflection of social ills. The National Institute of Education (NIE) study concluded that schools can do much to reduce school violence and disruption through such policies as: (1) increasing efforts in student governance and rule enforcement, (2) treating students fairly and equally, (3) improving the relevance of subject matter to suit students' interests and needs, and (4) having smaller classes, with teachers instructing a smaller number of different students (National Institute of Education, 1977: A13–A14).

The study also found that outsiders are not responsible for most problems of school crime and violence. Except for cases of trespassing and incidents of breaking and entering, between 74 and 98 percent of all offenses are committed by youngsters enrolled in the school. This finding is contrary to the claim of many that school dropouts and outsiders are responsible for most school crime.

If indeed school crime is primarily an internal problem, then schools are responsible for improving the school climate, student discipline policies, and other changes that may reduce crime and disruption. The Safe School Study found that many variables that are not under the school's control (such as unemployment, poverty, and neighborhood conditions) are not very important in school crime. School variables such as class size, pupil:teacher ratio, and the principal's firmness, fairness, and consistency of discipline may be more important in curbing school crime. The finding that nonstudents are not the cause of most school crime has a direct bearing on the types of security programs that school districts and individual schools should develop. If school administrators instituted security programs with the belief that their schools were more at risk from outside trespassers, then those programs may be misdirected and ineffective. The overall implications of school crime as an internal problem are that schools may have less to fear from the type of neighborhood in which they are located. According to this view, schools can do much to reduce disruption, crime, and violence, but they are also responsible for dealing with their own crime problems.

A Community Problem

Viewing school crime as an *external problem* regards the school in the context of the community. Bill Larson, assistant superintendent of the St. Paul, Minnesota, schools, supported that view and described schools as a "microcosm of society." He noted that problems and issues that happen in the community and on the streets invariably spill into the schools (Levy, 1995: 12A). The integral relationship between schools and the community is apparent to many experts. Nancy Riestenberg, violence-prevention specialist for the Minnesota Department of Education, noted that schools reflect what is going on in our culture. Whatever is happening in a town, city, or state will also happen in a school (Levy, 1995: 12A). James Q. Wilson (1977) noted that crime does not occur in the schools in isolation from crime in the rest of society. Much of what is called "crime in the schools" is really crime committed by young persons who happen to be enrolled in a school or who happen to commit the crime on the way to or from school (Wilson, 1977: 48). Gold and Moles (1978) analyzed data from the 1972 National Survey of Youth (a self-report survey of 1,395 boys and girls 11–18 years old) and concluded that delinquent behavior that occurs in school is not an isolated phenomenon, but is the same kind of behavior committed outside of school and tends to be committed by the same individuals. They claim that less delinquency occurs in school in proportion to the amount of time spent there, since youths spend about 20 percent of their waking hours in school, but report that 13 percent of their offenses are committed in school (Gold and Moles, 1978: 115).

Viewing school crime as an external problem begins with the premise that school crime is inseparable from and a function of crime in the community. The implications of this view are that school officials are not solely responsible for disorder and crime and that school crime-prevention strategies are likely to be ineffective without the cooperation and assistance of leaders and policymakers in the community, law enforcement, other justice officials, and parents. On the other hand, viewing school crime as an internal problem is to place the blame squarely on the schools and to hold schools responsible for solving what may be more of a community problem. McDermott (1983) noted two consequences of holding schools responsible for disorder and crime. First, the blame is placed solely on the schools or, more precisely, on school officials, administrators, and teachers. Second, solutions are almost always school related and include demands for better teachers, smaller classes, fair and equal treatment of students, relevant subject matter in courses, and tighter discipline (1983: 278). Policies such as these may surely help minimize school disruption, and of course they are positive steps toward quality education beyond any effect they may have on school crime. However, if school crime is primarily a reflection of crime in the community, then relying on improved teaching and discipline may not significantly reduce levels of school crime. McDermott argued that crime in schools does not exist apart from crime in the community, which has important implications for school crime-prevention efforts. She suggested that concentrating efforts in the school may not have a significant impact in the long run on schools located in high-crime communities. Tighter security, stricter rule enforcement, and student discipline are necessary first steps in reducing crime and disorder in schools but may have little effect on the surrounding community. School "zero-tolerance" policies that result in high rates of suspensions and expulsions are short-term fixes, but ultimately result in displacing troublemakers out on the street with nothing to do.

School crime as a reflection of community crime receives support from other researchers. In a reanalysis of the Safe School Study data, Gottfredson and Gottfredson (1985) presented evidence that school crime was as much a reflection of community disorganization and crime as it was caused by internal school problems. Analyses of data from the School Crime Supplement (SCS) of the National Crime Victimization Survey (NCVS) show that fear of being attacked at school is related to reports of street gangs at school and to how students get to and from school. Similar studies have shown that students who walk to school are more likely to fear being attacked than students on school buses and that those on buses report more fear than students getting to school by car (Pearson and Toby, 1991). A longitudinal analysis using NCVS data examined victimization of juveniles in schools, homes, and streets or parks. More assaults, robberies, and larcenies occurred in homes than in schools or streets and parks (Parker et al., 1991). The authors concluded that one of the causes of victimization in schools is the community surrounding the school, and they suggest that increases or decreases in victimization rates outside schools will be reflected by increases or decreases inside of schools. Parker et al. (1991) emphasized, however, that their results did not suggest that school administrators should ignore factors inside the school that may have an impact on this problem. School officials have more control over what happens in school than they do over what happens away from school grounds or what students are like when they come into the school.

The consensus from the research is that viewing school crime as an internal problem is incomplete and inaccurate. Concentrating crime-prevention efforts only on the school is not likely to have a long-term significant impact, especially for schools located in high-crime communities. School policies that focus on tighter security, more strict discipline, and similar crime-control approaches may well reduce disruption and crime in the school, but simply displace the problems to the community. Likewise, suspending or expelling disruptive students without referral to an alternative program simply puts them out on the street with nothing to do. If concerted efforts aimed at both school and community crime are not made, schools will continue to face problems of disruption, crime, and victimization in the hallways and on the school grounds. Crime in schools must be seen as an extension of crime in the community, so we must view it as a larger social problem. It is not just the responsibility of the school board, administrators, and teachers. Prevention of crime in both the school and the community is the responsibility of citizens, parents, and students, as well as police and juvenile court officials.

The Challenges Faced by Schools

We have documented and discussed the extent and frequency of school crime in previous chapters. We reviewed explanations and theories of the causes of delinquency, with a focus on those theories that included students' school experiences including academic performance, behavior, truancy, and dropout. A number of criminologists have blamed schools for academic failure, school disorder, and delinquency. In this chapter we examine school factors that have been found to be related to, and may cause, disorder and delinquency. There are four factors to keep in mind to provide a proper context and foundation for a discussion of the role of schools in the community and in crime: (1) the role of the school as an important *social institution*, (2) its role as an instrument for *social change*, (3) the *expectations and demands* placed upon schools, and (4) the claim that schools are often a *source of juvenile delinquency*.

An Important Social Institution

From a broad perspective, the public education of all citizens is viewed as essential in a democratic society. Along with the family, the school is important for the socialization of young people. In addition to providing knowledge and skills for effective living and working, schools are expected to instill in young people the values that contribute to an ordered and productive society. Education has played an important role in developing America. The framers of our Constitution, in forging a democratic form of government, understood early on that this radical experiment in government for the people and by the people would not succeed without an informed, educated citizenry. Thomas Jefferson and Benjamin Franklin, among others, advocated strongly for the development of schools that were publicly supported. America's leaders have placed high expectations on education in its role as an important social institution in a democratic society.

John Dewey became well known as an educational reformer when he published *The School and Society* in 1899. Dewey established a Laboratory School at the University of Chicago in 1896 to develop and test his educational ideas (Rippa, 1980). Like leaders before him, Dewey recognized the importance of public education in a democracy. Because of changes in society, he believed that the schools must take on some of the former functions of the home. He called for a more active role of the child in education and teaching styles that would encourage thinking and problem solving. Dewey was optimistic that education could improve students' lives and eliminate social problems.

Demands on Education for Social Change

Schools have been expected to serve as the primary institution for social change. A major function of the schools during the influx of immigrants in the early twentieth century was to socialize immigrant children, introducing them to American values. The school teacher was forced to become a parent substitute for many immigrant children. The living conditions of many early immigrants were deplorable. Jacob Riis, a police reporter and crusading journalist, was appalled by the physical squalor and poverty in the New York City tenement houses and the parental neglect of children who roamed the streets poorly clothed. Writing in 1892, Riis stated that the community, for its own protection, had a duty to train children to be good Americans and useful citizens (Rippa, 1980: 173). School leaders responded to many similar demands to assist needy children by developing special schools and educational programs in cities across the country where immigrants were working and struggling. By the turn of the 20th century schools were struggling to meet the demands of business and industry, immigration, and the social effects of urbanism. The idea that schools should be instruments of social change and take on responsibilities beyond basic education has been promoted by the U.S. Congress and has resulted in considerable legislation. One of the earliest congressional initiatives was the Smith–Hughes Act promoting vocational education in high schools (Maeroff, 1982: 9).

America underwent dramatic changes in the twentieth century, and education has been a central part of those changes. In addition to meeting educational demands, schools assumed responsibilities in the realm of personal development, formerly undertaken by the family and the church. The social and political problems of the 1960s and 1970s presented challenges to educational institutions. While schools were being asked to assist students in personal and social adjustment, the challenges of the space age brought criticism that American schools had weak academic standards.

Expectations and Demands on Schools

Serious questions have been raised as to whether schools really make much difference in the lives and attainments of students. Several writers in the 1960s and 1970s claimed that schools made little difference. Coleman (1966) questioned whether equal funding and resources for schools could produce equal students. Jencks et al. (1972) reanalyzed the Coleman data and other data and concluded that additional school expenditures and resources would make very little difference in students' academic performance. Examples of book titles illustrate the critical approach taken by many writers: *The Underachieving School, Death at an Early Age*, and *Pedagogy of the Oppressed* (Rutter, 1983: 2). Other critics of the American educational system have charged that it has perpetrated a literacy hoax on students and their parents. Educators are giving fewer assignments, standards are down, grades are up, and students end up with fewer skills (Copperman, 1980: 16). The 88th and 89th Congresses, with the prodding of President Lyndon Johnson, passed legislation that gave unprecedented support for education. Among the goals of the legislation was using the schools to address social problems such as poverty, unemployment, crime, violence, and racial discrimination. At the White House Conference on Education in 1965, Vice President Hubert Humphrey said that our country would achieve historical acclaim for using its educational system to overcome problems of illiteracy, unemployment, crime and violence, and even war among nations (Goodlad, 1984: 4, 33). Barely more than a decade after those optimistic expectations, legislators and the public were calling for school reform to "get back to basics" and to raise educational standards. American youth were falling behind in school achievement, particularly math scores, but also in reading and writing skills. At the same time that more has been expected of schools, changes in American society have meant that there is less support for public education. Declining birth rates and growing numbers of older Americans means that fewer individuals are directly involved in our school system, largely accounting for the failure of tax increases for education in many parts of the country. The success of public education depends on the public. It is difficult to convince a majority of citizens that the relationship exists and that schools require their support. It is more difficult when many people believe that schools are failing to fulfill their role and that raising school taxes is not the answer.

Although schools have been given responsibilities other than teaching reading, writing, and arithmetic, the criterion on which schools are evaluated is still academics. Books critical of schools bear titles such as *Why Johnny Can't Read*, *Crisis in Education*, *Educational Wastelands*, and *Crisis in the Classroom*, and Goodlad (1984) notes that public criticism of schools accompanied a general loss of faith in government and the justice system. This was a dramatic change from the optimistic expectation that public education would help bring about economic and social change. Although not necessarily unrealistic, it is clearly an unfulfilled expectation for many Americans. The commitment to educational opportunities and excellence for all students falls short of our expectations, particularly if we measure that commitment by the limited state and federal resources allocated for public education.

Some are critical of the numerous responsibilities placed upon schools in addition to their primary function of education. Maeroff (1982) questioned the unrealistic expectations placed on schools, noting that society has habitually turned to schools to help solve our social dilemmas. We have come to expect schools to absorb responsibilities that were traditionally vested in the home, in the church, in the hospitals, in the workplace, and in other institutions. In the apparent belief that nearly every task that involves children and youth is best handled by schools, they have been given responsibilities such as addressing the nutritional needs of children, alcohol and drug abuse education, driver education, and even health care and disease prevention through required innoculations (see Maeroff, 1982: 10f.). These extra demands make it even more difficult for schools to accomplish their primary responsibility—educating youth.

The Public Schools as a Source of Delinquency

Public schools have not only failed to meet the expectations of social change, vocational preparation, and academics, they have been cited as a source of delinquency. In the Task Force Report on Juvenile Delinquency and Youth Crime, Schafer and Polk (1967) noted several practices and deficiencies within the school system that tend to promote delinquency. They cited evidence suggesting that delinquency results in part from adverse or negative school experiences, and that defects within the educational system contribute to these negative experiences, increasing the probability of delinquent behavior (1967: 223). Schafer and Polk asserted that because of its important role in the lives of youth, the school has the potential to partly offset or neutralize the pressures toward delinquency that may originate in the family and community. They proposed a number of recommendations for educational changes that they believed would alleviate the school–delinquency problem. McPartland and McDill (1977) echoed the charge that schools are partially responsible for crime and violence and that schools can aggravate the problem or reduce it depending on the quality of teaching and disciplinary practices. School violence, they believed, could be reduced through reforms in school structure (1977: 21).

Schools appear to be facing insurmountable difficulties. Teachers and administrators find it increasingly difficult to carry out their educational function because of the growing problem of disorder and crime in schools. At the same time they are charged with being a source of crime because of their ineffectiveness in teaching and disciplining students. Our society has placed high demands and expectations on schools, some of which may be unrealistic. Furthermore, we might question whether it is fair to hold schools responsible for delinquent behavior that more often has its source in family and community problems. Yet, as a major social institution, schools do play an important role in youth development. Youths who for a number of reasons do not succeed in school often face problems of unemployment, poverty, and crime.

Several school conditions, including educational failure, perceived lack of payoff of education, and low commitment to education, contribute to juvenile delinquency (Schafer and Polk, 1972). In short, school conditions that lead to failure also indirectly lead to delinquency. Schafer and Polk acknowledged that one reason for low scholastic performance among lower-income children is that home influences are such that they enter school with serious deficiencies that are all but impossible for the school to overcome. Nevertheless, they argued that the school itself contributes to failure by not designing its program, curriculum, and instructional techniques to account for and effectively offset these deficiencies (Schafer and Polk, 1972: 182). The conditions believed to contribute to school failure and delinquency are summarized in Table 6–1.

Claims of a relationship between academic failure and delinquency remain applicable today, and many of these conditions continue to exist in many American public schools. There is certainly a correlation between school failure and delinquency, but it is more difficult to establish a causal relationship. Theories and explanations of delinquency include the school as a factor in delinquent conduct (see Chapter 3), and research on truancy and dropout supports a relationship with delinquency for some youths in certain circumstances (see Chapter 5). Research evidence is mixed as to whether educational failure causes juvenile delinquency. Some of the school conditions noted by Schafer and Polk (1972) more than three decades ago deserve further examination. A "belief in the limited potential of disadvantaged pupils" may be inherent in the practice of grouping or "tracking" students. School tracking and educational funding continue to be issues that may affect academic success and contribute to delinquency. Research on school climate and disorder has noted a correlation with victimization in schools and the quality of relationships between parents, the community, and racial groups. These are similar to the school conditions noted by Schafer and Polk in Table 6–1.

Table 6–1
School Conditions Contributing to Educational Failure and Juvenile Delinquency

•Belief in limited potential of disadvantaged pupils

•Irrelevant instruction

•Inappropriate teaching methods

•Testing, grouping, and "tracking"

•Inadequate compensatory and remedial education

•Inferior teachers and facilities in low income schools

•School-community distance

•Economic and racial segregation

Source: Schafer, Walter and Polk, Kenneth 1972. "School Conditions Contributing to Delinquency." Pp. 185–208 in W. E. Schafer and K. Polk, eds., *Schools and Delinquency*. Englewood Cliffs, NJ: Prentice-Hall.

School Tracking and Delinquency

Claims that schools are a cause of delinquency fall into one of two categories of criminological theories: strain theory and labeling theory (see Chapter 3). Strain theorists contend that youths who become frustrated by the academic failure and the demands of school
are likely to leave school or act out with delinquent behavior. Labeling theory holds
that placing students in low-level "tracks" or labeling them as failures or troublemakers
increases the likelihood of their engaging in delinquency.

Kenneth Polk (1982b) described a process by which delinquency results from
students' school experience, family support, social class, and academic performance. Polk
emphasized the "gate-keeping" function of schools, by which elite positions and credentials are conferred on some students while others are assigned lower status and lower credentials. Because the educational system is competitive, there are both winners and losers.
Unfortunately, the wins and losses are not randomly distributed, but are greatly dependent
on family background factors. Students are more likely losers in school if they belong to
a lower social class, are members of a minority group, speak a different language, or live in
the wrong part of town (Polk, 1982b: 228). Some students come to school more prepared
and with more competencies to face the competitive academic environment.

Polk argued that this process carries over to the school authorities' responses to student deviance and disruption in school. Teachers and principals often respond differently
to incidents of student disruption and rule violations. Deviant behavior of "good" students
is often overlooked, and even when students who are doing well are caught for disruption
or school rule violations, future problem behavior is generally minimized by the threat
that it could jeopardize their academic career. Promising students are also rewarded with
more opportunities for involvement in school activities. Students who perform poorly may
be singled out for disruptive behavior and excluded from school activities, resulting in
reduced bonds with the school. Polk provided data supporting relationships between family background, school performance, and deviance; school performance and adult success;
and the labels attached by schools and juvenile courts and the likelihood of juvenile and
adult criminality (Polk, 1982b: 229–230).

School Funding and Educational Inequality

Public education depends on adequate funding and resources in order to provide well-qualified
teachers and facilities. Citizens have been increasingly reluctant to support education with
more tax dollars. Many are quick to criticize the quality of education but unwilling to
pay for it, claiming that education quality has little to do with financial resources. Quality
public education, like other goods and services, comes with a price tag. There are vast
differences between school districts in terms of funding, physical resources, and education quality. The method of financing public education in America—the local property
tax—is poorly suited to today's educational needs. The significant differences in property
tax bases and rates among school districts means that the quality of education that a child
receives depends on residential location. Each state is free to develop its own method of
paying for public schools. The U.S. Constitution does not mention education and did not
spell out any specific guarantees for equality of education. Just as there are wide differences between states in the public financing of education, there are vast differences within

a given state: regional variations and differences between urban, suburban, and rural schools. The largest portion of real estate taxes goes to the support of public schools, and home-owners are well aware of the differences in property tax rates and the quality of schools. Home buyers generally try to buy a home in the best neighborhood with the best school district that is still within their financial means. Higher tax rates do not guarantee better schools, however. Tax rates vary considerably among communities, and property tax revenues also vary according to the kind of properties included in a district. Living in a community with a large utility plant or shopping center, for example, means that children will attend schools with much more tax base than the children in a neighboring community without such tax-generating properties.

School-funding inequities were not recognized by the courts until the 1970s. For most of America's history, the fact that public education differed from one place to another as a result of differences in property taxes was considered as natural as community differences. Inferior schools were viewed as being an unfortunate but natural result of deteriorating, poor communities. The acceptance of inequities in school funding based on differences in property taxes is grounded in the importance of property as a symbol of wealth in America. Only recently have some school administrators, lawmakers, and courts begun to raise the issue that the present system of financing schools on local prop-erty taxes is an inequitable and impractical method of assuring quality education for all children.

Challenges to School Funding

Arthur Wise (1968) was one of the first to claim that public school-funding formulas deny children in poor communities equal opportunities to education. As a law school student at the University of Chicago in 1964, Wise conducted legal research that led him to conclude that school-funding formulas based on unequal property taxes violated the constitution. Within 4 years he had documented his views in a book entitled *Rich Schools, Poor Schools*, arguing that basing school funding on property taxes is to deny children in poor communities equal protection of the law as guaranteed by the 14th Amendment. Thirty years later the legal theory developed by the young law school student has helped change the shape of school finance in more than half the states in this country. Jonathan Kozol (1991) renewed the challenge to unequal school funding in documenting the "sav-age inequalities" among selected rich and poor school districts in the nation. The issue of equality in education was initially raised in the U.S. Supreme Court case of *Brown v. Board of Education of Topeka* [347 U.S. 483, 14 S.Ct. 686 (1954)]. The Court concluded that children were being deprived of equal educational opportunity because of segre-gation. Following the *Brown* case there have been several federal court decisions that have affected virtually every important aspect of school policy, including the issue of unequal pupil expenditures among school districts. In *Hobson v. Hansen* [269 F. Supp. 401 (D.D.C. 1967)] a federal court ruled that per pupil expenditures for teachers' salaries in the Washington, DC, school district must be equalized. Problems with equity of school fund-ing have been apparent in several states, but court decisions have not ruled consistently against all states with an inequity in school funding. Courts in New Jersey, California, and Connecticut presumed a relationship between educational cost and quality, reason-ing that disparities in funding caused disparities in quality that in turn contributed to unequal educational opportunities. Federal courts in Texas, Idaho, Oregon, and Washington, on the other hand, did not presume that costs and quality were causally related (see Reutter, 1982).

Two court cases in California and Texas illustrate the variations in court rulings. In *Serrano v. Priest* [5 Cal. 3d 584, 96 Cal. Rptr. 601, 487 P. 2d 1241 (1971)] the California supreme court ruled that the state's school funding policy discriminated against pupils in property-poor districts, and therefore they did not receive the equal protection of the laws of the state. With this precedent in mind, plaintiffs challenging unequal funding in Texas were greatly disappointed by a federal court ruling in *San Antonio v. Rodriquez* [411 U.S. 1, 93 S.Ct. 1278 (1973)]. The court ruled that although there were inequities in the Texas school financing system, it did not violate the equal protection clause of the Fourteenth Amendment to the U.S. Constitution. The court in this case reasoned that the state's funding for local schools provided at least a minimum level of funding and that no students were deprived of educational opportunities. The fight for equitable school funding has a long history in San Antonio. The original suit was filed by Demetrio Rodriguez and other parents of students in the Edgewood School District, located on the west side of San Antonio, a property-poor area populated mostly by lower-income Mexican American families living in small homes and housing projects. The administrators and parents of the Edgewood district were assisted in their legal efforts by the Mexican American Legal Defense Fund (MALDEF) and were joined in a subsequent lawsuit by other property-poor districts throughout Texas. Their persistence paid off when a state district court judge declared in *Edgewood I.S.D. v. Kirby* [804 S.W. 2d 491 (Tex. 1991)] that the Texas system of school financing discriminated against students in property-poor districts and was unconstitutional. Judge Clark declared that "education is a fundamental right for each of our citizens. Equality of access to funds is the key and is one of the requirements of this fundamental right" (Hall, 1987: 9), and he ordered that the current system be abandoned. Judge Clark cited the following state funding disparities in making his ruling:

•Wealthy and poor districts can be found in the same county. Edgewood, for example, had $38,854 of property value per student, whereas Alamo Heights (an upper-class suburban district) had $570,109 per student.

•Texas had 3 million public school children. The million in districts at the upper range of property wealth had more than 2½ times as much property wealth to support their schools as the million in the bottom range.

•The wealthiest school district had more than $14 million in taxable property wealth per student, whereas the poorest district had only $20,000.

•The average tax rate in the state's 100 poorest districts was 74 cents compared with 47 cents in the 100 wealthiest (Hall, 1987: 8).

The fact that taxpayers in the poor districts generally pay higher tax rates than those in wealthier districts highlights the inequities of many state school-funding programs. The inequality is amplified further when the lower values of taxable properties in poor districts yield less expenditure per pupil than in wealthier districts. Courts have closely scrutinized the fairness of state school-financing systems in the past decade. The disparities between rich and poor districts were considered so great that the funding methods in several states have been struck down as unconstitutional. In addition to the Texas case cited above, state school financing systems were struck down in Montana, Kentucky, and New Jersey (Katz, 1991: 20), and litigation has been ongoing for the past few years in at least 19 other states.

The New Jersey supreme court noted disparities in educational opportunities and found that poor urban districts provided inadequate instruction in core curriculum subjects and were neglecting special educational needs. The court ruled that children in poor districts were entitled to per-pupil expenditures comparable to those in more affluent districts, regardless of property values or tax rates (see Katz, 1991: 21). The Kentucky supreme court made the most sweeping decision when it struck down the state's school finance system and all of its education statutes and regulations. The state legislature responded by changing the entire school system, reducing the role of the state education department, giving more control to local schools, and adding $1.3 billion to school funding over the following 2 years.

Legislative Challenges to School Funding

Equalizing funding among school districts throughout each state is not a simple, straightforward process. Taxpayers in wealthier districts are often more willing to approve higher tax rates for better school facilities and higher teacher salaries. Thus as more state funding goes to the poorer districts, wealthier districts have increased their local funding, which has the effect of continuing the disparity in per pupil expenditures. Some states, such as Colorado, have taken the controversial step of placing a cap on expenditures by local school districts. Spending caps achieve equality among rich and poor districts, but they often do so by penalizing the better school districts, cutting back on programs or reducing teacher salaries. Policymakers have questioned the practice of forced cutbacks in funding for the best school districts. Some argue that there ought to be districts that serve as models of quality education. Without them, wealthier families are more likely to leave the public school system and send their children to private schools (Katz, 1991).

Achieving equality of school funding by depending on more state funding for poor districts is a major concern, particularly with so many demands on state funding and the tendency to shift more responsibility to local governments. The dilemma in the school-funding issue is whether we can have a world-class education system and equal spending across school districts (see Katz, 1991: 22). Without question it takes more than equal education opportunities to help students attain more equal achievement levels in school. There is evidence that giving equal opportunities to persons through educational and community restructuring does make a difference. Beginning in the late 1970s, 4,000 low-income Chicago families were relocated to middle-class, often white neighborhoods throughout the city and 50 suburbs. The youths reported being happier in their new surroundings. Early studies by the Northwestern University Center for Urban Affairs showed that more of the adults became employed, and the high school graduation rate was 95 percent, with slightly more than half going on to college. The students were nearly twice as likely as those who stayed in the inner city to find jobs. It appears that integration and more equal education and employment opportunities can affect the future achievements of both students and their families (Alter, 1992: 55).

School Reform and At-Risk Students

School reform is an issue that has drawn even more attention than the issue of school funding. In the 1950s the Russian launching of the Sputnik satellite launched an outcry of criticism against America's education system, claiming that we were not adequately preparing our students to compete in the developing scientific technologies. President Reagan's National Commission on Excellence in Education echoed many of the same concerns in its 1983 report, which opened with this statement:

> Our nation is at risk. Our once unchallenged preeminence in commerce, industry, science, and technological innovation is being overtaken by competitors throughout the world (National Commission on Excellence in Education, 1983: 5).

Other commissions at both the federal and state levels have criticized the quality of public education. Some criticism was related to the "liberalization" of the curriculum, in which students could enroll in a wide variety of electives at the expense of focusing sufficiently on core courses. Beyond assigning blame, however, there is cause for concern when we consider that students' academic achievement has been declining. Scores on the Scholastic Aptitude Test (SAT), generally considered a reliable measure of overall academic achievement of college-bound high school seniors in the United States, have declined since 1966, except for small increases in 1984 and 1985. Data from the National Assessment of Educational Progress also confirm a decrease in students' mathematical knowledge and reading skills since the 1970s (Stevens and Wood, 1987: 350).

Commission recommendations for responding to the "crisis" in education, detailed in *A Nation at Risk* (National Commission on Excellence in Education, 1983), are similar to educational reform measures dating back to the 1950s and those coming out of a number of state education commissions calling for reforms. The Commission recommendations included: (1) curricula should focus more on the educational basics; (2) grading standards, entrance admissions scores for colleges and universities, and textbook rigor should all be increased; (3) more time should be spent in school as well as on homework; (4) teaching quality should be increased, and payment should be based on merit; and (5) education leaders at the local, state, and federal levels should become more effective leaders for change and reform (National Commission on Excellence in Education, 1983).

Mortimer Adler (1982), Ernest Boyer (1983), and John Goodlad (1984) have questioned some of the education reform recommendations and whether it is realistically possible for schools to offer so much for all students, particularly as so much is expected of the schools. Schools have been criticized for failing to properly educate all students in the basic skills, while at the same time they have been expected to take on what have traditionally been the responsibilities of families, churches, and other institutions charged with educating and socializing youth (Boyer, 1983: 63). Adler, Boyer, and Goodlad argue that "less is better" when it comes to educational goals and objectives. Adler believes that all children are entitled to the same quality of education. Basic schooling for all students should be general and liberal, not specialized and vocational, thus preparing persons for earning a living, being a citizen, and leading a good life (Adler, 1982: 4). Boyer's proposals are similar to Adler's, with four essential goals of public schools: (1) developing a student's ability to think critically and communicate effectively, (2) developing an understanding of shared cultural histories, (3) preparing students for work, and (4) helping students fulfill social and civic obligations through community and social service (Boyer, 1983: 282). Goodlad, like Boyer and Adler, argues that much of what schools are currently attempting to do should be the shared responsibility of the community at large. Education is so important and so much is expected of education that Goodlad believes that the task should not be left up only to the schools (Goodlad, 1984: 46). All three argue that education should become an integral part of the community. The family and the community must be willing to assume many of the tasks now carried out by schools in order for schooling to once again be a primarily educative function. Their proposals have not gone without criticism: Adler for his assumption that knowledge can elevate the quality of life, and Boyer and Goodlad for their failure to specify exactly how some of the school's functions can be assumed by the community (see Stevens and Wood, 1987: 353).

Not all academics who have examined the quality of education have come to such a gloomy conclusion about the effectiveness of schools. Michael Rutter (1983) reviewed a large number of studies on the effects of schools and arrived at a considerably more optimistic outlook. One reason for the critical views of schools was the narrow, limited criteria used for measuring effectiveness. Rutter argued that multiple indicators of school effectiveness are required, including scholastic attainment, classroom behavior, absenteeism, attitudes toward learning, continuation in education, employment, and social functioning (1983: 5–8). Schools vary in the effects that they have on students. Rutter noted that some of the school features that seem to be most responsible for positive effects on students include resources and school buildings, school size and class size, organizational structure, composition of the student body, the amount of academic emphasis, classroom management, discipline and pupil conditions, pupil participation and responsibility and staff organization (Rutter, 1983: 15–24).

School Programs and Teaching Strategies

There are wide variations among schools in the kinds of programs and teaching strategies used and the intensity with which the teaching staff applies them. Research on ability grouping at the secondary level indicates that it is ineffective and may have negative effects, and assigning students to different levels of the same course has no consistent positive or negative effects on students of high, average, or low ability (Slavin, 1990: 494). Promoting students who have not made satisfactory achievement has received criticism, and yet research provides no evidence that retention is more beneficial than promotion (Jackson, 1975). Holmes and Matthews (1984) concluded from a meta-analysis of 44 studies that retention is not helpful. Promoted students did better in school achievement than the retained group, and nonpromotion actually had negative effects on students (1984: 89). Robert Slavin and Nancy Madden (1989) reviewed research on programs for students at risk and found that while pull-out programs that were diagnostic and prescriptive may keep students from falling further behind, they are not really effective. They found that special education programs seldom bring students up to an acceptable level of school performance, but that early intervention, continuous progress, cooperative learning, remedial tutoring, and computer-assisted instruction programs have been effective (Slavin and Madden, 1989). Some special programs for at-risk students are effective at the preschool and elementary levels, but not at the secondary level. Dropout-prevention programs that have been successful generally at the secondary level are characterized by student success in school, positive student–adult relationships, relevance of school experience, and reduction in outside interference from gang-related activities and drug use (McLaughlin and Talbert, 1990). McLaughlin and Talbert (1990) found that a personalized school environment that included an ethic of caring made a difference in at-risk students' achievement. They noted that a personalized school environment is a matter of organizational design in schools and is not limited to individual teachers' practices and values.

J. David Hawkins and Tony Lam (1987) tested a model of classroom-based instructional strategies designed to assist in delinquency prevention. Their model consisted of three instructional strategies: proactive classroom management, interactive teaching, and cooperative learning (1987: 250–251). Implementation of the strategies after one year did not lead to consistent differences in the perceptions of experimental and control students, but there were some promising trends. Students were more likely to engage in learning activities and less likely to be off-task in the classroom, they spent more time on homework, they developed greater educational aspirations and expectations for themselves, and they were less likely to be suspended or expelled from school when their teachers used these instructional strategies (1987: 268). Hawkins and Lam (1987) believe that experimental teaching strategies could help create a classroom environment that increases the opportunities for involvement and skill development for more students.

The Role of Parents in School Achievement

The role of parents in helping their children succeed in school and avoid delinquent behavior has been documented in criminological and educational research. Sara Lawrence Lightfoot (1978) in her book *Worlds Apart: Relationships Between Families and Schools* noted that cultural developments had separated the home and the school—the two main social institutions important in children's lives. She observed parents and teachers carrying out their separate roles with little contact with each other. Researchers in education and child development have done little to reduce such fragmentation, as they tend to focus their scholarly efforts on the child either in the school or in the home. This barrier between parents and teachers has not gone unnoticed by teachers and school administrators, who frequently complain about the lack of interest and support shown by parents in regard to their children's school performance. There is evidence, however, that educators do little to cultivate a closer working relationship with parents. Henry Becker and Joyce Epstein (1982) surveyed 3,700 teachers in Maryland in respect to their involvement with parents. According to their findings, only a few teachers initiated interactions with parents beyond what was minimally expected of them, they did not seem to know how to work with parents, and many avoided using strategies that involved informal learning activities for students in the home, believing they would be too difficult for parents to handle. Fewer than 10 percent of the teachers in this sample requested parental cooperation (Becker and Epstein, 1982). Much more could and should be done by educators to encourage parental involvement in their children's education. Part of the problem seems to be a failure to recognize the changes occurring in the American family. Fewer children are living with both biological parents. Some share time with both parents, individually and at different residences, following a divorce settlement that involves joint custody. A study cosponsored by the National Association of Elementary School Principals and the Charles F. Kettering Foundation concluded that schools play an important role in the lives of single parents and their children and that they must be recognized as a valid family unit (Maeroff, 1982: 212). According to findings of a survey of 1,200 single parents in 47 states by the National Committee for Citizens in Education, fewer than 5 percent of noncustodial parents received information about school activities from the school, and fewer than 7 percent got a copy of their child's report card from the school (Maeroff, 1982: 212). Maeroff (1982: 213) had two suggestions for educators: (1) stop using the term "broken home," and do not assume that children of single parents will have problems in school performance and behavior, and (2) maintain records of the names and addresses of both parents following divorce, and send identical reports to both of them.

Research indicates that family structure and parental involvement make a difference in students' school performance. Results from a nationally representative sample of students in the High School and Beyond (HSB) study showed that children who live with single parents or stepparents during adolescence receive less encouragement and less help with schoolwork than children who live with both natural parents (Astone and McLanahan, 1991). An earlier analysis of the HSB study showed that parental involvement has an important direct and positive effect on students' grades (Fehrman et al., 1987). It is clear that students perform better in school when parents are involved. Because parental involvement encourages and reinforces proper behavior, students with involved parents may display less antisocial behavior and perform better academically (Astone and McLanahan, 1991).

Parent Involvement in School Decisions

A separate but related issue is that of parents' and citizens' involvement in school decisions regarding curriculum, activities, and policies. Not only do most parents have little involvement in their children's school performance, there is also little parental or citizen involvement in school policymaking decisions. Maeroff is critical of parents who tend to sit back and let their schoolboard members get involved for them. He contended that taxpayers are simply too willing to delegate all responsibility for the schools to the few people who are willing to take on the burden of school board service (Maeroff, 1982: 213). Few non–board members attend the schoolboard meetings, and there is little communication between the public and board members. The result is that few taxpayers have any idea of what is happening in the schools.

Teachers and administrators complain about parents' lack of interest and involvement in their children's school performance and parents' lack of support for educators in dealing with students' attendance and behavior problems. On the other hand, there is evidence that educators and school administrators do not welcome parental involvement in school policies and decisions. Many teachers and school administrators believe that parents have neither the right nor the expertise to exert all influence on the schools (Maeroff, 1982: 208). Most schools make no effort to involve parents in the selection or assignment of teachers or principals, curriculum development, the selection of textbooks, or regulations regarding dress and behavior. Nancy Chavkin and David Williams (1987) surveyed parents and school administrators in six southwestern states and reported that parents expressed an interest in participating in more school decisions than educators believed would be useful. Many educators may avoid parents' input on hiring, curriculum, and textbook selection out of a belief that few have the qualifications and background to contribute meaningfully in such decisions. Most school districts generally make an effort to inform students and their parents about regulations regarding dress and behavior and the consequences for violating school rules. Students and parents are seldom involved in the process of developing school codes and sanctions, however.

There is ample evidence that codes of conduct are more likely to be supported when those affected have a role in their development. This is a point that cannot be underscored enough. Since some of the teachers' most vocal complaints relate to students' dress and behavior in school and the lack of parental support for school discipline, it stands to reason that every effort to gain student and parental support is to the teachers' and principals' advantage. Most parents will still be reluctant to become more involved because of time constraints and because they view education as the primary responsibility of the paid professionals—the teachers and principals.

Students' Responsibility

Students clearly bear equal responsibility for their own academic success. No learning can take place unless the student is receptive and actively engaged in the learning process. The desire for knowledge and curiosity about the world around us is not inherent in all students, however. Young people vary greatly in their personal interest and motivation for learning. It is therefore incumbent upon parents, caregivers, and teachers to instill within young people a desire to learn, to share the enjoyment of learning, and to make reading and learning fun. It is one thing to insist that students be responsible for active involvement in the education process, but in reality too few students have been encouraged by their parents to pursue education seriously. Too few parents are positive role models for the value of education. Books, newspapers, and informative magazines are increasingly rare in many homes. Television viewing has taken the place of reading and has replaced lively and informative conversations over the dinner table (few families even sit down for meals together). It is unlikely that we will see many changes in active family support for education, so the primary responsibility still falls upon the schools. One promising strategy is for schools to implement programs to improve family–school relationships. Bruce Ryan and Gerald Adams (1995) recommended a family–school relationships model that takes into account different family patterns and contexts, encouraging within-the-family learning processes, support and encouragement for learning and homework, monitoring of attendance and homework, and being available to talk about school concerns and problems.

This chapter addresses school structure and policies as they relate primarily to disorder and delinquency. Readers who are interested in learning more about effective teaching strategies and educational interventions directed toward improving students' academic achievement are encouraged to refer to a volume of research and literature in the education field. The remainder of this chapter is focused on addressing school climate and conditions that may contribute to disorder, delinquency, and unsafe conditions that interrupt the education process and place students and teachers at risk of victimization.

Do Schools Cause Failure—and Delinquency?

Critics of public education have cited the significant number of American students who are functioning far below their grade level, the unacceptable graduation rates, and the number of dropouts. Factors often noted as causes of poor school performance are the disparities in school funding, unequal educational opportunities, and school reforms resulting in underachievement and failure of many students. Many critics have charged that schools not only are responsible for academic failure, but cause delinquency. Articles entitled "Schools and the Delinquency Experience" (Polk, 1982b) and "How the School and Teachers Create Deviants" (Kelly, 1977) drew more negative attention to the schools, raising the question of whether there were, in fact, "delinquent schools" that significantly influence delinquency rates among youth (Wenk, 1975). It was not suggested that schools were the direct causes of delinquency, rather that schools that fail to actively involve all students in the education process—especially marginal, at-risk students—contribute to their failure to be properly educated, trained, and prepared with skills to succeed in life and work. Many schools do not offer equal educational opportunities, resulting in the failure of disproportionate numbers of inner-city, minority, and lower-class students. School failure is linked to behavioral problems in the school and delinquency in the community. The response of teachers and school officials to low-achieving and disorderly students is another way that schools may contribute to delinquency, according to some critics. Misconduct in school generally precedes misconduct in the community, and the manner in which schools react to misconduct may determine whether it will be followed by delinquency (Wenk, 1975). Critics of school policies and disciplinary practices, such as corporal punishment, maintain that such practices may lead to victimization of students by teachers and administrators. Strict "zero-tolerance" school discipline policies combined with overly intrusive law enforcement procedures in schools may contribute to student misbehavior (Hyman and Perone, 1998).

Schools and Delinquency Prevention

We have noted that schools are a reflection of society. As important social institutions, schools are a part of the community and reflect both the best and the worst aspects of any community. They give the community pride and identity, but some schools may also reflect the divisiveness, segregation, and inequality that characterize some communities. The nature of the community, its people, and its leaders can limit the potential of schools; in spite of the professionalism and determination of some very dedicated school administrators and teachers, it is often difficult for them to overcome some of the obstacles that stand in the way of creating a positive learning environment.

School variables are one of the most significant correlates in any study of delinquency. Youths involved in delinquency also misbehave in school. They do not like school, they do not do well in school, and they are frequently truant from school. Michael Gottfredson and Travis Hirschi (1990) attribute the school-delinquency correlations to the school's system of rewards and restraints and the student's abilities and level of self-control. For most young people school contributes to pro-social behavior and delinquency prevention. The school deters delinquent conduct in several ways. It requires students to be at a certain place at a certain time, it expects compliance with rules and expectations when they are not under direct surveillance, and it requires them to be quiet, physically inactive, and attentive. The school promotes pro-social behavior through positive reinforcement. It rewards punctuality, the completion of homework, and good conduct, and it rewards academic competence through positive reports and praise from teachers, advancement through the school system, and official and public recognition through graduation with a diploma. In these ways the school serves as a system for socializing youth and preventing delinquency (Gottfredson and Hirschi, 1990). These school rewards and sanctions, however, depend a great deal on parents for their success. The school cannot very well sanction students for not complying with its behavioral expectations or reward them for good schoolwork without parents and families who are supportive of educational goals and means. Gottfredson and Hirschi acknowledge that school sanctions do not affect the behavior of all children equally. Students who do poorly in school do not experience the rewards of academic accomplishments and are unlikely to be restrained by threats of suspension or expulsion for misbehavior. The school is a demanding and structured place, and students lacking parental and peer support find it more difficult to meet the demands. Delinquents therefore tend to leave the structured school environment and place themselves more at risk of joblessness, personal and social problems, and criminal behavior (Gottfredson and Hirschi, 1990).

School Climate and Disorder

School disorder has been of concern since the origin of public schools. School climate theories have received increasing attention in the studies of school disorder (Welsh, 2001). Schools possess a unique "climate," unique to each organization and partly dependent upon the school staff, student body, and classroom processes. School climate is the "feel" of the school as perceived by students and teachers; it affects the quality of communication among teachers, students, and administrators, and it affects many student outcomes (Anderson, 1982). Variables such as communication patterns, norms about what is appropriate or how things should be done, role relationships and role perceptions, patterns of influence, and rewards and sanctions are part of the climate of a school. Two basic indicators of a healthy school climate are effective learning and personal satisfaction; schools with an unhealthy climate may have job dissatisfaction, alienation, and frustration (Fox et al., 1975). A positive and productive school climate contributes to a school effectively meeting its educational goals and objectives. Five components of effective schools have been identified: strong administrative leadership, high expectations for student achievement, an orderly atmosphere conducive to learning, an emphasis on basic skills acquisition, and frequent monitoring of pupil progress (Pink, 1984). Effective schools have more positive outcomes in student retention and achievement and may have significant potential for delinquency prevention. If schooling is more meaningful and rewarding, students have more to gain by engaging in pro-social rather than disorderly or delinquent behavior (Pink, 1984). School climate is significant in the extent to which schools are effective in maintaining a safe and orderly environment in which students can learn and achieve. A negative or dysfunctional school climate has been associated with school disorder and reduced quality of education (National Commission on Excellence in Education, 1983; Gottfredson and Gottfredson, 1985). Student disorder detracts from time that can be devoted to classroom instruction. The Safe School Study of the National Institute of Education (1978) reported that school administration and policies make an important contribution to the level of disorder in schools. Policies that reduce school disorder included reducing the size and impersonality of schools, making school discipline more systematic, decreasing arbitrariness and student frustration, improving school reward structures, increasing the relevance of schooling, and decreasing students' sense of powerlessness and alienation (Gottfredson and Gottfredson, 1985). Schools with the worst discipline problems shared common characteristics: rules were unclear, unfair, or inconsistently enforced; rules were enforced ambiguously or indirectly, such as lowering grades for misconduct; teachers and principals did not know the rules or disagreed on disciplinary responses; teachers ignored misconduct; and students did not recognize the legitimacy of the rules (Gottfredson and Gottfredson, 1985).

Measuring School Climate

School climate affects the job satisfaction of school staff and the quality of education and student outcomes. In recognition of its importance, education researchers developed instruments to assess school climate as a first step toward improving the working and teaching environment in schools (Fox et al., 1975). Fox and associates (1975) developed diagnostic instruments designed to assess several aspects of the school organization and climate, including teachers' and principals' perceptions of their roles and performance, classroom innovations, personal and educational goals, and parents' opinions. Gottfredson et al. developed a method of assessment of the school organization with a more directed focus on school safety and delinquency prevention. Gottfredson (1999) developed the Effective School Battery (ESB) to assess school climate. The instrument was also designed to identify a school's strengths and weaknesses and to help administrators develop and evaluate improvement programs that may improve school effectiveness and safety. The ESB has been administered to more than 14,000 students in about 70 schools, representing various regions of the United States, in urban and rural areas, and with students varying in age and race. The reliability and validity of the ESB scales have been established, assuring fairly accurate measures of school climate and effectiveness and the ability to make comparisons among schools. The ESB provides two kinds of information about the school: (1) it describes students' and teachers' perceptions about the climate of the school (the "psychosocial climate"), and (2) it describes student and teacher characteristics (the "school population"). Students and teachers complete a survey instrument, and the combined scores produce two profiles for the school: one for the nine psychosocial scales, and one for the student and teacher characteristics. The student and teacher scales are summarized in Table 6–2.

Students' School Climate Scales

Safety is a 13-item scale asking if students stay away from any of a list of places in the school, if they feel safe at school, or if they fear that someone will hurt them at school, or on their way to or from school. *Respect for students* is a scale that measures the extent to which students feel degraded or treated with respect and dignity in the school environment. Items include "Teachers treat students with respect" and "Teachers do things to make students feel put down." *Planning and action* is a scale to assess whether students believe that the school engages in experimenting and problem solving, or whether change is resisted. Items include "The teachers and principal make plans to solve problems" and "This school hardly tries anything new." *Fairness* is a scale with three items: "The rules are fair," "The punishment for breaking rules is the same for everyone," and "The principal is fair." Research has shown a positive correlation for schools in which rules are considered fair and clear and school orderliness (NIE, 1978; Gottfredson and Gottfredson, 1985). *Clarity* is intended to assess whether students believe rules are clear. Items ask students whether everyone knows what the rules are, whether the teachers and principal let students know what is expected, and whether the principal is firm. *Student influence* in the way a school is run is assumed to have positive outcomes, and many schools seek student participation in planning and decision making (G. Gottfredson, 1999). Items include: "Students have little say in how the school is run," "Students have helped to make the school rules," and "Students are seldom asked to help solve a school problem."

Table 6–2
The Effective School Battery (ESB) Student and Teacher Scales

Climate Scales Based on Student Reports with Example Questions	*Climate Scales Based on Teacher Reports with Example Questions*
Safety: "Do you feel safe at school? Do you avoid any places in school? Do you fear someone will hurt you at school?"	**Safety**. "How safe are the classrooms? . . . the halls? . . . the restrooms?"
Respect for Students: "Teachers treat students with respect. Teachers do things to make students feel put down."	**Morale**. "Is the faculty frustrated? Our problems in this school are so big that it is unrealistic to expect teachers to make much of a dent in them."
Planning and Action. "The teachers and principal make plans to solve problems. This school hardly tries anything new."	**Planning and Action**. "How often do you work on a planning committee with other teachers? Is the teaching faculty open to change?"
Fairness. "The rules are fair. The punishment for breaking rules is the same for everyone. The principal is fair."	**Smooth Administration**. "Simple procedures exist for the acquisition and use of resources. There is little teacher–administration tension. The principal is open."
Clarity. "Everyone knows what the rules are. The teachers and principal let students know what is expected. The principal is firm."	**Resources for Instruction**. Items on teaching supplies, space, availability of resources, extra settings for instruction.
Student Influence. "Students have little say in how the school is run. Students have helped to make the school rules. Students are seldom asked to help solve a school problem."	**School Race Relations**. Items on race relations from teachers point of view, how different groups get along.
	Involvement of Parents and Community. Items on parent and community involvement, parent influence on policies or practices, parent assistance, relations between parents and teachers, community receptiveness.
	Student Influence. "I often change my lesson plans based on students' suggestions. Teachers and students work together to make rules about behavior in the classroom."
	Use of Grades as a Sanction. Items on use of grades as a response to misconduct, teachers' knowledge of the extent of this practice.

Source: Adapted from Gottfredson, G. D. 1999. *The Effective School Battery: User's Manual*. Ellicott City, MD: Gottfredson Associates, Inc., pp. 40–41. The ESB is a copyrighted instrument (originally 1984), available from Gottfredson Associates, Inc., 11444 Old Frederick Road, Marriottsville, MD 21104-1521; (410) 442-3770; http://www.Gottfredson.com.

Teachers' School Climate Scales

A 10-item *safety* scale assesses teachers' perceptions of the safety of their school and asks them to indicate, for example, how safe the classrooms, the hallways, and the restrooms are. There is evidence that staff *morale* is associated with school effectiveness

(G. Gottfredson, 1984). This scale includes items that ask for teachers' response as to whether the faculty are frustrated, or problems in the school are so big that teachers can do little to improve them. *Planning and action* includes items that ask: "How often do you work on a planning committee with other teachers?" and "Is the teaching faculty open to change?" Previous research suggests that the way a school is run is important in understanding the climate and in preventing disruption (Gottfredson and Gottfredson, 1985). *Smooth administration* assesses administrative leadership and includes items such as: "Simple procedures exist for the acquisition and use of resources," "There is little teacher–administration tension," and "The principal is open." The *resources for instruction* scale includes items on teaching supplies, space, availability of resources, and extra settings for instruction. The *school race relations* scale includes two items on race relations from teachers' point of view and how different groups get along. Gottfredson (1999) noted that a goal of many school improvement programs is to increase the *involvement of parents and community*. Items on this scale measure the extent of parent and community involvement, parental influence on policies or practices, parent assistance, relations between parents and teachers, and community receptiveness. *Student influence* may contribute to organizational change and decrease students' alienation and sense of powerlessness (Gottfredson, 1999). Teachers are asked whether they may change their lesson plans based on students' suggestions and whether teachers and students work together to make rules about behavior in the classroom.

Applications of School Climate Measures

The use of an assessment tool such as the ESB can help school administrators address school disorder and victimization. Assessment of school climate is an essential first step to guide administrators in making policy decisions and school organization. School climate measures similar to those used in the ESB were used to examine school factors related to victimization incidents in a large nationally representative sample of public secondary schools. Measures of student perceptions of the fairness and clarity of rules, student influence, and good race relations were found to be correlated with the extent of teacher victimization (Gottfredson and Gottfredson, 1985). They found that psychosocial climate influenced victimization rates even when community and school characteristics were held constant. The results are important because they show that it is possible to measure school characteristics associated with victimization, many of which may be changed with school improvement efforts.

School reorganization is an important policy decision being made in school districts throughout the nation. As population demographics of cities change, some schools face decline in enrollment while others face overcrowded schools. Population changes force districts to close some schools and to consolidate others to meet changes in enrollment and limited financial resources. Restructuring of grade levels also occurs, with some districts moving to a "middle school" that places 6th, 7th, and 8th graders together rather than the traditional junior high serving 7th, 8th, and 9th graders. The most common structure has been the 4-year high school serving grades 9–12. School climate scores from a nationally representative sample of public schools indicated that traditional junior high schools (grades 7–9) and grade 8 and 9 junior high schools were higher in delinquent youth culture and in teacher punishment orientation than middle schools (grades 6–8) and grade 7 and 8 junior high schools. Three-year high schools (grades 10–12) had more positive climates than 4-year (9–12) high schools (Gottfredson, 1999: 58). The school climate measures indicate that removing 9th graders from a junior high school would make it a more pleasant place, but adding a 9th grade to a 3-year high school would make it a less pleasant place. Junior high schools in general have a less positive school climate. This is important to consider when reorganizing or restructuring schools, and assessment of school climate under various school grade structures is important when making those decisions.

The ESB was used as a measure to evaluate an organization development approach to reducing school disorder (Gottfredson, 1987a). Researchers and school staff worked together in a 3-year effort to reduce disorder in a troubled Baltimore school. The interventions combined classroom management innovations, instructional innovations, and programs to improve parent and community support. Evaluations using the ESB indicated that the organization development approach created a stronger school by increasing staff morale, cohesiveness, cooperation, innovative planning, and action that resulted in reducing disorder and delinquency.

Research on School Climate and School Disorder

The term "school disorder" has been used to refer to a variety of problem behaviors in schools, including classroom disruptions, verbal harassment and threats directed at teachers and other students, school security incidents, school rule violations resulting in suspension or expulsion, and incidents of student and teacher victimization (Welsh, 2001). Disorderly behavior has always been a problem in schools, and it shows no sign of decreasing. In the School Survey on Crime and Safety, a nationally representative sample of school principals was asked how often certain disciplinary problems occurred. Examples of *disorderly behaviors* included bullying, classroom disorder, student verbal abuse and acts of disrespect for teachers, and racial tensions that happened daily or once a week. More than one-fourth (29 percent) of the school principals reported daily or weekly bullying, 19 percent reported acts of disrespect for teachers, 13 percent verbal abuse of teachers, and 3 percent reported racial tensions and widespread classroom disorder (DeVoe et al., 2004: 48). More than half (54 percent) of principals reported taking *serious disciplinary actions* such as suspensions lasting 5 days or more, expulsions, or transfers to specialized schools. Most (35 percent) of these were for fights, 22 percent for threats, 18 percent for insubordination, 20 percent for possession or use of illegal drugs or alcohol, 10 percent for the distribution of illegal drugs, 19 percent for possession of weapons other than firearms, and 4 percent for the possession or a firearm or explosive device (DeVoe et al., 2004: 28). *Students' reports of being bullied* provide another indicator of an unsafe school climate, although the extent of bullying varies among studies. The National Institute of Child Health and Human Development conducted the Health Behavior of School-Aged Children (HBSC) to examine students in from the 6th to 10th grades who were perpetrators and victims of bullying (Nansel et al., 2001). The HBSC study found that 24 percent of students reported being bullied once or twice, 8.5 percent were bullied sometimes, and 8.4 percent of students reported being bullied weekly. The greater frequency of bullying reports may be explained by the broader definition of bullying (including verbal teasing) and including incidents occurring both at and away from school. The SCS of the NCVS defines bullying as "being picked on or made to do things you didn't want to do like give them money" (Addington et al., 2002: 193). That definition of bullying is fairly narrow and excludes other threatening behaviors such as "peer harassment" (Juvonen and Graham, 2001). Fewer than 1 in 10 (7 percent) students reported being bullied at school in the past 6 months according to the SCS (DeVoe et al., 2004: 20). The problem of bullying is greater among middle-school and junior high school students, however. In 2003, 14 percent of 6th graders and 7 percent of 9th graders reported being bullied. In the same year, rural students (10 percent) were more likely than urban or suburban students (7 percent) to be bullied at school (DeVoe et al., 2004: 20). Other SCS findings indicate that 6 percent of students aged 12–18 reported being *afraid of being attacked* at school or on the way to and from school, a decrease from 12 percent in the 1995 survey. Fear of attack varied by race/ethnicity and grade level, however. Black students (11 percent) and Hispanic students (10 percent) were more afraid than white students (4 percent), and sixth graders (10 percent) were more afraid than 9th graders (6 percent) or 12th graders (4 percent) (DeVoe et al., 2004: 40). School violence, whether perceived, observed, or experienced, can make students fearful and affect their readiness and ability to learn. Students' concerns about being vulnerable to attacks have a detrimental effect on the school environment (Elliott et al., 1998b). Fear of being attacked leads many students to *avoid places in school*. In 2003, 4 percent of students reported that they avoided one or more places in school. Avoidance also varied by race/ethnicity: 3 percent of white students reporting avoiding certain places, but 5 percent of black students and 6 percent of Hispanic students reported avoiding places in school (DeVoe et al., 2004: 42). Three final indicators of a disorderly and unsafe school environment are the presence of hate-related words or seeing hate-related graffiti, use of alcohol at school, and drug use and availability at school. In 2003, 12 percent of students reported that someone at school had used *hate-related words* against them, and more than one-third (36 percent) had seen *hate-related graffiti* at school. The SCS asked whether someone at school had called them a derogatory word having to do with race, religion, ethnicity, disability, gender, or sexual orientation during the previous 6 months. Discriminatory behavior in schools can create a hostile environment that is not conducive to learning. In 2003 5 percent of students reported that within the previous 30 days they had at least one drink of alcohol on school property, 6 percent reported using marijuana on school property, and 29 percent of students reported that someone had offered, sold, or given them an illegal drug on school property in the previous 12 months (DeVoe et al., 2004: 50–54).

Researchers have examined the factors involved in crime and violence in schools with the goal of developing effective prevention strategies. Previous research and school-based delinquency-prevention programs were targeted at individual students. That trend stands in marked contrast to explanations and theories of the causes of crime in the community that focused on social structural factors and social processes. More recent studies have examined the relationships among community, school climate, and other school factors and how these may influence school disorder. Researchers have expanded upon previous research to examine the relative contributions of individual student variables and community and school variables to explain school disorder.

School Size and Resources. Student enrollment and per-pupil expenditures are aspects of school climate that have been associated with school disorder. We have noted the significant differences in funding between states and school districts throughout the nation. School funding and per-pupil expenditures provide the basis for resources. Low operating budgets limit the availability of classroom materials for teachers and students and place restrictions on administrators to hire and retain the most qualified teachers with adequate salaries. School size and limited resources have been associated with school climate and disorder (Gottfredson and Gottfredson, 1985). Others have found mixed results for the effect of school size on school disorder. School size likely interacts with other school climate factors to influence disorder. Welsh, Stokes, and Greene (2000) found a small direct effect of school size on school crime incidents, and suggested that the effects of school size were mediated by school stability, an aspect of which we have defined as school culture. Data from the School Survey on Crime and Safety shows that as school size increased, so did the likelihood of schools reporting disorder and discipline problems. Principals in 26 percent of schools with 1,000 or more students reported student verbal abuse of teachers, compared to 14 percent of schools with 500–999 students, 10 percent of schools with 300–499 students, and 7 percent of schools with fewer than 300 students (DeVoe et al., 2004: 48).

Community Factors and School Disorder. School location is associated with students' perceptions of safety. Student responses to the SCS indicated that students in urban schools (10 percent) were more likely than students in suburban or rural schools (5 percent) to fear being attacked at school or on the way to and from school (DeVoe et al., 2004: 40). More urban students (6 percent) reported that they avoided certain places in school than suburban (4 percent) or rural (3 percent) students (DeVoe et al., 2004: 42). More students in urban schools also reported being called hate-related words and seeing hate-related graffiti. Factors associated with risk of school violence include poverty, inner-city residence, and living in a family and a community in which violence is common (Anderson, 1998). Individual student variables also explain a great deal of school violence. A study of large urban school districts found that community-level factors such as community crime rates and residential mobility explained only a small portion (4–5 percent) of the variation in school disorder beyond the 16 percent of the variation accounted for by individual-level variables in the schools studied (Welsh et al., 1999). These findings also show the limited effects of school size, suggesting that the influence of community factors on school disorder appear to be mediated to a considerable extent by aspects of school culture. An analysis of data from the School Safety and Discipline component of the 1993 National Household and Education Survey found that community variables had some effect on school victimization rates, but risk levels were associated more with the presence of likely offenders at school and students with more self-reported delinquent friends (Schreck et al., 2003). A study designed to examine the influence of institutional and community factors on disorder in Philadelphia public schools found that the neighborhoods immediately surrounding schools have a stronger influence on school disorder than the communities from which students are drawn (Welsh et al., 2000). The effects of community variables (such as poverty) on school disorder were strongly mediated by school stability. Schools with consistent, fair, and firm supervision and discipline appear to be more effective in reducing school disorder, regardless of the student population or the community.

Welsh (2001) explored the effects of several dimensions of school climate and individual student characteristics on five different measures of school disorder (misconduct, safety, avoidance, offending, and victimization) based on student self-report measures. He found that schools vary significantly in school disorder and that the variations were related more to individual students' characteristics and perceptions than to school-level factors. He suggested that school disorder can be reduced by the efforts of school administrators, teachers, parents, students, and community groups through appropriate pre-vention and intervention strategies. For example, school-based efforts at violence prevention that attempt to increase students' school efforts, encourage positive associations, and demon-strate that obeying the rules will result in valued rewards may reduce students' miscon-duct. Many school-based interventions addressing such needs are being developed and evaluated (Elliott et al., 1998a). Welsh (2001) emphasized that schools should assess their own climates to determine which factors (e.g., student characteristics vs. school climate) may be contributing to disorder before administrators proceed to develop and implement any school-based programs designed to reduce violence.

Stewart (2003) examined the extent to which individual- and school-level factors explain variation in school misbehavior by analyzing data from the National Education Longitudinal Study (NELS) on a nationally representative sample of high school students (10,578 students from 528 high schools) (Ingles et al., 1998). Individual-level variables include school attachment, commitment, involvement, and belief in school rules (Hirschi, 1969; Stewart, 2003). School-level characteristics include the proportion of nonwhite students, school size, school poverty, school location, school climate, and school culture (Anderson, 1982; Gottfredson and Gottfredson, 1985; Welsh, 2001). Results showed that higher levels of school attachment, school commitment, and belief in school rules are associated with lower levels of misbehavior in school. Students who care about and feel supported by their teachers and friends are more likely to feel an attachment and com-mitment to their school and to behave in an orderly and acceptable manner. Consistent with previous research, Stewart found that students who had positive peer associations, involved parents, and high grade point averages and who came from higher-income families were less likely to engage in school misbehavior. School size and location were also found to be associated with higher levels of school misbehavior, supporting findings of previous research. It appears that the effects of school size and location may reflect the architectural design of schools; that is, urban schools are built vertically and consist of more floor levels and isolated stairwells, thus having more unsupervised areas that offer a greater opportunity for students to misbehave (Astor et al., 1999; Stewart, 2003).

School Community and Disorder. Positive social relations among neighbors and "neighborhood collective efficacy" have been found to increase informal social controls and lead to reduced levels of crime. Allison Payne (2004) applied this idea to school crime in a study designed to examine whether communal school organization might explain the extent of disorder in schools. "Communal school organization" refers to the organization of a school as a community and includes positive relationships between administrators, teachers, and students; common goals and norms; and a sense of collaboration and involvement. Previous research has shown that schools that are communally organized have more positive student attitudes, better teacher morale, and less student disorder (Payne, 2004). Payne used data from the National Study of Delinquency Prevention in Schools based on a nationally representative sample of more than 1,200 schools (Gottfredson et al., 2004). The results indicated that communally organized schools had a significant relationship with student bonding, delinquency, and victimization of students and teach-ers. First, schools with higher levels of communal school organization had lower rates of school disorder. Schools that were more communally organized had lower levels of teacher victimization. Second, schools with higher levels of communal school organization had higher levels of student bonding. Third, schools with high levels of student bonding had lower rates of delinquency and victimization. Fourth, communal school organization had a stronger negative effect on school disorder in schools with higher levels of student racial heterogeneity than in schools with lower levels of student racial heterogeneity.

These findings support those of previous research on the effects of school size and climate on school disorder. Larger schools have lower levels of communal school organization. It is more difficult for schools to develop a sense of community when there are more students. There are fewer opportunities for active participation and collaboration among students and teachers in larger schools. Schools with greater student:teacher ratios also have lower levels of student bonding. Teachers who are responsible for a large number of students are less able to create strong attachments with individual students. Larger schools with higher student:teacher ratios also have higher levels of disorder. Teachers are unable to effectively monitor and supervise a larger number of students, and there are more opportunities for students in larger schools to engage in delinquency (Payne, 2004).

Policy Implications for School Crime Prevention

The positive effects of school climate and communal school organization have significant potential for improving school-based delinquency-prevention strategies. Interventions are directed not at individual students, but toward improving the school organization, which includes (1) positive relationships between administrators, teachers, and students; (2) common goals and norms; and (3) a sense of collaboration and involvement. Strategies that strengthen the communal organization and climate of the school can in turn increase student bonding, counter the negative effects of racial heterogeneity, and lead to reductions in disorder, delinquency, and victimization. Perhaps the most important applications of these findings are twofold: (1) The answers to school safety and crime reduction come *not* primarily through more formal social controls, police presence, and security devices (Schreck et al., 2003), but through improving informal social controls (Payne, 2004). (2) The findings of the effects of school climate and communal organization direct our attention to what school administrators and teachers can do to reduce school crime. Strategies to improve relationships among administrators, teachers, and students are likely to improve the school climate, reduce disorder and delinquency, make schools safe places in which to learn, and enhance teachers' ability to help students meet educational goals.

Summary

The way in which schools are structured and organized and the strategies used by teachers in the educational process all affect the quality of students' educational experiences. School disorder and violence are associated with community factors, size and location of schools, school resources, and school climate. Many criminologists have contended that schools are partially to blame for the failure and resultant delinquency of some students. Educational researchers have emphasized the role of families and parents, the community, and students' peers that place them at risk of failure and delinquency. Improvement in school organization, climate, teaching, and discipline strategies may be effective in helping at-risk students perform better academically and reducing disorder and delinquency.

7

Explaining and Responding to School Violence

Violent shooting incidents at schools involving multiple fatalities have garnered more media coverage and public attention than most other types of violent crimes in the United States. School shootings that result in deaths and serious injuries are shocking for at least two reasons: first, they occur relatively infrequently, and second, we expect schools to be safe havens, free of the dangers of street crime. Because school shooting incidents are rare and shocking events, they are newsworthy and therefore draw extensive media coverage. Such coverage of scattered incidents of school violence spread over several years and widely separated geographical locations has had the effect of distorting the actual incidence and probability of similar tragedies occurring in other states, cities, and local schools. Research shows that school shootings are rare events, and resulting fatalities represent only a fraction of the number of young people who are victims of homicide each year (Lawrence and Mueller, 2003). The Federal Bureau of Investigation (FBI) reports the number of homicides involving juveniles, but does not report homicides according to the location of the crime. "School-associated deaths" are reported annually by the National School Safety Center (NSSC) (2005) and have been reported in studies published in the *Journal of the American Medical Association* (Kachur et al., 1996). School shooting incidents involving multiple victims are summarized in Table 7-1.

The rate of juvenile homicides increased in the 1980s, but has since decreased. A number of factors account for the former: the emergence of crack cocaine, economic forces, guns, and gang activity (Fox and Levin, 2001). Adult offenders are responsible for most homicides, and only a very small proportion of juvenile delinquents commit violent crimes. According to Fox and Levin (2001), the group dynamics of young offenders distinguishes them from older killers. What distinguishes juvenile murders from those committed by older killers is the senseless character of murders committed by youth. Children and teenagers

Table 7–1

A Sample of School Shootings Involving Multiple Fatalities in the United States, 1974–2005[a]

Date	Location	Alleged Perpetrator (Age)	Victims
Dec. 1974	Olean, NY	Anthony Barbaro (18)	3
May 1992	Olivehurst, CA	Eric Houston (20)	3
Jan. 1993	Grayson, KY	Scott Pennington (17)	2
Oct. 1995	Blackville, SC	Toby Sincino (16)	3
Feb. 1996	Moses Lake, Wa.	Barry Loukaitis (14)	3
Feb. 1997	Bethel, Alaska	Evan Ramsey (16)	2
Oct. 1997	Pearl, MS	Luke Woodham	3
Dec. 1997	W. Paducah, KY	Michael Carneal (14)	3
Mar. 1998	Jonesboro, Ark.	Andrew Golden (11) Mitchell Johnson (13)	5
Apr. 1998	Pomona, Ca.	Unknown gang member(s)	2
May 1998	Springfield, Or.	Kip Kinkel (15)	4
Apr. 1999	Littleton, Co.	Eric Harris (18) Dylan Klebold (17)	15
Mar. 2001	Santee, CA	Charles Andrew Williams (15)	2
Apr. 2002	Red Lion, PA	James Sheets (14)	2
Sept. 2003	San Diego, CA	William Hoffine (58) (killed son, Evan Nash, 14)	2
Sept. 2003	Cold Spring, MN	Jason McLaughlin (15)	2
Mar. 2005	Red Lake, MN	Jeff Weiss (17)	8

[a] The listed cases are those involving multiple fatalities in "school-associated violent deaths," including suicides, that occur in or around schools, on the way to or from school, or at school events. Does not include incidents involving nonstudents (e.g., domestic, adults). Victims may include students, teachers, other school staff, and passers-by.

Sources: Adapted from Newman, 2004; National School Safety Center, 2005.

are impulsive, and those who kill often do so for what most adults would regard as trivial reasons, such as for being picked on, teased, or put down.

Homicides committed at schools reached a peak in 1993, with 54 deaths (Lawrence and Mueller, 2003; National School Safety Center, 2005). Since that year, killings at schools have leveled off and even decreased. The school shootings at Columbine High School claimed 15 lives (13 homicides and 2 suicides), but the total school-associated deaths during the 1998–1999 school year was 26, just half of the peak year of 1992–1993 (Lawrence and Mueller, 2003; National School Safety Center, 2005). School-associated deaths nevertheless generate a great deal of fear among the public (Addington et al., 2001) and result in demands on school administrators and law enforcement officials to do more to prevent weapon possession and violence at school.

Explaining and Predicting Youth Violence

Criminologists have attempted to identify the most important predictors of youth violence. A large proportion of serious and violent delinquency is committed by a relatively small number of juvenile offenders. Identification of those young offenders most at risk of serious offending opens the possibility of early intervention and prevention strategies. Lipsey and Derzon (1998) examined predictors of serious or violent delinquency and determined through meta-analysis the predictor variables that had the strongest empirical associations with subsequent violence at various ages. Their results suggest that disrupting early patterns of antisocial behavior and negative peer support is a promising strategy for preventing violence and serious delinquency (Lipsey and Derzon, 1998). Many predictors of violent behavior are also predictors of other problems, such as substance abuse, delinquency, and school dropout. Identifying risk factors for youth violence therefore shows promise for targeting and preventing multiple problem behaviors (Hawkins et al., 2000).

The Office of Juvenile Justice and Delinquency Prevention (OJJDP) brought together 22 researchers as part of the Study Group on Serious and Violent Juvenile Offenders. The group examined 66 studies that were also included in the meta-analysis of Lipsey and Derzon (1998) and identified the most significant predictors of juvenile violence. They focused on those predictors that could be changed through prevention strategies. The factors related to juvenile violence were organized in five major areas and are summarized in Table 7–2.

The violence predictors identified by the researchers have all been documented in empirical studies and through longitudinal research. Children and youth who have been exposed to the conditions summarized in Table 7–2 are at a higher risk to engage in violent behavior. The risk factors vary by age groups, and some factors are more important than others in predicting violence. Youths who are exposed to more risk factors are more likely to engage in violent behavior. Many of the factors are predictors of other problems such as substance abuse, school dropout, and nonviolent delinquency (Hawkins et al., 1998, 2000).

Identifying Youth at Risk of School Violence

National interest in the problem of school violence prompted public officials and school administrators to find ways to prevent similar tragedies. The question that immediately came to mind were whether the school shooting incidents could have been predicted and prevented. Were there some warning signs that should have been apparent to those close to the shooters days or even weeks before the shootings? Newspaper and television stories following several school shooting incidents highlighted interviews with students, parents, teachers, and law enforcement officials. The shooters were identified as troubled individuals who were often isolated from the main student population and sometimes showed signs of being troubled. Some had even made verbal threats or similar indications that hinted at the potential for violence. In hindsight, following the shootings, these signs seemed obvious to the casual viewers. Most students and teachers, however, did not expect those verbal threats to actually be carried out. Many students make threats, but few act on them.

The various strategies for identifying potential violent offenders vary, ranging from "profiling" to "risk assessment," "threat assessment," and "warning signs." The terms are often used interchangeably by various writers without a clear definition of the meaning, the methods used, or the accuracy and limitations of any given strategy. School shootings have been studied closely by psychologists (Dwyer et al., 1998; Borum, 2000), by FBI crime investigation experts (O'Toole, 1999), by Secret Service agents who have developed expertise in threat assessment (Reddy et al., 2000), and by social scientists in detailed and comprehensive case studies of the family backgrounds of the shooters (Newman, 2004).

Table 7–2
Predictors of Juvenile Violence

Individual Factors	Family Factors	Community and Neighborhood Factors	School Factors	Peer-Related Factors
Pregnancy and delivery complications	Parental criminality	Poverty	Academic failure	Delinquent siblings
Low resting heart rate	Child maltreatment	Community disorganization	Low bonding to school	Delinquent peers
Internalizing disorders	Poor family management practices	Availability of drugs and firearms	Truancy and dropping out of school	Gang membership
Hyperactivity, concentration problems, restlessness, risk taking	Low levels of parental involvement	Neighborhood adults involved in crime	Frequent school transitions	Peer-related factors
Aggressiveness	Poor family bonding and family conflict	Exposure to violence and racial prejudice		
Early initiation of violent behavior	Parental attitudes favorable to substance use and violence			
Involvement in other forms of antisocial behavior	Parent–child separation			
Beliefs and attitudes favorable to deviant or antisocial behavior				

Source: Adapted from Hawkins, J. D., T. I. Herrenkohl, D. P. Farrington, D. Brewer, R. F. Catalano, T. W. Harachi, and L. Cothern. 2000. "Predictors of Youth Violence." *OJJDP Juvenile Justice Bulletin*. Washington, DC: U.S. Department of Justice.

Criminal Profiling

Criminal profiling is a process of inferring distinctive personality characteristics of individuals responsible for committing crimes (Turvey, 1999). Profiling involves gathering pieces of information and evidence from various crime scenes and looking for any patterns that could help to determine the characteristics of a specific, individual offender. The major goals of profiling are to provide the criminal justice system with social and psychological assessments of offenders, evaluations of belongings found in the possession of suspected offenders, and suggestions and strategies for interviewing suspected offenders when they are apprehended (Holmes and Holmes, 1996: 3). Criminal profiling is multidisciplinary, drawing from the studies of criminal behavior (criminology), mental illness (psychology and psychiatry), and physical evidence (biology and chemistry). According to Turvey (1999), criminal profiling relies on both inductive and deductive reasoning for developing a profile of a criminal based on evidence. The *inductive* method uses a comparative, correlation, or statistical process relying upon subjective expertise. For example, profilers work from the premise that most known serial murderers are Caucasian, male, and operate within a comfort zone. The *deductive* method is a forensic-evidence–based, process-oriented method of investigative reasoning about the behavior patterns of a particular offender. Deductive criminal profiling develops a profile by working from general evidence to attempting to identify a specific offender. Crime scene characteristics and offender behavioral evidence patterns gathered from a series of crimes help to develop a profile of a single offender (Turvey, 1999). This method is retrospective in that it works from a crime scene investigation backward to infer the type of person who committed the crime (Reddy et al., 2001). Profiling involves social scientific processes, including deductive and inductive reasoning, collection of evidence, and drawing tentative conclusions based on that evidence and reasoning. Like social science and statistical analysis, profiling is highly probabilistic; that is, conclusions and predictions based on analysis of the evidence can never be made with 100 percent confidence. The FBI's research on the reliability and validity of profiling acknowledges a high rate of error. In a study of 192 cases in which profiling was used, 88 cases were solved. Of those 88, in only 17 percent did a profile help in the identification of a suspect (Holmes and Holmes, 1996: 44).

Profiling School Shooters

Criminal profiling is significantly different from attempting to predict whether a given student is likely to perpetrate a school shooting. Profiling is applied following a series of violent crimes to identify the characteristics or behavioral patterns of a criminal. Attempting to identify potentially violent students before the occurrence of a violent school shooting does not fit the traditional definition of criminal profiling. Criminal profiling has been extended to attempt "prospective" identification of potential criminals. Rather than working backward from a crime to identify a suspect, prospective profiling tries to predict the future likelihood that a crime may be committed, such as a school shooting (Reddy et al., 2001). Researchers have developed a profile of students who carry handguns to school. Kingery, Pruitt, and Heuberger (1996) surveyed a sample of 8th- and 10th-grade students in Texas ($N = 879$) and described the characteristics of the 85 students (10 percent) had carried a gun to school: they carried a gun out of fear or anger, experienced elevated rates of repeated victimization, and were more likely to enter dangerous situations repeatedly and more likely to have used crack cocaine. They had less instruction on preventing violence and less knowledge about means of avoiding fighting, and felt an obligation to fight in a variety of situations.

The FBI examined the characteristics of the suspects involved in six school shooting cases that occurred in 1997 and 1998 in Pearl, Mississippi; Stamps and Jonesboro, Arkansas; Edinboro, Pennsylvania; Springfield, Oregon; and Paducah, Kentucky (Band and Harpold, 1999). Experts from the FBI's Behavioral Science Unit, with assistance of agents from their Little Rock office and the Arkansas state police, developed an offender profile of the shooters involved in those cases. The FBI's offender profile of school shooters is summarized in Table 7–3.

Profiling school shooters presents many challenges and has been criticized for inaccuracy and lack of validity (Reddy et al., 2001). The number of students involved in school shooting incidents is a small fraction of the total number of juvenile homicides, so we

Table 7–3
FBI "Offender Profile" of School Shooters

Suspects were white males under 18 years old with mass or spree murderer traits.

Sought to defend narcissistic views or favorable beliefs about themselves, while at they same time they had low self-esteem.

Experienced a precipitating event (e.g., a failed romance) that resulted in depression and suicidal thoughts that turned homicidal.

Lacked, or perceived a lack of, family support. Two suspects killed one or both parents.

Felt rejected by others and sought revenge or retaliation for real or perceived wrongs done to them.

Acquired firearms owned by a family member or someone they knew.

Perceived that they were different from others; disliked those who different (i.e., self-loathing); needed recognition; when they did not receive positive recognition, they sought negative recognition.

Had a history of expressing anger or displaying minor acts of aggressive physical contact at school.

Had a history of mental health treatment.

Seemed to have trouble with their parents, though no apparent evidence of parental abuse existed.

Were influenced by satanic or cult-type belief systems or philosophical works.

Listened to songs that promote violence.

Appeared to be loners, average students, and sloppy or unkempt in dress.

Seemed to be influenced or used by other manipulative students to commit extreme acts of violence.

Appeared isolated from others, seeking notoriety by attempting to "copycat" other previous school shootings but wanting to do it better than the last shooter.

Had a propensity to dislike popular students or students who bully others.

Expressed interest in previous killings.

Felt powerless and may have committed acts of violence to assert power over others.

Openly expressed a desire to kill others.

Exhibited no remorse after the killings.

Source: Band, Stephen R. and Joseph A. Harpold. 1999. "School Violence: Lessons Learned." *FBI Law Enforcement Bulletin* 68(9):9.

have only a small number of cases upon which to build a profile. Attempting to profile potential school shooters involves predicting both the shooter and the general location of the shooting. Criminal profiling does not attempt to predict the location of a violent crime. Serious questions have been raised about the problems in attempting to "profile" students who are believed likely to commit school violence (Reddy et al., 2000). Mulvey and Cauffman (2001) noted three obstacles to predicting school violence: (1) the behavior being predicted is a rare event; (2) the event being predicted is embedded in a social and trans-actional sequence of events; and (3) the individuals being assessed are adolescents, whose characters are often not yet fully formed.

Profiling also raises many legal issues in regard to the validity and use of profiles as social science evidence originally intended for crime investigations. Profiling in a school setting is different from its use in criminal investigations and airport searches, as it raises issues of potential discrimination, search and seizure, and privacy rights (Bailey, 2001). Courts would question the use of profiles to identify potentially violent students in schools on constitutional grounds and on reasonableness standards. Because profiles are likely to miss many potentially violent youth and include too many innocent youth, Bailey questions the usefulness of profiles in a school setting. Profiling students likely to use a weapon in school violence is also problematic because of the small number of cases on which to develop a profile. A profile of students involved in school shootings over the past 10 or more years would be based on so few cases that it would have no statistical predictive value (Aultmann-Bettridge et al., 2000; Borum, 2000) and would therefore be likely to produce many "false-positives." Some students may resemble the profile of a school shooter, but in fact will not act out with violence.

Attempting to profile violent students is different from predicting youth violence based on a "risk-factor" approach. The purpose of identifying risk factors is to identify individuals who may be at risk of general youth violence; it does not attempt to predict a specific type of violent offender such as a school shooter. Risk factors are based on empirical research, with statistical data and analyses to support the findings. The primary purpose of risk factors is to identify youths who have a greater need for some special interventions and could benefit from preventive strategies. Considerable empirical research has been conducted on risk factors in attempts to predict youth violence, as discussed above (Lipsey and Derzon, 1998; Hawkins et al., 2000) and summarized in Table 7–2.

Warning Signs

Warning signs of possible youth violence have been developed by several organizations. The use of checklists or instruments by trained and licensed mental health professionals to identify violence potential is also referred to as "guided professional judgment" or "structured clinical assessment" (Borum, 2000; Reddy et al., 2001). The U.S. Department of Education (Dwyer et al., 1998) developed *Early Warning*, *Timely Response*, a guide to maintaining safe schools. The guide is a synthesis of an extensive knowledge base on violence and violence prevention, drawing from research funded by several federal offices. According to the authors, the warning signs in the guide are supported by empirical data or expert consensus. The document was reviewed for accuracy by an interdisciplinary panel including researchers and practitioners involved in youth violence (Dwyer et al., 1998: 32). The authors offer several notes of caution to assure that these warning signs are not treated as profiles of violent students: (1) none of the warning signs alone is sufficient for predicting aggression and violence; (2) they are not equally significant and they are not presented in order of seriousness; and (3) it is inappropriate and even potentially harmful to use the early warning signs as a checklist against which to match individual children (Dwyer et al., 1998: 8). The early warning signs are offered only as an aid in identifying and referring children who may need help. School staff and students should use the early warning signs only for purposes of identification and referral to mental health experts, and only trained professionals should make diagnoses in consultation with the child's parents or guardian. The Department of Education early warning signs are summarized in Table 7–4.

Dwyer, Osher, and Warger (1998) emphasized that the early warning signs were offered only as an aid in identifying and referring children who may need help. School staff

Table 7–4
Early Warning, Timely Response: Warning Signs Compiled by the U.S.
Department of Education

Social withdrawal

Excessive feelings of isolation and being alone

Excessive feelings of rejection

Being a victim of violence

Feelings of being picked on and persecuted

Low school interest and poor academic performance

Expression of violence in writings and drawings

Uncontrolled anger

Patterns of impulsive and chronic hitting, intimidating, and bullying behaviors

History of discipline problems

Past history of violent and aggressive behavior

Intolerance for differences and prejudicial attitudes

Drug use and alcohol use

Affiliation with gangs

Inappropriate access to, possession of, and use of firearms

Serious threats of violence

Source: Dwyer, Kevin P., David Osher, and Cynthia Warger. 1998. *Early Warning, Timely Response: A Guide to Safe Schools.* Washington, DC: U.S. Department of Education, pp. 8–11.

members are encouraged to look and listen for these early warning signs among their students. The warning signs are not intended as indicators for official intervention or for labeling students. Only a trained professional such as a school counselor, psychologist, or social worker should make diagnoses in consultation with the child's parents or guardian. They are not supported by extensive research or statistical analyses, however, so may not be reliable as predictors of violent behavior.

A list of warning signs compiled The American Psychological Association (APA, 2000) contains warning signs indicative of the possibility or potential for violence. The APA warning signs are summarized in Table 7–5.

The APA suggests that when warning signs for violence are recognized in an individual, the information should be passed along to a family member or a trusted official or professional, such as a guidance counselor, teacher, school psychologist, coach, member of clergy, or school resource officer.

The International Association of Chiefs of Police (IACP) compiled a list of warning signs of potential violence as a guide for preventing and responding to school violence (Kramen et al., 1999). The authors emphasize that these signs simply mean that a child appears to be troubled and that violent behavior might be one of the possible outcomes. Kramen and coauthors note that the list of warning signs is not intended to stigmatize children or predict that they will be violent just because they are at risk for such behavior. They suggest that responses include referral to appropriate professionals such as counselors,

Table 7–5
Warning Signs of Youth Violence

If you see these immediate warning signs, violence is a serious possibility:	*If you notice the following signs over a period of time, the potential for violence exists:*
Loss of temper on a daily basis	A history of violent or aggressive behavior
Frequent physical fighting	Serious drug or alcohol use
Significant vandalism or property damage	Gang membership or strong desire to be in a gang
Increase in use of drugs or alcohol	Access to or fascination with weapons, especially guns
Increase in risk-taking behavior	Threatening others regularly
Detailed plans to commit acts of violence	Trouble controlling feelings like anger
Announcing threats or plans for hurting others	Withdrawal from friends and usual activities
Enjoying hurting animals	Feeling rejected or alone
Carrying a weapon	Having been a victim of bullying
	Feeling constantly disrespected
	Poor school performance
	Failing to acknowledge the feelings or rights of others
	History of discipline problems or frequent run-ins with authority

Source: American Psychological Association. 2000. *Warning Signs*. Washington, DC: American Psychological Association. Online: http://www.helping.apa.org

law enforcement, or mental health agencies. The IACP list of warning signs is summarized in Table 7–6.

The NSSC (1998) compiled a checklist of the characteristics of youth who have caused school-associated violent deaths based on tracking school-associated violent deaths in the United States from 1992–1998. NSSC identified twenty behaviors that may indicate a youth's potential for harming him/herself or others. The NSSC checklist is summarized in Table 7–7.

The NSSC notes that there is no foolproof system for identifying potentially dangerous students who might harm themselves or others. The checklist is intended as a starting point to alert school administrators, teachers, and support staff to address needs of troubled students through meetings with parents, provision of school counseling, guidance and mentoring services, and referrals to appropriate community health/social services, and law enforcement personnel (National School Safety Center, 1998).

Threat Assessment

A third approach for predicting school violence is threat assessment (Borum, 2000; Burns et al., 2001; Reddy et al., 2001). Threat assessment refers to a fact-based method of assessing the risk posed by an individual whose communication or behavior has raised

Table 7–6
IACP Identifying Warning Signs of Potential Violence

Has engaged in violent behavior in the past

Has tantrums and angry outbursts abnormal for the child's age

Continues exhibiting antisocial behaviors

Forms and/or maintains friendships with others who have engaged in problem behaviors

Often engages in name calling, cursing, or abusive language

Has brought a weapon or has threatened to bring one to school

Consistently makes violent threats when angry

Has a substance abuse problem

Is frequently truant, or been suspended frequently

Seems preoccupied with weapons or violence, especially with killing humans more than target practice or hunting

Has few or no close friends

Has a sudden decrease in academic performance and/or interest in school activities

Is abusive to animals

Has too little parental supervision

Has been a victim of abuse or neglect

Has repeatedly witnessed domestic abuse/violence

Has experienced trauma or loss in home or community

Pays no attention to the feelings or rights of others

Intimidates others

Has been a victim of intimidation by others

Dwells on perceived slights, rejection, mistreatment by others; blames others, is vengeful

Preoccupied with TV shows, movies, video games, reading materials or music expressing violence

Reflects excessive anger in writing projects

Is involved in a gang or antisocial group

Seems depressed/withdrawn; has exhibited severe mood or behavior swings

Expresses sadistic, violent, prejudicial, or intolerant attitudes

Has threatened or actually attempted suicide or acts of self-mutilation

Has engaged in violent behavior in the past

Source: Kramen, Alissa J., Kelly R. Massey, and Howard W. Timm. 1999. *Guide for Preventing and Responding to School Violence.* Alexandria, VA: International Association of Chiefs of Police.

concerns and official attention. A specific threat against another individual or group of persons that indicates a potential for targeted violence is an example. The initial steps of threat assessment may begin as students have become more sensitized to the potential for violence and have reported their observations and concerns to officials. A distinction is made, however, between persons who make threats and those who actually pose a risk of violence (Borum, 2001; Reddy et al., 2001). Many students are characterized by risk factors, but may not pose an actual threat of violence; and even those who have made

Table 7–7

NSSC Checklist of Characteristics of Youth Who Have Caused School-Associated Violent Deaths

1. Has a history of tantrums and uncontrollable angry outbursts
2. Characteristically resorts to name calling, cursing or abusive language
3. Habitually makes violent threats when angry
4. Has previously brought a weapon to school
5. Has a background of serious disciplinary problems at school and in the community
6. Has a background if drug, alcohol, or other substance abuse or dependency
7. Is on the fringe of his/her peer groups with few or no close friends
8. Is preoccupied with weapons, explosives, or other incendiary devices
9. Has previously been truant, suspended or expelled from school
10. Displays cruelty to animals
11. Has little or no supervision and support from parents or a caring adult
12. Has witnessed or been a victim of abuse or neglect in the home
13. Has been bullied and/or bullies or intimidates peers or younger children
14. Tends to blame others for difficulties and problems s/he causes her/himself
15. Consistently prefers TV shows, movies, or music expressing violent themes and acts
16. Prefers reading materials dealing with violent themes, rituals, and abuse
17. Reflects anger, frustration, and the dark side of life in school essays or writing projects
18. Is involved with a gang or an antisocial group on the fringe of peer acceptance
19. Is often depressed and/or has significant mood swings
20. Has threatened or attempted suicide

Source: National School Safety Center. 1998. *Checklist of Characteristics of Youth Who Have Caused School-Associated Violent Deaths.* Westlake Village, CA: National School Safety Center.

threats may not pose an actual risk of acting on that threat. According to Borum (2001), three basic principles underlie the threat assessment approach:

1. Targeted violence is the result of an observable process of thinking and behavior that moves through various stages of planning and preparation.
2. Violence stems from an interaction among the potential attacker, past stressful events, a current situation, and the target.
3. A key to investigating and resolving threat-assessment cases is identification of the subject's "attack-related" behaviors (Borum, 2001: 1278).

An investigator conducting a threat assessment in a particular case generally asks questions and gathers information focused on (1) motivation for the behavior that brought attention, (2) communication about ideas and intentions, (3) unusual interest in targeted violence, (4) evidence of attack-related behaviors and planning, (5) mental condition, (6) level of mental clarity and organization to form and carry out a plan, (7) recent losses, including status or respect, (8) consistency between communications and behaviors, (9) concern by others about the person's potential for harm, and (10) factors in the person's life or environment that may increase the likelihood of an attack (Reddy et al., 2001: 169). The U.S. Secret Service has applied the knowledge gained from years of identifying individuals who may pose a threat to the president of the United States to the assessment of students who may pose a threat to school safety (Reddy et al., 2000).

The FBI has also supported threat assessment for identifying students who may pose a risk of school violence (O'Toole, 1999). Following the shootings at Columbine High

School, the Critical Incident Response Group (CIRG) and the National Center for the Analysis of Violent Crime (NCAVC) of the FBI sponsored a symposium to study cases of school shootings in order to better understand what precipitated the events. Attendees included more than 100 educators, administrators, mental health professionals, law enforcement officers, and prosecutors. Recommendations for factors to focus on in threat assessments of school shooters were (1) specific, plausible details, (2) the emotional content of a threat, and (3) precipitating stressors. A four-part assessment model was recommended, including (1) the personality of the student, (2) family dynamics, (3) school dynamics, and (4) social dynamics (O'Toole, 1999: 10).

The Reliability and Validity of Profiles and Warning Signs

Profiles, warning signs, and risk-assessment tools for identifying and predicting school violence are recent developments that have not been subjected to tests of reliability or validity. There are questions about the usefulness or accuracy of some of the lists of warning signs or violence indicators. Some may in fact be harmful when predictions result in false-positives. A closer examination of profiling, risk and threat assessment, and warning signs is necessary to assess their relative strengths and limitations. Table 7–8 presents a list of 26 characteristics, profiles, or warning signs from five of the lists discussed above. The characteristics in the table were included on at least two or more of the agencies' lists.

The characteristics or warning signs most frequently listed (included on four of the lists) were uncontrolled anger; drug/alcohol use or abuse; member of a gang, cult, or anti-social group; and feelings of rejection. Twelve characteristics were included on three of the lists. These related generally to bullying, a history of violence and discipline problems, and weapons. Only five of the original 20 characteristics of the FBI offender profile matched or were sufficiently similar to be included with those identified by other agencies. The FBI profiles were developed by law enforcement officers at a regional meeting in Arkansas, who based the them on six shooting cases. The other three lists (APA, IACP, and U.S. Department of Education) of characteristics or warning signs were developed by multi-disciplinary groups of experts including educators and mental health professionals; the NSSC list is based on more than 200 school-associated deaths from 1992 to 1998.

Aultmann-Bettridge, Elliott, and Huizinga (2000) compiled a list of 10 school violence indicators containing 57 characteristics (five of the lists were summarized earlier in this chapter). They then compared the list with the predictors identified in the meta-analysis of youth violence predictors by Lipsey and Derzon (1998). No one characteristic was found on all 10 lists. Elimination of the profile lists from the analysis resulted in slightly more agreement of indicators on the lists, but there was still considerable divergence. A comparison of the characteristics with findings of the Denver Youth Survey (DYS) (a longitudinal study of problem behavior, 1988–1999) indicated 25 characteristics that matched DYS variables. A discriminant analysis to test for predictive validity of the 25 best indicators revealed that 28 percent of the future offenders would be correctly identified, with a 4 percent false-positive rate; an analysis using the upper 10 percent of risk (those scoring high on six or more factors) found that 43 percent of future offenders would be correctly identified, but there would be a 22 percent false-positive rate. Aultmann-Bettridge, Elliott, and Huizinga (2000) concluded that using a checklist approach to identify higher-risk offenders improves prediction, but the false positive rate is higher than desired. They expressed concern that the lists of warning signs and risk factors made available to schools

Table 7–8

Comparison of Characteristics, Profiles, or Warning Signs of School Violence Risk

Characteristics, "Profile," or "Warning Signs" of Violence Potential or Risk	"Characteristic," "Profile", or "Warning Sign" Included in the List = X[a]				
	APA	FBI	IACP	NSSC	USDOE
Anger—uncontrolled	X		X	X	X
Animal cruelty/abuse	X		X		
Bullying/Aggressive behavior—verbal abuse of others	X		X	X	
Bullying/Aggressive behavior—threatens others (general)	X		X	X	
Bullying—victim	X		X	X	
Domestic violence (exposure to, witnessed)			X	X	
Drug/Alcohol use and/or abuse	X		X	X	X
Depression and mood swings			X	X	
Empathy (lack of empathy skills)	X		X		
Expresses violence in writings, artwork, etc.			X	X	X
History of discipline problems (general)	X			X	X
History of violent or aggressive behavior	X		X		X
Intolerance (prejudice or dislike of those who are different)		X	X		X
Member of gang, cult, antisocial group (incl. delinquent peer group)	X	X	X	X	
Parental involvement/monitoring (low)			X	X	
Precipitating event (psychological trauma that may or did trigger violence)		X	X		
Rejection (perceived or real rejection by peers/family; or no close friends; loner)	X		X	X	X
School failure (poor academic performance)	X		X		X
Social isolation (feelings of loneliness; lack of friends)		X	X	X	
Suspended/Expelled/Truant in the past (history of school discipline problems)		X	X	X	
Threats (previous)—suicide (threat or attempt)			X	X	
Threats (previous)—violence or terrorist threat	X		X		X
TV/Entertainment (preferences for violent themes)			X	X	
Weapons—brought weapon to school	X		X	X	
Weapons—access to, general ("inappropriate access to")	X				X
Weapons—talks about/preoccupied with	X		X	X	

[a] The list of characteristics, profile factors, or warning signs includes those that were included on two or more of the lists of agencies.

APA: American Psychological Association; FBI: Federal Bureau of Investigation; IACP: International Association of Chiefs of Police; NSSC: National School Safety Center; USDOE: U.S. Department of Education.

Sources: Dwyer et al., 1998; National School Safety Center, 1998; Band and Harpold, 1999; Kramen et al., 1999; American Psychological Association, 2000; Aultmann-Bettridge et al., 2000.

are widely divergent and not strongly supported by empirical evidence. Many of the lists do not address the issue of labeling or stigmatizing students who may fit a risk profile, but not pose an actual risk of violence. It is clear that more empirical research is needed to determine the predictive validity of school violence assessment tools.

A Theory of School Shootings

The research and literature on school shootings have focused on the individual shooters through profiles, warning signs, and personal characteristics. Identifying student risk factors is one step toward explaining violent behavior and describing some of the characteristics of those most prone to violence. Focusing on the individual student without examining the larger context, however, provides an incomplete picture of school violence origins. We noted in Chapter 6 that school culture and school environment are important variables for understanding school violence. School and community factors are equally important for explaining and understanding school shootings. Theories of juvenile delinquency include individual explanations that focus on biochemical and psychological factors as well as sociological explanations of the effects of social structure and social processes on delinquent behavior. Any explanations for school violence must also consider the effects of individual and social factors. The literature and studies on school shootings have offered several hypotheses to explain this most tragic form of school violence, citing factors like bullying, copycatting, family problems, gun culture, media violence, mental illness, and peer relations. Despite a growing body of literature on school violence, there have been few efforts to develop a theoretical explanation that includes the multitude of factors associated with violent behavior at school.

Research that exemplifies some of the best efforts toward developing a theory of school violence is that of Gottfredson and Gottfredson (1985) in *Victimization in Schools* and the edited volume on *Violence in American Schools* by Elliott, Hamburg, and Williams (1998a). The most recent theory examines the combination of factors that best explain "rampage school shootings" (Newman, 2004). The theory is based on in-depth interviews with individuals affected by two school shooting incidents (one involving Michael Carneal in December, 1997, in Kentucky, and a second involving Mitchell Johnson and Andrew Golden in March, 1998, in Arkansas). Newman and her student associates conducted the interviews in Heath, Kentucky, and Westside, Arkansas, with 163 persons including victims' families, classmates, teachers, school administrators, police, lawyers, court officials, psychologists, family members, friends, newspaper and television reporters, and church congregation members who were familiar with the victims and family members. Based on their interviews and reviews of other cases and research on school shootings, Newman proposed five conditions (necessary but not sufficient) for rampage school shootings:

1. The shooter perceives himself as extremely marginal in the social world that matters most to him.
2. School shooters suffer from psychosocial problems that magnify the impact of marginality.
3. "Cultural scripts" that are prescriptions for behavior must be available to lead the way toward an armed attack. The shooter believes that unleashing an attack on teachers and classmates will resolve his dilemmas, and the script provides an image of what the shooter wants to become.

4. There must be a failure of surveillance systems intended to identify troubled teens before their problems become extreme.

5. There must be an availability of guns, so that a youth can obtain unsupervised access to a weapon (Newman, 2004: 229–230).

Newman emphasizes that this theory, made up of necessary but not sufficient conditions, limits the population of children or communities in which multiple or "rampage" school shootings tend to occur. It is not a profile and is not intended to predict which students will erupt into gun violence or which schools and communities will be next. Because school shootings are relatively rare, it is difficult to impossible to develop a theory that has any predictive validity. As noted in Table 7–1, school shootings are spread geographically throughout the United States. No particular region has been more vulnerable than any other. One factor connected to school shootings involving multiple victims is population density. The majority (60 percent) of the incidents involving multiple victims have occurred in rural communities, 32 percent in suburbs, and only 8 percent in urban areas (Newman, 2004: 235). This is no accident, according to Newman, for "big cities offer a larger variety of social niches—escape hatches—than small, tight-knit communities where boys who fail to live up to masculine ideals may be ostracized" (2004: 235). Smaller schools in smaller communities, where most students, parents, and other community members know each other, may magnify some students' feelings of social marginalization and limit their ability to act out their feelings in other socially deviant but nonviolent ways. The theory does not explicitly highlight population density as an explanatory factor, nor does it attempt to explain or predict the locations of future violent school shootings. Newman's theory is nevertheless one step toward identifying troubled children before they explode and toward developing policies to address the problems of bullying, social marginalization, and easy accessibility of firearms to decrease the prevalence of rampage shootings.

Preventing School Violence

The Columbine High School shootings made school violence a high priority for preventive action. The tragedy prompted school and justice officials to take all necessary actions to prevent school violence. Most profiles and warning lists were developed shortly after Columbine. School officials were under pressure to do something immediately in response to the perceived threat of violence throughout the nation's school system. The news media's focus on school violence heightened public concerns (Lawrence and Mueller, 2003), and the possibility of legal liability for failure to maintain safe schools was a motivating factor in school administrators' decisions to implement immediate and highly visible violence-prevention strategies (Kramen, 1999: 43–46).

School Security and Safe School Policies

School administrators have proposed or implemented a variety of policies and programs, including physical security devices, school police and security officers, training school personnel, and requiring students to carry identification cards and clear backpacks and to comply with dress codes—even uniforms in some cases. According to the 2002 *Indicators of School Crime and Safety*, 8 percent of public schools reported some metal detector checks of students, and 10 percent of schools reported having police stationed at their schools at least part-time (DeVoe et al., 2002). Using law enforcement and security hardware to reduce violence is understandable and does show that the school is doing something. Metal detectors and security cameras have severe limitations, however, and may provide a false sense of security. Students can get weapons into schools in spite of metal detectors, and the devices cannot stop shootings that occur outside schools and on school buses (Fox and Levin, 2001; Lawrence and Mueller, 2003).

The need for effective school security strategies was recognized long before Columbine and other school shooting incidents (see Blauvelt, 1981). School security needs have changed over the years, however, from an emphasis on protecting school property from theft and vandalism (Hylton, 1996) to safeguarding the safety of students and teachers (Trump, 1998, 2000). Following the Columbine shootings, Trump (2000) highlighted the shifts in school security trends as terrorist-type threats such as homemade bombs, anthrax scares, and semi-automatic weapons surfaced in schools. School security today requires carefully developed risk assessment and security and safety plans (Stephens, 1998; Trump, 2000).

Zero-Tolerance Policies

Most schools (94 percent) have instituted zero-tolerance policies for weapons, alcohol, or drugs, resulting in more than 5,000 expulsions and more than 8,000 suspensions of 5 or more days (DeVoe et al., 2002: 135). Zero-tolerance policies are intended to send a strong message to students that weapons in schools will not be tolerated, and they may account at least partly for a reported decrease in weapons at school. The percentage of students who reported carrying a weapon to school declined from 12 percent in 1993 to 6 percent in 2001 (DeVoe et al., 2003: 34). School administrators have been criticized, however, for applying zero-tolerance policies too rigidly. Cases in which the policy was applied narrowly and with literally "no tolerance" have resulted in the suspension of elementary school children in Georgia for making a list of people they wanted to hurt (including the Spice Girls and Barney, the purple toy dinosaur), a girl in Colorado who brought a lunch bag to school that contained an apple and a paring knife, and a second grader in Maryland who made a gun out of construction paper (Fox and Levin, 2001: 96). The National Center for Education Statistics found that schools that had implemented zero-tolerance policies for as long as 4 years were still less safe than those without such policies (Skiba and Peterson, 1999). Despite their questionable effectiveness, most schools have been quick to adopt the hard-line zero-tolerance policies, whereas fewer (59 percent) schools reported to have included violence-prevention programs in the curriculum (DeVoe et al., 2002: 135). Skiba and Peterson (1999) suggest that programmatic prevention and effective discipline policies are viable alternatives to zero-tolerance policies.

Most of the focus of violence-prevention programs has been directed toward either identifying at-risk students through warning signs or beefing up security through hardware and law enforcement presence. A violence-prevention strategy that focuses primarily on identifying troubled students is based on the assumption that poor parental supervision, family conflict, exposure to media violence, and parental abuse is primarily to blame. Focusing on the individual child also ignores the fact that threats and violence are the results of relationships and interactions among peers (Fox and Levin, 2001). School and community factors that may contribute to school violence have been largely ignored. There is abundant research evidence that school climate and environment account for a great deal of school disorder (see Chapter 6). Violence-prevention strategies must also examine what the schools could have done to prevent the tragic shootings. Many students who brought a weapon to school stated that they did so for self-protection (Kingery et al., 1999; Addington et al., 2002: 35). A significant portion of school violence is caused by students retaliating for threats and prior victimization and taking self-defense into their own hands because they do not believe teachers and school officials can protect them (Devine, 1996). Many students do not report being victims of bullying and threats because they do not believe school officials respond to their complaints or do enough to ensure a safe school environment.

An Integrated Approach to Violence Prevention

We have emphasized that school violence is not an isolated problem, but is closely related to community factors as well as school climate, organization, and environment. Prevention of violence requires a more comprehensive approach than identifying troubled students, placing more police in schools, and adopting more punitive sanctions. Elliott, Hamburg, and Williams (1998b), recommending an integrated approach to violence prevention, suggested four theoretical perspectives for studying school violence and for promoting prevention strategies:

1. *Social-ecological perspective*: Examines the role of social context in generating and shaping attitudes, beliefs, and behavior by studying the personal past history, personal traits, and dispositions of individuals as they interact with the social setting such as in schools.
2. *Life-course perspective*: Overcomes the limitations of cross-sectional designs by following the same individual from early childhood through adolescence to identify factors that promote aggressiveness and violence.
3. *Developmental perspective*: Recognizes that violence is not only destructive behavior, but also affects the school and community environments, interfering with normal learning processes and normal adolescent development. This perspective also emphasizes that mastery of youth development tasks can act as a protective factor to prevent violence and promote healthy adaptation to life in many social settings.
4. *Public health model*: Emphasizes a prevention strategy that utilizes a series of steps: identifying sources of the problem, identifying risk and protective factors, regular surveillance and tracking of the problem, designing community-based interventions, monitoring and evaluation, and public education to share information about the strategies (Elliott et al., 1998b: 18–20).

Responding to violence as a public health problem recognizes the significant economic, medical, and personal costs of violent injuries and deaths. A public health approach to violence prevention directs resources at identifying the causes and risk factors related to youth violence (Rosenberg and Fenley, 1991); and directs community resources to develop preventive strategies, similar to public health campaigns to reduce smoking and drunk driving, and to promote seat belt use and safe driving (Hamburg, 1998). Federal government initiatives for responding to youth violence as a public health issue include the Office of Disease Prevention and Health Promotion (2001) and the "Safe Schools, Healthy Students" initiative (Substance Abuse and Mental Health Services Administration, 2005).

Summary

Violent shooting incidents at schools involving multiple fatalities have garnered more media coverage and public attention than most other types of violent crimes in the United States.

School shootings that result in deaths and serious injuries are shocking because they occur infrequently and because we expect schools to be safe havens free of the dangers of street crime. Numerous efforts to predict which students are at risk of committing school violence and why have produced warning signs, profiles, and threat or risk assessment approaches. Because school shootings are so rare, however, it is very difficult to develop a method of identifying potential school shooters that has any predictive validity. Most school violence-prevention efforts have been directed toward identifying at-risk students through warning signs or toward beefing up security through hardware and law enforcement presence. School and community factors that may contribute to school violence have been largely ignored. In addition to identifying troubled students who may need mental health services, violence prevention must also examine the school climate and environment that may contribute to disorder and violence and develop problem-solving strategies to reduce and resolve conflict that may erupt in violent incidents.

8

School Law and Students' Rights

During the 1999–2000 school year more than 1 million serious disciplinary actions were taken against students involving about 54 percent of public schools in the United States. A majority (83 percent) of the disciplinary actions were suspensions of 5 days or more, 11 percent were expulsions from school, and 7 percent were transfers to specialized schools (DeVoe et al., 2004: 28). About 20 percent of schools took disciplinary actions for possession of drugs or alcohol in school, 4 percent for possession of a firearm and 19 percent for weapons other than firearms; 35 percent for fights, 22 percent for threats, and 18 percent for insubordination (DeVoe et al., 2004: 28). Lack of discipline and control ranked just behind lack of financial support in a national survey asking respondents what were the biggest problems facing public schools; use of drugs, fighting, violence, and gangs were also among the problems most cited by survey respondents (Rose and Gallup, 2004: 44).

Many believe that school discipline problems are attributable to an overemphasis on students' rights—that the balance has shifted from teachers' authority to students' rights. Despite court decisions that have recognized students' rights in school disciplinary matters, teachers and principals have been given wide authority and power in supervising students and regulating their conduct. Most school districts have regulations and discipline policies that are clearly spelled out to teachers, parents, and students in handbooks and policy manuals. Some teachers nevertheless choose to ignore and not intervene in student disruptions and school rule violations because they believe that school administrators will not support their disciplinary actions or that they will face legal challenges by students and their parents (Devine, 1996). Most school administrators and many teachers will at some time in their careers be involved in a lawsuit or legal challenge (Chandler, 1992). Many educators lack sufficient knowledge of Supreme Court decisions that affect them with regard to maintaining discipline and order (Reglin, 1992).

Students' Rights in School

The issue of students' rights has emerged as a focus of attention in concerns about mis-conduct in schools.[1] Many school officials and citizens are convinced that the growing problems of student disruption and general lack of respect for authorities are attributable directly to an overemphasis on students' rights. Students do have rights; they do not "shed their rights at the schoolhouse gate." The U.S. Supreme Court in *Tinker v. Des Moines* reminded educators and school boards that schools may not be operated in a totalitarian manner with absolute authority over students:

> It can hardly be argued that either students or teachers shed their constitutional rights . . . at the schoolhouse gate. . . . In our system, state-operated schools may not be enclaves of total-itarianism. School officials do not possess absolute authority over their students. Students in school as well as out of school are "persons" under our Constitutions. They are possessed of fundamental rights which the State must respect . . . [Justice Abe Fortas, *Tinker v. Des Moines Independent Community School District*, 309 U.S. at 506, 511, (1969)].

The authority of school principals and school boards in developing and enforcing school rules must take into consideration students' rights and responsibilities relating to school rules. State and federal courts have determined what is considered to be reasonable and fair enforcement of rules, and a number of decisions by the courts have extended legal protection to students against school sanctions that have been deemed unreasonable and unconstitutional.

The increase in violence, drugs, and weapons in schools has prompted school officials to take all reasonable steps to assure a safe learning environment for students and teachers. Rather than view students' rights as impeding school officials' authority, it is more appropriate to view the rights and responsibilities of students and educators in a broader context. An emphasis on the balance of the rights and responsibilities of students and teachers is especially appropriate in an educational setting. Treating students as young citizens of the community, with rights and responsibilities, is an invaluable lesson in prep-aration for life in a democratic society. Many students (and their parents) are quick to demand their rights. Responsibilities go hand in hand with rights, and schools have an opportunity to teach students that the former must be learned before the latter may be enjoyed (Wilkinson, 1996: 313).

Given the demands for equal rights among disadvantaged groups such as minor-ities and women over the past few decades, it should not be surprising that students have also exerted their rights under the U.S. Constitution. Most school administrators and many teachers will at some time in their career be involved in a lawsuit or legal challenge (see Chandler, 1992). Although there is evidence that many educators lack sufficient knowledge of Supreme Court decisions affecting them (Reglin, 1992), most school districts have worked to develop policies and regulations that are clear and to communicate them to teachers, parents, and students. Certainly one of the benefits of the increase in litigation involving schools is the development of clear policies and guidelines and better efforts in com-municating them to students and parents.

Teachers and principals are given wide authority and power in supervising students and regulating their conduct. The authority of school officials is not absolute, however, and their actions in enforcing school rules and disciplining students must at all times be reasonable. The courts have given school boards and officials considerable discretion in establishing and enforcing regulations, but they have also closely examined school policies to assure reasonableness and fairness. School rules are considered reasonable if they contribute to advancing the educational process, and they are generally considered to be fair and sufficiently clear if they provide students with adequate information as to what is expected of them and are stated in a way that persons of common intelligence are not required to guess at their meaning (Alexander and Alexander, 2005). In addition to relating directly to the educational process, school rules are usually upheld by courts if they use terminology that parents and students would ordinarily understand. School regulations do not have to be formally adopted and published, and the absence of formally adopted rules may not prohibit formal action by school officials, but the formal adoption and publication of rules will certainly be more convincing to courts in showing that a given rule was necessary and was enforced fairly.

Common Law and the Student

Various court decisions over the years have established what is referred to as a "common law of the school" (Alexander and Alexander, 2005). Under the common law as defined through various court decisions, both teachers and students have certain rights and responsibilities. These mutual rights and responsibilities have their basis in what is necessary for schools to fulfill their educational objectives and meet the expectations that society places on schools. The courts have generally recognized that teachers have a great responsibility to educate students and therefore have given teachers considerable latitude in controlling student conduct in order to maintain a positive learning environment in the classroom. Teachers have what has been referred to as "inherent authority" in their role as educators. "Inherent" means that the teacher's authority is not limited to that which is spelled out literally in school policies, regulations, and handbooks. By virtue of the special teacher–student relationship, the teacher also has an obligation to promote the harmony of the school by requiring discipline while protecting and advancing the interest of the child (Alexander and Alexander, 2005). In a ruling more than a century ago, the Wisconsin Supreme Court enunciated the extent of the teacher's authority.

> While the principal or teacher in charge of a public school is subordinate to the school board . . . and must enforce rules and regulations adopted by the board . . . he does not derive all his power and authority in the school and over his pupils from the affirmative action of the board. He stands for the time being *in loco parentis* to his pupils, and because of that relation, he must necessarily exercise authority over them in many things concerning which the board may have remained silent [*State ex rel. Burpee v. Burton*, 45 Wis. 150, 30 Am. Rep. 706, (1878)].

Students also have a responsibility to conduct themselves in a manner that assists school officials to fulfill the educational function of the school. Thus, while students enjoy their rights to a public education, they are expected at the same time to conduct themselves in a way that will not interfere with the educational goals of teachers or other students. This means that individual student rights in the school are subordinate to the rights of teachers and other students to pursue educational goals uninterrupted and in a safe environment. The Wisconsin Supreme Court also defined students' responsibilities in the same case cited above.

> In the school, as in the family, there exist on the part of the pupils the obligations of obedience to lawful commands, subordination, civil deportment, respect for the rights of other pupils

and fidelity to duty. These obligations are inherent in any proper school system, and constitute
. . . the common law, and is subject, whether it has or has not been reenacted by the district
board in the form of written rules and regulations. Indeed it would seem impossible to frame
rules which would cover all cases of insubordination and all acts of vicious tendency which
the teacher is liable to encounter daily and hourly [*State ex rel. Burpee v. Burton*, 45 Wis.
150, 30 Am. Rep. 706, (1878)].

The school is often referred to as a community, and indeed the rights and responsibilities of students and teachers are very similar to those of citizens in society. Some reduction of individual rights and freedoms may be necessary in order for the community to
harmoniously meet its objectives. Political philosophers such as Hobbes and Rousseau
have referred to the "social contract," whereby individual rights and duties are balanced
for the common good of the community. The same concept may be correctly applied to
the balance of rights and responsibilities of teachers and students in public schools. An
early ruling by a court in Missouri illustrates this balance of rights and responsibilities.

The teacher of a school as to the children of his school, while under his care, occupies, for
the time being, the position of parent or guardian, and it is his right and duty not only to
enforce discipline to preserve order and to teach, but also to look after the morals, the
reasonably necessary to preserve and conserve all these interests . . . [*State v. Randall*, 79
Mo. App 226, (1899)].

Reasonableness of School Rules

School rules must be reasonable, meaning that they must be related to educational
objectives and the discipline or sanctions for violation of the rules must not be unfair or
excessive. "Reasonableness" is a central concept in the law and is a major test for whether
rules and regulations will stand up in court. Rules that are reasonable would generally
meet the test of being proper, rational, and fair. Unreasonable sanctions may be characterized as those that are immoderate, excessive, and unsuitable to the particular conditions
or circumstances (Alexander and Alexander, 2005: 432). The authority of teachers and school
officials in responding to a multitude of different behaviors and examples of misconduct
under a variety of circumstances cannot possibly be spelled out exactly in written rules
and regulations. Courts have therefore allowed for considerable flexibility in determining
what is reasonable as teachers and school officials take disciplinary actions.

In Loco Parentis

The English translation of the Latin term *in loco parentis* is literally "in the place of
the parent." The concept originated from English law, giving schoolmasters parental-like
authority over students. Teachers' and school officials' roles as authorities and guardians
of students are limited to school functions and activities and must be limited to what is
considered reasonable. While there are limitations, the intent of the *in loco parentis*
doctrine under the law has been to help define the school–student relationship and to help
maintain an orderly environment that is conducive to meeting educational goals. The courts
have generally taken a broad view of school power when interpreting the extent of *in
loco parentis*. In *Baker v. Owen* [395 F. Supp. 294 (M.D. N.C. 1975), aff'd 423 U.S. 907
(1975)] the plaintiff parents had told local school officials that they did not want their
child subjected to corporal punishment. Despite the parents' wishes, their child was given

two licks with a desk drawer divider that was just thicker than a ruler. The court accepted the parents' argument that the Fourteenth Amendment supports the right of a parent to determine and choose the means of discipline of children, but that right was superseded by the greater state interest in maintaining school discipline. The court's decision is consistent with the model of school power prevailing today. The broad view of schools' power under *in loco parentis* holds that school authority flows exclusively from an explicit or implicit delegation of authority from parents and is rooted in the state's independent power to educate and discipline students (see Imbrogno, 2000).

School Reporting of Student Problems

The school has been a central part of the socialization of children, in addition to its primary function of education. Schools have been required to supplement (if not supplant) the role of parents in many areas. In accordance with the doctrine of *in loco parentis*, school personnel have been charged with the responsibility of not only educating children, but also safeguarding health conditions, including dental, hearing, and vision problems; requiring vaccinations; and noting any signs that indicate the child has been a victim of physical abuse.

Reporting Child Abuse. The 1974 federal Child Abuse Prevention and Treatment Act included a provision that medical personnel and other professionals, including school teachers and officials, were required to report suspected instances of child abuse and neglect. State statutes also require the reporting of child abuse. The statutes grant immunity to reporters of child abuse and neglect from criminal and civil liability "if the report *is made in good faith*" (Alexander and Alexander, 2005: 477). In a 1985 Oregon case, *McDonald v. State, By and Through CSD* (71 Or. App. 751, 694 P.2d 569), the court dismissed the parents' complaint after their child was removed from their custody based on reports of suspected child abuse by a teacher and principal. Child abuse allegations were later ruled without grounds and the parents regained custody of their child. The court ruled that the principals and teacher had acted in good faith and had reasonable grounds to report the suspected child abuse.

In order to ensure that medical professionals, law enforcement officials, lawyers, and teachers will comply with statutes requiring reporting of suspected child abuse or neglect, most state laws include a criminal penalty or civil liability for failure to report. Statutes requiring the reporting of suspected abuse include statements such as "reason to believe," so a teacher who may be charged with failure to report suspected child abuse should be prepared to show that there was no reason to believe that child abuse or neglect had occurred (Alexander and Alexander, 2005: 478).

Reporting Substance Abuse. Using the child abuse reporting statute as a model, the Minnesota state legislature adopted several drug abuse–reporting statutes for schools. These statutes imposed responsibilities on teachers to report the use of drugs by students, established chemical preassessment teams, and required reports from local law enforcement agencies. Under Minnesota Statutes Sec. 121A.29 (subd.1), teachers who know or have a reason to believe that a student is using, possessing, or transferring alcohol or a controlled substance while on school premises or involved in school-related activities are required to notify the school's chemical abuse preassessment team. Law enforcement agencies are also required to report any drug incident involving a student within the agency's jurisdiction to the chemical abuse preassessment team in the school where the student is enrolled (Minn. Stat. 121A.28).

The chemical abuse preassessment team is a school committee appointed by the superintendent composed of teachers, administrators, and, when possible, a school nurse, counselor, school psychologist, social worker, or chemical abuse specialist. The group is expected to review each case and within 45 days make a determination whether to provide the student and parents with information about school and community services in connection with chemical abuse. The teacher and police reports are not grounds for violation of school rules or official legal action. The intent of the statute is to provide information and assistance to students and their parents.

School Records and Privacy

Maintaining safe schools requires cooperative working relations between schools and youth-serving agencies, including the police department, child-protective services, juvenile court, and probation office. The resistance to open communication and sharing of information between schools and justice agencies has posed problems for developing effective strategies for working with delinquent youth. Communication and sharing of information among agency personnel is essential to deliver services to at-risk and troubled youth. Educators who notice early signs of delinquency or have critical information about youths involved in the juvenile justice system can help other agencies develop effective intervention strategies by sharing information. Information about school attendance, behavior, and academic performance is important for a probation officer to include in a predisposition report to assist in judicial decision making. It is equally important for law enforcement and juvenile court officials to provide some information to educators about some juveniles with whom they are working. As discussed above relating to the Minnesota statutes requiring notification of students' drug abuse, the intent of the law is to provide assistance to students and their parents. Education is considered of critical importance in the rehabilitation process of adjudicated juvenile offenders. One of the probation conditions ordered by a juvenile court judge is that the juvenile on probation attend school regularly and obey all school rules. This information is shared with educators by juvenile probation officers, with the expectation that teachers, school counselors, and the principal will assist in the probation supervision and treatment process. Juvenile officials should also notify school personnel when a student is being returned to school after release from a detention facility or training school, so that needed support services can help the student succeed. Information sharing and communication among law enforcement, juvenile probation, and school officials is important to ensure public safety and to improve the cooperative efforts of agencies working with youth.

Educators and juvenile justice officials have an extensive history of refusing to share information with each other (Lawrence, 1995). Educators and juvenile court officials have typically been reluctant to share school records and court information because they have a legitimate concern about the privacy rights of students and their families. They are also constrained by laws and policies. Privacy and confidentiality policies and statutes have placed limits on record sharing between juvenile justice and school personnel. Juvenile court hearings have traditionally been closed to the public, and court records have not been open for public inspection, except by court order. Representatives of both agencies have been restrictive in their interpretation and practice of privacy laws, therefore recent legislation has spelled out more clearly under what circumstances and with whom juvenile court records and school records may be shared.

All public schools are subject to the Family Educational Rights and Privacy Act (FERPA) (20 U.S.C. § 1232g), a federal law that governs the disclosure of information from education records. FERPA was enacted in 1974 to protect the privacy interest of students and parents by setting record-keeping standards that were designed to discourage abusive and unjustified disclosure of a student's education records (Laney, 1996). In 1994 Congress passed the Improving America's Schools Act (IASA) (Public Law 103–382), which amended FERPA to promote more active information sharing by educators. FERPA specifically allows educators to:

•Share information with juvenile justice agencies after obtaining prior consent from the juvenile's parent or guardian.

•Share information, without prior parental consent, under the following circumstances:

  •when the disclosure is made in compliance with a court order or lawfully issued subpoena

  •if the educational agency is initiating legal action against the student or the student's parent and has made reasonable effort to give prior notice

  •when information about disciplinary action taken against a student is being provided to other schools that have a significant interesting the behavior of the student

  •if the information is needed by a juvenile justice agency that is providing services to the student, prior to adjudication, as authorized by state law

  •when the record disclosed is a law enforcement record created and maintained by the law enforcement unit of the educational agency or institution

  •when the disclosure is in connection with an emergency and is necessary to protect the health or safety of the student or other individuals (Laney, 1996; Medaris et al., 1997)

These provisions allow school personnel to share records and information on students under specified circumstances. Schools are thereby encouraged to play an important role in delinquency prevention by helping to identify at-risk youth. Schools can also work more cooperatively with juvenile court services either prior to a child's involvement in serious or violent crime or following adjudication. Research conducted prior to implementation of the amended FERPA indicated low levels of communication, information sharing, and cooperation between juvenile court and school officials (Lawrence, 1995). The revised provisions of FERPA have facilitated more communication and information sharing on a case-by-case basis to identify and provide services to at-risk and troubled students. The open sharing of information and records is a matter of concern to many, however, because the information could become available to school resource officers for use in a criminal investigation (Beger, 2003). The current practice of hiring more police and security officers to maintain order and safety in schools increases the probability of this occurring. State lawmakers have passed legislation that mandates information sharing between law enforcement and the school, including personal information gathered by school counselors. The intent is to protect teachers and students, but the laws may also violate students' right to privacy and result in more punishment than treatment for students in need of services (Vail, 1997). At least 41 states require school officials to report students who violate certain disciplinary rules to law enforcement agencies (Advancement Project/Civil Rights

Project, 2000). The provisions of FERPA outlined above allow schools to share information with police officials. The courts are split as to whether students' disciplinary files are protected under FERPA (Rosenzweig, 2002). Despite the majority opinion in *Earls* that results of drug testing in the school were disclosed only to school personnel who had a "need to know" and not to police officials, Beger (2003) and others remain skeptical that results of school drug tests will remain confidential.

Freedom of Speech and Expression

School officials are charged with the responsibility to provide a quality education for students in a safe environment that is conducive to learning. What students say and express in written communication and how they dress sometimes interfere with educational objectives. The First Amendment rights relating to freedom of speech and expression are more misunderstood and less clear than, for example, the Fourth Amendment relating to unreasonable search and seizure. The U.S. Supreme Court has used the test of "material and substantial disruption" to determine whether a school can deny a student the right of freedom of expression. In the case of *Tinker v. Des Moines Independent Community School District* [393 U.S. 503, 89 S.Ct. 733 (1969)], the Supreme Court ruled that students wearing black armbands to protest the Vietnam War did not pose a substantial disruption to the educational process, and the school officials violated the students' right to freedom of expression. In the more recent case of *Bethel School District No. 403 v. Fraser* [478 U.S. 675, 106 S.Ct. 3159 (1986)], the Supreme Court supported the school officials' suspension of a student who made a lewd speech full of sexual innuendos that offended the teachers and other students of the school. The Court thus made a distinction between the "political message" in the *Tinker* case and expression that includes vulgar and offensive terms (see Alexander and Alexander, 2005: 317). The two cases also serve as contrasting examples of how the First Amendment right to freedom of expression may have positive educational value. In the *Tinker* case, the silent protest of the Vietnam War (i.e., wearing black arm bands) presented an opportunity for organized class discussions that may have positive educational value. School officials, teachers, and students could also choose not to recognize the students making the silent protest, whose actions did not interfere with the educational process or the rights of other students. In contrast, the delivery of an indecent speech containing vulgar and offensive terms can hardly be said to have any positive educational value, so the Bethel School District was justified in curtailing the student's right to freedom of expression.

Student appearance as freedom of expression pertains to the issue of whether school officials may regulate students' dress and personal appearance, including haircuts. Students and parents have relied on the First Amendment and the equal protection clause of the Fourteenth Amendment to contest school regulations regarding student attire, and available court cases reveal a lack of consensus as to whether various dress styles pose a "material and substantial disruption" of the educational process. Students wearing gang colors and paraphernalia in some schools pose a potential risk and disruption, and some schools have considered policies that ban the wearing of gang-related clothing. No court cases to date have tested the legality of any bans, however.

School regulations banning unkempt or long hair have been challenged in some court cases, but school officials are hard-pressed to prove that the length or style of students' hair would significantly disrupt the school educational process. A federal appellate court refused to become involved in haircut disputes, writing that "we refuse to take our judicial clippers to this hairy issue" (Alexander and Alexander, 2005: 318). Federal Circuit courts of appeals have been involved in considerable litigation regarding school regulations on student hairstyles, but the rulings are not consistent. Some courts have determined that hairstyles may be a distraction in schools and could be regulated; other courts have ruled that hairstyles are constitutionally protected. Some federal judges have expressed indignation at having to rule on matters relating to hairstyles, in light of full court calendars with weightier criminal and civil matters. Despite ruling in favor of one school district's good grooming rule, the federal court nevertheless noted that the entire problem seemed minuscule in light of other matters involving the school system (Alexander and Alexander, 2005: 318).

Constitutional Due Process

The Fourteenth Amendment to the United States Constitution provides that no state shall deprive a person of life, liberty, or property without due process of law. This post–Civil War amendment has come to be of special importance as it applies the rights guaranteed to citizens under the federal constitution to actions of state and local agencies of government. Thus, for example, the right against unreasonable search and seizure (Fourth Amendment), against self-incrimination (Fifth Amendment), and the right to legal counsel and to a fair and impartial hearing (Sixth Amendment) are all applied to the state government agencies through the Fourteenth Amendment. A state may therefore deprive a person of life, liberty, or property as long as the individual is given due process.

There are two kinds of due process: procedural and substantive due process. *Procedural due process* means that a constitutionally prescribed procedure must be followed before a person may be deprived of life, liberty, or property. The United States Supreme Court has identified three components that comprise procedural due process. First, the person must be given proper notice that he is about to be deprived of life, liberty, or property; second, the person must be given an opportunity to be heard and present his side of the issue or case; and third, the person is entitled to a fair hearing. The procedures prescribed for and expected to be followed by all police and court officials, including probation officers, routinely include careful measures to assure that no persons are stopped, questioned, temporarily detained, or taken into custody for law violations unless these three procedures are provided for in the process. It is now (or should be) common practice for school officials to include these three procedures when any student is deprived of the liberty to attend school or deprived of property such as illegal substances or weapons.

Substantive due process refers to the objectives and appropriateness of legal interventions. To satisfy this constitutional requirement, before a state may deprive someone of liberty or property, it must show that the objective and methods used are reasonable and appropriate for accomplishing the objective. An Arizona court defined substantive due process:

> The phrase "due process of law," when applied to substantive rights . . . means that the state is without power to deprive a person of life, liberty or property by an act having no reasonable relation to any proper governmental purpose, or which is so far beyond the necessity of

case as to be an arbitrary exercise of governmental power [*Valley National Bank of Phoenix v. Glover*, 62 Ariz. 538, 159 P.2d 292, (1945)].

Substantive due process is a major factor in court decisions relating to corporal punishment in schools. Courts have upheld the right of school authorities to use physical punishment as a means of discipline. Corporal punishment in schools has not been found to violate the Eighth Amendment against cruel and unusual punishment as long as school officials can show that the punishment is not excessive and reasonably relates to educational objectives. We will discuss corporal punishment in more depth later in this chapter.

Suspension and Expulsion

Courts have applied the due process clause of the Fourteenth Amendment to school disciplinary actions that include suspension or expulsion of students. "Expulsion" refers to action taken by a school board to prohibit a student from attending a given school for up to the remainder of that school year. "Suspension" refers to action taken by a school board to prohibit a student from attending school for a shorter period of time, generally no longer than 10 school days. Under substantive due process, the school policy should clearly state the grounds for dismissal. The school board should be able to show that dismissal of any student in a given case is justifiable and appropriate in order to fulfill educational objectives of the school and that the dismissal is not excessive in light of the circumstances of the case. Procedural due process requires written notice to the student giving the grounds for suspension or expulsion and describing the hearing process and a statement summarizing the school officials' decision and the evidence or facts on which the decision was based.

The Supreme Court on Suspensions

The United States Supreme Court ruling in *Goss v. Lopez* [419 U.S. 565, 95 S.Ct. 729 (1975)] detailed the procedural due process requirements for temporary suspension of students. Administrators of the Columbus, Ohio, Public School System (CPSS) appealed the judgment of a federal court that had ruled that various high school students in the CPSS (including the principal appellee, Dwight Lopez) were denied due process of law contrary to the Fourteenth Amendment because they were temporarily suspended without a hearing. Ohio law provided that a principal could suspend a pupil for up to 10 days for misconduct or expel the student. In either case, the student's parents were to be notified within 24 hours and given reasons for the action. In the case of expulsion (but not suspension), the pupil or his or her parents could appeal the decision to the school board and receive a hearing. Neither the CPSS nor the individual high schools involved had written procedures regarding suspensions. At the time of the case they only had a regulation that referred to the state statute. The procedure was limited to formally or informally describing the conduct for which suspension could be imposed. Six of the nine students who had appealed the school system's decisions to the federal court had been suspended for disruptive or disobedient conduct; another was immediately suspended for attacking a police officer who was attempting to remove him from the auditorium where he had been demonstrating. One student was arrested along with other students for demonstrating at a high school, taken to the police station, and released without being formally charged. Before that student returned to school the following day, she was notified that she had been suspended for a 10-day period. No one from the school testified regarding the incident, and there was no record detailing on what basis the principal made the decision. Dwight Lopez was suspended in connection with a disturbance in the lunchroom that involved some physical damage to school property. Lopez testified that he was not a party to the destructive conduct but was an innocent bystander. No one from the school testified regarding the incident, and there was no recorded evidence indicating the official basis for concluding otherwise. Lopez never had a hearing. On the basis of the evidence, the federal court had declared that the students were denied due process of law because they were suspended without a hearing prior to the suspension or within a reasonable time after being suspended. The U.S. Supreme Court upheld the ruling of the federal court.

The Constitutional Right to Education.   School officials in *Goss* had argued that because there is no constitutional right to an education at public expense, the due process clause does not protect against expulsions from a public school system. The Court drew upon previous rulings to refute that argument, noting that the due process clause forbidding deprivations of liberty applies where "a person's good name, reputation, honor, or integrity is at stake because of what the government is doing to him" [*Wisconsin v. Constantineau*, 400 U.S. 433, 437; 91 S.Ct. 507, 510 (1971)]. The Court in *Goss* noted that misconduct charges and suspension could "seriously damage the students' standing with their fellow pupils and their teachers as well as interfere with later opportunities for higher education and employment" [419 U.S. 565 at 567; 95 S.Ct. 729 at 731(1975)].

School officials had also argued that the due process clause only comes into play when the state subjects students to a "severe detriment or grievous loss" and that a 10-day suspension is neither severe nor grievous. The Court noted that because "education is perhaps the most important function of state and local governments" [*Brown v. Board of Education*, 347 U.S. 483, 493; 74 S.Ct. 686, 691 (1954)], exclusion from the educational process for even a 10-day period is a serious sanction in the life of a child.

The Court required a written notice and a hearing as part of the suspension and expulsion process in order to avoid unfair or mistaken exclusion from the educational process. The Court noted in the *Goss* case that the due process clause does not shield students from suspensions that are imposed properly, and the justices noted the reasons and importance of a fair hearing and decision process.

> The concern would be mostly academic if the disciplinary process were a totally accurate, unerring process, never mistaken and never unfair. Unfortunately, that is not the case, and no one suggests that it is. Disciplinarians, although proceeding in utmost good faith, frequently act on the reports and advice of others; and the . . . facts and the nature of the conduct under challenge are often disputed. The risk of error is not at all trivial, and it should be guarded against if that may be done without prohibitive cost or interference with the educational process [*Goss v. Lopez*, 419 U.S. 565 at 568; 95 S.Ct. 729 at 732(1975)].

The Court noted that suspensions are a necessary tool to maintain order in schools and may be a valuable educational device if the process is done fairly and there is communication between school officials and students: "(I)t would be a strange disciplinary system in an education institution if no communication was sought by the disciplinarian with the student in an effort to inform him of his dereliction and to let him tell his side of the story in order to make sure that an injustice is not done" [*Goss v. Lopez*, 419 U.S. 565

at 568; 95 S.Ct. 729 at 732(1975)]. The Court required these steps to meet due process requirements: that the student be given oral or written notice of the charges against him, an explanation of the evidence the authorities have, and an opportunity to present his side of the story. The Court did not require a delay between the time of the notice and the hearing. An informal hearing could be held minutes after the alleged misconduct had occurred. Emphasis was placed on telling the student what he was accused of doing and the basis for the accusation and giving the student an opportunity to explain his version of the facts. Exceptions were allowed in cases where a student's presence poses a continuing danger to persons or property or an ongoing threat of disrupting the educational process. In such cases the notice and hearing should follow the student's removal as soon as possible.

The Court in *Goss v. Lopez* did not impose on school officials due process requirements that were unrealistically formal, time-consuming, or inappropriate in an educational setting. The requirements were no more than what a fair-minded school board and principal might expect of themselves in enforcing school regulations. In this case the Court only addressed suspensions of 10 days or less, and it stopped short of requiring the right to counsel and the student's right to confront and cross-examine witnesses or call his own witnesses. Expulsions or longer suspensions would likely require more formal procedures.

Grounds for Expulsion or Suspension

The U.S. Supreme Court has noted that suspension and expulsion are indeed not minor sanctions to be taken lightly. They may in fact have significant consequences on a pupil's future educational and employment endeavors. School boards and officials should therefore be certain that dismissal of a student has a direct relation to furthering educational goals and that they have made a good-faith effort to provide an alternative educational program for the offending student. The Pupil Fair Dismissal Act of Minnesota provides an example of the latter:

> No school shall dismiss any pupil without attempting to provide alternative programs of education prior to dismissal proceedings, except where it appears that the pupil will create an immediate and substantial danger to self or to surrounding persons or property. Such programs may include special tutoring, modification of the curriculum for the pupil, placement in a special class or assistance from other agencies (Minn. Stat. Ann., Sec. 127.29, Subd.1).

The grounds for dismissal should be clearly stated in writing and distributed to students and parents with clear explanations of the expectations and possible consequences for their violation. In Minnesota a pupil may be dismissed on the following grounds:

  (a) Willful violation of any reasonable school board regulation. Such regulation must be clear and definite to provide note to pupils that they must conform their conduct to its requirements;
  (b) Willful conduct which materially and substantially disrupts the rights of others to an education;
  (c) Willful conduct which endangers the pupil or other pupils, or the property of the school (Minn. Stat. Ann., Sec. 127.9 Subd.2).

Procedures for Suspension and Expulsion

School boards and officials must follow at least the minimum procedures detailed by the U.S. Supreme Court in the case of *Goss v. Lopez*. These include an informal conference with the student and a written statement of the facts and the grounds for the suspension decision. The period of suspension may not exceed 10 school days. Before school officials can expel a student for the remainder of a school year, there must be a written notice of its intent; a statement of the facts; a formal hearing, to include witnesses; and the student's right to legal counsel, to confront and cross-examine the witnesses, to present his or her own evidence. A formal record must be made of the hearing. The suspension and expulsion procedures required in the state of Minnesota are summarized in Table 8–1.

Table 8–1
Procedures for Suspension and Expulsion of Students

Suspension Procedures
1. No suspension from school shall be imposed without an informal administrative conference with the pupil, except where it appears that the pupil will create an immediate and substantial danger to him/herself or other persons, or to property.
2. A written notice containing the grounds for suspension, a brief statement of the facts, a description of the testimony, a readmission plan, and a copy of the statute shall be given to the pupil at or before the suspension is to take effect.

Expulsion Procedures
1. No expulsion shall be imposed without a *hearing* (unless waived by the pupil and parent or guardian).
2. Written notice of the intent to expel shall:

    •Be sent to the pupil and parent or guardian by certified mail;

    •Contain a complete statement of the facts, a list of the witnesses, a description of their testimony; state the date, time, and place of the hearing; and include a copy of the statute;

    •Describe alternative educational programs available to the pupil prior to beginning expulsion proceedings;

    •Inform the pupil and parent/guardian of the right to have legal counsel; examine the pupil's records before the hearing; present evidence; and confront and cross-examine witnesses.

3. The hearing shall be scheduled within ten days at a time and place reasonably convenient to pupil and parent/guardian; and shall be closed unless the pupil or parent/guardian request an open hearing.
4. The pupil shall have a right to representation, including legal counsel; and if financially unable to retain counsel, the school board shall advise the pupil's parent/guardian of available legal assistance.
5. The hearing shall take place before an independent hearing officer; a member or committee of the school board; or the full school board, as determined by the school board.
6. The proceedings of the hearing shall be recorded and testimony shall be given under oath.
7. The pupil, parent/guardian, or representative shall have access to all school records or employee who may have evidence upon which the action may be based; they may confront and cross-examine any witness testifying for the school system; and shall have the right to present evidence and testimony. The pupil cannot be compelled to testify.
8. The recommendation of the hearing officer or school board member or committee shall be based solely upon substantial evidence presented at the hearing, and given within two days.
9. The decision by the school board shall be rendered within five days after the recommendation, and shall be in writing, giving the facts upon which the decision is made.

Source: Minnesota Stat. Ann. 127.30, 127.31.

Zero Tolerance for Weapon Possession

Federal law requires that school districts adopt discipline policies providing for expulsion of students who are in possession of a firearm on school grounds [18 USC 922(q)]. The applicable law in the state of Minnesota is:

> . . . (A) school board must expel for a period of at least one year a pupil who is determined to have brought a firearm to school except the board may modify this expulsion requirement for a pupil on a case-by-case basis. For the purposes of this section, firearm is as defined in United States Code, title 18, sec. 921 (Minn. Statutes Sec. 121A.44).

The law has been mandated for all states in an effort to prevent the repeat of school shooting incidents and to assure some interstate uniformity and consistency in the law prohibiting firearms in schools. Further clarification is necessary regarding the definition of a firearm and other deadly weapons, "look-alikes," and zero tolerance.

Dangerous Weapons. Under the statute a "dangerous weapon" means any firearm, whether loaded or unloaded, or any device designed as a weapon and capable of producing death or great bodily harm, or any flammable liquid or other device that is intended to or may cause death or great bodily harm. The Minnesota statute (121A.44, Subd.1d) defines as a felony the possession or storage of a dangerous weapon on school property, and a person who uses or "brandishes" a replica firearm or a BB gun on school property is guilty of a felony. A student who possesses or stores a replica firearm or BB gun on school property is guilty of a gross misdemeanor. There are some questions as to whether a knife is a dangerous weapon, specifically regarding the length of the blade. Federal law defines an unlawful knife as one with a blade in excess of 2½ inches.

Exceptions to the dangerous weapons law are peace officers, military personnel, and students participating in military training; persons who have a permit to carry a firearm; firearm safety or marksmanship courses; firearms used by a ceremonial color guard; a gun or knife show on school property; or having written permission of the principal.

Possession of "Look-Alikes." Research findings on violence and victimization in schools indicate that the fear of being attacked and the perception of danger create an environment that is not conducive to learning. Many students stay at home and miss school because of a fear of being victimized. The presence of weapons poses a serious breech of school security, and realistic replicas of firearms are threats to students' feelings of safety and security. Legislators and school boards have debated the issue of "look-alike" weapons. After extensive discussion, the Minnesota legislature did not criminalize and include in the statute the possession of something that did not pose a risk of injury or harm to individuals. Most school districts do, however, include a prohibition against look-alike weapons as objects that are not allowed in schools, and offenders are punished under school disciplinary policies.

Zero Tolerance: A Critical Assessment. Zero-tolerance policies have been required by federal statute as a response to firearms in and around public schools. Many schools, however, have extended zero-tolerance policies to a wide range of minor infractions (Brady, 2002), including for alcohol or drugs, resulting in more than 5,000 expulsions and more than 8,000 suspensions of 5 or more days for weapons or minor infractions (DeVoe et al., 2002: 135). School administrators have been criticized for applying zero-tolerance policies too rigidly (as noted in Chapter 7). Students have been expelled or suspended under zero tolerance for dress code violations, profanity, excessive absenteeism, and shoving matches (Black, 1999; Insley, 2001). Narrow and rigid "no-tolerance" policies have resulted in the suspension of elementary school children in Georgia for making a list of people they wanted to hurt (including the Spice Girls and Barney, the purple toy dinosaur), a girl in Colorado who brought a wrong lunch bag to school that contained an apple and a paring knife, and a second grader in Maryland who made a gun out of construction paper (Fox and Levin, 2001: 96). Skiba and Peterson (1999) note that the National Center for Education Statistics found that schools with zero-tolerance policies are still less safe than those without such policies, and they suggest that programmatic prevention, screening and early identification, and effective discipline policies are viable alternatives to zero tolerance.

Automatic or zero-tolerance disciplinary policies do not serve the best interests of the students, teachers, administrators, or school districts. Each disciplinary decision relating to possession of a weapon should be based on the facts of the case and the student. School officials should use discretion in determining appropriate discipline in each case.

Unfair and Unequal Application of Suspensions

Educators and others have raised concerns about the overrepresentation of minority youth among students who have been suspended or expelled from school under zero-tolerance policies (Skiba and Peterson, 2000; Peden, 2001; Beger, 2003). A Harvard University Civil Rights Project reported that African American students comprised just 17 percent of the students enrolled in public schools, but represented 33 percent of out-of-school suspensions for zero tolerance (Advancement Project/Civil rights Project, 2000). Students identified as troublemakers are routinely targeted for suspension or transfer to another school or to an alternative school (Bowditch, 1993). The same factors that predict dropout (frequent absences, truancies, or suspensions, failing classes, and being overage in grade) (see Chapter 5) are the indicators that disciplinarians use to define troublemakers and that lead to suspensions, disciplinary transfers, and involuntary drops. Bowditch (1993) concluded that the preferred option of many school officials dealing with troublemakers is to push them out rather than work at correction and retention. Observations such as these raise serious concerns about the equity and fairness of zero-tolerance policies and resulting suspensions and expulsions.

Corporal Punishment

Corporal punishment has been described as the use of physical force intended to cause a child to feel pain, but not to cause injury, for the purpose of correction or control of a child's behavior (Straus, 1994), and as used in the schools it has been defined as the infliction of pain or confinement as a penalty for an offense committed by a student (Hyman 1990). Corporal punishment is not, by definition, self-defense by teachers and principals against attacks by students. Proponents of corporal punishment argue that it is often necessary to control students and maintain order and discipline in schools. Without the use or threat of corporal punishment, proponents argue, teachers would be powerless to control students, especially those who might otherwise threaten them. Opponents counter this claim by noting that most corporal punishment is not used in situations where a teacher is threatened or assaulted by a student. It is more often used against students who may have talked in class without permission or disobeyed a school rule. Corporal punishment is not generally used with students who pose a threat to the safety of teachers or other students or to school property. Far from threatening a teacher or principal, students who receive corporal punishment are often so compliant as to bend over in order to "take their licks."

In further support of the statement that corporal punishment is not self-defense, states that forbid the use of corporal punishment do allow the use of force in specific situations, such as to quell a disturbance or to protect oneself, property, or another person or to protect a student from self-injury (see Hyman, 1990: 14). All states and school districts that forbid corporal punishment recognize the right of teachers to protect themselves against assaults by students.

In states and schools that still use corporal punishment, the wooden paddle is the most common method of administering it. Several other methods and instruments have been used: rubber hoses, leather straps and belts, switches, sticks, rods, ropes, and plastic baseball bats. Punching, slapping, kicking, shaking students, and grabbing them while pushing them hard up against a wall or locker are other popular methods of getting students' attention (see Hyman, 1990: 11).

History of Corporal Punishment

Corporal punishment has been common in American homes and schools since the Colonial period. The use of physical means to discipline students has been justified by the belief that it is necessary to get their attention and obtain compliance with school rules. A Biblical and religious justification has provided corporal punishment with a solid base of support in America. Early immigrants to America brought with them the belief that proper discipline of children included whippings in order to restrain their inherent immorality and sinful nature. A common support of spanking maintained that to "spare the rod" was to "spoil the child," a saying attributed to Solomon in the old Testament book of Proverbs (13:24): "He that spareth the rod hateth his son, but he that loveth him chasteneth him." Corporal punishment made a natural transition from the home to the classroom with the support of parents and teachers and school administrators who believed that whippings and a few strikes with a ruler were necessary to keep order and discipline students.

Falk (1941) traced the history of corporal punishment in America, noting its widespread use through the Colonial period and the nineteenth century and into the twentieth century. The use of corporal punishment in schools was legal in every state except New Jersey (Falk, 1941: 1, 124). Support for corporal punishment is a reflection of the role of government as authoritarian and a view of students as amenable to order and control only through fear and physical threats. The use of corporal punishment has diminished significantly in most parts of the country. Proponents still argue that the threat of corporal punishment is often necessary, and that removing the option of corporal punishment in schools would surely mean trading social order for chaos. Corporal punishment has been considered synonymous with school discipline and order in many schools in America, especially throughout the southern United States and more conservative regions, where fundamental religious traditions are strong (Society for Adolescent Medicine, 1992; Imbrogno, 2000).

The Effectiveness and Consequences of Corporal Punishment

Effectiveness as a Form of Discipline. There is not, nor will there likely ever be, any available research evidence on the effectiveness of corporal punishment in controlling student behavior. Ethical limitations on testing its effects on students preclude such research.

In order to examine the effectiveness corporal punishment as a disciplinary tool, it would be necessary to randomly assign misbehaving students to paddling and nonpaddling groups, with pre- and post- measures of behavior (see Hyman and Wise, 1979: 349). The problems in methodology are obvious. Although many Americans are supportive of corporal punishment as one means of school discipline, it is unlikely that research on the subject would receive widespread support or funding. Controls for the protection of human subjects in research would preclude research support by funding agencies and research organizations. Much of the available research on corporal punishment is therefore limited to survey research and analysis of existing discipline records. We do not therefore have solid research evidence of the effectiveness of corporal punishment as a form of discipline, and available research results are mixed.

Research on the effectiveness of corporal punishment is basically limited to survey research that examines the opinions of samples of principals, teachers, and parents on the effectiveness and support of this type of punishment. A survey of 1,278 principals, 972 teachers, and 558 parents in 292 Pennsylvania school districts showed that a majority of the subjects believed that corporal punishment (1) does change behavior, (2) helps students learn self-discipline, (3) is less harmful than humiliation, and (4) is necessary for some students (Reardon and Reynolds, 1979. A survey of 232 principals representing 10 school districts in 10 states found that a majority of them believe that corporal punishment is effective in maintaining general discipline, reducing specific behavior problems, and improving teacher morale (Rose, 1984). Rust and Kinnard (1983) administered a survey and a personality scale to a sample of Tennessee principals and teachers who used corporal punishment and found that supporters were close-minded, neurotic, had fewer years of teaching experience, were impulsive, and likely subjects of corporal punishment as students. In general, supporters have argued that corporal punishment teaches children to learn to obey and, to respect authority and that it builds students' character (Imbrogno, 2000). Proponents also suggest that corporal punishment supports the right of all students to receive an education uninterrupted by disruptive students, and that it is preferable to other disciplinary measures, such as suspension from school, that lack an educational component (Imbrogno, 2000).

A review of the research on corporal punishment in schools concluded that the weight of the evidence indicates that it is not only ineffective, but likely counterproductive (Bongiovanni, 1979). The available research showed that corporal punishment was ineffective in producing any long-lasting behavior change; potentially harmful to students, school personnel, and property; and impractical considering the controls required for it to be effective. Bongiovanni also cited the potential for negative side effects such as increased social disruption and maintained that corporal punishment appears to be contrary to the educational role of school personnel and not in the best interests and welfare of the students. Given that corporal punishment is time-consuming and must adhere to a set of guidelines and limitations, any possible reduction in disorderly behavior does not seem to be justified by its use (Bongiovanni, 1979: 367).

The Society for Adolescent Medicine (1992) concluded from a review of research studies that there is no clear evidence that corporal punishment offers better discipline or control in the classroom, and it has never been shown to enhance moral character development, social skills, or self-control skills. There is no research support for the belief that corporal punishment increases a student's respect for teachers or other authority figures in general or improves the teacher's classroom control. The Society noted that there are many effective alternatives to corporal punishment, such as behavior modification and positive reinforcement techniques, and it is possible for school authorities to learn these techniques and for children to benefit from them (Society for Adolescent Medicine, 1992).

 The Effects and Consequences of Corporal Punishment. Social scientists have noted a number of adverse and negative consequences of corporal punishment (see Table 8–2). Welsh (1979) observed many juvenile delinquents through clinical observations and found that corporal punishment produces fear and then anger, and the level of reported aggressive behavior in males is a function of the severity of their corporal punishment histories. Straus (1991) found that corporal punishment may produce conformity in the immediate situation, but it tends to increase deviance and delinquency in the long run. A number of researchers link corporal punishment to increased aggressiveness and violence during both childhood and adulthood (Imbrogno, 2000: 131). Corporal punishment may legitimize violence in the eyes of the child through a social learning process; that is, children tend to imitate aggressive behavior, especially when the aggressive behavior (corporal punishment) is being administered by an authority figure, such as parents or teachers, whom they are taught to emulate (Straus, 1994).

 Criticism of corporal punishment is based primarily on its psychological impact on children and students. Symptoms may include problems with memory, concentration, sleep disturbances, and somatic complaints (Hyman, 1990). Other studies suggest that corporal punishment can create feelings of alienation, depression, and suicidal thoughts that last long into adulthood (Imbrogno, 2000: 131) and may generate feelings of rage and indignation (Straus, 1994). The Society for Adolescent Medicine (1992) noted that researchers have suggested that corporal punishment creates an educational environment that is punitive and unproductive. The Society takes the position that corporal punishment amounts to physical and mental abuse and cites evidence that students who are victims or witnesses of corporal punishment can develop low self-esteem, magnified guilt feelings, and anxiety symptoms (Society for Adolescent Medicine, 1992). Medical complications from corporal punishment include abrasions, severe muscle injury, extensive hematomas, whiplash damage, and arm or leg injury. Studies also indicate that students who were victims of corporal punishment may have difficulty sleeping, fatigue, feelings of sadness and worthlessness, suicidal thoughts, anxiety episodes, increased anger with feelings of resentment and outbursts of aggression, deteriorating peer relationships, difficulty with concentration, lowered school achievement, antisocial behavior, dislike of authority, school avoidance, and dropout (Society for Adolescent Medicine, 1992). Physicians have expressed concern about the detrimental effects of corporal punishment, particularly on the physical, mental, and emotional health of children and youth, and have actively sought to abolish its use in public schools (Society for Adolescent Medicine, 1992; American Academy of Child and Adolescent Psychiatry, 1997).

Current Policies and Practices

 During the 1999–2000 school year, a total of 342,038 students were reported to be subjects of corporal punishment in U.S. public schools in the 23 states that allow corporal punishment (U.S. Department of Education, 2003). This represents a drop of 7 percent from the previous survey conducted 2 years earlier. Twenty years ago it was estimated that more than 1 million children were hit by teachers and principals annually and that 10,000–20,000 students sustained injuries serious enough to require medical attention

Table 8–2
Corporal Punishment in U.S. Public Schools, 1999–2000

State	No. of Students Hit	Percent of all Students	State	No. of Students Hit	Percent of all Students
Alabama	39,197	5.4	Mississippi	48,627	9.8
Arizona	632	<0.1	Missouri	9,223	1.0
Arkansas	40,437	9.1	New Mexico	2,205	0.7
Colorado	260	<0.1	North Carolina	5,717	0.5
Delaware	65	0.1	Ohio	1.085	0.1
Florida	11,405	0.5	Oklahoma	17,764	2.9
Georgia	25,189	1.8	Pennsylvania	407	<0.1
Idaho	23	<0.1	South Carolina	3,631	0.5
Indiana	2,221	0.2	Tennessee	38,373	4.2
Kansas	99	<0.1	Texas	73,994	1.9
Kentucky	2,797	0.4	Wyoming	8	0.7
Louisiana	18,672	2.6			

Source: U.S. Dept. of Education, Office of Civil Rights. 2003.

2000 Elementary and Secondary School Civil Rights Compliance Report. Compiled by the National Coalition to Abolish Corporal Punishment in Schools, Columbus, Ohio. http://www.stophitting.com.

(Goodlad 1984). Table 8–2 reports the number of students subjected to corporal punishment in those states that still allowed the practice during the 1999–2000 school year.

The top 10 states, by rank order and percentage of students hit by educators, during the 1999–2000 school year are: Mississippi (9.8 percent), Arkansas (9.1), Alabama (5.4), Tennessee (4.2), Oklahoma (2.9), Louisiana (2.6), Texas (1.9), Georgia (1.8), Missouri (1.0), and New Mexico (0.7). Blacks comprise 17 percent of students, but received 39 percent of corporal punishment, whereas whites make up 62 percent of students, but received 53 percent of corporal punishment. Teachers in Texas accounted for 22 percent of administrators of corporal punishment in the United States, and in Mississippi, one out of every 10 children was struck with a paddle by a teacher (U.S. Department of Education, 2003). The practice of corporal punishment is clearly more predominant in the southern United States than elsewhere. Welsh (1979) suggested that the more aggressive a culture, the more probable the members of that culture will be found to utilize corporal punishment as their chief socialization technique (Welsh, 1979: 133). Based on a review of newspaper editorial opinions, McDowell and Friedman (1979) found that support for corporal punishment was correlated with lower educational expenditures, fewer school support personnel, percent of school dropouts, and percent illiteracy.

There is now a movement in the United States to ban corporal punishment in schools entirely, but sponsors of such a ban face stiff resistance. In one national opinion poll 48 percent of Americans answered affirmatively when asked: "Do you agree with teachers being allowed to inflict corporal punishment?" Forty-four percent of the sample disagreed; 8 percent registered no opinion (Hyman, 1990). Prohibitions against corporal punishment stem at least in part from the belief that while physical punishment may produce short-run conformity, it increases the probability of problem behavior, such as delinquency, in the long run (Straus et al., 1991: 133–154). A majority of the states (28) plus the District of Columbia now prohibit corporal punishment in public schools. New Jersey was the first state to ban corporal punishment, having prohibited its use as early as 1867, and Delaware

Table 8–3
U.S. States That Ban Corporal Punishment and Year Legislation Was Adopted

State	Year	State	Year
Alaska	1989	Nevada	1993
California	1986	New Hampshire	1983
Connecticut	1989	New Jersey	1867
Delaware	2003	New York	1985
District of Columbia	1977	North Dakota	1989
Hawaii	1973	Oregon	1989
Illinois	1993	Rhode Island	a
Iowa	1989	South Dakota	1990
Maine	1975	Utah	1992
Maryland	1993	Vermont	1985
Massachusetts	1971	Virginia	1989
Michigan	1989	Washington	1993
Minnesota	1989	West Virginia	1994
Montana	1991	Wisconsin	1988
Nebraska	1988		

a   Banned by all local school boards.

Source: National Coalition to Abolish Corporal Punishment in Schools, Columbus, Ohio. http://www.stophitting.com.

passed legislation banning corporal punishment in 2003. The states in which corporal punishment in public schools is prohibited and the year in which the legislation was adopted are listed in Table 8–3.

Every industrialized nation in the world except for the United States, Canada, and one state in Australia prohibits corporal punishment. Many nations have banned corporal punishment for more than 100 years; others that have passed laws more recently indicate a worldwide trend toward eliminating corporal punishment. In addition to all European countries and the United Kingdom, other nations that have banned corporal punishment include Russia (1917), Turkey (1923), China (1949), and South Africa (1996) (National Coalition to Abolish Corporal Punishment in Schools, 2005).

Physicians and psychiatrists have actively sought to abolish corporal punishment use in public schools. The American Academy of Child and Adolescent Psychiatry (1997) opposes the use of corporal punishment in schools and joins with the American Medical Association, the National Education Association, and the American Bar Association in calling for an end to this form of punishment. The American Academy of Pediatrics (2000) urges parents, educators, school administrators, school board members, and legislators to seek legal prohibition by all states of corporal punishment in schools and to encourage the use of alternative methods of managing student behavior. The Society for Adolescent Medicine (2003) concluded that corporal punishment in schools is an ineffective, dangerous, and unacceptable method of discipline; it reinforces the notion that physical aggression is an acceptable and effective means of eliminating unwanted behavior in our society, and therefore it should be banned and replaced by nonviolent means of classroom control.

Given the rising level of violence among youth in communities and schools, corporal punishment seems to be an inappropriate means of responding to school rule violations.

We are trying to teach youth to avoid violence as a way of problem solving and that communication, mediation, and nonconfrontational means are better alternatives to settling differences. Opponents believe that it is time for school officials throughout America to recognize that physical force and infliction of pain is not the way to solve school problems. There is reason to believe, however, that laws banning corporal punishment in American schools will not be forthcoming any time soon, particularly in those states and regions where it continues to be viewed as a necessary and effective means of discipline. There is pressure from child's rights advocates in the international community for the United States to join other nations in supporting the United Nations (UN). Convention on the rights of the child, which supports a worldwide ban on corporal punishment in schools. According to Imbrogno (2000), the United States is the only democratic, industrialized nation to not ratify the UN. Convention. He offers several reasons why he believes the United States is unlikely to ratify the international agreement: corporal punishment has a long history in U.S. schools and supporters believe that corporal punishment is justified on Biblical and religious grounds and it is a necessary form of punishment to maintain school discipline (Imbrogno, 2000). If this is the case we are not likely to see a national ban on corporal punishment in schools in the near future.

Constitutionality of Corporal Punishment

The U.S. Supreme Court considered the constitutionality of corporal punishment in the 1977 decision of *Ingraham v. Wright* [97 S.Ct. 1401 (1977)]. The Court held that the punishments administered to students at Drew Junior High School (Dade County, Florida, Oct. 1970) did not violate the Eighth Amendment of the Constitution against cruel and unusual punishment. Fourteen-year-old James Ingraham, an 8th grader, was paddled so severely that a resulting hemotoma required doctor's care and prescriptions of pain pills, a laxative, sleep pills and ice packs, and advice to stay home for at least a week. The Court also held that the due process clause of the Fourteenth Amendment to the Constitution does not require notification of charges and an informal hearing prior to the infliction of corporal punishment. The petitioners in the case argued that public school children could legally be whipped by teachers, but convicted criminals are protected against beatings in jails and prisons under the Eighth Amendment that protects citizens against cruel and unusual punishment. A federal court in *Jackson v. Bishop* [404 F.2d 571 (1968)] ruled that the use of the strap in Arkansas state penitentiaries violated the Eighth Amendment, and "offends contemporary concepts of decency and human dignity and . . . it also violates those standards of good conscience and fundamental fairness . . ." (404 F.2d at 580, 1968). Despite this ruling, the U.S. Supreme Court held less than a decade later that corporal punishment in schools was not unconstitutional.

Justice Powell, writing for the majority (a 5-to-4 decision), supported the use of corporal punishment in schools based on common law and traditional societal attitudes, noting that corporal punishment in schools has a long tradition, dating from early colonial days. He acknowledged that corporal punishment has been abandoned as a means of punishing criminal offenders, but noted that "the practice continues to play a role in the public education of school children in most parts of the country. . . . Professional and public opinion is sharply divided on the practice. . . . Yet we can discern no trend towards its elimination" (*Ingraham v. Wright*, 97 S.Ct. at 1407).

Since the *Ingraham* case, several more states have passed legislation banning the use of corporal punishment in schools. Nevertheless, the practice continues in U.S. schools, particularly in the South. Lee (1979) suggested that students and their parents not look to the courts for meaningful protection against the abuses of corporal punishment in schools. She suggested they should assess the political climate in their communities and organize around discipline issues, pushing for elimination of corporal punishment from their school systems and for substitution of humanistic alternatives.

Search and Seizure

The Fourth Amendment to the U.S. Constitution provides for "the right of people to be secure in their persons, houses, papers, and effects" and for the right "against unreasonable searches and seizures." School officials are frequently confronted with the question of whether to search a student's pockets, book bag, purse, locker, or automobile. Educators must often make an instant decision whether to initiate a search, particularly in cases of bomb threats and dangerous weapons, in order to protect the safety of students and teachers. The Fourth Amendment as applied to persons conducting searches generally pertains to law enforcement, court, and security officers. The right of school officials to search students depends upon whether any illegal evidence seized may be turned over to law enforcement officers and used as evidence in juvenile or criminal prosecution. In that case, a search warrant would be required.

The Fourth Amendment in Schools

There are three parts to the Fourth Amendment as applied to students' rights in school. First, students have a right to privacy ("to be secure in their persons, papers and effects"); second, they have a right against unreasonable searches and seizures; and third, any search must be specific as to the location of the search and what is being sought. The courts have not required school officials to show probable cause for a search or to obtain a search warrant from a judge before initiating a search. They must have "reasonable suspicion" before conducting a search, but this requirement is less rigorous than the requirement of "probable cause," which is required for police to obtain a search warrant (see Alexander and Alexander, 2005). "Reasonable suspicion" means that school officials must have some facts or knowledge that provide reasonable grounds to search, and a school search may only be conducted if it is necessary to fulfill educational objectives. Thus, a student's freedom from unreasonable search and seizure must be weighed against the need for school officials to maintain order, discipline, and a safe learning environment.

New Jersey v. T.L.O.

The U.S. Supreme Court in the case of *New Jersey v. T.L.O.* [105 S.Ct. 733 (1985)] defined students' Fourth Amendment rights and provided guidelines for officials in conducting school searches. The case originated when a teacher at a New Jersey high school found two girls smoking in the restroom. The teacher took them to the principal's office because smoking in restrooms was in violation of a school rule. When questioned by the assistant vice principal, T.L.O., a 14-year-old freshman, denied that she had been smoking and claimed that she did not smoke at all. The vice principal demanded to see her purse, and upon opening it he found a pack of cigarettes and also noticed a package of cigarette rolling papers that are commonly associated with the use of marijuana. A further search of the purse produced some marijuana, a pipe, plastic bags, a substantial amount of money, an index card containing a list of students who apparently owed her money, and two letters that implicated her in marijuana dealing. The evidence was turned over to the police and she was charged with delinquent conduct. The juvenile court denied her motion to suppress the evidence found in her purse, held that the search was reasonable, and adjudged her delinquent. The state appellate court affirmed the juvenile court's finding, but the New Jersey Supreme Court reversed, ordered that the evidence found in her purse be suppressed, and held that the search was unreasonable.

On appeal, the U.S. Supreme Court ruled that the Fourth Amendment prohibition against unreasonable searches and seizures does apply to school officials, who are acting as representatives of the state. Students do have expectations of privacy when they bring to school a variety of legitimate, noncontraband items, but the Court noted that school officials have an equally important need to maintain a safe and orderly learning environment. In balancing students' Fourth Amendment rights and school officials' responsibilities, the Court ruled that school officials do not need to obtain a warrant before searching a student as long as the search was reasonable in light of educational objectives and not excessively intrusive in light of the student's age and sex and the nature of the violation (Id. at 736).

A "Reasonable" Search

The Court cited two considerations in determining whether a warrantless search was "reasonable" or not. First, "one must consider whether the . . . action was justified as its inception" and, second, "one must determine whether the search . . . was reasonably related in scope to the circumstances which justified the interference in the first place" (Id. at 744). The first involves justification or grounds for initiating the search, while the second relates to the intrusiveness of the search (see Alexander and Alexander, 1992: 339–340). In one case, a school administrator had heard reports that a student was involved in drugs. A search of the student's locker and car revealed drugs and was found reasonable and constitutional [*State v. Slattery*, 56 Wn.App. 820, 787 P.2d 932 (1990)]. In another case a student's car was searched and cocaine was found after the assistant principal noticed that the student smelled of alcohol, walked unsteadily, had slurred speech, glassy eyes, and a flushed face. The court found that the observations were sufficient to support reasonable suspicion [*Shamberg v. State*, 762 P.2d 488, Alaska App. (1988)]. School officials must also be able to justify the extensiveness and intrusiveness of searches, and show that there was reasonable suspicion. In one case in which money was missing from a schoolroom, a teacher searched the books of two students and then required them to remove their shoes. The court found the search to be reasonable and not excessively intrusive, because the two students had been alone in the room where the stolen money disappeared [*Wynn v. Board of Education of Vestabia Hills*, 508 So. 2d 1170, Ala. (1987)].

Beyond *T.L.O.*—Expanded Search Powers

The Court in *T.L.O.* held that when the purpose of a search was to maintain a safe environment conducive to learning, it falls within the category of the "special needs" exception to the warrant and probable cause requirements. Since *T.L.O.*, courts have expanded the special needs doctrine to areas beyond those considered in the original case, including searches conducted by law enforcement officials (Vaughn and del Carmen, 1997). The U.S. Supreme Court expanded school search powers 10 years after *T.L.O.* in *Vernonia School District 47J v. Acton* [515 U.S. 646 (1995)]. The Court allowed the consideration of special circumstances to give school officials the right to conduct random searches without reasonable individual suspicion. After experiencing several instances of drug possession and use at school, the Vernonia school district had instituted a policy that required students who wanted to participate in extracurricular sports to sign a form consenting to random urinalysis testing to search for drug use among student athletes. The Court upheld the policy, resting the decision on three factors: (1) school officials may determine that "special needs" exist to conduct random searches for the use of drugs that place students at risk of personal harm and safety; (2) students in sports programs have a lower expectation of privacy than students who do not participate (the Court noted in *Acton* that student athletes dress and undress and shower together); and (3) the Court ruled that the method of the search, collecting urine, was not overly intrusive, since the samples were collected by the students themselves in the privacy of enclosed stalls. The "special needs" argument was extended in *Board of Education of Independent School District No. 92 of Pottawatomie County v. Earls*, [536 U.S. 822 (2002)], in which Justice Thomas argued that "special needs" may justify searches of students involved in extracurricular activities. (The case is discussed in more detail below under "Drug Testing").

Search Guidelines for Principals

The courts have recognized the need for school officials to maintain a positive and safe learning environment in schools and therefore have required only "reasonable suspicion" rather than the more stringent standard of "probable cause" for student searches. Courts nevertheless hold firmly to the need for officials to show that reasonable grounds existed to justify a search. Alexander and Alexander (2005) have offered some guidelines for school officials in determining whether a search is justified:

1. Students do have a right to privacy of their persons, papers, and effects.
2. The courts will consider the seriousness of the offense and the extent to which a search intrudes on a student's privacy.
3. Reasonable suspicion requires that the school official have some specific facts or circumstances regarding the particular situation, including the background of the student, to justify a search for items that are in violation of school rules.
4. While a warrant is not required, a school official must have knowledge of the alleged violation, where illegal contraband is presumably located, and the identity of the student alleged to be in violation (Alexander and Alexander, 2005: 401).

In determining whether a school search is "reasonable," the courts have weighed heavily on the use of the evidence seized. A search in which the evidence is used only for school disciplinary measures, and not shared with justice officials, may be justified based only on "reasonable suspicion."

Rulings on Types of School Searches

Locker Searches

The U.S. Supreme Court has recognized that even a limited search of students "is a substantial invasion of privacy," although the Court has not addressed the question of whether students have a reasonable expectation of privacy in their lockers or desks [*New Jersey v. T.L.O.* 105 S.Ct. at 741(1985)]. A number of state courts have considered the issue of locker searches, and the majority have held that students have a legitimate expectation of privacy in regard to their lockers (Bjorklun, 1994). This would indicate that a locker could only be searched when school officials have reasonable suspicion that an individual student may have concealed illegal contraband in a locker under the standard set forth in the *T.L.O.* decision. Random locker searches, according to this decision, would be in violation of the Fourth Amendment.

The Massachusetts Supreme Court held that students have an expectation of privacy in their school lockers, but only if there was no "express understanding to the contrary" [*Commonwealth v. Snyder*, 413 Mass. 521, 597 N.E. 2d 1363, 1366 (1992)]. This condition has implications for random locker searches without prior individualized reasonable suspicion, and it was applied in a ruling by the Wisconsin Supreme Court in 1993 [*In Interest of Isaiah B.*, 176 Wis.2d 639, 500 N.W. 2d 637 (1993)] (see also Bjorklun, 1994: 1070). A random locker search was conducted at Madison High School in Milwaukee after six incidents involving guns had been investigated by school officials within a one-month period in the fall of 1990. In one incident, students reported that they were shot at as they left the school following a basketball game. In another incident multiple gunshots were heard by students as they were leaving school grounds following a near riot after a school dance. The following week school officials received reports of guns in the school, on school buses, and rumors that a shootout was inevitable. Because of the fear and tension and the risk to students' safety, the principal ordered a random search of school lockers. About 75–100 of the school lockers were searched, including that of Isaiah B.'s, where school security found a handgun and a packet of cocaine in his coat pocket. Based on the evidence, he was adjudicated delinquent in juvenile court. He challenged the adjudication based on the absence of individualized suspicion for the search of his locker; he had no history of prior weapons violations, nor was there any evidence of his involvement in the recent gun incidents at the school. The Wisconsin Supreme Court ruled that the random locker search was not in violation of the Fourth Amendment, because the Milwaukee public school system had a written policy and students had been informed that the school system had ownership and control of school lockers. The policy in the *Milwaukee Public School Handbook* states:

> School lockers are the property of Milwaukee Public Schools. At no time does the Milwaukee school district relinquish its exclusive control of lockers provided for the convenience of students. Periodic general inspections of lockers may be conducted by school authorities for any reason at any time, without notice, without student consent, and without a search warrant (cited in Bjorklun, 1994: 1071).

The court noted that students might have a reasonable expectation of privacy in their lockers if schools do not have a policy explicitly stating otherwise, such as the Milwaukee school policy. Schools may adopt such a policy, and when they do and clearly inform students of the policy, random searches of school lockers are not in violation of the Fourth Amendment.

The U.S. Supreme Court implied (in a footnote) in the *T.L.O.* decision that individualized suspicion is not always a prerequisite to a search if less than ordinary conditions exist. Since *T.L.O.* the Court has upheld random drug testing of railway employees and border guards where no individualized suspicion was present. The rationale in these rulings was that the government's interest in public safety and the need to discover potential threats to safety made such searches permissible. Bjorklun (1994) noted that the presence of weapons and drugs in schools is a less than ordinary condition, and the need to make schools safe justifies random locker searches without individualized suspicion. This is not unlike the justifiable searches of all persons entering an airplane boarding area, a courtroom, or a school building using metal detectors. The prevalence of weapons in society and the resulting threat to public safety has unfortunately necessitated more infringements on everyone's freedom. In response to weapons and drug problems, Zirkel (1994) noted that society has moved "to a warlike view of alcohol, drugs, and violence in the schools. Reflecting this change, courts have started to sacrifice the individualized aspect of reasonable suspicion . . ." (Zirkel, 1994: 729). Sanchez (1992) analyzed 18 cases dealing with searches of students in schools. The courts declared that the searches in only three of the cases were invalid, and 15 led to criminal or delinquency proceedings. Sanchez concluded that as school officials are increasingly faced with students carrying weapons and dealing in drugs, state courts have expanded the power of school officials to conduct searches. It is apparent that more school systems will adopt policies and announce to students that lockers are school property and may be opened and searched whenever school officials believe it is necessary.

Drug Testing

The presence of alcohol and other drugs in school adversely affect the school environment and school safety. Substance use and possession may lead to other more serious crimes in and around schools. In 2001, 5 percent of students reported that they had consumed at least one alcoholic drink on school property in the past 30 days, 29 percent of all students in grades 9–12 reported that drugs were made available to them on school property (someone had offered, sold, or given them an illegal drug), and 5 percent of students reported using marijuana on school property (DeVoe et al., 2003: 46–50).

School officials are concerned about drugs in the school and their effects on students and some have begun to resort to drug testing programs to control the problem. Precedent exists for drug testing in the workplace, as private businesses and state and federal government agencies have used drug testing to deter drug use among employees, particularly where job safety was clearly at risk. In 1989 the U.S. Supreme Court ruled on two cases, *Skinner v. Railway Labor Executives Ass'n* (489 U.S. 602, 109 S.Ct. 1402) and *National Treasury Employees Union v. Von Raab* (489 U.S. 656, 109 S.Ct. 1384), involving drug testing of railway employees and customs service employees. The court ruled that a drug or alcohol test—whether a blood, urine, or breath test—is a search, but the tests were upheld because of the government's interest in protecting public safety (preventing accidents among railway workers and because customs officers carry firearms). Because of the public safety interest, no individualized suspicion was required before ordering mandatory drug tests of these workers. The *Skinner* and *Von Raab* cases involved drug tests of employees, but the rulings have been extended to public school situations involving students. The Seventh Circuit Court of Appeals ruled in the 1988 case of *Schaill v. Tippecanoe County School Corporation* (864 F.2d 1309) that random drug testing of students who participated in interscholastic programs did not violate their Fourth Amendment rights. An important factor in the decision was the procedure for assuring the student due process if the test results were positive. The student and his or her parent or guardian could obtain a second lab test at a laboratory of their choice and could present evidence and an explanation for the positive results, such as the student's use of other legal medications.

Similar testing procedures were upheld in *Brooks v. East Chambers Consolidated Independent School District* [730 F.Supp. 759 (S.D.Tex 1989); 930 F.2d 915 (5th Cir. 1991)]; in the 1995 U.S. Supreme Court case of *Vernonia School District v. Acton* (115 S.Ct. 2386); and in *Board of Education of Independent School District No. 92 of Pottawatomie County v. Earls* [536 U.S. 822 (2002)]. All three cases involved students who participated in extracurricular activities. Students were tested at the beginning of the school year and by random selection the rest of the year.

In the *Vernonia* case, the parents of James Acton filed suit after he was denied participation in football because they refused to sign consent forms for mandatory drug testing. School district officials resorted to the drug testing policy to curb a growing drug problem in the schools. Vernonia is a small logging community in Oregon where school sports are important in the town's life and student athletes are admired in the schools and the community. School officials began to notice a sharp increase in drug use among students, accompanied by an increase in disciplinary problems. Students were rude during class, and outbursts of profanity were more common. The number of disciplinary referrals increased, and several students were suspended (Id. at 2388). Many of the problem students were athletes. Administrators and coaches were concerned about student athletes' drug abuse, and evidence was presented of the effects of drugs on coordination, performance, and safety among athletes. The school district initially responded to the drug problem by offering special classes, speakers, and presentations in an effort to prevent the drug abuse. When those efforts had little effect, district officials proposed the drug testing policy to parents for their input and feedback. Parents who attended a meeting gave their unanimous approval, and the school approved the policy. Under the policy, all students participating in interscholastic sports would be tested at the beginning of the season for their sport, and a 10 percent of student athletes, selected randomly, would be tested weekly. The expressed purpose of the policy was to "prevent student athletes from using drugs, to protect their health and safety, and to provide drug users with assistance programs" (Id. at 2389). The U.S. Supreme Court upheld the policy with a 6–3 decision handed down June 26, 1995.

The Court extended the right of schools to conduct random drug testing of students other than athletes in the 2002 *Earls* case. The school district of Tecumseh, Oklahoma, adopted a drug testing policy that required all students who wanted to participate in any extracurricular activities to consent to random urinalysis tests. The student plaintiffs in this case were not student athletes, but members of the choir, marching band, and academic team. Writing for the Court majority opinion in *Board of Education of Independent School District No. 92 of Pottawatomie County v. Earls*, [536 U.S. 822 (2002)], Justice Thomas argued that "special needs" may justify the searches among students in activities beyond those required of all students; second, students in extracurricular activities have a lower expectation of privacy; third, the method of the search was minimally intrusive on students' privacy; and fourth, the designation of "special needs" does not require the school district to show a pervasive drug problem to justify random suspicionless drug testing. Evidence collected in the search was kept private and not turned over to any agencies of the justice system. Student safety is the important factor for both athletes and nonathletes.

The Supreme Court has used a number of criteria to determine the legality of drug testing programs: whether (1) there is a compelling need; (2) the programs have a limited scope and achievable goals; (3) less intrusive methods in schools have been tried; (4) students have diminished expectations of privacy; (5) there are limitations on officials' discretion in selecting students for testing; and (6) the testing is intended to enforce school rules and not for evidence in criminal prosecution (Bjorklun, 1993: 918–923). The Court determined that the Vernonia school district policy met these criteria. The increase in students' drug use, disciplinary problems, and threats to safety in athletics presented a compelling need. The Court in both the *Schaill* and *Vernonia* cases noted that students who voluntarily participate in athletics have a diminished expectation of privacy for a variety of reasons, including "communal undress" in locker rooms and showers, required physical examinations, and state high school athletic rules prohibiting smoking, drinking, and drug use (Bjorklun, 1993: 921). The drug testing policy had been instituted only after less intrusive methods proved unsuccessful, and the testing policy was limited in its scope and intended only to prevent students' drug abuse, not for gathering evidence for criminal prosecution.

Justice O'Connor, joined by Justices Stevens and Souter, wrote a dissenting opinion, noting that "millions of . . . students who participate in interscholastic sports, an overwhelming majority of whom have given school officials no reason whatsoever to suspect they use drugs at school, are open to an intrusive bodily search" (Id. at 2397). The majority decision of the Supreme Court clearly goes beyond the Court's decision in *T.L.O.* that school officials must have individualized suspicion that a student search would likely reveal evidence of the student's violation of the law or school rules. Justice Scalia, writing for the majority, justified drug testing without individualized suspicion by noting that "deterring drug use by our Nation's schoolchildren is at least as important as enhancing efficient enforcement of the Nation's laws against the importation of drugs. . . . And . . . the effects of a drug-infested school are visited not just upon the users, but upon the entire student body and faculty, as the educational process is disrupted" (115 S.Ct. at 2395).

Canine Searches

Because of an increase in the possession and use of drugs in schools, officials have turned to K–9 police officers to bring their dogs into the school to sniff out drugs. This practice has generally been limited to urban schools, and many officials are hesitant to resort to this intrusive type of drug detection. Courts have expressed some reservations about accepting evidence from canine searches in schools (see Alexander and Alexander, 2005).

The Tenth Circuit Court of Appeals in *Zamora v. Pomeroy* [639 F.2d 662 (1981)] ruled that using dogs for an exploratory sniffing of lockers was permissible. At the beginning of the year the schools had given notice that the lockers were joint possessions of the school and the student and might be periodically opened. That notice and the need for officials to maintain a proper educational environment led the court to determine that locker inspections were not unreasonable under the Fourth Amendment. The Seventh Circuit Court held in *Doe v. Renfrow* [631 F.2d 91; 635 F.2d 582 (1980)] that school officials stood *in loco parentis* and could use dogs to sniff out drugs, because there was less expectation of privacy in the public schools and because officials had a duty to maintain a positive educational environment. Alexander and Alexander (2005) note that this decision may be contrary to the U.S. Supreme Court decision in *New Jersey v. T.L.O.*, which limited the application of *in loco parentis*.

Courts have been reluctant to accept canine searches in schools under some circumstances. A federal district court ruled in *Jones v. Latexo Independent School District* [499

F. Supp. 223 (E.D. Tex. 1980)] that using dogs to sniff both students and automobiles was in violation of the Fourth Amendment. The court ruled that without individual suspicions, the sniffing of students was too intrusive and not reasonable, and because students did not have access to their automobiles during the school day, the school officials' interest in sniffing the cars was minimal and not reasonable. The Fifth Circuit Court addressed two questions in *Horton v. Goose Creek Independent School District* [690 F.2d 470 (5th Cir. 1982)]: first, whether the sniff of a drug-detecting drug was a "search" under the Fourth Amendment, and second, whether the Fourth Amendment protects students against searches by school officials who are trying to maintain a safe educational environment that is conducive to learning (690 F.2d at 475). The court ruled, first, that a dog sniffing lockers and cars did not constitute a search and thus no further inquiry needed to be made as to its reasonableness (690 F.2d at 477). Regarding the second question, the court held that school officials may search students if they have reasonable cause. A personal canine search of students, however, was considered to be overly intrusive into a student's "dignity and personal security" and could not be justified under the Fourth Amendment without prior individualized suspicion (690 F.2d at 481–2). In *B.C. v. Plumas Unified School District* [192 F.3d 1260 (9th Cir. 1999)] the court held that a canine search without individual suspicion was unreasonable. School officials had asked students to wait outside their classroom while a trained canine sniffed backpacks, jackets, and other belongings that the students left in the room. The court ruled that the canine sniffing was a search and that the search was unreasonable because there were no reported drug instances in the school.

Courts may be more willing to allow canine searches justified on safety concerns. A routine canine search of an Alabama high school parking lot by law enforcement officials in conjunction with school officials led to the discovery of two knives in a student's car, in violation of the school's weapons policy. The student, an athlete and Honor Society member with hopes of attending the Naval Academy, was suspended from school for 3 days and then sent to an alternative school for 45 days. The student's stepfather appealed the case on his behalf to the Federal District Court, claiming a violation of due process and an unreasonable search under the Fourth Amendment. The court in *Marner v. Eufaula City School Board* [204 F. Supp. 2d 1318 (M.D. Ala. 2002)] rejected the claims, reasoning that the routine and even-handed policy of the school district was intended to ensure the safety of students and was not in violation of the Constitution.

The goal of most school principals is simply to keep drugs out of schools, so strict policies are put in place and communicated clearly to students and their parents at the beginning of each school year, with the threat of suspension or expulsion for violation of the drug policy. Robert Rubel, an author of several books and articles on school crime, personally conveyed one rather "innovative" method of using drug-sniffing dogs in school without violating any court restrictions. While conducting training seminars for school administrators, Rubel related the story of one principal, who announced over the school intercom just before the lunch hour that a K–9 officer and his drug-sniffing dog would be at the school after the lunch hour "just for a visit and to sniff out some student lockers." Immediately after the lunch bell rang, there was a flurry of activity, with some students rushing to their lockers, then to the restrooms, followed by a flushing of toilets! When the officer and his dog arrived, no drugs were found, but they had a nice visit with the students—and the principal had the satisfaction of knowing that, at least for the rest of that day, the school was very likely free of drugs. This strategy would not result in seizing evidence that could result in disciplinary school suspensions or official legal actions. It does, however, accomplish the overall goal of school officials: to rid schools of drugs. As a simple deterrent strategy, it also avoids the legal question of admissibility of evidence gained through canine searches.

Metal Detector Searches

According to the Youth Risk Behavior Survey (YRBS) conducted from 1993 to 2001, between 7 and 9 percent of students in grades 9–12 reported being threatened or injured with a weapon such as a gun, knife, or club (DeVoe et al., 2003: 12); and 6 percent of students reported carrying a weapon to school (DeVoe et al., 2003: 34). School officials in many urban schools have initiated the use of metal detectors as a response to the problem. According to Garcia (2003), up to 15 percent of large urban schools in the United States have resorted to using metal detectors in order to curb the presence of weapons and to provide a safe learning environment.

There are legal and policy questions involved in the use of metal detectors or scanning devices in schools (see Johnson, 1993). Federal courts have approved suspicionless searches using hand-held and walk-through metal detectors in airport boarding areas and courthouses, but neither the U.S. Supreme Court nor the lower federal courts have made a specific ruling on suspicionless searches of students using metal detectors. A New York State appellate court in *People v. Dukes*, [151 Misc. 295, 580 N.Y.S. 2d 850 (1992)] approved the use of metal detectors to search students at random as they entered the lobby of a Manhattan public high school, reasoning that "the governmental interest underlying this type of search is equal to if not greater than the interest justifying the airport and courthouse searches." The court noted that a fatal shooting in a Brooklyn high school a few months earlier and confiscation of more than 2,000 weapons from students during the 1990–1991 school year underscored its decision. Special police officers from a school safety task force set up several metal detector scanning posts in the lobby of Washington Irving High School one morning in May 1991. Signs announcing a search for weapons were posted outside the building, and students had been informed at the beginning of the school year that searches would take place. The officers conducted the search in a uniform manner under written guidelines adopted a few years earlier by former Chancellor Richard E. Green. The stated purpose of the search was to prevent students from bringing weapons into the schools. All students entering the school were subject to the search, although the officers could choose to limit the search by a random selection of students. Officers explained the scanning process and asked the student to place any bags on a table and remove all metal objects from his or her pockets. The officer passed a metal scanner over bags and from the student's feet to head, without touching the student's body. Students were searched by officers of the same sex. If any metal activated the scanning device, the student was again asked to remove any metal objects from the bag or his or her person. If the device was activated after a second scan, the student was escorted to a private area. Before conducting a pat-down search, the officer asked the student for a third time to remove any metal objects [580 N.Y.S. 2d at 850–51(1992)].

Courts consider metal-detector searches in airports and courthouses to be "administrative searches" and have held them to be reasonable when the intrusion on an individual's privacy is no greater than necessary to justify the governmental interest in public safety. An administrative search is not connected with probable cause or the issuing of a warrant.

It is designed to protect the public and is directed at a group or class of people rather than at a particular person. The court acknowledged that one way in which an administrative search of a student at school differs from that of a passenger in an airport is the subject's voluntary consent: the passenger may walk away and not board the plane, but the student is required by law to attend school. The New York court nevertheless held that "consent is hardly a necessary component of a valid administrative search" and was "satisfied that the guidelines are minimally intrusive despite the absence of a consent provision" [*People v. Dukes*, N.Y.S. 2d at 851–53(1992)].

The Superior Court of Pennsylvania upheld metal detector searches in a 1995 case involving students at University High School in Philadelphia (*In the Interest of F.B.*, 658 A. 2d 1378). Because of a high violence rate in the local schools, the Philadelphia school district resorted to metal-detector scans and publicized the search policy through letters informing parents and students. The court ruled that the searches did not violate students' Fourth Amendment rights, because they were given prior notice. No individualized suspicion was necessary because the searches were part of a regulatory plan to ensure safety of students and were announced with signs posted on the front door, and all students or a randomly selected number of students were subjected to the searches, which were conducted in a uniform manner.

Only a relatively small number of schools, primarily in urban areas, have resorted to the use of metal detectors, generally in response to growing problems of violence and students carrying guns. There are a number of considerations that should be carefully weighed by school boards before initiating a metal detector policy (Johnson, 1993: 4–5). First, metal detectors in schools are likely to raise public relations problems and costly litigation; second, in addition to legal expenses, metal-detector searches require expenditures for public information materials, staff training, the detection equipment, and some administrative overhead; third, some parents, students, and staff are likely to strongly oppose the intrusion on students' dignity and privacy; and fourth, most school districts will find it difficult to demonstrate any convincing need for metal detector searches. Johnson (1993) noted that the Texas Association of School Boards has not developed a model policy for using metal detectors for searching students for weapons, and the legal division of the state board does not recommend that a school district adopt a metal-detector policy except in schools with a documented problem of several weapon-related incidents that seems to justify such a program.

As senior staff attorney for the Texas Association of School Boards, Johnson has several recommendations for districts that decide to proceed with a metal-detector policy:

•Collect factual documentation regarding weapon-related incidents involving students in or around schools.

•Work to gain student, staff, and community agreement on the need for such a policy and their participation in its development.

•Develop search procedures that are as economical and as nonintrusive as possible.

•Develop a policy that incorporates the features of the search program in *People v. Dukes*, and with consultation from the school district's attorney.

•Before implementing the search policy, give plenty of notice to students, parents, and staff about the purpose of the policy and the techniques to be used, along with the district's plans for disciplining (or reporting to law enforcement authorities) students found to be in violation of the district's policy against carrying weapons.

•Provide training and precise written instructions for all administrators and school officials conducting the search procedures (Johnson, 1993: 6–7).

The cost and time required for schools to conduct metal-detector searches will necessarily limit their use primarily to large schools that have prior experiences with students carrying weapons. School boards and administrators are under pressure to take all reasonable means to assure safe schools, however, and metal detectors are a choice for many of them. The courts have generally supported the use of metal detectors, following the *Dukes* case, finding that no individualized suspicion was necessary. Recent cases in which metal detectors revealed a weapon and were upheld by courts include two high schools in Philadelphia [*In the Interest of S.S.*, 680 A. 2d 1172 (Pa. Super. 1996); and *In re F.B.* 658 A. 2d 1378 (Pa.Super.Ct. 1995), aff'd 726 A. 2d 361 (Pa. 1999)], the Los Angeles Unified School District [*People v. Latasha W.*, 70 Ca. Rptr. 2d 886 (Cal Ct. App. 1998)], and a Florida secondary school [*State v. J.A.*, 679 So. 2d 316 (Fla. App. 1996)].

Strip Searches

Because of the intrusive nature of strip searches, the courts have determined that strip searches require more than just reasonable suspicion. School officials should have probable cause that the student is in possession of illegal substances or a weapon that may threaten the safety of other students. The Second Circuit Court of Appeals in *M.M. v. Anker* [607 F.2d 588 (2d Cir. 1979)] ruled that as the intrusiveness of a search intensifies, as with a strip search, the justification for the search should require that probable cause be present (the same standard as that required for criminal prosecution). A New York court held that a teacher violated the Fourth Amendment rights of students who were strip-searched after some money was missing in a classroom. The search did not meet the test of even individualized reasonable suspicion, because there was no observed act or evidence to indicate which student, if any, might have taken the money. Further, a strip-search was considered excessively intrusive when the expressed purpose was to locate a missing three dollars [*Bellnier v. Lund* 438 F.Supp. 47 (N.D.N.Y. 1977)]. Combining canine searches and strip-searches has also come under critical scrutiny. The Seventh Circuit Court held that school officials violated a student's constitutional rights when they used dogs to detect drug odors and then strip-searched the student. The officials did not have reasonable suspicion or probable cause to justify the intrusive search. The court condemned this nude search of a 13-year-old child and considered it worse than a violation of constitutional rights: "It is a violation of any known principal of human decency. Apart from any constitutional readings and rulings, simple common sense would indicate that the conduct of the school officials in permitting such a nude search was not only unlawful but outrageous under settled indisputable principles of law" [*Doe v. Renfrow* 631 F.2d 91 (7th Cir. 1980)].

Despite the fact that legal scholars and most courts generally considered strip-searches in schools to be illegal, there is evidence that some lower courts are willing to support strip-searches in schools for safety reasons. In the *Williams* case a Sixth Circuit Court upheld the strip-search of a female student for drugs [*Williams by Williams v. Ellington*, 936 F.2d 881 (6th Cir. 1991)]. This was a radical departure from previous rulings in the 1970s. No other court had been willing to uphold such an intrusive search. Strip-searches that were upheld were only minimally intrusive, involving only the removal of outer garments such as jackets or shoes. Following *Williams*, two other lower courts upheld very intrusive searches of students. Those cases both involved male high school students, and the searches were for drugs. In *Widener*, school officials asked a former student to remove his jeans after they observed him acting "sluggish" and detected what they believed to be a marijuana smell. The court ruled that the search was reasonable [*Widener v. Frye*, 809 F. Supp. 35 (S.D. Ohio 1992)]. In *Cornfield*, a male student suspected of carrying drugs was required to remove all of his clothing, including his underwear. Because there was reasonable individual suspicion, the courts also ruled this search reasonable [*Cornfield v. Consolidated High School District 230*, 991 R.2d 1316 (7th Cir. 1993)]. The strip-search in both cases was conducted in the presence of male school officials, and no drugs were found in either case.

The more recent court decisions regarding strip-searches in schools have dealt primarily with drug searches, but some have dealt with suspected theft of money or property. In a West Virginia case [*State v. Mark Anthony B.*, 433 S.E. 2d 41 (W. Va. 1993)] the court overturned a strip-search for $100 because money did not pose the same sort of danger as drugs, but in a Kansas case [*Singleton v. Bd. of Educ. U.S.D. 500*, 894 F. Supp. 386 (D. Kan. 1995)] the court ruled that a pat-down and strip-search of a male student's crotch area for $150 was legal. The assistant principal conducted the search after a woman accused the 13-year-old middle school student of stealing the money from the front seat of her car. The court ruled the search was legal in light of the student's age, sex, and the nature of the wrongdoing.

Despite an apparent willingness of lower courts to allow such intrusive searches in schools, they are only permissible where there is reasonable, individualized suspicion. A federal district court in South Dakota ruled in *Konop v. Northwestern School District* [26 F. Supp 2d 1189 (D.S.D. 1998)] that a strip-search of two 8th-grade girls for stolen money was not reasonable. The male principal asked a female music teacher to conduct a strip-search. The girls were crying as they were told to remove their underwear, pants, and bras, but felt that they could not refuse. The principal later determined that the money found ($14 and $10, respectively) was not the stolen money. In *Kennedy v. Dexter Consolidated Schools* [10 P.3d 115 (NM 2002)] the New Mexico Supreme Court ruled that the strip search of 10 students for a missing ring was unconstitutional because the group was too large for each of the students to be individually suspect. A court in *Thomas v. Roberts* [261 F.3d 1160 (11th Cir. 2001)] reemphasized the importance of individualized suspicion. A 5th grader at the West Clayton Elementary School in Georgia brought an envelope to school containing $26 that he had raised selling candy for a school trip. He laid the envelope on a table near the teacher's desk, and it was later missing. The teacher and a D.A.R.E. officer who was there to teach a class conducted strip searches of the whole class. The 11th Circuit Court ruled that a strip search of a class for missing money was unconstitutional because there was no individualized suspicion.

School officials must carefully consider whether a strip search is justified based on school safety, even if they believe they have reasonable suspicion to conduct a search. Courts have ruled that school officials are not immune from liability under Section 1983 of the U.S. Civil Code. A U.S. district court in Indiana held that conducting a strip search of a class of 7th-grade girls for a missing $4.50 was not legal [*Oliver v. McClung* 919 F. Supp. 1206 (N.D. Ind.1995)]. The court ruled that the school board and superintendent were not held liable for damages because the search was not a policy or customary practice in the school, but the principal, food service worker, and teacher were liable under Section 1983 because a strip-search for such a small amount of money was clearly a constitutional violation. A federal district court in Pennsylvania ruled in *Sostarecz v. Misko*, [E.D. pa. mar. 26, 1998] (1999) that a strip-search by the school nurse was not reasonable after she had determined that the student's vital signs showed no instance of drug use, and the court refused summary judgment regarding the Section 1983 claims against the nurse.

In response to concerns about strip searching, seven states (California, Iowa, New Jersey, North Carolina, Oklahoma, Washington, and Wisconsin) have passed laws prohibiting administrators from conducting strip searches in public schools (Stefkovich and Rossow, 2003).

The Exclusionary Rule and School Searches

School officials are mainly concerned with enforcing school rules and policies that aim to assure a safe school environment. The objective of the policies is not primarily the criminal prosecution of students. The issue of the exclusionary rule has been raised because illegal substances or weapons that have been seized in public schools may be turned over to law enforcement officials. In *Weeks v. United States* [232 U.S. 383, 34 S.Ct. 341 (1914)], the Supreme Court ruled that evidence seized without a warrant can not be used in federal courts for prosecution. In *Mapp v. Ohio* [367 U.S. 643, 81 S.Ct. 1684 (1961)], the exclusionary rule was extended to ban illegally seized evidence in state courts. Several cases have addressed the application of the exclusionary rule to public schools, and the courts have generally not applied the rule, thus allowing materials seized by school officials to be used in a criminal or juvenile court prosecution (Alexander and Alexander, 2005: 403).

Arguments Against Applying the Exclusionary Rule

Those who argue against applying the rule to school searches note that it may lead to compromised school safety and more cumbersome adjudication and would not deter constitutional violations in the school setting (Mitchell, 1998: 1222–1226). Others have questioned the wisdom of introducing excessive formal legal guidelines and restrictions in the school disciplinary process. Wilkinson (1996) noted that all decisions made by any persons always involve discretion, and he questioned whether principals and teachers would abuse discretion, given that troublesome students are given several chances. Teachers have to deal with disruptions to maintain respect, and to open up the school discipline process to judicial oversight would infringe upon principals' and teachers' ability to take the necessary steps to maintain classroom order and to teach effectively. Student legal challenges to school disciplinary procedures are increasingly common. Wilkinson is concerned that litigation weakens school authority and puts it in a position of having to justify itself and tends to undermine parental and educational authority (1996: 313).

Arguments in Favor of the Exclusionary Rule

The question remains whether student searches originally intended to maintain order and discipline in school may be turned over to law enforcement authorities for formal adjudication. We are reminded of the words of Justice Fortas in *Tinker* that students do not "shed their constitutional rights at the schoolhouse gate." Our review of previous cases makes it clear that teachers and principals have conducted illegal searches of students. Those who argue in favor of application of the exclusionary rule in schools cite the rule's deterrent effect against illegal searches, that it is the only viable alternative to protect students' rights, and that it maintains judicial and administrative integrity (Mitchell, 1998).

Balancing Students' Rights with School Safety

Mitchell (1998) has proposed an alternative approach intended to balance students' rights with school safety. Under the proposal, school officials would be educated about students' rights as outlined by the Supreme Court, and a school official would face some consequences if a students' rights were violated in the process of applying disciplinary actions. The proposed plan includes five points:

1. *A Standard*: A search is allowed only if a school official reasonably suspects that evidence violating the law or school policy will be found; the search must not exceed the original objective and may not be excessively intrusive, considering the age and gender of the student.
2. *Training and Education*: School officials will be instructed on the search and seizure law and receive yearly refresher courses.
3. *Reporting Procedure*: All searches and seizures must be reported to the school district administrator for review.
4. *Violations*: Officials who violate the standards may be subject to one or more disciplinary actions: additional training and education, administrative leave, suspension of pay, or other effective deterrent action.
5. *Notice*: School officials must provide regular notification to students and parents of the school's disciplinary policies and procedures (Mitchell, 1998: 1232–1233). The weak or questionable part of the proposal plan is whether or how school districts would actually respond to violations of the standards. It is doubtful whether school officials would subject teachers to disciplinary actions when the teachers believed they were acting in the best interests of student safety and maintaining an orderly school environment.

Court Decisions on the Exclusionary Rule in Schools

The Eighth Circuit Court of Appeals in *Thompson v. Carthage School District* [87 F.3d 979 (8th Cir. 1996)] did find, however, that the exclusionary rule does apply to illegal searches conducted by school officials. The Thompson case involved a school principal who patted down a 9th-grade student, Ramone Lea, on suspicion that he was carrying a firearm on school grounds. The search did not produce a gun, but it did turn up a small quantity of crack cocaine. Following a disciplinary hearing, Lea was expelled for the remainder of the school year. Upon appeal, the circuit court held Lea's expulsion to be wrongful and awarded him $10,000 in damages for the illegal search under section 1983. The court expressed concern that application of the exclusionary rule in schools could "deter educators from undertaking disciplinary proceedings that are needed to keep the schools safe," but the court went on to assert that the impact of the exclusionary rule is mitigated by the fact that "school officials are not law enforcement officers, and thus do not occupy a role whose mission is closely analogous to that of police officers" (Jones, 1997: 390). The case settled the question as to whether the exclusionary rule applied to searches conducted by a school principal, but the question was less clear as to whether school resource officers are school officials or law enforcement officers. We will address that issue in Chapter 9 in a discussion of the role of police officers in schools.

When determining the appropriate level of suspicion required for searches in schools, one factor considered by the courts is the underlying purpose of the search. If the purpose is to uncover evidence that the student has violated school rules, courts typically have employed the lesser standard of reasonable suspicion (see Stefkovich and Miller, 1999). If, on the other hand, the purpose is to investigate a criminal violation, courts will often require probable cause. Criminal violations and school rule violations are of course not mutually exclusive. Criminal law violations typically also violate school rules, but school rule violations do not necessarily constitute criminal law violations.

Safety concerns are another important factor in the permissibility of searches. The courts seem willing to grant school and law enforcement officials more flexibility to conduct searches when faced with potentially dangerous situations without sacrificing the more lenient and flexible reasonable suspicion standard. Court decisions in California, New York, and Wisconsin have upheld searches based on the overriding need to maintain safety of all students in schools.

Safe Schools: Required by Law?

Nearly 30 states have adopted legislation that either requires or recommends safe school planning, according to Ronald Stephens, director of the NSSC. The State of California has had legislation in place for more than 20 years declaring that students and staff of public schools have a right to safe schools, as part of the "Declaration of Rights" in the California Constitution (Article 1, Sec. 28). The California Appellate Court in the case of *In re Alexander B.* [(220 Cal. App. 3d 1572 (1990)] upheld a police search based on reasonable suspicion when the school's dean directed officers to search a group of students after receiving a report that one of the them had a weapon. The court defended the ruling based on the California state constitution, which reads in part that "All students and staff of public . . . schools have the inalienable right to attend campuses which are safe, secure and peaceful" (see also *People v. Butler* [725 N.Y.S. 2d 534 [N.Y. Sup. Ct. 2001)]. A Wisconsin court held in a similar case that "School officials not only educate students . . . but they have a responsibility to protect those students and their teachers from behavior that threatens their safety and the integrity of the learning process" [*In re Angelia D.B.* 564 N.W. 2d 685 (Wis.1997)]. The protection of all students and the maintenance of a safe school environment have been recognized by the courts as being of primary importance, and school officials have been given wide latitude in carrying out their responsibility of maintaining safe schools, even when it involves conducting reasonable searches.

Civil Litigation and the Effect on Schools

School officials are now under pressure from legislative mandates and from a concern to avoid civil litigation to maintain safe schools. Nearly every major school shooting incident, with few exceptions, has resulted in litigation (Stephens, 2005). School officials have a legal obligation to take action when students pose a danger to other students (Bailey, 2001), although the courts have been reluctant to find school officials liable in school violence cases (Herman and Finn, 2002). The U.S. Supreme Court commented on school officials' duty to address school violence in *Davis v. Monroe County Bd. of Educ.* [526

U.S. 629 (1999)]. The Court put school personnel on notice that they can be held responsible for failing to exercise reasonable care to protect students from harm. Emphasis is placed on responding to threats from students who have engaged in violent activities in the past. Current case law indicates that indicators of potential violence need to be taken seriously, and courts are supporting the temporary removal from school of students who exhibit indicators of potentially violent behavior. A federal district court in *Brian A. v. Stroudsburg Area School District* [141 F. Supp. 2d 502 (M.D. Pa. 2001)] upheld school officials' decision to expel a student for *writing a note* stating "there's a bomb in this school bang bang!!" The court upheld the expulsion as a reasonable response to a bomb threat because the student was on probation for a previous incident that involved blowing up a shed on the property of another school.

The courts have ruled on the appropriateness of school disciplinary actions for *verbal threats* made by a student. In *Lovell v. Poway Unified School District* [90 F.3d 367 (9th Cir. 1996)], a federal appeals court upheld the suspension of a 15-year-old student who verbally threatened to shoot her school counselor because she was dissatisfied with her schedule. The student appealed her suspension, stating that the threat was merely a figure of speech that she did not intend to be taken as a literal threat, and she had immediately apologized for her inappropriate outburst. The student had not acted in a physically threatening manner, but the counselor reported that she felt threatened and had witnessed the student's outbursts and lack of impulse control on previous occasions. The court supported the suspension, stating that "in light of the violence prevalent in schools today, school officials are justified in taking very seriously student threats against faculty or other students" (p. 372). Verbal and written threats from students are unfortunately too common, and courts have considered students' constitutional rights and whether threats of violence made in school settings are believable. Some courts are finding that for a threat to be believable and therefore punishable, the threat must meet the "true threat" test (as in *Lovell v. Poway*. A true threat is one that a reasonable person in the same circumstances would believe to be a serious and unambiguous expression of intent to do harm based on the language and context of the threat (Herman and Finn, 2002: 48). An application of the true threat test was illustrated in the case of *D.G. v. Independent School District No. 11, Tulsa County, Oklahoma* [2000 U.S. Dist. Lexis 12199 (N.D. Okla. 2000)]. An 11th-grade student had *written a poem* about killing a specific teacher. The student explained that she was upset with the teacher at the time and wrote the poem to express her frustration, but did not intend for the teacher to see the poem. Neither the teacher nor the school administrator considered the threat to be a true threat because the student had never made any threats or acted out violently. The school had a zero-tolerance policy for student threats however, so the student was suspended. The court held that the student's suspension was appropriate while the threat was being investigated but added that once a psychologist determined that the threat was not a true threat, the school violated the student's constitutional rights by not allowing her to return to school. In a similar case in *LaVine v. Blaine School District* [257 F.3d 981 (9th Cir. 2001)], a student sued school officials after being expelled because of a poem he wrote. An English teacher was concerned about the suicidal and homicidal imagery that described a school shooting with multiple fatalities, the shooter feeling no remorse, then shooting himself. The incident occurred shortly after a school shooting in nearby Springfield, Oregon, so the teacher was concerned and notified the school counselor. The counselor was aware that the student had previously had suicidal thoughts, was having serious problems at home, had broken up with his girlfriend and was reportedly stalking her, and had a discipline record that included a fight and an incident of insubordination to a teacher. The principal expelled the student based on these facts, but he was readmitted after a psychiatric evaluation determined that he could safely return to school. The student's father nevertheless sued the school officials, claiming that the expulsion violated his son's constitutional rights. The court upheld the school's decision to expel the student pending an evaluation to determine whether he was a danger to himself or others. In supporting the school officials' actions, the court reflected on recent school shootings that had focused attention on what school and law enforcement officials could do to prevent such tragedies, and declared that "the school had a duty to prevent any potential violence on campus" (*LaVine v. Blaine School District*, 2001, p. 989).

As the professional field of school safety develops, it is increasingly important for schools to remain current with "best practices," not necessarily to guarantee the best and safest schools, but to follow operative guidelines as to what is "reasonable and standard care" (Stephens, 2005). Ron Stephens, executive director of the NSSC, has noted that it is important for all schools to have safe school plans, supervision plans, a crisis plan, a working partnership with local law enforcement, staff training about safety, and appropriate student support services. Schools that take prudent measures to protect students and school staff members from potentially violent students and to maintain a safe school can avoid costly litigation and the tragic consequences of school violence. The courts have given wide latitude to school officials in taking reasonable actions to maintain safe schools.

In conclusion, we are witnessing a struggle between the rights of students and the need to maintain safe and drug-free schools. The U.S. Supreme Court in the 1969 case of *Tinker* ruled that students do not "shed their constitutional rights at the schoolhouse gate," and they are entitled to protection under the Fourth Amendment. Despite efforts to recognize students' privacy rights, they have been outweighed by public and official concern over drugs and violence in schools. The courts have increasingly leaned more toward suspicionless drug testing and police searches in schools. Police had been allowed to search students only where there was probable cause, but the courts have lowered the standards necessary to conduct a search and have expanded the authority of school officials to test students for drugs. The U.S. Supreme Court has moved beyond *T.L.O.* in giving schools more authority under the doctrine of *in loco parentis*, allowing more liberal drug testing under the rulings in *Acton* and *Earls*. Justice Scalia wrote in *Acton* that students are under the "temporary custody of the State as Schoolmaster" (p. 652), and in *Earls* the Court emphasized the custodial and tutelage responsibilities of schools. The lower courts have likewise taken a tougher version of *in loco parentis* in authorizing searches without probable cause under the "special needs" rationale. Schools increasingly resemble prisons, where there is little expectation of privacy, and despite acknowledging some Fourth Amendment rights, search and seizure will generally be upheld as reasonable and constitutional (Mello, 2002; Beger; 2003). Accompanying the judicial support for police and school officials to maintain safe and drug-free schools is the tendency for disciplinary matters to be handled more formally. Student misbehavior has traditionally been handled informally by educators, with various in-school sanctions. With a greater police presence in schools, many cases of student misconduct are now handled more formally with police involvement and may result in automatic suspension, expulsion, or referral to a law enforcement agency or court. We address the police role in school crime in the next chapter.

Summary

Students do not in the words of Justice Abe Fortas, "shed their constitutional rights at the schoolhouse gate." As citizens, students enjoy the same constitutional rights as all Americans. The courts have also determined, however, that school officials may develop and enforce policies with the intent to make schools safe and healthy places with a positive educational environment where all students can pursue their education. Constitutional rights embodied in the First and Fourth Amendments guaranteeing students freedom of expression and freedom from unreasonable search and seizure have been applied by the courts with the intention of balancing students' rights with the responsibility of school officials to provide safe schools. Concerns about an increase in drugs and violence in schools have prompted courts to broaden school officials' search authorities and limited students' privacy rights.

Acknowledgments

The assistance of some legal experts and scholars in writing this chapter is greatly appreciated and acknowledged. Thanks to Judge Kristena LaMar, Multnomah County (Portland, OR) Circuit Court Judge; to Janet Steverson, Lewis & Clark Law School; to C.W. Seefeldt, St. Cloud State University; and to David Mueller, Boise State University, for their helpful comments on this chapter.

9

The Police
and Juvenile Crime

Police officers are the most visible officials in the criminal justice system. They introduce citizens to the justice process. That introduction ranges from taking a report from a victim or witness to a crime, issuing a traffic citation, and questioning or taking into custody a suspect in a misdemeanor or felony offense. For juveniles, the police role is considered especially important, as young persons' views and attitudes toward police are shaped by their first encounter with a law enforcement officer. In 2002, law enforcement agencies in the United States made an estimated 2.3 million arrests of persons under age 18. Juveniles accounted for 17 percent of all arrests and 15 percent of arrests for violent crimes (Snyder, 2004).

Police Roles and Responsibilities

Police officers actually perform three roles in fulfilling their law enforcement responsibilities: law enforcement, order maintenance, and service (Wilson, 1968). The public and the police themselves have viewed the law enforcement function as the primary and most important task, and little attention was given to the others, which were considered less important, and not "real law enforcement."

Law Enforcement

The traditional law enforcement role of police is to detect and investigate crimes and to apprehend those responsible for committing crimes. The police attempt to detect crimes through regular police patrols and by responding to complaints of victims. Special techniques are necessary to detect so-called victimless crimes (more appropriately termed "consensual" crimes, because persons involved are willing participants). To detect crimes such as drug dealing, gambling, and prostitution, police work as undercover officers to make arrests where the crimes are less visible to the public and where there are no victim reports. The law enforcement role includes enforcement of traffic laws and parking violations, and it is here that officers have the most interaction with the general public as law enforcers. To finalize their law enforcement role and ensure that suspects are brought to trial, police engage in interrogation of suspects, collection of physical evidence at a crime scene, and presentation of that evidence at trial.

Order Maintenance

The order-maintenance function of police involves crowd control, such as during parades, large public gatherings, music concerts, sports events in indoor and outdoor stadiums or patrolling on foot, on horseback, or in small or large vehicles, on streets, sidewalks, and in public parks. The order-maintenance function parallels the law enforcement role when officers intervene to control disorderly behavior. The order-maintenance role is less clear (both to the public and to many police) than the law enforcement role, mainly because the behaviors being controlled are less clearly defined. Disorderly behavior, for example, generally refers to behavior that disturbs the public peace, but the exact definition and an officer's determination whether the behavior warrants official intervention depends on the neighborhood and the time at which the disturbance occurs. The officer's role may be that of telling guests at a loud party to quite down or dispersing a group of juveniles who are loitering on a street corner or in front of a business establishment.

Service Function

The third role of police is that of providing services to the public. This includes providing aid or assistance to persons in need, such as calling a tow truck for a stranded motorist, transporting abandoned or neglected children to a hospital or shelter facility, or delivering a baby whose parents did not make it to the hospital on time. The service function often results in a combination of functions, such as when one officer transports abandoned children to a shelter and another officer locates the parent(s) and initiates a child abuse investigation (a law enforcement function). The service function more recently has come to include an education component, such as when police are assigned to schools to assist in the education of children as to the dangers of drugs and how to avoid drug abuse.

These three roles of police differ in a number of dimensions: criminal versus noncriminal, urgent versus routine, and dangerous versus relatively safe (Dorne and Gewerth, 1995). Police officers have differing views of the importance of the various roles and do not undertake these three functions with equal degrees of enthusiasm. Officers view the law enforcement function as the primary role, whereas order-maintenance and service tasks have typically been regarded with mixed feelings, ranging from ambivalence to disdain (Moore, 1992). Police are permitted to exercise a great deal of discretion in their duties; that is, they have the ability to choose between different courses of action, depending on their particular assignment.

Police Discretion and Police Roles

Employees in many organizations are given some discretionary authority and flexibility in carrying out job functions. In most organizations however, discretion among personnel at the lower levels is very limited, and flexibility in decision-making expands as one moves through up the organization. In police organizations the opposite is true; discretionary authority among police is greater at the lowest levels of the organization, giving the line-level police officer on patrol a considerable amount of discretion in carrying out and discharging his or her duties (Goldstein, 1977). In other organizations the actions of personnel are under close scrutiny. In police organizations, officers on patrol are out of sight of their superiors, and the low visibility means they are frequently beyond the commanding officers' control. Because of the considerable amount of discretion, much research and writing has been devoted to studying and understanding the nature of police discretion.

The nature of police discretion varies with different police roles. In law enforcement situations, police must resolve whether a crime occurred and whether there is sufficient evidence to justify stopping a suspect for questioning, taking into custody, or making an arrest. Officers receive extensive training in the law enforcement function, including thorough education on the legal statutes and the appropriate legal interventions they are authorized to make for law violations. Order-maintenance situations leave more room for police discretion, as public order and disorderly conduct are not as clearly defined. It is difficult or sometimes impossible to determine, for example, whether a loud exchange of words on the street, in a public gathering, or in a home amounts to a violation of the public order. It may depend, in fact, on the context and circumstances of the verbal exchange. Police decision making and discretion in the service function is equally difficult. The police role in service situations has generally not been discussed in police training manuals or in books and research articles on policing (Moore, 1992). Many police regard calls for service, such as rendering first aid or helping a stranded motorist, as a waste of time and interference with the real job of policing. Some police would maintain that calls for service are better handled by other agencies and individuals.

A number of arguments have been made for reevaluating the negative attitude toward the service function of police: (1) police response to requests for service might result in more effective law enforcement; (2) response to such calls may prevent a crime later; (3) response to service calls helps establish a positive community presence; and (4) response to service helps enhance the flow of information from community sources and aids in crime detection and prevention (Moore, 1992). The emergence of community policing has diminished to a great extent some of the earlier sense of frustration and resistance of police officers in fulfilling service functions. Community policing includes emphases on police–community relations, citizen input, team policing, crime problem solving, and crime prevention (see Cordner, 2005). With the emergence of community policing, officers have come to more readily accept that order maintenance and service functions are important functions of law enforcement. Police agencies that have adopted a community policing perspective accept and recognize that all three functions are equally important in carrying out effective police operations. Programs such as Drug Awareness Resistance Education (D.A.R.E.) and School Resource Officers (discussed later in this chapter) support community policing and offer a combination of service, order maintenance, and law enforcement functions.

Special Police Roles with Juveniles

The service functions of policing take on a special emphasis in relation to juveniles. Police are expected to protect children and to prevent delinquency (Sanborn and Salerno,

2005). Child protection may involve intervening in suspected cases of child neglect (being left at home alone or left inside a vehicle in cold or hot weather conditions), endangering a child's safety (failure to use a car seat or seat belts), or child abuse such as physical punishment that may involve serious injury or even death. Child neglect and abuse have been shown to have a relationship with status offenses such as runaway, which in turn often lead to more serious delinquency. The primary reason for the inclusion of status offenses in all juvenile codes in fact is for child protection and delinquency prevention. Laws giving police the authority to intervene in noncriminal behaviors such as runaway, truancy, and curfew violations are intended to protect them and prevent worse delinquent behavior. The child-protection and delinquency-prevention roles are primarily a service function of police, but are an essential part of law enforcement with juveniles, particularly in a community policing context. The child development and community policing model in New Haven, Connecticut, is a prime example of how police can forge a collaborative working relationship with public schools and mental health services to protect children from violence and identify and refer children involved in predelinquent activities (Marans and Schaefer, 1998).

Police Officers in Schools

Police have played an important role in assisting schools with law enforcement responsibilities. Officers on routine police patrol are involved in incidents ranging from truancy to juvenile crimes such as drug and weapon possession and student fights and assaults. Officers regularly drive by schools during night and weekend patrols to prevent burglary and vandalism to school property. Police departments have taken an active role in developing delinquency prevention programs since the early part of this century. The Police Athletic League (P.A.L.), for example, has an extensive history of established activities and programs in cities throughout the United States. Police presence in schools is an extension of delinquency-prevention efforts throughout the community. The role of police in schools has changed and become more prevalent in recent years. In 1996–1997, six percent of public schools reported having police or other law enforcement representatives stationed 30 hours or more at the school in a typical week during the school year; 12 percent did not have police at the school, but made them available as needed; and 78 percent of schools did not have any officers stationed at their schools (DeVoe et al., 2002: 136). Principals reported a greater presence of police in their schools in the 2000 School Survey on Crime and Safety. Schools that regularly used paid law enforcement or security were less likely to experience a violent incident than those that did not regularly have officers in the schools (62 percent vs. 80 percent) (Miller and Chandler, 2003: 18).

D.A.R.E.

One of the most recent and well-known prevention programs is the D.A.R.E. program, which has been implemented in schools throughout the United States. Originally begun by the Los Angeles Police Department, D.A.R.E. programs have been established in large and smaller cities throughout the country. Special juvenile officers undergo several weeks of training in order to be a D.A.R.E. officer and present the structured curriculum of educational materials to primarily 5th and 6th graders. Research on D.A.R.E. programs shows mixed results when evaluated on the basis of long-term drug and delinquency prevention

(Harmon, 1993; Ennett et al., 1994; Rosenbaum et al., 1994). D.A.R.E. programs never-theless are widely supported by educators and by police departments that sponsor the officers who conduct the courses. (D.A.R.E. is discussed in more depth in Chapter 12.)

School Resource Officers

Many school administrators have employed police officers full-time or part-time dur-ing school hours. The practice is more common in inner-city urban schools or in schools that have experienced an increase in juvenile crime activity. The costs are generally shared with the local police department, and the specific duties and responsibilities are agreed upon by the police department and the school system. The origin of police-school liaison officers has been traced to Liverpool, England, in 1951. The concept was soon introduced to North America, as the Flint, Michigan, school district hired police officers in 1958 and schools in British Columbia, Canada, began placing police-school liaison officers in many schools in 1972 (LaLonde, 1995: 20). School liaison officers in Canada are not armed and place more emphasis on the crime-prevention and educational role than on law enforce-ment and patrol functions (LaLonde, 1995). In summary, school liaison officers may:

•Counsel, advise, and talk informally with students

•Teach classes on alcohol and drug use prevention

•Advise school personnel and students on security precautions

•Offer safety and crime prevention education to students, staff, and parents

•Work to improve the safety and security of the school

•Gain students' trust and be aware of bullying behavior, harassment, alcohol and drug use, and gang activities

•Investigate, document, and record critical incidents

•Serve as a liaison between the school and the criminal justice system (LaLonde, 1995)

School police officers in the United States fulfill all of the above roles, but they are now usually called school resource officers (SROs). The Omnibus Crime Control and Safe Streets Act of 1968 (Part Q, Title I) defines the SRO as "a career law enforcement officer, with sworn authority, deployed in community-oriented policing, and assigned by the employ-ing police department or agency to work in collaboration with school and community-based organizations." In contrast with officers in Canada, SROs in the United States generally focus on traditional police functions and are usually armed, although not all officers may be in uniform. They patrol school grounds, parking lots, hallways, stairways and bathrooms; check student identification; handle trespassers, class cutters and truants; investigate criminal complaints; handle disruptive students; and prevent disturbances at after-school activities (Blauvelt, 1990: 6). Police assigned to schools also provide services beyond tra-ditional law enforcement functions. They are available to counsel students and faculty on crime and security issues and improve school safety and prevent crime through educational programs. Experts have recommended that school administrators should carefully assess the frequency and seriousness of crime and disruption in their schools before determining whether to hire police or security professionals (Blauvelt, 1990). School administrators and police officials should develop mutually agreeable policies for the specific duties and responsibilities of the school liaison officers. Larger metropolitan schools districts have developed an independent school district police force (Dorn, 2004). Regardless of the exact structure of the SRO program, the important factor is the selection of highly qualified officers and proper training for working in schools. The U.S. Department of Justice recently funded $68 million to be awarded through the Office of Community Oriented Policing Services (COPS) to hire and train 599 SROs in 289 communities throughout the nation (Girouard, 2001). The special funding is in recognition that the SRO's multifaceted role as law enforcement officer, counselor, teachers and liaison between law enforcement, schools, families, and the community requires training beyond that traditionally offered in police academies (Girouard, 2001).

SROs have been effective in helping to control disciplinary problems and school crime. A study comparing incidents before and after the placement of officers in schools showed a significant reduction in the number of crimes and disciplinary infractions and in suspensions related to such incidents (Johnson, 1999). Studies have found that SROs reduce the time and effort that school administrators and teachers spend addressing illegal and disruptive behavior; they support educational objectives through classroom presentations (Atkinson, 2001); they counsel students on behavioral and attitudinal issues relating to school security and delinquency prevention (Benigni, 2004); and they help provide a safe environment in public schools (May et al., 2004). SROs may be instrumental in helping to reduce the number of crime incidents in the neighborhood around schools and during nonschool hours. SROs have been able to obtain valuable information through their communication with students, which has helped in the investigation of crimes in the community. The most effective programs emphasize close working relationships between police, school staff, and students and clear communication regarding the police role, policies, and actions to be taken in crime incidents.

Do SROs "Criminalize" School Discipline?

Some researchers have expressed concerns about the greater participation of law enforcement and juvenile justice professionals in the schools, fearing that the presence of police and security officers in schools may actually interfere with student learning. In a study of New York City public schools, Devine (1996) concluded that fortress-like security is bad for students, for teachers, and for the educational process. Teachers complained about not being able to teach because of the loud noises of two-way radios of the officers in the hallways. Principals also expressed concerns about what was perceived by some as an unclear order of authority. Police who are employees of the local law enforcement agency report to their superiors, not to the school principal or superintendent, and this may create problems (Devine, 1996). Another concern is that the presence of SROs tends to result in their taking over disciplinary functions that have traditionally been a responsibility of teachers and principals. Because of concerns about safety, schools have become more dependent on the police to intervene not only in criminal matters, but also in disciplinary matters that used to be handled by teachers. Dohrn (2001) contends that incidents such as a minor tussle between students or locker graffiti might result in an arrest and possible prosecution, rather than school discipline utilizing a teachable moment and conflict resolution. A combination of school policies designed to reduce violence and the presence of police officers has had the effect of "criminalizing" a broad range of student misconduct that presents no real threat to school safety (Beger, 2003). The presence of SROs has had the effect of absolving teachers and principals of their responsibility for problem students. Behaviors that were once viewed as troublesome, disruptive, violations of school rules may now be handled more formally as a law enforcement matter (Bazemore et al., 2004). In too many cases the informal authority and decision-making discretion of educational professionals have been replaced by the formal controls of police. Giving precedence to formal control by school resource officers tends to weaken and replace the informal controls of education professionals. As police have been willing to exert more formal controls in schools, school officials seem to have gotten the message that social control is no longer their primary responsibility (Clear and Karp, 1999; Bazemore et al., 2004).

Police and Juvenile Offenders

Police are the first, and often the only, contact that most young people have with the juvenile justice system. Police are charged with preventing crime and enforcing the law. They are given the authority to arrest and to use physical force. Society entrusts a great deal of authority to police, but also expects a lot from them: from public safety, to detection of crimes, to apprehension of offenders, and all of this without violating constitutional rights. In reality, traditional police patrol does little to prevent crime. Police in most cases react to crime after it has already happened, responding to citizen calls, reporting to crime scenes, conducting investigations, and tracking and apprehending offenders. The fact that police are called upon for many services besides law enforcement makes their job even more difficult. Police handle many noncriminal matters, referred to as status offenses, such as incorrigibility (disobeying parents), running away, curfew violations, and truancy as well as nondelinquent juvenile matters such as neglect, abuse, and missing persons reports. Most urban police departments have special police units or juvenile bureaus for handling the increasing number of juvenile cases. Duties of special juvenile officers include taking missing children reports; examining runaway cases; investigating juvenile crimes; contacting and interviewing juveniles, their parents, school officials, and complainants regarding the circumstances of an offense; maintaining juvenile records; and appearing in juvenile court.

Juveniles are less predictable than adults and often exhibit less respect for the authority of officers. The immaturity of many youngsters means that they are more vulnerable to the "dares" of others, and they often engage in deviant behavior when in the company of their peers. Many young people view the police officer on patrol not as a deterrent to delinquent behavior, but as a challenge to avoid detection and confrontation while loitering at night or engaging in behaviors ranging from petty mischief to property damage and vandalism to more serious crimes of theft and assaults. The immaturity of youth, coupled with limited parental supervision and negative peer influence, presents special problems for police officers, who frequently encounter juveniles with little respect for law and authority. Juveniles also present a special problem for police because they are less cognizant of the consequences of their actions and the effects of their delinquent behavior on their victims, their parents and families, their peers, and themselves.

Police-Juvenile Relations

Juvenile crime presents a difficult challenge for police. Police officers encounter a wide variety of deviant and delinquent behavior among children and youth, ranging from minor status offenses to serious crimes. The majority of police encounters with juveniles are in response to minor offenses that involve an order maintenance function of law enforcement (Friedman et al., 2004). Regardless of the seriousness of the behavior, however, the nature of the police–juvenile encounter can make a significant difference on police–juvenile relations. Sherman (1997a) noted that police themselves often create a risk factor for crime by using "bad manners." Research evidence indicates that the less respectful police are toward suspects and citizens in general, the less people obey the law (Sherman, 1997a: 8-1). Juveniles are critical of police practices such as stopping and questioning them and asking them to "move on" and not loiter on street corners, parking lots, or in front of stores. African American and Hispanic youths and those living in urban areas are more critical of police than white students or those living in suburban or rural areas (Taylor et al., 2001). Students often have ambivalent or mixed feelings about police. Taylor et al. (2001) found that a majority of students believed that police are friendly and hard working, but they also believed that officers are racially prejudiced and dishonest. They did not believe that police officers contribute directly to the negative feelings, however. The reasons for juveniles' negative attitudes toward police are likely the inevitable result of police officers' fair but unpopular restrictions on young people's behaviors (Taylor, et al., 2001). Lieber, Nalla, and Farnsworth (1998) suggested that community policing practices and problem-oriented policing can positively influence youths' perceptions of police, but Hurst and Frank (2000) noted that attempting to involve youths in community-oriented policing is a challenge because of their negative views and disapproval of many police functions. Friedman and associates (2004) have noted that both police and youths' demeanors affect the perceived nature and outcomes of their encounters, so there is reason to believe that juveniles' negativity toward the police might have triggered officer disrespect, which in turn feeds juveniles' negative attitudes. In short, they believe that police–juvenile interactions are a two-way street. Young people react to how police officers treat them, and officers often respond in kind to juveniles' disrespectful behavior. Working with juveniles is a challenge, and police departments do well to provide officers with cultural awareness training to enhance their skills in working and interacting with juveniles (Friedman et al., 2004). Schools can also educate students about police responsibilities and procedures and the appropriate responses when interacting with police. D.A.R.E. and SROs have an opportunity to improve juvenile–police relations through better understanding of police roles and functions.

Police Decisions and Use of Discretion

Police have considerable discretionary power in handling juvenile matters, ranging from reprimand and release to transporting a juvenile to detention and referral to juvenile court. Discretion is important in police work, because the officer's decision to intervene in any suspected law violation is the first stage in the juvenile justice process. Officers use their discretion in deciding whether or not to take official actions with offending juveniles or simply order them to "move on," "break it up," or "get on home." Most police contact with juveniles is nonofficial, and police make an arrest and take juveniles into custody in only a small percentage of cases. In a study of police responses with juveniles in two cities, Myers (2002) found that police took juveniles into custody in only 13 percent of their encounters with them. Most of the police–juvenile encounters involved noncriminal matters, such as public disorder (22 percent), traffic offense (14 percent), nonviolent conflicts (9 percent), and suspicious situations (7 percent), and about one-fourth (27 percent) involved violent or nonviolent crimes (Myers, 2002: 123). A national report of juvenile arrests in 2002 revealed that 18 percent of arrests that could have been processed in the juvenile justice system were handled by police within the agency, and the majority were referred to the juvenile court (73 percent), with a small number referred directly to the criminal court (7 percent) (Snyder, 2004). The proportion of arrests referred to juvenile court has increased in the past 10 years, but that proportion is similar in cities, suburban counties, and rural counties.

Critics believe that police abuse their broad discretionary powers and base their decisions on factors other than the offense. Factors such as sex, race, socioeconomic status, and individual characteristics of the offender have been shown to make a difference in police officers' decisions as to whether or not to take official actions. Girls are less likely than boys to be arrested and referred to juvenile court, but they are often referred more than boys for status offenses such as running away or disobeying parents (Armstrong, 1977; Chesney-Lind, 1977). Researchers have reported differing results on the importance of race in police discretion. Some studies report few differences when controlling for offense seriousness and prior record. African Americans and other minority youths seem to be involved in more frequent and serious offenses than whites, so it is difficult to determine whether they are singled out more by police for official action. There is some evidence of racial bias, however, because minority youths have more often been targeted by police for official intervention (Wolfgang et al., 1972: 252). Some critics of police discretion also contend that lower-class youths are processed into the justice system for the same offenses for which middle- or upper-class juveniles are simply reprimanded and released to their parents. Police and juvenile officers justify this use of discretion on the basis that middle- and upper-class youths are more likely to be corrected without referral to the justice system because their parents have the resources to provide their children with the necessary supervision and corrective services. Merry Morash (1984) found that an older juvenile with a prior record who fits the image of a serious delinquent is more likely to be referred by police to the juvenile court. A juvenile's demeanor and attitude make a difference in a police officer's use of discretion. A youth who is polite and respectful is more likely to get off with a reprimand, while a negative and hostile attitude is likely to result in a court referral (Piliavin and Briar, 1964; Lundman et al., 1990). In addition to the characteristics and demeanor of the juvenile, police are also influenced by public pressure and press coverage. Newspaper articles that emphasize youth gangs and violence tend to heighten public fears and concern about juvenile crime, resulting in pressure on police to arrest and process juveniles to court.

Race as a Factor in Juvenile Arrests

The issue of race is a major concern in the criminal and juvenile justice systems. It is an undisputed fact that racial and ethnic minorities (especially African Americans) are disproportionately represented at each stage of the system: in police arrests, in jails and detention centers, in courts, and in correctional facilities. Research studies are mixed, however, as to whether that disproportionate representation is a result of racial bias in police arrest, prosecutors' decisions, and judicial sentencing (see, e.g., Wilbanks, 1987; Conley, 1994; Wordes et al., 1994). Black youth are overrepresented in juvenile arrests compared to their proportion of the population. Of all juvenile arrests for violent crimes in 2002, 55 percent involved white youth (Hispanics are an ethnic group and classified as whites) and 43 percent involved black youth; for property crime arrests the proportions were 70 percent whites and 27 percent black youth (Snyder, 2004: 9). The rate of arrests for violent crimes (per 100,000 juveniles in the racial group) in 2002 was much greater for blacks (736) than for whites (196), and the same differences existed for property crime arrests (2,448 for blacks vs. 1,308 for whites) (Snyder, 2002: 9). From 1980 through 2002 the black–white disparity in juvenile arrest rates for violent crimes declined.

The question remains: Is the overrepresentation of black juveniles in police arrest rates a result of racial bias, or is it a result of the greater involvement of black youths in violent crimes that are more likely to be reported, detected, and result in a police arrest? To answer this question, Pope and Snyder (2003) analyzed National Incident-Based Reporting System (NIBRS) data from law enforcement agencies in 17 states. They made no claim that the states were nationally representative, but the data used in the final analysis did represent a large sample of 102,905 juvenile offenders. The results of the study are interesting, because they found no significant effects of race in police arrest decisions, and they were able to identify some characteristics that differentiated between the crimes of white and nonwhite juvenile offenders. Compared to nonwhites, white juvenile offenders were:

• Less likely to have multiple victims
• More likely to act alone
• More likely to commit crimes indoors
• Less likely to possess a nonpersonal weapon (firearm, knife, or club)
• Less likely to offend against adults
• Equally likely to offend against females
• Less likely to offend against members of another race
• Equally likely to injure victims
• More likely to commit crimes against family members, equally likely to commit crimes against acquaintances, but less likely to commit crimes against strangers (Pope and Snyder, 2003: 4)

The findings revealed that the crime incident characteristics that increased the odds of arrest for violent crimes were largely the same for white and nonwhite offenders, with one important exception: victim's race was correlated with arrest probability for nonwhite juvenile offenders, but not for white offenders. A nonwhite juvenile offender was therefore more likely to be arrested if the victim was white than if the victim was nonwhite. The authors acknowledged that more research must be conducted on police arrest patterns using larger samples that may be more representative of the nation. It is quite possible that arrest patterns may differ among states and within regions of states and the nation.

Race and ethnic background may be a factor in police decisions to arrest juvenile offenders, but based on research evidence it is clear that several other factors influence officers' decisions. The factors influencing police officers' decisions to arrest a juvenile or to take less formal actions without court referral include relate to the:

• Offense (seriousness, type, time of day, gang-related, use of weapon)
• Youth's record or status (prior police contact or arrest, school record, probation status)

•Offender (age, gender, race, social class, demeanor)

•Complainant (present at the scene, desire to prosecute, age, gender, and race)

•Location of the offense (type of neighborhood, low- or high-crime area)

•Parents (attitude, present at the scene or at home, concern, and ability to supervise)

•Officer (training and experience, view of justice system and diversion, workload)

•Police department (enforcement policies, community policing, or problem-solving emphasis) (Sanborn and Salerno, 2005: 137–139)

Police discretion is necessary, and the juvenile justice system could not function without some use of discretion. Juvenile courts in urban areas have a backlog of cases, probation officers' caseloads are too heavy for them to provide adequate supervision, and correctional facilities are becoming overcrowded. The system must concentrate on those juvenile offenders who pose the greatest risk and need official intervention to prevent further offending.

Police Diversion and Status Offenders

Diversion of minor juvenile offenders and deinstitutionalization of status offenders have been promoted as effective delinquency-prevention strategies by federal legislation for the past two decades. The Juvenile Justice and Delinquency Prevention (JJDP) Act of 1974 promoted the diversion of juvenile offenders from the justice system and referral of those youths requiring intervention to community-based programs. *Diversion* had been recommended by the 1967 President's Commission on Law Enforcement and Administration of Justice as a process of referring minor juvenile offenders to community treatment programs in lieu of formal juvenile justice processing. Criminologists argued that processing minor offenders through the justice system had a stigmatizing effect that was likely to perpetuate rather than reduce the chance of further delinquent behavior. Many experts noted that too much was expected of the juvenile court system. Some believed that court referrals should be restricted to juvenile offenses that would be crimes if committed by adults. Status offenders should be diverted to agencies outside the formal justice process, which would provide services to meet the needs of at-risk children. Youth Service Bureaus (YSBs) were among the diversion agencies developed through federal funding to provide an alternative source for police referral of minor status offenders. These programs offer counseling, job treatment, educational help, job assistance, and recreational opportunities for youth.

Deinstitutionalization of status offenders (DSO) was a major provision of the JJDP Act. The Act required states to provide that juveniles who were charged with offenses that would not be criminal if committed by an adult not be placed in juvenile detention or correctional facilities, but rather in shelter facilities. Amendments to the original act (in 1977, 1980, and 1992) required that states receiving JJDP Act grant funds provide assurance that they were taking action to remove status offenders and nonoffenders from detention and correctional facilities and not detaining juveniles in adult jails (see Holden and Kapler, 1995). Solomon Kobrin and Malcolm Klein (1982) conducted a national evaluation of DSO programs and found mixed results. One problem was the definition of status offenders. They found that "pure" status offenders were relatively rare; most status offenders had prior delinquent experiences. Some areas limited their programs to pure status offenders, so many otherwise eligible youth were not served by the programs. Another problem was "net widening." In some areas the number of juveniles referred to court actually increased, and many youngsters whose behavior did not justify police intervention were referred to diversion programs. Thus, many status offenders who would have previously been handled by police or intake probation officers through a "reprimand and release" were drawn into diversion or DSO programs. Diversion and alternatives to detention programs have for the most part been effective in reforming the juvenile justice system. Anne Schneider (1985b) conducted a comprehensive national evaluation of DSO programs and found that they were successful in significantly reducing the number of status offenders in detention and institutions. Diversion and DSO are not a panacea for delinquency prevention, but shelters and foster care are as effective and much less expensive than detention and juvenile institutions (see Holden and Kapler, 1995; Raley, 1995).

Alternatives to Police Arrest and Custody

A police officer may refer a minor offender to a youth services bureau, a community agency such as a big brother or big sister program, or a similar delinquency-prevention program. In the majority of cases where police have reason to believe that a juvenile has committed an offense, the youth will be taken to the police department juvenile bureau for questioning, may be fingerprinted and photographed, and then be taken to the intake unit of the juvenile probation department where a decision will be made whether to detain the youth or release to the parents.

•*Questioning, warning and release in the community*: The least severe sanction is when an officer questions a youth for a possible minor offense and gives a warning and reprimand on the street without taking formal actions.

•*Station adjustment*: Police may take a youth into custody and to the station, record the alleged minor offense and actions taken, give the youth an official reprimand, and release the youth to the parents. The parents are generally contacted first and may be present when the youth is reprimanded. In smaller cities the youth may be placed under police supervision for a short period of time.

•*Referral to a diversion agency*: Police may release and refer a juvenile to a YSB, big brother/big sister program, runaway center, or a mental health agency. Diverting minor offenders from the juvenile justice system to a YSB that provides counseling and social services is considered preferable for many first-time offenders and troubled youths.

•*Issuing a citation and referring to juvenile court*: The police officer can issue a citation and refer the youth to juvenile court. The intake probation officer accepts the referral, contacts the parents if the police have not already done so, and releases the youth to the parents on the condition that they will report to the court when ordered to do so. The intake officer then determines whether a formal delinquency petition should be filed. In some states the decision is made by the prosecuting attorney assigned to the juvenile court.

•*Taking to a detention center or shelter home*: The police officer can issue a citation, refer the youth to the juvenile court, and take him or her to a detention center. The intake officer at the detention center then decides whether to hold the juvenile or release him or her to the parents. Juveniles are detained when they are considered dangerous, when there is a lack of parental supervision, or when there is a high probability that they will not report to the court when ordered to do so. If a detention center is felt to be too restrictive and an appropriate parent or foster home is not available, the youth may be placed in a shelter care facility, which might be either a private home or a group home. Most states now provide for a detention hearing within a day after the youth's referral in which a judge or referree must determine whether there is sufficient reason to continue to detain the juvenile. In cities without a separate juvenile detention center, juveniles who cannot be released to their parents are confined in a separate section of the county jail or may be transported to a juvenile facility in another county. There has been a national effort to remove juveniles from adult jails. Removing juveniles from their homes and detaining them in juvenile centers is considered a last resort.

The Special Case of Curfew Laws

Many cities have implemented curfew laws in an effort to get young people off the streets at night, reduce their opportunities to get into trouble, and therefore prevent delinquency. Curfew laws generally apply only to youths under the age of 16, and the hours during which they are required to be off the streets may vary according to age (the limit may be 10 p.m. for those under 14 and 11 p.m. or midnight for those aged 15 or 16, for example). Violation of curfew laws is a status offense, illegal only for those of juvenile age, and not punishable by referral to juvenile court. Police responses to curfew violations vary, but may include a warning to get home, telephoning the parents, delivering the youth to their home in a patrol car, or bringing the youth to a shelter, where parents are asked to come and pick them up. Evidence of the effectiveness of curfew laws varies, with some researchers claiming that juvenile crime is reduced (McDowall et al., 2000), while others found no evidence of crime reduction that could be explained by the curfew (Reynolds et al., 2000). Curfew laws may have little effect on juvenile crime because there is evidence that a significant proportion of juvenile crimes occur immediately after school hours (3 p.m.) and before 6 p.m. (Sickmund et al., 1997). Some cities have attempted to enforce daytime, after-school curfews, but these present countless problems in affecting youth who are not or would not engage in criminal activity (Bannister et al., 2001).

Police and Juveniles' Legal Rights

The law of arrest or taking into custody is generally the same for juveniles as for adults. A police officer must have "probable cause" to believe that the suspected juvenile has committed an offense. Probable cause requires more than mere suspicion, but not absolute certainty to take a suspect into custody. Juveniles, like adults, have certain procedural rights after being taken into custody, particularly with regard to searches and interrogations.

The Fourth Amendment right against unlawful search and seizure applies when a police officer stops a juvenile for questioning as a suspect in a crime. We discussed in Chapter 8 the procedures required for police officers and school officials to conduct a search of student's bookbags or pockets for unlawful drugs or weapons. The legal procedures governing search and seizure of a juvenile who is a suspect in a crime are essentially the same as that for adults. A police officer is allowed to conduct a pat-down search for weapons that suspects in a crime may be carrying. If other illegal substances such as drugs are found during a search for weapons, the search and seizure will generally be held admissible in court. In circumstances where a juvenile is not a suspect in a crime and has not consented to have his or her person or property searched, then police must obtain a valid search warrant.

Under the U.S. Supreme Court case of *Miranda v. Arizona* (384 U.S. 436) police officers are required to notify suspects of their rights before interrogation, their right to remain silent and that anything they say may be held against them in court, and their right to speak with an attorney. The 1967 Supreme Court case of *In re Gault* (387 U.S. 1) made the right against self-incrimination and right to counsel applicable to juveniles, but failed to specify whether a juvenile could waive the Miranda rights intelligently and knowingly. The 1979 Supreme Court case of *Fare v. Michael C.* (442 U.S. 23) applied the "totality of circumstances" standard to the interrogation of juveniles. The case involved a juvenile who asked for his probation officer, but not an attorney, while being interrogated by police. When his request was denied he continued to willingly talk to police, thus implicating himself in the crime. The Supreme Court ruled that Michael C. appeared to understand his rights, and his conviction was upheld by a narrow 5–4 decision. The Court thus applied the *Miranda* ruling the same way for juveniles as for adults: juveniles may remain silent or ask for an attorney, but not for a probation officer. Despite the Supreme Court decision regarding juvenile interrogation, most state jurisdictions now require police to give juveniles a Miranda warning prior to any custodial interrogation (see Sanborn and Salerno, 2005).

Implicit in the Miranda warning is a constitutional requirement that all confessions and statements be given voluntarily (Sanborn and Salerno, 2005). Police interrogation of juveniles therefore involves four important issues and concerns: (1) whether a juvenile has made an informed and voluntary consent to give an confession or statement; (2) whether juveniles who are told by their parents to talk to the police have voluntarily waived their rights; (3) whether the questioning of juveniles in school is a "custodial" interrogation; and (4) whether school resource officers are school officials or police officials.

First, a number of studies have examined the issue of juveniles' understanding of their constitutional rights. Thomas Grisso (1981) conducted research on a sample of juveniles who had been questioned by police in St. Louis. Although most of them had waived their Miranda rights, Grisso found that most of those 16 years of age or younger did not adequately understand their Miranda rights in order to make an informed, intelligent waiver. Many jurisdictions now require that a parent, legal guardian, or attorney be present during any police questioning before any confession is admissible in court. The Supreme Court ruling in the *Gault* case also required that the parents be immediately informed when a juvenile is taken into custody, either by the officer who took the juvenile into custody, the juvenile bureau officer, or the court intake officer.

Second, Sanborn and Salerno (2005) have noted that when juveniles talk to police after being told to do so by their parents, they may be doing so involuntarily, and yet appellate courts have refused to declare these waivers involuntary. The fact that statements to police could be used to convict juveniles in criminal court is a matter of concern. The parents' intentions may be for their child to be honest, held accountable, and/or receive needed control and supervision, but an overriding concern is that juveniles' rights not be ignored in the process.

A third issue is whether the questioning of juveniles in school is a "custodial" interrogation that should require a Miranda warning by school officials. Our discussion of students' rights above (and in the previous chapter) suggests that the answer is a simple one: only police officials are required to give a Miranda warning. The U.S. Supreme Court ruling in *T.L.O.* has not provided a final and definitive answer to the question, however. Two factors that prompt a requirement for a Miranda warning are present in the questioning of a student in school: custody and a police agent. First, students are legally required to attend school and to remain in school, and therefore arguably are in quasi-custody. Second, the *T.L.O.* decision suggested that school officials are quasi-police and have the authority to take actions similar to police officials to maintain order and safety in schools. Sanborn and Salerno (2005: 149) argue that the quasi-control status of students and the quasi-police status of school officials make seem to make "quasi-Miranda" warnings necessary for questioning students. The fourth and final point is an extension of this third point: Are police officers school officials or police officials?

Are SROs School Officials or Police Officials?

We have noted the different standards required for a search by police officers as compared with school principals as determined by the U.S. Supreme Court in *T.L.O.* One of the first cases to address the distinctions between school resource officers and school officials was *People v. Dilworth* (661 N.E. 2d310 [Ill 1996]). *In Dilworth*, a school liaison officer confiscated a flashlight from a student, searched it, and discovered a powdery substance that was later determined to be cocaine. At trial the student moved to suppress the cocaine evidence, arguing that the search was a violation of the Fourth and Fourteenth Amendments. In its ruling the court outlined three basic categories of school searches that involve police officers: (1) those in which school officials initiate the search and act with minimal officer involvement, (2) those involving a school police or liaison officer acting on his or her own authority, and (3) those in which outside police initiate a search. The court reasoned that the first two types of searches typically permit the lesser search standard of reasonable suspicion, whereas the third typically requires probable cause.

The court in *Dilworth* upheld the search based on reasonable suspicion. It relied heavily on the Supreme Court's own language in *T.L.O.* permitting reasonable suspicion searches of students by "a teacher or other school official." Because the officer was assigned to the school on a full-time basis, he was recognized as a "school official." A dissenting opinion in the case, however, argued that the officer in question should not have been construed as a school official for Fourth Amendment purposes because his primary responsibility (as a police officer) was to investigate and prevent criminal activity. Four points were made in support of the dissent: (1) the officer arrested the student and took him to the police station; (2) he was not a member of the school's security staff (which the school did have); (3) although he was listed in the school handbook as a member of the support staff, he was in fact a police officer assigned to city patrol to investigate and prevent criminal activity; and (4) he acted as a police officer in the case: chasing, detaining, searching, arresting, and interrogating the suspect (after a Miranda warning).

The Dilworth case raises more questions than it answers. Courts have therefore looked to at least four factors to help determine whether student searches in school require the high standard of probable cause or only reasonable suspicion (Mueller et al., 2005). First, courts have considered officers' terms of employment and areas of responsibility to clarify their status and to determine whether they are school employees or police department employees. This approach has unfortunately not satisfactorily answered that question. Pinard (2003: 1084) has noted that even when officers assigned to a school are responsible to a law enforcement agency, some courts have declared them to be comparable to school officials and therefore allowed them to search students based only on reasonable suspicion.

The second factor that courts consider when determining the appropriate level of suspicion required for searches involving school resource officers is the underlying purpose of the search. If the purpose is to uncover evidence that the student has violated school rules, courts typically employ the lesser standard of reasonable suspicion (see Stefkovich and Miller, 1999). If, however, the purpose is to investigate a criminal violation, courts often require probable cause. Criminal and school rule violations are, of course, not mutually exclusive. Criminal law violations are also violations of school rules, but school rule violations do not necessarily constitute criminal law violations. This distinction does help reduce the tendency for officers to become school disciplinarians. Law enforcement officers arguably should focus on law violations, and not on lesser matters.

A third issue courts have considered is the level and extent of the officer's involvement in the search. For example, did the officer initiate the search on his or her own without the knowledge or consent of school administrators? If a school administrator, in the presence of an officer, conducted a search, what role did the officer play during the search? Rulings in this area generally indicate that as the officer's involvement and participation in the search increases, so too does the likelihood that courts will require the higher standard of probable cause (see *F.P. v. State*, 528 So. 3d 1253 [Fla. Dist Ct. App. 1998]; *State v. Twayne H.*, 933 P.2d 251 [N.M. Ct App. 1997]). Conversely, when the officer's participation is minimal, the reasonable suspicion standard will often suffice (see *State v. N.G.B.*, 806 So. 2d 567 [Fla. Dist. Ct. App. 2002]).

Safety concerns are a fourth factor in determining the legality of a school search. Courts have been willing to grant school officials "a certain degree of flexibility" to seek the assistance of law enforcement officers when faced with potentially dangerous situations without sacrificing the more lenient and flexible reasonable suspicion standard. For example, in the case of *In re Alexander B.* (220 Cal. App. 3d. 1572 [1990]), the California Appellate Court upheld a police search based on reasonable suspicion when the school's dean directed officers to search a group of students after receiving a report that one of them had a weapon. Here the court defended its ruling by pointing to the California state constitution, which reads in part that "All students and staff of public . . . schools have the inalienable right to attend campuses which are safe, secure and peaceful." In a similar case, a Wisconsin court held that "school officials not only educate students . . . but they have a responsibility to protect those students and their teachers from behavior that threatens their safety and the integrity of the learning process" (*In re Angelia D.B.* 564 N.W. 2d 685 [Wis. 1997]). In summary, various state courts have been willing to apply the reasonable suspicion standard to searches performed by school resource officers when the search is conducted at the behest of a school official. This may actually be an appropriate standard given that (1) most of the searches in question involve students in possession of weapons at school and (2) school officials are not presumed to have the necessary skills and training to deal with such dangerous situations.

School Safety Versus Privacy Rights

It has become readily apparent that students, like the general public, have been expected to give up more and more privacy rights for safety concerns. Recent events have tipped the balance on security versus privacy. In the wake of airplane hijackings and the terrorist attacks on New York and Washington, DC (9/11/2001), passengers now undergo rigorous security checks at airports. School shooting incidents have had a similar effect on school security. There is no question about the vital importance of public and school safety, and although many complain about lengthy security clearances and personal inconvenience, few challenge them. We have noted the range and intensity of school law enforcement and security procedures put in place recently in schools throughout the United States, many of them without clear evidence of need or effectiveness. The courts have generally supported the trend toward safety over privacy rights.

The U.S. Court of Appeals in the case of *Shade v. City of Farmington* (309 F.3d 1054, [8th Cir., 2002]) provides an example of how far they are willing to tilt the balance of safety over privacy rights. In *Shade*, a group of students were being transported by bus from their alternative technical school to an auto body repair shop in a neighboring community. Along the way, appellant Shade attempted to open an orange juice container with a knife he borrowed from another student. The bus driver witnessed Shade with the knife and upon arriving at the auto body shop the bus driver telephoned the school resource office. The officer subsequently searched all the males on the bus; the knife was located (on its owner) and was confiscated. Shade was the person charged with possessing a dangerous weapon on school property and he was expelled. On appeal, the U.S. Court of Appeals upheld the search even though it was based only on reasonable suspicion and conducted off school grounds. Safety concerns are clearly not only of high priority in schools but extend to school transportation and activities away from campus; the presence of SROs and law enforcement has resulted in school rule violations being handled as official legal sanctions rather than school disciplinary actions (Mueller et al., 2005). Critics (see e.g., Beger, 2003; Bazemore et al., 2004) have questioned the current trend of law enforcement taking over the discipline functions in schools. This trend is not universal, and many law enforcement and juvenile probation agencies are working with schools to implement a more balanced approach such as restorative justice, conflict resolution (see Chapter 12).

Fingerprinting, Photographing, and Records

Juvenile justice procedures following an arrest and taking into custody are different from those for adult offenders, particularly in regard to fingerprinting, photographing, and maintaining records. Restrictions have been placed on those procedures with juveniles. Juvenile justice philosophy recognizes the immaturity of youth and that offenses committed as juveniles should not be held against them after becoming adults. Restrictions on fingerprint and photo records are intended for the purpose of not treating juvenile offenders as criminals, to reduce the stigma that may be attached to such records, and to minimize the adverse effects of a juvenile offense on a young person's schooling and employment opportunities. Some state juvenile codes require that judges approve the fingerprinting and photographing of juveniles, particularly before the court has entered an adjudication decision. Some state juvenile statutes limit these procedures to juveniles arrested for felony crimes, and others leave the decision to individual police department policy. The National Advisory Commission on Criminal Justice Standards and Goals (1977) recommended that juvenile fingerprints and photographs be taken only for evidence and investigation of specific crimes, that they be used and recorded only by the local police department and not sent to a central records depository such as the FBI, and that they be destroyed once the investigation is complete or when the juvenile is no longer under juvenile court supervision. Some of the original precautions against treating juveniles differently from adults and keeping all juvenile records separate are currently being examined and questioned as many juvenile justice procedures are becoming "criminalized" (see Feld, 1993, Feld, 1999: 233). Several changes have occurred since the 1990s in juvenile court procedures, resulting in fewer restrictions on juvenile records, as lawmakers have moved to treat serious juvenile offenders more like adult criminals. At least 16 states have abolished the court order requirement for fingerprints and photos of arrested juveniles, lowered or eliminated the age requirement, increased the types of eligible offenses, and even required prints and photos of juvenile offenders in some cases (Sanborn and Salerno, 2005: 150). We will discuss in the next chapter how the lifting of restrictions on juvenile records may have far-reaching consequences, as those records are increasingly being used to enhance young adult offenders' sentences in criminal court.

Summary

The juvenile justice process differs from the legal process for adults in a number of key areas. Police respond differently to younger, minor juvenile offenders and are actively involved in a variety of delinquency-prevention programs. Police work with juveniles presents special challenges for law enforcement, given the immaturity and impulsive nature of youth and the fact that their minority age status and limited understanding of the legal process requires special procedures for taking into custody, interrogation, and searches. Law enforcement agencies have been actively involved in delinquency-prevention efforts in communities and schools, and these have been somewhat effective in helping to improve relations between youth and police, possibly reducing some delinquent involvement. Law enforcement presence in schools has increased dramatically throughout the United States. SROs initially began with an educational emphasis, but their role has evolved into one that is now focused more on school security and discipline. The police role in juvenile crime and in schools will continue to evolve and develop in response to statutory and case law, community policing initiatives, and collaborative agreements with the community and the schools.

10

The Juvenile Court

History and Development of the Juvenile Court

The first juvenile court in the United States was established in Chicago, Illinois, in 1899. The juvenile justice system was established on the principle of individualized justice and focused on rehabilitation of youthful offenders. While due process protections were considered important, they were considered secondary in importance given the court's emphasis on care, treatment, and rehabilitation for juveniles. It was believed that youths could be held responsible for their unlawful behavior and society could be protected through an informal justice system that focused on treatment and "the best interests of the child." For the majority of juvenile offenders, this approach is still considered to be appropriate and effective. The majority of juvenile crimes range from status offenses to property offenses and drug offenses.

The original intentions of the juvenile court were to act in the best interests of the child in an informal, caring environment. These intentions, however, often led to arbitrary decisions. Under the guise of treatment and rehabilitation, juveniles often received sentences that were longer and more punitive than if they were an adults and had committed a comparable offense. The practice continued for more than 50 years until the procedural informality of the juvenile court was questioned by the United States Supreme Court in the case of *Kent v. United States*, 383 U.S. 541, 566 (1966), noting that a child receives "neither the protections accorded to adults nor the solicitous care and regenerative treatment postulated for children" (Id. at 566), and the informal procedures were condemned in the case of *In re Gault* (387 U.S. 1, 1967). The Court mandated several legal procedures that were common to the criminal court, such as formal written notice of the charge against the young offender and the right to notice and counsel, to question witnesses, and to protection against self-incrimination.

A century after the origin of the juvenile court there is considerable debate over the goals and legal procedures for dealing with juvenile offenders. The juvenile justice system has come under increasing scrutiny as juveniles are increasingly involved in violent crimes, school violence, gang-related violence, and assaults with weapons resulting in fatalities and serious injuries. Despite the fact that juveniles are involved in a relatively small number of murders each year, violent crime committed by juveniles elicits widespread media coverage. The public and political/legislative response to juvenile violence has been to demand more accountability and punishment resembling that of the criminal justice system. The Supreme Court decisions that began with the 1966 *Kent* case were intended to correct what Justice Abe Fortas referred to as juveniles' receiving the "worst of both worlds"—neither due process protection, nor the helpful treatment that was promised (383 U.S. 541, at 566). The legal changes that began in response to the Supreme Court's *Kent* and *Gault* decisions have had some unintended consequences, however. Barry Feld (2003) has argued that the changes have culminated in "get-tough" law reforms directed at juvenile offenders, and the more punitive legal reforms fall disproportionately on minority juvenile offenders. One century after the development of the first juvenile court, the system faces a multitude of challenges and questions, particularly in the form of prosecutorial and legislative waiver of juvenile offenders and transfers to adult criminal court. We will examine those issues and questions following an overview of the juvenile court process.

Juvenile Court Procedures

Court Intake Procedure

Referrals to the juvenile court are usually made by a police officer, but they may also be made by school officials and truant officers. The intake unit of the court serves as a preliminary screening process. The intake procedure is done by one or more probation officers, who determine whether a petition should be filed for adjudication of delinquency. In some jurisdictions the decision whether to file a delinquency petition is made in consultation with the prosecutor. The intake procedure is important in the juvenile court process, because many courts have promoted the policy that it is in the best interests of the juvenile and the community to place the youngster under "informal adjustment," a type of short-term unofficial supervision or make a referral to social services or a community agency. Many court officials believe that unless the juvenile has committed a serious offense or has a prior record, it is better to handle the case informally, short of adjudication and formal probation.

When a case is referred to the intake unit of the juvenile court, the intake officer must verify the juvenile's age to determine that the court has jurisdiction over the case. The officer will also review the report of the police officer, or other referring agency, to ascertain that it is an appropriate referral to the court. The next step is to conduct a preliminary investigation to determine whether the case may best be processed informally or petitioned to the court. The officer generally interviews the juvenile and the parent(s) or legal guardian and may contact the complainant in the case, school officials, or other parties who may provide relevant information about the juvenile and the particular case. In many jurisdictions the prosecuting attorney makes the legal decision as to whether the alleged offense should be adjudicated in court and whether there is sufficient evidence to do so. The case is dismissed if the court does not have jurisdiction, the case is weak, or the intake officer's preliminary investigation raises questions about the need to file a petition for delinquency. Informal adjustment is recommended for status offenders and for juveniles charged with minor offenses. The intake officer may require a short period of supervision or payment of restitution for damaged or stolen property or may refer the juvenile to a social agency or youth services bureau for guidance and supervision. The case may be dismissed at that point or remain open pending the juvenile's positive adjustment.

Adjudication Hearing

The adjudication hearing is the fact-finding part of the hearing. The judge will first determine if the juvenile understands his or her rights, and the charges are read by the prosecuting attorney. The judge asks the juvenile if he or she understands the charges and wishes to be represented by legal counsel as well as whether he or she wants a full hearing or is willing to waive that right and accept the adjudication of delinquency (similar to a guilty plea). Many urban juvenile courts require the appearance of officers and witnesses only for full hearings in order to streamline the court docket. If the juvenile wants a full hearing, the adjudication is then rescheduled so that the police officer, complainant, and any witnesses can be present to testify. The adjudication hearing would also be rescheduled for juveniles requesting a jury trial, although few states provide for the right to a jury trial for juveniles. The U.S. Supreme Court ruled in the 1971 case of *McKiever v. Pennsylvania* (403 U.S. 528) that it was not a constitutional right in juvenile proceedings, and jury trials are rare even in those states that provide for them.

In the 1967 *Gault* decision, the Supreme Court held that juveniles and their parents must be given adequate notice in writing of the charge, the right to legal counsel, and written notice of when they are to appear in court. The ideals stated in that case have yet to make a significant impact on juvenile court practices throughout the nation. Feld (1988a) studied legal representation in six midwestern states and reported that in three of them only about one-half or fewer of the juveniles charged and adjudicated were represented by legal counsel. The American Bar Association–Institute of Judicial Administration recommended that juveniles should have the right to effective counsel at all stages of the proceedings and that this right should be mandatory and not waiveable (1980b: 81). Juveniles are allowed to waive their right to legal counsel in many jurisdictions. The Minnesota statute (Sec. 260.155), for example, states that: "Waiver of any right . . . must be an express waiver intelligently made by the child after the child has been fully and effectively informed of the right being waived." The court must determine if a juvenile who waived the rights fully understood the rights and was capable of making an informed, voluntary waiver.

Serious questions have been raised as to whether juveniles can make an informed, intelligent, and voluntary waiver of their 5th and 6th Amendment rights regarding self-incrimination, legal counsel, and to due process rights in a full hearing. There is evidence in fact that many juveniles do not have adequate knowledge and understanding of the law to make an informed waiver of their rights (Feld, 1989; Bishop, 2004). We noted in the previous chapter the concerns regarding juveniles' waiver of their Miranda rights during police questioning. In a sample of St. Louis youth who had been questioned by police, Grisso (1981) found that most of those 14 years and under and one-third to one-half of the 15- and 16-year-olds lacked the necessary competence to waive their rights to silence and counsel (1981: 194). In a partial replication of Grisso's research, Lawrence (1983) conducted interviews and collected survey data from a sample of youths, their parents, attorneys, and probation officers immediately following their appearance in juvenile court. A third of the juveniles had only a poor understanding, and fewer than one-half had only a fair understanding of their right to remain silent and to have legal counsel. There was no significant difference in legal understanding between the juveniles and their parents. This raises doubts about whether parents can make an intelligent, informed waiver of their child's legal rights. The study was conducted in an urban juvenile court in a south-western state that requires all juveniles who appear in court to be accompanied by an attorney. Lawrence assessed the roles of attorneys and probation officers and found that probation officers often play a more important role in explaining juveniles' legal rights, primarily because they had spent more time with the youth before the court hearing and were more aware of their level of legal understanding. Based on the finding that attorneys seemed to overestimate the extent of juvenile clients' understanding of their legal rights and the court process, some recommendations were made:

> [T]he appointment of legal counsel at an earlier point in the juvenile justice process is recommended as a means of enhancing juveniles' understanding of the law and the legal process, and ensuring that any waiver of their legal rights is an informed waiver with a full understanding of the possible consequences of the waiver. Earlier appointment of legal counsel would also reduce the wide variation in the quality of legal counsel and the amount of time attorneys are able to spend in case preparation (Lawrence, 1983: 57).

Barry Feld (1989) examined a sample of juveniles against whom petitions were filed for delinquency and status offenses in Minnesota in 1986 and found that more than half of the juveniles did not have lawyers. He was particularly concerned that nearly one-third of juveniles who received out-of-home placement and more than one-fourth of those incarcerated in secure institutions were not represented by legal counsel (1989: 1323). The U.S. Supreme Court in the 1979 case of *Scott v. Illinois* (440 U.S. 367) and the Minnesota Supreme Court in the 1967 case of *State v. Borst* (154 N.W. 2d 888) held that it was not proper to incarcerate an adult offender without legal representation or without a valid waiver of counsel. In many cases juveniles are clearly receiving less justice and more punishment than adult offenders. Feld (1989) questioned whether the typical Miranda advisory and the following waiver of rights under the "totality of the circumstances" is sufficient to assure a valid waiver of counsel by juveniles. The issue is further complicated by the finding that juveniles who are represented by counsel tend to receive more severe dispositions than nonrepresented juveniles (Bortner, 1982; Feld, 1988). A number of possible explanations have been suggested for this finding (see Feld, 1988: 419–420), but clearly more research is needed on the question of legal representation for juveniles.

Disposition Hearing

Once the juvenile has been adjudicated delinquent, the next stage in the court process is the disposition, comparable to the sentencing phase in adult criminal court. Juvenile court proceedings are considered "bifurcated" in the sense that the adjudication and disposition hearings are separate. Separating the hearings allows time for the probation officer to write a social history or predispositional report to assist the court in decision making. It has been common practice in many courts for the disposition hearing to proceed immediately following adjudication. In this case, the probation officer has completed the predisposition report prior to both hearings. The disposition hearing is more informal than the adjudication hearing. The judge asks for the probation officer's report, which is based on interviews with the child and the parents and may include information from school officials, other social service agencies, and mental health professionals. The report examines such factors as the child's family structure and quality of parental supervision; peer relationships; attendance, grades, and behavior in school; participation in school and community activities; degree of maturity and responsibility; attitude toward authority figures; and previous court or police involvement. The disposition hearing may include testimony and cross-examination of the probation officer and any other persons who have provided information in the report. Juveniles may have legal counsel and may challenge the facts and information presented in the predisposition report. The most important factors in the disposition hearing are the seriousness of the offense and the juvenile's prior record. The social background information contained in the probation officer's report and the dispositional options available to the court are also important factors in the court disposition.

The dispositional alternatives available to juvenile courts vary considerably, with urban courts having more options available. The primary alternatives include:

1. *Dismissal*: Even though there may have been sufficient evidence to adjudicate a juvenile, a judge can dismiss the case if there is insufficient evidence that the child needs formal supervision by the court.

2. *Court diversion alternatives*: Many state juvenile codes now include provisions that allow for suspension of the formal adjudication or disposition process, and the juvenile may be supervised under "informal adjustment" by a community agency (preadjudication) or by a probation officer (predispositional). The case may be terminated after 6 months of successful adjustment, or may be returned to court for adjudication and disposition. Mediation is an alternative for resolving conflicts and disputes outside the courtroom. Mediation can take place as an alternative to trial and adjudication or, after a finding of guilt, to determine the disposition and often to establish restitution conditions. Mediation sessions are arranged for victims who are willing to meet with the offender and are facilitated by a trained mediator. The Victim Offender Reconciliation Program (VORP) is a form of mediation that has operated in a number of courts for more than two decades (see Coates, 1990). If a settlement is reached, the mediator writes out the terms of the agreement, and both parties sign it. If the parties cannot make an agreement, the case may be referred back to the court. There are several benefits of mediation: (1) victims have an important role in the process, with an opportunity to express feelings associated with the crime and the impact of the damages and costs of the crime; (2) the offender is confronted with the responsibility for the crime, the impact on the victim, and has an opportunity to make restitution for the wrongful actions; (3) court backlogs can be reduced, and judges have an additional sentencing tool that is often more effective than court-ordered conditions. There is some evidence that offenders involved in mediation are more likely to satisfactorily fulfill restitution conditions and are less likely to reoffend.

3. *Probation*: The child may be released to the parents with orders to report to a probation officer. Probation supervision includes several conditions and rules that must be followed, including an order to attend school regularly and obey all school rules and regulations. Juveniles with a history of behavioral or academic performance problems in school may be ordered to attend an alternative school. The juvenile may be ordered to pay restitution or complete community service restitution or participate in counseling or treatment programs for specific identified needs.

4. *Placement in community residential programs*: The court may order placement in a residential facility or foster care if there is evidence of inadequate parental supervision or poor parent–child relations. Such placements are short-term and in nonsecure residential programs. The court may also order temporary placement in a mental health facility or a residential drug and alcohol treatment facility.

5. *Institutional commitment*: Juveniles who are considered a risk to the community may be committed to more secure facilities, often called "training schools." These are generally administered and operated by the state and range from minimum-security schools with open campuses and cottage-like settings to medium- or maximum-security correctional facilities for juveniles or young adults. The latter are generally considered a last resort and are reserved for youths who have committed serious crimes or who failed to adjust in a number of other juvenile programs. Institutional commitment may be for a fixed term or for an indefinite term up to the juvenile's twenty-first birthday. Recent legislation in some states allows courts to extend the jurisdiction over juveniles. Under an "extended juvenile jurisdiction" statute, youths who are convicted of violent crimes may be transferred to an adult correctional facility at a given age (usually 18 or 21).

Juvenile Transfers to Adult Court

Juveniles who commit serious or violent offenses may be tried as adults in criminal court. "Waiver," "certification," and "transfer" are terms used to describe this process, meaning that juvenile court jurisdiction is waived, the juvenile is certified as an adult, and the case is transferred to criminal court. Traditionally, in the juvenile system all cases must initially be filed in juvenile court, which has exclusive, original jurisdiction over minors. This is still the case in most jurisdictions, but recent "get-tough" legislation in some states has led to statutory or automatic transfer of chronic or violent juvenile offenders (see Torbet et al., 1996; Sridharan et al., 2004). In most states the juvenile court alone has the authority to waive jurisdiction and transfer a juvenile to adult criminal court. The waiver decision essentially is a choice between punishment in adult criminal court or rehabilitation in juvenile court (Podkopacz and Feld, 1996). The juvenile court must determine whether the seriousness of the present offense and the juvenile's prior record justify transferring the case to criminal court.

There are three routes by which a juvenile case may be transferred to criminal court: statutory exclusion, judicial waiver, and prosecutorial discretion (Feld, 1993: 233–243; Sickmund, 1994). All states provide for the transfer of more serious juvenile offenders by one or more of these methods. Juveniles are transferred to criminal court in many states by statutory exclusion. Although this is not generally thought of as a form of juvenile transfer, many juveniles under 18 years of age are tried in adult criminal court because some state legislatures have established the maximum age for juvenile court jurisdiction at 16 or 15, rather than age 17 as in most states (see Sickmund, 1994: 4; Szymanski, 1994). Some states (29 in 1999) automatically exclude cases from juvenile court that meet specific age and offense criteria; other states (15 in 1999) allow prosecutors to file certain juvenile cases directly in criminal court (Puzzanchera, 2003).

Judicial waiver is usually requested by the prosecuting attorney and is granted by the court after a hearing, in accordance with two U.S. Supreme Court cases. In the 1966 case of *Kent v. United States* (383 U.S. 541), the Supreme Court reversed the conviction of a 16-year-old who had been tried as an adult. The waiver to adult court was ruled invalid because the juvenile was denied a hearing with assistance of legal counsel, and no written statement was made giving reasons for the waiver to criminal court. In *Kent* the Supreme Court expressed concerns that the *parens patriae* philosophy of the juvenile court had led to questionable legal practices that were arbitrary and unfair.

In the 1975 case of *Breed v. Jones* (421 U.S. 519) the Court ruled that it was in violation of the double jeopardy clause of the Fourteenth Amendment to prosecute a juvenile in criminal court following adjudicatory proceedings in juvenile court. The purpose of the hearing, therefore, is not to determine guilt or innocence, but to assess the juveniles' threat to public safety and amenability to treatment under the juvenile justice system. Under most waiver statutes, the juvenile court judge considers such factors as the circumstances and seriousness of the alleged offense, prior adjudications, and age and maturity of the youth.

Judicial waivers were exceptionally rare in juvenile court through the 1970s, when the focus of the court was on the needs and "best interests" of the child. That traditional juvenile justice philosophy began to change in the 1980s and 1990s to more focus on the criminal acts of juvenile offenders and a presumed need for more coercive intervention. Waivers increased 68 percent from 1988 to 1992, when an estimated 11,700 (2 percent of juvenile court cases) were waived and transferred to criminal court (Sickmund, 1994: 1). The number of delinquency cases judicially waived to criminal court peaked in 1994 with 12,100 cases and then declined to 8,300 cases waived in 1990 and 7,500 cases waived in 1999, representing less than 1 percent of the approximately 1.7 million formally processed delinquency cases in 1999 (Puzzanchera, 2003: 1). The proportion of formally processed cases waived to criminal court varied by offense. In 1999, 2,500 (34 percent) of the 7,500 cases waived to criminal court were person offenses, 1,200 (16 percent) of drug offense cases were waived, and 3,000 (40 percent) of property offenses cases were waived to criminal court (Puzzanchera, 2003: 1). This raises the question of whether transfer decisions are in fact fulfilling the stated purpose of waiver as a need for public safety.

The provision for prosecutorial discretion adopted by some states allows prosecutors to file certain juvenile cases in either juvenile or criminal court (see Torbet et al., 1996; Sridharan et al., 2004). This represents a dramatic departure from the practice as specified in *Kent*, in which juvenile court judges were to determine a youth's "amenability to treatment" in the juvenile justice and corrections process. The waiver hearing generally has included social background information compiled by a probation officer and often a psychological assessment. Critics of prosecutorial waiver have expressed concerns about whether prosecutors' decisions will rely on any supporting evidence and be guided by any criteria or will be based solely on the present charge and prior record. Feld (2004) noted that jurisdictional waiver represents a type of sentencing decision, that is, whether to treat a youth as a juvenile or as an adult. The practice of allowing elected prosecutors (who are subject to political pressure and are not likely to rely on any social background information) to make the important decision of jurisdictional waiver therefore raises many sentencing policy questions (Feld, 2004: 600).

Are Juveniles Different from Adults?

A basic principle underlying the separate system of justice for juveniles is that they are different from adults. This principle is not disputed for most juvenile offenses and offenders. The difference between adult and juvenile offenders becomes blurred in cases of older juveniles who commit serious crimes (Zimring, 1998b). Regardless of the age of the offender, however, a fundamental legal premise in the justice system requires that a crime must include both an act and an intent to commit the act (the *actus reus* and *mens rea*). The offender must be shown to have caused harm and be culpable for the offense. The principle of fundamental fairness was demonstrated in a recent U.S. Supreme Court ruling that banned the execution of mentally retarded persons who had committed murder. In support of the reduced culpability of mental retarded defendants the Court held that:

> (They) frequently know the difference between right and wrong and are competent to stand trial. Because of their impairments, however, by definition they have diminished capacities to understand and process mistakes and learn from experience, to engage in logical reasoning, to control impulses, and to understand the reactions of others. . . . Their deficiencies do not warrant an exemption from criminal sanctions, but they do diminish their personal culpability [*Atkins v. Virginia*, 536 U.S. 304, 318(2002)].

The Court's reasoning in relation to the mentally retarded is similar to reasons given for the reduced culpability of young people. All western nations, including the United States, have separate systems of justice for juveniles based on the understanding that juveniles are less mature than adults and therefore are less culpable (Zimring, 2000).

Research from the field of developmental psychology shows that there is ample evidence and support for the reduced culpability of juveniles based on their lower level of maturity. Youths deserve to be treated as less culpable for a number of reasons (see Zimring, 1998b, 2000; Feld, 1999: 306–313; Bishop, 2004: 635–636): (1) their lower cognitive development means that they do not process information and consider alternatives as well as adults; (2) adolescent judgment and emotional and social maturity are not as well developed as in adults; (3) young people are less aware of risks and are more likely to take risks that may result in harm to themselves and others; (4) youths have a different sense of time than adults, and think more in terms of short-term rather than long-term consequences; (5) juveniles are more vulnerable to peer pressure than adults; (6) youths make poorer judgments because they have less experience in decision making; and (7) recent research in neuroscience indicates that portions of the brain responsible for impulse control and decision making are underdeveloped in addlescents compared to adults.

The American Bar Association (ABA) (2004) has recognized the reduced culpability of youth based on differences in brain development between adults and juveniles. Based on neuroscientific studies of brain development in adolescents, the ABA supports the assertion that adolescents are less morally culpable for their actions than competent adults and are more capable of change and rehabilitation. The ideal of not holding violent juveniles as accountable and blameworthy as adults is difficult for many to accept. This is especially true for juveniles who are physically as big and strong as adults. Appearance and physical size may be deceiving, however. The appearance of physical maturity does not mean that an adolescent has the same reasoning capacity as an adult. Research reported by the ABA (2004) indicates that because of slower development of parts of the brain that support clear reasoning and decision making, youths often rely on emotional parts of the brain. Another misconception is that commission of a serious crime is a sign of maturity. It is unfortunate that some children and adolescents commit serious crimes and cause serious harm. Murder and violent crimes are not exclusively adult activities, however, and it is illogical to reason that a youth who kills is more mature than a youth who steals (Bishop, 2004). It is understandable that the crime of murder triggers a desire for punishment, retribution, and vengeance. It is no more appropriate to hold an adolescent accountable for murder the same as an adult, however, than it is to hold a mentally retarded offender accountable the same as a person of normal, average intelligence. The fact that adolescents are less mature than adults does not excuse them from punishment for violent crimes. It does, however, lessen their culpability and therefore the level of punishment. For this reason it is important to have a fair and just process of determining through a hearing whether a juvenile offender is "amenable to treatment" in the juvenile system or may be held accountable for a crime the same as an adult. The ABA (2004) reminds us that the concept of adolescents being less mature and less culpable is not new. We refer to those under 18 as minors and juveniles for a reason: they are less than adult.

Do Juvenile Transfers Make a Difference?

The stated purpose of juvenile transfers is for public safety, so the policy is presumably directed toward those serious juvenile offenders who are believed to be not "amenable to treatment" in the juvenile justice system. A number of studies have examined the question of whether transfers do in fact make a difference. There is evidence that many juveniles waived to adult court are not the most dangerous or serious offenders. Bortner (1986) examined 214 remanded juveniles and found that they were not more dangerous or intractable than nonremanded juveniles. Her analysis suggested that their remand did not enhance public safety, and she concluded that political and organizational factors accounted for the increased number of remands. There is evidence that criminal courts have given less severe sentences to waived juveniles than if those young offenders had been tried in juvenile court. Donna Hamparian and associates (1982) found that most of the juveniles transferred to adult court in 1978 received fines or probation, and the small number who were incarcerated received sentences of one year or less. Donna Bishop and associates (1989) examined the practice of prosecutorial waivers in Florida and found that few of the juveniles transferred were dangerous or repeat offenders for whom the waiver would be justified. They found that a lack of statutory guidelines and the ease of prosecutorial waiver without judicial oversight accounted for many inappropriate cases being transferred to criminal court (Bishop et al., 1989: 198).

Legislative changes that provide for more juvenile transfers were made with the goal of reducing juvenile crime. Rising juvenile crime rates in the 1970s led many to assume that the juvenile system had failed and that it was too lenient and ineffective in deterring juvenile crime. It is generally taken for granted by politicians and the public that getting tougher with harsher punishment is an effective response to crime. Media accounts of violent juvenile offenders tend to portray them as incorrigible young criminals who view juvenile laws, the court, and corrections system as "soft" on crime. Based on limited empirical evidence of what works in juvenile justice, state legislatures have revised juvenile codes with an emphasis on offender accountability, punishment, and public safety. Most of the states have revised their juvenile codes to make it easier to transfer young offenders to the criminal courts (Feld, 1995; Torbet et al., 1996). Does the transfer of juveniles to criminal court make a difference? Research on the effects of the harsher juvenile code revisions indicates that the effects have not been in the intended direction. A study that compared matched samples of juveniles, some of whom were transferred and others not, showed that transfer actually resulted in increased short-term recidivism rates (Bishop et al., 1996). Despite being incarcerated for longer periods of time, the transferred youths committed more offenses. Even when controlling for time at risk, the rate of reoffending in the transfer group was significantly higher, and they were more likely to commit a subsequent felony offense. More of the nontransfer youths improved their behavior over time. The authors concluded that juvenile transfer did not have a deterrent effect and removal from the streets through incapacitation did not result in improved public safety (Bishop et al., 1996).

Juvenile transfer policies have disproportionately affected black youth. Juvenile arrests disproportionately involve minorities. Of juvenile arrests for violent crimes in 2002, 55 percent involved whites and 43 percent involved blacks (Snyder, 2004). Despite the fact that white youths account for more than half of the violent crime arrests, violent crime has become associated more with black youths. Feld (2003) maintains that media reports and conservative political reactions have resulted in associating crime with racial minorities, specifically young black males. Media reports tend to focus on crimes that are considered more "newsworthy," resulting in disproportionate coverage of urban street crime. The media therefore exaggerates the true extent of violent crime and presents a distorted picture of criminals (Surette, 1998). Media news coverage has overreported and over-emphasized the role of minority youth in violent crime (Dorfman and Schiraldi, 2001). Crime policies are a central political agenda, and the public and political perceptions of race and youth crime were inevitably a part of the incentive behind the "get-tough" reforms of juvenile statutes (Zimring, 1998a). Feld (2003) has argued that media coverage, racial factors, and a conservative political agenda played a major role in punitive changes in juvenile justice laws and practices that have had a disproportionate impact on racial minorities.

Other research has indicated that juveniles waived to criminal court have received more severe sentences than if they had been retained in juvenile court, but there are significant disparities in the sentences for property and personal offenses and between adult and juvenile courts (Rudman et al., 1986; Podkopacz and Feld, 1996). In a study of the criminal court data from the Pennsylvania Commission on Sentencing, Kurlychek and Johnson (2004) found that juvenile offenders transferred to adult court were sentenced more severely than their young adult counterparts. Their juvenile status did not act as a mitigating factor, but rather seemed to aggravate the sentence. Because prosecutorial decisions to transfer do not include an assessment of maturity or culpability, one might expect that criminal courts would at least take those factors into account when sentencing young offenders (Bishop, 2004). Contrary to youthfulness being a mitigating factor, the transferred juveniles received what Kurlycheck and Johnson referred to as a "juvenile penalty" (2004: 506).

Research evidence suggests that judicial waiver may have little more than symbolic value, relaying a message to the public that something is being done about violent juvenile crime. Legislative reforms that include "get-tough" provisions for juvenile offenders seem to have been driven more by political rhetoric than sound research. Slogans such as "if you're old enough to do the crime, you're old enough to do the time" resonate strongly with voters. Juvenile waiver and transfer, however, may not accomplish much in terms of reducing the growing number of serious and violent juvenile offenders. It does remove more serious offenders from the juvenile system, but there are questions whether the adult system is equipped to handle a growing number of youthful offenders. Rudman et al. (1986) believe that waiver creates new problems for adult corrections and that it may be counterproductive to sentence juvenile offenders to several years of punishment with adult offenders rather than a few years of treatment in the juvenile system. According to Rudman et al. (1986), the effectiveness of juvenile justice system responses to violent youth will be improved not by removing them but rather by developing appropriate dispositional alternatives for the juvenile court. These might include increasing the age for juvenile corrections jurisdiction and improving the quality of services in secure juvenile corrections institutions. These alternatives would have more immediate impact on violent juvenile crime than simply transferring the problem to already overburdened criminal courts and correctional facilities. Zimring (1998b) contends that transfer of juvenile homicide cases to criminal court simply relocates these difficult problems. It does not solve them.

There is some evidence that juvenile transfers may be waning in popularity. The number of juvenile transfers in the United States has declined steadily in the past decade, as noted earlier (Puzzanchera, 2003). Donna Bishop (2004) cites several reasons for the reduction in juvenile transfers to criminal court: (1) there is less public support for simplistic, punitive responses to youth crime, particularly as we become aware of the monetary costs and ineffectiveness of transfers; (2) some state legislatures have actually reduced the number of crimes that are subject to prosecutorial transfer decisions; and (3) professionals in the juvenile justice system have responded to evaluation research and begun to develop new and more effective juvenile corrections programs and intervention strategies (Bishop, 2004: 641). As with all justice policies and practices, juvenile transfer is an issue that demands further evaluative research to determine its appropriateness in responding to juvenile crime. It is important for legislators to consider policies for responding to juvenile crime that are most effective in producing long-term benefits for the protection of the community and change for juvenile offenders.

"Blended Sentencing": An Alternative to Transfers

Several states have developed an alternative to certification, waiver, and transfer of juvenile offenders to adult criminal court. The states of Arkansas, Illinois, Kansas, Minnesota, and Montana, for example, have revised their juvenile codes to include what is referred to as extended juvenile jurisdiction (EJJ) prosecution. This is often referred to as "blended sentencing," or what Sanborn and Salerno (2005) refer to as "transfer to juvenile court's second tier" (2005: 295). An EJJ proceeding is generally used for a serious or violent juvenile offender who would meet the criteria for transfer to criminal court. In processing a case as EJJ, a youth is given a hearing before a juvenile court judge to determine the appropriateness of transferring the case to criminal court. The disposition in an EJJ case is a combined or "blended" sentence. The youth is given both a juvenile court disposition and an adult sentence, but the adult sentence is stayed or suspended, while the juvenile court disposition is implemented. According to the Minnesota statute, for example (Section 260B.130), the adult criminal sentence is stayed on the condition that the juvenile not violate the provisions of the disposition order and not commit a new offense. The juvenile disposition in most cases is commitment to a juvenile correctional facility or placement in a private residential treatment center, followed by a period of aftercare supervision until the young offender's twenty-first birthday. If the juvenile violates the conditions of the stayed sentence, typically by committing a new offense, the court may revoke the stay and require that the offender be taken into custody. The juvenile is then given written notice of the reasons for the revocation of the stayed sentence and may have a hearing with representation of legal counsel if the revocation is challenged. If there are sufficient reasons to revoke the stay of the suspended adult sentence, the court treats the offender as an adult and the adult sentence is implemented, with no credit given for the time served in juvenile facility custody (Minn. Stat. 260B.130, subd. 5). The extended juvenile jurisdiction process has a number of advantages over immediate transfer to criminal court. First, the young offender is placed in a juvenile corrections or treatment facility, rather than with adults in a prison setting. Second, the juvenile has the opportunity to receive necessary correctional and treatment services that are more available in juvenile corrections than in adult corrections. Third, the juvenile is not exposed to the "criminogenic" environment of adult correctional facilities. Fourth, the juvenile is given another chance to prove that he or she may be "amenable to treatment" within the juvenile justice system and may be released earlier than an adult sentence and not pose a risk to public safety. Research on the results of "blended sentencing" or extended juvenile jurisdiction is limited. Initial results indicate that the policies do provide an alternative to juvenile transfer to criminal court, but may not significantly reduce the number of youthful offenders who are incarcerated.

Podkopacz and Feld (2001) found that nearly half (48 percent) of youths who received an EJJ sentence were revoked and a majority of the revocations were not the result of new criminal charges. Judges sent nearly as many youths to jail or prison following EJJ revocations as they did directly through certification proceedings. Additional research is needed to evaluate the effects of EJJ prosecution and whether the results are significantly different from sentences resulting from juvenile transfer.

Juvenile Records

Throughout the history of the juvenile justice system, juvenile court records have been kept separate from criminal court records, and juvenile records could not be used later as part of the criminal history when a person was being sentenced for a felony crime committed as an adult. In keeping with juvenile justice philosophy, it was felt that crimes committed as an immature and less responsible juvenile should not be held against a person once he or she becomes an adult. One of the changes accompanying the more punitive and control-oriented justice process has been to allow access to juvenile records for young adults charged with violent crimes. Feld (1999) has noted that expanded uses of juveniles' prior records to enhance the criminal court sentences of young adult offenders raise troubling issues because of the inferior quality of procedural justice according to which juveniles were found guilty and adjudicated in the juvenile court (1999: 234).

Juvenile records have traditionally not been open to the public and are available only by court order (Sanborn and Salerno, 2005: 405ff.). One of the developments in the "get-tough" era of juvenile justice, however, has been an increased accessibility of juvenile records to selected persons or institutions that arguably may have a right or need to know. We discussed in Chapter 8 the right of schools to receive juvenile court information about students who are enrolled in the school. Several states have amended juvenile codes to require disclosure of juvenile court records of students, especially if it is a school-related offense, and some states insist that the superintendent and principal share records with teachers, SROs, and other school staff who will come into contact with the student (Sanborn and Salerno, 2005: 406).

In some jurisdictions, victims may request limited juvenile court information about cases in which they were involved. In Minnesota, for example, the victim may request information about the juvenile offender and the court disposition "unless it reasonably appears that the request is prompted by a desire on the part of the requester to engage in unlawful activities" (Minn. Stat. 260B.171, subd.4).

Sealing and Expunging Juvenile Records

Many state juvenile codes provide for the sealing or expunging of court records after the juvenile has satisfactorily fulfilled the conditions of correctional supervision as ordered by the court and the case has been successfully terminated. In addition to having successfully completed the terms of the juvenile court disposition, most state laws also require a period of time to have expired during which the juvenile has not been involved in further law violations. Sealing or expungement is not an automatic process. The juvenile must make a formal request to the court to have the court record sealed or expunged according to the particular state law. Factors that the court may consider in determining whether to grant a request to seal or expunge a record include whether the person has satisfactorily completed all terms of supervision, including restitution; whether the minimum amount of time has passed since termination of supervision (ranging from 1 to 2 years or more); whether the person has been arrested, charged, or convicted of subsequent offenses; whether the youth has been rehabilitated; and whether the youth is no longer a threat to public safety (see Sanborn and Salerno, 2005: 407).

The End of the "Ultimate Punishment" for Juveniles

The death penalty for juveniles convicted of murder has been a controversial issue. The United States has until recently been one of few nations in the world—the only democratic, industrialized nation—to allow the execution of juveniles convicted of murder. Since 1973, a total of 228 juvenile death sentences has been imposed, 22 (14 percent) of which resulted in execution and 134 (86 percent) of which were reversed or commuted (Streib, 2005). The rate at which that small number of states allows the death penalty for juveniles under 18 has been declining for years. In 1988 the U.S. Supreme Court in *Thompson v. Oklahoma* (487 U.S. 815) held that execution of juvenile offenders under age 16 violated the Eighth Amendment against cruel and unusual punishment. The next year (1989) the Court held in *Stanford v. Kentucky* (492 U.S. 361) that the execution of juvenile offenders 16 and 17 years of age was not unconstitutional (see del Carmen, Parker, and Reddington, 1998). Fifteen more years passed before the Supreme Court in 2005 in *Roper v. Simmons* [543 U.S. (forthcoming)] put an end to the execution of all juvenile offenders under 18 years of age. In a close 5–4 majority opinion, the Court drew upon the earlier decision in *Atkins v. Virginia* (536 U.S. 304) forbidding execution of the mentally retarded. In *Roper* the Court held that:

> Rejection of the imposition of the death penalty on juvenile offenders under 18 is required by the Eighth Amendment. Capital punishment must be limited to those offenders who commit "a narrow category of the most serious crimes" and whose extreme culpability makes them "the most deserving of execution" [*Atkins v. Virginia*, 536 U.S. at 319; and *Roper v. Simmons*, 543 U.S. forthcoming].

The decision was based in part on the earlier *Thompson* decision and rested on what the Court recognized as three general differences between juveniles under 18 and adults and why juvenile offenders cannot be classified among the "worst offenders." First, because juveniles are susceptible to immature and irresponsible behavior, it means that "their irresponsible conduct is not as morally reprehensible as that of an adult" [*Roper v. Simmons*, 543 U.S. (forthcoming); *Thompson v. Oklahoma*, 487 U.S. 815, at 835]. Second, the Court reasoned that because juveniles still struggle to define their own identity means that "it is less supportable to conclude that even a heinous crime committed by a juvenile is evidence of irretrievably depraved character" [543 U.S. (forthcoming)]. Third, because the Court recognized juveniles' diminished culpability compared with adults over 18, then (similar to the mentally retarded in *Atkins*) "neither of the two penological justifications for the death penalty—retribution and deterrence of capital crimes by prospective offenders . . . provides adequate justification for imposing that penalty on juveniles" [543 U.S. (forthcoming)]. In ruling against the death penalty for juvenile murderers, the justices acknowledged that they could not deny or overlook the brutal crimes that too many juvenile offenders have committed. While the state may no longer execute those juveniles under 18 for murder, the Court added a reminder that "the State can exact forfeiture of some of the most basic liberties" [543 U.S. (forthcoming)], that is, a life sentence in prison. The *Roper* decision will have an impact on 22 states: 10 specified the minimum age for the death penalty at 16 years, 5 at 17 years, and 7 established no minimum age. Of the 38 states that authorize capital punishment, 16 of the states and the federal judicial system had already specified 18 years as the minimum age for execution (Bonzcar and Snell, 2004).

Juvenile Court Trends and Reforms

The juvenile court has come under criticism from two sides: those who want more control and punishment to hold juvenile offenders accountable and those who point to social problems that contribute to delinquency. Conservatives contend that the court is "soft on crime" when it adopts the traditional goal of treating juvenile offenders, rather than holding them accountable for their crimes. Conservatives believe that giving repeat offenders too many chances through diversion programs and community treatment alternatives sends a message to them and the community that we do not take juvenile crime seriously. Juvenile training schools are criticized for their open, private school–like setting, and conservatives believe some juveniles should be confined for longer sentences in a more punitive setting.

Liberal critics express concern about the social problems and lack of equal opportunities and resources for disadvantaged youth that place many at risk of involvement in gangs, drug use, and delinquency. Liberals claim that transfers to criminal court, and even formal processing through the juvenile justice system, often aggravates the problems and that institutional confinement in detention centers and training schools only serves to further criminalize juveniles. Judicial critics denounce the lack of procedural safeguards and uniformity in the informal juvenile court process, with many juveniles receiving more punitive sanctions than adults for minor offenses that would result in no more than a fine in adult court.

Practitioners in the juvenile justice system also express dissatisfaction and disagree among themselves. Police and prosecutors want tougher sanctions for juvenile offenders and fewer "second chances" through diversion programs and community alternatives. Probation officers contend that a large group of juvenile offenders have special needs that can be met through treatment and supervision in the community. Given their knowledge of the social and family background of referred juveniles, probation officers are reluctant to take a punitive approach except as a last resort after treatment alternatives have failed.

The criticisms leveled against the juvenile court from all sides stem in part from the judicial and legislative changes that have transformed the juvenile court from what was originally intended as a social rehabilitation welfare agency into what Feld (1999) has referred to as a "scaled-down, second-class criminal court for young people" (1999: 286). The criticisms also underscore the reality that the juvenile court cannot be both a court of law and an agency for individual and social change. The probation officers, attorneys, and judges who see the hundreds of young offenders pass through the courts each week readily acknowledge the numerous social problems that characterize them, none of which are their fault. Most juvenile offenders and their families encounter lack of proper nutrition and health care, housing problems, lack of employment opportunities, and unequal access to quality schools. The sole reason that juveniles appear before the court, however is for the commission of a crime, so any compassion or mitigation of a disposition based on a youth's social disadvantages is secondary to his or her legal status as a young law violator (see Feld, 1999: 295). The juvenile court's first responsibility is to impose legal sanctions and attempt to prevent further delinquent behavior—cannot fulfill the traditional promise of juvenile rehabilitation (Feld, 1999: 296; and Grubb and Lazerson, 1982: 179). Changing many of the conditions that lead to juvenile delinquency is not the responsibility of the juvenile court, but lies with society, families, schools, other social institutions, and government social policies.

Juvenile Court Changes

The juvenile court has undergone significant changes and reforms. The reform movement began with the U.S. Supreme Court decisions of *Kent*, *In re Gault*, and *In re Winship* in the 1960s, in which the Court required for juveniles most of the same due process protections provided for adults in criminal courts. Juveniles were provided notice of the charges, right to counsel, and protection against self-incrimination and unlawful searches. Another step in juvenile court reform involved efforts to remove status offenders from formal adjudication and commitment to detention centers and juvenile institutions. Juvenile lockups and training schools housed many youths whose only crime was disobeying their parents, running away, or school truancy. Advocates of such practices argued that involvement in status offenses was the first step toward more serious delinquency and early intervention might prevent serious delinquency. Opponents noted the unfairness of punishing youths for minor deviant behavior and voiced concerns about the adverse effects on status offenders being housed with older, hard-core juvenile offenders. The President's Commission on Law Enforcement and Administration of Justice (1967) recommended narrowing the range of offenses going before the juvenile court, and groups such as the American Bar Association–Institute of Judicial Administration (1982) called for an end to adjudicating and incarcerating status offenders in juvenile institutions.

Despite the changes that were implemented following *Gault* and *Kent*, children and youth appearing before juvenile court still do not have the same constitutional safeguards as adults in criminal court (Feld, 1999: 287; Sanborn and Salerno, 2005: 503). Juvenile laws still allow officials to intervene in noncriminal behavior including incorrigibility, runaway, and truancy. Parents may lose custody when their delinquent child is put under state custody for placement in a juvenile facility. The juvenile justice system may retain control of children beyond their 18th birthday when they become adults. Juvenile justice advocates would point to the positive side of the system. Juvenile justice interventions are justified based on multiple goals that range from prevention, to treatment, to public safety. Preventing status offenders from becoming more serious delinquents is still considered a viable function of the court. Research does indicate that parental disobedience, leaving home without permission, and school truancy are precursors of delinquent behavior. Juvenile treatment programs that focus on substance abuse prevention, education, and skill development have been effective in reducing delinquency. Finally, the need for control and public safety remains true for a relatively small number of chronic and violent juvenile offenders.

Abolish or "Rehabilitate" the Juvenile Court?

The current focus of discussion concerning juvenile court reform revolves around the very purpose of the juvenile court. The question at issue is whether the primary purpose of the juvenile court is punishment or treatment. Most of the states have revised their juvenile codes and redefined the purpose of the juvenile court, deemphasizing rehabilitation and placing more importance on public protection and safety (Feld, 1995; Torbet et al., 1996). Barry Feld (1993) has argued that judicial and legislative changes have "criminalized" the juvenile court. The juvenile court reforms have altered the court's jurisdiction over status offenders, who are diverted from the system, and serious offenders, who are increasingly transferred to adult criminal court. He contends that there are fewer differences between the two courts. In much the same manner as criminal courts, juvenile courts now tend to punish youths for their offenses rather than treat them for their needs (Feld, 1993: 197). Beyond being punished for their crimes, however, Feld argues that the procedural safeguards that are standard in criminal courts would be beneficial to juveniles. Juvenile offenders receive an inferior quality of justice in juvenile courts, and this practice has been rationalized and justified because "they are only children" (1993: 267). Feld believes that a separate juvenile court must be based on more than simply a treatment-versus-punishment rationale, and he contends that "the current juvenile court provides neither therapy nor justice and cannot be rehabilitated" (Feld, 1999: 297).

Feld has therefore argued for abolition of the juvenile court as we know it. A more formal criminal court hearing would ensure that juvenile offenders receive the same due process safeguards and constitutional rights as adults in criminal court. Juveniles would only be treated differently at the sentencing phase, when they would receive a "youth discount" in consideration of their lower level of maturity and culpability (Feld, 1999: 317). The concept of a youth discount is not new or unique. Other juvenile justice policy groups, such as the ABA and Institute of Judicial Administration (IJA) (1980), have recommended a similar policy. The ABA–IJA noted that age is a relevant factor in determining the juvenile's level of responsibility for breaking the law and for establishing an appropriate sentence or disposition in juvenile court (1980a: 35). In addition to a "youth discount" in sentencing, Feld recommends that youths who are sentenced to an institution be placed in separate correctional facilities for youthful offenders (1999: 326). (We will discuss juvenile corrections in Chapter 11.)

Abolition of the juvenile court is unlikely in the near future, but juvenile justice experts welcome the ongoing reforms and agree that more changes are needed. Supporters of the current juvenile court acknowledge that juveniles receive "unequal" and "duel" processing in court, not the same quality of due process as adults, for the purpose of both punishment and rehabilitation (Sanborn and Salerno, 2005). They also emphasize that not everything about juvenile justice is negative or unfair, especially when juvenile courts do pursue the best interests of the youthful offender and make positive efforts to provide beneficial interventions and programs aimed at offender change. The juvenile court in most cases does take into account the child's needs and risks and aims to arrive at a disposition that will best facilitate offender change and public safety. Juvenile justice still does focus on both the youthful offender and the offense. "In short, juvenile justice is *still* largely about who the youth is (in addition to what the youth has done)" (Sanborn and Salerno, 2005: 503). The concept of individualized justice risks differential treatment according to gender, race, and social class despite the intention of a court disposition based on perceived risks or needs of youthful offenders. Sanborn and Salerno (2005: 504) suggest that maintaining the rehabilitative purpose of juvenile court may require acceptance of some unequal processing in order to assist families who cannot or will not help resolve their child's problems. This is not to say that juvenile court dispositions based on race are acceptable, however, but that racial minorities and lower-class youth who come before the court often have problems for which resources and services available through the court may provide some relief.

The juvenile justice system must be vigilant in preventing the influence of racism in differential sentencing of juvenile offenders. The federal government, through the Office of Juvenile Justice and Delinquency Prevention, has made the elimination of disproportionate minority confinement a high priority. Feld (1999, 2003) has repeatedly emphasized the tendency of the individualized juvenile justice system to produce racial disparities in sentencing youthful offenders. Juvenile court officials must be vigilant to not repeat some of the same unfair treatment that is prevalent in many schools because African American students are often treated harshly and unfairly by school officials in dealing with discipline and truancy problems (Ferguson, 2000) (see Chapter 5).

Those who support the juvenile court believe that it can still provide a fair and just legal process and rehabilitative services better than would be available in the criminal court (Sanborn and Salerno, 2005). The majority of juvenile offenders—who have not committed serious, violent crimes and who do not have lengthy records—will continue to benefit from the treatment-oriented juvenile court. For violent and chronic juvenile offenders, the options of transfer and blended sentencing are still available. Correctional and treatment services available as juvenile court dispositions are more properly tailored to meet the needs of most juvenile offenders. Professionals in the juvenile justice system have responded to evaluation research and have begun to develop new and more effective juvenile corrections programs and intervention strategies (Bishop, 2004: 641).

American citizens look to the police and the courts to solve the nation's juvenile crime problem. As juvenile crime has become more rampant and a disproportionate number of young people commit violent crimes, citizens have demanded tougher laws from their legislators. In an effort to show that "something is being done," legislators have enacted more severe punishment for juvenile offenders. It is important to remember, however, that there are "limits to the criminal sanction" (Packer, 1975). Police and the courts cannot prevent crime or the root causes of juvenile delinquency. They can only respond to criminal violations after they occur. Focusing all of our attention on laws and their enforcement is not an adequate approach for reducing the social and family problems that lead to juvenile delinquency (see Feld, 1995: 980–982). The Minnesota Task Force that recommended changes in juvenile laws emphasized that

> juvenile crime is directly related to the quality of life in a community—not to the degree of punishment handed out by the government. . . . The inter-relationships among family, religion, health care, education, housing, employment, community values, and crime mean that all segments of the community must play an active role in combating juvenile delinquency (Advisory Task Force on the Juvenile Justice System, 1994: 16).

As long as society relies solely on tougher laws and their enforcement to respond to juvenile crime, we are unlikely to see any changes in the current trends of increasing numbers of young people who are committing crimes. Legal institutions will continue to respond to the juvenile crime problem, but social institutions such as the family, schools, and community agencies are essential for helping prevent the problem before it occurs. We will discuss delinquency-prevention programs and strategies in Chapter 12, following our discussion of juvenile corrections in Chapter 11.

Summary

The juvenile justice process differs from the legal process for adults in a number of key areas. The juvenile court was established more than 100 years ago to process juvenile cases separately from adults in recognition of the fact that juveniles are different from adult offenders in terms of maturity and understanding of the law, their legal rights, and the judicial process. The juvenile court has undergone several changes following a number of U.S. Supreme Court decisions and a desire of the public and lawmakers to treat serious juvenile offenders more like adults. Some legal experts have also argued for improving the quality of justice in juvenile court proceedings by implementing more of the formal due process safeguards common to the criminal court. It is unlikely that the juvenile court will be abolished or changed dramatically, however, for it continues to be the focal point of the juvenile justice system.

11

Juvenile Corrections

The third component of the juvenile justice system, after law enforcement and the juvenile court, is juvenile corrections. Following adjudication in juvenile court, juvenile offenders are referred to a correctional agency by a juvenile court judge's order. The juvenile court disposition (see Chapter 10) varies according to the risk level and needs of the juvenile offender, as established in a predisposition report by a probation officer. The guiding principles of the juvenile justice system have been to make judicial decisions that are "in the best interests of the child" and use the "least restrictive" dispositional alternatives that fulfill the goals of correctional treatment and public safety. There are two types of juvenile corrections: community corrections and institutional corrections. *Community corrections* refers to supervision in the community on *juvenile probation* and may be combined with other alternatives to incarceration such as fines, restitution, and community service. The choice of available alternatives and programs varies in different jurisdictions, but the majority of juvenile offenders are placed on juvenile probation. *Institutional corrections* refers to placement in secure or semi-secure institutional and residential facilities, including temporary detention centers or juvenile shelters, state training schools, public or private residential facilities, group homes, and wilderness camps.

Residential Programs and Institutional Corrections

According to the Census of Juveniles in Residential Placement (CJRP) in 1999, a total of 134,011 juveniles were held in 2,939 facilities (Sickmund, 2004). Some of the characteristics of the juveniles and the residential facilities in which they were held are as follows:

•Most (78 percent) of the residents were held for delinquency offenses.

•A small proportion (4 percent) of the residents were status offenders.

•Some residents (19 percent) were not charged with or adjudicated for an offense, but were held for reasons such as abuse, neglect, emotional disturbance, or mental retardation.

•There were more private facilities (1,794) than public facilities (1,136), but more juveniles (71 percent) were held in public facilities than in private ones (29 percent).

•The number of delinquent offenders in residential facilities increased 5 percent from 1997 to 1999 and 50 percent from 1991 to 1999.

•The U.S. rate of custody for juvenile offenders was 371 per 100,000 juveniles in the population.

•The rate of custody among the states varied widely, from 96 to 632 per 10,000 juveniles.

•Minority youths (62 percent) accounted for a significantly disproportionate part of the juvenile facility population compared with whites (38 percent).

•An additional 7,600 youths younger than 18 were held in adult jails, and 5,600 youths under age 18 were in state adult prison systems (Sickmund, 2004: 3–19).

The average length of stay for juveniles in a residential facility is about 4 months; the average yearly cost for custody in a public facility was more than $32,000 in 1998; and private facilities had increased in average annual costs to over $45,000 in 1995 (Smith, 1998: 537). Placement in a residential facility is generally used only for the most serious or chronic juvenile offenders, who require secure confinement and treatment. There are exceptions, however, as illustrated by the 25,000 (19 percent) confined youth who were not charged or adjudicated for an offense. Residential placement is costly compared with community corrections, and it is uncertain whether the education, training, and treatment received in juvenile institutions are effective in reducing delinquent behavior.

History and Development of Juvenile Corrections

Juvenile corrections has a long history in America, beginning with the development of houses of refuge and probation in the nineteenth century (see Chapter 2). Juveniles are confined in correctional facilities separate from adults, but many of the "training schools" in which thousands of children are confined differ very little from prisons for adult criminals. The goal of juvenile corrections is to prevent young offenders from becoming adult criminals, but juvenile correctional institutions have had the unintended effect of becoming "schools for crime." Many incarcerated adult felons report that they were institutionalized as youths. Severe punishment of young offenders appears to have little effect in deterring them from crime, and may in fact promote more criminality as young adults. Major efforts in the 1970s led to a movement to deinstitutionalize young offenders and to remove all status offenders from juvenile institutions. There has been a long nationwide effort to develop a variety of community treatment programs for juvenile offenders. Those efforts seem to have stalled somewhat in the 1990s, however, with public demands for a "get-tough" approach to what was perceived to be a youth crime plague.

Juvenile institutions have existed in the United States since 1825, when the first House of Refuge opened for delinquent youths in New York. Other Houses of Refuge in Boston and Philadelphia were soon established, and these were followed shortly thereafter by reform schools for vagrant and delinquent juveniles. State reform schools opened in Massachusetts in 1847, in New York in 1853, and in Ohio in 1857; the first State Industrial

School for Girls was opened in Massachusetts in 1856 (Law Enforcement Assistance Administration, 1976: 65). The *cottage system* was developed later in the nineteenth century as a humane improvement over the crowded houses of refuge in the cities. The cottage system housed smaller groups of juveniles in separate buildings in a rural campus setting. These later came to be known as *training schools* or *industrial schools*, which exist to the present as the primary form of juvenile correction facilities in this country. It was assumed that by removing juvenile offenders from the criminogenic conditions of the cities, they would be reformed through exposure to a simple rural lifestyle. Required attendance in school classes and vocational training was intended to teach the wayward youths work skills and habits.

Juvenile training schools came under criticism in the 1960s and 1970s as reformers highlighted their inhumane conditions, claiming that housing minor juvenile offenders with more serious and violent offenders made the facilities nothing more than "schools for crime." Jerome Miller received national attention in the early 1970s when, as director of the Massachusetts juvenile corrections agency, he closed all the training schools. Juveniles were placed in alternative public and private residential programs. Research evaluating the effects of closing the state schools indicated that the reform did not result in an increase in delinquency in the state (Coates et al., 1978; Schwartz, 1989: 100). Barry Krisberg and James Austin (1993) reported that a cost analysis of the Massachusetts system compared with other state juvenile corrections systems indicated that the Massachusetts system was cost-effective while providing public safety and offender rehabilitation (1993: 163). The Massachusetts experience has been closely followed, and many other states have considered reforms similar to those initiated by Jerome Miller.

Incarceration of juvenile offenders is very costly and does little to reduce crime rates. Krisberg and Austin (1993) suggest that a better use of tax dollars might be neighborhood-based crime-prevention efforts directed at reducing child abuse, school dropout rates, youth unemployment, and drug dealing. The tremendous increase in the number of offenders being sentenced to correctional institutions has placed enormous demands on state and federal budgets. The cost of building and operating correctional institutions means that states have had to cut back on other expenditures. From 1960 to 1985, state and local spending per capita increased 218 percent for corrections, significantly more than the increase for hospitals and health care (119 percent), police (73 percent), or education (56 percent) (Bureau of Justice Statistics, 1988: 120). Increasing the proportion of taxpayer dollars that go to corrections more than the rate of spending for education presents a troubling dilemma. We seem to be taking dollars from school classrooms to pay for more prison cells (Lawrence, 1995a). Research evidence indicates that a better use of taxpayer dollars is to invest in educational programs that have been shown to be effective in reducing delinquency and concentrate correctional spending on community-based programs that are more cost-effective than incarceration, while still providing for public safety.

Detention Centers

Juvenile detention centers, also called juvenile halls or shelters, were established around the turn of the twentieth century to serve as an alternative to placing juveniles in adult jails. City, county, or state governments administer detention centers, although most are run by the county in conjunction with child welfare departments or juvenile courts. Detention centers serve as a temporary holding facility for juveniles who need to be detained for their own safety or that of the community. They may be held temporarily after arrest and referral to the probation intake unit pending release to their parents. Juveniles are usually detained for a week or less, with exceptional cases being held up to 3–4 weeks. The juvenile codes of most states require a detention hearing to be held before a child is held more than 1 or 2 days. The physical environment of many metropolitan juvenile detention centers resembles that of many adult jails. The facilities are usually adjacent to the probation offices and hearing rooms of the juvenile court, but are usually of concrete and steel construction with small individual cells or rooms containing a bed, toilet, and sink. If the cell has a window, it is a small opening that allows some natural light into the tiny room. Detention centers are built and programmed almost entirely around custody and security concerns. Educational, recreational, and treatment programs are secondary. This emphasis is justified by the short-term nature of detention and the focus on custody and security. Several county and regional detention centers built in the past few years feature a modular living arrangement that is less institutional in appearance, with space designed for educational, recreational, and treatment programs.

Correctional Institutions for Juveniles

Larger states such as California, Illinois, Ohio, New York, and Texas have several training schools and account for nearly half of all juveniles held in public long-term facilities (Snyder and Sickmund, 1995: 168). Many states have developed coeducational facilities, with separate cottages for girls and boys but with shared participation in education, vocational, and treatment programs.

The physical structure of juvenile training schools varies from cottage settings to open dormitories, and maximum security facilities may house residents in individual cells. The secure training schools have an institutional appearance inside and out, with high fences surrounding them, locked doors, and screens or bars on windows. Residents' movements throughout the facility are restricted and closely supervised by the staff. The living quarters of the medium security cottage and dormitory-style facilities are more homelike, but they offer little privacy for residents. Medium security training schools often are surrounded by fences, and therefore resemble maximum security juvenile facilities. Few juvenile training schools are minimum security; most juveniles are sent to a training school because they need restricted confinement.

Juvenile training schools represent the most punitive sanction available in the juvenile justice system. Removing youths from their families, communities, and public school is a significant punishment for many of them. They live under close 24-hour supervision with strict rules and discipline. Serious violations of the rules, especially fighting and assaults, result in short-term commitment to disciplinary segregation, which is a secure detention setting within the training school. Staff members maintain discipline among the residents by withholding privileges or extending the length of stay for those who violate any rules.

Training School Programs

Many training schools do have some good programs, including medical and dental care, an accredited school, vocational training, recreation, and treatment programs.

Rehabilitation is still the primary purpose of juvenile training schools. The treatment methods that are used most widely are behavior modification, guided group interaction, transactional analysis, reality therapy, and positive peer culture. Efforts are made to prepare the juveniles for return to their families and communities. Juveniles who have made satisfactory adjustment and are within a few weeks of their release may be allowed to make home visits or take part in work-release programs in the community. The goal of rehabilitation has seldom been achieved in most juvenile training schools. Studies indicate that few of the programs being used in training schools are effective in preventing future delinquency, although there is some evidence that institutional treatment may work with some youth. Carol Garrett (1985) reviewed more than 100 studies conducted between 1960 and 1983 on juvenile corrections treatment programs such as counseling, behavior modification, and life-skill improvement. Garrett found no single treatment strategy that was most effective, but she concluded that the majority of interventions did show change in a positive direction. On the other hand, Steven Lab and John Whitehead (1988) analyzed juvenile correctional research done from 1975 to 1984 and concluded that treatment has little impact on recidivism. One problem seems to be that the programs themselves are not being used effectively (Whitehead and Lab, 1989). The youth workers and counselors of juvenile training schools face the dilemma of trying to adapt programs to a diverse and varied juvenile offender population. The institutional setting in which the primary concern is control of some of the most serious delinquents presents a challenge for the correctional staff in fulfilling educational and treatment goals.

Abuse and Oppression

Despite the goals of treatment, juvenile training schools remain institutional settings marked by oppressiveness and fear. As states confine dangerous juvenile offenders together with younger, smaller, or less serious offenders in the same institution, even the closest supervision and the best programs have little positive effects. Training school staff members are often powerless to prevent incidents of inmate abuse by other inmates (Feld, 1977). Bartollas, Miller, and Dinitz (1976) examined victimization in a maximum security juvenile institution in Columbus, Ohio. In this training school, which inmates called a "jungle," 90 percent of the residents were involved in abusing other inmates or were victims of abuse. Juveniles who are confined in training schools find the institutional environment oppressive and stressful. Despite any good intentions of treatment or "training," staff must first be concerned about maintaining security and close supervision among the residents. Wooden (1976) documented multiple examples of abuse of juvenile inmates by oppressive correctional workers in state training schools. Many state training schools resemble adult prisons with security precautions such as restriction of movement throughout the facility, regimented schedules, and occasional strip searches for contraband. Adaptation to the institutional setting becomes a higher priority than treatment for the juvenile residents. Gaining acceptance from their peers in the institution is of more immediate importance than working toward a positive adjustment to the community. The inmate subculture in training schools presents a more serious problem with the introduction of youth gangs in many juvenile institutions throughout the nation.

Coeducational training schools have been developed in many states as a way to humanize and normalize juvenile institutions. They have been effective in some respects, but training school staff must still deal with close supervision and security issues while trying to implement treatment programs among a juvenile population more concerned with adapting in an oppressive institutional environment. Unfortunately, little can be positively stated about juvenile training schools. Punishment does not work to change juvenile offenders, and the punitive setting of most training schools is more likely to make juveniles worse than to result in any positive change. Training school personnel face limitations in correcting juvenile offenders because they cannot make any impact in the areas where juvenile crime begins: the community, the home, peers, and schools. The least-restrictive model remains the more appropriate correctional strategy. Policymakers must balance public safety concerns with the need to reintegrate wayward juveniles with the community and social institutions such as the schools.

Other Community Programs

The main types of community-based programs are group homes, foster care, and day treatment programs. Group homes, also referred to as "halfway houses," are small residential facilities in the community that are designed to house about 10–25 youths. Group homes serve as an alternative to incarceration or a short-term community placement for youth on probation or after-care supervision, and they serve as "halfway houses" for youths needing semi-secure placement. Foster care programs offer temporary placement for juveniles who must be removed from their own homes. Foster parents provide shelter, food, and clothing for neglected, abused, or delinquent children. Local or state governments provide subsidies to foster parents to cover their expenses. It is difficult to find people willing to serve as foster parents, especially for delinquent youngsters. Foster care places considerable stress on a home, because many delinquent youth have experienced abusive parental relationships and are therefore distrustful and rebellious toward foster parents. Foster care is a better placement alternative for youths who must be removed from their biological parents. Foster parents are able to provide temporary shelter with more consistent, firm supervision than troubled juveniles may have been receiving in their own homes. Short-term placement with foster parents gives more time for probation officers to seek other placement alternatives. Day treatment programs are nonresidential programs that offer delinquent youths a variety of educational, counseling, recreational, and training activities. They are less expensive to operate because they are nonresidential and require fewer staff members.

Boot Camps

Boot camps were developed as part of the trend toward more harsh treatment for juvenile offenders. Boot camps, also referred to as "shock incarceration," are alternatives to training school incarceration, where youths are housed for periods of 3–6 months in facilities that resemble military training camps (Whitehead and Lab, 2004). Officers resembling a drill instructors supervise the residents, and each day begins with calisthenics, running, and conditioning exercises. Proponents of boot camps believe that the focus on military-type discipline and physical training will be effective in changing the attitudes and bad habits of many chronic juvenile offenders. Boot camps have also been promoted as a way to reduce crowding in correctional facilities and to reduce costs. Research results on the effectiveness of boot camps are mixed. Some residents have responded well to the discipline and training, but Mackenzie (1994) found that any positive results of boot camps are not from the military atmosphere but from educational and rehabilitative programming. An evaluation of three boot camps indicated that recidivism rates were no better than for juvenile offenders in other correctional programs, and the costs per day were similar to costs of juvenile institutions, although the overall costs were less because juvenile offenders spent less time in boot camps (Peters et al., 1997). The researchers concluded that boot camps are no more effective than many other juvenile corrections programs, but do serve the purpose of offering a more punitive alternative than probation, while not increasing the population of juvenile correctional facilities.

Wilderness Camps

A viable institutional alternative for juvenile offenders is the type of outdoor education and training program known as wilderness camps. The goals of wilderness programs are to help youths gain self-confidence and self-reliance by placing them in outdoor settings and challenging them with new physical tasks that appear impossible, especially for metropolitan juvenile offenders who are unfamiliar with wilderness settings (Greenwood and Zimring, 1985). Wilderness programs attempt to accomplish their goals through backpacking in wilderness areas, high-altitude camping, mountain hiking, rock climbing, and rappelling from platforms, trees, or cliffs. Participants first receive training in basic skills, then participate in an expedition, and finally are tested in a solo experience. The wilderness experience lasts 3–4 weeks.

VisionQuest is a survival program based in Tucson, Arizona. The program contracts with juvenile courts and takes juveniles who are committed to the program from California, Pennsylvania, and several other states. VisionQuest programs, lasting 12–18 months, include wilderness camps, cross-country travel on a wagon train, or a voyage on a large sailboat. Participants are closely supervised and rigorously challenged emotionally, intellectually, and physically. VisionQuest has attracted some controversy for its confrontational style with juveniles who do not perform up to expectations, slack off, or act out (Greenwood and Zimring, 1985).

Several states have developed wilderness camps as alternatives to placement in a correctional facility. The state of Minnesota has operated a camp for offenders who have failed to comply with probation conditions, but who do not need secure placement in the state training school. Thistledew Camp, located between two lakes in a remote forest area of northern Minnesota, features a unique educational facility intended to serve delinquent youth who have experienced failure in the home, school, and community. Education is provided for youths at all levels, and all classroom teachers are certified in learning disabilities (LDs) or emotional/behavioral disorders (EBDs) to provide optimum services for students with special needs. About a third of the time at Thistledew Camp is devoted to Challenge, an outdoor wilderness survival program. Challenge is a high-adventure wilderness experience designed to build individual self-confidence, develop leadership abilities, and teach the importance of a group effort. Residents receive training and instruction in the use of equipment and basic wilderness techniques. Expeditions are conducted throughout the year and geared to the seasons. Treks include canoeing, backpacking, rock climbing, cross-country skiing, and traveling by snowshoe. Expeditions are planned to be rugged and difficult in order to build self-confidence and to teach the importance of teamwork. "Solo camping" is a final phase of Challenge. Camping alone in an isolated area for 3 days and nights, residents experience loneliness, hunger, and cold, and they learn how to handle those situations in a self-reliant manner (Minnesota Department of Corrections, 2004).

Wilderness programs are also used in conjunction with probation supervision. Staffed by probation officers and lay volunteers, wilderness probation involves juveniles in outdoor expeditions to give them a sense of confidence and purpose (Callahan, 1985). Counseling and group therapy are combined with day hikes and a wilderness experience. The programs provide an opportunity for juveniles on probation to confront difficulties in their lives and to attain some personal satisfaction. Wilderness programs have been effective in producing positive changes in juvenile offenders, but research shows mixed results as to their effectiveness in reducing recidivism. Lipsey, Wilson, and Cothern (2000) found that wilderness and challenge programs were not effective in reducing recidivism among serious juvenile offenders. Programs that combine education, skills development, and counseling show more positive results (Lipsey et al., 2000).

Disproportionate Minority Confinement

Minority youths accounted for 7 in 10 (65 percent) of juveniles held in custody for a violent offense in 1999 (Sickmund, 2004). Blacks (39 percent) and Hispanics (18 percent) outnumbered whites (38 percent) among the juvenile offenders held in residential placement in 1999. The proportion of minority youths committed to public facilities nationwide (66 percent) was nearly twice that of the juvenile population (34 percent). In six states and the District of Columbia, the minority proportion of the total population of juvenile offenders in residential placement was greater than 75 percent. Custody rates present a dramatic picture of disproportionate minority confinement. For every 100,000 black juveniles in the United States, 1,004 were in a residential placement in 1999 compared with 485 Hispanics and 212 whites per 100,000 in the general population (Sickmund, 2004: 10).

Three factors may explain disproportionate minority confinement (DMC): overrepresentation, disparity, and discrimination (Sickmund, 2004). Overrepresentation means that the proportion of a group in the justice system is larger than the proportion in the general population. Disparity means that the chance of being arrested, detained, or adjudicated differs for different groups of youth. Discrimination means that justice officials treat one group of juveniles differently because of gender, race, or ethnicity. Discrimination is a possible explanation for disparity and overrepresentation of minority youth in the justice system. If racial and ethnic discrimination exists, minorities are more likely to be arrested by police, referred to court intake, petitioned for formal processing, adjudicated delinquent, and placed in a residential facility. Differential decision making throughout the juvenile justice system by police, probation, and court officials may account for minority overrepresentation. Disparity and overrepresentation may, on the other hand, be the result of minority members committing disproportionately more crimes than white ones or being involved in more serious crimes that come to the attention of police and are more likely to be processed through the justice system. Thus, minority overrepresentation in the justice system and in confinement may be explained by behavioral and legal factors, rather than by discrimination (Sickmund, 2004).

Minority youths are disproportionately represented at every stage of the juvenile justice process (Pope and Feyerherm, 1995). Police arrests involve a disproportionate number of minority youths, especially for more serious violent crimes (Snyder, 2004) (see Chapter 1), and a disproportionate number of minority youths are represented in juvenile court cases (Puzzanchera et al., 2003) (see Chapter 1). Results of self-report measures show that delinquent behavior is spread equally among youths of all social classes and racial/ethnic groups, and in fact white middle-class youths report involvement in offenses such as drug violations to a greater extent than lower-class and minority youths (Elliott et al., 1985) (see Chapter 1). Data from victimization surveys have indicated that the violent offending rate for black juveniles was four times higher than for white juveniles during the years 1992–1998 (Lynch, 2002; Sickmund, 2004). There is evidence, however, that victims report a higher rate of serious/violent offenses committed by African Americans compared to white and Hispanic youths (Rubin, 2001).

Research evidence confirms that minority youths receive more severe juvenile court dispositions than do white youths, even after controlling for legal variables. In California, African American youths comprise 8.7 percent of the population but 37 percent of youths in confinement. Police arrest black youths at rates 2.2 times greater than their share of the population, and judges sentence them to juvenile institutions at rates 4.6 times greater than white youths (Krisberg and Austin, 1993: 123–125). Among youths referred for violent crimes, California juvenile courts detained almost two-thirds (64.7 percent) of black youths compared with fewer than half (47.1 percent) of white juveniles and sentenced to juvenile institutions 11.4 percent of black youths compared with 9.4 percent of Latino and only 3.4 percent of white youths (Krisberg and Austin, 1993: 125). The authors concluded that race clearly plays at least an indirect role in juvenile court decision making, and African Americans are disproportionately represented throughout the system, particularly in detention centers and state training schools. Analyses of juvenile court dispositions in Florida showed a consistent pattern of unequal treatment. Bishop and Frazier (1996) found that nonwhite youths were more likely than comparable white youths to be recommended for petition to court, to be held in detention prior to the court hearing, to be formally processed in juvenile court, and to receive the most restrictive court dispositions. More recent studies have found mixed results for differential treatment of minority youths in the juvenile justice system. In a study of the arrests of juveniles for violent crimes, Pope and Snyder (2003) found no differences in the overall likelihood of arrest of white and nonwhite juveniles after controlling for legal factors and characteristics of the crime incident such as the victim and extent of injury. Others have suggested that arrest rates for serious/violent crimes are similar for blacks and whites because police exercise little discretion in handling the more serious offenses. More police discretion is allowed with minor offenses, however, with the result that African American youths are arrested more often for minor offenses than are similarly offending white youths. Black youths, therefore, may be more likely than whites to get arrest records for offenses such as drug crimes, curfew, and truancy violations (Rubin, 2001). Arrest records and prior delinquent histories are among the legal factors that make confinement more likely.

Racially disproportionate rates of arrest and confinement may not be a benign result of juvenile justice officials' decision making based on youths who presumably need more intervention and social control. Barry Feld (1999) has argued that the juvenile court was designed and intended to discriminate between white middle-class children and the children of poor and immigrant parents, and it should come as no surprise that arrests and confinement are racially disproportionate.

If young people's real needs differ because of social circumstances, such as poverty or a single-parent household that correlate strongly with race, then the ideology of "individualized treatment" necessarily will have a racially disparate impact. Racial disproportionality in a system designed to differentiate on the basis of social structural, economic, or personal circumstances should come as no surprise. But in a society formally committed to racial equality, punitive sentences based on social and personal attributes that produce a disparate racial impact implicate the legitimacy, fairness, and justice of the process (Feld, 1999: 265).

David Cole (1999) has argued that while our criminal justice system is based theoretically on equality before the law, the practices and administration of justice are in fact "predicated on the exploitation of inequality." He contends that we have not simply ignored the effects of inequality in the justice process, or tried but failed to achieve equality in administering justice. Rather, he contends that *our criminal justice system affirmatively depends on inequality. Absent race and class disparities, the privileged among us could not enjoy as much constitutional protection of our liberties as we do; and without those disparities, we could not afford the policy of mass incarceration that we have pursued over the past two decades*" (Cole, 1999: 5; italics in original). Cole cites the example of how the "war on drugs" shifted attention from the users of drugs to the dealers and sellers. In the 1960s the use of marijuana spread from being a ghetto problem, where it was used by the lower class, to widespread use on college campuses. Laws and practices then changed to focus more on the dealers and sellers than on users. The same might be said for the spread of cocaine use since the 1990s, in which many users are middle- and upper-class persons, but a significant number of dealers and sellers are lower-class minorities. Cole (1999) noted that police and prosecutors began to leave users alone, and instead targeted dealers and sellers. He contends that when the criminal law begins to affect the children of the white majority, our response is not to get tough, but rather to get lenient. Americans maintain a harsh tough-on-crime attitude as long as the burden of punishment falls disproportionately on minority populations. "The white majority could not possibly maintain its current attitude toward crime and punishment were the burden of punishment felt by the same white majority that prescribes it" (Cole, 1999: 153).

Drug abuse is a problem that has serious consequences, including health problems, school failure and dropout, unemployment, family problems, and criminal sanctions. The question is not whether the "war on drugs" was the most effective approach for control and prevention of drugs. The issue is the unfair and unequal application of the laws regarding the possession, use, and selling of illegal drugs. The enforcement of drug laws by police and the courts have contributed to the disproportionate confinement of minority offenders.

Federal Government Response to DMC

Disproportionate minority confinement has not gone unnoticed by the federal government. In 1988, Congress amended the Juvenile Justice and Delinquency Prevention (JJDP) Act of 1974 (Public Law 93–415, 42 U.S.C. 5601) to require states to address disproportionate minority confinement in their state plans. In 2002, Congress broadened the concept of disproportionate minority confinement to include disproportionate minority contact at all stages of the juvenile justice system. The JJDP Act requires that states determine whether the proportion of minorities in the justice system and in confinement exceeded their proportion in the population, to document the extent of the problem, and to demonstrate efforts to reduce it where it exists (Hsia et al., 2004). Most states have responded to the federal mandate, taking steps to assess state levels of disproportionate minority confinement. Several factors have been identified that contribute to differential decision making throughout the juvenile justice system and to disproportionate minority confinement:

•Racial stereotyping and cultural insensitivity

•Lack of alternatives to detention and incarceration

•Misuse of discretionary authority in implementing laws and policies

•Lack of culturally and linguistically appropriate services (Krisberg and Austin, 1993: 129–132; Hsia et al., 2004: 12)

School Problems and Social Factors and DMC

In response to the JJDP Act, 10 states have identified school problems as factors contributing to disproportionate minority confinement. The lack of educational resources in minority neighborhood schools, the failure of schools to engage minority students and their families, the inability to prevent early and high rates of school dropout among minority students, and the resulting failure of minority students and their families to fully participate in the school system contribute to school failure, involvement in delinquency, and the likelihood of confinement (Hsia et al., 2004: 12).

Thirteen states identified poverty, substance abuse, lack of job opportunities, and high crime rates in predominantly minority neighborhoods, placing minority youth at higher risk for delinquent behaviors. Eleven states found that a disproportionate number of youth in confinement came from low-income, single-parent (mostly female-headed) households, with low-paying jobs or unsteady employment. Family disintegration, diminished family values, substance abuse, and insufficient supervision contribute to delinquent behavior and are factors in court officials' decisions to confine youth where they will receive more supervision and treatment (Hsia et al., 2004: 13).

Rubin (2001) has contended that juvenile justice decision makers in every community must closely examine every step of the process to reduce DMC. He offered several suggestions for reducing minority overrepresentation in the juvenile justice system and in confinement: (1) examine law enforcement interventions and use interventions prior to arrest; (2) examine detention intake; (3) examine changes in probation intake, prosecutor diversion and formal petitioning practices; (4) examine probation practices and expectations; (5) examine practices in community corrections programs, institutions and aftercare; and (6) examine defense counsel and judicial practices (Rubin, 2001: 15–16).

From Deinstitutionalization to "Get-Tough" Policies

Dramatic changes have taken place in juvenile corrections in the past few decades. Juvenile corrections policies have gone from deinstitutionalization to a "get-tough" approach, with a return to greater use of institutions. Juvenile justice administrators and corrections officials recognized two decades ago that committing delinquents together in isolated training schools away from the community was not an effective long-range answer to juvenile crime. Thus began a trend toward deinstitutionalization or "decarceration" and greater use of community correctional alternatives. That trend was curtailed and then reversed in the 1990s. Policymakers have been pressured by public demands to "do something" about youth involvement in drugs, gangs, and violent crime. The usual response has been to "get tough" on crime and criminals, which usually means a return to incarceration of offenders. Statistics indicate that after a decade of decarceration efforts, the number of juveniles being incarcerated has increased. From 1985 to 1989 the average daily population and total census count of juveniles in public facilities increased 14 percent and the juvenile custody rate per 100,000 increased 19 percent (Allen-Hagen, 1991: 2). According to the CJRP in 1999, a total of 134,011 juveniles was held in 2,939 facilities, and the number of delinquent offenders in residential facilities increased 5 percent from 1997 to 1999 and 50 percent from 1991 to 1999 (Sickmund, 2004). The increasing number of adjudicated youths sent to juvenile corrections facilities does not even include the increasing number who are waived to criminal court, tried as adults, and often sent to adult institutions. Juvenile corrections policies in the 1990s were dominated by a more conservative, control-oriented philosophy.

The commitment to rehabilitation of offenders began to shift by the 1970s, in part due to a widely publicized report by Robert Martinson (1974) (see Lipton et al., 1975) in which he argued that rehabilitation programs have not had an effect on recidivism. Martinson's conclusions that "nothing works" in corrections had a great national impact, despite the fact that Ted Palmer (1975) wrote a detailed rebuttal questioning Martinson's findings, and Martinson (1979) himself retracted some of his earlier premature and exaggerated conclusions. The demise of the rehabilitative ideal actually had less to do with whether correctional programs were effective in changing offenders and more to do with a shift in the viewpoints of the public and politicians regarding crime and criminals. Cullen and Gilbert (1982) suggested that crime-control policies reflect lawmakers' ideological assumptions about the causes of crime and the most effective strategies to reduce crime. Garland (2001) contended that cultural patterns structure how the public and politicians feel about offenders. The politics of the 1980s produced a greater division between the jobless and the employed, between blacks and whites, and between the affluent suburbs and the struggling inner cities; social problems such as violence, street crime, and drug abuse became worse. Accompanying these political and social changes was the view that punishing individuals for criminal and delinquent behavior was more appropriate than rehabilitation and change strategies. Contrary to the views of positivist criminologists that crime was caused by individual and social problems over which an individual had little control, law violators were now seen as evil individuals who deserved to be punished. Crime was not seen as a sign of need or deprivation, but was viewed as a rational choice by persons who lacked discipline and self-control who needed to be deterred and deserved to be punished harshly (Garland, 2001: 102). Garland (2001) noted that the term that best describes this new conservative crime control policy is "zero tolerance." Intolerance of crime and criminals has pervaded society and legislative chambers, communities and school hallways, and the proposed solutions are harsh discipline and punishment.

There are signs that rehabilitation is making a comeback (Cullen, 2005). A return to the rehabilitative ideal (see Allen, 1981) is not necessarily a result of a softening of attitudes toward crime and criminals, but a realization that attempting to control crime through incarceration is costly and produces no significant reduction in crime rates. Although there is considerable disagreement as to whether training schools and prisons are an effective deterrent to crime, many criminal justice experts point to research evidence that greater use of incarceration may increase rather than decrease crime rates (Garland, 2001). Cullen and associates have conducted studies on public opinions about rehabilitation and found that Americans still strongly support the view that efforts should be made to rehabilitate offenders (Cullen et al., 2000; Cullen, 2005). There is evidence of significant public and legislative support for rehabilitation of juvenile offenders, who are still generally seen as more amenable to treatment than adult offenders. The exceptions are the serious and chronic juvenile offenders who are likely to face waiver to criminal court or extended juvenile jurisdiction prosecution (as discussed in the previous chapter). The majority of juvenile offenders may receive some rehabilitative interventions on juvenile probation and community supervision.

Juvenile Probation and Community Corrections

Probation is the most common form of community supervision and treatment in the juvenile justice system. Probation supervision may be combined with orders of restitution, temporary placement in a residential facility, and participation in a treatment program. Juveniles are placed on probation under specified conditions or court orders that must be followed. Failure to comply with probation conditions may result in revocation of probation and placement in a residential or institutional facility. A variety of "intermediate sanctions" have been developed to provide more public safety than regular probation, while being less intrusive and expensive than correctional institutions. These alternatives to incarceration include intensive probation supervision, electronic monitoring, and home detention.

History of Juvenile Probation

The concept of probation was originally developed through the efforts of John Augustus, a Boston boot maker who persuaded a judge in 1841 to release an offender to him for supervision in the community rather than sentence him to prison. Augustus worked with hundreds of offenders and set the stage for probation as we know it today (Sieh, 1993). As the first probation officer, John Augustus developed many of the probation strategies that continue to be used in probation today: investigation and screening, supervision, educational and employment services, and providing guidance and assistance.

The State of Massachusetts followed up on the work of Augustus and established a visiting probation agent system in 1869. Probation was developed statewide in Massachusetts by 1890, and many other states adopted probation statutes soon thereafter. What began as a volunteer movement became the most common correctional alternative, funded and administered by the courts or by state or local government. Today juvenile probation is administered by either the juvenile court or a group of courts in the jurisdiction, state or local department of youth services, a department of social services, or some combination of these (McShane and Krause, 1993: 67; Torbet, 1996). In either organizational context, the juvenile court judge and the probation staff have a close working relationship. Today virtually all counties in the nation have juvenile probation services, although in some remote rural counties a single probation officer may serve multiple counties and have the responsibility of covering a wide geographical area. Larger metropolitan juvenile probation departments are administered by a chief probation officer, with one or more assistants overseeing specialized units within the department. Larger departments may have units specializing in intake services, investigation and writing the predisposition report, a field supervision unit, and detention services.

Probation Goals and Objectives

Probation is the primary form of community supervision and treatment in the juvenile justice system. There are four components of juvenile probation:

1. As a legal disposition juveniles are under court supervision with conditions and rules with which they must comply before being released.
2. As an alternative to incarceration probation is a nonpunitive disposition that emphasizes correctional treatment and reintegration of juvenile offenders.
3. Probation is a subsystem of the juvenile justice system.
4. As a court service agency, probation officers conduct investigations for the court, supervise juveniles, and provide services that are helpful to youth, their families and the community (National Advisory Commission on Criminal Justice Standards and Goals, 1973: 312).

Probation is the most common disposition used by juvenile court judges. As an alternative to incarceration, probation has a number of advantages over institutional commitment or residential care. Probation is a privilege, however, and not a right (del Carmen, 1985). Juvenile court judges emphasize to young offenders the conditions that must be met in order to remain on probation and be successfully terminated rather than face revocation and possible commitment to a correctional facility. Probation has been criticized as a lenient sentence that provides little supervision or close monitoring of offenders. Community corrections experts have countered such criticism and noted the multiple advantages of probation: (1) reintegration of offenders in the community while under court orders and supervision; (2) furthering the goals of justice and protecting the community from further delinquent behavior; (3) monitoring probation conditions and providing services to help change offenders and meet probation objectives; (4) retaining young offenders in the community, with their families, in public or alternative schools, and thus avoiding the difficulties of reintegration; and (5) avoiding the fiscal costs and the negative influence and stigma of commitment to a correctional facility (see Latessa and Allen, 2003: 101–102).

The Practice of Probation. In practice, probation is basically an agreement between the juvenile court and the young offender. The adjudicated delinquent agrees to comply with the court orders and probation conditions and is released to his or her parents. In cases where the probation officer's investigation has indicated that parental supervision is lacking, the youth may be placed with a legal guardian, foster parents, or in a group home. In either case, the placement is less punitive than commitment to a juvenile institution. The time period for probation supervision is generally for an indefinite period of time, but it usually does not exceed 2 years. Each probation case is reviewed periodically to assure that some progress is being made, treatment goals are being met, and to assure that the juvenile is not kept on probation unnecessarily. If a juvenile is not complying with probation conditions, the probation officer is expected to take the case before the judge, who may choose to revise the probation conditions or order the youth referred to a different placement, including commitment to a more secure setting if he or she seems to present a danger to self or community.

Probation Officer Responsibilities

Intake. The *intake officer* is responsible for accepting referrals from the police and in some cases from the schools, parents, or other social agencies. The intake officer must verify that the department has jurisdiction in each case. This involves determining from a written report of the referring officer that the child is allegedly in violation of a provision in the state juvenile code. The range of forbidden juvenile behavior is quite broad, ranging from status offenses such as disobeying parents and running away to felony offenses. The intake officer must also verify the child's date of birth to ascertain that the department has jurisdiction. State juvenile codes vary, but most legal definitions of juvenile cite ages of 10–17 years. The intake officer must immediately inform the parents of the referral and decide whether to turn the child over to the parents pending further action or temporarily detain him or her. Options available include a "reprimand and release," diversion and referral to a community agency for informal supervision and intervention, and working with school officials to place students with learning and/or behavioral problems in an alternative school. These referrals are informal and voluntary, but they may be accompanied by the threat of more formal action if the youth is not cooperative. Under the "least restrictive" philosophy of the juvenile justice system, the goal of probation agencies is to divert minor juvenile offenders from processing through the juvenile court, and refer them to other agencies for short-term intervention and guidance. Diversion is considered most appropriate for status offenders and youth who have allegedly committed minor property crimes. The intake officer serves a screening function, separating those cases that seem appropriate for diversion from cases that should be petitioned to juvenile court. The decision of whether to file a petition for adjudication is made in consultation with the county or state prosecuting attorney.

Investigation and Predisposition Report. Delinquency petitions are filed by a district attorney (prosecutor) in cases of juveniles referred for violent crimes, more serious property offenses, and those with persistent minor offenses. When the decision has been made to take a case to court, it will be referred to an investigation unit pending appearance in the juvenile court. In juvenile courts that use a bifurcated hearing (separate adjudication and disposition stages), the probation officer will conduct an investigation and write a predisposition report after the child has been adjudicated in the fact-finding part of the hearing. Many courts combine the adjudication and disposition parts of the hearing, so the report must be prepared beforehand and ready for the judge to read if the youth was found delinquent in the adjudication phase of the hearing. In either case, the probation officer generally has at least 30 days to complete the social history report. As part of the investigation, the probation officer will interview the youth and his or her parents, will review current and past arrest records, may request a psychological evaluation, and may review reports or interview officials from social agencies and schools. The probation officer's investigation will involve at least one interview with the youth and parents in the probation office and include at least one visit to the home and often a visit or a phone call to the child's school.

Considerable importance is placed on the predisposition report, as it represents the primary source of background information on the juvenile and is considered invaluable for the judge in making the most appropriate dispositional decision. The importance accorded to the report varies with different judges, however. Some judges request a complete report from the probation officer, which may include a risk assessment, a recommended supervision and treatment plan with specific goals, and possibly a recommended contractual agreement between the youth (which may include the parents) and the court. Other judges may prefer a brief summary statement of the youth's background and may place equal or greater importance on the legal circumstances of the case. Since probation officers serve the court, they understandably will write the kind of report that the juvenile court judge prefers. Probation officers also come to know the particular legal philosophy of the judge and whether he or she leans more toward a punitive or treatment philosophy for juvenile offenders. There is evidence that presentence reports reflect probation officers' attitudes (Katz, 1982), and some analyses of the judicial process suggest that officers' recommendations simply reflect what they believe the judge wants to hear (Carter and Wilkins, 1967; Blumberg, 1973: 283). Predisposition reports present an accurate picture of the youth and the family background, but the recommendations often may simply reflect what the judge has been known to prefer in similar cases. Probation officers have thus been referred to as "judicial civil servants," who are not given full recognition by judges and attorneys in the courtroom, but are now acquiring professional status through more specialized education and training, and whose investigative services are recognized as being invaluable in most courts (Lawrence, 1984).

Supervision and Monitoring Probation Conditions. The third major function of a probation officer is to provide supervision of offenders in the community. When a juvenile court judge sentences a youth to probation, the probation officer generally meets with the youth and his or her parents to explain the rules and conditions of probation, answer any questions about the term of probation and the court's expectations, and ensure that they understand the importance of complying with the probation conditions. The length of time that a juvenile is on probation varies from state to state. Juvenile probation is generally an indeterminate sentence, and probation officers may recommend to the court that probation be terminated after 2 years or less if the juvenile has successfully complied with the conditions and not been rearrested. For older youths or those in need of more supervision, probation may continue for an indefinite period of time until the youth reaches the age of majority, usually 17 or 18 (Sanborn and Salerno, 2005).

The probation officer performs an important role in clarifying and emphasizing the statements and any warnings made by the judge during the hearing. This is particularly true when a child and his or her parents are hesitant to ask the judge or attorney any questions during the tense moments of a court hearing. Most hearings are brief, perfunctory proceedings, often lasting 5–10 minutes or less, and thus the juvenile and the parents may not understand the full significance of the legal proceeding. The probation officer is often more helpful than a defense attorney in explaining the significance of the juvenile court hearing (Lawrence, 1983). The officer explains the rules and conditions of probation and emphasizes the importance of complying with each of them, including reporting regularly to the probation office. Special probation conditions require additional explanation, especially if the court has ordered restitution payments to victims or community service restitution, avoiding drinking or drug use, and participation in drug-treatment programs. Juvenile probation officers face a special challenge in supervising delinquents, because they usually receive little assistance and support from the parents and family. Many juvenile offenders do not have a very good relationship with their parent(s), and they show little respect for their parents' authority. Families of delinquents are often characterized by parental negligence or abuse, inconsistent discipline, poor communication, and poor parenting skills. Probation supervision is more difficult without solid parental and family support. Under those rare but ideal conditions, parents can play an important role in helping a youth comply with probation conditions by in closely supervising their child and communicating regularly with the probation officer. Parental support is especially important in closely monitoring the child's school attendance and behavior, peer associations, and compliance with curfew requirements. Probation officers must perform a dual role of encouraging, helping, and assisting the young offender to make a positive adjustment, while also acting as an authority figure who will report probation violations to the court.

Probation Officer Roles

In carrying out the supervision responsibility, probation officers fulfill three major roles and functions: casework management, treatment, and surveillance. *Casework management* involves maintaining current files on each juvenile in a caseload averaging 40 or more cases (Torbet, 1996). In addition to the police offense reports and social history report, the case file includes periodic contact reports of every personal visit and telephone call regarding the juvenile. Contacts are made with each juvenile once a week to once a month or less, depending on the intensity level of supervision needed. Documentation in the juvenile's file is important. Cases are often managed by more than one caseworker, or may be transferred to another officer who is less familiar with the case. If the probation officer files a court petition for revocation of probation, he or she may be called to testify to the violations of probation conditions including the exact dates, circumstances, and details of the violations. Paperwork and file management are sources of frustration and complaints among probation officers, but are an important part of the job responsibilities (Lawrence, 1984).

Casework management has developed and evolved considerably since the early days of probation, but the principles and challenges remain the same. John Augustus, the father of probation, was careful to select only those offenders who were believed to be amenable to treatment and change, The casework management task now usually includes some form of classification procedure to determine the risk and needs of offenders. A number of risk and needs assessment instruments have been developed to assist with identifying offenders' needs, classifying them according to their level of risk and supervision level (see Latessa and Allen, 2003: 296–312).

The *treatment* function of a juvenile probation officer focuses on his or her role as a caseworker or counselor. We have noted the importance of working with the parents and families of juvenile delinquents. One of the most difficult challenges faced by probation officers is the large number of juveniles from dysfunctional families. Parents have often lost control and the respect of their child—the parent–child relationship has deteriorated to the point that the youth has become incorrigible, refusing to comply with the parents' demands. Many parents have never learned to use effective communication and management strategies. Juvenile probation officers commonly emphasize that they "work with as many delinquent parents as they do delinquent children!" Because a poor parent–child relationship is one of the major problems faced by probation officers in working with delinquents, some educational background in family counseling, social work, or general counseling skills has traditionally been one of the job requirements for juvenile probation. Training seminars in family intervention and guidance are provided for many juvenile officers around the nation, and probation conferences often include at least one session on the subject. Because the minimum educational requirement for probation officers is a 4-year college degree, they are not expected to provide professional counseling services, nor are they qualified to do so. One of their responsibilities is to identify problems that require further professional treatment and then refer the child and family to mental health services for family counseling and guidance.

Recognition in the 1970s that juvenile probation officers had neither the expertise nor the time to provide professional counseling and treatment led to an emphasis on the probation officer as *resource broker* or *resource manager* rather than counselor. The National Advisory Commission on Criminal Justice Standards and Goals recommended that probation agencies should "redefine the role of probation officer from caseworker to community resource manager" (1973: 320). As a resource broker or manager, the officer's responsibility is to assess the juvenile's needs and then make appropriate referrals to other social agencies that can best provide the needed services. The resource broker model of probation is most appropriate in metropolitan jurisdictions where there are more available agencies and resources for referral. Juveniles on probation in smaller communities with fewer available resources, however, are likely to receive only the extent of counseling and guidance that the probation officers themselves are able to provide.

The *surveillance* function requires the probation officer to closely monitor juveniles to make certain that they are complying with the probation conditions. This may be accomplished through questions directed at the juvenile during office visits, and when suspicions arise the officer will generally verify the juvenile's compliance through telephone calls or personal visits to the juvenile's home or school. The surveillance function is much like that of a police officer, and probation officers have the authority to take probationers into custody for violating conditions of probation. Some probation officers carry a badge, handcuffs, and even a handgun; although the latter is more common among adult probation officers with high-risk caseloads in metropolitan areas. The surveillance function of juvenile probation is not emphasized as much as it is in adult probation. Juvenile probation officers generally focus on youths' compliance with probation conditions and depends on police officers to arrest, investigate, and report the commission of a new crime by the juvenile. For juveniles suspected of continued illegal drug use, however, probation agencies may require drug testing. Violation of probation conditions is considered a "technical violation," and officers have more latitude in whether to file for revocation of probation than when a youth is rearrested by police for a new crime. In either case, probation revocation is not automatic, however, and the juvenile is entitled to a revocation hearing under due process guidelines established by the U.S. Supreme Court in the 1972 case of *Morrissey v. Brewer* (408 U.S. 471, 92 S.Ct. 2593). If the judge finds that there is sufficient evidence that probation conditions have been violated, he or she may revoke probation and commit the juvenile to a state training school or may choose a range of less punitive alternatives, including more intensive probation supervision with more restrictive conditions or temporary placement in a semi-secure group home placement.

Probation Officer Role Conflict

Probation officers are charged with helping offenders to change, but as officers of the court they are also expected to monitor compliance with court orders. The two roles represent treatment versus surveillance—acting as a counselor or social worker one moment, and a law enforcement officer the next. Probation officers experience "role conflict" in attempting to fulfill both functions at the same time (Lawrence, 1984; Latessa and Allen, 2003). Attention to both responsibilities is necessary, however. An important role of the probation agency is to help probationers adjust to problems at home, school, and in the community. They are also responsible for complying with probation rules and avoiding further delinquent involvement. Probation administrators responded to problems of role definition and conflict more than 30 years ago through research and training designed to clarify probation officer roles. O'Leary and Duffee (1973) developed a "correctional policy model" to illustrate how correctional agents' decisions and policies place great emphasis on the offender (such as rehabilitation) or great emphasis on the community (such as reform or reintegration). A correctional policy inventory administered to a large sample of correctional administrators, middle managers, and line officers indicated significant differences in their individual roles and policies in working with clients. They concluded that role differences are understandable and acceptable, provided that correctional workers are aware of the different roles and strive to maintain some balance in working for both offender change and community protection. O'Leary (1973) developed a "juvenile justice policy model" and inventory that applied the original model to persons working with juvenile offenders. Juvenile justice officials in the course of their duties perform four different roles: restraint, reform, rehabilitation, and reintegration. The choice of roles varies depending on officials' personal preference, as well as what is perceived to be the most appropriate role to meet offender risks and needs in each particular case. The correctional and juvenile justice policy inventories have been instrumental in probation officer training, helping officers recognize and deal with role conflict. Louis Tomaino (1975) developed a similar model to describe the "five faces of probation supervision." Tomaino noted that probation officers' supervisory practices with offenders vary between a concern for control and a concern for rehabilitation, representing a conflict in roles. He suggested that the most effective supervision approach is the "have-it-make-sense" face. Probationers will obey laws and probation rules when it makes sense to them and when they realize that a law-abiding life best meets their needs. Probation officers should be open but firm and focus on the content of communications with probationers (Tomaino, 1975). Considerable research has been conducted on the dilemmas and difficulties presented by probation officer role conflict (see Latessa and Allen, 2003: 258–263). The nature of the job requirements means that some role conflict will always be present, but education and training can minimize the adverse effects of role conflict on correctional workers and probation officers.

Balanced and Restorative Approach

Many probation departments have taken a "balanced approach" to probation supervision, utilizing a logical consequences model whereby juveniles are held accountable for antisocial behavior. Maloney, Romig, and Armstrong (1988) noted that the purpose of the balanced approach to juvenile probation is to protect the community from delinquency, to make offenders accountable for delinquent acts, and to ensure that juvenile offenders leave the system with more skills to live productively and responsibly in society (1989: 10). Many juvenile probation agencies throughout the United States have adopted the balanced approach, where attention is given equally to the community, the victim, and the juvenile offender (Maloney et al., 1988). Probation officers like the balanced approach with emphasis on the logical consequences model, because it helps to alleviate much of the role conflict experienced by officers trying to fulfill treatment and surveillance functions. Adopting a logical consequences approach in probation supervision reminds juveniles to take probation seriously and encourages more of them to be less resistant and more open to a cooperative working relationship with their probation officer. The balanced approach places emphasis on three programming priorities: offender accountability, competency development, and community protection (Bazemore and Umbreit, 1994: 3). Through restitution and community service, offenders are required to make amends to victims and the community. Community protection is increased through closer surveillance and by directing juvenile offenders' time and energy into more productive activities during nonschool hours. The goal of competency development recognizes the need to help juvenile offenders develop skills, get work experience, interact with conventional adults, earn money, and take part in productive activities. Advocates of the balanced approach emphasize the importance of community organizations working together with juvenile justice professionals and offenders (Bazemore and Umbreit, 1994).

Intermediate Sanctions in Juvenile Corrections

The juvenile court judge traditionally had only two main options when sentencing adjudicated delinquents: probation or commitment to a juvenile institution. Many offenders require more supervision than regular probation, but do not require the constant and costly surveillance provided by a secure correctional facility. The concept of "intermediate sanctions" was developed to provide supervision and correctional services that are literally "between prison and probation" (Morris and Tonry, 1990). Examples of intermediate sanctions that have been implemented in juvenile corrections include intensive probation supervision, day reporting centers, electronic monitoring, and restitution programs. They are commonly used within probation agencies as a part of and in addition to probation supervision. There is evidence that intermediate sanctions are more successful than regular probation supervision and have advantages over institutional commitment in that they are less expensive and avoid severing ties between the juvenile's family and the community (Latessa and Allen, 2003: 329–365).

Intensive Probation Supervision. Probation has been criticized for being too lenient and for providing only minimal supervision. There is no question that many juveniles need more supervision than is possible for a probation officer with a large caseload to provide. Intensive supervision programs have been adopted by many probation agencies as an alternative to sending high-risk juveniles to a correctional institution (Byrne, 1986). A small number of cases (usually no more than 15–25) are assigned to a probation officer, who is expected to make daily contacts and to closely monitor their daily activities. The recidivism rates of juveniles on intensive probation supervision are often higher than those on regular probation, but that is due at least in part to the higher-risk juveniles in the programs and the fact that the officer's close surveillance often detects probation violations that may go unnoticed on regular probation supervision. Even if intensive supervision is no more effective in reducing recidivism of high-risk juvenile offenders, the cost benefits (about one-third that of confinement) make it a desirable alternative to incarceration (Latessa, 1986).

Day Reporting Centers. Day reporting centers have been implemented as an alternative means of assisting probation officers to keep up with the task of monitoring probation clients through personal visits. It is not possible for most probation officers to personally see each of their clients with a caseload of 40 or more cases. Day reporting centers were developed to monitor a larger number of probationers with a smaller number of officers. Offenders in the program are court ordered to report in person to a reporting center, to provide a schedule of planned activities, and to participate in designated activities. Offenders must also call the centers by phone throughout the day, and can also expect random phone calls from the center staff during the day and at home following curfew (Gowdy, 1993). In addition to monitoring probationers' activities, day reporting centers offer a variety of services, including job skills training and placement, drug abuse education, and counseling. Research evidence indicates that day reporting centers have been effective in providing closer monitoring of probation clients without significantly increasing the cost of probation services (Latessa and Allen, 2003: 339–343).

Electronic Monitoring and House Arrest. Juveniles may be placed on probation under special conditions requiring that they remain in their home at all times except for school, employment, or medical reasons. House arrest may be coupled with frequent random phone calls or personal visits or electronic monitoring. In this technological innovation, probationers are fitted with a nonremovable monitoring device attached to their ankle that signals the probation department's computerized monitoring station if the offender leaves the house (see Ball and Lilly, 1986; Petersilia, 1986; Schmidt, 1986; Charles, 1986). The monitoring device is connected to the telephone in the house and makes random phone calls to verify the probationer's presence. Some monitoring devices can detect through a voice analysis if someone other than the probationer responds to the call, and some have a breath analyzer to detect whether the subject has been drinking alcohol. Electronic monitoring has the advantage of operating as an effective alternative to incarceration in a detention center at less than half the cost. Joseph Vaughn (1989) conducted a survey of eight juvenile electronic monitoring programs and found that most were successful in reducing the number of days that juveniles spent in detention; the youths were able to participate in school and work activities during the time they were not confined to their homes. Vaughn found, however, that the treatment benefits of electronic monitoring programs still remain in question. Recent evaluations of electronic monitoring have found little evidence that it has a positive impact on offender recidivism (Latessa and Allen, 2003: 351).

Restitution Programs. One of the goals of community corrections is to hold offenders accountable and to recognize the harm they have done. Restitution programs represent a way for juvenile offenders to literally "pay for" their crimes while on probation. Restitution can take two forms: monetary or service restitution, either to the victim or to the community (Schneider, 1985a; Schneider and Warner, 1989). Under monetary restitution the probationer may be ordered to reimburse the victim of the crime for property damages or the medical costs of personal injury. In the second form, a juvenile may be required to provide some service directly to the victim or to the community. Victim restitution is done with the consent of the victim, and service restitution is usually done under the supervision of a probation officer. Juvenile restitution programs existed in more than 400 jurisdictions throughout the nation, and by 1985 most states had legislation authorizing such programs as part of probation (Schneider, 1989).

Four goals of restitution programs have been identified:

1. Holding juveniles accountable
2. Providing reparation to victims

3. Treating and rehabilitating juveniles
4. Punishing juveniles (Schneider, 1985a: 1)

Restitution programs are usually a part of probation and ordered as a probation condition. They may also be implemented at other stages of the juvenile justice process, such as part of a diversion program or as a method of informal adjustment at probation intake. In support of the goals identified above, restitution offers alternative sentencing options for the court (see Newton, 1979: 435–468). It directs attention to the forgotten persons in the justice process—the victims—and provides monetary compensation or service to them. It is rehabilitative in that the juvenile has an opportunity to compensate the victim for injury or damages, and encourages him or her to be accountable for wrongful actions and become a productive member of society. Restitution is not the same as retribution, which is the belief that offenders must be made to pay for their crimes through punishment. It does meet the dual objectives of rehabilitation and retribution, however, and may improve the public's attitude toward offenders and the justice system because offenders literally pay something back to the victim and to the community, taking responsibility for their actions (Galaway, 1989). Restitution has been criticized as being an unfair and unrealistic expectation for juvenile offenders at a time when unemployment rates are high for all youths (Staples, 1989). For that reason, community service restitution programs, under the supervision of a probation officer or volunteer worker, are more widely used than monetary restitution. Evaluations of restitution programs indicate that they are quite effective as a treatment alternative. Schneider (1986) evaluated programs in four states and found that the program participants had lower recidivism rates than control groups of youths placed on regular probation. The differences were not dramatic (10 percent in recidivism rates in some comparisons), but the restitution programs did seem to result in more positive attitudes among many juveniles (Schneider, 1986: 550). The National Center for Juvenile Justice studied 6,336 probation cases in Utah, which has a statewide restitution program (Butts and Snyder, 1992). In more than half (3,215 or 51 percent) of the cases, restitution was ordered as part of probation. Results of the study showed a significant relationship between the use of restitution and recidivism. Restitution combined with probation was associated with lower recidivism rates one year later, as 32 percent of restitution cases recidivated, and 38 percent of those not paying restitution were involved in new court referrals within one year (Butts and Snyder, 1992: 4). The results of the study suggest that the use of restitution as part of probation is associated with significantly less recidivism among some juvenile offenders. Restitution programs have been recognized as representing the best practices for juvenile court and probation, as they focus on offender accountability and offer an opportunity for juvenile offenders to make reparations to the victim and the community (Kurlychek et al., 1999).

Reexamining Community Corrections Models

Community corrections has undergone many changes in the past two decades. The emphasis on rehabilitation that focused on offenders' needs and problems has given way to greater concerns for public safety and attention to victims. The changes are due in part to increases in crime and more high-risk offenders being sentenced to community corrections programs. Questions have been raised about the effectiveness of rehabilitation and whether it is even a realistic or primary goal of corrections. Community corrections was founded on three models that distinguished it from institutional corrections: diversion, advocacy, and reintegration (Lawrence, 1991a). *Diversion* of less serious or first-time offenders from formal judicial processing to alternative community programming was considered more appropriate for the child and the community. Youths received helpful intervention without the stigma and adverse effects of more punitive sanctions and at less cost to taxpayers. Community corrections agents adopted an *advocacy* role in assisting young offenders through referrals to community resources, educational programs, and employment opportunities. *Reintegration* was the ultimate goal of community corrections in recognition that many offenders are persons who have been alienated from mainstream society and social institutions. Many delinquents are school dropouts or have been "pushed out" of school because of misbehavior and poor performance. Many young offenders lack the education, job skills, and labor market credentials to compete in mainstream society. Reintegration is directed at change in both offenders and the community, through opportunities and resources such as alternative schools, job training, and employment (see O'Leary and Duffee, 1971; Lawrence, 1991a).

We have witnessed a demise of the original community corrections models. Although many treatment programs have shown positive results, the role of rehabilitation has been questioned (Lipton et al., 1975; Allen, 1981). A growing public intolerance of crime, coupled with the belief that community corrections cannot control crime, has resulted in demands for greater use of jails and prisons. Politicians have rushed to embrace punishment rather than community interventions (Garland, 2001). "Getting tough on crime" has become a sure way to gain voter approval. Probation and community corrections have become identified as too lenient and "soft on crime." The readiness of politicians to increase prison sentences but not allocate sufficient funds to corrections departments has resulted in overcrowded prisons and overflowing probation caseloads that render meaningful supervision impossible. The emphasis in corrections is now more on controlling and punishing the offender than on reintegrating him or her into the community.

The original community corrections models have given way to emphases on just deserts, adversary, and restitution (Lawrence, 1991a). Court sanctions based on *just deserts* are now more important than diversion from the system. Sentencing guidelines in many states are based on a just-deserts model, focusing more on the crime than on the criminal (von Hirsch, 1976). Community corrections agents now view themselves more as *adversaries* of the offender than as advocates. The change came about in large part because probation has been criticized for being too lenient and is often viewed as "getting off" rather than as a judicial sanction in its own right. Excessively large probation caseloads have placed unrealistic demands on officers and make probation supervision meaningless. Corrections departments have responded by developing intensive supervision probation (ISP) programs (Byrne, 1986; Petersilia, 1990). In contrast to an advocacy role, the probation officer's role with intensive supervision is in control, surveillance, and monitoring the offender's compliance with probation rules. Offender *restitution* is now more important than offender reintegration. It became readily apparent that victims were the forgotten persons in the criminal justice process. Restitution is a means by which victims and the community may be repaid for the wrongs suffered at the hands of offenders. Restitution programs have been a welcome addition to community corrections, but they will be most effective when they incorporate goals of offender change and reintegration.

Community corrections programs will be more effective by integrating the old and new community corrections models (Lawrence, 1991a). Integrating diversion and deserts, advocacy and adversary roles, and reintegration and restitution is difficult, but not impossible. Crime control and offender reintegration are both necessary ingredients of effective community corrections. Community corrections programs must assure protection for the general public and also offer chances for offenders to free themselves from a no-win criminal lifestyle. Intermediate sanctions offer the necessary degree of control, but equal importance must be given to reintegrating the offender in the community. An effective corrections policy would strive for a balance between punishment and rehabilitation and between emphasis on community protection and offender change. Crime-control strategies and punitive sanctions alone are short-term solutions that further alienate offenders from the community. On the other hand, treatment programs that fail to address offender accountability or the realities and demands of a productive, crime-free lifestyle will not reduce criminal involvement.

"Reintegrative Shaming" in Community Corrections

Community corrections should continue to focus on reintegration, but must also adopt strategies whereby offenders are confronted with the wrongfulness of crime and the damage done to victims and the community. Most corrections experts acknowledge that emphasis must be placed on making the juvenile justice and corrections processes more meaningful and consequential. I have argued for a community corrections model that incorporates internalization, shaming, and reintegration (Lawrence, 1991a: 459–461). "Internalization" is the strategy of behavior change on which a reintegration correctional policy was based (Kelman, 1958; O'Leary and Duffee, 1971). Efforts to reform offenders by force and threats of punishment require constant surveillance and place unrealistic demands on corrections agents. True behavior change means that offenders have internalized community standards and values. To accomplish true reintegration requires changes in the offender and the community. In addition to offender change, reintegration seeks community support to provide opportunities and resources for offenders. Under a reintegration policy, community corrections agents would be involved with community institutions such as schools, businesses, churches, and civic organizations. Equal emphasis would be placed on offender accountability, community protection, and opportunities for education, training and employment.

"Reintegrative shaming" was first described by Braithwaite (1989) as one method of criminal punishment, involving a process by which the community may express disapproval of law violations, followed by reacceptance into the community of law-abiding citizens. The more common form of punishment is stigmatization, whereby the offender is labeled for lawbreaking and the person rather than the behavior is rejected (Braithwaite, 1989: 55). By stigmatizing law violators, we treat them as outcasts, which generally results in high crime rates. Reintegrative shaming is based on a "family model" in which punishment is administered by supportive family members. Braithwaite argued that his theory of offender punishment explains crime variations better than other theories and that it explains the lower crime rates in countries like Japan that emphasize public shaming and acknowledgement of responsibility followed by reacceptance of the wrong-doers (1989: 84–97, 164–145).

There are clearly dangers with advocating a shaming strategy for corrections in America. Images come to mind of historic colonial sanctions such as the ducking stool, the scarlet letter, the stocks and pillory. Many persons today support public shaming practices as

effective crime deterrents, but they omit the reintegrative element of acceptance and support by the community. Karp (1998) has questioned the practice of shaming tactics and
contends that they are ineffective and may be counterproductive in producing any positive offender change. Ordering persons convicted of driving while intoxicated to display
bumper stickers announcing their conviction may be a well-intended effort to shame them
into compliance, but may stigmatize and alienate them from the community. Supporters
of corporal punishment and paddling in schools justify its use as an effective device for
shaming misbehaving students and deterring further misconduct. Beyond the questionable
practice of using physical force to change behavior, however, paddling as punishment is
more stigmatization than reintegrative shaming. Requiring law violators to make public
apologies in a newspaper may be a better example of reintegrative shaming if it is accompanied by an opportunity to make restitution and if the community responds with for-
giveness and acceptance. Gaining compliance from persons, in society or in schools,
requires more than stigmatizing punishment. Reintegrative shaming seeks to encourage
offenders to accept responsibility and to internalize laws and community expectations and
then works toward acceptance and support of them. Under a reintegrative shaming approach,
getting offenders to internalize laws and societal expectations is accompanied by efforts
to involve them positively in the community. Juvenile probation officers might bring together
representatives of the offender's school, employer, and other concerned groups to attend
the court hearing and offer opinions of how they might be able to contribute to monitoring the offender's behavior and assist in his or her rehabilitation (Braithwaite, 1989: 173).
A community-based juvenile justice policy might effectively include shaming penalties
provided that they are accompanied by acceptance and reintegration into the community
(Cole, 1999: 195). The objectives are to increase the level of informal social control and
to achieve reintegration of the offender and community organizations.

Restorative Justice

Reintegrative emphases in community corrections are embodied in restitution programs
that involve "paying for crime" and encouraging reacceptance by the victim and the
community. Victim-offender reconciliation programs (VORPs) combine the concept of
restitution and traditional justice principles that when a person wrongs another, he or she
has a responsibility to make amends to the victim and to society. VORPs extend this principle by actually bringing the victim and the offender together in a face-to-face meeting.
The goals of VORPs include humanizing the justice process through face-to-face mediation, emphasizing offender accountability, providing for victim restitution, improving community understanding of crime and justice, and providing an alternative to incarceration
(Coates, 1990: 126). Findings from a survey of 240 juvenile justice agencies that have
a victim–offender mediation program indicated that the programs are widespread and
functioning well and were well supprted by the community and those working with the
juveniles, and the program components were considered to be very successful (Hughes
and Schneider, 1989).

The concept of "restorative justice" has emerged as a viable means of attaining offender
accountability and change and is viewed as a way to involve offenders, victims, and the
community together in responding to crime (Galaway and Hudson, 1990; Bazemore and
Umbreit, 1995). Restorative justice presents an alternative to the traditional retributive
justice approach that views crime as a violation against the laws of the state and places

total responsibility on the state for punishing and correcting the offender. Restorative justice is neither punitive nor lenient. Crime is viewed as an act against another person or the community, and victims and the community are equally important in helping to resolve the crime problem (Bazemore and Umbreit, 1994: 6–7). Restorative justice sanctions can provide meaningful consequences for crime, confront offenders, denounce delinquent behavior, and give offenders the message that such behavior is unacceptable (Bazemore and Umbreit, 1995: 302).

A comprehensive community corrections approach is one that facilitates change in offenders, the justice process, and the community. Correctional programs that include community service, restitution, and victim–offender reconciliation are meaningful sanctions that avoid stigmatization, but make offenders accountable while still being reintegrated with the community.

Safety Issues in Community Corrections

Probation officer safety is a growing concern as officers are expected to supervise a larger number of serious or chronic offenders with a history of violence (Lindner and Del Castillo, 1994). Research has indicated that a significant number of probation and parole officers have been victims of intimidation, threats, and physical assaults. Parsonage and Bushey (1989) found that 38 percent of probation/parole staff in Pennsylvania reported victimization; when controlling for officers who actively supervise cases the victimization rate rose to 50 percent. In a survey of state and county probation and parole agents in Minnesota, 19 percent reported being a victim of one or more physical assaults during their career, and 4 percent were victims in the past year; 74 percent reported being verbally or physically threatened one or more times during their career, and 37 percent reported such victimizations in the past year (Arola and Lawrence, 1999). Victimization incidents against officers occurred during visits to the offender's residence, in the probation office, and in a jail or detention center. Victimization experiences have significant adverse effects on community corrections officers, including personal stress, reduced sense of trust in offenders, fear on the job, reduced self-confidence, and being less sensitive to probation clients (Arola and Lawrence, 1999). Probation officers' safety concerns have prompted a number of precautions and changes, including more physical security devices in probation offices; training in conflict management, crisis intervention, and self-defense; and conducting field visits with two probation officers or with police–probation officer teams (Arola and Lawrence, 1999).

Effectiveness of Juvenile Corrections

The traditional measure of effectiveness in corrections has been based on recidivism, which variously refers to a new arrest, a new conviction, or return to prison. There is no unanimous agreement on how to assess correctional outcome, but using a new arrest as a measure of recidivism has clear limitations (Latessa and Allen, 2003: 471). Violations of probation conditions ("technical violations") and state and federal laws are the primary measures of probation and parole outcomes. Corrections researchers believe, however, that success or failure should be viewed on a continuum using multiple indicators rather than a dichotomous win–lose criterion. Petersilia (1993) has recommended that community corrections should be assessed according to several performance indicators that are based on clearly stated goals, methods, and activities. Five goals of community corrections that should be included in an assessment of outcome are:

1. Assess offender's suitability for placement
2. Enforce court-ordered sanctions
3. Protect the community
4. Assist offenders to change
5. Restore crime victims (Petersilia, 1993: 78–79)

Evaluating effectiveness according to these five goals takes into account the multiple roles and responsibilities of probation officers, including investigation, supervision, and monitoring of court orders, including restitution payments to victims. Multiple performance indicators are included to assess the performance of corrections professionals and the responses of offenders to correctional services and supervision. Number of days employed, vocational education, school attendance, and the number of drug- and alcohol-free days are included as performance indicators in addition to the number of arrests and technical violations (Petersilia, 1993: 78–79).

Measures of the effectiveness of juvenile corrections should also assess the quality of programs, including those conducted in institutions and public and private residential facilities and those providing supervision and treatment in the community (Latessa and Allen, 2003). While assessment of program effectiveness is important, corrections researchers acknowledge that recidivism remains the most common measure of the effectiveness of corrections programs. A meta-analysis of 200 experimental or quasi-experimental studies of institutional and community corrections interventions for serious juvenile offenders showed that three types of treatment had the strongest and most consistent evidence of reducing recidivism: interpersonal skills training, individual counseling, and behavioral programs (Lipsey et al., 2000). Lipsey et al. (2000) found that community-based programs showed greater reductions in recidivism than institutional programs. Offenders in nonsecure community supervision programs do commit some new crimes, but the fact that they do as well or better than youths sent to training schools and released to aftercare supervision suggests that community supervision presents no more risk to public safety and recidivism than incarceration. Research on get-tough measures such as Scared Straight programs, boot camps, and intensive supervision has indicated that harsher measures, without additional educational or skills training components, do not reduce recidivism (Whitehead and Lab, 2004: 299).

Cullen, Eck, and Lowenkamp (2002) have proposed a new paradigm for effective probation and parole supervision, which they have called "environmental corrections." The new supervision strategies would be based on environmental criminology, a theory that links crime causation and crime reduction to the presence or absence of opportunities to commit crime. Cullen and associates (2002) believe that probation and parole officers would be more effective if they worked closely with offenders, family and community members, and the police in order to reduce offenders' opportunities and temptations to commit crime. In addition to maintaining the usual responsibilities of assessment and investigation, probation and parole officers would use a problem-solving approach in supervising offenders to help them avoid the opportunities and temptations that lead to offending. Cullen et al. (2002) acknowledge that, while this new approach is based on sound criminological theory, considerable efforts are needed to put it into practice. A new problem-solving approach for probation and parole officers engaged in "environmental corrections" will add to their responsibilities, but may improve community supervision and be more cost effective.

Limitations of Juvenile Corrections for Delinquency Prevention

Corrections has a long history in which a wide variety of approaches have been tried, ranging from punishment to different methods of treatment interventions. Considerable debate has ensued around the question of whether correctional programs have been effective in changing offenders (Martinson, 1974). Murray and Cox (1979) argued that juvenile institutions have a "suppression effect" and have been a more effective deterrent to delinquency than community-based corrections programs. Further analyses have raised questions about that conclusion, however, with evidence indicating that community-based treatment may be as effective as institutionalization (Lundman, 1986). There is still much to be learned about the effectiveness of juvenile corrections programs in changing the delinquent.

Juvenile corrections has several limitations as a primary source of delinquency prevention for a number of reasons. It is always a "reactive" approach, not "proactive" or preventive. The juvenile court can only intervene after a juvenile's delinquent involvement is serious or persistent enough to warrant police arrest and referral. Delinquency prevention is generally more effective at an early age, before the onset of more serious behavior (Hawkins and Lishner, 1987a).

Correctional agencies may actually promote rather than prevent delinquency by bringing offenders together and isolating them from the community. Frank Tannenbaum (1938) claimed that juvenile correctional institutions were "schools for crime," where young offenders' delinquent tendencies often became worse. Criminologists have suggested that group interventions such as Positive Peer Culture and Guided Group Interaction used in juvenile institutions may actually maintain and enhance delinquent behavior of the youth (Elliott et al., 1985: 149; Gottfredson, 1987: 710).

The factors that generate and influence delinquent behavior usually lie within the community, the family, and the school—factors that are, for the most part, beyond the power of correctional agencies to change. True delinquency prevention requires a coordinated and consolidated effort of the entire community (see Sherman et al., 1997). A proactive approach to delinquency prevention must include communitywide efforts to address unequal educational opportunities, unemployment, poverty, and racism. This requires the combined efforts of legislative bodies with the support of citizens. True delinquency prevention requires some long-range, expensive legislative programs that many voters would not accept. Many voters are more willing to spend billions of dollars on building and operating correctional institutions, believing that incarceration and punishment are the best means to crime control. Some evidence suggests that we may be taking money from school classrooms and pouring it into prison cells. Comparisons of state and federal expenditures for corrections and for education indicate that there have been significant increases in funds going to corrections, while the amount of state and federal dollars going to education has remained stable or actually declined in recent years (Lawrence, 1995a). Correctional programs and alternatives do need to expand. Most state prison systems need to provide additional space and hire more officers to house and supervise the growing numbers of sentenced offenders. Cutting back on educational funds while spending more money for prisons or training schools, however, is not the answer to crime prevention. Institutions are only a short-term, reactive approach to juvenile crime. Young people with inadequate schooling face the grim realities of unemployment and poverty and are tempted by drug dealing, gang involvement, and other criminal activities. The threat of punitive sanctions has little deterrent effect on desperate youth who foresee little future for themselves. True delinquency prevention must offer more opportunities for at-risk youth to experience positive alternatives and to succeed in productive social and economic roles. The African saying that "it takes a whole village to raise a child" has never been more true than when applied to the need for total community involvement in delinquency prevention.

Juvenile Corrections and Schools

Schools play an important role in delinquency prevention and can support the objectives of community corrections agencies. School officials and juvenile probation officers are responsible for dealing with many of the same youth, and yet few efforts have been made to improve the interorganizational relations between them. Many schools rely on police and security officers to patrol school grounds and the hallways. Police respond to incidents of drug and weapon possession in schools or to investigate other criminal incidents. There is less communication and cooperation between juvenile probation and parole (or aftercare) officers and school officials however. This is unfortunate, because schools and corrections agencies rely on each other to achieve common objectives, such as reducing truancy, dropout, and delinquent involvement (Ingersoll and LeBoeuf, 1997). Students who have been adjudicated delinquent are generally ordered to attend school and obey school regulations. School attendance and participation in school activities can be beneficial in helping delinquent youth refrain from further delinquent involvement. For youth returning from placement in a state training school or other public or private residential placement, returning to school is essential for successful reintegration in the community. A majority of juvenile offenders who return from placement do not return to school (Roy-Stevens, 2004). Altschuler, Armstrong, and MacKenzie (1999) have noted the importance of community reintegration for youth returning from residential placement (see also Kurlychek et al., 1999).

Cooperation Among Community, Corrections, and Schools

Delinquency is a community problem that requires a total community effort to solve. Trying to get different organizations to work together in delinquency prevention efforts, however, has traditionally faced difficulties. Walter Miller (1958b) noted that a major barrier to delinquency prevention was conflict and disagreement among institutions. Miller's description of one community's concern about juvenile gang violence more than 30 years ago is true in many cities today. Although most community organizations agreed there was a problem, they disagreed on how to deal with the problem. The police, courts, probation, social welfare agencies, churches, and schools all disagreed and accused each other of improper actions. Differences revolved around the causes of delinquency and the methods for dealing with it (Miller, 1958b: 22–23). Reid (1964) concluded that interagency coordination in delinquency prevention and control is more likely when there are shared goals, complementary resources, and when the time and effort of coordination is seen as worthwhile to each agency (1964: 421–427). Agencies that deal with problem youth frequently have less than optimal interorganizational relations. Social welfare and probation agencies were found to have the highest level of conflict and the lowest level of coordination in one study comparing relations among juvenile probation, police, social welfare, mental health, and school officials (Hall et al., 1981). Results of a study of school teachers, principals, and probation officers in three different cities revealed significant conflict over goals and methods of delinquency prevention (Lawrence, 1995b). School officials and probation officers expressed sharply divided opinions on matters pertaining to judicial procedures, sharing of school and court records, and appropriate probation supervision strategies for delinquent students in schools (Lawrence, 1995b: 10–12). There clearly is a need for school and probation officials to develop better interorganizational relations. Schools and community corrections agencies would improve their ability to deal with delinquent students if they improved working relationships. This might include:

•Informal personal meetings between school and probation officials

•Exchange of resources such as meeting rooms, offices, or personnel

•Joint planning in programs and activities for at-risk and delinquent students

•Written agreements and policies regarding the sharing of school and court records, students' probation status and educational progress, and supervision and disciplinary policies (see Lawrence, 1995b: 5; and Oliver, 1991: 950)

Some promising approaches have been developed in which schools join with district attorneys' offices, law enforcement, probation, and social services agencies in an attempt to reduce truancy and dropout. Schools and juvenile corrections agencies have also developed programs to assist in the reintegration of youth making a transition to the community and returning to school after release from a correctional facility (Ingersoll and LeBoeuf, 1997).

Positive Examples of School-Probation Programs

Several juvenile probation and school partnerships have been developed throughout the United States. School-based probation is a supervision model in which the juvenile probation officer works directly in the school rather than out of the traditional courthouse office (Kurlychek et al., 1999). The Yuba County (Marysville, California) probation department developed the Truancy Intervention Program and the Probation and Schools Success Program (PASS) with the local school district and has probation officers located in various community schools. The Community School Program was developed in Monterey County, California, by the probation department and school district to address the educational needs of youth who have dropped out or been expelled. A probation officer works with teachers in the Community School Program. A contract that specifies expectations for attendance, proper attire, conduct, and productivity is developed among each student, the parents, and school personnel. The Clark County (Jefferson, Indiana) probation department has a volunteer school liaison officer to provide services and keep lines of communication open between the probation agency and the school (see National School Safety Center, 1995). In a program combining police and probation, the Fresno (California) police department and Fresno county probation department joined forces to bring integrated police and probation services to the seven high schools in the school district (West and Fries, 1995).

The Pennsylvania Commission on Crime and Delinquency has supported a School-Based Probation Services Program through grants to probation agencies and schools (Clouser, 1995). The Lehigh county probation department worked with the Allentown school district to place full-time juvenile probation officers in public schools. The goals of the program are to:

•Strengthen cooperation and communication between schools and the probation department

•Inform teachers about the duties, functions, and limitations of the juvenile justice system

•Provide an alternative approach for suspended students and behavioral problems

•Act as a liaison between the school district, juvenile probation agency, police departments, and the youths' families

•Confront drug abuse by having juvenile justice officials train teachers on signs of abuse (National School Safety Center, 1995: 1)

The duties of the school-based probation officer include providing the school with a list of the students who are on probation supervision, monitoring the attendance and behavior of probation clients, and intervening in behavioral problems with probation clients.

Funding for the program has come from the Pennsylvania Juvenile Court Judges' Commission and the Pennsylvania Commission on Crime and Delinquency. More than $885,000 was provided in 1993 to 17 counties (including Lehigh County) for developing and operating school-based probation programs. As of 1995 the Commission had provided a total of nearly $3.5 million in federal funds from the Office of Juvenile Justice and Delinquency Prevention to support 35 school-based probation programs throughout the Commonwealth of Pennsylvania. Pennsylvania is now leading the way in school-based probation, with more than 150 juvenile probation officers in its schools (Rubin, 1999: 2).

Evaluations of the School-Based Probation Services Program indicate that it has been successful. Officials in Pittsburgh reported a one-year reduction of 22 percent in residential placements and 7 percent in day treatment programs. Data from Lehigh County showed dramatic changes in the school behavior and performance of the middle-school youths served by the program: detentions and suspensions dropped 4 percent; tardiness dropped 9.5 percent; absenteeism was down 15 percent; dropouts were reduced by 29 percent; and grade averages increased 4.1 percent. School officials and students have responded positively to the program. Although the probation officers work directly only with students assigned to school-based probation, school officials reported that their presence has reduced the incidence of behavioral problems among the student body in general (Rubin, 1999: 12).

One of the concerns in developing the school-based probation program was the ability of the school district and probation department to share relevant information and records while maintaining confidentiality of sensitive information. The school and juvenile court records are kept separately by schools and probation agencies in order to maintain confidentiality and to assure that a child is not unfairly labeled or stigmatized. Information is shared only on an as-needed basis between teachers and probation officers, and the sharing of information is specified in written agreements between the school district and probation departments.

Another concern of the school-based probation program was the role definition of the probation officer. Precautions were taken to ensure that the officers' role was limited to working directly only with juveniles who were under the jurisdiction and supervision of the juvenile court. There was a concern that officers placed in the schools might observe delinquent behavior, resulting in additional referrals to the justice system. The Pennsylvania Commission addressed this concern by requiring school-based probation officers to work only with youths already on juvenile probation and not serve as discipline officers for the entire student body.

Schools and probation agencies clearly stand to benefit from better interagency relations and sharing of goals and resources. Schools contribute to probation objectives through special efforts and programs aimed at retaining probation clients in school. School involvement and educational attainment are major factors in crime reduction, as young offenders receive the education and skills essential for employment and a productive lifestyle. Probation agencies contribute to safer schools where teachers and students have less fear of crime when court orders and school rules are strictly enforced. School-based probation may also benefit other students by allowing probation officers to have contact with youth in various roles as mentors, advisors, and classroom speakers (Peterson, 2002). The development of better working relations between school and probation officials is a necessary first step in getting the whole community involved in preventing delinquency and correcting young offenders.

Summary

Juvenile corrections agencies are charged with carrying out the sentence imposed by the court. Corrections encompasses a wide variety of programs, ranging from traditional training schools and probation supervision to innovative programs such as restitution, mediation, and restorative justice emphases that incorporate offender accountability and concern for the victim. Corrections agents often experience "role conflict" in supervising delinquents as they exercise their authority enforcing court orders, while at the same time attempting to be change agents for young offenders. Effective corrections programs must work closely with parents and families, school officials, and community agencies in a collaborated effort to help change delinquent youth and reintegrate them into society.

12

School-Based Programs
for Delinquency Prevention

School crime is a serious problem that affects the entire community beyond the school hallways. Schools historically have always experienced some problems with disruptive students, and bullying, pushing, hitting, and verbal teasing have been a part of most persons' school experience. Schools in the past were relatively safe havens, however, that were insulated from the crime and violence on city streets. The problem has become worse in the past few decades, as verbal threats, harassment, and assaults are now more common. Students and teachers experience incidents of school violence weekly. School crime is a pervasive problem, affecting not only urban, inner-city schools, but also elementary, middle schools, and junior and senior high schools throughout the country. Our nation has been shocked by multiple school shootings, and numerous students are killed every year through such tragedies. School crime is a pervasive problem that has a significant impact on communities and schools. School violence and the fear of victimization in schools adversely affect students and teachers and interfere with the ability to learn in a safe school environment. Disruptive and threatening behavior makes learning difficult if not impossible. In the previous chapters we have examined the extent of juvenile crime in communities and in schools and the causes and correlates of juvenile crime, with emphasis on school-related factors, and we have reviewed the justice system responses to delinquent behavior. In this final chapter we review the role of school-based programs directed at delinquency prevention.

Crime Control Versus Crime Prevention

There have traditionally been two ways to deal with juvenile crime: prevention and control (Hawkins and Weis, 1985). Prevention refers to actions taken to stop illegal behavior before it ever occurs. Control refers to reactions to violations of the law and takes place in response to delinquent behavior. Juvenile justice agencies including police, juvenile courts, probation, community corrections agencies, and correctional institutions respond to juvenile crime after it has occurred. Crime control and punishment are the primary goals of the justice system. Juvenile justice agencies are engaged in prevention strategies as well as control and punishment, however. Sherman (1997b) has noted that it is a mistake to view prevention and punishment as mutually exclusive. Rather, he suggests that criminology views crime prevention as a result, while punishment is just one possible tool for achieving that result. Crime prevention may be more appropriately defined not by the agencies involved or by the intentions, but by the consequences. Thus, interventions by justice agencies or preventive efforts by community institutions may be assessed in terms of a reduction in the number of crimes, criminal offenders, or the amount of harm (Sherman, 1997b: 2-3).

Defining Crime Prevention

School crime affects students who have been personally victimized, but it also has a serious impact on students who witness violence and on students and teachers who fear for their own safety at school. Crime prevention should therefore include efforts to reduce the fear of crime. A more inclusive definition of crime prevention is offered by Steven Lab: "crime prevention entails any action designed to reduce the actual level of crime and/or the perceived fear of crime" (Lab, 2004: 23). Lab also distinguishes between control and prevention and divides crime prevention into three approaches similar to those found in public health models of disease prevention. Primary prevention includes approaches such as environmental design, neighborhood watch, and private security; secondary prevention includes community policing, substance abuse prevention, and school crime prevention (Lab, 2004: 25). Secondary prevention deals with predelinquents and deviant behavior that often leads to more serious criminal activity. Teachers and school staff are among the first persons to observe this behavior. Schools play an important role in secondary prevention by identifying problem children and youth and providing early interventions for those problems (Lab, 2004).

School-based delinquency prevention may be defined as an intervention or program that is designed to reduce or prevent delinquency, that takes place in a school building, and that is implemented by school staff or other specialists under the authority of the school administration (Gottfredson et al., 2002: 162). Examples of school-based programs include classroom instruction or other classroom activities, schoolwide organizational or environmental changes, and modifying teacher or school administrator behaviors and instructional practices (Gottfredson, 2001).

Desired Outcomes for School-Based Programs

School-based programs are directed at multiple factors and causes of crime and victimization. Program evaluations therefore include multiple outcome measures to assess the effectiveness of the school-based strategies. Denise Gottfredson (2001) has summarized the common outcome measures used in studies of school-based prevention in five categories:

•*Problem behaviors* (delinquency, alcohol and other drug use, conduct problems, truancy, and dropout)

•*Individual characteristics, attitudes, beliefs, and experiences* (association with delinquent peers, academic performance, cognitive ability, social competencies, or skills)

•*Personality disposition, attitude, belief, or intention* (emotional stability, psychological health, self-control)

•*School and classroom characteristics* (rules, norms, expectations for behavior, responsiveness to behavior)

•*Family characteristics* (parental supervision, family or parental behavior management practices)
(D. Gottfredson, 2001: 103)

Denise Gottfredson and associates (1997, 2001, 2002) have reviewed numerous school-based prevention programs to determine their effectiveness in producing the desired outcomes summarized above. The National Study of Delinquency Prevention in Schools (Gottfredson et al., 2004) found that the typical school operates 14 different activities concurrently in an attempt to prevent or reduce problem behavior or improve school safety. The development and implementation of these vary significantly, however, and most of these school programs have been implemented with poor quality (Gottfredson et al., 2004). Many of the programs have the potential for reducing school crime and victimization, but schools need to assure that the programs are implemented as intended and that school staff are trained and involved and receive adequate resources and administrative support (Gottfredson, et al., 2002).

Theoretical Bases for School-Based Delinquency Prevention

Delinquent behavior is associated with academic failure and school problems. Most major criminological explanations of delinquency include some school factors that may contribute to delinquent behavior. Strain theorists (Cohen, 1955) have argued that students who disrupt class and engage in delinquent behavior do so in response to frustration and "strain" at not being able to meet academic expectations and demands of schools. Opportunity-structure theorists (Cloward and Ohlin, 1960) have argued that lower-class students are denied equal access to goals and opportunities in society, such as equal quality education and employment opportunities. The lack of equal resources and opportunities leads many youths to engage in delinquent behavior as a means of attaining the goals. According to strain theory, the school is seen as a middle-class institution with expectations and demands that lower-class students feel they cannot successfully achieve. Many youths turn to delinquency out of frustration, feelings of failure, and low self-esteem. School absenteeism, truancy, and dropout are often indicators of students' frustration and perceived inability to meet educational demands. Researchers have established an association between poor academic achievement, disruptive behavior, delinquency, and dropout (Elliott and Voss, 1974). Despite some disagreement on the causal order of dropout and delinquency, there clearly is a relationship between academic failure, dropping out of school, and delinquency (Thornberry et al., 1985; Jarjoura, 1993).

Social control theorists (Hirschi, 1969) have identified the importance of schools as a social bond that helps to insulate youth from the likelihood of delinquent involvement. Students who do not like school and are not involved in school activities are more likely to become involved in delinquent behavior. In contrast, students who are committed to educational goals and who see the value of education have a greater probability of avoiding delinquent involvement. Positive school experiences and involvement in school activities is an important social bond that helps overcome the disadvantages faced by lower-class youth and even the negative influence of delinquent peers (Lawrence, 1991b).

The relationship between schools and delinquency is complex. School experiences contribute to the causes of delinquency for many youth. Lack of school resources and exclusionary school policies result in alienating many youth who become delinquents. It is clear, however, that schools have considerable potential as a valuable source of delinquency prevention (Catalano et al., 1998). Children and youths spend a significant portion of their time in school. Students spend as much as 18 percent of their waking hours in school for 12 years (Gottfredson et al., 2002: 159). No other organization has such frequent and in-depth access to children and youth for such a long time. Teachers and school staff persons spend a considerable amount of time with students and are often the first professionals able to identify problem behaviors and offer guidance and services for students who show early signs of delinquent behavior (Dryfoos, 1990). The structured school environment in which school officials impose rules and expectations for behavior is important for instilling students' self-discipline and helps to reduce the possibility of delinquent behavior. Research shows that schools that have good discipline policies with clearly stated rules that are enforced firmly and fairly experience less crime and victimization (Gottfredson and Gottfredson, 1985). Schools that are managed well, with adequate resources, clearly stated goals, and good communication among teachers and administrators experience less disruption and crime (Gottfredson et al., 2002). Schools that are most effective at delivering quality instruction, minimizing disruption and victimization, and implementing delinquency-prevention programs have been described as having a positive "communal organization." This concept refers to the organization of a school as a community and includes positive relationships between administrators, teachers, and students; common goals and norms; and a sense of collaboration and involvement. Previous research has shown that schools that are communally organized have more positive student attitudes, better teacher morale, and less student disorder (Payne, 2004). School variables such as organization and climate, discipline management, clear communication, and teacher morale are related to school crime and violence, and therefore changes and improvements in those areas may reduce school crime (Gottfredson, 2001; Gottfredson et al., 2002). The school setting offers a convenient place to provide delinquency-prevention programs in addition to the regular school curriculum.

Some Directions for School Crime Prevention

Crime in schools and in the communities around schools is related to multiple causes and factors. The most effective and efficient crime-prevention approaches are based on sound theory and research. School violence prevention requires careful assessment, planning, resources, and additional funding. The federal government has assisted in these efforts through the U.S. Departments of Education, Health and Human Services, and Justice. Organizations devoted to school violence prevention that have been funded by the Justice Department in the past 10 years include the National School Safety Center (Ron Stephens, director); the Center for the Study and Prevention of Violence (Delbert Elliott, director); and the Hamilton Fish Institute (Paul Kingery, director and Jim Derzon, associate director). These organizations have partnered with universities to support school violence-prevention initiatives such as research and resource materials, national satellite broadcasts and videoconferences, and technical assistance.

The best practices focus crime-prevention strategies at the sources of the problem. In developing a comprehensive framework for school violence prevention, the Hamilton Fish Institute (2000) recommended starting with a careful examination of the people, relationships, resources, activities, facilities, and surrounding neighborhoods that make up the school community. The comprehensive framework includes six categories of areas that should be addressed in school violence prevention:

•*Administrative approaches*: Effective principals with leadership skills; engaging, effective academic programs; disciplinary code that is clearly communicated and enforced consistently and impartially, with consequences for inappropriate behaviors; reinforcement for positive behavior; training teachers in classroom discipline; monitoring and reporting of serious violent behaviors.

•*School security*: Monitor all areas of school buildings and grounds; assure sufficient interior and exterior lighting; redesign spaces to remove blind spots; restrict access to inappropriate individuals; remind all students, teachers, and staff of the responsibility for observing and reporting violent behavior; and effective use of security personnel, security devices, and police.

•*Schoolwide education in violence prevention*: Provide education and skills training to reduce anger, bullying, and violent behavior; offer opportunities for students to practice social skills and resist negative pressures from peers; integrate age-appropriate learning materials into the curriculum; use banners, posters, and special events to supplement violence-prevention curricula.

•*Counseling*: Be cognizant of the emotional needs, fears, and stressors of students; expand counseling services for perpetrators, victims, and witnesses of violence; refer students for diagnostic services and psychotherapeutic interventions; provide teachers and staff with information to aid in identifying and responding to disruptive and violent behaviors.

•*Alternative education*: Provide alternative programs for students expelled or suspended for weapons carrying or violent acts; use specially-trained school staff, offer individualized instruction, low student:teacher ratios and innovative presentations; include training in anger management, nonviolent communication, conflict resolution, and use of mediation.

•*Community involvement*: Offer *parents* training in communication, establishing rules and discipline, proper safeguarding of weapons in the home, family management, and skills to reduce the stress and challenges of raising children; develop clear communication and working relationships with *police, juvenile probation, mental health* agencies, and other social service agencies; encourage businesses to offer financial support for programs and services, training programs for job skills and internships for students, and offer employees training in parenting and family management, and flexible scheduling for employees with school children; develop partnerships with local government, community organizations, and faith-based organizations to help prevent youth violence (Hamilton Fish Institute, 2000).

School safety programs have been included as part of the comprehensive strategy for serious and violent juvenile offenders of the Office of Juvenile Justice and Delinquency Prevention (OJJDP). Juvenile accountability programs are part of that strategy, and one of the goals is to promote school safety by increasing students' accountability for their behavior (Decker, 2000). Students who violate the law need to be held accountable for their offenses through consequences or sanctions proportionate to the offense. Accountability in a school setting means expecting students to comply with school rules and regulations that also support community standards of behavior. Key elements of effective accountability-based programs are an emphasis on student involvement and accountability, meaningful responses to school misconduct and law violations, and graduated sanctions appropriate to the seriousness of the misconduct (Decker, 2000). Effective school-based juvenile accountability programs have integrated the work of school resource officers, school-based probation officers, alternative education programs, and skills training to help students make good choices and avoid the risk of violence.

Resources for violence-prevention programs vary greatly in availability and quality among communities and school districts. It is important for school administrators and juvenile justice officials to assess the violence prevention needs for each school and develop a comprehensive plan based on available resources. The Hamilton Fish Institute (2000) has recommended seven steps for schools to follow in order to implement a violence-prevention program that matches the needs and resources of a given school: (1) unite schools with their communities in the effort to prevent violence; (2) identify and measure the problem; (3) set goals and objectives; (4) identify appropriate strategies; (5) implement a comprehensive plan; (6) measure the success of the effort; and (7) revise strategies based on the evaluation (Hamilton Fish Institute, 2000: 6).

In this section we review the school-based crime-prevention strategies that have received the most attention through research and publications. These strategies address school structure and climate, classroom management and instruction, conflict management and resolution, and vocational and employment programs.

School Structure and Climate

School crime is related somewhat to the extent of crime in the neighborhood surrounding schools, but more clearly to the structure of the school itself and to the climate of the school. Research evidence on these factors offers some direction for effective crime-prevention strategies and interventions.

Neighborhood Crime. There is evidence that crime in schools is related to crime in the neighborhood surrounding schools. According to the Safe School Study and more recent analyses of the school crime problem, the amount of crime in the neighborhood around the school is a factor in school crime and violence (National Institute of Education, 1978: 111–113; Gottfredson and Gottfredson, 1985). The presence of gangs, drug dealing, and violence in the school's attendance area tends to increase the level of disruption and violence within the school. The more crime and violence to which students are exposed outside of the school, the greater the problems in the school. A school's proximity to students' homes can make it a convenient target for vandalism. The presence of nonstudent youths around the school also increases the risk of property loss. Other research has failed to show a clear and direct relationship between neighborhood crime and school crime. Lab and Clark (1996) found little relationship between the level of violence in a school and the nature of the surrounding community. Indeed, many schools in high-crime areas are stable and safe havens for learning, while students in many suburban and small city schools have experienced school violence. The neighborhood environment does contribute to school disorder, but in an indirect way; and the strongest predictors of school crime are school factors such as size, structure, and student achievement levels (Welsh et al., 1999). Current research supports the focus on school-based violence prevention and the importance of focusing on school structure and climate. School administrators can do very little to change the conditions and criminal incidents in the neighborhood surrounding the school. They can, however, take security precautions to make school grounds a safe zone and develop firm and consistent disciplinary policies that will reduce the level of disruption and delinquent behavior inside school buildings. Regular communication and coordination with local law enforcement agencies will help to keep police informed about law violations and concentrate police patrols in trouble spots around schools.

School Size and Structure. The size and physical structure of schools are factors in crime and disruption. The probability of victimization is greater if the teacher has classes with more than 30 students (National Institute of Education, 1978: 111). Larger schools and schools with larger classes tend to have more violence and vandalism. Research indicates that large, overcrowded schools suffer chronic disorder more than those with student bodies small enough to manage. School size and student:teacher ratios are important factors in controlling the level of violence in schools (Anderson, 1998).

Larger schools have lower levels of student involvement in school activities. Roger Barker and Page Gump (1964) conducted research on big and small schools and noted an interesting paradox. Although large schools offer more opportunities for extracurricular activities than do small schools, a significantly greater proportion of students in smaller schools participate. They explained this paradox in terms of "undermanning." Because smaller schools' activities are short of students, they actively recruit more students to participate. For example, a school of 500 students has to recruit 5 percent, or 25 male students, to fill a football roster. This means that more students, regardless of their abilities, will participate. A large school with 3,000 students could field a football team with fewer than 1 percent of its students. The smaller schools cannot compete athletically with larger schools and may not win many championships, but by involving more students they win out on what is undoubtedly more important for students: involvement and overall school achievement (Barker and Gump, 1964: 64–74).

Marcus Felson (1994) compared urban schools in the past ("convergent city schools") with the present "divergent metropolitan schools." City schools in the past had perhaps 600 secondary school students, with 20 teachers supervising 20 homerooms of 30 students each. About 300 of the students were males. Youths from outside the school would likely be recognized as such, and any student who committed a crime would be recognized by name or described to teachers to find out his name. About 1 percent, or 6 students, would be most difficult to control, and not too numerous for teachers to control. In contrast, the larger divergent metropolitan school of 3,000 students has some 300 teachers supervising 100 homerooms of 30 students each. With 1,500 males it becomes difficult for teachers and other students to recognize who does and does not belong and equally difficult to recognize and identify students who commit crimes in school. The 1 percent of students who are most difficult to control numbers at least 30 students, a formidable number who can easily interfere with the educational process and present serious security risks (Felson, 1994: 93–95). The physical size and setting of smaller schools present fewer problems with security and control. The buildings are more compact, and the smaller number of halls and stairwells are easy to watch. Large school buildings that are spread out present special difficulties in controlling entry points. Longer hallways, more of them, and more stairwells connecting two and three stories present security risks for students and teachers.

Schools are built today to accommodate a growing number of students, with efficiency in mind. It is more efficient for school districts to build a smaller number of large schools. Smaller schools cannot provide teachers and students with as many learning resources as efficiently as larger schools. Given taxpayers' concerns about the cost of education, it is unlikely that we will see any trends toward building smaller schools. An alternative to physically restructuring schools is the "schools-within-a-school" concept (Gottfredson and Gottfredson, 1985: 172; Hawkins and Weis, 1985: 85; Gottfredson, 1997: 5–26). Under this plan, large schools are divided into smaller units. The schools may be subdivided by educational structures, with students, teachers, guidance counselors, and administrators in separate units, or by dividing academic and extracurricular activities. The schools-within-a-school plan aims to provide more attention to individual students and to increase opportunities for students to take initiative and get recognition. Proponents believe this type of school restructuring will increase and improve student–teacher interaction and result in more active participation among students. The plan would support the control theory of delinquency prevention as it is expected to result in greater involvement in school, greater commitment to education, and positive attachments between students and teachers.

School planners would be well advised to consider school safety and violence prevention more than large size and efficiency when building new school structures. Schools are safer when they are smaller, more manageable, and free of dangerous stairwells and locker rooms that make it nearly impossible to maintain close surveillance and supervision. Better school building designs would facilitate communication among teachers, administrators, and students and allow hall monitors and security staff to observe student behavior, report problems, and summon help on short notice (Anderson, 1998: 359). Attempts to legislate effective schools from the state level have been unsuccessful, and more attention has now shifted to encouraging reform at the local school district level. A movement referred to as "school restructuring" reform proceeds on the belief that effective reforms must begin at the local school level with input from the local community and groups of teachers, principals, and parents working together to reform their schools (Gottfredson, 2001).

Metal Detectors, Security Cameras, and Other Physical Security. One of the first demands made by the public and legislators following a school shooting incident is for more physical security devices, especially metal detectors. According to Garcia (2003), up to 15 percent of large urban schools in the United States have resorted to using metal detectors in order to curb the presence of weapons and to provide a safe learning environment. Other security measures include surveillance cameras in hallways, restricted access to certain parts of the school, better lighting inside and outside the school building, and the use of photo identification cards for students. Security measures have some positive effect in reducing school violence (Anderson, 1998), but there are legal and policy questions involved in the use of metal detectors or scanning devices in schools (see Johnson, 1993) (see Chapter 8). Robert Rubel and Peter Blauvelt (1994) have recommended that school administrators make a careful assessment of school security needs. A physical security assessment of school grounds and buildings should include the number and location of entrances and exits; lighting around the buildings and parking lot; detailed recording of all incidents of assault, theft, and vandalism; and inventory control of all school supplies and equipment. School administrators must determine whether law enforcement or security personnel should be hired to patrol the school buildings and grounds and, if so, how they are to be selected and trained.

A survey of New York City high school students showed that students in schools with a metal detector were about half as likely to carry a gun, knife, or other weapon to school as were students in schools without a metal detector (Catalano et al., 1998). The researchers noted, however, that metal-detector programs may have only a site-specific impact on weapon carrying, and do not appear to influence weapon carrying in other settings. Physical security devices are important considerations in schools that have a serious problem with weapon possession, but administrators must recognize the limitations of metal detectors and other security devices and consider the costs and procedural factors in deploying metal detector searches on all persons entering the school building. The most effective approach to school safety and violence reduction comes not through more formal social controls, police presence, and security devices (Schreck et al., 2003), but through improving informal social controls (Payne, 2004).

School Climate. Before school administrators introduce policies relating to discipline and crime prevention, it is important to conduct a thorough assessment of school climate, orderliness, and safety. Welsh (2001) emphasized that administrators should assess the school climate to determine which factors (e.g., student characteristics vs. school climate) may be contributing to disorder before proceeding to develop and implement any school-based programs designed to reduce violence. Time, effort, and valuable resources may be wasted if policies and programs are instituted before a careful assessment of needs and problems. Measuring the extent and nature of school disruption is a clear indicator that administrators care about school safety and orderliness (Gottfredson and Gottfredson, 1985: 197). Schools have come under general pressure from parents, politicians, and the media to "do something" about the problems of disruption and crime. The extent and seriousness of the problems vary considerably from school to school, however. Periodic assessments will help to pinpoint any problem areas so that appropriate policies can be instituted. Schools regularly assess students' academic performance and overall educational achievement, and teachers are assessed as to their effectiveness in the classroom. Schools could benefit greatly by including regular measures of school climate, orderliness, and safety. There are a number of ways in which schools can closely monitor the number and types of disruptive incidents. Measures can also include teachers' and students' perceptions of school climate and safety (see Gottfredson and Gottfredson, 1985; Welsh, 2001).

Assessment of school climate and safety requires the full support of school administrators, who are sometimes hesitant about collecting data that may place the school in a negative light and could be used against them in litigation. Gottfredson and Gottfredson suggest that legislative action may be necessary to mandate periodic assessment of school climate, with the added provision that the required monitoring implies no private right of action (1985: 196). Legislation may also be necessary to ensure that schools have sufficient resources to conduct periodic assessments and develop programs to improve school safety.

Teachers and administrators should work together to help identify school safety and discipline issues that are in need of improvement and then implement policies and activities to specifically address those needs. Through cooperative efforts in developing specific policies and procedures directed at identified needs, teachers will see that administrators are serious about improving school safety and discipline. Developing consistent expectations for student behaviors and clear policies and procedures for responding to rule violations will help to improve the school climate. Students are more likely to view school policies as being fair and equitable and see that administrators are serious about maintaining a safe and orderly school environment (Hawkins and Weis, 1985: 89–90; Gottfredson and Gottfredson, 1985; Gottfredson, 2001).

School Governance and Discipline. The quality of school governance and clear and consistent discipline policies are important factors for preventing school disruption. A firm, fair, and consistent system for running a school seems to be a key factor in reducing violence. Where the rules are known and where they are firmly and fairly enforced, less violence occurs. Good coordination between the faculty and administration also promotes a better school atmosphere. Schools run with clear, explicit rules that are firmly and uniformly enforced are marked by less disruption. Schools in which there is coordination between teachers and principals have more consistent discipline policies, the teachers feel more confident that the school administrators will back them up, and they get along better with the administration. School principals must be clear and firm in enforcing rules, especially as they face questions and lack of support from parents of problem students. When teachers are confused about school policies, or when administrators do not uniformly enforce the policies, students are given mixed signals and respond by testing the limits of educators through disruptive behavior. Firm enforcement of school policies does not mean that schools should be run in authoritarian ways, however, or with sanctions that deny students their dignity. Sanctions can be effective without being harsh, and rewards can be as effective as punishments in getting students to conform (Gottfredson and Gottfredson, 1985: 173). Students should be disciplined and corrected, but not alienated from the school community. Experience shows that if students perceive a hostile or author-itarian attitude on the part of the teachers and principals, disruption and vandalism may result. There is evidence that student involvement in setting school policies and discipline procedures may be effective in reducing disruption and rule violations (Hawkins and Weis, 1985: 87). Student involvement in school policies and governance is hypothesized on the premise that it will increase student attachment to school and promote positive peer pressure to reduce disruption and create a positive and safe learning environment. The practice of allowing students to be involved in establishing discipline policies and deter-mining fair punishments has been referred to as "humanistic" discipline. Research indi-cates that all discipline measures reduce victimization in school, but humanistic policies appear to be more effective than coercive ones (Lab and Clark, 1996).

Classroom Management and Instruction

More than half of the most effective school-based delinquency-prevention programs involve classroom instruction and are designed to improve discipline management and to establish clear norms and expectations for behavior (Gottfredson, 2001; Gottfredson et al., 2002).

Effective Classroom Management. Teachers make a difference in the lives of young people, and some teachers are more effective than others in maintaining discipline and order in the classroom and in nurturing a positive learning environment. To accom-plish this task in some school settings takes a great deal of patience and perseverance. Teachers are faced daily with overwhelming challenges. Many students do not want to learn. Maintaining discipline among students often requires more time and energy than teaching, and many students are increasingly reluctant to respect teachers' authority. The skillful and experienced teacher must constantly decide how best to get students engaged and involved in learning and must use a variety of techniques to maintain an orderly classroom that is conducive to learning. Techniques including behavior modification, humanistic interventions, and teaching prosocial values and behaviors have been promoted as means by which educators can reduce disruption, aggression, and violence in the schools and the community (Goldstein et al., 1984). In an evaluation of several studies of class-room management and student behavior change, Denise Gottfredson and associates (2002) found that these methods had a positive effect on problem behavior.

Enhanced Methods of Classroom Instruction. J. David Hawkins and his associates at the Seattle Social Development Project at the University of Washington have developed, implemented, and tested the effects of classroom-based instructional practices intended to improve student academic achievement and bonding to school and positive peers and reduce disruption and delinquent behavior (Hawkins and Weis, 1985; Hawkins and Lam, 1987; Hawkins and Lishner, 1987a, 1987b). Three general principles for delinquency prevention were identified by Hawkins and Weis: (1) To be effective, prevention efforts should focus on the causes of delinquency; (2) there are multiple correlates and causes of delinquency that derive variously from the family, school, peers, and community; and (3) delinquency results from experiences during the process of social development, in the family, school, and with peers, so different prevention efforts are required at different stages in youths' social development (1985: 77–78). The "social development model" is an integration of control theory (Hirschi, 1969) and social learning theory (Akers, 1985). According to the model, the development of social bonds to conventional persons inhibits delinquent involvements. There are three conditions that seem to be necessary for develop-ment of social bonds: opportunities for involvement, skills, and reinforcements (Hawkins and Lishner, 1987; Hawkins and Lam, 1987). According to the model, delinquency can be prevented only when youths have the opportunities to interact with conventional peers and adults and to be involved in conventional activities. Such interactions and involve-ments are expected to lead to positive social bonds when youth experience them positively and gain the necessary skills and when there are rewards for positive involvement in the community and in schools.

The social development model has been applied and evaluated in school settings. Hawkins and Lam (1987) examined the effects of teaching practices on classroom behaviors, academic achievement, school bonding, and school-related delinquent and antisocial behavior in a study of more than 1,000 7th-grade students in Seattle. They implemented and evaluated three classroom-based instructional strategies: proactive classroom manage-ment, interactive teaching, and cooperative learning (Hawkins and Lam, 1987: 250–251). *Proactive classroom management* is aimed at establishing an environment that is conducive to learning, promotes appropriate student behavior, and minimizes student disruption. Teachers give clear instructions for student behavior and recognize and reward coopera-tive student efforts. *Interactive teaching* is based on the premise that all students can and will develop the skills necessary to succeed in the classroom. Components include devel-oping a mental set, clear objectives, checking for understanding, remediation, and assess-ment. Students must master learning objectives before proceeding to more advanced work. Grades are determined by mastery and improvement over past performance, rather than comparison with other students. Interactive teaching seeks to expand opportunities for students' success and enhance their perception of their own competence and commitment to education. *Cooperative learning* involves small groups of students of differing abilities and backgrounds working together. Team scores are based on individual students' improvement over past performance, so each student contributes to the teams' overall achieve-ment. Students in cooperative classrooms seem to exhibit better mastery of learning tasks, are motivated, and have more positive attitudes toward teachers and schools than students in competitive or individualistic classrooms (Hawkins and Lam, 1987: 251). Using cooperative learning seeks to develop more interaction among students across racial and social class lines, reduce alienation, and reduce attachments with delinquent peers.

The teaching practices used in this project revealed positive results. Students in the experimental group engaged in more behaviors associated with academic success and in fewer behaviors associated with academic failure. The teaching practices resulted in lower rates of classroom misbehavior and fewer suspensions and expulsions. Students in the experimental group appeared to benefit from the special teaching practices. They were more likely to engage in learning activities, less likely to be off task in the classroom, spent more time on homework, liked math classes better, and developed greater educational aspirations and expectations for themselves (Hawkins and Lam, 1987: 268). The authors acknowledged that it is unclear whether many schools and teachers will adopt and consistently support these special teaching practices; and it is not clear whether the positive results will continue beyond the 1 year in which students were observed in this study. More research is needed to determine the long-term effects of special teaching practices on the classroom environment and on students. Current applications of the Social Development Model involve integrating school-based programs with community involvement in a program called "Communities That Care" (Catalano et al., 1998).

Conflict Management and Resolution

Preventing Bullying at School. Bullying has been a regular occurrence in schools since early colonial days (Crews and Counts, 1997), and it was considered a devious but normal part of childhood and adolescent behavior. Most Americans, including many school personnel, in fact did not consider bullying a serious problem until the past few years, when it became apparent that bullying had long-term serious consequences and was related to other serious behavior. Only in the past several decades has bullying been the subject of systematic research. Initial research on bullying was confined mostly to Scandinavia with the work of Dan Olweus (1978), but bullying among schoolchildren has now been the subject of research in England, Japan, the Netherlands, Australia, Canada, and the United States (Farrington, 1993). Based on surveys of more than 150,000 Norwegian students, an estimated 15 percent (1 in 7) of students in grades 1 through 9 are involved in bully/victim problems (about 9 percent as victims and 7 percent as bullies) (Olweus, 1994: 1). According to Olweus, data from other countries indicate that the bullying problem exists outside Norway with similar or even higher prevalence rates.

Bullying occurs among both boys and girls, although many more boys than girls bully others. A high percentage of girls report that they are bullied mainly by boys, but a somewhat higher percentage of boys are victims of bullying. Bullying among boys is mostly physical. Girls typically use more subtle and indirect forms of harassment, such as slandering, spreading rumors, exclusion from the group, and manipulating friendships (Olweus, 1994). All of these behaviors are included in the definition of bullying as the repeated oppression, either physical or psychological, of a less powerful person by a more powerful one (Farrington, 1993: 381).

Three myths about bullying have been challenged by research findings of Dan Olweus. First, many believe that bullying problems are more common in large schools or large classes. Empirical data indicate that the size of the class or school has little to do with the frequency or seriousness of bullying. Second, bullying behavior is often thought to be a reaction to school failure and frustration. Research data do not support a causal relationship between poor grades and school failure. Third, it is commonly believed that physical characteristics make some youth more vulnerable to bullying, for example, that students who are fat, have red hair, wear glasses, or speak in an unusual manner are more likely to be victims of bullying. This belief also has not been supported by research (Olweus, 1994).

Victims of bullying tend to be more anxious and insecure than students in general. They are often cautious, sensitive, quiet, have low self-esteem, are often lonely, and have few close friends at school. Bullies have a positive attitude toward violence and are characterized by impulsivity and a need to dominate others. They are usually physically stronger than most other boys, they use violence and aggression more than most students, and they express little empathy for victims. Contrary to the belief that bullying is a reaction to underlying insecurity, research indicates that bullies have little anxiety or insecurity, and they do not suffer from poor self-esteem (Olweus, 1994).

Bullying is not something that can be ignored or treated as simply normal adolescent behavior. Many children suffer greatly from bullying. Some respond by withdrawing and staying home from school. Others become more aggressive themselves. There are documented cases of suicide among victims of bullying. School-based bullying-prevention programs have proven to be effective in reducing this behavior. Evaluation results from a program involving 2,500 students in 42 schools in Bergen, Norway, indicated that bullying decreased by 50 percent (Olweus, 1991; Gottfredson, 2001). An effective anti-bullying program requires that efforts be directed at students in primary and secondary grade levels, teachers, and parents. A school program to prevent bullying should include the following:

•Increase awareness of the bully/victim problem. Assess the extent of the problem in each school through an anonymous survey of students.

•Present an in-service training session for school personnel on the bullying problem; present results of the survey; compare with national and international data on bullying; and explain the characteristics of victims and bullies.

•Organize a parent–teacher meeting to inform parents about bullying and what the school is doing to prevent it. Provide parents with the information presented to teachers. Show a video on bullying (the National School Safety Center has produced one), and solicit parents' input on preventing bullying.

•Develop clear rules against bullying, including a definition of bullying and the various oppressive and harassing behaviors that are forbidden. Enforce the rules with appropriate sanctions that are agreed upon by school personnel, parents, and students.

•School personnel should provide adequate supervision on school grounds during recess; in school hallways, stairways, restrooms and areas where students are must vulnerable to bullying. Provide support and protection for the victims, and help them develop friendships.

•Teachers should discuss bullying with students in class, and use role-playing exercises and video presentations. Teachers should talk to identified bullies, their victims, and their parents (see Olweus, 1994: 4; Farrington, 1993: 425–426).

The problem of bullying and peer harassment in school has now become the subject of considerable research. Educational researchers and school psychologists have conducted extensive research on peer victimization in schools, including how to assess and measure the problem, identifying the perpetrators and victims, the correlates and consequences, and the development and implementation of effective prevention programs to reduce bullying (Juvonen and Graham, 2001). Perhaps more than any other single topic related to school crime, research on the causes, consequences, and prevention of bullying is an international effort, including experts such as Dan Olweus of Norway, David Farrington of the United Kingdom, and Ken Rigby of Australia. Rigby (2001) has documented the serious mental health consequences of peer victimization and recommended a "whole school approach" to reducing the problem. A review of the worldwide representation of contributors to Juvonen and Graham's (2001) edited work on peer harassment in school attests to the international nature of the problem of school bullying and to the serious commitment of educational researchers to confronting bullying and developing effective prevention strategies.

School-Based Violence-Prevention Programs. The rate of serious violent crimes committed by high school–aged youths with a weapon has increased dramatically. Several violence-prevention programs have been developed in the past few years to teach anger management and conflict resolution skills to youths. In 1992 nearly half of all murder victims were related to (12 percent) or acquainted with (35 percent) their assailants, and 29 percent of all murders were the result of an argument. Most were committed impulsively, and about half of all perpetrators or victims had consumed alcohol before the homicide (DeJong, 1994: xi).

The nature of violent crime has led some to view the growing problem of violence from a public health perspective as well as from the criminal justice perspective (Rosenberg and Fenley, 1991; Elliott et al., 1998b). Criminal justice professionals concern themselves with investigation, arrest, prosecution, and conviction. Public health officials, on the other hand, approach health problems in terms of the interaction between persons, the agent, and the environment. The environment that contributes to violence as a public health problem includes social, cultural, and institutional forces. Violence is often the product of the inability of families and communities to transmit positive values to young people and to teach nonviolent conflict resolution skills. The agents of violence are the weapons that are so readily available to young people, and the public health focus has increased efforts to restrict the sales of firearms, and especially limit their availability to young people. School-based violence prevention programs are based on the premise that violence is a learned behavior, and that children must be taught nonviolent means of resolving conflict.

The Resolving Conflict Creatively Program (RCCP) is a school-based conflict resolution and mediation program sponsored by the New York City Public Schools and Educators for Social Responsibility—Metro. The K–12 program was begun in 1985 and has operated in 180 elementary, junior high, and high schools in New York City, with 3,000 teachers and 70,000 students participating (DeJong, 1994: 19). RCCP's year-long curriculum concentrates on active listening, assertiveness (as opposed to aggressiveness or passivity), expression of feelings, perspective-taking, cooperation, and negotiation. Teachers are encouraged to include at least one "peace lesson" each week, to use "teachable moments" related to classroom situations or world events, and to infuse conflict resolution lessons into the regular academic program. Teachers strive to give their students a new image of what their world can be by creating a "peaceable school." In order to most effectively teach the RCCP curriculum, educators must learn a new set of skills for resolving conflict and adopt a new style of classroom management, sharing power with students so that they can learn how to deal with their own disputes. RCCP recently began a pilot program for parents, in which a few parents per school are trained to lead workshops for other parents on intergroup relations, family communication, and conflict resolution. By the end of 1994, nearly 300 parents had received training (DeJong, 1994: 29).

The Violence Prevention Project (VPP) is a community-based outreach and education project in Boston. The project was implemented in 1986 and was run by the Boston Department of Health and Hospitals as part of its Health Promotion Program for Urban Youth. Providing the educational foundation for the Violence Prevention Project is the "Violence Prevention Curriculum for Adolescents," developed by Dr. Deborah Prothrow-Stith (1987; Prothrow-Stith et al., 1987). The primary message of VPP is that violence is a learned behavior and is therefore preventable. The project directs attention to the acceptance of violence in American culture. There are elements of American culture that promote the use of violence to resolve conflict not as a last resort, but as a first option. When parents teach their children to stand up to bullies by fighting, they promote violent behavior. When peers encourage each other to respond to any verbal insult, even mild ones, with verbal and physical threats and fighting, they promote violence. When the entertainment industry continues to produce films and television shows that depict violence as the hero's way to resolve conflict, they promote violence in a manner that has become very difficult to overcome. The goal of the VPP is to reduce students' acceptance of violence by helping them to discover that whatever gains fighting might bring are far outweighed by the risk of serious injury or death. The VPP teaches staff members from community-based youth agencies how to use lessons from the high school curriculum in their own violence-prevention programs. The community education program of VPP was combined with a mass media campaign to raise public awareness of adolescent violence. The campaign featured a series of public service announcements on the role of peer pressure and the responsibility that friends have for helping to defuse conflict situations. The Advertising Club of Boston produced radio and television announcements with the theme "Friends for Life Don't Let Friends Fight." VPP's peer leadership program has used a small group of youth leaders to do conflict resolution and violence prevention work among their peers. VPP also organized a coalition of service providers, teachers and school administrators, juvenile justice officials, parents, and other community residents. Organizers believe that such coalitions are more likely to start their own violence prevention activities, which are a key objective of the VPP (DeJong, 1994: 36).

Beacons of Hope is a program of school-based community centers in New York City. Originally implemented in 1991 by a New York City mayoral commission, the program grew to include 37 centers located in each of the 32 school districts in the city. The program was designed to help residents, particularly youths, avoid crime and violence and to solve community problems. Services provided have included mentoring, tutoring, employment training and counseling, and cultural and recreational activities. The services are aimed at addressing the risk factors associated with crime and violence by strengthening protective factors such as bonding with role models and developing healthy peer groups. Beacons of Hope centers have included antiviolence programs and campaigns, conflict resolution training, public education about drugs, substance abuse treatment, community beautification projects, and Police Athletic League (P.A.L.) activities in which youth play basketball and interact informally with local police officers (National Institute of

Justice, 1996: 6). Average daily attendance in the after-school programs has been about 120–150 elementary and/or intermediate school students. Outcome measures indicate some improvements in school attendance, improved cognitive skills of program participants, improved relationships between youth and adults in the community, reduced drug activity, and fewer youth congregating on street corners in the Beacons' vicinities (National Institute of Justice, 1996).

Alternative Schools

Alternative education has become widely accepted as a means for preventing school dropout and delinquency. School districts throughout the nation have recognized the need to develop alternative educational programs for students who are not achieving in the regular classroom and often disrupt the learning environment. Alternative education programs are structured and operated in a variety of different ways. Alternative education programs range from remedial reading and math programs for students with academic problems to in-school suspension for disruptive students (Hawkins and Wall, 1980: 2). Alternative schools are designed to create a more positive learning environment through lower teacher:student ratios, individualized self-paced instruction, and classrooms that are less structured and less competitive (Raywid, 1983). A self-paced curriculum and informal classroom structure enable teachers to provide more individualized instruction. A review of several empirical studies of alternative schools revealed that small school size, a supportive and noncompetitive environment, and a student-centered curriculum were the characteristics most associated with success of the programs (Young, 1990). Students in alternative schools generally work under less pressure and competition from other students because their academic progress is measured by their own individual achievement rather than in comparison with other students in the class (Gold and Mann, 1984). Denise Gottfredson (1987) noted that many alternative educational programs have been developed for disruptive and delinquent students because such programs will purportedly help improve their self-esteem, their attitudes toward school, attendance, and academic performance and reduce their delinquent involvement. Stephen Cox, William Davidson, and Tim Bynum (1995) conducted a meta-analysis of 57 evaluative studies of alternative education programs. The results of their study suggested that alternative education programs can have a small positive effect on school performance, school attitude, and self-esteem. Their analysis indicated, however, that alternative schools have not been effective in reducing delinquent behavior. They suggested that even though alternative schools promote positive school attitudes, their effect on school performance and self-esteem is not large enough to influence delinquent behavior. Even though the students liked going to the alternative school and seemed to have better academic performance, those improvements were not sufficient to overcome other influences (such as family problems and peer influences) that may have had a greater effect on delinquency (Cox et al., 1995: 229). It appears that alternative schools that are targeted at specific problem students have a greater impact than schools with a mix of students with different problems and needs. The school structure and curriculum can be more easily adapted for a more clearly defined student population.

The varied nature of alternative school programs makes it difficult to conduct a meaningful evaluation (Gottfredson, 2001: 154). More research is needed to determine whether alternative schools may have a significant impact on delinquent students and to identify specific components of alternative education programs that may be most effective. A variation on alternative schools is the above-mentioned "school within the school" concept. Denise Gottfredson (1997, 2001) reviewed two programs that place high-risk students into smaller groups within the school. The School Transitional Environment Project (STEP) kept high-risk students in small groups for their home room period and classes, and the teacher offered more support, including counseling and guidance. The Student Training Through Urban Strategies (STATUS) program grouped high-risk students for classes that included law-related education and teaching methods that emphasized active student participation. Program evaluations indicated that participating students had reduced levels of delinquency and drug use, greater attachment to school, better academic performance, and lower dropout rates (Gottfredson, 2001: 145–147).

Vocational and Employment Programs

Relevance of Education for Life and Work. The degree of student commitment to education is an important factor in whether students comply with teacher expectations or engage in disruptive behavior. Perceived irrelevancy of education is a factor that has been identified as important in the school-delinquency connection (Schafer and Polk, 1967: 231–232). Many students do not understand the importance of reading, writing, and math skills in getting a job and doing well in the workplace. Schools and the business community can do more to impress upon students the importance of education for life and work. Simply telling them that education is important is not enough for many students. Teachers can include work-related problems and examples in school lesson plans and can invite a variety of employers to speak to their classes about the skills required for the workplace. Many employers do not in fact recognize school performance as being important in screening job applicants. James Rosenbaum (1989) has noted that surveys of employers have shown that grades and test scores are important when hiring college graduates, but not high school graduates. Many employers do not even request school transcripts, and some consider participation in extracurricular activities more important than grades. Rosenbaum (1989) emphasized that students who are not motivated by personal standards or parental pressure to excel in school have little incentive to do well, because schoolwork does not really affect the jobs they will get after high school. When students perceive that school tasks, demands, and rewards have no payoff for them in the future, the school experience becomes meaningless for them. They feel no commitment to education, no incentives for achieving academically, and have little to lose by disrupting the classroom environment. Students need to feel that their courses are relevant and that school attendance and performance will make a difference for their immediate and future employment prospects. Disruptive students are often those who have given up on school, do not care about grades, find courses irrelevant, and feel that nothing they do makes any difference. Some students take out their frustration through disruption in the classroom or violence against teachers or other students. Caring about grades and seeing relevance in education is an important step toward commitment to school and to each student's own future.

A major function of schools is that of developing youths' cognitive and social skills. Many school-based prevention programs focus on student skill development. Life skills training helps young people in communication skills, decision making, and conflict resolution. Developing these skills will help them improve interpersonal relations with family members, teachers, and peers (Hawkins and Weis, 1985: 88). Some believe that schools should help young people develop social skills just as they do cognitive skills. Young people with better social skills will find that interactions with conventional others are more rewarding, and they are more likely to develop attachments to positive persons. Social skills also contribute to students' academic success and commitment to schools (Hawkins and Weis, 1985: 88).

School and Business Cooperation in Education. Schools and the business community can enhance students' perception of the relevance of education by placing more emphasis on preparing students for the work world. Offering students career and employment information would help improve their commitment to and expectations of attaining legitimate employment. Improving students' commitment to gainful employment will in turn help increase their commitment to schooling as a necessary step toward employment. One method for including this in the school curriculum is "experiential prevocational training and exploration" in which students are introduced to several career options and the required skills and training for them (Hawkins and Weis, 1985: 89). The training can begin in classrooms and includes field trips to various work sites. Improving students' social and vocational knowledge and skills has significant potential for increasing their commitment to education and reducing the likelihood of their delinquent involvement.

James Rosenbaum (1989) examined the Japanese model of school–employer relationships and identified several ways in which schools and employers can work together in the United States. To motivate students and bolster teachers' authority, employers can show students that some desirable jobs are available to them, hire students before they leave school, and hire students based on their grades. Schools can help to better prepare students for employment and bolster teachers' authority by adopting similar practices that help emphasize the relationship between school and employment: maintain strong ties to employers; advise employers and students and help match qualified students with employers; make evaluations of students, grading systems, and transcripts available to employers in a clear and understandable form (see Rosenbaum, 1989: 40).

Collaborative efforts between schools and employers will help to prepare students with the skills needed for the workplace, show that there is a direct relationship between school performance and employment, and increase the rewards for students to attend school regularly and apply themselves. The Boston Compact is an example of high schools working together to improve student achievement by developing linkages with employers. Boston businesses promised to hire more youth if the Boston public schools worked to improve student academic achievement. Employers increased job opportunities for Boston's high school graduates, but the schools have not done as well at improving students' attendance or school achievement (Rosenbaum, 1989: 15). Some Boston high schools and employers have extended the original Boston Compact initiative, however, and have informally agreed to use grades, teacher evaluations, and attendance to select students for some jobs (Rosenbaum, 1989). As part of a comprehensive framework for school violence prevention, the Hamilton Fish Institute (2000) has recognized the valuable resources that businesses can offer for school-based prevention efforts. Businesses can offer financial support for programs and services, facilities for events, safe places for students traveling to and from school, training programs for job skills, leadership and organizational skills, and jobs and internships for students. Business representatives can have a presence in the schools by donating computers or services, directly offering programs, or participating in meetings (Hamilton Fish Institute, 2000: 14).

Federal Government Role in Delinquency Prevention

Juvenile crime is a local problem with roots that can be traced to the family, peers, community factors, and schools. Responding to juvenile crime and preventing delinquency are likewise the primary responsibility of local police, juvenile justice officials, community agencies, and local schools. The federal government has provided delinquency-prevention assistance to local schools and agencies primarily through measures, data analyses, and reports on the extent of crime and violence and through funding and technical assistance for program development (Lawrence, 2002). School administrators and law enforcement officials have turned to federal agencies for technical assistance, funding, and additional resources to assist in juvenile crime prevention. The federal government has played an important role in delinquency prevention especially over the past 40 years. One of the first major federal government initiatives in juvenile delinquency assessment and prevention was the 1967 President's Commission on Law Enforcement and Administration of Justice, which produced a series of reports, one of which was the "Task Force Report: Juvenile Delinquency and Youth Crime" (President's Commission on Law Enforcement and Administration of Justice, 1967).

The Juvenile Justice and Delinquency Prevention Act of 1974 established a dual function philosophy for juvenile justice that separated formal legal control from prevention. Federal, state, and local governments are interested in delinquency prevention. The OJJDP is the arm of the U.S. Department of Justice responsible for disseminating information about delinquency prevention and control. Under the 1974 Act, the juvenile court is limited in its role of delinquency prevention and formally deals only with juveniles who have engaged in delinquent acts that are considered crimes if committed by adults. The 1974 Act called for deinstitutionalization of status offenders and removal of status offenders from the juvenile court. Crime prevention is not the primary role of the juvenile court, but is considered the responsibility of the community, which includes families and the schools.

Limiting the juvenile court to a control function does not mean that delinquency prevention is less important. Rather, the division of responsibility is an acknowledgement that delinquency prevention is more appropriately done by social institutions such as families and schools. Delinquency prevention has long been recognized as the most important means of dealing with crime. The Task Force Report on Juvenile Delinquency of the President's Commission on Law Enforcement and Administration of Justice (1967) focused on the importance of prevention, and noted that

the most promising and . . . important method of dealing with crime is by preventing it. . . . The Commission doubts that even a vastly improved criminal justice system can substantially reduce crime if society fails to make it possible for each of its citizens to feel a personal stake in it—in the good life that it can provide and in the law and order that are prerequisite to such a life. . . .

Clearly it is with young people that prevention efforts are most needed and hold the most promise. It is simply more critical that young people be kept from crime, for they are the Nation's future, and their conduct will affect society for a long time to come. They are not yet set in their ways; they are still developing, still subject to the influence of the socializing institutions that structure . . . their environment: Family, school, gang, recreation program, job market. But that influence, to do the most good, must come before the youth has become involved in the formal criminal justice system (The President's Commission on Law Enforcement and Administration of Justice, 1967: 41).

Since the 1960s the federal government has invested millions of dollars in delinquency-prevention efforts. In asking the U.S. Justice Department to report on the effectiveness of its crime prevention efforts, the U.S. Congress adopted a broad definition of crime prevention when it requested a report on the reduction of *risk factors* for crime (such as gang membership) and increases in *protective factors* (such as high school completion), which is considered primary prevention (Sherman, 1997b: 2-3). Denise Gottfredson (1997) noted that the amount of federal expenditures on school-based substance abuse- and crime-prevention efforts are very modest compared with the federal funds allocated for policing and prison construction. The single largest federal expenditure on school-based prevention has been for the Safe and Drug-Free Schools and Communities that have been administered by the U.S. Department of Education. Programs that have been operated with these funds include teacher and staff training, curriculum development, governors' state and local programs such as Drug Abuse Resistance Education (D.A.R.E.), and high-risk youth programs. The U.S. Department of Justice shares funding of D.A.R.E. programs and also has provided funding for Gang Resistance Education and Training (G.R.E.A.T.), Cities in Schools (CIS), and Law-Related Education (LRE) (Gottfredson, 1997: 5).

The federal government has played a leading role in school crime prevention by providing funding and technical assistance for schools and agencies to develop and implement prevention programs at the local level. The U.S. Departments of Education and Justice have assisted in measuring and reporting on school crime and safety (DeVoe et al., 2004). The annual reports serve an important function for providing the most accurate and reliable assessments of the problem. Both of these reports provide a sound basis for information on school crime and safety and point out the importance of maintaining accurate measures. The reports provide a more accurate basis to guide policymakers and practitioners in developing effective programs and policies to prevent school crime and violence.

School-Based Prevention: Some Model Programs

A large number of school-based delinquency-prevention programs have been developed and implemented during the past few decades. These programs range from early interventions for at-risk students in elementary schools to curricular additions that include all students to programs aimed at students who have been identified as being at high risk for delinquency (Hawkins and Denise Lishner, 1987a). School-based programs also provide health and social services as well as recreational opportunities in local schools (Dryfoos, 1994). The OJJDP has documented a number of delinquency-prevention programs throughout the United States, many of which are school-based programs (see Howell, 1995; Office of Juvenile Justice and Delinquency Prevention, 1995). Some of the outstanding school-based prevention programs that have been more widely publicized are reviewed in this section. These programs vary as to the available information on the specific design and method of implementation, and not all programs have conducted or reported on efforts to monitor and evaluate program outcomes.

The Perry Preschool Project. One of the oldest school-based delinquency-prevention programs is the Perry Preschool Project in Ypsilanti, Michigan (Berrueta-Clement et al., 1987). Originally developed in 1962, the project was designed to prevent educational failure among students who were identified as being at-risk of school dropout. The program concentrated in a lower socioeconomic, predominantly black, neighborhood in Ypsilanti,

Michigan. Less than one in five parents of the students in the program had completed high school, compared to one in two nationally. About half of the families were headed by a single adult. In two out of five families no parent was employed, and those who were employed worked in jobs classified as unskilled labor. Half of the families received welfare assistance, compared to only one in twenty families nationwide.

The Perry Preschool program was an organized educational program directed at the intellectual and social development of young children. Teachers on the staff had received in-service training and worked in teams with extensive managerial support. The staff:child ratio was about one adult for every five to seven children in the program. Children attended preschool for 2 school years at ages 3 and 4. Classes were conducted for 2½ hours each morning 5 days a week; the school year ran from October through May. In addition, teachers visited mothers and children in the home for 2½ hours each week (Berrueta-Clement et al., 1987: 224). The program is based on the premise that a major link between early preschool intervention and later misbehavior and delinquency is through school failure. Through the Perry Preschool project, children who are at risk of educational failure have an opportunity to achieve success in early schooling. Early school success is linked to later success and higher attainment in school and, in turn, is related to reduced involvement in misbehavior and delinquency.

The program has been evaluated annually among students aged 4–11, and at 14, 15, and 19 years of age. The measures collected for the last three age groups included school records, interviews, and juvenile and adult arrest and court records. Outcome measures were collected on students from the preschool program and a matched control group. Overall, the preschool program resulted in a significant reduction in the number of youths who were later arrested or charged with crimes—31 percent compared to 51 percent—and the program resulted in lower numbers of self-reported offenses. Participants in the preschool program were more likely to graduate from high school and to undertake some kind of postsecondary education or vocational training, more likely to be working at the age of 19, and less likely to have received some form of welfare assistance (Berrueta-Clement et al., 1987: 231–234). The Perry Preschool project is clear evidence that early preschool intervention with an at-risk population of children can have very significant results in delinquency prevention.

Cities in Schools Program. The CIS program is a public–private partnership that has operated in more than 30 cities. The program was developed to reduce school violence, prevent students from dropping out, and provide more successful school experiences among inner-city students who often fail in school (Murray et al., 1980; see Hawkins and Lishner, 1987; Office of Juvenile Justice and Delinquency Prevention, 1989: 82–83). Students are referred to a CIS program because of low academic achievement, poor attendance, disruptive behavior, or family problems. Students were offered academic support, counseling, cultural enrichment activities, and other human services. Caseworkers monitored each student's progress and well-being. Students and school staff were grouped into school "families" to provide positive support networks. A 3-year study compared treatment and control students at three different sites. Outcomes at two of the sites showed mostly negative results, but students in one site showed positive results, including more personal control, increased attention and effort in the classroom, more success in interpersonal relations and in learning situations, better reading skills, and better attendance (Murray et al., 1980). Although program evaluations have shown mixed results, the CIS concept has produced some excellent programs that have made a difference for many high-risk youth.

School Action Effectiveness Study. A project that evaluated 17 alternative education programs for 6th- to 12th-grade students in high-crime communities was conducted by Gary and Denise Gottfredson (1986). The alternative education programs were based on the assumption that school structure and organization contribute to the failure of many students, that school failure reduces students' commitment to conventional values, and in turn increases the likelihood of delinquent involvement. Project developers believed that some changes in school organization might help reduce disruptive classroom behavior, absenteeism, dropout, and delinquency. Interventions varied among the alternative education programs but included peer counseling, leadership training, parent involvement, skills classes, token economies, vocational education, and school climate improvement. Positive results were noted in some of the alternative programs, including better school safety, less teacher victimization, slightly less delinquency, decreases in student alienation, and improved self-concept (Gottfredson and Gottfredson, 1986; and see Hawkins and Lishner, 1987).

Project PATHE. PATHE ("Positive Action Through Holistic Education") was a 3-year delinquency-prevention program implemented by the Charleston County, South Carolina, public schools between 1980 and 1983 (Gottfredson, 1986). The program combined an environmental change approach with direct intervention for high-risk youths to reduce delinquent behavior and increase educational attainment. The program involved school staff, students, and community members in planning and implementing a comprehensive school improvement effort, changed disciplinary procedures, and enhanced the school program with activities that were directed at improving achievement and creating a more positive school climate. The program was implemented in four middle schools and three high schools. One middle school and one high school were included in a study as comparisons to assess year-to-year differences in the program. The program resulted in small but measurable reductions in delinquent behavior and misconduct. Students in the program were suspended less often and reported less involvement in delinquent behavior and drug-related activities. School attendance increased in the high schools, but dropped slightly in the middle schools. The PATHE program improved general school climate and discipline management, and school safety improved in all the schools. The program increased the academic success experiences of the students, and significantly more students in the program graduated from high school. Denise Gottfredson noted that the improved school climate in the PATHE programs seemed to be responsible for students' increased sense of belonging in the school and for students' greater level of attachment to the school (1986: 726). School climate was defined as teachers' perceptions of the way the school is managed, teacher and student perceptions of school safety, staff morale, and improved discipline management. The program did not result in reduced delinquent behavior among the high-risk students but did increase their commitment to education as indicated by the rates of dropout, retention, graduation, and achievement test scores. The PATHE program suggests that altering the school organization can be an effective approach to delinquency prevention. Effective steps that schools can take are to involve the school staff, students, and community members in planning and implementing change; retrain school staff; make changes in the curriculum and discipline procedures in the school; and create clear standards for implementing performance. These are lofty goals for schools to achieve, but these changes can help reduce the risk of involvement in delinquent activities for the general school population (Gottfredson, 1986: 728, 2001).

Law-Related Education. A delinquency-prevention approach that has gained widespread acceptance throughout the United States involves a variety of additions to the regular school curriculum to promote prosocial attitudes and behaviors. The most prominent of these curriculum approaches and the one most evaluated is LRE. LRE seeks to help students understand rights and responsibilities that are part of everyday life. The program teaches youth about good citizenship, encourages them to become more accountable for their actions, and attempts to develop respect for the law. LRE added a drug component to the curriculum in 1988 to stress to youth that they will be held accountable for illegal drug use. Since 1978, the OJJDP has funded a national LRE effort through grants to five organizations: the American Bar Association, Center for Civic Education, Constitutional Rights Foundation, the National Institute for Citizen Education in the Law, and the Phi Alpha Delta Public Service Center. In 1989–1990 LRE was active in 43 states. The National Training and Dissemination Program (NTDP) provides coordination for statewide LRE programs, but the success of LRE depends on the initiative of local citizens, educators, and justice professionals. Since 1984, LRE programs have been conducted in 670 school districts, training some 52,000 teachers and resource persons to reach an estimated 2.4 million students (Office of Juvenile Justice and Delinquency Prevention, 1990: 4).

LRE is based on the premise that helping young people recognize that they have a stake in their future is crucial if they are to become law-abiding, responsible citizens (Office of Juvenile Justice and Delinquency Prevention, 1990). One way to do this is to teach them about the law, the legal system, and their rights and responsibilities as citizens. LRE seeks to help young people grasp the importance of laws and their relationship to everyday life and problems. The programs include a curriculum for elementary through high school students. LRE is intended to help students understand why rules exist and why it is important that rules are obeyed. The curriculum also teaches them how the courts work and why citizens who break the law must be held accountable for their illegal activities. The educational focus of LRE is on civil, criminal, and constitutional themes relating to such familiar topics as consumer protection, housing law, voting rights, child custody, spouse and child abuse, and traffic laws. LRE curricula include scenarios that illustrate key constitutional issues such as search and seizure, indentured servitude, political asylum, and freedom of speech, the press, and religion. The programs engage students in debating issues that directly involve them and require careful application of the Constitution, such as drunk driving, drug testing on the job and in the schools, handgun registration, environmental protection laws, and computer crimes. Effective LRE programs engage students in lively debates about school locker searches for drugs or weapons; about freedom of the press in student publications; or in mock trials for drunk driving, theft, assault, and murder. LRE directs students' attention to the necessity of a balance between rights and responsibilities and how rule violations and weapon and drug possession disrupt the school environment and threaten the safety of all students. By teaching students about the law through active, personal engagement, it is hoped that they will gain a deeper understanding that will in turn promote positive attitudes toward the law and prosocial behavior.

James W. Fox, Kevin Minor, and William Pelkey (1994) examined the perceptions of juvenile offenders who participated in Kentucky's LRE diversion program. The state Juvenile Services Division received funds in 1990 from the National Training and Dissemination Program to introduce law-related education as a diversion option. All delinquents and status offenders aged 12–17 who meet the criteria for diversion are eligible to participate in LRE. The Kentucky program consists of the LRE curriculum noted above, and coverage is also given to drug education and community issues. Trained staff also rely on active learning techniques, field trips, and interactive presentations from resource persons such as law enforcement officers, attorneys and judges. Fox and associates examined pretest and posttest data for 33 juvenile offenders diverted into a LRE program and a control group of 28 public school students (total $N = 61$). Information was gathered on the number of LRE subjects who were referred for a new offense within one year following completion of the program. Data were also collected on juveniles' perceptions of themselves, their parents, their neighbors, their best friends, judges, teachers, and the police. The LRE group had significant pretest-to-posttest improvements in perceptions of police officers, themselves, parents, and teachers, but the posttest perceptions of LRE subjects did not significantly differ from the perceptions of control subjects on any scale. Only six (10.5 percent) of the LRE participants were referred for one offense each in the year following the program. The researchers acknowledge that the quasi-experimental design does not allow definite cause–effect conclusions to be drawn, but the results do suggest that LRE may be a viable addition to a juvenile diversion program. Denise Gottfredson (1997, 2001) suggested that law-related education will probably not reduce delinquency when used in isolation, but when used together with classroom organization and management the outcomes are better.

Drug Awareness Resistance Education. Drug abuse prevention has received considerable attention as an addition to the school curriculum, especially as alcohol and drug use are increasingly seen as being among the biggest problems faced by schools and communities. In 1986 the U.S. Congress passed the Drug-Free Schools and Communities Act to promote drug abuse education and prevention throughout the nation. Millions of federal dollars have been allocated to assist in state and local drug-prevention efforts. In many states, schools are required by law to have drug education programs.

D.A.R.E. is the best-known and most widely disseminated school-based drug-prevention program in the United States. It was originally developed in 1983 by the Los Angeles Police Department in cooperation with the Los Angeles Unified School District. D.A.R.E. programs now operate in all 50 states and in six foreign countries (Rosenbaum et al., 1994: 6). D.A.R.E. is unique for its collaborative effort between education and law enforcement and for the use of trained, uniformed police officers in the classroom to teach a highly structured drug-prevention curriculum. The program targets students in their last years of elementary school, usually the 5th or 6th grade. The D.A.R.E. program is focused on this age group because it is assumed that these students are most receptive to antidrug messages and are entering the drug experimentation phase where intervention may be most beneficial. D.A.R.E. officers receive 80 hours of instruction in classroom management, teaching strategies, communication skills, adolescent development, drug information, and the D.A.R.E. lessons. D.A.R.E. officers are closely observed by the classroom teacher and by periodic visits from an experienced D.A.R.E. officer to ensure that the curriculum is being delivered consistently and well. The law enforcement agency pays for the officer's training, salary, and the instructional materials, which include student workbooks, visual aids, and graduation certificates. Officers teach the D.A.R.E. curriculum in one-hour sessions for 17 weeks. Teaching strategies include lectures, workbook exercises, question and answer sessions, audiovisual materials, and role-playing sessions. The strategies support the objective of D.A.R.E., to teach peer-resistance skills by offering students several ways to say "no" to drugs. D.A.R.E. is a comprehensive program that includes a variety of teaching objectives including the effects and consequences of using alcohol, marijuana, and other drugs; media influences and advertising techniques for tobacco and alcohol; and assertiveness skills and strategies for resisting peer pressure to use drugs (Rosenbaum et al., 1994: 8).

The results of empirical studies evaluating the effects of D.A.R.E. programs do not show that the programs have a consistent or significant impact on students' drug use, however. Michele Harmon (1993) examined the effectiveness of the D.A.R.E. program in Charleston County, South Carolina, using a quasi-experimental design. A sample of 341 D.A.R.E. students and 367 comparison students were administered pre- and posttests to compare the effects of the program on such variables as school attachment and commitment, belief in prosocial norms, self-esteem, assertiveness, attitudes about substance use, beliefs regarding the police, and their drug use. Students in the D.A.R.E. group used alcohol less, had higher levels of belief in prosocial norms, reported less association with drug-using peers, showed an increase in attitudes against substance use, and were more assertive. However, no significant effects were found for self-reported cigarette, tobacco, or marijuana use in the last year; frequency of any drug use in the past month; and coping strategies, attitudes about police, school attachment and commitment, and rebellious behavior.

Susan Ennett, Nancy Tobler, Christopher Ringwalt, and Robert Flewelling (1994) conducted a meta-analysis of several D.A.R.E. program outcome evaluations. Eight evaluation studies representing six states and one Canadian province met their criteria of studies that used a control group, pretest–posttest design, and quantitative outcome measures. Each of the studies had evaluated a statewide or local D.A.R.E. program and included at least 10 schools with sample sizes of 500–2,000 students. The meta-analysis examined six outcome measures, including knowledge about drugs, attitudes about drug use, social skills, self-esteem, attitude toward police, and drug use. The outcomes of the D.A.R.E. programs were compared with school-based drug use–prevention programs in a control group of schools. The results of the meta-analysis indicated that the D.A.R.E. programs had very little effect on the outcome variables measured and were smaller than other drug-prevention programs using interactive techniques. Except for tobacco use, the effects of the D.A.R.E. programs were slight and not statistically significant. Ennett and associates noted that some features of D.A.R.E. may be more effective in school districts where the D.A.R.E. curricula for younger and older students are in place, and its impact on community law enforcement relations may have important benefits. The results showing D.A.R.E.'s limited influence on adolescent drug use behavior contrasts with the popularity and prevalence of the program. The authors cautioned that expectations for the D.A.R.E. program to significantly change adolescent drug use should not be overstated (Ennett et al., 1994: 1399).

Dennis Rosenbaum and associates (1994) evaluated the D.A.R.E. program in 12 urban and suburban schools in Illinois involving 1,584 students. A matched group of 24 schools were selected for the study. Twelve schools were randomly assigned to receive D.A.R.E., and 12 served as controls for comparison. The D.A.R.E. program had no statistically significant overall impact on students' use of alcohol or cigarettes about one year after completion of the program. The only statistically significant main effect of D.A.R.E. was on perceived media influences regarding the portrayal of beer drinking: more of the D.A.R.E. students' recognized the media's portrayal of beer drinking as desirable. The program appeared to have some effect in encouraging females to quit using alcohol but seemed to have the opposite effect for males. The apparent failure of D.A.R.E. to produce any measurable differences on students' drug attitudes and use raises questions about the value of D.A.R.E. programs spending time on issues that are not directly related to substance use. Rosenbaum and associates (1994) suggested that greater attention be given in drug-prevention programs to changing students' inaccurate perceptions concerning the extent to which drugs are used and sanctioned by peers. The overall decline in the prevalence of drug use among the school-age population raises the question of whether factors other than school-based drug-prevention programs are responsible for the decline, or the evaluation measures are simply not precise enough to detect the effectiveness of school programs (Rosenbaum et al., 1994: 27). It is possible that the decline in drug use may be attributable to the current emphases on the health risks of drug use, declining social acceptance, and the fact that youth are getting these messages from multiple sources, including the media, parents, family members and their peers. Rosenbaum and associates (1994) concluded that as a society we are doing something right in preventing drug abuse among youth, but research results do not clearly show that positive results are attained by school-based drug education. A review of D.A.R.E. programs also led Denise Gottfredson (1997, 2001) to conclude that they do not work to reduce substance use. She suggested that the program's content, teaching methods, and use of uniformed police officers rather than teachers might explain the weak evaluations; and added that the D.A.R.E. curriculum is unlikely to reduce substance use without instruction that is more focused on social competency development (1997: 5–35).

Gang Resistance Education and Training. A delinquency-prevention program called G.R.E.A.T. is aimed at reducing gang membership based on an enhancement of the regular school curriculum, much like the D.A.R.E. program. G.R.E.A.T. and D.A.R.E. in fact have many features in common, from their origins in police departments to their delivery by uniformed police officers in the school classroom. In 1991 the Phoenix, Arizona, police department initiated a pilot project with seven school districts in the Phoenix metropolitan area to provide youth in the lower grades with the skills necessary to resist becoming gang members. After a pilot study involving nearly 4,000 students, the police department took the program to the entire Phoenix area, targeting 4th and 7th grade students. After about a year of operation, the police department entered into a collaborative agreement with the Bureau of Alcohol, Tobacco and Firearms (ATF) to sponsor and train the police instructors for national distribution of the program (Winfree et al., 1996).

The G.R.E.A.T. program is designed to teach youths to set goals for themselves, how to resist peer pressure, how to resolve conflicts, and how gangs can affect the quality of their lives (Esbensen, 2000). The program is taught by uniformed police officers over 9 consecutive weeks during the school year. The program targets 7th-grade students, although some schools have offered it to 6- and 8-graders, and there is a 3rd- and 4th-grade component and a summer program component. These age groups were targeted based on a belief that many youths are predisposed toward gang membership at those levels, and much gang recruitment occurs in the middle school and even the later elementary school levels (McEvoy, 1990). The program curriculum consists of eight parts, with such topics and objectives as:

•Crimes, victims, and their impact on the school and neighborhood

•How cultural differences affect the school and the neighborhood

•Conflict resolution

•Meeting basic needs without joining a gang

•How drugs affect the individual, the school, and the neighborhood

•Responsibilities of students in the school and the neighborhood

•Goal setting: how to set short- and long-term goals (Winfree et al., 1996)

Police officer–instructors are provided with detailed lesson plans that have clearly stated purposes and goals and serve as instructional guides. Classroom teachers are also provided a copy of the curriculum and are expected to remain in the classroom during the officer's instructional presentation. Students who complete the program receive a certificate at the tenth week. Since its development in 1991, the G.R.E.A.T. program has been adopted by many other law enforcement agencies. A comprehensive evaluation of G.R.E.A.T. in 11 sites involving nearly 6,000 students indicated that students had more pro-social attitudes and lower rates of some types of delinquent behavior than a comparison group of students (Esbensen and Osgood, 1999). Overall, the program has had modest positive effects on adolescents' delinquency risk factors (delinquent peer associations, attitudes toward police, awareness of the negative consequences of gang involvement), but no significant effects on youth involvement in gangs or delinquent behavior (Esbensen, 2004). The program does have wide support from parents, law enforcement, and educators. It is evident that the G.R.E.A.T. program must be combined with other educational programs before it can have significant effects on students' involvement in gangs and delinquency.

Summary of School-Based Delinquency Prevention

Funding and implementation of school-based delinquency-prevention programs have expanded and grown significantly in the past decade. Legislators and policymakers at the state and federal levels have responded to the growing problem of school crime and violence and recognize that schools are among the best locations for implementing delinquency-prevention programs. This adds to the already complex and demanding tasks of educators, but the responsibility of educating students cannot be accomplished until we can ensure a safe and healthy learning environment.

Measuring and evaluating the impact that programs have on crime and delinquency is always a difficult and challenging task. Many programs have included a method for monitoring program outcomes in the original design and implementation. Program assessments are unfortunately not a regular part of all programs, and many programs lack careful monitoring for quality implementation of activities and program objectives (Gottfredson, 2001). At the minimum, it is important for all programs to specifically define the goals and objectives, the target population, and some desired outcomes of the program and to collect information and data to assess the impact of the program in meeting its objectives. Program administrators must include mechanisms for monitoring and assessment of the program if they want to improve their chances for receiving further support and funding from government agencies and foundations.

School-based delinquency-prevention programs continue to develop and evolve, and funding opportunities for safe school initiatives are regular agenda items among state and federal agencies. Educators, law enforcement, juvenile justice, and mental health professionals are developing and implementing effective delinquency-prevention programs.

The National Study of Delinquency Prevention in Schools (Gottfredson, 2004) has shown that most schools have numerous programs in operation, but they vary greatly in quality of implementation and effectiveness. A great deal of emphasis has been placed on "get-tough" crime-prevention strategies, particularly in response to the widely publicized school shooting incidents. The initial response to school violence has generally been to hire police and security officers, install metal detectors and surveillance cameras, require identification badges, and change student policies regarding backpacks and use of school lockers. The use of "zero-tolerance" policies and suspension or expulsion from school has also increased significantly. Few studies have been conducted on the effectiveness of "get-tough" policies, but the available research indicates that they may have few positive effects (Gottfredson et al., 2002) and may even increase students' fear of victimization (Schreck et al., 2003). Comprehensive strategies for school violence prevention must offer more than "get-tough" approaches focused on security and formal controls and must place equal emphasis on improving school climate and organization, supporting the role of school staff in working with students and utilizing school curricula and classroom programs to promote students' social skills and decision making (see Catalano et al., 1998; Elliott et al., 1998b; Hamilton Fish Institute, 2000; Mihalic et al., 2001; D. Gottfredson, 2001; G. Gottfredson, 2004).

Recommendations for Educators, Justice Officials, and Policymakers

School crime and violence are problems with causes as varied as the troubled students who engage in such behaviors. No one program or strategy will be sufficient to deal with school crime. As we study school problems and juvenile delinquency, we are struck by the complexity of the problem. We cannot study crime and delinquency in the schools apart from crime and delinquency in the community. Crime is a multifaceted problem with roots in the family and is influenced by peer associations and community problems. Young people who grow up without close parental ties and supervision are at risk of negative associations with antisocial peers and are more likely to experience problems in school and to engage in delinquent behavior. I have outlined in this book the problem of juvenile delinquency and crime in schools and the role of schools in delinquency prevention. Schools are often criticized for educational failure, while at the same time they are expected to take on more of the responsibilities for the overall social development of young people. The general reluctance of the American public to provide adequate funding and resources to support public education presents an additional challenge for educators, who are expected to do more with less.

Schools are meeting the challenge. School retention and graduation rates are showing some improvement. Teachers and administrators are confronting and making progress toward overcoming the problems of disruption, crime, and violence in schools throughout the United States and other countries. Educators are implementing new school curricula and special programs to improve students' academic performance and reduce delinquent involvement in schools. Controlling school crime and providing a safe school environment for all students is a never-ending process, but one that demands our highest commitment and priority.

Strong and effective leadership of school administrators is essential for maintaining a safe school environment. It is important for school administrators to develop cooperative interagency relations. A major impediment against effective delinquency prevention in most cities is the absence of cooperative interagency relations between school districts and community agencies. School crime prevention depends on the collaborative efforts of law enforcement, the juvenile court, juvenile probation, and social service agencies.

Many school districts have developed comprehensive and effective delinquency-prevention programs. A great deal of effort is required, and it is essential to get the cooperative participation of students, parents, and community representatives. It is important to recognize that there are no easy and simple answers to providing a quality education for all young people in a safe school environment, free of crime and violence. In conclusion, I offer the following policy recommendations for school administrators, justice officials, community and business leaders, policymakers, and legislators. These recommendations are based on findings of the school-based delinquency-prevention programs presented here, based on reviews and evaluative research of numerous school-based delinquency-prevention programs.

Recommendations for Preventing School Crime and Violence

•School administrators and law enforcement officials should carefully monitor and keep records on the nature and extent of school crime incidents.

•School boards and administrators should seek input from teachers, parents, and students to develop a clear statement of school policies and regulations and the sanctions that students should expect for criminal behavior and violations of school rules.

•Administrators and teachers should strive to develop a communal school environment with good communication and positive working relations among staff to promote a healthy and safe learning environment.

•School districts should consider various options to reduce disruption and crime, including restructuring, reducing school size, and providing more resources and technical assistance for schools with the highest risks of problems.

•Administrators should carefully assess the need for physical security devices and law enforcement or security officers and place equal emphasis on developing informal social controls to reduce school crime and violence.

•School administrators and teachers should take every opportunity to improve their skills in discipline, classroom management, and conflict mediation, through available training sessions.

•Schools should implement promising strategies to reduce school disorder by developing model disciplinary procedures, increasing instructional resources, and offering a range of educational programs so that all students have the opportunity and incentives to succeed in school.

•Administrators should study the conditions under which effective programs are achieved and should monitor the implementation and evaluate the outcomes of the programs.

•Law enforcement and juvenile court officials should make every effort to assist schools in delinquency prevention, cooperate with their efforts, and communicate periodically regarding school policies and crime-prevention programs.

•Business and community leaders should work closely with schools and justice agencies in crime-prevention efforts, offer employment-training opportunities, offer incentives for student-employee attendance and achievement, and offer internship and employment positions on schedules appropriate for students.

•Special emphasis should be focused on developing interagency relations between school administrators, law enforcement and justice officials, and community leaders and meeting regularly to discuss mutual concerns, monitor progress, and engage in joint program planning.

•State and federal legislators and policymakers must recognize the important role that education plays in reducing crime and delinquency and should increase funding for education at levels that are proportionate to the funding increases for police, jails, and prisons.

•We must recognize that spectacular results cannot be expected immediately. We should expect some failures and be skeptical about claims that there is a single best solution to school crime. Program evaluations of good efforts do not always produce positive results. We must learn from each effort, design and implement new programs, and evaluate them.

•We should persist in our efforts. There is ample evidence that school-based delinquency-prevention programs can succeed, especially when they have the support of legislators and government agencies, criminal justice agencies, community leaders, parents, and students.

Summary

School crime and disruption is a serious problem with multiple causes. Law enforcement, the juvenile court, and juvenile corrections are not primarily intended for crime prevention. They can only respond to crime after it occurs. True delinquency-prevention efforts must begin in the family, the schools, and the community. Several school-based delinquency-prevention programs have been implemented, and many show promise in helping to improve student attendance and school performance and reducing their involvement in substance use and delinquent behavior. The task of providing safe schools that are free of crime, drugs, and weapons demands the consolidated efforts of the entire community. The goal of safe schools cannot be met without the aid of the federal and state governments and the coordinated efforts of school administrators, law enforcement officials, community leaders, parents, and students.

References

Action for Children Commission. 1992. *Kids Can't Wait: Action for Minnesota's Children.* St. Paul, MN: Action for Children Commission.

Addington, L., S. A. Ruddy, A. K. Miller, J. F. DeVoe, and K. A. Chandler. 2002. *Are America's Schools Safe? Students Speak Out: 1999 School Crime Supplement.* Washington, DC: National Center for Education Statistics.

Adler, Freda. 1975. *Sisters in Crime.* New York: McGraw-Hill.

Adler, Mortimer. 1982. *The Paideia Proposal.* New York: Macmillan.

Advancement Project/Civil Rights Project. 2000. *Opportunities Suspended: The Devastating Consequences of Zero Tolerance and School Discipline Policies.* Cambridge, MA: Harvard University Press.

Advisory Task Force on the Juvenile Justice System. 1994. *Final Report.* St. Paul, MN: Minnesota Supreme Court.

Ageton, Suzanne S., and Delbert S. Elliott. 1974. "The Effects of Legal Processing on Delinquent Orientations." *Social Problems* 22:87–100.

Agnew, Robert. 1985. "A Revised Strain Theory of Delinquency." *Social Forces* 64:151–167.

Agnew, Robert. 1991. "The Interactive Effects of Peer Variables on Delinquency." *Criminology* 29:47–72.

Agnew, Robert. 1992. "Foundation for a General Strain Theory of Crime and Delinquency." *Criminology* 30:47–87.

Agnew, Robert, and Helene Raskin White. 1992. "An Empirical Test of General Strain Theory." *Criminology* 30:475–499.

Aichhorn, August. 1936. *Wayward Youth.* New York: Viking Press.

Akers, Ronald L. 1985. *Deviant Behavior: A Social Learning Approach*, 3rd ed. Belmont, CA: Wadsworth Publishing.

Akers, Ronald. 1990. "Rational Choice, Deterrence, and Social Learning Theory in Criminology." *Journal of Criminal Law and Criminology* 81:653–676.

Akiba, Motoko. 2002. "Student Victimization: National and School System Effects on School Violence in 37 Nations." *American Educational Research Journal* 39(4):829–853.

Alexander, Karl L., Gary Natriello, and Aaron M. Pallas. 1985. "For Whom the School Bell Tolls: The Impact of Dropping Out on Cognitive Performance." *American Sociological Review* 50:409–420.

Alexander, Kern, and M. David Alexander. 2005. *American Public School Law*, 6th ed. St. Paul, MN: West Publishing Co.

Alfaro, J. D. 1981. "Report on the Relationship Between Child Abuse and Neglect and Later Socially Deviant Behavior." In R. J. Hunter and Y. E. Walker, eds., *Exploring the Relationship Between Child Abuse and Delinquency.* Montclair, NJ: Allanheld, Osmun.

Allen, Francis A. 1981. *The Decline of the Rehabilitative Ideal.* New Haven: Yale University Press.

Allen-Hagen, Barbara. 1991. *Children in Custody 1989.* Washington, DC: Office of Juvenile Justice and Delinquency Prevention.

Alpert, Geoffrey P., and Roger G. Dunham. 1986. "Keeping Academically Marginal Youths in School: A Prediction Model." *Youth and Society* 17:346–361.

Alter, Jonathan. 1992. "The Body Count at Home." *Newsweek* 120(Dec. 28):55.

Altschuler, David M., Troy L. Armstrong, and Doris L. MacKenzie. 1999. *Reintegration, Supervised Release, and Intensive Aftercare*. Washington, DC: U.S. Department of Justice.

Altschuler, David M., and Paul J. Brounstein. 1991. "Patterns of Drug Use, Drug Trafficking, and Other Delinquency Among Inner-City Adolescent Males in Washington, D.C." *Criminology* 19:589–622.

American Bar Association. 2004. *Juvenile Justice Center: Adolescence, Brain Development, and Legal Culpability*. Washington, DC: American Bar Association. [Online: http://www.abanet.org/crimjust/juvjus/Adolescence.pdf]

American Bar Association-Institute of Judicial Administration. 1980a. *Juvenile Justice Standards Relating to Dispositions*. Cambridge, MA: Ballinger.

American Bar Association-Institute of Judicial Administration. 1980b. *Juvenile Justice Standards Relating to Pretrial Court Proceedings*. Cambridge, MA: Ballinger.

American Bar Association-Institute of Judicial Administration. 1982. *Juvenile Standards Relating to Non-criminal Misbehavior*. Cambridge, MA: Ballinger.

American Academy of Child & Adolescent Psychiatry. 1997. *Policy Statement: Corporal Punishment in Schools* (Approved June, 1988). Washington, DC: American Academy of Child & Adolescent Psychiatry. (online: www.aacap.org/publications/policy/ps14.htm)

American Academy of Pediatrics. 2000. "Policy Statement: Corporal Punishment in Schools." *Pediatrics* 106(2):343.

American Psychological Association. 2000. *Warning Signs*. Washington, DC: American Psychological Association. [Online: http://www.helping.apa.org]

Anderson, Carolyn S. 1982. "The Search for School Climate: A Review of the Literature." *Review of Educational Research* 52(3):368–420.

Anderson, David C. 1998. "Curriculum, Culture and Community: The Challenge of School Violence." Pp. 317–363 in M. Tonry and M. H. Moore, eds., *Youth Violence*, Vol. 24. Chicago: University of Chicago Press.

Anderson, M., J. Kaufman, T. Simon, L. Barrios, L. Paulozzi, G. Ryan, R. Hammond, W. Modzeleski, T. Feucht, and L. Potter. 2001. "School-Associated Violent Deaths in the United States, 1994–1999." *Journal of the American Medical Association* 286:2695–2702.

Arenson, Karen W. 2004. "More Youths Opt for G.E.D., Skirting High-School Hurdle." *New York Times* (May 15). (Available online: http://www.nytimes.com/w004/05/15/education/15GED.html]

Armstrong, Gail. 1977. "Females Under the Law—Protected but Unequal." *Crime and Delinquency* 23:109–120.

Arnette, J. L., and M. C. Walsleben. 1998. *Combating Fear and Restoring Safety in Schools*. Washington, DC: U.S. Department of Justice.

Arola, Teryl, and Richard Lawrence. 1999. "Assessing Probation Officer Assaults and Responding to Officer Safety Concerns." *Perspectives* 23(3):32–35.

Arum, R., and I. R. Beattie. 1999. "High School Experience and the Risk of Adult Incarceration." *Criminology* 37:515–540.

Astone, N. M., and S. S. McLanahan. 1991. "Family Structure, Parental Practices and High School Completion." *American Sociological Review* 56:309–320.

Astor, R. A., H. A. Meyer, and W. J. Behre. 1999. "Unowned Places and Times: Maps and Interviews About Violence in High Schools." *American Educational Research Journal* 36:3–42.

Atkinson, Anne J. 2001. "School Resource Officers: Making Schools Safer and More Effective." *Police Chief* 68(3):55–57, 60–62.

Aultmann-Bettridge, Tanya, Delbert S. Elliott, and David Huizinga. 2000. "Predicting School Violence: Analyzing the Validity and Reliability of Violent Student 'Profiles'". Paper presented at the American Society of Criminology, San Francisco.

Bailey, Kirk A. 2001. "Legal Implications of Profiling Students for Violence." *Psychology in the Schools* 38(2):141–155.

Baker, Keith, and Robert J. Rubel, eds. 1980. *Violence and Crime in the Schools*. Lexington, MA: Lexington Books.

Baker, Myriam L., Jane N. Sigmon, and M. Elaine Nugent. 2001. "Truancy Reduction: Keeping Students in School." *OJJDP Juvenile Justice Bulletin.* Washington, DC: U.S. Department of Justice.

Ball, Richard, and J. Robert Lilly. 1986. "A Theoretical Examination of Home Incarceration." *Federal Probation* 50:17–25.

Band, Stephen R., and Joseph A. Harpold. 1999. "School Violence: Lessons Learned." *FBI Law Enforcement Bulletin* 68(9):9–15.

Bandura, Albert. 1977. *Social Learning Theory.* Englewood Cliffs, N.J.: Prentice-Hall.

Bannister, A. J., David L. Carter, and J. Schafer. 2001. "A National Police Survey on Juvenile Curfews." *Journal of Criminal Justice* 29:233–240.

Barker, Roger G., and Page V. Gump, eds. 1964. *Big School, Small School.* Stanford, CA: Stanford University Press.

Bartollas, Clemens. 1993. *Juvenile Delinquency*, 3rd ed. New York: Macmillan.

Bartollas, Clemens, Stuart J. Miller, and Simon Dinitz. 1976. *Juvenile Victimization: The Institutional Paradox.* New York: Halsted Press, A Sage Publication.

Bastian, Lisa D., and Bruce M. Taylor. 1991. *School Crime: A National Crime Victimization Survey Report.* Washington, DC: U.S. Department of Justice.

Battin, S., K. G. Hill, R. Abbott, R. F. Catalano, and J. D. Hawkins. 1998. "The Contribution of Gang Membership to Delinquency Beyond Delinquent Friends." *Criminology* 36(1):93–115.

Bavolek, Stephen J. 2000. "The Nurturing Parenting Programs," OJJDP Juvenile Justice Bulletin. Washington, DC: U.S. Department of Justice.

Bayh, Birch. 1977. *Challenge for the Third Century: Education in a Safe Environment—Final Report on the Nature and Prevention of School Violence and Vandalism.* Washington, DC: U.S. Government Printing Office.

Bazemore, Gordon, Jeanne B. Stinchcomb, and Leslie A. Leip. 2004. "Scared Smart or Bored Straight? Testing Deterrence Logic in an Evaluation of Police-Led Truancy Intervention." *Justice Quarterly* 21(2):269–299.

Bazemore, Gordon, and Mark S. Umbreit. 1994. *Balanced and Restorative Justice: Program Summary.* Washington, DC: Office of Juvenile Justice and Delinquency Prevention.

Bazemore, Gordon, and Mark Umbreit. 1995. "Rethinking the Sanctioning Function in Juvenile Court: Retributive or Restorative Responses to Youth Crime." *Crime & Delinquency* 41:296–316.

Becker, Henry J., and Joyce L. Epstein. 1982. "Parent Involvement: A Survey of Teacher Practices." *Elementary School Journal* 83:85–102.

Becker, Howard S. 1963. *The Outsiders.* New York: The Free Press.

Beger, Randall R. 2003. "The 'Worst of Both Worlds': School Security and the Disappearing Fourth Amendment Rights of Students." *Criminal Justice Review* 28(2):336–354.

Bell, Allison J., Lee A. Rosen, and Dionne Dynlacht. 1994. "Truancy Intervention." *Journal of Research and Development in Education* 27:203–211.

Benigni, Mark D. 2004. "Need for School Resource Officers." *FBI Law Enforcement Bulletin* 73(5):22–24.

Berg, Ian, Imogen Brown, and Roy Hullin. 1988. *Off School, In Court: An Experimental and Psychiatric Investigation of Severe School Attendance Problems.* New York: Springer-Verlag.

Bergsmann, Ilene R. 1989. "The Forgotten Few: Juvenile Female Offenders." *Federal Probation* 53:73–78.

Bernard, Thomas J. 1992. *The Cycle of Juvenile Justice.* New York: Oxford University Press.

Berrueta-Clement, John R., Lawrence J. Schweinhart, William S. Barnett, and David P. Weikart. 1987. "The Effects of Early Educational Intervention on Crime and Delinquency in Adolescence and Early Adulthood." Pp. 220–240 in J. D. Burchard and S. N. Burchard, eds., *Prevention of Delinquent Behavior.* Newbury Park, CA: Sage Publications.

Bishop, Donna M. 1996. "Race Effects in Juvenile Justice Decision-Making: Findings of a Statewide Analysis." *Journal of Criminal Law and Criminology* 86:392–413.

Bishop, Donna M. 2004. "Reaction Essay: Injustice and Irrationality in Contemporary Youth Policy." *Criminology & Public Policy* 4(3):633–644.

Bishop, Donna M., Charles E. Frazier, and John C. Henretta. 1989. "Prosecutorial Waiver: Case Study of a Questionable Reform." *Crime & Delinquency* 35:179–201.

Bishop, Donna M., Charles E. Frazier, Lonn Lanza-Kaduce, and Lawrence Winner. 1996. "The Transfer of Juveniles to Criminal Court: Does It Make a Difference?" *Crime & Delinquency* 42(2):171–191.

Bjorklun, Eugene C. 1993. "Drug Testing High School Athletes and the Fourth Amendment." *Education Law Reporter* 83:913–925.

Bjorklun, Eugene C. 1994. "School Locker Searches and the Fourth Amendment." *Education Law Reporter* 92:1065–1073.

Black, Susan. 1999. "Locked Out Research: Why Suspension and Expulsion Should be Your Court of Last Resort." *American School Board Journal* 186(1):34–37.

Blauvelt, Peter. 1981. *Effective Strategies for School Security.* Reston, VA: National Association of Secondary School Principals.

Blauvelt, Peter D. 1990. "School Security: 'Who You Gonna Call?'" *School Safety* (Fall):4–8.

Blumberg, Abraham. 1979. *Criminal Justice: Issues and Ironies*, 2nd ed. New York: New Viewpoints.

Bonczar, Thomas P., and Tracy L. Snell. 2004. "Capital Punishment, 2003," Bureau of Justice Statistics Bulletin. Washington, DC: U.S. Department of Justice.

Borum, Randy. 2000. "Assessing Violence Risk Among Youth." *Journal of Clinical Psychology* 56(10):1263–1288.

Borum, Randy, Robert Fein, Bryan Vossekuil, and John Berglund. 1999. "Threat Assessment: Defining an Approach for Evaluating Risk of Targeted Violence." *Behavioral Sciences and the Law* 17:323–337.

Bongiovanni, Anthony F. 1979. "An Analysis of Research on Punishment and Its Relation to the Use of Corporal Punishment in the Schools." Pp. 351–372 in I. A. Hyman and J. H. Wise, eds., *Corporal Punishment in American Education.* Philadelphia: Temple University Press.

Bortner, M. A. 1982. *Inside a Juvenile Court: The Tarnished Ideal of Individualized Justice.* New York: New York University Press.

Bortner, M. A. 1986. "Traditional Rhetoric, Organizational Realities: Remand of Juveniles to Adult Court." *Crime & Delinquency* 32:53–73.

Bowditch, Christine. 1993. "Getting Rid of Troublemakers: High School Disciplinary Procedures and the Production of Dropouts." *Social Problems* 40(4):493–509.

Boyer, Ernest. 1983. *High School: A Report on Secondary Education in America.* New York: Harper & Row.

Brady, K. P. 2002. "Zero Tolerance or (In)tolerance? Weaponless School Violence, Due Process, and the Law of Student Suspensions and Expulsions: An Examination of *Fuller v. Decatur Public School Board of Education School District*." *Brigham Young University Education & Law Journal* 21:159–209.

Braithwaite, John. 1989. *Crime, Shame and Reintegration.* Cambridge, UK: Cambridge University Press.

Broadhurst. D. D. 1980. "The Effect of Child Abuse and Neglect in the School-Aged Child." Pp. 19–41 in R. Volpe, M. Breton, and J. Mitton, eds., *The Maltreatment of the School-Aged Child.* Lexington, MA: Heath.

Bronfenbrenner, Urie. 1970. *Two Worlds of Childhood: U.S. and U.S.S.R.* New York: Russell Sage Foundation.

Bryan, Bruce A., Gerald R. Adams, Thomas P. Gullotta, Roger P. Weissberg, and Robert L. Hampton, eds. 1995. *The Family-School Connection: Theory Research, and Practice.* Thousand Oaks, CA: Sage Publications.

Buckley, William E. 1988. "Estimated Prevalence of Anabolic Steroid Use Among Male High School Seniors." *Journal of the American Medical Association* 260:3441–3445.

Bureau of Justice Statistics. 1988. *Report to the National on Crime and Justice*, 2nd ed. Washington, DC: U.S. Department of Justice.

Bureau of Labor Statistics. 2001. *A Profile of the Working Poor, 1999.* Report 947. Washington, DC: U.S. Department of Labor.

Burgess, Robert J., Jr. and Ronald L. Akers. 1966. "A Differential Association-Reinforcement Theory of Criminal Behavior." *Social Problems* 14:128–147.

Burkett, Stephen R., and Bruce O. Warren. 1987. "Religiosity, Peer Associations and Adolescent Marijuana Use: A Panel Study of Underlying Causal Structures." *Criminology* 25:109–125.

Burns, Matthew K., Vincent J. Dean, and Susan Jacob-Timm. 2001. "Assessment of Violence Potential Among School Children: Beyond Profiling." *Psychology in the Schools* 38(3):239–247.

Butts, Jeffrey A., and Howard N. Snyder. 1992. *OJJDP Update on Research: Restitution and Juvenile Recidivism*. Washington, DC: U.S. Department of Justice.

Byrne, James. 1986. "The Control Controversy: A Preliminary Examination of Intensive Probation Supervision Programs in the United States." *Federal Probation* 50:4–16.

Callahan, Robert. 1985. "Wilderness Probation: A Decade Later." *Juvenile & Family Court Journal* 36:31–35.

Campbell, Anne. 1990. "Female Participation in Gangs." Pp. 163–182 in C. R. Huff, ed., *Gangs in America*. Newbury Park, CA: Sage Publications.

Cantelon, Sharon and Donni LeBoeuf. 1997. "Keeping Young People in School: Community Programs That Work." *OJJDP Juvenile Justice Bulletin*. Washington, DC: U.S. Department of Justice.

Canter, Rachelle. 1982. "Sex Differences in Self-Report Delinquency." *Criminology* 20:373–393.

Carter, Robert M., and Leslie T. Wilkins. 1967. "Some Factors in Sentencing Policy." *Journal of Criminal Law, Criminology, and Police Science* 58:503–514.

Catalano, Richard F., Michael W. Arthur, J. David Hawkins, Lisa Bergland, and Jeffrey J. Olson. 1998. "Comprehensive Community- and School-Based Interventions to Prevent Antisocial Behavior." Pp. 248–283 in R. Loeber and D. P. Farrington, eds., *Serious & Violence Juvenile Offenders: Risk Factors and Successful Interventions*. Thousand Oaks, CA: Sage Publications.

Cernkovich, Stephen, and Peggy Giordano. 1979. "A Comparative Analysis of Male and Female Delinquency." *Sociological Quarterly* 20:131–145.

Cernkovich, Stephen A., and Peggy C. Giordano. 1987. "Family Relationships and Delinquency." *Criminology* 25:295–321.

Chandler, Gary L. 1992. "Due Process Rights of High School Students." *High School Journal* 75:137–143.

Charles, Michael. 1989. "The Development of a Juvenile Electronic Monitoring Program." *Federal Probation* 53:3–12.

Chavkin, Nancy F., and David L. Williams. 1987. "Enhancing Parent Involvement: Guidelines for Access to an Important Resource for School Administrators." *Education and Urban Society* 19:164–184.

Chesney-Lind, Meda. 1977. "Judicial Paternalism and the Female Status Offender." *Crime and Delinquency* 23:121–130.

Chesney-Lind, Meda. 1989. "Girls' Crime and Woman's Place: Toward a Feminist Model of Female Delinquency." *Crime & Delinquency* 1989:5–29.

Chesney-Lind, Meda. 1995. "Girls, Delinquency, and Juvenile Justice: Toward a Feminist Theory of Young Women's Crime." Pp. 71–88 in B. R. Price and N. Sokoloff, eds., *The Criminal Justice System and Women*. New York: McGraw-Hill.

Chesney-Lind, Meda, and Randall G. Shelden. 1998. *Girls, Delinquency, and Juvenile Justice* 2nd ed. Belmont, CA: West/Wadsworth.

Clear, Todd, and David Karp. 1999. *The Community Justice Ideal: Preventing Crime and Achieving Justice*. Boulder, CO: Westview Press.

Clouser, Megan. 1995. "School-Based Juvenile Probation." *Pennsylvania Progress* 2(1):1–6.

Cloward, Richard, and Lloyd Ohlin. 1960. *Delinquency and Opportunity*. New York: The Free Press.

Coates, Robert B. 1990. "Victim-Offender Reconciliation Programs in North America: An Assessment." Pp. 125–134 in B. Galaway and J. Hudson, eds., *Criminal Justice, Restitution, and Reconciliation*. Monsey, NY: Criminal Justice Press.

Coates, Robert B., A. D. Miller, and Lloyd E. Ohlin. 1978. *Diversity in a Youth Correctional System: Handling Delinquents in Massachusetts*. Cambridge, MA: Ballinger.

Cohen, Albert. 1955. *Delinquent Boys*. New York: The Free Press.

Cohen, Lawrence, and Marcus Felson. 1979. "Social Change and Crime Rate Trends: A Routine Activities Approach." *American Sociological Review* 44:588–608.

Cole, David. 1999. *No Equal Justice: Race and Class in the American Criminal Justice System*. New York: The New Press.

Coleman, James S. 1966. "Equal Schools or Equal Students?" *The Public Interest* 4:70–75.

Colvin, Mark, and John Pauly. 1983. "A Critique of Criminology: Toward an Integrated Structural-Marxist Theory of Delinquency Prevention." *American Journal of Sociology* 89:513–551.

Conger, J. J., and W. C. Miller. 1966. *Personality, Social Class, and Delinquency.* New York: Wiley.

Conley, D. J. 1994. "Adding Color to a Black and White Picture: Using Qualitative Data to Explain Disproportionality in the Juvenile Justice System." *Journal of Research in Crime and Delinquency* 31(2):135–148.

Copperman, Paul. 1980. *The Literacy Hoax.* New York: William Morrow Co.

Cordner, Gary W. 2005. "Community Policing: Elements and Effects." Pp. 401–418 in R. G. Dunham and G. P. Alpert, eds., *Critical Issues in Policing.* Long Grove, IL: Waveland Press.

Cornish, Derek B., and Ronald V. Clarke, eds. 1986. *The Reasoning Criminal: Rational Choice Perspectives on Offending.* New York: Springer-Verlag.

Cox, Stephen M., William S. Davidson, and Timothy S. Bynum. 1995. "A Meta-Analytic Assessment of Delinquency-Related Outcomes of Alternative Education Programs." *Crime & Delinquency* 41:219–234.

Cox, S. M., J. J. Conrad, and J. M. Allen. 2003. *Juvenile Justice: A Guide to Theory and Practice,* 5th ed. New York: McGraw-Hill.

Crews, Gordon A., and M. Reid Counts. 1997. *The Evolution of School Disturbance in America: Colonial Times to Modern Day.* Westport, CT: Praeger Publishers.

Cullen, Francis T. 2005. "The Twelve People Who Saved Rehabilitation: How the Science of Criminology Made a Difference: The American Society of Criminology 2004 Presidential Address." *Criminology* 43(1):1–42.

Cullen, Francis T., John E. Eck, and Christopher T. Lowenkamp. 2002. "Environmental Corrections—A New Paradigm for Effective Probation and Parole Supervision." *Federal Probation* 66(2):28–37.

Cullen, Francis T., Bonnie S. Fisher, and Brandon K. Applegate. 2000. "Public Opinion About Punishment and Corrections." Pp. 1–79 in M. Tonry, ed., *Crime and Justice: A Review of Research,* Vol. 27. Chicago: University of Chicago Press.

Cullen, Francis T., and Karen Gilbert. 1982. *Reaffirming Rehabilitation.* Cincinnati: Anderson Publishing Co.

Curry, G. David, Richard A. Ball, and Robert J. Fox. 1994. "Gang Crime and Law Enforcement Recordkeeping," National Institute of Justice Research in Brief. Washington, DC: U.S. Department of Justice.

Curry, G. David, and Irving A. Spergel. 1988. "Gang Homicide, Delinquency, and Community." *Criminology* 26:381–405.

Curtis, G. C. 1963. "Violence Breeds Violence—Perhaps?" *American Journal of Psychiatry* 120:386–387.

Datesman, Susan K., and Frank R. Scarpitti. 1975. "Female Delinquency and Broken Homes: A Re-Assessment." *Criminology* 13:33–55.

Davis, Samuel M. 1980. *Rights of Juveniles: The Juvenile Justice System,* 2nd ed. New York: Clark Boardman Co.

Decker, Scott H. 2000. "Increasing School Safety Through Juvenile Accountability Programs," JAIBG Bulletin. Washington, DC: U.S. Department of Justice.

DeJong, William. 1994. *Preventing Interpersonal Violence Among Youth: An Introduction to School, Community, and Mass Media Strategies.* Washington, DC: National Institute of Justice.

del Carmen, Rolando V. 1985. "Legal Issues and Liabilities in Community Corrections." Pp. 47–70 in L. F. Travis III, ed., *Probation, Parole, and Community Corrections: A Reader.* Prospect Heights, IL: Waveland Press.

del Carmen, Rolando V., Mary Parker, and Fran P. Reddington. 1998. *Briefs of Leading Cases in Juvenile Justice.* Cincinnati: Anderson Publishing.

Devine, John. 1996. *Maximum Security: The Culture of Violence in Inner-City Schools.* Chicago: The University of Chicago Press.

DeVoe, J. F., K. Peter, P. Kaufman, A. Miller, M. Noonan, T. D. Snyder, and K. Baum. 2004. *Indicators of School Crime and Safety: 2004.* Washington, DC: U.S. Departments of Education and Justice.

DeVoe, J. F., K. Peter, P. Kaufman, S. A. Ruddy, A. K. Miller, M. Planty, T. D. Snyder, and M. R. Rand. 2003. *Indicators of School and Safety: 2003.* Washington, DC: U.S. Departments and Education and Justice.

DeVoe, J. F., S. A. Ruddy, A. K. Miller, M. Planty, K. Peter, P. Kaufman, T. D. Snyder, D. T. Duhart, and M. R. Rand. 2002. *Indicators of School Crime and Safety: 2002.* Washington, DC: U.S. Departments of Education and Justice.

Dorfman, L., and Schiraldi, V. 2001. *Off Balance: Youth, Race and Crime in the News.* Building Blocks for Youth. [http:www.buildingblocksforyouth.org/]

Dorn, Michael. 2004. "How to Start an SRO Program: School Resource Officers Serve as Important Liaisons Between Police Departments and Local Schools." *Police* 28(10):16–18, 22–24.

Dorne, Clifford, and Kenneth Gewerth. 1995. *American Juvenile Justice: Cases, Legislation and Comments.* Bethesda, MD: Austin & Winfield, Publishers.

Drennon-Gala, Don. 1995. *Delinquency and High School Dropouts.* New York: University Press of America.

Dryfoos, Joy. 1990. *Adolescents at Risk.* New York: Oxford University Press.

Dryfoos, Joy G. 1994. *Full-Service Schools.* San Francisco: Jossey-Bass, Inc.

Dunham, R. G., and G. P. Alpert. 1987. "Keeping Juvenile Delinquents in School: A Prediction Model." *Adolescence* 22:45–57.

Dwyer, Kevin P., David Osher, and Cynthia Warger. 1998. *Early Warning, Timely Response: A Guide to Safe Schools.* Washington, DC: U.S. Department of Education.

Dynarski, Mark and Philip Gleason. 1999. *How Can We Help? Lessons From Federal Dropout Prevention Programs.* Princeton, NJ: Mathematica Policy Research, Inc.

Ekstrom, Ruth B., M. E. Goertz, J. M. Pollack, and D. A. Rock. 1986. "Who Drops Out of High School and Why? Findings from a National Study." *Teachers College Record* 87:356–373.

Elliott, Delbert S. 1994. "Serious Violent Offenders: Onset, Developmental Course, and Termination." *Criminology* 32:1–21.

Elliott, Delbert S., Suzanne S. Ageton, and Rachell J. Canter. 1979. "An Integrated Theoretical Perspective on Delinquent Behavior." *Journal of Research in Crime and Delinquency* 16:3–27.

Elliott, Delbert S., Beatrix A. Hamburg, and Kirk R. Williams, eds. 1998a. *Violence in American Schools.* New York: Cambridge University Press.

Elliott, Delbert S., Beatrix A. Hamburg, and Kirk R. Williams. 1998b. "Violence in American Schools: An Overview." Pp. 3–28 in D. S. Elliott, B. Hamburg, and K. R. Williams, eds., *Violence in American Schools.* Cambridge, UK: Cambridge University Press.

Elliott, Delbert S., David Huizinga, and Suzanne E. Ageton. 1985. *Explaining Delinquency and Drug Use.* Beverly Hills, CA: Sage Publications.

Elliott, Delbert S., and Harwin H. Voss. 1974. *Delinquency and Dropout.* Lexington, MA: Lexington Books.

Ennett, Susan T., Nancy S. Tobler, Christopher L. Rngwalt, and Robert L. Flewelling. 1994. "How Effective is Drug Abuse Resistance Education? A Meta-Analysis of Project DARE Outcome Evaluations." *American Journal of Public Health* 84:1394–1401.

Esbensen, Finn-Aage. 2000. "Preventing Adolescent Gang Involvement," OJJDP Juvenile Justice Bulletin. Washington, DC: U.S. Department of Justice.

Esbensen, Finn-Aage. 2004. "Evaluating G.R.E.A.T.: A School-Based Gang Prevention Program," NIJ Research for Policy. Washington, DC: U.S. Department of Justice.

Esbensen, Finn-Aage, and Elizabeth P. Deschenes. 1998. "A Multisite Examination of Youth Gang Membership: Does Gender Matter?" *Criminology* 36(4):799–828.

Esbensen, Finn-Aage, and David Huizinga. 1993. "Gangs, Drugs, and Delinquency in a Survey of Urban Youth." *Criminology* 31(4):565–589.

Esbensen, Finn-Aage, David Huizinga, and Anne W. Weiher. 1995. "Gang and Non-gang Youth: Differences in Explanatory Factors." Pp. 192–201 in M. W. Klein, C. L. Maxson, and J. Miller, eds., *The Modern Gang Reader.* Los Angeles: Roxbury Publishing Co.

Esbensen, Finn-Aage, and D. Wayne Osgood. 1999. "Gang Resistance Education and Training (G.R.E.A.T.): Results From the National Evaluation." *Journal of Research in Crime and Delinquency* 36(2):194–225.

Esbensen, Finn-Aage, and L. Thomas Winfree. 1998. "Race and Gender Differences Between Gang and Non-gang Youth: Results from a Multisite Survey." *Justice Quarterly* 15(3):505–526.

Fagan, Jeffrey. 1989. "The Social Organization of Drug Use and Drug Dealing Among Urban Gangs." *Criminology* 27:633–669.

Fagan, Jeffrey. 1990. "Social Processes of Delinquency and Drug Use Among Urban Gangs." Pp. 183–219 in C. Ronald Huff, ed., *Gangs in America*. Newbury Park, Calif.: Sage.

Fagan, Jeffrey, Karen V. Hansen, and Martin Jang. 1983. "Profiles of Chronically Violent Delinquents: Empirical Test of an Integrated Theory." Pp. 91–119 in J. Kleugel, ed., *Evaluating Juvenile Justice*. Beverly Hills, CA: Sage Publications.

Fagan, Jeffrey, and Edward Pabon. 1990. "Contributions of Delinquency and Substance Use to School Dropout Among Inner-City Youths." *Youth & Society* 21:306–354.

Fagan, Jeffrey, and Sandra Wexler. 1987. "Family Origins of Violent Delinquents." *Criminology* 25:643–669.

Falk, Herbert A. 1941. *Corporal Punishment*. New York: Columbia University Press.

Farnworth, Margaret, and Michael J. Leiber. 1989. "Strain Theory Revisited: Economic Goals, Educational Means, and Delinquency." *American Sociological Review* 54:263–274.

Farrington, David. 1980. "Truancy, Delinquency, the Home and the School." Pp. 49–63 in Lionel Hersov and Ian Berg, eds., *Out of School: Modern Perspectives in Truancy and School Refusal*. New York: John Wiley & Sons.

Farrington, David P. 1993. "Understanding and Preventing Bullying." Pp. 381–458 in M. Tonry, ed., *Crime and Justice: A Review of Research*, Vol. 17. Chicago: The University of Chicago Press.

Farrington, David. 1998. "Predictors, Causes, and Correlates of Male Youth Violence." Pp. 421–475 in M. Tonry and M. H. Moore, eds., *Youth Violence*. Chicago: The University of Chicago Press.

Farrington, D., B. Gallagher, L. Morley, R. St. Ledger, and D. West. 1986. "Unemployment, School Leaving, and Crime." *British Journal of Criminology* 26:335–356.

Faust, F. N., and P. J. Brantingham. 1979. *Juvenile Justice Philosophy: Readings, Cases and Comments*, 2nd ed. St. Paul, MN: West Publishing Co.

Federal Bureau of Investigation. 2005. *Crime in the United States, 2004*. Washington, DC: U.S. Department of Justice.

Fehrman, P. G., T. Z. Keith, and T. M. Teimers. 1987. "Home Influence on School Learning: Direct and Indirect Effects of Parental Involvement on High School Grades." *Journal of Educational Research* 80:330–337.

Feld, Barry C. 1977. *Neutralizing Inmate Violence: The Juvenile Offender in Institutions*. Cambridge, MA: Ballinger.

Feld, Barry C. 1988a. "*In re Gault* Revisited: A Cross-State Comparison of the Right to Counsel in Juvenile Court." *Crime & Delinquency* 34:393–424.

Feld, Barry C. 1988b. "Juvenile Court Meets the Principle of Offense: Punishment, Treatment, and the Difference it Makes." *Boston University Law Review* 68:821–915.

Feld, Barry C. 1989. "The Right to Counsel in Juvenile Court: An Empirical Study of When Lawyers Appear and the Difference They Make." *The Journal of Criminal Law & Criminology* 79:1185–1346.

Feld, Barry C. 1993. "Criminalizing the American Juvenile Court." Pp. 197–280 in M. Tonry, ed., *Crime & Justice: An Annual Review of Research*. Chicago: The University of Chicago Press.

Feld, Barry C. 1995. "Violent Youth and Public Policy: A Case Study of Juvenile Justice Law Reform." *Minnesota Law Review* 79:965–1128.

Feld, Barry C. 1999. *Bad Kids: Race and the Transformation of the Juvenile Court*. New York: Oxford University Press.

Feld, Barry. 2003. "The Politics of Race and Juvenile Justice: The 'Due Process Revolution' and the Conservation Reaction." *Justice Quarterly* 20:765–800.

Feld, Barry. 2004. "Editorial Introduction: Juvenile Transfer." *Criminology & Public Policy* 4(3):599–603.

Felson, Marcus. 1986. "Linking Criminal Choices, Routine Activities, Informal Control, and Criminal Outcomes." Pp. 119–128 in D. B. Cornish and R. V. Clarke, eds., *The Reasoning Criminal*. New York: Springer-Verlag.

Felson, Marcus. 1994. *Crime and Everyday Life*. Thousand Oaks, CA: Pine Forge Press.

Ferguson, Ann A. 2000. *Bad Boys: Public Schools in the Making of Black Masculinity*. Ann Arbor, MI: University of Michigan Press.

Fine, M. 1986. "Why Urban Adolescents Drop Into and Out of Public High School." *Teachers College Record* 87:393–409.

Fishbein, Diana. 1990. "Biological Perspectives in Criminology." *Criminology* 28:27–72.

Flanagan, Timothy and Edmund McGarrell. 1986. *Sourcebook of Criminal Justice Statistics 1985*. Washington, DC: U.S. Department of Justice.

Fleisher, Mark. 1995. *Beggars and Thieves*. Madison: University of Wisconsin Press.

Foster, J. D., Simon Dinitz, and Walter C. Reckless. 1972. "Perceptions of Stigma Following Public Intervention for Delinquent Behavior." *Social Problems* 20:202–209.

Fox, James Alan, and Jack Levin. 2001. *The Will to Kill: Making Sense of Senseless Murder*. Boston: Allyn and Bacon.

Fox, James W., Kevin I. Minor, and William L. Pelkey. 1994. "The Relationship Between Law-Related Education Diversion and Juvenile Offenders' Social- and Self-Perceptions." *American Journal of Criminal Justice* 19:401–418.

Fox, R. S., R. Schmuck, E. Van Egmond, M. Rivto, and C. Jung. 1975. *Diagnosing Professional Climates of Schools*. Fairfax, VA: Learning Resources Corporation.

Friedman, Warren, Arthur J. Lurigio, Richard Greenleaf, and Stephanie Albertson. 2004. "Encounters Between Police Officers and Youths: The Social Costs of Disrespect." *Journal of Crime & Justice* 27(2):1–25.

Fritsch, Eric J., Tory J. Caeti, and Robert W. Taylor. 1999. "Gang Suppression Through Saturation Patrol, Aggressive Curfew, and Truancy Enforcement: A Quasi-Experimental Test of the Dallas Anti-Gang Initiative." *Crime & Delinquency* 45(1):122–139.

Galaway, Burt. 1989. "Restitution as Innovation or Unfilled Promise." *Federal Probation* 52:3–15.

Galaway, Burt, and Joe Hudson, eds. 1990. *Criminal Justice, Restitution, and Reconciliation*. Monsey, NY: Criminal Justice Press.

Garcia, C. A. 2003 "School Safety Technology in America: Current Use and Perceived Effectiveness." *Criminal Justice Policy Review* 14(1):30–54.

Garland, David. 2001. *The Culture of Control: Crime and Social Order in Contemporary Society*. Chicago: University of Chicago Press.

Garrett, Carol. 1985. "Effects of Residential Treatment on Adjudicated Delinquents: A Meta-Analysis." *Journal of Research in Crime and Delinquency* 22:287–308.

Garry, Ellen M. 1996. "Truancy: First Step to a Lifetime of Problems," OJJDP Juvenile Justice Bulletin. Washington, DC: U.S. Department of Justice.

Gelles, Richard, and Murray Straus. 1988. *Intimate Violence*. New York: Simon and Schuster.

General Accounting Office. 2002. *School Dropouts: Education Could Play a Stronger Role in Identifying and Disseminating Promising Prevention Strategies*. Washington, DC: United States General Accounting Office.

Gibbs, Jack P. 1966. "Conceptions of Deviant Behavior: The Old and the New." *Pacific Sociological Review* 9:9–14.

Gillespie, Mark. 2000. "School Violence Still a Worry for American Parents." *Gallup Poll Monthly* 415:47–50.

Giordano, Peggy. 1978. "Girls, Guys and Gangs: The Changing Social Context of Female Delinquency." *Journal of Criminal Law and Criminology* 69(1):126–132.

Giordano, Peggy, and Stephen Cernkovich. 1979. "On Complicating the Relationship Between Liberation and Delinquency." *Social Problems* 26:467–481.

Giordano, Peggy C., Stephen A. Cernkovich, and M. D. Pugh. 1986. "Friendship and Delinquency." *American Journal of Sociology* 91:1170–1202.

Girouard, Cathy. 2001. "School Resource Officer Training Program," OJJDP Fact Sheet. Washington, DC: U.S. Department of Justice.

Glueck, Sheldon, and Eleanor Glueck. 1950. *Unraveling Juvenile Delinquency*. Cambridge, MA: Harvard University Press.

Goddard, Henry. 1920. *Efficiency and Levels of Intelligence*. Princeton, NJ: Princeton University Press.

Gold, Martin, and David W. Mann. 1984. *Expelled to a Friendlier Place: A Study of Alternative Schools*. Ann Arbor: University of Michigan Press.

Gold, Martin, and Oliver C. Moles. 1978. "Delinquency and Violence in Schools and the Community." Pp. 111–124 in J. A. Inciardi and A. E. Pottieger, eds., *Violent Crime: Historical and Contemporary Issues*. Beverly Hills, CA: Sage Publications.

Goldstein, Arnold P., Steven J. Apter, and Berj Harootunian. 1984. *School Violence.* Englewood Cliffs, NJ: Prentice-Hall, Inc.

Goldstein, Herman. 1977. *Policing a Free Society.* Cambridge, MA: Ballinger Publishing.

Goodlad, John. 1984. *A Place Called School.* New York: McGraw-Hill.

Gordon, Robert A. 1987. "SES versus IQ in the Race-IQ-Delinquency Model." *The International Journal of Sociology and Social Policy* 7:30–96.

Gottfredson, Denise C. 1986. "An Empirical Test of School-Based Environmental and Individual Interventions to Reduce the Risk of Delinquent Behavior." *Criminology* 24:705–31.

Gottfredson, Denise C. 1987a. "An Evaluation of an Organization Development Approach to Reducing School Disorder." *Evaluation Review* 11(6):739–763.

Gottfredson, Denise C. 1987b. "Examining the Potential for Delinquency Prevention Through Alternative Education." *Today's Delinquent* 6:87–100.

Gottfredson, Denise C. 1997. "School-Based Crime Prevention." Pp. 5-1–5-74 in Sherman, L. W., D. Gottfredson, D. MacKenzie, J. Eck, P. Reuter, and S. Bushway, eds., *Preventing Crime: What Works, What Doesn't, What's Promising.* Washington, DC: U.S. Department of Justice.

Gottfredson, Denise C. 2001. *Schools and Delinquency.* Cambridge, UK: Cambridge University Press.

Gottfredson, Denise C., and Gary D. Gottfredson. 1986. *The School Action Effectiveness Study: Final Report. Center for Social Organization of Schools.* Baltimore: The Johns Hopkins University.

Gottfredson, Denise C., David B. Wilson, and Stacy S. Najaka. 2002. "The Schools." Pp. 149–189 in J. Q. Wilson and J. Petersilia, eds., *Crime: Public Policies for Crime Control.* Oakland, CA: ICS Press.

Gottfredson, Gary D. 1987. "Peer Group Intervention to Reduce the Risk of Delinquent Behavior: A Selective Review and a New Evaluation." *Criminology* 25:671–714.

Gottfredson, Gary D. 1999. *The Effective School Battery: User's Manual.* Ellicott City, MD: Gottfredson Associates, Inc.

Gottfredson, Gary D., and Denise C. Gottfredson. 1985. *Victimization in Schools.* New York: Plenum Press.

Gottfredson, Gary D., and Denise C. Gottfredson. 2001. *Gang Problems and Gang Programs in a National Sample of Schools.* Ellicott City, MD: Gottfredson Associates, Inc.

Gottfredson, G., D. C. Gottfredson, E. R. Czeh, D. Cantor, S. B. Crosse, and I. Hantman. 2004. "Toward Safe and Orderly Schools—The National Study of Delinquency Prevention in Schools." National Institute of Justice Research in Brief. Washington, DC: U.S. Department of Justice.

Gottfredson, Michael R., and Travis Hirschi. 1990. *A General Theory of Crime.* Stanford, CA: Stanford University Press.

Gove, Walter R., and Richard D. Crutchfield. 1982. "The Family and Juvenile Delinquency." *The Sociological Quarterly* 23:301–319.

Gowdy, Vernon B. 1993. *Intermediate Sanctions.* Washington, DC: U.S. Department of Justice.

Gray, Ellen. 1988. "The Link Between Child Abuse and Juvenile Delinquency: What We Know and Recommendations for Policy and Research." Pp. 109–123 in G. T. Hotaling, D. Finkelhor, J. T. Kirkpatrick, and M. A. Straus, eds., *Family Abuse and Its Consequences.* Newbury Park, CA: Sage Publications, 1988.

Greenberg, David. 1977. "Delinquency and the Age Structure of Society." *Contemporary Crises* 1:189–223.

Greenwood, Peter, and Franklin Zimring. 1985. *One More Chance: The Pursuit of Promising Intervention Strategies for Chronic Juvenile Offenders.* Santa Monica, CA: RAND Corp.

Grisso, Thomas. 1981. *Juveniles' Waiver of Rights: Legal and Psychological Competence.* New York: Plenum Press.

Grubb, W. Norton, and Marvin Lazerson. 1982. *Broken Promises: How Americans Fail Their Children.* New York: Basic Books.

Hagan, John, A. R. Gillis, and John Simpson. 1985. "The Class Structure of Gender and Delinquency: Toward a Power-Control Theory of Common Delinquent Behavior." *American Journal of Sociology* 90(6):1151–1178.

Hagan, John, John Simpson, and A. R. Gillis. 1987. "Class in the Household: A Power-Control Theory of Gender and Delinquency." *American Journal of Sociology* 92(4):788–816.

Hall, Ginger. 1987. "State school fund plan ruled illegal." *San Antonio Express-News* (April 30):1,8–9.

Hall, Richard H., John P. Clark, Peggy C. Giordano, Paul V. Johnson, and Martha Van Roekel. 1981. "Patterns of Inter-organizational Relationships." Pp. 477–494 in O. Grusky and G. A. Miller, eds., *The Sociology of Organizations*. New York: The Free Press.

Hamburg, Margaret A. 1998. "Youth Violence Is a Public Health Concern," Pp. 31–54 in D. S. Elliot, M. A. Hamburg, and K. R. Williams, eds., *Violence in American Schools*. Cambridge, UK: Cambridge University Press.

Hamilton Fish Institute. 2000. *Comprehensive Framework for School Violence Prevention*. Washington, DC: Hamilton Fish Institute.

Hamparian, D. M., L. K. Estep, S. M. Muntean, R. R. Priestino, R. G. Swisher, P. L. Wallace, and J. L. White. 1982. *Youth in Adult Courts: Between Two Worlds*. Washington, DC: U.S. Department of Justice.

Haney, Craig, and Philip G. Zimbardo. 1975. "It's Tough to Tell a High School from a Prison." *Psychology Today* (June):26, 29–30, 106.

Hantman, I., G. Bairu, A. Barwick, B. Smith, B. Mack, S. Meston, L. Rocks, and B. James. 2002. *Safety in Numbers: Collecting and Using Crime, Violence and Discipline Incident Data to Make a Difference in Schools*. Washington, DC: U.S. Department of Education.

Harmon, Michele A. 1993. "Reducing the Risk of Drug Involvement Among Early Adolescents: An Evaluation of Drug Abuse Resistance Education (DARE)." *Evaluation Review* 17:221–239.

Hartnagel, Timothy and Harvey Krahn. 1989. "High School Dropouts, Labor Market Success, and Criminal Behavior." *Youth and Society*, 20:416–444.

Hawkins, J. David, and Denise M. Lishner. 1987a. "Etiology and Prevention of Antisocial Behavior in Children and Adolescents." Pp. 263–282 in D. H. Crowell, I. M. Evans, and C. R. O'Donnell, eds., *Childhood Aggression and Violence: Sources of Influence, Prevention and Control*. New York: Plenum Press.

Hawkins, J. David, and Denise M. Lishner. 1987b. "Schooling and Delinquency." Pp. 179–221 in E. H. Johnson, ed., *Handbook on Crime and Delinquency Prevention*. New York: Greenwood Press.

Hawkins, J. David, R. F. Catalano, G. Jones, and D. Fine. 1987. "Delinquency Prevention Through Parent Training: Results and Issues from Work in Progress." Pp. 186–203 in J. Q. Wilson and G. C. Loury, eds., *From Children to Citizens*, Vol. 3: *Families, Schools, and Delinquency Prevention*. New York: Springer-Verlag.

Hawkins, J. David, David P. Farrington, and Richard F. Catalano. 1998. "Reducing Violence Through the Schools." Pp. 188–216 in D. S. Elliott, B. A. Hamburg, and K. R. Williams, eds., *Violence in American Schools*. New York: Cambridge University Press.

Hawkins, J. D., T. I. Herrenkohl, D. P. Farrington, D. Brewer, R. F. Catalano, T. W. Harachi, and L. Cothern. 2000. "Predictors of Youth Violence," OJJDP Juvenile Justice Bulletin. Washington, DC: U.S. Department of Justice.

Hawkins, J. David, and Tony Lam. 1987. "Teacher Practices, Social Development, and Delinquency." Pp. 241–274 in J. D. Burchard and S. N. Burchard, eds., *Prevention of Delinquent Behavior*. Newbury Park, CA: Sage Publications.

Hawkins, J. David, Paul A. Pastro, Jr., Michelle Bell, and Sheila Morrison. 1980. *Reports of the National Juvenile Justice Assessment Centers: A Typology of Cause-Focused Strategies of Delinquency Prevention*. Washington, DC: U.S. Department of Justice.

Hawkins, J. David, and John S. Wall. 1980. *Alternative Education: Exploring the Delinquency Prevention Potential*. Washington, DC: U.S. Department of Justice.

Hawkins, J. David, and Joseph G. Weis. 1985. "The Social Development Model: An Integrated Approach to Delinquency Prevention." *Journal of Primary Prevention* 6:73–97.

Haynie, D., B. Simons-Morton, K. H. Beck, T. Shattuck, and A. D. Crump. 1999. "Associations Between Parent Awareness, Monitoring, Enforcement and Adolescent Involvement with Alcohol." *Health Education Research* 14(6):765–775.

Heaviside, Sheila, Rowand Cassandra, Catrina Williams, Elizabeth Farris, Shelley Burns, and Edith McArthur. 1998. *Violence and Discipline Problems in U.S. Public Schools: 1996–97*. Washington, DC: U.S. Department of Education.

Helfer, R. E., and C. H. Kempe, eds. 1976. *Child Abuse and Neglect: The Family and the Community.* Cambridge, MA: Ballinger Publishing Co.

Hennepin County Home School. 1993. *Juvenile Sex Offender Program.* Minneapolis, MN: Hennepin County Home School.

Hepburn, John R. 1977. "The Impact of Police Intervention Upon Juvenile Delinquents." *Criminology* 15:235–262.

Hermann, Mary A., and Abbe Finn. 2002. "An Ethical and Legal perspective on the Role of School Counselors Preventing Violence in Schools." *Professional School Counseling* 6(1):46–54.

Hill, K. G., J. C. Howell, J. D. Hawkins, and S. R. Battin-Pearson. 1999. "Childhood Risk Factors for Adolescent Gang Membership: Results from the Seattle Social Development Project." *Journal of Research in Crime and Delinquency* 36(3):300–322.

Hindelang, Michael J. 1973. "Causes of Delinquency: A Partial Replication and Extension." *Social Problems* 21:471–487.

Hirschi, Travis. 1969. *Causes of Delinquency.* Berkeley, CA: University of California Press.

Hirschi, Travis. 1983. "Crime and the Family." Pp. 53–68 in J. Q. Wilson, ed., *Crime and Public Policy.* San Francisco: ICS Press.

Hirschi, Travis. 1986. "On the Compatibility of Rational Choice and Social Control Theories of Crime." Pp. 105–118 in D. B. Cornish and R. V. Clarke, eds., *The Reasoning Criminal.* New York: Springer-Verlag.

Hirschi, Travis, and Michael Hindelang. 1977. "Intelligence and Delinquency: A Revisionist Review." *American Sociological Review* 42:471–486.

Hoffer, Abraham. 1975. "The Relation of Crime to Nutrition." *Humanist in Canada* 8:3–9.

Holden, Gwen A., and Robert A. Kapler. 1995. "Deinstitutionalizing Status Offenders: A Record of Progress." *Juvenile Justice (OJJDP)* 2(Fall/Winter):3–10.

Holmes, C. Thomas, and Kenneth M. Matthews. 1984. "The Effects of Nonpromotion on Elementary and Junior High School Pupils: A Meta-Analysis." *Review of Educational Research* 54:225–236.

Holmes, Ronald M., and Stephen T. Holmes. 1996. *Profiling Violent Crimes: An Investigative Tool* 2nd ed. Thousand Oaks, CA: Sage Publications.

Horowitz, R. 1990. "Sociological Perspectives on Gangs: Conflicting Definitions and Concepts." Pp. 37–54 in C. R. Huff, ed., *Gangs in America.* Newbury Park, CA: Sage Publications.

Howell, James C., ed. 1995. *Guide for Implementing the Comprehensive Strategy for Serious, Violent, and Chronic Juvenile Offenders.* Washington, DC: Office of Juvenile Justice and Delinquency Prevention, U.S. Department of Justice.

Howell, James C., and James P. Lynch. 2000. "Youth Gangs in Schools," OJJDP Juvenile Justice Bulletin. Washington, DC: U.S. Department of Justice.

Hsia, Heidi M., George S. Bridges, and Rosalie McHale. 2004. *Disproportionate Minority Confinement 2002 Update Summary.* Washington, DC: U.S. Department of Justice.

Huff, C. Ronald. 1989. "Youth Gangs and Public Policy." *Crime & Delinquency* 35(4):524–537.

Huff, C. Ronald, ed. 1990. *Gangs in America.* Newbury Park, CA: Sage Publications.

Hughes, Stella P., and Anne L. Schneider. 1989. "Victim-Offender Mediation: A Survey of Program Characteristics and Perceptions of Effectiveness." *Crime & Delinquency* 35:217–233.

Huizinga, David, Finn-Aage Esbensen, and Anne W. Weiher. 1991. "Are There Multiple Paths to Delinquency?" *The Journal of Criminal Law & Criminology* 82(1):83–118.

Huizinga, David, Rolf Loeber, and Terence Thornberry. 1994. *Urban Delinquency and Substance Abuse: Initial Findings.* Washington, DC: Office of Juvenile Justice and Delinquency Prevention.

Huizinga, David, Rolf Loeber, and Terrance Thornberry. 1995. *Urban Delinquency and Substance Abuse: Initial Findings.* Washington, DC: Office of Juvenile Justice and Delinquency Prevention.

Huizinga, David, Scott Menard, and Delbert Elliott. 1989. "Delinquency and Drug Use: Temporal and Developmental Patterns." *Justice Quarterly* 6:419–455.

Hurst, Yolander G., and James Frank. 2000. "How Kids View Cops: The Nature of Juvenile Attitudes Toward the Police." *Journal of Criminal Justice* 28(3):189–202.

Hylton, J. Barry. 1996. *Safe Schools: A Security and Loss Prevention Plan.* Boston: Butterworth-Heinemann.

Hyman, Irwin A. 1990. *Reading, Writing, and the Hickory Stick.* Lexington, MA: D.C. Heath and Co.

Hyman, Irwin A., and Donna C. Perone. 1998. "The Other Side of School Violence: Educator Policies and Practices That May Contribute to Student Misbehavior." *Journal of School Psychology* 36(1):7–27.

Hyman, Irwin A., and James H. Wise, eds. 1979. *Corporal Punishment in American Education.* Philadelphia: Temple University Press.

Imbrogno, Andre R. 2000. "Corporal Punishment in America's Public Schools and the U. N. Convention on the Rights of the Child: A Case for Nonratification." *Journal of Law & Education* 29:125–147.

Ingersoll, Sarah, and Donni LeBoeuf. 1997. "Reaching Out to Youth Out of the Education Mainstream," OJJDP Juvenile Justice Bulletin. Washington, DC: U.S. Department of Justice.

Insley, A. C. 2001. "Comment: Suspending and Expelling Children from Educational Opportunity: Time to Reevaluate Zero Tolerance Policies." *American University Law Review* 50:1039–1077.

Jackson, G. B. 1975. "The Research Evidence on Grade Retention." *Review of Educational Research* 45:613–635.

Jarjoura, G. Roger. 1993. "Does Dropping Out of School Enhance Delinquent Involvement? Results from a Large-Scale National Probability Sample." *Criminology* 31:149–171.

Jarjoura, G. Roger. 1996. "The Conditional Effect of Social Class on the Dropout-Delinquency Relationship." *Journal of Research in Crime and Delinquency* 33(2):232–255.

Jencks, C., M. Smith, H. Acland, M. J. Bane, D. Cohen, M. Gintis, B. Heyns, and S. Michelson. 1972. *Inequality: A Reassessment of the Effect of Family and Schooling in America.* New York: Basic Books.

Jensen, Gary F. 1973. "Inner Containment and Delinquency." *Criminology* 64:464–470.

Jensen, Gary F., and Dean G. Rojek. 1992. *Juvenile Delinquency,* 2nd ed. Lexington, MA: D.C. Heath.

Johnson, Ida M. 1999. "School Violence: The Effectiveness of a School Resource Officer Program in a Southern City." *Journal of Criminal Justice* 27(2):173–192.

Johnson, Richard E. 1979. *Juvenile Delinquency and Its Origins.* Cambridge, UK: Cambridge University Press.

Johnson, Richard E. 1986. "Family Structure and Delinquency: General Patterns and Gender Differences." *Criminology* 24:65–84.

Johnson, Richard E., Anastasio C. Marcos, and Stephen J. Bahr. 1987. "The Role of Peers in the Complex Etiology of Adolescent Drug Use." *Criminology* 25:323–340.

Johnson, Robert S. 1993. "Metal Detectors in Public Schools: A Policy Perspective." *Education Law Reporter* 80:1–7.

Jones, D. Shane. 1997. "Application of the 'Exclusionary Rule' to Bar Use or Illegally Seized Evidence in Civil School Disciplinary Proceedings." *Washington University Journal of Urban and Contemporary Law* 52:375–397.

Josephson, W. L. 1987. "Television Violence and Children's Aggression." *Journal of Personality and Social Psychology* 53:882–890.

Juvonen, Jaana, and Sandra Graham, eds. 2001. *Peer Harassment in School: The Plight of the Vulnerable and Victimized.* New York: The Guilford Press.

Kachur, S. P., Stennies, G. M., Powell, K. E., Modzeleski, W., Stephens, R., Murphy, R., Kresnow, M., Sleet, D., and Lowry, R. 1996. "School-associated violent deaths in the United States, 1992 to 1994." *Journal of the American Medical Association,* 275(22), 1729–1733.

Karp, David R. 1998. "The Judicial and Judicious Use of Shame Penalties." *Crime & Delinquency* 44(2):277–294.

Katz, Janet. 1982. "The Attitudes and Decisions of Probation Officers." *Criminal Justice and Behavior* 9:455–475.

Katz, Jeffrey L. 1991. "The Search for Equity in School Funding." *Governing* (August):20–22.

Kaufman, Phillip, Martha Naomi Alt, and Christopher D. Chapman. 2001. *Dropout Rates in the United States: 2000.* Washington, DC: National Center for Education Statistics.

Kelly, Delos H. 1977. "How the School and Teachers Create Deviants." *Contemporary Education* 48(4):202–205.

Kelly, Delos H., and Winthrop D. Grove. 1981. "Teachers' Nominations and the Productin of Academic 'Misfits'." *Education* 101:246–263.

Kelly, Delos H., and William T. Pink. 1982. "School Crime and Individual Responsibility: The Perpetuation of a Myth?" *The Urban Review* 14(1):47–63.

Kelman, Herbert. 1958. "Compliance, Identification, and Internalization: Three Processes of Attitude Change." *Journal of Conflict Resolution* 2:51–60.

Kempe, C. H., R. S. Kempe, F. N. Silverman, B. F. Steele, W. Droegemueller, and H. K. Silver. 1962. "The Battered-Child Syndrome." *Journal of the American Medical Association* 181:17–24.

Kempe, Ruth S., and C. Henry Kempe. 1978. *Child Abuse*. Cambridge, MA: Harvard University Press.

Kingery, P. M., B. E. Pruitt, and G. Heuberger. 1996. "A Profile of Rural Texas Adolescents Who Carry Handguns to School." *Journal of School Health* 66(1):18–22.

Kirkegaard-Sorensen, Lis, and Sarnoff A. Mednick. 1977. "A Prospective Study of Predictors of Criminality: Intelligence." In S. A. Mednick and K. O. Christiansen, eds., *Biosocial Basis of Criminal Behavior*. New York: Gardner.

Klinteberg, Britt A. F., David Magnusson, and Daisy Schalling. 1989. "Hyperactive Behavior in Childhood and Adult Impulsivity: A Longitudinal Study of Male Subjects." *Personality and Individual Differences* 10(1):43–49.

Kobrin, Solomon, and Malcolm W. Klein. 1982. *National Evaluation of the Deinstitutionalization of Status Offender Programs: Executive Summary*. Washington, DC: U.S. Department of Justice.

Kohlberg, Lawrence. 1964. "Development of Moral Character and Moral Ideology." In Martin Hoffman and Lois Hoffman, eds., *Review of Child Development Research*, Vol. 1. New York: Russell Sage Foundation.

Konopka, Gisela. 1966. *The Adolescent Girls in Conflict*. Englewood Cliffs, NJ: Prentice-Hall.

Kozol, Jonathan. 1991. *Savage Inequalities*. New York: HarperCollins Publishers.

Kramen, Alissa J., Kelly R. Massey, and Howard W. Timm. 1999. *Guide for Preventing and Responding to School Violence*. Alexandria, VA: International Association of Chiefs of Police.

Kratcoski, Peter C. 1982. "Child Abuse and Violence Against the Family." *Child Welfare* 61:445–455.

Krisberg, Barry, and James F. Austin. 1993. *Reinventing Juvenile Justice*. Newbury Park, CA: Sage Publications.

Krohn, Marvin, Terence Thornberry, Lori Collins-Hall, and Alan Lizotte. 1995. "School Dropout, Delinquent Behavior, and Drug Use." Pp. 163–183 in H. Kaplan, ed., *Drugs, Crime and Other Deviant Adaptations: Longitudinal Studies*. New York: Plenum Press.

Kumpfer, Karol L. and Rose Alvarado. 1998. "Effective Family Strengthening Interventions." *OJJDP Juvenile Justice Bulletin*. Washington, DC: U.S. Department of Justice.

Kurlychek, Megan C., and Brian D. Johnson. 2004. "The Juvenile Penalty: A Comparison of Juvenile and Young Adult Sentencing Outcomes in Criminal Court." *Criminology* 42(2):485–515.

Kurlychek, Megan, Patricia Torbet, and Melanie Bozynski. 1999. "Focus on Accountability: Best Practices for Juvenile Court and Probation," JAIBG Bulletin. Washington, DC: U.S. Department of Justice.

Lab, Steven P. 2004. *Crime Prevention: Approaches, Practices and Evaluations*, 5th ed. Cincinnati: Anderson Publishing.

Lab, Steven, and Richard Clark. 1996. *Discipline, Control and School Crime: Identifying Effective Intervention Strategies*. Washington, DC: U.S. Department of Justice.

Lab, Steven, and John Whitehead. 1988. "Analysis of Juvenile Correctional Treatment." Crime & Delinquency 34:60–83.

LaLonde, Mark. 1995. "The Canadian Experience: School Policing Perspective." *School Safety* (Fall):20–21.

Laney, Ronald. 1996. "Information Sharing and the Family Educational Rights and Privacy Act," OJJDP Fact Sheet. Washington, DC: U.S. Department of Justice.

Latessa, Edward. 1986. "The Cost Effectiveness of Intensive Supervision." *Federal Probation* 50:70–74.

Latessa, Edward J., and Harry E. Allen. 2003. *Corrections in the Community*, 3rd ed. Cincinnati: Anderson Publishing Co.

Laub, J. H. and R. J. Sampson. 1988. "Unraveling Families and Delinquency: A Reanalysis of the Gluecks' Data." *Criminology* 26:355–379.

Law Enforcement Assistance Administration. 1976. *Two Hundred Years of American Criminal Justice: An LEAA Bicentennial Study.* Washington, DC: U.S. Department of Justice.

Lawrence, Richard. 1983. "The Role of Legal Counsel in Juveniles' Understanding of Their Rights." *Juvenile & Family Court Journal* 34(4):49–58.

Lawrence, Richard. 1984. "Professionals or Judicial Civil Servants? An Examination of the Probation Officer's Role." *Federal Probation* 48(4):14–21.

Lawrence, Richard. 1985. "School Performance, Containment Theory, and Delinquent Behavior." *Youth and Society* 17:69–95.

Lawrence, Richard. 1991a. "Reexamining Community Corrections Models." *Crime and Delinquency* 37(3):449–464.

Lawrence, Richard. 1991b. "School Performance, Peers and Delinquency: Implications for Juvenile Justice." *Juvenile & Family Court Journal* 42(3):59–69.

Lawrence, Richard. 1995a. "Classrooms vs. Prison Cells: Funding Policies for Education and Corrections." *Journal of Crime & Justice* 18:113–126.

Lawrence, Richard. 1995b. "Controlling School Crime: An Examination of Inter-organizational Relations of School and Juvenile Justice Professionals." *Juvenile and Family Court Journal* 46(3):3–15.

Lawrence, Richard. 1998. "School Crime, School Discipline: A Study of Individual and Institutional Factors in School Crime Incidents and Disciplinary Actions Taken." Paper presented at the American Society of Criminology, Washington, DC.

Lawrence, Richard. 2002. "Invited Commentary: The Federal Government's Role in Measuring and Reporting on School Crime and Safety." *Educational Statistics Quarterly* 4(4) [http://nces/ed/gov/pubs2003/quarterly/winter/q2_3.asp]

Lawrence, Richard, and David Mueller. 2003. "School Shootings and the Man-Bites-Dog Criterion of Newsworthiness." *Youth Violence and Juvenile Justice* 1(4):330–345.

Lee, Virginia. 1979. "A Legal Analysis of Ingraham v. Wright." Pp. 173–195 in I. A. Hyman and J. A. Wise, *Corporal Punishment in American Education.* Philadelphia: Temple University Press.

Lehr, Camilla A., Anastasia Hansen, Mary F. Sinclair, and Sandra L. Christensen. 2003. "Moving Beyond Dropout Towards School Completion: An Integrative Review of Data-Based Interventions." *School Psychology Review* 32(3):342–364.

Lemert, Edwin M. 1951. *Social Pathology.* New York: McGraw-Hill.

Levin, H. M. 1972. *The Effects of Dropping Out. U.S. Senate Select Committee on Equal Educational Opportunity.* Washington, DC: U.S. Government Printing Office.

Levy, Paul. 1995. "Today's Lesson: Safety at School." *Minneapolis Star-Tribune* (Sept. 3):12A.

Lieber, Michael J., Mahesh K. Nalla, and Margaret Farnworth. 1998. "Explaining Juveniles' Attitudes Toward the Police." *Justice Quarterly* 15(1):151–174.

Lightfoot, Sara Lawrence. 1978. *Worlds Apart: Relationships Between Families and Schools.* New York: Basic Books.

Lillard, Dean R., and Philip P. DeCicca. 2001. "Higher Standards, More Dropouts? Evidence Within and Across Time." *Economics of Education Review* 20(5):49–73.

Lincoln, Alan J., and Murray Straus. 1985. *Crime and the Family.* Springfield, IL: Charles C Thomas.

Linden, Eric, and James C. Hackler. 1973. "Affective Ties and Delinquency." *Pacific Sociological Review* 16:27–46.

Lindner, Charles, and Vincent Del Castillo. 1994. "Staff Safety Issues in Probation." *The Justice Professional* 8(2):37–53.

Lipsey, Mark W., and James H. Derzon. 1998. "Predictors of Violent or Serious Delinquency in Adolescence and Early Adulthood: A Synthesis of Longitudinal Research." Pp. 86–105 in R. Loeber and D. Farrington, eds., *Serious and Violent Juvenile Offenders: Risk Factors and Successful Interventions.* Thousand Oaks, CA: Sage.

Lipsey, Mark W., David B. Wilson, and Lynn Cothern. 2000. "Effective Intervention for Serious Juvenile Offenders," OJJDP Juvenile Justice Bulletin. Washington, DC: U.S. Department of Justice.

Lipsitt, Paul D., Stephen L. Buka, and Lewis P. Lipsitt. 1990. "Early Intelligence Scores and Subsequent Delinquency: A Prospective Study." *The American Journal of Family Therapy* 18:197–208.

Lipton, Douglas, Robert Martinson, and Judith Wilks. 1975. *The Effectiveness of Correctional Treatment: A Survey of Treatment Evaluation Studies.* New York: Praeger.

Liska, Allen E., and Mark D. Reed. 1985. "Ties to Conventional Institutions and Delinquency: Estimating Reciprocal Effects." *American Sociological Review* 50:547–560.

Loeber, Rolf. 1988. *Crime File: Families and Crime*. Washington, DC: National Institute of Justice.

Loeber, Rolf, and Magda Stouthamer-Loeber. 1986. "Family Factors as Correlates and Predictors of Juvenile Conduct Problems and Delinquency." Pp. 29–149 in M. Tonry and N. Morris, eds., *Crime and Justice: An Annual Review of Research*, Vol. 7. Chicago: University of Chicago Press.

Lombroso, Cesare. 1920. *The Female Offender*. New York: Appleton.

Low, W. Y., S. N. Zulkifli, K. Yusof, S. Batumalail, and K. W. Aye. 1996. "The Drug Abuse Problem in Peninsular Malysia: Parent and Child Differences in Knowledge, Attitudes and Perceptions." *Drug and Alcohol Dependence* 42(2):105–115.

Lucas, Samuel R. 1999. *Tracking Inequality: Stratification and Mobility in American High Schools*. New York: Teachers College Press.

Lugaila, T. 1998. *Marital Status and Living Arrangements: March 1998 (Update)*. U.S. Census Bureau Current Population Survey Report P20-514. Washington, DC: U.S. Government Printing Office.

Lundman, Richard J. 1986. "Beyond Probation: Assessing the Generalizability of the Delinquency Suppression Effect Measures Reported by Murray and Cox." *Crime & Delinquency* 32:134–147.

Lundman, Richard J., Richard F. Sykes, and John P. Clark. 1990. "Police Control of Juveniles: A Replication." Pp. 107–115 in R. A. Weisheit and R. G. Culbertson, eds., *Juvenile Delinquency: A Justice Perspective*, 2nd ed. Prospect Heights, IL: Waveland Press.

Lynch, James P. 2002. "Trends in Juvenile Violent Offending: An Analysis of Victim Survey Data," OJJDP Juvenile Justice Bulletin. Washington, DC: U.S. Department of Justice.

MacKenzie, Doris L. 1994. "Results of a Multisite Study of Boot Camp Prisons." *Federal Probation* 58(2):60–66.

Maddan, Sean, and William Hallahan. 2002. "Corporal Punishment in the 21st Century: An Examination of Supreme Court Decisions in the 1990s to Predict the Reemergence of Flagellance." *Journal of Crime and Justice* 25(2):97–120.

Maeroff, Gene I. 1982. *Don't Blame the Kids*. New York: McGraw-Hill.

Maguin, E., and R. Loeber. 1996. "Academic Performance and Delinquency." Pp. 145–264 in M. Tonry, Ed., *Crime and Justice: An Annual Review of Research*, Vol. 20. Chicago: University of Chicago Press.

Males, M. (2000). *Kids and Guns: How Politicians, Experts, and the Media Fabricate Fear of Youth*. Monroe, ME: Common Courage Press.

Malmgren, K., R. D. Abbott, and J. D. Hawkins. 1999. "Learning Disabilities and Delinquency: Rethinking the Link." *Journal of Learning Disabilities* 32:194–200.

Maloney, Dennis, Dennis Romig, and Troy Armstrong. 1988. "The Balanced Approach to Juvenile Probation." *Juvenile and Family Court Journal* 39:1–49.

Mann, Dale. 1987. "Can We Help Dropouts? Thinking About the Undoable." Pp. 3–20 in G. Natriello, ed., *School Dropouts: Patterns and Policies*. New York: Teachers College Press.

Marans, Steven, and Mark Schaefer. 1998. "Community Police, Schools, and Mental Health: The Challenge of Collaboration." Pp. 312–347 in D. S. Elliott, B. A. Hamburg, and K. R. Williams, eds., *Violence in American Schools*. New York: Cambridge University Press.

Martinson, Robert. 1974. "What Works? Questions and Answers About Prison Reform." *Public Interest* 35:22–54.

Martinson, Robert. 1979. "New Findings, New Views: A Note of Caution Regarding Sentencing Reform." *Hofstra Law Review* 7:243–258.

Matsueda, Ross L., and Karen Heimer. 1987. "Race, Family Structure, and Delinquency: A Test of Differential Association and Social Control Theories." *American Sociological Review* 52:826–840.

Matthews, Jay. 2003. "Federal Law's Effect: Raised Expectations." *Washington Post* (Jan. 14, 2003). Washington, DC: Washington Post. [http://edworkforce.house.gov]

Matza, David. 1964. *Delinquency and Drift*. New York: John Wiley & Sons.

Maurer, Adah. 1981. *Paddles Away: A Psychological Study of Physical Punishment in Schools*. Palo Alto, CA: R & E Research Associates, Inc.

Maxon, C. L., M. L. Whitlock, and M. W. Klein. 1998. "Vulnerability to Street Gang Membership: Implications for Practice." *Social Service Review* 72:70–91.

May, David C., Stephen D. Fessel, and Shannon Means. 2004. "Predictors of Principals' Perceptions of School Resource Officer Effectiveness in Kentucky." *American Journal of Criminal Justice* 29(1):75–93.

McCardle, Lynn, and Diana Fishbein. 1989. "The Self-Reported Effects of PCP on Human Aggression." *Addictive Behaviors* 4:465–472.

McCluskey, Cynthia P., Timothy S. Bynum, and Justin W. Patchin. 2004. "Reducing Chronic Absenteeism: An Assessment of an Early Truancy Initiative." *Crime & Delinquency* 50(2):214–234.

McCord, Joan. 1982. "A Longitudinal view of the Relationship Between Paternal Absence and Crime." Pp. 113–128 in J. Gunn and D. P. Farrington, eds., *Abnormal Offenders, Delinquency, and the Criminal Justice System.* Chichester, UK: John Wiley & Sons Ltd.

McCord, Joan. 1983. "A Forty-Year Perspective on Effects of Child Abuse and Neglect." *Child Abuse and Neglect* 7:265–270.

McDermott, Joan. 1983. "Crime in the School and in the Community: Offenders, Victims, and Fearful Youths." *Crime & Delinquency* 29:270–282.

McDill, E. L. G. Natrello, and A. Pallas. 1987. "The High Costs of High Standards: School Reform and Dropouts." Pp. 183–209 in W. T. Denton, ed., *Dropouts, Pushouts, and Other Casualties.* Bloomington, IN: Phi Delta Kappa.

McDowell, E. and R. Friedman. 1979. "An Analysis of Editorial Opinions Regarding Corporal Punishment: Some Dynamics of Regional Differences. In I. A. Hyman and J. H. Wise, eds., *Corporal Punishment in American Education.* Philadelphia: Temple University Press.

McDowell, E., Colin Loftin, and B. Wiersema. 2000. "The Impact of Youth Curfew Laws on Juvenile Crime Rates." *Crime & Delinquency* 46:76–91.

McEvoy, Alan. 1990. "Combating Gang Activities in Schools." *Education Digest* 56:31–34.

McLaughlin, Milbrey W. and Joan Talbert. 1990. "Constructing a Personalized School Environment." *Phi Delta Kappan* 72(3):230–235.

McPartland, James M. 1994. "Dropout Prevention in Theory and Practice." Pp. 255–276 in R. J. Rossi, ed., *Schools and Students at Risk: Context and Framework for Positive Change.* New York: Teachers College Press.

McPartland, James M., and Edward L. McDill, eds. 1977. *Violence in Schools: Perspectives, Programs and Positions.* Lexington, MA: Lexington Books.

McPartland, James M., and Robert E. Slavin. 1990. *Policy Perspectives: Increasing Achievement of At-Risk Students at Each Grade Level.* Washington, DC: U.S. Department of Education.

McShane, Marilyn D., and Wesley Krause. 1993. *Community Corrections.* New York: Macmillan.

Medaris, Michael L., Ellen Campbell, and Bernard James. 1997. *Sharing Information: A Guide to the Family Educational Rights and Privacy Act and Participation in Juvenile Justice Programs.* Washington, DC: U.S. Department of Justice.

Mello, M. 2002. "Friendly Fire: Privacy vs. Security After September 11." *Criminal Law Bulletin* 38:367–395.

Menard, Scott, and Barbara J. Morse. 1984. "A Structuralist Critique of the IQ-Delinquency Hypothesis: Theory and Evidence." *American Journal of Sociology* 89:1347–1378.

Mennell, Robert M. 1972. "Origins of the Juvenile Court: Changing Perspectives on the Legal Rights of Juvenile Delinquents." *Crime and Delinquency* 18:68–78.

Merton, Robert K. 1957. *Social Theory and Social Structure.* New York: Free Press.

Mihalic, Sharon, Katherine Irwin, Delbert Elliott, Abigail Fagan, and Diane Hansen. 2001. "Blueprints for Violence Prevention," OJJDP Juvenile Justice Bulletin. Washington, DC: U.S. Department of Justice.

Miller, Amanda, and Kathryn Chandler. 2003. *Violence in U.S. Public Schools: 2000 School Survey on Crime and Safety.* Washington, DC: U.S. Department of Education.

Miller, George. 2002. *New "No Child Left Behind" Regulations Fundamentally Flawed: Could Increase Dropout Rate for Poor and Minority Children.* Washington, DC: Committee on Education and the Workforce.

Miller, Walter. 1958a. "Lower Class Culture as a Generating Milieu of Gang Delinquency." *Journal of Social Issues* 14:5–19.

Miller, Walter. 1958b. "Inter-Institutional Conflict as a Major Impediment to Delinquency Prevention." *Human Organization* 17:20–23.

Minnesota Department of Corrections. 2004. *Thistledew Camp.* St. Paul, MN: Minnesota Department of Corrections. [http://www.doc.state.mn.us/facilities/Thistledew.htm]

Mitchell, J. Chad. 1998. "An Alternative Approach to the Fourth Amendment in Public Schools: Balancing Students' Rights with School Safety." *B.Y.U. Law Review* 3:1207–1241.

Moffitt, Terrie E. 1990. "Juvenile Delinquency and Attention Deficit Disorder: Boys' Developmental Trajectories from Age 3 to Age 15." *Child Development* 61:893–910.

Moffitt, Terrie E. 1993. "Adolescence-Limited and Life-Course-Persistent Antisocial Behavior: A Developmental Taxonomy." *Psychological Review* 100(4):674–701.

Moffitt, Terrie E., William F. Gabrielli, Sarnoff A. Mednick, and Fini Schulsinger. 1981. "Socio-economic Status, IQ, and Delinquency." *Journal of Abnormal Psychology* 90(2):152–156.

Moore, Mark H. 1992. "Problem-Solving and Community Policing." Pp. 99–158 in M. Tonry and N. Morris, eds., *Crime and Justice: An Annual Review of Research*, Vol. 15, *Modern Policing.* Chicago: University of Chicago Press.

Morash, Merry. 1984. "Establishment of a Juvenile Police Record." *Criminology* 22:97–111.

Morash, Merry. 1986. "Gender, Peer Group Experiences, and Seriousness of Delinquency." *Journal of Research in Crime and Delinquency* 25:43–61.

Morash, Merry, and Meda Chesney-Lind. 1991. "A Reformulation and Partial Test of the Power Control Theory of Delinquency." *Justice Quarterly* 8:347–377.

Morris, Norval, and Michael Tonry. 1990. *Between Prison and Probation.* New York: Oxford University Press.

Mueller, David, and Andrew Giacomazzi. 2003. "Reeling in Disengaged Students: An Assessment of a Countywide Juvenile Court Attendance program." *Juvenile and Family Court Journal* 54(2):25–39.

Mueller, David, Cody Stoddard, and Richard Lawrence. 2005. "The Constitutionalization of School Discipline: Balancing Students' Rights with School Safety." Paper presented at the Academy of Criminal Justice Sciences annual meeting, Chicago.

Mulvey, Edward P., and Elizabeth Cauffman. 2001. "The Inherent Limits of Predicting School Violence." *American Psychologist* 56(10):797–802.

Murray, C. A., B. B. Bourgue, R. S. Harnar, J. C. Hersey, S. R. Murray, D. D. Overbey, and E. S. Stotsky. 1980. *The National Evaluation of the Cities in Schools Program Report No. 3.* Washington, DC: National Institute of Education.

Murray, Charles, and Louis Cox. 1979. *Beyond Probation.* Beverly Hills, CA: Sage Publications.

Myers, Stephanie M. 2002. *Police Encounters with Juvenile Suspects: Explaining the Use of Authority and Provision of Support.* Washington, DC: National Institute of Justice.

Nansel, T. R., M. Overpeck, R. S. Pilla, W. J. Ruan, B. Simons-Morton, and P. Scheidt. 2001. "Bullying Behaviors Among U.S. Youth: Prevalence and Association with Psychosocial Adjustment." *Journal of the American Medical Association* 285(16):2094–2100.

National Advisory Commission on Criminal Justice Standards and Goals. 1973. *Corrections.* Washington, DC: U.S. Government Printing Office.

National Advisory Commission on Criminal Justice Standards and Goals. 1976. *Juvenile Justice and Delinquency Prevention.* Washington, DC: U.S. Department of Justice.

National Center for Education Statistics. 1993. *National Household Education Survey.* Washington, DC: U.S. Department of Education.

National Center for Education Statistics. 1995. *Statistical Perspectives: Gangs and Victimization at School.* Washington, DC: U.S. Department of Education.

National Clearinghouse on Child Abuse and Neglect Information. 1998. *Child Maltreatment 1996: Reports From the States to the National Child Abuse and Neglect Data System.* Washington, DC: U.S. Government Printing Office.

National Coalition to Abolish Corporal Punishment in Schools. 2005. *Worldwide Bans on Corporal Punishment.* Columbus, Ohio: National Coalition to Abolish Corporal Punishment in Schools. [online: http://stophitting.com/disatschool/facts.php]

National Commission on Excellence in Education. 1983. *A Nation at Risk: The Imperative for Educational Reform*. Washington, DC: U.S. Government Printing Office.

National Education Association. 1972. *Report of the Task Force on Corporal Punishment*. Washington, DC: National Education Association.

National Institute on Drug Abuse. 1991. *National Household Survey on Drug Abuse: Highlights 1990*. Washington, DC: Government Printing Office.

National Institute of Education. 1977. *Violent Schools—Safe Schools: The Safe School Study Report to the Congress—Executive Summary*. Washington, DC: U.S. Department of Health, Education and Welfare.

National Institute of Education. 1978. *Violent Schools—Safe Schools: The Safe School Study Report to the Congress*, Vol. I. Washington, DC: U.S. Department of Health, Education and Welfare.

National Institute of Justice. 1996. *Beacons of Hope: New York City's School-Based Community Centers*. Washington, DC: U.S. Department of Justice.

National Juvenile Justice Assessment Centers. 1981. *Juvenile Delinquency Prevention: A Compendium of Thirty-Six Program Models*. Washington, DC: U.S. Department of Justice.

National School Safety Center. 1990. *School Safety Check Book*. Westlake Village, CA: National School Safety Center.

National School Safety Center. 1993. *Safe School Planning*. Westlake Village, CA: National School Safety Center.

National School Safety Center. 1994. "Full-Service Schools: One-stop Health and Social Services." *School Safety Update* (Oct.):1–4.

National School Safety Center. 1995a. "Promising Strategies for Juvenile Crime Prevention." *School Safety Update* (Feb.):5.

National School Safety Center. 1995b. "School-Based Juvenile Probation: Everyone Benefits." *School Safety Update* (Dec.):1–4.

National School Safety Center. 1998. *Checklist of Characteristics of Youth Who Have Caused School-Associated Violent Deaths*. Westlake Village, CA: National School Safety Center

National School Safety Center. 2005. *School-Associated Violent Deaths*. Westlake Village, CA: National School Safety Center. [Online: http://www.nssc1.org]

National Youth Gang Center. 2000. *1998 National Youth Gang Survey*. Washington, DC: U.S. Department of Justice.

Needleman, Herbert, Charles Gunnoe, Alan Leviton, Robert Reed, Henry Peresie, Cornelius Maher, and Peter Barrett. 1979. "Deficits in Psychologic and Classroom Performance of Children with Elevated Dentine Lead Levels." *The New England Journal of Medicine* 300:689–695.

Needleman, Herbert, Julie Riess, Michael Tobin, Gretchen Biesecker, and Joel Greenhouse. 1996. "Bone Lead Levels and Delinquent Behavior." *Journal of the American Medical Association* 275:363–369.

Needleman, Herbert, Alan Schell, David Bellenger, Alan Leviton, and Elizabeth Allred. 1990. "The Long-Term Effects of Exposure to Low Doses of Lead in Children." *New England Journal of Medicine* 322:83–88.

Nettler, Gwynn. 1984. *Explaining Crime*, 3rd ed. New York: McGraw-Hill.

Newman, Katherine S. 2004. *Rampage: The Social Roots of School Shootings*. New York: Basic Books.

Newton, Anne. 1979. "Sentencing to Community Service and Restitution." *Criminal Justice Abstracts* (Sept.):435–468.

Nye, F. Ivan. 1958. *Family Relationships and Delinquent Behavior*. New York: John Wiley and Sons.

Oakes, Jeannie. 1985. *Keeping Track: How Schools Structure Inequality*. New Haven, CT: Yale University Press.

Office of Disease Prevention and Health Promotion. 2001. "Youth Violence is a Public Health Issue." *CDC Fact Sheet*. Washington, DC: U.S. Department of Health and Human Services. [http://odphp.osophs.dhhs.gov/pubs/prevrpt/01spring/Spring2001PR.htm]

Office of Juvenile Justice and Delinquency Prevention. 1990. "Education in the Law: Promoting Citizenship in the Schools," OJJDP Update on Programs. Washington, DC: U.S. Department of Justice.

Office of Juvenile Justice and Delinquency Prevention. 1995. *Delinquency Prevention Works: Program Summary*. Washington, DC: U.S. Department of Justice.

Office of National Drug Control Policy. 2003. "Juveniles and Drugs," Fact Sheet. Washington, DC: Executive Office of the President. [Online: http://www.whitehousedrugpolicy.gov]

Office of National Drug Control Policy. 2004. "Juveniles and Drugs," Drug Facts. Washington, DC: Executive Office of the President. [Online: http://www.whitehousedrugpolicy.gov]

Offord, David R. 1982. "Family Backgrounds of Male and Female Delinquents." Pp. 129–151 in J. Gunn and D. P. Farrington, eds., *Abnormal Offenders, Delinquency, and the Criminal Justice System*. Chichester, UK: John Wiley & Sons Ltd.

Offord, D. R., K. Sullivan, N. Allen, and N. Abrams. 1979. "Delinquency and Hyperactivity." *The Journal of Nervous and Mental Disease* 167(12):734–741.

O'Leary, Vincent. 1973. *Juvenile Justice Policy Inventory*. San Francisco: National Council on Crime and Delinquency.

O'Leary, Vincent, and David Duffee. 1971. "Correctional Policy Models: A Classification of Goals Designed for Change." *Crime & Delinquency* 17:373–386.

Oliver, Christine. 1991. "Network Relations and Loss of Organizational Autonomy." *Human Relations* 44:943–961.

Olweus, Dan. 1978. *Aggression in the Schools*. London: Hemisphere Publishing Corporation.

Olweus, Dan. 1980. "Familial and Temperamental Determinants of Aggressive Behaviour in Adolescent Boys: A Causal Analysis." *Developmental Psychology* 16:644–660.

Olweus, Dan. 1991. "Bully/Victim Problems Among Schoolchildren: Basic Facts and Effects of a School Based Intervention Program." Pp. 411–448 in D. J. Pepler and K. H. Rubin, eds., *The Development and Treatment of Childhood Aggression*. Hillsdale, NJ: Lawrence Erlbaum.

Olweus, Dan. 1994. "Bullying: Too Little Love, Too Much Freedom." *School Safety Update* (May): 1–4.

Orpinas, P., N. Murray, and S. Kelder. 1999. "Parental Influences on Students' Aggressive Behaviors and Weapon Carrying." *Health Education & Behavior* 26(6):768–781.

O'Toole, Mary Ellen. 1999. *The School Shooter: A Threat Assessment Perspective*. Quantico, VA: FBI Academy.

Packer, Herbert L. 1968. *The Limits of the Criminal Sanction*. Stanford, CA: Stanford University Press.

Pallas, Aaron M. 1987. "School Dropouts in the United States." Pp. 158–174 in W. T. Denton, ed., *Dropouts, Pushouts, and Other Casualties*. Bloomington, IN: Phi Delta Kappa.

Palmer, Ted. 1975. "Martinson Revisited." *Journal of Research in Crime and Delinquency* 12:133–152.

Parker, Robert N., William R. Smith, D. Randall Smith, and Jackson Toby. 1991. "Trends in Victimization in Schools and Elsewhere, 1974–1981." *Journal of Quantitative Criminology* 7:3–17.

Parsonage, William H., and W. Conway Bushey. 1989. "The Victimization of Probation and Parole Workers in the Line of Duty: An Exploratory Study." *Criminal Justice Policy Review* 2(4):372–391

Pasternack, Robert, and Reid Lyon. 1982. "Clinical and Empirical Identification of Learning Disabled Juvenile Delinquents." *Journal of Correctional Education* 33(2):7–13.

Paternoster, Raymond, and Paul Mazerolle. 1994. "General Strain Theory and Delinquency: A Replication and Extension." *Journal of Research in Crime and Delinquency* 31:235–263.

Patterson, Gerald R. 1986. "Performance Models for Antisocial Boys." *American Psychologist* 41:432–444.

Patterson, Gerald R., and Thomas J. Dishion. 1985. "Contributions of Families and Peers to Delinquency." *Criminology* 23:63–79.

Patterson, Gerald R., and Magda Stouthamer-Loeber. 1984. "The Correlation of Family Management Practices and Delinquency." *Child Development* 55:1299–1307.

Payne, Allison Ann. 2004. *School Community and Disorder: Communal Schools, Student Bonding, Delinquency, and Victimization*. New York: LFB Scholarly Publishing.

Pearson, Frank S., and Jackson Toby. 1991. "Fear of School-Related Predatory Crime." *Sociology and Social Research* 75:117–125.

Peden, J. M. 2001. "Through a Glass Darkly: Educating with Zero Tolerance." *Kansas Journal of Law & Public Policy* 10:369–398.

Peters, M., D. Thomas, and C. Zamberlan. 1997. *Boot Camps for Juvenile Offenders: Program Summary*. Washington, DC: U.S. Department of Justice.

Petersilia, Joan. 1986. "Exploring the Option of House Arrest." *Federal Probation* 50:50–56.

Petersilia, Joan. 1990. "Conditions that Permit Intensive Supervision Programs to Survive." *Crime & Delinquency* 36:126–45.

Petersilia, Joan. 1993. "Measuring the Performance of Community Corrections." Pp. 61–84 in *BJS-Princeton Project, Performance Measures for the Criminal Justice System*. Washington, DC: U.S. Department of Justice.

Peterson, Reece L. 2002. "School-Based Probation Officers," The Safe & Responsive Schools Project. Washington, DC: U.S. Department of Education.

Piaget, Jean. 1932. *The Moral Judgment of the Child*. London: Kegan Paul.

Piliavin, Irvin, and Scott Briar. 1964. "Police Encounters with Juveniles." *American Journal of Sociology* 70:206–214.

Pinard, M. 2003. "From the Classroom to the Courtroom: Reassessing Fourth Amendment Standards in Public School Searches Involving Law Enforcement Authorities." *Arizona Law Review* 45:1067–1125.

Pink, William T. 1984. "Schools, Youth, and Justice." *Crime & Delinquency* 30(3):439–461.

Pisciotta, Alexander W. 1982. "Saving the Children: The Promise and Practice of *Parens Patriae*, 1838–98." *Crime & Delinquency* 28(3):410–425.

Platt, Anthony. 1974. "The Triumph of Benevolence: The Origins of the Juvenile Justice System in the United States." In R. Quinney, ed., *Criminal Justice in America: A Critical Understanding*. Boston: Little, Brown.

Podboy, John W., and William A. Mallory. 1978. "The Diagnosis of Specific Learning Disabilities in a Juvenile Delinquent Population." *Federal Probation* 42:26–33.

Podkopacz, Marcy R., and Barry C. Feld. 1996. "The End of the Line: An Empirical Study of Judicial Waiver." *The Journal of Criminal Law and Criminology* 86:449–492.

Podkopacz, Marcy R., and Barry C. Feld. 2001. "The Backdoor to Prison: Waiver Reform, Blended Sentencing, and the Law of Unintended Consequences." *Journal of Criminal Law and Criminology* 91:997–1071.

Polk, Kenneth. 1982a. "Curriculum Tracking and Delinquency: Some Observations." *American Sociological Review* 48:282–284.

Polk, Kenneth. 1982b. "Schools and the Delinquency Experience." Pp. 227–232 in D. Rojek and G. Jensen, eds., *Readings in Juvenile Delinquency*. Lexington, MA: D.C. Heath.

Polk, Kenneth, Dean Frease, and F. Lynn Richmond. 1974. "Social Class, School Experience, and Delinquency." *Criminology* 12(1):84–96.

Pollak, Otto. 1950. *The Criminality of Women*. Philadelphia: University of Pennsylvania Press.

Pope, Carl E. 1988. "The Family, Delinquency, and Crime." Pp. 108–228 in E. W. Nunnally, C. S. Chilman, and F. M. Cox, eds., *Mental Illness, Delinquency, Addictions, and Neglect*. Newbury Park, CA: Sage Publications.

Pope, Carl E., and William Feyerherm. 1995. *Minorities and the Juvenile Justice System: Research Summary*. Washington, DC: U.S. Department of Justice.

Pope, Carl E., and Howard N. Snyder. 2003. "Race as a Factor in Juvenile Arrests," OJJDP Juvenile Justice Bulletin. Washington, DC: U.S. Department of Justice.

Post, Charles H. 1981. "The Link Between Learning Disabilities and Juvenile Delinquency: Cause, Effect and 'Present Solutions'." *Juvenile & Family Court Journal* 31:58–68.

President's Commission on Law Enforcement and Administration of Justice. 1967. *Task Force Report: Juvenile Delinquency and Youth Crime*. Washington, DC: U.S. Government Printing Office.

Prothrow-Stith, Deborah. 1987. *Violence Prevention Curriculum for Adolescents*. Newton, MA: Education Development Center.

Prothrow-Stith, D., H. Spivak, and A. J. Hausman. 1987. "The Violence Prevention Project: A Public Health Approach." *Science, Technology, and Human Values* 12:67–69.

Puzzanchera, Charles M. 2003. "Delinquency Cases Waived to Criminal Court, 1990–1999," OJJDP Fact Sheet. Washington, DC: U.S. Department of Justice.

Puzzanchera, Charles, Anne L. Stahl, Terrence A. Finnegan, Nancy Tierney, and Howard N. Snyder. 2003. *Juvenile Court Statistics 1999*. Pittsburgh, PA: National Center for Juvenile Justice.

Puzzanchera, Charles, Anne L. Stahl, Terrence A. Finnegan, Nancy Tierney, and Howard N. Snyder. 2004. *Juvenile Court Statistics 2000*. Pittsburgh, PA: National Center for Juvenile Justice.

Quinney, Richard. 1974. *Criminal Justice in America: A Critical Understanding.* Boston: Little, Brown.

Raley, Gordon A. 1995. "The JJDP Act: A Second Look." *Juvenile Justice (OJJDP)* 2(Fall/Winter):11–18.

Rankin, Joseph H. 1977. "The Family Context of Delinquency." *Social Problems* 30:466–479.

Rankin, Joseph H. 1980. "School Factors and Delinquency: Interactions by Age and Sex." *Sociology and Social Research* 64(3):420–434.

Rankin, Joseph H., and Roger Kern. 1994. "Parental Attachments and Delinquency." *Criminology* 32:495–515.

Raywid, Mary A. 1983. "Alternative Schools as a Model for Public Education." *Theory Into Practice* 22:190–197.

Reardon, F. J. and R. N. Reynolds. 1979. "A Survey of Attitudes Toward Corporal Punishment in Pennsylvania Schools." In I. A. Hyman and J. H. Wise, eds., *Corporal Punishment in American Education.* Philadelphia: Temple University Press.

Reckless, Walter C. 1961. "A New Theory of Delinquency and Crime." *Federal Probation* 25:42–46.

Reckless, Walter C., Simon Dinitz, and Barbara Kay. 1956. "Self Concept as an Insulator Against Delinquency." *American Sociological Review* 21:744–746.

Reddy, Marisa, Randy Borum, John Berglund, Bryan Vossekuil, Robert Fein, and William Modzeleski. 2001. "Evaluating Risk for Targeted Violence in Schools: Comparing Risk Assessment, Threat Assessment, and Other Approaches." *Psychology in the Schools* 38(2):157–172.

Reddy, Marisa, Randy Borum, Bryan Vossekuil, Robert Fein, John Berglund, and William Modzeleski. 2000. *Evaluating Risk for Targeted Violence in Schools: Comparing Risk Assessment, Threat Assessment, and Other Approaches.* Washington, DC: U.S. Secret Service.

Redl, Fritz, and David Wineman. 1951. *Children Who Hate.* New York: The Free Press.

Reglin, Gary L. 1992. "Public School Educators' Knowledge of Selected Supreme Court Decisions Affecting Daily Public School Operations." *Journal of Educational Administration* 30(2):26–31.

Reid, W. 1964. "Interagency Coordination in Delinquency Prevention and Control." *Social Service Review* 38(1):418–428.

Reiman, Jeffrey. 1990. *The Rich Get Richer and the Poor Get Prison: Ideology, Class, and Criminal Justice,* 3rd ed. New York: Macmillan.

Reutter, E. Edmund, Jr. 1982. *The Supreme Court's Impact on Public Education.* Bloomington, IN: Phi Delta Kappa and National Organization of Legal Problems of Education.

Reynolds, K. Michael, Ruth Seydlitz, and Pamela Jenkins. 2000. "Do Juvenile Curfew Laws Work? A Time Series Analysis of the New Orleans Law." *Justice Quarterly* 17(1):205–230.

Riesman, David. 1950. *The Lonely Crowd.* New Haven, CT: Yale University Press.

Rigby, Ken. 1993. "School Children's Perceptions of Their Families and Parents as a Function of Peer Relations." *Journal of Genetic Psychology,* 154(4):501–512.

Rigby, Ken. 2001. "Health Consequences of Bullying and Its Prevention in Schools." Pp. 310–331 in J. Juvonen and S. Graham, eds., *Peer Harassment in School.* New York: The Guilford Press.

Rippa, S. Alexander. 1980. *Education in a Free Society: An American History,* 4th ed. New York: Longman.

Robins, See N., and Kathryn S. Ratcliff. 1980. "The Long-Term Outcome of Truancy." Pp. 65–83 in Lionel Hersov and Ian Berg, eds., *Out of School: Modern Perspectives in Truancy and School Refusal.* New York: John Wiley & Sons.

Romer, D., Jamieson, K. H., and deCoteau, N. J. 1998. "The Treatment of Persons of Color in Local Television News: Ethnic Blame Discourse or Realistic Group Conflict?" *Communication Research,* 25(3):286–305.

Rose, Lowell C., and Alec M. Gallup. 2004. *The 36ᵗʰ Annual Phi Delta Kappa/Gallup Poll of the Public's Attitudes Toward the Public Schools.* Bloomington, IN: Phi Delta Kappa International. [http://www.pdkintl.org/kappan/k0409pol.htm]

Rose, Terry L. 1984. "Current Uses of Corporal Punishment in American Public Schools." *Journal of Educational Psychology* 76:427–441.

Rosen, Lawrence. 1985. "Family and Delinquency: Structure or Function." *Criminology* 23:553–573.

Rosenbaum, Dennis P., Robert L. Flewelling, Susan L. Bailey, Chris L. Ringwalt, and Deanna L. Wilkinson. 1994. "Cops in the Classroom: A Longitudinal Evaluation of Drug Abuse Resistance Education (DARE)." *Journal of Research in Crime and Delinquency* 31:3–31.

Rosenbaum, J. E. 1976. *Making Inequality: The Hidden Curriculum of the High School.* New York: Wiley.

Rosenbaum, James E. 1989. "What if Good Jobs Depended on Good Grades?" *American Educator* 13(Winter):10–15, 40, 42–43.

Rosenbaum, Jill L., and James R. Lasley. 1990. "School, Community Context, and Delinquency: Rethinking the Gender Gap." *Justice Quarterly* 7(3):493–513.

Rosenberg, Mark L. and Mary A. Fenley, eds. 1991. *Violence in America: A Public Health Approach.* New York: Oxford University Press.

Rosenzweig, E. M. 2002. "Comment: Please Don't Tell. The Question of Confidentiality in Student Disciplinary Records Under FERPA and the Crime Awareness and Campus Security Act." *Emory Law Journal* 51:447–481.

Rowe, David C., and D. Wayne Osgood. 1984. "Heredity and Sociological Theories of Delinquency: A Reconsideration." *American Sociological Review* 49:526–540.

Roy-Stevens, Cora. 2004. "Overcoming Barriers to School Reentry," OJJDP Fact Sheet. Washington, DC: U.S. Department of Justice.

Rubel, Robert. 1977. *The Unruly School: Disorder, Disruptions, and Crimes.* Lexington, MA: Lexington Books.

Rubel, Robert J., and Peter D. Blauvelt. 1994. "How Safe Are Your Schools?" *The American School Board Journal* (Jan.):28–31.

Rubin, H. Ted. 1999. "School-Based Probation Officers in Pittsburgh: A New and Different School-Juvenile Court Partnership." *Juvenile Justice Update* 5(3):1–2, 10–13.

Rubin, H. Ted. 2001. "A Community Imperative: Curbing Minority Overrepresentation in the Juvenile Justice System." *Juvenile Justice Update* 7(2):1–2, 14–16.

Rudman, Cary, Eliot Hartstone, Jeffrey Fagan, and Melinda Moore. 1986. "Violent Youth in Adult Court: Process and Punishment." *Crime & Delinquency* 32:75–96.

Rumberger, Russell W. 1983. "Dropping Out of High School: The Influence of Race, Sex, and Family Background." *American Educational Research Journal* 20:199–220.

Rumberger, Russell W. 1987. "High School Dropouts: A Review of Issues and Evidence." *Review of Educational Research* 57:101–122.

Rumberger, Russell W. 1995. "Dropping Out of Middle School: A Multilevel Analysis of Students and Schools." *American Educational Research Journal* 32:583–625.

Rust, James O., and Karen Q. Kinnard. 1983. "Personality Characteristics of the Users of Corporal Punishment in the Schools." *Journal of School Psychology* 21:91–105.

Rutter, Michael. 1983. "School Effects on Pupil Progress: Research Findings and Policy Implications." *Child Development* 54:1–29

Ryan, Bruce A., and Gerald R. Adams. 1995. "The Family-School Relationships Model." Pp. 3–28 in B. A. Ryan, G. R. Adams, T. P. Gullotta, R. P. Weissberg, and R. L. Hampton, eds., *The Family School Connection: Theory, Research and Practice.* Thousand Oaks, CA: Sage Publications.

Sampson, Robert J., and John H. Laub. 1997. "A Life-Course Theory of Cumulative Disadvantage and the Stability of Delinquency." Pp. 133–155 in T. P. Thornberry, ed., *Developmental Theories of Crime and Delinquency.* New Brunswick, NJ: Transaction Publishers.

Sanborn, Joseph, and Anthony W. Salerno. 2005. *The Juvenile Justice System: Law and Process.* Los Angeles: Roxbury Publishing Co.

Sanchez, J. M. 1992. "Expelling the Fourth Amendment from American Schools: Students' Rights Six Years After T.L.O." *Journal of Law and Education* 21(3):381–413.

Schafer, Walter E. 1972. "Deviance in the Public School: An Interactional View." Pp. 145–163 in K. Polk and W. E. Schafer, eds., *Schools and Delinquency.* Englewood Cliffs, NJ: Prentice-Hall, Inc.

Schafer, Walter, Carol Olexa, and Kenneth Polk. 1972. "Programmed for Social Class: Tracking in High School." Pp. 33–54 in K. Polk and W. E. Schafer, eds., *Schools and Delinquency.* Englewood Cliffs, NJ: Prentice-Hall.

Schafer, Walter E., and Kenneth Polk. 1967. "Delinquency and the Schools." Pp. 222–277 in *Task Force Report: Juvenile Delinquency and Youth Crime*. Washington, DC: U.S. Government Printing Office.

Schafer, Walter E., and Kenneth Polk. 1972. "School Conditions Contributing to Delinquency." Pp. 181–238 in K. Polk and W. E. Schafer, eds., *Schools and Delinquency*. Englewood Cliffs, NJ: Prentice-Hall, Inc.

Schargel, Franklin J., and Jay Smink. 2001. *Strategies to Help Solve Our School Dropout Problem*. Larchmont, NY: Eye on Education.

Schauss, Alexander. 1981. *Diet, Crime, and Delinquency*. Berkeley, CA: Parker House.

Schmidt, Annesley. 1986. "Electronic Monitors." *Federal Probation* 50:56–60.

Schneider, Anne L. 1985a. *Guide to Juvenile Restitution*. Washington, DC: U.S. Department of Justice.

Schneider, Anne L. 1985b. *The Impact of Deinstitutionalization on Recidivism and Secure Confinement of Status Offenders*. Washington, DC: U.S. Department of Justice.

Schneider, Anne L. 1986. "Restitution and Recidivism Rates of Juvenile Offenders: Results from Four Experimental Studies." *Criminology* 24:533–552.

Schneider, Anne L., and Jean Warner. 1989. *National Trends in Juvenile Restitution Programming*. Washington, DC: U.S. Department of Justice.

Schoenthaler, Stephen, and Walter Doraz. 1983. "Types of Offenses Which Can Be Reduced in an Institutional Setting Using Nutritional Intervention." *International Journal of Biosocial Research* 4:74–84.

Schoenthaler, Stephen, Walter Doraz, and James Wakefield. 1986. "The Impact of a Low Food Additive and Sucrose Diet on Academic Performance in 803 New York City Public Schools." *International Journal of Biosocial Research* 8:185–195.

Schreck, Christopher J., J. Mitchell Miller, and Chris L. Gibson. 2003. "Trouble in the School Yard: A Study of the Risk Factors of Victimization at School." *Crime & Delinquency* 49(3):460–484.

Schuesler, Karl, and Donald Cressey. 1955. "Personality Characteristics of Criminals." *American Journal of Sociology* 55:476–484.

Schwartz, Ira. 1989. *(In)Justice for Juveniles*. Lexington, MA: Lexington Books.

Schwendinger, Herman, and Julia Schwendinger. 1985. *Adolescent Subcultures and Delinquency*. New York: Praeger Publshers.

Shaw, Clifford R., and Henry D. McKay. 1942. *Juvenile Delinquency and Urban Areas*. Chicago: University of Chicago Press.

Shaw, Margaret. 2001. *Promoting Safety in Schools: International Experience and Action*. Washington, DC: U.S. Department of Justice.

Sheldon, William. 1949. *Varieties of Delinquent Youth*. New York: Harper & Row.

Sherman, Lawrence W. 1997a. "Policing for Crime Prevention." Pp. 8-1–8-58 in L. W. Sherman, D. Gottfredson, D. MacKenzie, J. Eck, P. Reuter, and S. Bushway, eds., *Preventing Crime: What Works, What Doesn't, What's Promising*. Washington, DC: U.S. Department of Justice.

Sherman, Lawrence W. 1997b. "Thinking About Crime Prevention." Pp. 2-1–2-32 in L. W. Sherman, D. Gottfredson, D. MacKenzie, J. Eck, P. Reuter, and S. Bushway, eds., *Preventing Crime: What Works, What Doesn't, What's Promising*. Washington, DC: U.S. Department of Justice.

Sherman, L. W., D. Gottfredson, D. MacKenzie, J. Eck, P. Reuter, and S. Bushway, eds. 1997. *Preventing Crime: What Works, What Doesn't, What's Promising*. Washington, DC: U.S. Department of Justice.

Shoemaker, Donald J. 2004. *Theories of Delinquency*, 5th ed. New York: Oxford University Press.

Sickmund, Melissa. 1994. "How Juveniles Get to Criminal Court," OJJDP Update on Statistics. Washington, DC: U.S. Department of Justice.

Sickmund, Melissa. 2004. "Juveniles in Corrections," Juvenile Offenders and Victims National Report Series Bulletin. Washington, DC: U.S. Department of Justice.

Sickmund, Melissa, Howard N. Snyder, and Eileen Poe-Yamagata. 1997. *Juvenile Offenders and Victims: 1997 Update on Violence*. Washington, DC: Office of Juvenile Justice and Delinquency Prevention.

Sieh, Edward W. 1993. "From Augustus to the Progressives: A Study of Probation's Formative years." *Federal Probation* 57(3):67–72.

Simon, Rita J. 1975. *Women and Crime*. Lexington, MA: D.C. Heath.

Simons, Ronald L. 1978. "The Meaning of the IQ-Delinquency Relationship." *American Sociological Review* 43:268–270.

Simons, Ronald L., Les B. Whitbeck, Rand D. Conger, and Katherine J. Conger. 1991. "Parenting Factors, Social Skills, and Value Commitments as Precursors to School Failure, Involvement with Deviant Peers, and Delinquent Behavior." *Journal of Youth and Adolescence* 20:645–664.

Simons, R. L., C. Wu, R. D. Conger, and F. O. Lorenz. 1994. "Two Routes to Delinquency: Differences Between Early and Late Starters in the Impact of Parenting and Deviant Peers." *Criminology* 32(2):247–272.

Skiba, Russ, and Reece Peterson. 1999. "The Dark Side of Zero Tolerance: Can Punishment Lead to Safe Schools?" *Phi Delta Kappan* 80(5):372–376, 381–382.

Skiba, Russ. J., and Reece L. Peterson. 2000. "School Discipline at a Crossroads: From Zero Tolerance to Early Response." *Exceptional Child* 66:335–346.

Skinner, B. F. 1953. *Science and Human Behavior*. New York: Macmillan Publishing Co.

Slavin, Robert E. 1990. "Achievement Effects of Ability Grouping in Secondary Schools: A Best-Evidence Synthesis." *Review of Educational Research* 60(3):471–499.

Slavin, Robert E., and Nancy A. Madden. 1989. "What Works for Students at Risk: A Research Synthesis." *Educational Leadership* 46:4–13.

Smith, Bradford. 1998. "Children in Custody: 20-Year Trends in Juvenile Detention, Correctional, and Shelter Facilities." *Crime & Delinquency* 44(4):526–543.

Snyder, Howard. 2002. "Juvenile Arrests 2000," Juvenile Justice Bulletin. Washington, DC: U.S. Department of Justice.

Snyder, Howard N. 2004. "Juvenile Arrests 2002," OJJDP Juvenile Justice Bulletin. Washington, DC: U.S. Department of Justice.

Snyder, Howard N. 2005. "Juvenile Arrests 2003," OJJDP Juvenile Justice Bulletin. Washington, DC: U.S. Department of Justice.

Snyder, Howard N., and Melissa Sickmund. 1995. *Juvenile Offenders and Victims: A National Report*. Washington, DC: Office of Juvenile Justice and Delinquency Prevention.

Snyder, Howard N., and Melissa Sickmund. 1999. *Juvenile Offenders and Victims: 1999 National Report*. Washington, DC: U.S. Department of Justice.

Society for Adolescent Medicine. 1992. "Corporal Punishment in the Schools: Position Paper of the Society for Adolescent Medicine." *Journal of Adolescent Health* 13:240–246.

Sorenson, S. B., J. G. P. Manz, and R. A. Berk. 1998. "News Media Coverage and the Epidemiology of Homicide." *American Journal of Public Health* 88:1510–1514.

Spergel, Irving, Ron Chance, Kenneth Ehrensaft, Thomas Regulus, Candice Kane, Robert Laseter, Alba Alexander, and Sandra Oh. 1994a. *Gang Suppression and Intervention: Community Models-Research Summary*. Washington, DC: Office of Juvenile Justice and Delinquency Prevention.

Spergel, Irving, David Curry, Ron Chance, Candice Kane, Ruth Ross, Alba Alexander, Edwina Simmons, and Sandra Oh. 1994b. *Gang Suppression and Intervention: Problem and Response: Research Summary*. Washington, DC: Office of Juvenile Justice and Delinquency Prevention.

Spivack, George, and Norma Cianci. 1987. "High-Risk Early Behavior Pattern and Later Delinquency." Pp. 44–74 in J. D. Burchard and S. N. Burchard, eds., *Prevention of Delinquent Behavior*. Newbury Park, CA: Sage Publications.

Sridharan, Sanjeev, Lynette Greenfield, and Baron Blakley. 2004. "A Study of Prosecutorial Certification Practice in Virginia." *Criminology and Public Policy* 4(3):605–632.

Stahl, Anne L. 2003. "Delinquency Cases in Juvenile Courts, 1999," OJJDP Fact Sheet. Washington, DC: U.S. Department of Justice.

Staples, William. 1986. "Restitution as a Sanction in Juvenile Court." *Crime & Delinquency* 32:177–185.

Steffensmeier, Darrell J., and Renee H. Steffensmeier. 1980. "Trends in Female Delinquency." *Criminology* 18(1):62–85.

Stefkovich, J. A., and J. A. Miller. 1999. "Law Enforcement Officers in Public Schools: Student Citizens in Safe Havens." *BYU Education and Law Journal* 1999(1):25–69. [http://www.law2.byu.edu/jel/v1999_1/html/stefkovich.htm]

Stefkovich, Jacqueline A., and Lawrence F. Rossow. 2004. "Search and Seizure in Public Schools: 2003 Update of Fourth Amendment Cases." *Illinois School Law Online* 24(3). [http://www.coe.ilstu.edu/eafdept/islq/islqarch.htm]

Steinberg, Laurence. 2000. "Youth Violence: Do Parents and Families Make a Difference?" *National Institute of Justice Journal* 2000(Apr.):30–38.

Steinberg, Laurence, B. Bradford Brown, and Sanford M. Dornbusch. 1996. *Beyond the Classroom: Why School Reform Has Failed and What Parents Need To Do*. New York: Touchstone/Simon and Schuster.

Stephens, Ron. 1998. "Safe School Planning." Pp. 253–289 in D. S. Elliott, B. A. Hamburg, and Kirk R. Williams, eds., *Violence in American Schools*. Cambridge, UK: Cambridge University Press.

Stephens, Ronald. 2005 (personal communication and correspondence.).

Stevens, Edward, Jr., and George H. Wood. 1987. *Justice, Ideology and Education*. New York: McGraw-Hill.

Steverson, Janet W., ed. 2002. *Children and the Law: The State and the Schooling of Children*, Vol. 2. Hamden, CT: Routledge.

Stewart, Eric A. 2003. "School Social Bonds, School Climate, and School Misbehavior: A Multi-level Analysis." *Justice Quarterly* 20(3):575–604.

Stinchcombe, Arthur L. 1964. *Rebellion in a High School*. Chicago: Quadrangle Books.

Straus, Murray A. 1991. "Discipline and Deviance: Physical Punishment of Children and Violence and Other Crime in Adulthood." *Social Problems* 38(20):131–154.

Straus, Murray A. 1994. *Beating the Devil Out of Them: Corporal Punishment in American Families*. New York: Lexington Books.

Straus, Murray A., Richard J. Gelles, and Susanne K. Steinmetz. 1980. *Behind Closed Doors: Violence in the American Family*. Garden City, NY: Anchor Press/Doubleday.

Streib, Victor L. 2005. *The Juvenile Death Penalty Today: Death Sentences and Executions for Juvenile Crimes*, Jan. 1, 1973–Dec. 31, 2004. (Online: http://www.law.onu.edu/faculty/streib/documents/JuvDeathDec2004.pdf)

Strother, Deborah Burnett, ed. 1991. *Learning to Fail: Case Studies of Students at Risk*. Bloomington, IN: Phi Delta Kappa.

Substance Abuse and Mental Health Services Administration. 2002. *Results from the 2001 National Household Survey on Drug Abuse: Volume I. Summary of National Findings*. Rockville, MD: National Clearinghouse for Alcohol and Drug Information.

Substance Abuse and Mental Health Services Administration. 2005. "Safe Schools, Healthy Students." Washington, DC: U.S. Department of Health and Human Services. [http://www.mentalhealth.samhsa.gov/safeschools/default.asp]

Surette, Ray. 1998. *Media, Crime and Criminal justice: Images and Realities*, 2nd ed. Pacific Grove, CA: Brooks/Cole.

Sutherland, Edwin H., and Donald R. Cressey. 1970. *Principles of Criminology*. New York: J.B. Lippincott.

Szymanski, Linda. 1994. *Upper Age of Juvenile Court Jurisdiction Statutes Analyses*. Pittsburgh, PA: National Center for Juvenile Justice.

Tannenbaum, Frank. 1938. *Crime and the Community*. New York: Columbia University Press.

Taras, Howard L., Barbara L. Frankowski, Jane W. McGrath, Cynthia J. Mears, Robert D. Murray, and Thomas L. Young. 2003. "Out-of-School Suspension and Expulsion." *Pediatrics* 112(5):1206–1209.

Taylor, T. J., K. B. Turner, F. Esbensen, and T. L. Winfree. 2001. "Coppin' an Attitude: Attitudinal Differences Among Juveniles Toward Police." *Journal of Criminal Justice* 29(4):295–305.

Tennenbaum, D. J. 1977. "Personality and Criminality: A Summary and Implications of the Literature." *Journal of Criminal Justice* 5:225–235.

Thomas, W. I. 1923. *The Unadjusted Girl*. New York: Harper.

Thornberry, Terence P. 1987. "Toward an Interactional Theory of Delinquency." *Criminology* 25:863–891.

Thornberry, Terence P., ed. 1997. *Developmental Theories of Crime and Delinquency*. New Brunswick, NJ: Transaction Publishers.

Thornberry, Terence P., Marvin D. Krohn, Alan J. Lizotte, and Denise Chard-Wierschem. 1993. "The Role of Juvenile Gangs in Facilitating Delinquent Behavior." *Journal of Research in Crime and Delinquency* 30(1):55–87.

Thornberry, Terence P., Melanie Moore, and R. L. Christenson. 1985. "The Effect of Dropping Out of High School on Subsequent Criminal Behavior." *Criminology* 23:3–18.

Thornberry, Terence P., Carolyn A. Smith, Craig Rivera, David Huizinga, and Magda Stouthamer-Loeber. 1999. "Family Disruption and Delinquency," OJJDP Juvenile Justice Bulletin. Washington, DC: U.S. Department of Justice.

Toby, Jackson. 1980. "Crime in American Schools." *Public Interest* 58:18–42.

Toby, Jackson. 1983. "Violence in School." Pp. 1–47 in M. Tonry and N. Morris, eds., *Crime and Justice: An Annual Review of Research*. Chicago: University of Chicago Press.

Toby, Jackson. 1994. "Everyday School Violence: How Disorder Fuels It." *American Educator* (Winter): 4–9, 44–48.

Toles, R., E. M. Schulz, and W. K. Rice. 1986. "A Study of Variation in Dropout Rates Attributable to Effects of High Schools." *Metropolitan Education* 2:30–38.

Tomaino, Louis. 1975. "The Five Faces of Probation." *Federal Probation* 39(4):41–46.

Torbet, Patricia, M. 1996. "Juvenile Probation: The Workhorse of the Juvenile Justice System," OJJDP Juvenile Justice Bulletin. Washington, DC: U.S. Department of Justice.

Torbet, Patricia, Richard Gable, Hunter Hurst IV, Imogene Montgomery, Linda Szymanski, and Douglas Thomas. 1996. *State Responses to Serious and Violent Juvenile Crime: Research Report*. Washington, DC: Office of Juvenile Justice and Delinquency Prevention.

Trulson, Chad, Ruth Triplett, and Clete Snell. 2001. "Social Control in a School Setting: Evaluating a School-Based Boot Camp." *Crime & Delinquency* 47(4):573–609.

Trump, Kenneth. 1998. *Practical School Security: Basic Guidelines for Safe and Secure Schools*. Thousand Oaks, CA: Corwin Press.

Trump, Kenneth. 2000. *Classroom Killers? Hallway Hostages? How Schools Can Prevent and Manage School Crises*. Thousand Oaks, CA: Corwin Press.

Turvey, Brent. 1999. *Criminal Profiling: An Introduction to Behavioral Evidence Analysis*. San Diego: Academic Press.

U.S. Census Bureau. 2003. *Poverty: 2002 Highlights*. Washington, DC: U.S. Department of Commerce. [Online: http:www.census.gov]

U.S. Department of Education Office for Civil Rights. 2003. *2000 Elementary and Secondary School Civil Rights Compliance Report*. Washington, DC: U.S. Department of Education.

U.S. Department of Justice. 1976. *Two Hundred Years of American Criminal Justice: An LEAA Bicentennial Study*. Washington, DC: Law Enforcement Assistance Administration.

U.S. Senate, Committee on the Judiciary. 1975. *Our Nation's Schools—A Report Card: "A" in School Violence and Vandalism. Preliminary Report of the Subcommittee to Investigate Juvenile Delinquency*. Washington, DC: U.S. Government Printing Office.

U.S. Senate, Committee on the Judiciary. 1976. *School Violence and Vandalism: Models and Strategies for Change. Hearing Before the Subcommittee to Investigate Juvenile Delinquency*. Washington, DC: U.S. Government Printing Office.

Vail, Kathleen. 1997. "Privacy Rights Versus Safety: Should School Juvenile Records Be Open to Schools?" *The American School Board Journal* 184(4):40–41.

Van Voorhis, Patricia, Frank T. Cullen, Richard A. Matthers, and C. Chenoweth Garner. 1988. "The Impact of Family Structure and Quality on Delinquency: A Comparative Assessment of Structural and Functional Factors." *Criminology* 26:235–261.

Vaughn, Joseph B. 1989. "A Survey of Juvenile Electronic Monitoring and Home Confinement Programs." *Juvenile and Family Court Journal* 40:1–36.

Vaughn, Michael S., and Rolando V. del Carmen. 1997. "The Fourth Amendment as a Tool of Actuarial Justice: The 'Special Needs' Exception to the Warrant and Probable Cause Requirements." *Crime & Delinquency* 43:78–103.

von Hirsch, Andrew. 1976. *Doing Justice*. New York: Hill & Wang.

Waldo, Gordon, and Simon Dinitz. 1967. "Personality Attributes of the Criminal: An Analysis of Research Studies 1950–1965." *Journal of Research in Crime and Delinquency* 4:185–201.

Walsh, Anthony. 1987. "Cognitive Functioning and Delinquency: Property Versus Violent Offenses." *International Journal of Offender Therapy & Comparative Criminology* 31:285–289.

Walters, Glenn D. 1992. "A Meta-Analysis of the Gene-Crime Relationship." *Criminology* 30:595–613.

Warr, Mark. 2000. "Public Perceptions of and Reactions to Crime." Pp. 13–31 in J. Sheley, ed., *Criminology: A Contemporary Handbook*, 3rd ed. Belmont, CA: Wadsworth.

Wehlage, Gary G. 1986. "At-Risk Students and the Need for High School Reform." *Education* 107:18–28.

Wehlage, Gary G., and Robert A. Rutter. 1986. "Dropping Out: How Much Do Schools Contribute to the Problem?" *Teachers College Record* 87:374–392.

Wehlage, Gary G., Robert A. Rutter, and A. Turnbaugh. 1987. "A Program Model for At-Risk High School Students." *Educational Leadership* 44:70–73.

Weiss, A., and Chermak, S. M. 1998. "The News Value of African-American Victims: An Examination of the Media's Presentation of Homicide." *Journal of Crime and Justice* 21(2):71–88.

Wells, L. Edward, and Joseph H. Rankin. 1986. "The Broken Homes Model of Delinquency: Analytic Issues." *Journal of Research in Crime and Delinquency* 23:68–93.

Wells, L. Edward, and Joseph H. Rankin. 1988. "Direct Parental Controls and Delinquency." *Criminology* 26:263–285.

Wells, L. Edward, and Joseph H. Rankin. 1991. "Families and Delinquency: A Meta-Analysis of the Impact of Broken Homes." *Social Problems* 38:71–93.

Welsh, Ralph S. 1979. "Severe Parental Punishment and Aggression: The Link between Corporal Punishment and Delinquency." Pp. 126–142 in I. A. Hyman and J. H. Wise, eds., *Corporal Punishment in American Education*. Philadelphia: Temple University Press.

Welsh, Wayne N. 2001. "Effects of Student and School Factors on Five Measures of School Disorder." *Justice Quarterly* 18(4):911–947.

Welsh, W. N., J. R. Greene, and P. H. Jenkins. 1999. "School Disorder: The Influence of Individual, Institutional and Community Factors." *Criminology* 37:73–115.

Welsh, W. N., R. Stokes, and J. R. Greene. 2000. "A Macro-Level Model of School Disorder." *Journal of Research in Crime and Delinquency* 37(3):243–283.

Wenk, Ernst A. 1975. "Juvenile Justice and the Public Schools: Mutual Benefit Through Educational Reform." *Juvenile Justice* 26:7–14.

West, D. J., and David P. Farrington. 1973. *Who Becomes Delinquent?* London: Heinemann.

West, Marty L., and John M. Fries. 1995. "Campus-Based Police/Probation Teams—Making Schools Safer." *Corrections Today* 57(5):144, 146, 148.

White, M. D., J. J. Fyfe, S. P. Campbell, and J. S. Goldkamp. 2001. "The School-Police Partnership: Identifying At-Risk Youth Through a Truant Recovery Program." *Evaluation Review* 25(5):507–532.

Whitehead, John T., and Steven P. Lab. 1989. "Meta-Analysis of Juvenile Correctional Treatment." *Journal of Research in Crime and Delinquency* 26:276–295.

Whitehead, John T., and Steven P. Lab. 2004. *Juvenile Justice: An Introduction*, 4th ed. Cincinnati: Anderson Publishing Co.

Wiatrowski, Michael D., Stephen Hansell, Charles R. Massey, and David L. Wilson. 1982. "Curriculum Tracking and Delinquency." *American Sociological Review* 47:151–160.

Widom, Cathy Spatz. 1989a. "Child Abuse, Neglect, and Violent Criminal Behavior." *Criminology* 27:251–270.

Widom, Cathy Spatz. 1989b. "Does Violence Beget Violence? A Critical Examination of the Literature." *Psychological Bulletin* 106:3–28.

Wilbanks, William. 1987. *The Myth of a Racist Criminal Justice System*. Pacific Grove, CA: Brooks/Cole Publishing Co.

Wilkinson, J. Harvie. 1996. "Constitutionalization of School Discipline: An Unnecessary and Counter-Productive Solution." *Michigan Law & Policy Review* 1:309–313.

Wilkinson, Karen. 1974. "The Broken Family and Juvenile Delinquency: Scientific Explanation of Ideology." *Social Problems* 21:726–739.

Wilkinson, Karen. 1980. "The Broken Home and Delinquent Behavior: An Alternative Interpretation of Contradictory Findings." Pp. 21–42 in T. Hirschi and M. Gottfredson, eds., *Understanding Crime: Current Theory and Research*. Beverly Hills, CA: Sage.

Wilson, James Q. 1968. *Varieties of Police Behavior*. Cambridge, MA: Harvard University Press.

Wilson, James Q. 1977. "Crime in Society and Schools." In J. M. McPartland and E. L. McDill, eds., *Violence in Schools*. Lexington, MA: D.C. Heath.

Wilson, James Q. 1983. "Crime and Public Policy." Pp. 273–290 in J. Q. Wilson, ed., *Crime and Public Policy*. San Francisco: ICS Press.

Wilson, James Q., and Richard J. Herrnstein. 1985. *Crime and Human Nature.* New York: Simon and Schuster.

Wilson, James Q., and Glen C. Loury, eds. 1987. *From Children to Citizens,* Vol. 3: *Families, Schools and Delinquency Prevention.* New York: Springer-Verlag.

Winfree, L. Thomas, Finn-Aage Esbensen, and D. Wayne Osgood. 1996. "Evaluating a School-Based Gang Prevention Program: A Theoretical Perspective." *Evaluation Review* 20:181–203.

Wise, Arthur E. 1968. *Rich Schools, Poor Schools.* Chicago: University of Chicago Press.

Wolfgang, Marvin F., Robert M. Figlio, and Thorsten Sellin. 1972. *Delinquency in a Birth Cohort.* Chicago: The University of Chicago Press.

Wooden, Kenneth. 1976. *Weeping in the Playtime of Others: America's Incarcerated Children.* New York: McGraw-Hill.

Wordes, M., Timothy C. Bynum, and Charles J. Corley. 1994. "Locking Up Youth: The Impact of Race on Detention Decisions." *Journal of Research in Crime and Delinquency* 31(2):149–165.

Wright, Kevin N., and Karen E. Wright. 1994. *Family Life, Delinquency, and Crime: A Policymaker's Guide.* Washington, DC: Office of Juvenile Justice and Delinquency Prevention.

Young, Beth A. 2003. *Public High School Dropouts and Completers From the Common Core of Data: School Year 2000–01.* Washington, DC: National Center for Education Statistics.

Young, Timothy W. 1990. *Public Alternative Education: Options and Choice for Today's Schools.* New York: Columbia University Press.

Zigler, Edward, and Nancy W. Hall. 1987. "The Implications of Early Intervention Efforts for the Primary Prevention of Juvenile Delinquency." Pp. 154–185 in J. Q. Wilson and G. C. Loury, eds., *From Children to Citizens,* Vol. 3: *Families, Schools and Delinquency Prevention.* New York: Springer-Verlag.

Zimmerman, Joel, William Rich, Ingo Keilitz, and Paul Broder. 1981. "Some Observations on the Link Between Learning Disabilities and Juvenile Delinquency." *Journal of Criminal Justice* 9:9–17.

Zimring, Franklin E. 1998. *American Youth Violence.* New York: Oxford University Press.

Zimring, Franklin E. 2000. "Penal Proportionality for the Young Offender: Notes on Immaturity, Capacity, and Diminished Responsibility." In T. Grisso and R. G. Schwartz, eds., *Youth on Trial: A Developmental Perspective on Juvenile Justice.* Chicago: University of Chicago press.

Zingraff, Matthew T., and Michael J. Belyea. 1986. "Child Abuse and Violent Crime." Pp. 49–63 in K. C. Haas and G. P. Alpert, eds., *The Dilemmas of Punishment.* Prospect Heights, IL: Waveland Press.

Zirkel, Perry A. 1994. "Another Search for Student Rights." *Phi Delta Kappan* 75:728–230.

Author Index

Subject Index